LEARNING LEGAL SKILLS AND REASONING

D1350301

Language skills, study skills, argument skills and legal knowledge are vital to every law student, professional lawyer and academic. *Learning Legal Skills and Reasoning* discusses the main sources of English law and explains how to work with legal texts in order to construct credible legal arguments which can be applied in coursework, exams or presentations.

Learning Legal Skills and Reasoning:

- Discusses how to find and understand sources of both domestic and European Union Law.
- Develops effective disciplined study techniques, including referencing, general reading, writing and oral skills and explains how to make good use of the university print and e-library.
- Contains chapters on writing law essays, problem questions and examinations, and on oral skills including presentations and mediation skills.

Packed full of practical examples and diagrams across the range of legal skills from language and research skills to mooting and negotiation, this textbook will be invaluable to law students seeking to acquire a range of discrete legal skills in order to use them together to produce competent assessed work.

Sharon Hanson is a Senior Lecturer in Law at Canterbury Christ Church University where she teaches Legal Method, Criminal Law and Employment Law. Her research interests lie in law and religion.

1 MAR 2024

WITHDRAWN

York St John University

3 8025 00645201 8

LEARNING LEGAL SKILLS AND REASONING

Sharon Hanson

YORK ST. JOHN
LIBRARY & INFORMATION
SERVICES

 Routledge
Taylor & Francis Group

LONDON AND NEW YORK

Fourth edition published 2016
by Routledge
2 Park Square, Milton Park, Abingdon, Oxon, OX14 4RN

and by Routledge
711 Third Avenue, New York, NY 10017

Routledge is an imprint of the Taylor & Francis Group, an informa business

© 2016 Sharon Hanson

The right of Sharon Hanson to be identified as author of this work has been asserted by her in accordance with sections 77 and 78 of the Copyright, Designs and Patents Act 1988.

All rights reserved. No part of this book may be reprinted or reproduced or utilised in any form or by any electronic, mechanical, or other means, now known or hereafter invented, including photocopying and recording, or in any information storage or retrieval system, without permission in writing from the publishers.

Trademark notice: Product or corporate names may be trademarks or registered trademarks, and are used only for identification and explanation without intent to infringe.

First edition published 1999 by Cavendish Publishing Ltd

Third edition published 2010 by Routledge

British Library Cataloguing-in-Publication Data
A catalogue record for this book is available from the British Library

Library of Congress Cataloging-in-Publication Data
Hanson, Sharon, LLB. author.
  [Legal method, skills and reasoning]
  Learning legal skills and reasoning / Sharon Hanson. — Fourth Edition.
    pages cm
  1. Law—Great Britain—Methodology. 2. Law—Great Britain—
Interpretation and construction. 3. Law—Great Britain—Language.
  4. Law—Methodology. I. Title.
   KD640.H36 2016
   340'.1—dc23
   2015016572

ISBN: 978-0-415-83020-1 (hbk)
ISBN: 978-0-415-83019-5 (pbk)
ISBN: 978-1-315-67847-4 (ebk)

Typeset in Helvetica Neue by Apex CoVantage, LLC

For the next generations; my children Amy and Ben Hanson, my niece Daisy Robinson and my nephew John O'Rourke.

CONTENTS

List of figures   *xxxi*
List of tables   *xxxv*
Preface   *xxxix*
Acknowledgements   *xli*
Introduction to the book   *1*

PART 1: SOURCES OF LAW   **7**

1   Domestic legislation   **9**
    Learning outcomes   9
    Introduction   10
    What is domestic legislation?   10
       Naming conventions for legislation   11
       The statute book   11
       Finding legislation   12
    What is Parliament?   14
       The House of Commons   14
       The House of Lords   14
       Royal Assent   14
       The power of government to create legislation   15
    Types of domestic legislation: primary and secondary   15
       Types of primary legislation   15
          Public General Acts   15
          Private Acts   15
          Hybrid Acts   16
          Orders in Council by virtue of the royal prerogative   16
          Private members' bills   16
          Introducing a private member's' bill in the House of Commons 16
          The ballot   16
          The ten minute rule (under House of Commons Standing
             Order 23)   17
          Presentation (House of Commons Standing Order 39)   17
          Introducing a private member's bill into the House of Lords   17

The procedures leading to the enactment of a Public General Act 17
Pre-legislative procedures for a Public General Bill 17
Public consultation, Green Papers and White Papers 18
Drafting of a Public General bill by parliamentary counsel 18
The parliamentary legislative timetable 19
The passage of a public bill through Parliament 19
Passage of a bill through the House of Commons 20
Passage of a bill through the House of Lords 22
Amendment consideration 22
Royal Assent 23
Date in force of the Act 23
Secondary legislation 23
Parliamentary control over secondary legislation 25
Procedure for making statutory instruments 26
The negative resolution procedure 26
The affirmative resolution procedure 27
The super-affirmative procedure 27
Debates to affirm or annul SIs 27
Other parliamentary procedures 27
Lists of statutory instruments laid before Parliament 28
Using legislation and understanding judicial statutory interpretation 28
Conclusion 29
Chapter summary 29

2 Domestic case law **31**
Learning outcomes 31
Introduction 32
The development of the common law 32
Development of equity 35
Custom 37
English law and the doctrine of precedent 38
The courts 38
Generic term applied to courts 40
Description of the main domestic courts 40
Appellate courts 40
Superior courts 42
Inferior courts 44
Tribunals 47
Courts outside the hierarchical system of the English legal system 48
The Judicial Committee of the Privy Council 48
The European Court of Human Rights 51
ECtHR 51
The Court of Justice of the European Union 51
CJEU 51

The hierarchy of the domestic courts (with reference to tribunals
        and European courts)   51
Chapter summary   54

3   European and international treaties   **57**
Learning outcomes   57
Introduction   58
Definition of a treaty   58
The legal effect of treaties when concluded between states   58
   Public international law (PIL)   58
   The International Court of Justice (ICJ)   59
   The Vienna Convention on the Law of Treaties 1969 (VCLT)   59
       The contractual approach to treaties adopted by the
              states under the Vienna Convention   59
Synonyms for a treaty   60
The subject matter of treaties   60
The form taken by written treaties   60
Standard issues to bear in mind when dealing with treaties   60
   The standard layout of a treaty   60
       The preamble   62
       The main body of a treaty   62
   Parties to a treaty   63
   The process of formalising an agreement of states to be
              bound by a treaty   63
       Signature   63
       Ratification   64
   The methods to minimise dissent in the negotiation process
              of a treaty   64
       Reservations: occur during negotiation of the treaty   64
   When is a treaty actually 'in force'?   66
   The legal effect of a treaty   66
       Monist position   66
       Dualist position   66
   Treaty names   67
   General procedures for changing (amending) treaties   67
   Protocols   67
   New treaties   68
   Accession treaties   68
   Procedures for a state to cease to be bound by a treaty:
              abrogation/denunciation   69
Official records of treaties – originals and certified copies   69
Conclusion   70
Chapter summary   70

4   **European Convention on Human Rights**   **71**
Learning outcomes   71
Introduction   72
Understanding the Council of Europe   72
   Background to the establishment of the Council of Europe   73
   The Council of Europe flag and anthem for Europe   74
The institutions of the Council of Europe   74
European Court of Human Rights (ECtHR)   74
Understanding the European Convention on Human Rights 1950   76
   Pilot judgments of the ECtHR   77
   Leaving the ECHR   77
   Protocols to the ECHR   78
      Derogations and reservations   78
The ECHR, its protocols and their legal impact on English law   78
   The UK and violations of the ECHR and its protocols   79
   The treaties office of the Council of Europe   80
The UK Human Rights Act 1998 (HRA)   80
   Background to the Human Rights Act 1998 and current concerns   81
   The key sections of the Human Rights Act 1998   81
Conclusion   85
Chapter summary   85
   Understanding the Council of Europe   85
   Understanding the European Convention on Human Rights   85
   Understanding the Human Rights Act 1998   86

5   **European Union law**   **87**
Learning outcomes   87
Introduction   88
Understanding the European Union (EU)   89
   What is the EU?   89
   The founding treaties of the EU   89
   European citizens   89
   Core functions of the EU   89
Understanding the development of the EU through its
      treaties 1957–2007   90
   The Treaty of Rome (No 2) 1957, date in force 1 January 1958   91
   The Brussels Treaty 1965 (The Merger Treaty), date in force
      1 July 1967   91
   The Single European Act 1986 (SEA), date in force 1 July 1987   93
   The Treaty of Maastricht 1992 (TEU), date in force 1 November 1993   93
   The Treaty of Amsterdam 1997, date in force 1 May 1999   94
   The Treaty of Nice 2001, date in force 1 February 2003   94
   The 'failed' Constitutional Treaty 2004   94
   The Treaty of Lisbon 2007   95
   The main treaties   95

The consolidated version of the two founding treaties 2010   95
Table of equivalences   97
EU enlargement   97
Understanding the institutions of the EU   97
The European Council: the key policy/political institution   98
The three key institutions for law making   98
The European Commission (the Commission)   99
Law making powers   100
Judicial powers   100
The Council of the European Union (also referred
    to as the 'council of ministers' or the 'council')   100
Powers of the Council   100
Warning: potential naming confusions concerning institutions   100
The European Parliament (EP)   101
Court of Justice of the European Union (CJEU)   101
Understanding the EU legal order and EU law   102
The EU legal order: the acquis communautaire   102
The sources of EU law   102
Primary law of the EU   103
Secondary law of the EU   103
General principles of EU law (developed by the Court of
    Justice)   105
Hierarchy of legal norms   105
The legal effect of EU primary and secondary EU law   105
Effect of EU law on member states   106
EU law that is 'directly applicable'   106
EU law that is binding 'as to outcome': directives   106
The effect of EU law on private organisations and
    individuals: direct effect   106
Enforcement of EU law   109
The role of the Commission   109
The role of the CJEU in enforcing EU law   109
Preliminary rulings   110
Institutions acting in excess of their powers (ultra vires)   111
Understanding the supremacy of EU law and the impact
    of EU law on the English legal system   111
What does the EU understand by the supremacy of EU law?   111
English law and the supremacy of EU law   112
Conclusion   115
Chapter summary   115

PART 2: FINDING LAW – EFFECTIVE LEGAL RESEARCH   117

6   How to get the most out of your university print
    and e-library   119
Learning outcomes   119

Introduction   120
The general structure and layout of university law holdings   122
   The main library catalogue   122
Types of print materials and their standard locations   123
   Reference   124
   Thin resources (pamphlets)   124
   Parliamentary papers   124
   Journals   125
   Law reports   125
   Legislation   125
   Books   126
The structure and layout of the electronic collection   126
   Accessing the e-library collection   126
Types of electronic materials and their standard locations   127
   Public domain sites: open access free internet electronic
      sources located outside the e-library   131
Primary texts of law (whether print or online)   131
   Primary legal materials – texts of the law   131
Secondary texts about law (whether print or online)   132
Conclusion   132
Chapter summary   132

7   **How to find domestic and European legislation**   **135**
Learning outcomes   135
Introduction   136
How to locate primary domestic legislation   137
   Terminology   137
      Primary legislation   137
      Secondary legislation   138
      Year of enactment   138
      Date in force   138
   How to understand citations for domestic legislation   139
      Citation of primary legislation: Public General Acts   139
      Citation of secondary legislation: statutory instruments   140
      Citations and referencing your work   140
   How to locate statutes in print form in the university library   140
      Chronological table of statutes   141
      Current law legislation citators (containing current law statutes
         citator)   141
      Current Law Statutes annotated (from 1994 to 2000 it was
         called Current Law Statutes)   142
      Halsbury's Statutes   142
      Halsbury's 'Is it in force?'   143
      Destination tables   143
      Halsbury's Statutes Citator   145

Index to the Statutes (1235–1990)   145
Law Reports: Statutes   145
Public General Acts and measures   145
How to locate statutes online   145
The main subscription sites   146
Public domain 'free' sites   146
Public domain site: www.legislation.gov.uk   146
Guided exercise: Race Relations Act 1976   148
Finding legislation in print and electronic formats   152
How to locate secondary legislation   154
How to locate draft primary and secondary legislation   155
Locating draft primary legislation   155
Using the Parliament website (www.parliament.uk)   156
Locating draft secondary legislation   157
Searching for legislation on a subscription site: Westlaw   157
Primary legislation search   159
Secondary legislation   163
European treaties and secondary legislation   164
Print   164
Online   165
Locating the European Convention on Human Rights (ECHR)
        and its protocols   166
How can a student retrieve out of date law and get their
        answers to questions about legislation wrong?   166
Secondary texts: out of date textbooks, articles, etc.   167
Primary texts: law reports   167
Legislation databases   168
Questions to test your understanding of finding legislation   168
Conclusion   168
Chapter summary   169
Domestic legislation   169
EU treaties and legislation   169
Hard copy   169
Online   169
European Convention on Human Rights   170
Answers to questions   170

8   How to find domestic and European cases   171
Learning outcomes   171
Introduction   172
Locating cases in the English legal system   172
Terminology   173
The development of law reporting in the English legal system   174
Note on unreported cases generally   176
Case summaries and full text cases   176

The hierarchy of the law reports   177
    What is the relationship of electronic forms to print forms
        of law cases?   178
Choosing your legal authorities   179
How to understand citations   179
    Neutral citations   179
Understanding law report citations of the private publishers   181
    Year dates and law reports   182
        Date of reporting a case contrasted with date of hearing
            a case   183
    Case names   183
        Criminal cases   183
        Civil cases   184
        Correctly citing law cases before and after 2001   184
    How to locate cases in the print collections when you
        do not know the citation   185
    How to locate cases online   185
Searching for cases using online databases   190
    Subscription sites   190
        Westlaw   190
    Lexis®Library   193
    BAILII   194
European cases   195
    Locating European Union law cases   196
        Locating cases in print collections   196
        Locating cases online   198
    Understanding EU case citations   198
    Locating ECHR law reports from the ECtHR part
        of the Council of Europe   198
        Print collection   198
        E-collections   199
Chapter summary   199
    Domestic cases   199
    European Union cases   200
    European Convention cases from the European Court
        of Human Rights   201
    Unreported cases   201

9   **How to find secondary material: texts about law**   **203**
Learning outcomes   203
Introduction   204
General issues relating to searching for secondary texts   205
Search strategies   206
    Journal articles   207
        What are journals?   207

Journal title abbreviations   207
Journal article citations   208
  Finding online journals using Westlaw   208
  Finding journals on Lawtel   211
  Finding journals on Lexis®Library   211
  Finding journals on HeinOnline (www.heinonline.org)   211
Books   212
  The library catalogue   212
  Using print only materials   212
  General note on module 'set textbooks'   213
Locating official documents   213
Command papers   214
  Online access to command papers   215
  Locating parliamentary papers   215
  Finding reports of parliamentary debates   215
  Using TSO official documents online   217
Good practice with internet retrieval and evaluation of open
    access material   217
  Who has posted this?   218
  Why have they posted it?   218
  When was this information posted?   218
Conclusion   220
Chapter summary   220
  General   220
  Journal articles   220
  Books   220
  Official documents   221

PART 3: READING AND UNDERSTANDING LAW   **223**

10 **How to read and understand domestic cases**   **225**
Learning outcomes   225
Introduction   226
Legal dispute resolution in court   226
Introducing precedent   227
  Persuasive precedents   227
    Relationship between legislation and precedent   228
  Requirements for an effective system of precedent   228
    Hierarchy of the courts   229
  Understanding the theory of the doctrine of precedent   229
    What does 'similar' mean?   229
    Finding, understanding and using the reasoning in a case 230
    The differing strengths of a precedent   232
    Handling precedent in a series of cases   233
  Interpreting precedent in practice   235
  The practical implementation of the doctrine of precedent   236

Handling law reports   236
  Engaging with the language of judgments   236
  Law reports at appellate level   238
  Reading a law report: a series of guided exercises
    on *George Mitchell (Chesterhall) Ltd v Finney*
    Lock Seeds [1983] 2 AC (*George Mitchell* case) 238
The anatomy of a law report   239
  Obtaining a general overview of the case   241
  The basic reading of the case   243
  Consideration of your summary for task 4   244
  How useful is summary 1?   245
  What is useful in summary 2   245
  How to break into difficult text   247
  Strategy 1   248
  Strategy 2   249
  Strategy 3   249
  How to engage in a detailed reading of the judgment
    in this case to assist with understanding
    and summarising   250
  Activity   253
  Constructing a usable case note   273
Conclusion   274
Chapter summary   275
Activity writing a usable case note: question 1   275

11   **How to read and understand domestic legislation**   **279**
Learning outcomes   279
Introduction   280
The layout of a statute   281
Using and handling a statute   281
  The overall structure of legislation   283
  The importance of careful research to ensure that the
    legislation you have is the latest version   288
  The importance of understanding the layout of individual
    sections and links between sections   289
  Locating the purpose of the section you are considering:
    exploring s 9 of the Equality Act 2010   289
  The explanatory notes re: s 9 of the Equality Act 2010   292
  Section 4 of the Equality Act 2010   292
  Understanding the impact of changes to statutes   293
  Activity: Questions on section 9   295
  Linking a series of sections due to their interconnections   296
  Reading s 13 of the Equality Act 2010   296
  Reading s 19 of the Equality Act 2010   297
  Activity   297

Consolidation exercise   299
Statutory interpretation   300
   The general idea of interpretation   301
   Judicial interpretation   301
The neutrality and objectivity of law   301
   The rules of statutory interpretation   302
   The three main rules of statutory interpretation   304
     The literal rule   305
     The golden rule   305
     The mischief rule   306
     The purposive rule   306
     The teleological approach   307
     Other aids to statutory interpretation   307
     Which rules of interpretation should be used, when,
       and in what order?   310
   Statutory interpretation and the European Convention on
       Human Rights   311
   Statutory interpretation and secondary legislation   312
   Summary to statutory interpretation   312
Conclusion   313
Chapter summary   313
Consolidation to Exercise (comparison between s 9 of the Equality
       Act 2010 and s 3 of the Race Relations Act 1976)   314

12   How to read and understand ECHR and EU law   315
Learning outcomes   315
Introduction   316
Section 1: Civil law legal systems   316
   Differences between civil law systems and the English
       common law legal system   317
Section 2: Understanding and reading EU law   317
The legal system of the EU: the acquis communautaire   318
   The nature of the trial process in the EU civil law legal
       system: the acquis communautaire   319
    What type of case gets to the CJEU?   319
   Requesting a preliminary ruling   320
    When should a state court seek a preliminary reference?   320
   Procedure to be followed by a domestic court in the English legal
       system when making a preliminary reference   322
   Guided exercise: Reading and understanding the case of *van Gend
       en Loos v Nederlandse Tariefcommissie* (Case 26/62)
       [1963] ECR 3 (van Gend en Loos) page 00095 (AGO
       page 00001).   323
   The initial reading of the judgment in Van Gend en Loos   324
   The second reading: the tabulated micro-analysis of the case   324

Comment on van Gend en Loos   338
Reading and understanding the primary and secondary law of the EU   339
   The anatomy of EU primary and secondary law   339
   Primary law of the EU: treaties   339
Secondary law of the EU: regulations, directives, decisions,
      recommendations, opinions and general principles of law
      established by the Court of Justice of the EU   341
   Regulations   342
   Directives   343
Reading and understanding the law relating to the European
      Convention on Human Rights (ECHR)   345
Understanding the structure and layout of the ECHR   345
The rights contained in the ECHR   346
   Adding new rights to the ECHR via protocols   348
   Making amendments and repeals to articles in the ECHR   349
The importance of up to date knowledge of the ECHR
      and its protocols   350
CJEU and Convention   350
Understanding ECtHR cases   350
   Procedure in court   350
Reports of cases   351
Understanding and reading cases in the ECtHR   351
The Human Rights Act 1998   353
Guiding you through aspects of reading the HRA   356
   The structure of the Human Rights Act   356
   The Convention rights   356
      Illustrative examples of issues raised by the ECHR
         in relation to UK cases   358
Conclusion   359
Chapter summary   360
   EU law   360
   Understanding the law relating to the ECHR   360
   Understanding the Human Rights Act 1998   360

PART 4: LEGAL REASONING SKILLS   361

13   How to construct an argument   363
Learning outcomes   363
Introduction   364
What is an argument?   364
   Developing your skills of argument   365
   Critical thinking   367
Problems and rules   372
   The nature of problems   372
   Solving problems   373
   The nature of rules   375
      Legal rules   376

Constructing arguments   377
How to argue   377
  Evidence   378
    The role of judicial judgments in argument construction   379
Logic   379
  Deduction   381
  Induction   382
  Analogous reasoning   384
Conclusion   384
Chapter summary   384

14 English legal reasoning: theory and practice   387

Learning outcomes   388
Introduction   388
Legal reasoning theory   388
  Natural law   389
  Positivism   389
  Legal realism   390
  The critical legal theory movement   391
English legal reasoning in practice   392
  Legal argument   392
    Argument by analogy   395
    The building blocks of an inductive argument   396
  Factual analysis   397
  Legal analysis   402
  The use of 'inference' in argument construction   403
How do you critique a deductive or inductive reasoning?   406
Attacking the major premise of a deductive argument   406
  How can the defence attack the major proposition?   406
  How can the defence attack the minor proposition?   407
  The importance of careful argument construction   408
Putting it all together: A guided case study: *R v Mary*   409
  (1) The charge   409
  (2) The governing legal rule   409
  (3) Evidence   409
  Statement 1: William   409
  Statement 2: Andrew   410
  Statement 3: Mary   410
  (1) Clarification of standpoint   410
  (2) Analysis of the legal rule   411
  (3) Analysis of the facts   411
Activity 14.1: Analysing the witness statements   411
  The analysis of *R v Mary*   413
  Element 1: Appropriates (*actus reus*)   413
  Element 2: Property   414
  Element 3: Belonging to another   414
  Element 4: Dishonesty (*mens rea*)   414

Element 5: With the intention to deprive permanently
    (*mens rea*)   416
Conclusion   416
Chapter summary   416

15 European legal reasoning   **419**
Learning outcomes   419
Introduction   420
The drafting of legislation in civilian legal systems   420
The general approach to legal reasoning and interpretation
    in civilian legal systems   421
The approach to reasoning and interpretation by the CJEU   422
Interpretation, legal reasoning and the multiplicity of
    languages in the EU   424
    Extra-legal strategies in decision making   426
        The style of EU judgments   427
        The use of past cases in the CJEU   427
Legal reasoning in the European Court of Human Rights   428
Conclusion   429
Chapter summary   429

PART 5: GENERAL ACADEMIC SKILLS   **431**
16 Study skills   **433**
Learning outcomes   433
Introduction   434
    Activity 16.1: What are your goals?   435
What is studying?   435
    Studying law at university   436
What is learning?   437
    How do you like to learn?   437
    Learning styles   437
        Cottrell's learning styles   438
        Kolb's learning styles   439
        Honey and Mumford's learning styles   439
    Which learning style should you use, and should you stick
        to one?   440
    Activity 16.2: Finding out your learning style   440
    Why should you know your learning style?   443
What is independent study?   443
How to develop habits of independent learning   444
The cycles, patterns and schedules of standard university study   445
    The pattern of your degree   445
        Modules   445

The cycle of the academic year   446
   Planning your weekly and termly timetable of taught classes
      and independent study   450
The range of skills required for successful legal study   455
   Competent understanding of the use of the electronic
      communication in your department   456
Making the best use of your department's teaching arrangements   457
   One to one learning opportunities with staff   458
      Lecturer office hours/drop in hour   458
   Lectures   458
Seminars/tutorials   459
   Working in groups with fellow students (formally and informally)   459
Personal development planning (PDP)   460
Conclusion   461
Chapter summary   461

17   General reading skills   463
Learning outcomes   463
Introduction   464
Reading skills   464
   Reading with a purpose   465
   The three main methods of approaching reading   466
      Scanning   466
      Skimming   466
      Detailed reading   467
   Reading speeds: how long does it take to read a text?   467
      Increasing reading speeds   467
      Activity 17.1: How to find out your reading speed for
         an academic text   468
      Activity 17.2: One method for increasing reading speeds,
         increasing 'eye fix'   470
   The four stages of reading: a strategy for efficient reading   472
      Activity 17.3: Reading exercise designed to allow you to use
         the reading strategy when reading an academic article:
         JJ Weiler 'The European Union belongs to its citizens:
         Three immodest proposals' (1997) 22 EL Rev 150–156   474
Guided demonstration of the reading strategy for JHH Weiler
      'The European Union belongs to its citizens'   475
   Stage 1: Preparation prior to reading   475
      Reader goal(s)/intention(s)   475
      Reader prediction of use and content of text   477
   Stage 2: Methods of reading   477
      Skimming   478
      Activity 17.4: Reading the whole of the introduction in our
         article   479
      Scanning   480

Metaphor   482
How does metaphor work – the source domain and
    the target domain of a metaphor   483
Alliteration   484
Example of the identification and interpretation of figurative
    language (alliteration, repetition and metaphor)   484
Metaphors in the article 'The European Union belongs
    to its citizens'   487
Activity 17.5: Beginning to read and understand metaphors
    Deciphering 'The proof of the pudding is in the eating'   487
Connecting and joining words/phrases   488
Activity 17.6: Being aware of cohesive and connecting words
    and phrases   488
Stage 3: Understanding what is being read   489
Guessing words/phrases you do not know   489
Guessing words by understanding the construction of
    English words (affixes)   489
Identifying ideas/arguments   492
Identifying overall text organisation   493
Stage 4: Evaluating what you are reading   493
How to evaluate the strength and weakness of argument
    presented   494
Evidence for an essay 'Does the European Union Belong
    to its Citizens?'   495
Conclusion   498
Chapter summary   499

18   **General writing skills**   **501**
Learning outcomes   501
Introduction   502
Developing your written voice: your writing style   502
Activity 18.1: Finding your voice   503
The requirements of formal academic language   504
An objective style should be used, that does not
    in any shape or form refer to the person of the writer   504
Gendered or gender neutral language?   505
Incorporating the work of others in your writing   505
The structure and organisation of written work   505
Grammar and punctuation   506
Grammar   506
What is grammar?   506
What are morphology and syntax?   507
Why is knowledge of basic grammar important?   508
What is punctuation?   508
Why is it important to use correct punctuation?   508

Vocabulary   516
  Extending your general vocabulary   516
  Extending your technical legal vocabulary   517
  Issues with spelling   517
    Use dictionaries and thesauruses   518
  Understanding the relationship between sentences and paragraphs   519
Writing notes   520
  Strategies for note taking   522
    What should notes contain?   522
  The structure of notes   523
    Linear text   523
    Diagrams   523
  Notes from verbal presentations   524
    Note taking symbols and abbreviations   526
    Questions arising in your mind as you write notes   527
    Note-making templates   528
Conclusion   528
Chapter summary   529

19 Referencing and avoiding plagiarism   531

Learning outcomes   531
Introduction   532
What is referencing?   533
  When should you reference?   533
  Referencing systems   535
    How to use the referencing tools in your word processing package   535
How to use the OSCOLA system of referencing   535
  How do I use OSCOLA?   536
    Where to place a raised numerical marker in your text   536
  Referencing primary source material   537
    What is a legal citation?   537
    UK cases   537
    Pinpoint referencing using cases   541
  Referencing secondary sources   542
    Books and journal articles   542
    Making direct and indirect references from books/articles   546
    Saving time? OSCOLA footnoting protocols when a full
        reference has already been given   548
    Compiling bibliographies, tables of cases and tables of
        statutes using OSCOLA   548
How to use the Harvard referencing system   550
The in-text reference   551
  In-text referencing protocols   551
Referencing UK cases and legislation in Harvard   554
Shortcuts in Harvard referencing   555

Plagiarism 555
What is plagiarism? 555
What is the sanction for plagiarism? 556
Conclusion 556
Chapter summary 557

20 General oral skills 559
Learning outcomes 559
Introduction 560
Oral skills exercises 560
Understanding 561
Managing the task 561
Overall task management 562
Time limits 564
Managing stress 564
Research 564
Understanding the question 564
Delivery 565
Body language 565
Team working 566
Conclusion 566
Chapter summary 567

PART 6: LAW ASSESSMENTS: WRITTEN AND ORAL 569

21 Writing law essays 571
Learning outcomes 571
Introduction 572
Characteristics of legal language 572
English words that have come to develop a special meaning in law 574
The importance of wider reading and careful note taking 574
What is an essay? 575
What is the purpose of an essay? 576
What standard formats are used for essay questions? 576
Structuring your essay 577
The function of the essay introduction 580
The main body of the text (body text) 580
The conclusion 581
Method for the preparation and construction of essays 581
Stage 1: Carefully reflect on the question 581
Stage 2: Search for relevant texts 586
Stage 3: Carefully read, make notes, organise and reflect
on the material collected 586
Law cases 586
Textbooks 586
Academic books and articles 587

Stage 4: Begin to form a view of possible arguments
    to be used to answer the question 587
Stage 5: Consider the strength of your argument 588
Stage 6: Begin to write the essay plan outline 589
  Introduction 589
  Body text 589
  Conclusion 589
Stage 7: Write the first draft of the essay 589
Stage 8: Write the final version of the essay 590
  A special note on presentation: editing, formatting and referencing 590
  Word limits and editing 591
Conclusion 591
Chapter summary 592

22 Writing answers to legal problem questions 593
Learning outcomes 593
Introduction 594
  What range of skills are tested and developed
    by problem questions? 595
  General academic study skills 595
  Legal reasoning skills 597
  Skills relating to legal problem solution 597
Methods for the preparation and construction of answers
    to problem questions 597
Methods for writing solutions to problem questions 598
The four general stages of problem solution methodology 598
  Stage 1: Identification of the legal issues arising from the
    facts in the problem question 600
  Identification of all relevant facts given in the problem question 600
  Identification of the primary and secondary legal issues
    raised by the facts 600
  Checking the capacity of the defendant or a litigant to be
    held liable 600
  Stage 2: Identification of all relevant legal rules 600
  Determine the relevant legal rules relating to any breach of law 600
  Stage 3: Application of relevant legal rules to the legal
    issues identified 601
  Carefully consider doubts/interpretational issues and ask
    yourself what you consider to be the appropriate
    response to them 601
  Discussion of applicable defences/mitigation 601
  Stage 4: Your determination of liability based on your
    prediction of the likely application of the law 601
The structure of your final written answer 601
  (1) Introduction 602
  (2) Main body: The worked out answer to problem question 602
  (3) Conclusion 602

A guided demonstration of the basics of the four stage problem
    solving method, using problem question 2 in
      Table 22.1 as an example   604
Stage 1: Identification of the legal issues arising from the facts
    in the problem question   604
Stage 2: Identification of all relevant legal rules   604
Stage 3: Application of relevant legal rules to the legal
    issues identified   606
Stage 4: Your determination of liability based on your
    prediction of the likely application of the law   608
Conclusion   609
Chapter summary   609

23 Examination strategies   **611**
Learning outcomes   611
Introduction   612
Find out about the structure of your exams   612
Drawing up a list of potentially examinable topics   614
Drawing together information on your examinable topics   615
Making an inventory of examinable topics so that you can
    choose your revision topics   615
Stress and exam performance   615
Assumptions about what exams are testing   618
Assumption 1: Exams are a test of how much information
    I can remember   618
Assumption 2: Exams are a test of the quality of my
    reasoning powers   619
Assumption 3: Exams are a test of my techniques for
    answering examination questions   620
Assumption 4: Exams are a test of how well I can take apart
    an examination question   620
Assumption 5: Exams test how quickly I can write in the
    time allowed   620
Assumption 6: Exams test how well I can argue   620
Assumption 7: Exams test how clever I am   621
What does your university lecturer expect you to demonstrate in
    your exam?   621
The art of careful exam preparation – revision   622
Preparing a revision timetable   623
Compiling the list of topics that you will revise   624
Assisting your memory   629
How long before the exam should I start revising?   631
Revision activities and how to keep motivated (boredom
    sabotages revision!)   631
The day of the examination   632
Strategies during the examination   632
(4) Structuring essays   633
(5) Structuring problem answers   633

Conclusion 634
Chapter summary 634

24 Presentation skills **637**
Learning outcomes 637
Introduction 638
The six stages of the presentation 638
(1) Understanding the nature of the task: what is a presentation? 638
(2) Managing the task 639
Time limits 639
(3) Research 639
Notes and sources 640
(4) Content of the presentation 641
Ensure that your presentation is relevant to the question 641
Ensure that you build competent arguments 641
(5) Delivery 642
Your voice 642
Using appropriate high quality audio-visual aids 644
Using useful presenter prompts 644
Team issues on delivery 644
Conclusion 644
Chapter summary 644
Ensure that your presentation is relevant to the questions 645
Ensure that you build competent arguments 645
Use appropriate high quality audio-visual aids 646
Use presenter prompts 646

25 Mooting skills **647**
Learning outcomes 647
Introduction 648
What is mooting? 648
'Why should I moot?' 648
But – I am too nervous to moot! 649
The roles of the various participants in a moot 649
The moot master 649
The judge 650
The clerk 650
Counsel 650
Senior and junior counsel 650
Counsel for the appellants 651
Counsel for the respondents 651
The general rules of engagement governing moots 651
Case limitation 652
Time limits 652
Turn taking in a moot, the 'order of submissions' 652
The 'right to reply' 653
Judicial questions to mooters 653

The skeleton argument 653
Bundles 654
Dress codes 654
Correct forms of address in relation to participants in the moot 654
Correct oral references to case citations 655
A model for mooting 655
Stage 1: Analysis of the moot problem 656
Which court? 656
Understanding the procedural history of the moot 656
Clarification of which party you are representing in the moot 656
Analysis of the facts 657
Issues of fact and issues of law 658
Court authorities 658
Analysis of the grounds of appeal 658
Stage 2: Legal research 658
Questions to inform your legal research 659
The statement of current law 659
Resources to be accessed 659
Construction of legal argument 661
Your legal argument 661
Preparing the content of your speech in court 662
Oral delivery 662
Using correct forms of address when mooting 663
Deliver your speech 667
Do not read it! 667
When delivering your speech do use prompt notes 667
Your tone of voice 667
Pacing of your speaking voice for the speech 668
Dealing with judicial interventions 668
'Practice makes perfect' 668
Conclusion 668
Chapter summary 669

26 **Negotiation skills** **671**
Learning outcomes 671
Introduction 672
What is negotiation? 672
Range of skills required for negotiation 672
The skills you bring with you to negotiation 673
The two main forms of negotiation 673
Positional negotiation 673
Principled negotiation 674
The process of a negotiation 674
Guided narrative on the stages in a negotiation 675
Pre-negotiation planning 676

First meeting with your team and becoming familiar
    with the client instructions   676
Second meeting with the team and allocation of tasks   676
Third team meeting and decisions concerning application
    of law, negotiating strategies and division of tasks
    in-negotiation   677
In-negotiation strategy   677
Post-negotiation critical review   679
   Agenda for post-negotiation review   679
   Team-working issues   679
   Individual issues   679
   The appropriateness of the negotiation strategy – pre-planning   679
Conclusion   680
Chapter summary   680

27 Mediation skills: Ben Waters   **683**
Learning outcomes   683
Introduction   684
What is mediation?   684
   The foundational principles of mediation   684
The mediation process   685
   The phases of mediation   686
   The four phases of a typical mediation   687
      Phase 1: Opening   687
      Phase 2: Exploration   688
      Phase 3: Bargaining   689
      Phase 4: Concluding   690
Mediation skills   692
   The skills you bring to mediation   692
      Positivity: [B] 2   692
      Questioning: [B] 3   694
      Listening skills: [B] 4   695
Activity 27.1: Reframing exercise   697
Conclusion   697
Chapter summary   698
Activity 27.1: Suggested answers   698

Conclusions   *701*
Further reading and useful websites   *705*
Index   *709*

FIGURES

I.1	The function of this 'how to' text	5
1.1	Correct reference to primary legislation	12
1.2	Synonyms for secondary legislation and types of secondary legislation	13
1.3	Types of secondary legislation	24
1.4	Statutory instruments: meaning of terms of art: laid, made, in force	26
1.5	Types of UK domestic legislation	27
2.1	UK court structure: also showing its relationship with the tribunals, the Privy Council and two key European courts	53
3.1	Standard issues to bear in mind when dealing with treaties	61
3.2	The layout of a treaty	62
3.3	Dualist and monist legal traditions	67
3.4	Changing a treaty	68
4.1	The institutions of the Council of Europe	75
4.2	Statutory duties imposed by ss 2–4, 6 and 19 of the HRA 1998	84
5.1	Areas you need to understand when dealing with European Union law	88
5.2	The legal competency of European Union law	90
5.3	EU treaties 1957–2007	92
5.4	The three pillars of the European Union	93
5.5	The key law making institutions of the EU	98
5.6	The three key institutions for law making	99
5.7	The general principles of EU law	104
5.8	Possible horizontal and vertical legal direct effect	107
5.9	Basic procedure for a preliminary ruling under Article 267 of TFEU	110
6.1	How the volume of different types of legal resources compare	121
6.2	A selection of legal resources available on the internet	128
6.3	A selection of the different types of legal internet sites	129
6.4	Types of resources in standard university library collections	130
7.1	Annotated screenshot of home page	147
7.2	Screenshot of retrieved Race Relations Act	149
7.3	Screenshot of changes to legislation results for the Race Relations Act 1976	150
7.4	Screenshot of changes to the Race Relations Act 1976, with entry noting its repeal highlighted	150
7.5	Screenshot of UK Statutory Instruments	155
7.6	Screenshot of the whereabouts of the Affordable Homes Bill 2014–2015	156
7.7	Screenshot of SIs sub divided by methods for approval	158

7.8   Screenshot of Statutory Instruments Lost No 14, 7 November 2014   158
7.9   Screenshot of the list of statutory instruments subject to the
       negative resolution   159
7.10   Annotated front page of Westlaw showing quick search boxes   160
7.11   Westlaw: retrieved results for a search of 'Race Relations Act'   161
7.12   Westlaw: advanced search page   162
7.13   Westlaw: result of search for versions of Race Relations Act 1976, s 3   162
7.14   Screenshot of Eur-lex home page   165
8.1   The types of generalist reports available in print and online   175
8.2   Constituent parts of a neutral citation   180
8.3   Court structure showing neutral citation abbreviations used for court and
       jurisdiction   180
8.4   Constituent parts of citation for a criminal case published in the ICLR
       Law Reports series   184
8.5   Constituent parts of citation for a civil case published in the ICLR Law
       Reports series   184
8.6   Retrieved results 1–3   191
8.7   Westlaw: Screenshot of login page   192
8.8   Westlaw: screenshot of detailed search in cases   192
8.9   Lexis®Library screenshot of quick find page   193
8.10   Lexis®Library screenshot of cases web page   194
8.11   Lexis®Library screenshot of retrieved cases   195
8.12   Bailii: Screenshot of sign in page   196
8.13   Case law search options   197
8.14   Bailii screenshot of retrieved case of George Mitchell v Finney Lock Seeds   197
8.15   The constituent parts of a European law report citation   199
9.1   Accessing Parliamentary Papers   216
9.2   Deconstructing the URL of the http://www.canterbury.ac.uk/induction
       /students website   219
10.1   UK court structure: with arrows showing hierarchical relationships   228
10.2   Q & As on similarities   230
10.3   Wambaugh's method for location of the precedent   231
10.4   Differing methods of finding the ratio   232
10.5   A flow chart to determine whether a previous reported law case
       (previous case) is a precedent for the case you are considering currently
       (current case)   234
10.6   Issues to be considered when handling law reports   237
10.7   The anatomy of a standard law report (using the George Mitchell case)   239
10.8   Anatomy of a law report: first two pages of ICLR Appeal Court law report of
       George Mitchell v Finney Lock Seeds [1983] 2 AC 803   240
10.9   Screenshot of George Mitchell v Finney Lock Seeds   240
10.10 Screenshot of retrieved case of George Mitchell v Finney Lock Seeds
       indicating anatomy of the report as shown   241
10.11 The basic framework of the law of contract   242
10.12 The procedural history of the case   246
10.13 Verbatim text of G & H of Lord Bridge's judgment on p 811 set out in
       different text layout to aid understanding   249
10.14 Verbatim text of Lord Bridge from page 811, with annotations to check
       for understanding   250
10.15 Annotation of Lord Bridge's paragraphs G & H p 811 of his judgment   251

10.16 The imposition of relabelling on the relevant condition 252
10.17 Layout of the modified s 55 of the Sale of Goods Act 1979 263
10.18 Revised diagram of section 55 264
10.19 Summary: court's rationale for decision 272
11.1 Skills required for understanding legislation 280
11.2 The different elements of a statute 282
11.3 Screenshot of arrangement of Equality Act 2010 284
11.4 pdf from Westlaw of original print version open at table of contents 285
11.5 Screenshot of the Equality Act 2010 showing part of the table of contents
     from www.legislation.gov.uk (accessed 29/10/14) 286
11.6 Screenshot of changes to s1 Equality Act from www.legislation.gov.uk
     (accessed 29/10/14) 286
11.7 The general layout of the Equality Act 2010 287
11.8 Tree diagram of s 9 of the Equality Act 2010 as originally enacted.
     Blue text indicates that a sub-section has subsequently been amended. 291
11.9 Layout of s 9 of the Equality Act 2010 292
11.10 Layout of s 19 298
11.11 Comparison of S3 RRA 1976 and s9 EA 2010 299
11.12 The three main official rules of statutory interpretation 304
12.1 Illustration of the basic layout of a regulation 343
12.2 Illustration of the basic layout of a directive 344
12.3 The layout of the ECHR 346
12.4 The layout of the human rights act 1998 357
13.1 The Latin, French and English meanings of 'to argue' 365
13.2 Different meanings of the word 'argument' as used in English 366
13.3 Skills required for good argument construction 367
13.4 Twining and Miers' problem-solving model 374
13.5 The definition of a rule 375
13.6 Classification of rules 376
13.7 A vocabulary of rule-making verbs 377
13.8 Definition of logic 380
13.9 The components of a deductive reasoning argument 382
13.10 Types of standard generalisations which can find their way into inductive
      argument 383
14.1 Section 1 of the Theft Act and the five required elements in the definition
     of theft 398
14.2 Basic argument for the prosecution in the case of *R v Anna* showing
     relationships between inductive and deductive reasoning 404
14.3 Arguments are based on propositions, evidence and proof 405
14.4 Evaluation of activity 412
16.1 The cycle of the academic year 447
17.1 Interconnection between the four stages of reading 476
17.2 Examples of figurative language 488
17.3 Weiler's argument in diagrammatic form 496
17.4 Comparing Weiler's argument with hypothetical other texts 497
17.5 Conclusion for a sample essay question 498
18.1 Example spray diagram using the keyword 'STUDY' 524
18.2 Example mind map using the keyword 'STUDY' 525
18.3 Screenshot of power point (ppt) printed in hand out mode 526
19.1 Checklist for when to reference source material 534

19.2   Examples of different placement of superscript footnote numerals in OSCOLA   536
19.3   Example reference 1: *Adler v George* [1964] 2 QB 7 (QB)   542
19.4   Example reference 2: *Evans v Amicus Healthcare Ltd* [2004]
       EWCA Civ 727; [2005] Fam 1   543
19.5   Example reference 3: *R v Moloney* [1985] 2 AC 905 (HL)   544
19.6   Example reference 4: *R v Rafferty* [2007] EWCA Crim 1846; [2008]
       Crim LR 218   545
19.7   Demonstration of insertion of short and long verbatim quotations in text   546
19.8   Correct pinpoint reference for book   546
19.9   Correct pinpoint reference for a journal article   546
19.10 Latin references as referencing shortcuts   549
20.1   Types of oral skills exercises   561
20.2   Summarises the nature of these six components   562
20.3   The inter related components of competent oral skills exercises   563
21.1   Examples of essay questions   577
21.2   Method for the preparation and construction of essays   582
21.3   Radial diagram for essay question 3   584
21.4   Annotated version of essay question 4   585
22.1   Four stage method of problem solution mapped against standard
       structure of written solution   603
22.2   First breakdown of problem question: Initial questions that will begin a
       breakdown of questions to form legal issues and lay the foundation of a
       search through relevant case law   605
22.3   Locating the contract   607
23.1   The range of skills that examiners look for   621
23.2   Revision session timing   624
23.3   Revision activities   631
23.4   Good habits on exam day   632
24.1   Eight initial questions flowing from a proper consideration of the
       demonstration presentation question: 'Should the English legal system
       allow a cultural defence as a valid plea in criminal cases?'   640
25.1   Model 1   652
25.2   Model 2   652
25.3   Model for approaching mooting   655
26.1   The three stages of negotiation   674
26.2   The basic macro-level of arrangements for the negotiation   675
26.3   The micro-dynamics of the negotiation   678
27.1   The dispute resolution continuum   685
27.2   Common civil/commercial mediation phases   686
27.3   Mediator skills   693

TABLES

2.1	An illustrative list of equitable maxims, remedies and rights	36
2.2	Range of references to role/hierarchy of court	40
2.3	Supreme Court, and the Court of Appeal: function judges and jurisdiction	43
2.4	Superior courts: High Court and Crown Court: role, judges, divisions and jurisdiction	45
2.5	Inferior courts: county court and magistrates' court: role, judges and jurisdiction	46
2.6	Tribunals tier system: role, adjudicators and jurisdiction	49
2.7	Privy council: function, role, judges, and jurisdiction	50
2.8	European Courts impacting the English legal system; role and jurisdiction	52
4.1	European Court of Human Rights: sittings, appointment of judges, jurisdiction, procedure, judgments and enforcement: ECHR requires all hearings to be in public	76
5.1	Chronological list of treaties developing the EU	96
5.2	Current treaties of the EU in force	97
5.3	Trying to avoid naming confusions!	101
5.4	Core sources of EU law	103
5.5	Hierarchy of legal norms	105
7.1	Quick reference: accessing primary legislation using print and electronic sources	152
7.2	Quick access: How to locate domestic secondary legislation (SI) in print and online	163
8.1	Technical meaning of key words/phrases used in relation to court cases and their reporting	173
8.2	Abbreviations for law reports published in print	182
8.3	Correctly citing law cases before and after 2001	185
8.4	How to locate law reports in print collections	186
8.5	How to locate law reports: online databases	188
9.1	Illustrative examples of journal, type, areas and abbreviations	208
9.2	Journal abbreviations	209
9.3	Full citation of journal articles	210
10.1	Comparing verbatim text of Lord Bridge's judgment in *George Mitchell v Finney Lock Seeds* illustrating accurate summarising of the range of legal issues and the argument as it is built by Lord Bridge	254
10.2	Information required for a case note	273

11.1	s 9 EA annotated	290
11.2		294
12.1	Guided reading (van Gend en Loos)	325
12.2	Guided reading: Annotated of the verbatim text of NV Algemene Transport-en Expeditie Onderneming van Gend & Loos v Netherlands Inland Revenue 1963 ECR Administration [1963] ECR 3	326
12.3	The layout of a treaty: standard layout	340
12.4	The standard layout of a regulation	342
12.5	The standard layout of a directive	345
12.6	ECHR Section I: Article 1 the General Obligation and Articles 2–18 the Convention rights consolidated version 2010 including Protocol 14	347
12.7	Absolute rights or unqualified rights, limited rights and qualified rights	348
12.8	Procedural history of *Al-Skeini and others v the United Kingdom* (Application no. 55721/07) taken from non-official private report (2011) 53 EHRR 18	354
16.1	Cottrell's learning styles	438
16.2	Kolb's learning styles	439
16.3	Honey and Mumford's learning styles	440
16.4	What is your style of learning, and what are you willing to try?	441
16.5	Typical academic cycle for a year 1 student on a degree divided into terms	448
16.6	Hypothetical year 1 subject showing teaching hours and independent study hours	451
16.7	Term 1 personal weekly timetable showing fixed points for attending taught sessions	453
16.8	The skills required for the successful study of law	455
17.1	A strategy for competent reading	472
17.2	The meaning of figurative language generally and its main forms: descriptions and examples	481
17.3	The constituent parts of English words	489
17.4	English affixes derived from other languages (mainly Latin, Greek and French) and used to construct English words	490
17.5	illustrates how the word stem, the core of the word, is also in many cases derived from other languages	491
17.6	Using translations of affixes to guess at the meanings of words	491
17.7	The evidence supporting propositions 1–3 forwarded by Weiler and the conclusion drawn	492
18.1	Grammar: Explanation of terms and detail concerning conventional use of grammar	509
18.2	Punctuation symbols: names, functions and examples	512
18.3	What do you do with an 'e'?	517
18.4	Understanding the role of sentences and paragraphs in the construction of writing	519
19.1	Types of material that will require referencing (non-exhaustive)	537
19.2	Making direct and indirect referencing decisions using OSCOLA	547
19.3	Single authors: Making direct and indirect referencing decisions using Harvard	552
19.4	Indirect reference to multiple authors	553
19.5	Multiple authors: Making reference to multiple texts by one author using Harvard	554
19.6	Dealing with the referencing of edited volumes	554

21.1	General: Latin abbreviations used in standard academic writing and legal writing	573
21.2	Definition of standard words used in essay instructions	578
22.1	Two specimen problem questions	596
22.2	Indication of the ranges of methods of the analysis of problem questions and indication of ideal structure of your final answer to problem question	599
23.1	A sample exam inventory chart	613
23.2	A sample hypothetical examinable topics inventory chart for criminal law	616
23.3	Testing your assumptions about exams	619
23.4	Sample revision timetable	625
23.5	Sample knowledge summary for examinable topics	628
23.6	Learning styles and memory tactics for enhancing your revision	630
25.1	Ordering of legal argument	664
25.2	Judicial titles in the Supreme Court	665
25.3	Judicial titles in the Court of Appeal	666

PREFACE

This new 27 chapter text, *Learning Legal Skills and Reasoning*, is based on the success of the 11 chapter *Legal Method, Skills and Reasoning*. Retaining the well-known user-friendly and practical approach of the previous text *Learning Legal Skills and Reasoning* contains 16 additional chapters exploring sources of law, general academic skills (writing, reading, referencing, speaking and study skills) and extending the original oral skills chapter into four chapters dealing with presentation and debating, mooting, negotiation and mediation.

The book reflects the need for new law undergraduates to grasp a broad range of skills and my commitment to delivering these in one manageable text retaining all that has gone before together with additions. The book enters into a direct dialogue with the reader, explaining how to understand and apply the full range of legal and academic skills required by law students. It covers basic issues of concern for many students as well as more sophisticated skills relating to arguing and reading the law.

Practical manuals do not aim to be encyclopaedic, and this one is no exception. It aims to engage the reader in a highly personalised conversation, at times presuming to voice their worst fears, 'What if I am not good enough?', 'What if I cannot understand?', 'What if I fail something?' At every point the book gives a context, and engages the student in a conversation about the matters under consideration. I retain my belief in the importance of diagrams to demonstrate interconnections that are not apparent from just reading or hearing narrative. They remain one of the particular characteristics of this text.

I am also particularly delighted that current colleagues at Canterbury Christ Church University have been able to be involved in the text. I am indebted to Dr Tobias Kliem, Senior Lecturer in Law for his careful consideration of the chapters on treaties and the EU. I am also extremely pleased that the director of our mediation clinic, Ben Waters, has been able to write the chapter on mediation. For the student there are a range of exercises and activities with suggested answers to test development of skills, together with glossaries of troublesome terms.

This book would not have been possible without the incredible support received from my editor Fiona Bridon and her assistant Emily Wells. I am indebted to you and the rest of the team.

ACKNOWLEDGEMENTS

The publishers would like to acknowledge the following publishers for kind permission for the use of their materials for this book:

Screenshots taken from Legislation.gov.uk reproduced under Open Government Licence v 3.0

Screenshots taken from parliament.uk site reproduced under Open Parliament Licence v 3.0

Screenshots taken from WESTLAW UK, reproduced with permission from THOMSON REUTERS (PROFESSIONAL) UK LIMITED

The European Union belongs to its citizens: Three immodest proposals by JJ Weiler, referenced with permission from THOMSON REUTERS (PROFESSIONAL) UK LIMITED

Screenshots taken from BAILII (www.bailii.org) reproduced with permission from BAILII Executive Director

Screenshot taken from EUR-Lex reproduced with permission from EUR-Lex

Screenshots taken from Lexis Library reproduced with permission from LexisNexis

INTRODUCTION

'The journey of a thousand miles starts with a single step'.

Lao Tzu

Careful thought has gone into the structure of this book. It can be approached in an order to suit the reader. As a whole it is designed to enable you to gain skills vital to the academic stage of legal education.

This is a method and skills book and it is therefore no substitute for texts in your substantive areas of study such as criminal law, the law of contract, or the English legal system. The book draws on a range of areas of law to demonstrate skills development and to alert you to some of the confusions and mistakes easily made. It is a book that bridges the gap between substantive legal subjects and the skills that need to be acquired in relation to:

Study skills	How to develop independent and highly efficient learning strategies
IT skills	How to engage with email, word processing, virtual learning environments, internet searches, e-library use, database manipulation
Language skills	How to competently understand and use ordinary English and legal English terminology
Critical thinking skills	How to develop the ability to constantly question, seeking the underlying assumptions behind arguments, taking nothing for granted, seeking evidences for your assertions, questioning your own positions
Legal research skills	How to find law and texts about law through highly effective library skills
Legal method skills	How to approach and handle legal rules
Argumentation skills	How to identify, construct and evaluate arguments

Reading skills	How to read legal rules, judges' opinions, academic critiques of law reports etc.
Writing skills	How to write notes, summaries, essays, legal problem solutions, exams, reports etc.
Speaking (oral) skills	How to engage in debating, mock trials (mooting), mediation, negotiation, presentation
Preparing for assessments	How to effectively prepare for and produce written and oral assessments

Successful legal study depends upon the simultaneous development of different, but complementary, skills. For example, knowing how to study, understand the sources of law, and where to find the law; how to analyse and critique the law, how to construct legal arguments and how to successfully engage in written and oral assessments. All of these issues are covered in this book which is divided into six parts.

Part 1: Sources of law

Part 2: Finding law – effective legal research

Part 3: Reading and understanding law

Part 4: Legal reasoning skills

Part 5: General academic skills

Part 6: Law assessments: written and oral

Throughout the book you will note that the primary focus is inevitably text based. It deals with *texts of law* (statutes, case law, treaties) and *texts about law* (textbooks, academic articles). This distinction between texts **OF** law and texts **ABOUT** law is important to grasp.

Texts of law set out the primary legal rules, while texts about law look at law from a range of perspectives, questioning and critiquing or just summarising the state of law. These are called secondary texts because they are basically commentaries about the legal rules in the texts of law.

As you gain competency in legal study and legal skills you will increase your critical ability to analyse law, this will sharpen your thinking, you will learn to ask questions, never taking anything for granted, looking for evidence to support arguments.

You may have found the above listing of the parts of the book daunting as it sets out the range of skills that you need to develop. However, it is better to be informed about the complex interconnectedness of your studies from the start. Too often, students are not clearly informed at the beginning of studies of the full extent of the skills required. They then wonder why they are not progressing, but it may be that while they will be good at the study of law eventually they initially need to develop skills of library usage, research, IT and personal time management.

Be warned, however: it is easy to forget the range of skills you need to work on, once you become too busy coping with information overload, the facts of cases, the words making up a legal rule, a definition, the translation of a Latin phrase used in law etc. You may think you cannot waste time trying to understand as well! Frequently, memorising becomes a comfortable tranquilliser protecting the student from the productive pain of fighting with incomprehension to reach a place of partial understanding. Sadly, within the discipline of law, successful memorising often merely ensures failure as the student knows it all and yet understands nothing.

The acquisition of knowledge without the ability to understand it and apply it is not studying it; it is just mindless rote learning. The **easy** part is acquiring knowledge – the **difficult** part of studying is understanding what you know and applying it. You would not pay to be advised by a lawyer who knew everything but understood nothing.

The majority of books on the market that deal with issues of legal skills and legal method (that is, the way in which legal rules are used to resolve certain types of disputes) do so in the context of legal process or legal theory. Inevitably, many of these books tend to be weighted in favour of explaining the English legal system, its processes, personnel and doctrines. They do not give time to an appreciation of how to engage with standard academic skills, how to break into texts, to read them and to understand them and how to construct arguments. This book recognises that in order to be successful in your legal studies you need to get inside legal rules, and fully appreciate their various dimensions.

This text acknowledges the complexities of legal rules, the importance of critique and the construction of legal arguments, and the need to develop excellent general academic skills, including study skills. But it also assists students, in a user-friendly manner, to make interrelationships within and between texts. It presents language clearly, and uses these interrelationships to allow the commencement of the task of understanding and reading the law, of seeing arguments, evaluating arguments and in turn assisting you to construct arguments.

Law is dynamic, not passive. Reading is dynamic, not passive as you will find out – it has to be as you need to enter into 'conversation' with what you are reading. Studying is also dynamic, not passive. Learning does not happen to you; it is something that you do.

Essentially, therefore, this is a book about practical matters, practical skills of studying, IT strategies, practical thinking and the acquisition of a range of practical legal, research, intellectual and presentational skills and, as such, relies on reader reflection and activity. But these practical matters are underpinned by Part 1 which sets out, in some detail in five chapters, the sources of law. Its practical nature means that it relies on your willingness to engage actively with the book. But its practicality is consistently aimed at developing critical thinking and allowing you to develop a complex understanding so that you can engage in highly competent analysis.

My objective in writing this book was to provide a usable manual: the text draws a map of your studies, it sets out the territory and also provides smaller maps to enable you to locate and understand legal texts and to reach a place of understanding where you can recall relevant memorised knowledge concerning general or specific contexts and apply it, or interpret it confidently with a clear comprehension of the interrelationships between rules, arguments and language, in the search for plausible solutions to real or imaginary problems.

This text is not a philosophical enquiry that asks why English law prefers the methods of reasoning it has adopted. Although such texts are of the utmost importance, they will mean more to the student who has first acquired a thorough competency in a narrow field of practical legal method and practical reason. Then, a philosophical argument will be appreciated, considered, evaluated and either accepted or rejected. This is not a theoretical text designed to discuss in detail the importance of a range of legal doctrines such as precedent, although you must also carefully study these. Further, this is not a book that critiques itself or engages in a post-modern reminder that what we know and see is only a chosen, constructed fragment of what may be the truth. Although self-critique is a valid enterprise, a fragmentary understanding of 'the whole' is all that can ever be grasped.

Intellectual understanding brings with it the ability to realise that we can only ever see part of the whole collection of stories that is the law. Therefore we should approach the study of law carefully, checking that our arguments and our criticisms are plausible. We need to constantly check that the arguments and criticisms of others are also plausible. Knowledge is essential but it is equally essential to think of the use of our knowledge in terms of it being a torch shining in the dark. There is a strong central beam of light which enables you to see well. But that beam of light fades through shadows to darkness and although we cannot see it we know that there is more 'out there'. Study is the same: there is always more we cannot see, and never will see. This should protect us from making assertions about the whole of law, for we cannot see it all. We do not understand it all.

This is above all a 'how to do' text, a practical manual. As such, bearing in mind the list of skills set out above that are necessary for legal studies it concerns itself primarily with the use of 12 areas identified in Figure 1. Carefully read the list as it constitutes your marching orders for the rest of the book and for your legal study.

The parts and chapters in this book can stand alone, or be used selectively to form a pathway for a particular need of study. For example, if you wished only to study about domestic legislation you can look at:

Part 1: Sources of law

- Chapter 1: Domestic legislation

Part 2: Finding law – effective legal research

- Chapter 6: How to get the most out of your university print and e-library

- Chapter 7: How to find domestic and European legislation

Part 3: Reading and understanding law

- Chapter 11: How to read and understand domestic legislation

---

HOW TO

1. Effectively engage in general study skills and become an independent and interdependent learner.
2. Effectively engage in general reading, writing and oral skills.
3. Effectively prepare for oral and written assessments and exams including using consistent referencing.
4. Engage in efficient legal research using your institution's library print and electronic collections.
5. Develop an awareness of the importance of understanding the influence and power of language; including how to effectively use legal dictionaries and glossaries.
6. Understand the European influence on English law.
7. Effectively use and deploy IT resources.
8. Find, understand, use and apply texts *of* law – primary textual sources of law (law cases; legislation (in the form of primary legislation or secondary, statutory instruments, bylaws, etc.), European Union legislation).
9. Connect texts *about* the law and texts *of* the law to construct arguments to produce plausible solutions to problems (real or hypothetical, in the form of essays, case studies, questions, practical problems).
10. Find, understand, use and apply a range of different texts *about* the law (secondary textual sources from the discipline of law and from other disciplines).
11. Identify the relationship of the text being read to those texts produced before or after it; make comprehensible their interrelationships.
12. Identify, construct and evaluate legal arguments.

Figure 1 The function of this 'how to' text

The last part of the book, Part 6: Law assessments: written and oral, contains seven chapters that concentrate on the deployment of a range of skills to engage in the finished products of writing differing types of coursework, engaging in oral skills and writing examinations.

The book will also draw attention to the fact that there is often more than one solution to a legal problem. Judges make choices when attempting to apply the law. The study of law is about critiquing the choices not made as well as the choices made.

The text as a whole will introduce you to the value of alternatives to purely textual explanations. An ability to comprehend diagrammatic explanations will be encouraged. The diagrams used are integral to the successful understanding of legal skills, legal method, legal reasoning and general academic skills as presented in this text.

They have been specifically designed to:

- provide a way of taking students to deeper levels of understanding;
- give a basic description or blueprint for an area;
- demonstrate interconnections between seemingly disconnected areas/texts/skills.

Diagrams present another way of seeing, and the sheer novelty value of seeing the interconnections in a diagram can sometimes be enough to change confusion into comprehension. It is hoped that students will begin to construct diagrams for themselves.

PART 1
SOURCES OF LAW

'The world can doubtless never be well known by theory: practice is absolutely necessary; but surely it is of great use . . . before set[ting] out for that country, full of mazes, windings, and turnings, to have at least a general map of it, made by some experienced traveller.'

Philipe Dormer Stanhope

A clear understanding of the different types of legal rule is a basic prerequisite for the competent exercise of legal skills and reasoning. The five chapters in Part 1 are designed to map the territory of law. They identify its sources, describe its creation, format and the limits of its jurisdiction.

Chapter 1 *Domestic legislation* defines and explains what legislation is, how it is created by Parliament and the formats used to set it out. The chapter also distinguishes between primary legislation (created by Parliament) and secondary legislation (created by office holders and groups on the delegated authority of Parliament). Time is also taken to explain the range of interchangeable words/phrases used when referring to legislation which can be confusing.

Chapter 2 *Domestic case law* gives you a basic appreciation of what common law or case law is, and the way in which it is created, developed, discussed and changed by the senior judges in the English courts. It describes the hierarchical structure of English courts and tribunals as well as their jurisdiction, staffing and development of the key doctrine of precedent by the senior judiciary. Precedent is discussed in detail in Chapter 10. The importance of three courts outside the hierarchy of the courts is also considered: the Privy Council, the Court of Justice of the European Union and the European Court of Human Rights.

Chapter 3 *European and international treaties* is designed to introduce students to the basic concept of treaties (formal agreements between nations) and discusses how they are created, amended, or terminated. It also considers the legal impact of treaties that have been entered into by the government, drawing distinctions between international law and English law. Time is taken to ensure the vocabulary used in treaties and about treaties is understood.

Chapter 4 *European Convention on Human Rights* looks at the European Convention on Human Rights, explaining its relationship to domestic human rights law. Human rights law is an increasingly important area of law globally. It is a key issue in political debate and has given rise to many controversies in the UK concerning judicial interpretations of both the European Convention on Human Rights (ECHR) 1951 created by the Council of Europe and the English Human Rights Act 1998 (HRA). Students of English law are often quite justly confused about the relationship between the ECHR and the HRA. The chapter explains in detail how the English legal system's human rights law originates outside the English legal system in European treaties. It also explains how parts of the ECHR have been given limited legal effect in the English legal system by the HRA. The chapter includes concentration on selected articles[1] of the ECHR and its protocols, as well as selected decisions of the European Court of Human Rights.

Chapter 5 *European Union law* is a source of law originating outside the English legal system in the founding treaties of the European Union (EU). These only have a legal effect inside the English legal system because the UK Parliament has allowed this through the enactment of legislation. EU law includes the treaties, legislation and the case law of the European Union and each area is discussed in this chapter.

---

1   A treaty is subdivided into numbered articles.

DOMESTIC LEGISLATION

1

LEARNING OUTCOMES

After reading this chapter you should be able to:

- Understand the structure and role of Parliament in the enactment of domestic legislation.
- Appreciate the role of government in proposing legislation.
- Be aware of the procedures that must be followed to create valid legislation.
- Understand the process of drafting legislation.
- Distinguish between primary and secondary legislation and be aware of its standard formats and subject matter.
- Be aware of the function of statutory interpretation.
- Understand the basic relationship between cases and legislation.

INTRODUCTION

Domestic legislation is created by Parliament or by the delegated authority of Parliament and it is the major source of legal rules in the English legal system. English legislation is referred to as 'domestic' to differentiate it from European Union (EU) legislation enacted by the institutions of the EU. EU legislation is a major source of English law but this is discussed in Chapter 5.

Primary and secondary domestic legislation are described and the standard method of creating them is set out. The standard layout of domestic legislation is also dealt with. A brief explanation of statutory interpretation by the judiciary is given; however, detailed discussion of this area is reserved for Chapter 11, which concentrates on the skills of reading, analysing and interpreting legislation.

WHAT IS DOMESTIC LEGISLATION?

Domestic legislation is the dominant form of law making in the English legal system and it is created by the authority of Parliament. It exists in two main forms, primary and secondary legislation. Primary legislation applies to the whole of the English legal system and is created by Parliament directly. It can deal with any subject matter that Parliament wishes.

Secondary legislation is created by others acting on powers delegated to them in primary legislation, which in these circumstances can be described as 'enabling' or 'parent' legislation. For example, an individual minister of state may be given powers to make changes to certain primary legislation. Or a professional body may be allowed to make legal rules affecting its members. A local council[1] can enact legal rules applicable only to the geographic area of the council. Secondary legislation is often described as an indirect form of law making and can be additionally referred to as delegated or subordinate legislation. It can be repealed or changed by primary legislation.

A good description of legislation has been given by Professors Twining and Miers who state that legislation can be used to encompass a wide variety of rules in 'fixed verbal form'.[2] When Parliament is exercising its authority to draft, scrutinise and enact legislation, it does so by agreeing a set of particular words to be used to communicate the rules. No other words can be used as they were not authorised.

Legislation is enacted in various timescales. Sometimes it is a reasonably well-considered response to a particular issue such as consumer protection. Sometimes legislation is quickly created as a reaction by Parliament to a crisis or public outcry or a one-off situation, for example, in response to an act of terrorism. On other occasions it is the end product of several years of public, political and expert consultation. The Equality Act 2010[3] (EA) is an example of legislation that was the outcome of several years of consultation.

Legislation can be enacted to create new legal rules on any matter. It can also be enacted to order and bring together existing law in a particular area, such as theft. It can

---

1   Technically referred to as a local authority (LA).
2   W Twining and D Miers *How to Do Things with Rules* (Cambridge University Press, 2010) 193.
3   c. 15 2010.

in this way bring together common law judge-made rules,[4] customary legal rules,[5] and/ or existing legislation into one statute. Consolidating legislation brings together disparate legislative provisions in different legislative acts and re-presents them in a logical order. There is no change made to that existing law. Codifying legislation restates legal rules previously contained in a range of places, the common law, customary law and legislation to promote clarity in a particular area of law.

Not all codifying legislation gets it right. A good example is the Theft Act 1968. It codified the common law and prior legislation in existence in the area of theft. However, a major problem with the old law was the definition of deception. The Theft Act 1968 failed to deal with this adequately and eventually the Theft Act 1978 was enacted to resolve the problem. That too proved inadequate in a range of areas and it was followed nearly 20 years later by the Theft (Amendment Act) 1996. Continuing issues around fraud and deception finally led to the Fraud Act 2006.[6]

Although each legislative act responds to particular issues, the finer details of the situations to which the rules will have to be applied will vary enormously. Therefore, a particular characteristic of primary legislation is that it is drafted in a general way, in order to be applicable to the widest possible range of situations. This often presents a major challenge to those drafting the legislation and to those who are subsequently called upon to interpret it.

Naming conventions for legislation

You need to learn when clusters of names actually refer to the same thing, as well as understand when names are used to denote differences between primary and secondary legislation. As well as understanding the names used to refer to enacted legislation you need to be familiar with descriptions of it prior to enactment. For example a legislative act is called a 'bill' at the drafting stage. As a bill can change dramatically as it goes through the processes of enactment, if legislation has been enacted the bill should not be consulted for a view of the up to date law. However, it can be an interesting historical record of what was left in and what was taken out of the legislation during the processes leading to enactment.

There are several phrases used to refer to primary and secondary legislation and these are set out in Figures 1.1 and 1.2.

Secondary legislation, like primary legislation, is covered by a range of synonyms, and can also be of several different types. Figure 1.2 sets out the main synonyms and types of secondary legislation.

The statute book

When considering legislation in other texts you will no doubt hear the phrase 'the statute book'. This is a reference to the totality of enacted legislation in the English legal system arranged chronologically. Each statute in any year is a chapter in the statute book. The

---

4   Explained in Chapter 2.
5   Ibid.
6   c. 35 2006.

1. SYNONYMS USED FOR GENERAL REFERENCE TO PRIMARY LEGISLATION:
A synonym is another word or phrase meaning the same thing

- An Act of Parliament
- An Act
- A legislative act
- A statute (which means decree)

PRIMARY LEGISLATION GIVING DELEGATED POWERS TO
LEGISLATE CAN BE REFERRED TO AS

The parent Act or the enabling Act

2. DIFFERENT TYPES OF PRIMARY LEGISLATION
There are also different types of primary legislation that need to be distinguished from each
other

- A Public General Act
- A private Act
- A private member's Act
- A hybrid Act
- Orders in Council

SINGULAR AND PLURAL FORMS FOR PRIMARY LEGISLATION

Students can be confused by plurals in this area; hopefully the following will help:
- The word 'legislation' is understood in the plural sense.
- If you want to refer to the singular you need to think in terms of a 'piece' of legislation. But the
  appropriate term would be legislative act.
- More commonly a singular reference is made to 'an Act', or 'the Act' or to the statute. The
  plural is denoted by the addition of an 's' to the relevant noun and changing the pronoun
  e.g. 'The Acts considered together provide', or 'these statutes provide'.

Figure 1.1 Correct reference to primary legislation

Equality Act 2010 has the full citation Equality Act 2010 c.15, with the lowercase 'c' being
an abbreviation for 'chapter'. From this we know it is the 15th statute enacted in 2010; it is
Chapter 15 of the statute book for 2010.

Finding legislation

Legislation can be found in many places: in handwritten collections, print collections[7] and
online collections held by libraries or institutions such as Parliament or the Courts. There
is only one online official site for UK legislation, which is free and can be located at www.
legislation.gov.uk. Other subscription-only online sites exist. Your library should be able to
give you access to some of these.

---

7   There are surviving parchment rolls of handwritten legislation dating from about 1299.

SECONDARY LEGISLATION	
SYNONYMS FOR SECONDARY LEGISLATION	
Subordinate legislation **OR** delegated legislation	
DIFFERENT TYPES OF SECONDARY LEGISLATION	

1. Bylaws
2. Orders **by** Council (The Privy Council)
3. Statutory Instruments
   (1) *Local*
   (2) *Public*
      (i) Hybrid statutory instruments
      (ii) Orders:
         (a) Commencement Orders
         (b) Orders **in** Council (The Privy Council)
            NB: Orders in Council here expressly excludes the use of the 'royal prerogative'; this is an instance of an order in council constituting primary legislation.
         (c) Regulatory Reform Orders
         (d) Remedial Orders
         (e) Special Procedure Orders
      (iii) Regulations
      (iv) Church Measures (of the Church of England)
4. Court Rules Committees

SINGULAR AND PLURAL FORMS FOR SECONDARY LEGISLATION	
Singular	**Plural**
Bylaw	Bylaws
An order in council	Orders by Council
Statutory instrument	Statutory instruments
Regulation	Regulations
Church measure	Church Measures

Figure 1.2 Synonyms for secondary legislation and types of secondary legislation

There are a range of publications that provide lawyers, students and researchers with lists of legislation; these are arranged either chronologically or by subject matter. We will look at these in more detail in Chapter 6 which is concerned with finding legislation. The domestic legislation currently in force has been created by Parliament over the past 700 years, but most of the legislation has been created since 1850.

WHAT IS PARLIAMENT?

Parliament is the main political and legal institution in the English legal system, and the only institution empowered to create primary legislation. It is made up of three elements. There are two Houses, the elected Members of Parliament (MPs) in the House of Commons (which is often referred to as the 'commons' or less often 'the lower house') and the non-elected Lords in the House of Lords (which is often just referred to as the Lords, and less often 'the upper house'). Both Houses of Parliament acting together must agree the exact wording of legislation. The third element is the monarch, who must give their Royal Assent to all legislation for it to be legitimately enacted. The monarch in our modern democracy does not have the ability to refuse.

The House of Commons

The House of Commons is currently composed of 650 Members of Parliament elected by members of the public who are eligible to vote and contains representatives from the four nations, England, Northern Ireland, Scotland and Wales. For this purpose they are divided into constituencies containing one MP. So everyone knows who is representing them in the House of Commons.

The number of MPs went down to 600 in the general election[8] on 7 May 2015. Since the Fixed Term Parliament Act 2011 general elections of all members of the House of Commons take place every five years. In practice the head of the government, the prime minister, has a two month leeway before or after the expiry of five years in which to hold the election. The only other way in which an earlier general election could take place would be if there was a successful vote of 'no-confidence' in the government passed in the Commons and no alternative government could be formed; or if a two-thirds majority of the House of Commons agreed to an early general election. If an MP resigns or dies a by-election is held to replace them.

The House of Lords

The House of Lords is composed of 777 unelected Lords who are eligible by virtue of their titles, or the office they hold. They have a delaying power over legislation but not a complete veto. Under the Parliament Act 1911 the delay was two years and by virtue of the Parliament Act 1949 it is now one year.

Royal Assent

There is also a final formal agreement to legislation given by the figurehead of the state, the monarch, currently Queen Elizabeth II. The convention is that the monarch does not refuse consent.

---

8   Parliamentary Voting System and Constituencies Act 2011.

The power of government to create legislation

Given the Lords can only delay, and the monarch cannot dissent, then it is correct to say that the practical centre of power is in the House of Commons. Furthermore as the government normally controls the majority in the Commons, due to it being the party with most votes in the Commons, it is the government that is the seat of power with only limited checks and balances on the exercise of that power.

TYPES OF DOMESTIC LEGISLATION: PRIMARY AND SECONDARY

So far we have noted that Parliament authorises the creation of a range of different types of legal rule generally subdivided into primary and secondary legislation, both of which are united by the fact that they are created in a fixed verbal form. The phrase 'fixed verbal form' means that only *those* words in that order with that punctuation (if any) were agreed by Parliament as containing the legal rule.[9]

There are two broad classifications of legislation into primary and secondary legislation. Both types of legislation are important and they will now be considered in turn.

Types of primary legislation

There are several types of legislative act that can become a primary Act of Parliament:

Public General Acts

These mostly originate through the daily work of government departments and affect the general public. Some may be the result of implementing electoral promises. On occasion they can be created in response to public concern over a controversial problem. Public General Acts comprise the vast majority of primary legislation and will therefore be our main area of focus.

Private Acts

These go through the same procedures in Parliament to become law as a Public General Act. But private Acts only contain rules applying to a specific geographical area, or to a particular institution, or even just one person. They do not apply to all members of the public.

Law relating to a single individual is usually concerned with name changes. In 1987 the term 'private Act in relation to name change' was changed to 'personal Act'. Not only can such a personal Act of Parliament be used to change a surname, but it can also be used to change a forename that was given to a person during a Christian ceremony of baptism. As you might imagine, the procedure for obtaining a private Act of Parliament is extremely expensive and rather complex.

Not surprisingly, such Acts are rare.

---

9   Although, as you will see in Chapter 11, judges interpreting words and phrases in court will often deal in the substitution of words.

Hybrid Acts

These affect the general public but additionally a smaller locality or group may well be particularly affected by the legislation in ways that may be onerous. The legislation is usually required to allow work of national benefit and importance to take place.

Orders in Council by virtue of the royal prerogative

This is an order made on the authority of the monarch. There are few examples of the royal prerogative today. A list would include appointments to the Church of England, heads of Crown Corporation and governors of British Overseas Territory. By tradition prime ministers use them for political appointments. In times of emergency the government can use Orders in Council as a quick response. They can be used to change the decision of courts that apply to British Overseas Territories without an Act of Parliament. Only a Public General Act can be used to reverse a domestic court's decision.

Private members' bills

A private member's bill is a type of public bill that is not introduced by the government but by an individual member of the House of Lords or the House of Commons. The only condition attaching to this right is that the person concerned must not be a government minister. Such bills are not exempt from the normal procedure for the enactment of an Act of Parliament. One of their values is allowing there to be a debate on an issue. A private member's bill that has not been enacted can have an impact on legislation that later comes from the government after serious issues have been aired in debate in the Houses of Parliament during the progress of the private members' bill.

Introducing a private members' bill in the House of Commons

There are several ways that such a bill can be introduced. In the House of Commons this is by success in a ballot, using 'the ten minute rule', or by 'presentation'.

The ballot

Each year there is a private member's ballot. Usually about 20 MPs are successful and it can be expected that the first seven drawn will get a hearing in the house. Success in a ballot is the best method of getting an issue timetabled for parliamentary debate. The bill is known as a 'Ballot Bill'. Often MPs will make it known that they are going into the ballot and are open to suggestions as to what bill they should support. Lobby groups who wish the enactment of specific legislation often try and persuade an MP to go into the ballot. But of course there is an element of chance! Ten Fridays in each parliamentary session are set aside for the debating of private member's bills.

A private member's bill that attracts government support could finally reach the statute book as a Public General Act, a private Act or a hybrid Act. Usually private member's bills fail to be enacted, technically referred to as 'lost'. In the past it has been government strategy to allow highly contentious issues to be debated as a private member's bill. It gauges support for the bill and if all looks well the government take it over.

The ten minute rule (under House of Commons Standing Order 23)[10]

The ten minute rule is a provision whereby MPs have ten minutes to set out their bill to the House. Another MP may give a short opposition response. It does at least get an issue aired in Parliament and allows a limited debate. This type of bill is known as a 'ten minute rule bill'. Often such a bill does not move beyond a first debate of issues.

Presentation (House of Commons Standing Order 39)

Presentation is acceptance of the fact that in theory any MP can propose a bill and the only prerequisite is that they give due notice of any intention to do so. The downside here is that there is no debate at all and just the title of the bill is read out.

Introducing a private member's bill into the House of Lords

The position in the House of Lords is different, and the bill is called a Lords private member's bill. If a Lord introduces a private bill it is treated in the same way as any other bill. Should such a bill complete its passage through the House of Lords an MP has to be found to support it. If support for the legislation is obtained, the bill will continue to the House of Commons. A Lords private member's bill is not privileged over a Commons bill coming to the House of Lords for debate and this means that in practice they do not get much debating time.

THE PROCEDURES LEADING TO THE ENACTMENT OF A PUBLIC GENERAL ACT

A primary legislative act, applying generally to all of the public within the state is called a Public General Act. The bulk of primary legislation is in the form of Public General Acts and therefore it is not surprising that our consideration will primarily focus on the Public General Act. Prior to enactment the draft legislation is called an act.

Procedures for enacting legislation can be broken down into four main areas:

- Pre-legislative procedures.
- The passage of the bill through Parliament.
- Royal Assent.
- The 'in force' date of the Act.

Pre-legislative procedures Public General Bill

Technically the processes before a bill is introduced in Parliament are collectively referred to as the pre-legislative procedures. These include getting the views of the public and institutions by informal or formal consultations; and drafting the legislation.

---

10 House of Commons standing rules: 'Standing Orders are written rules formulated by each House to regulate its own proceedings. They cover, for example, how business is arranged and conducted, the behaviour of MPs and members of the House of Lords during debates, and rules relating to committees. Some Standing Orders are temporary and only last until the end of a session or a parliament. There are around 150 Standing Orders relating to parliamentary business and public bills, and about 250 relating to private business'. http://www.parliament.uk/about/how/roles/customs Accessed 10/07/2014.

Public consultation, Green Papers and White Papers

Ideas about proposals for future legislation usually go through a consultation period, and on some occasions, a thorough pre-legislative scrutiny by experts in the field. Modern government relies on consultation prior to bills being drafted to see if it will obtain support from those affected, the so-called 'stakeholders'. Negative feedback will not necessarily stop a government forwarding proposed legislation but it will make it think carefully about its proposals before proceeding.

The relevant government department or minister of state may publish a completely exploratory report asking for general views, which is bound in a green cover and referred to as a Green Paper. Or it may issue a discussion paper with an attached prospective bill to generate more specific comment. Bound in white, this is called a White Paper. Both are called 'command' papers from the header in each which states:

> 'Presented to Parliament by the Secretary of State for . . . by Command of Her Majesty'.

For example, the coalition government published its White Paper, 'Water for Life', on 8 December 2011.[11] The government department publishing this White Paper was Environment, Food and Rural Affairs (EFRA). Each government department has its own select committee and EFRA's select committee[12] voiced their concerns over matters in the proposed legislation. They undertook an inquiry into the White Paper and published their findings on 5 July 2012. Shortly after this the government published a draft Water Bill. A set period of time is usually given for responses to a consultation.

The public is usually given a number of months to reply to a call for views on issues in White and Green Papers, and some organisations are explicitly invited to respond to proposals. All such responses are published in Hansard[13] as government papers.

The parliamentary outreach programme also runs free 'Public Bill workshops' to let members of the public know how to engage with proposals for legislation.[14] These include online opportunities to respond.

Drafting of a Public General bill by parliamentary counsel

Government bills are drafted by the Office of Parliamentary Counsel. All those working in the Office of Parliamentary Counsel (an office dating back to 1869) are lawyers and employed as civil servants.

Before the Office of Parliamentary Counsel will accept instructions from a government department to draft a bill it must have a European Convention on Human Rights

---

11 Ref: PB13689.
12 Each government department has an assigned select committee.
13 Hansard is responsible for ensuring the verbatim notation of all parliamentary debates and proceedings in commit as well as a range of other parliamentary papers. Publication is by the Stationery Office (TSO).
14 http://www.parliament.uk/get-involved/outreach-and-training/public-bill-workshops/ accessed 18 April 2013.

Memorandum[15] stating that the proposed legislation is compatible with the Convention. This memo, formally a statement of compatibility, must be printed on the front of the bill. A bill can still be drafted and journey through Parliament in the absence of a memorandum of compatibility. There would need to be a most compelling reason given by government for choosing to go ahead anyway.

It is the civil servants in the relevant government department promoting the bill that instruct parliamentary counsel to draft the bill. When full instructions are sent to parliamentary counsel the relevant government department should also inform them of any existing judicial interpretation of legislation that may be relevant to understanding what the law might currently be. Also, the department should lay out any legal concepts that they are using in instructing the drafting of the bill. Parliamentary counsel also expects the instructions to include alerts when there are any arrangements in the bill proposing to give secondary legislative powers to another person or institution. Counsel will then advise the relevant government department, or a minister, whether what they wish to do is possible from a technical, legal perspective.

The bill is divided into small parts called clauses. Linked clauses are usually put together. These clauses become sections if the bill becomes an Act.

The parliamentary legislative timetable

At the commencement of each parliamentary session the monarch gives a speech written by 'her government' outlining the legislation planned for the current session. Government control of the parliamentary legislative timetable is absolutely key to the success of government bills.

Two cabinet committees determine which bills will be presented and when.

'The legislation committee' is responsible for the timing of bills in the current Parliament and is responsible for drawing up a programme from the Queen's speech. The 'future legislation committee' determines the bills to go forward in the next session of Parliament.

The passage of a public bill through Parliament

Once the legislation has been drafted then it has to face a strict series of procedures as it travels through Parliament. Each public bill has three readings, a committee stage and a report stage, in both Houses of Parliament. After the committee stage a report is sent to the relevant House on changes to the bill. A bill can be introduced initially in either House although most are introduced into the House of Commons. However, the House of Commons can, after the elapse of set periods of time, ignore the dissent of the House of Lords using the Parliament Acts 1911 and 1949. These Acts curtailed the powers of the House of Lords by only allowing them a delaying power of up to a year; after that it receives the Royal Assent and becomes an Act. Prior to the enactment of the Parliament Acts, the House of Lords could completely veto legislation and it would be lost.[16]

---

15 See Human Rights Act 1998 c. 42, s 19(1)(a) – this is technically referred to as a memorandum of compatibility.
16 The delay was initially two years in the 1911 legislation which was reduced to one year in the 1949 legislation.

Passage of a bill through the House of Commons

First reading

This is a mere formality; the only requirement is that the short title[17] of the bill is read out in the House. Each bill, and subsequently each Act, has a long title set out in its preamble (see later in the chapter)[18] and a short title which is determined by a section (sections are explained later in this chapter) in the Act and this is the title by which it is known. A time is then set for a second reading. Conventionally this should be after the passing of two weekends.

Second reading

This is a full debate in the House of the issues raised by the legislation. The relevant minister or spokesperson will introduce the bill. This is immediately followed by the 'official' opposition[19] shadow minister or spokesperson responding. After this a general debate opens up, and at the end of the debate there is a vote to determine if the bill can continue its passage through the House. The bill must receive a 50 per cent majority of those voting to continue on its way. MPs do not have to be in the debating chamber of the House to vote. They can slip into the chamber near the time for a vote.

Voting procedures

Immediately the time for voting arrives the Speaker of the House of Commons[21] will ask all members present in the Commons chamber to simultaneously call out their agreement or dissent to the bill.[20] This is a noisy event. The Speaker will then gauge from what he or she has heard if the bill has majority support or not. If it is unclear the Speaker will call for a vote by 'division'.

It is called a division because the House physically divides for the purposes of voting. All MPs are asked to show their support or dissent by either walking out of the chamber into one of two areas, called division lobbies. One lobby is the 'ayes' (yes) lobby and the other the 'noes' lobby.[21] Any MP can vote in the Commons lobbies, but they cannot vote in the House of Lords and vice versa. You can only vote in the House of which you are a member.

Division bells ring for eight minutes to allow MPs to arrive from elsewhere in the area of Parliament. The bells are placed in a range of places within Parliament and its precincts. The sound of the bell for House of Lords divisions is different to that of the Commons. TV screens around Parliament and surrounding parliamentary and government buildings also

---

17 See below for details of the short title. Each bill and subsequent Act has a long and a short title. These matters are discussed in detail in Chapter 11.

18 A bill is divided into clauses which become sections in the Act.

19 The political party not in government in the House of Commons with the largest number of MPs is the official opposition. They appoint MPs to 'shadow' government ministers, the 'shadow minister'. They will respond to them in debates.

20 In the House of Lords it is the Lord Speaker who deals with this matter.

21 In the House of Lords the Lords walk through the 'bar' and the lobbies are known as 'consent' and 'not consent'.

indicate that a division is taking place.[22] When the bell stops, the door to the chamber is locked. No one can gain access to vote if they have been locked out.

Clerks note the name of the MP as they vote by simply walking through the relevant division lobby. Those acting as 'tellers' of the vote to the Speaker count the MPs through from the chamber into the division lobby and the Speaker announces the result. If there is a tied vote then the Speaker has the casting vote (this is a very rare occurrence). This authority belongs to the Speaker because of a constitutional convention[23] known as Speaker Denison's rule.[24]

A constitutional convention is a practice that is so honoured and well used within Parliament that it has to be followed. The rule here is that the Speaker must maintain the status quo by voting in favour of the government.

The division lobby process does not take much time, around 15–20 minutes. However, it is also possible to have a deferred division which allows MPs to vote at a convenient time during a limited timescale. The votes in a deferred division remain public to match the lobby/bar procedures for accountability. This can be seen to mirror the first vote after any debate when MPs shout out their views from their seat on the benches. The 'division list' is a list of the way in which each Member of Parliament voted and is published the next day in Hansard, and posted on the Parliament website.

Committee stage

A bill that successfully passes the second reading is sent to a public bill committee composed of 16–50 MPs chosen to maintain the political representation of the parties in the House. So the government will usually have a majority in committee, with the next highest number of places going to the official opposition. It is usually hoped that a bill can go to committee within a few weeks of the second reading. But the parliamentary timetable is always full and the wait may be longer. Amendments to clauses can be put forward by committee members. However, only the Chair of the committee can decide which amendments are discussed. A list of amendments to the bills in committee is published each day. Votes are taken clause by clause, after detailed scrutiny, and every clause must be either:

- agreed;
- agreed as amended; or
- removed.

If the bill is amended then it is reprinted and there is a report stage back to the House.

Report stage

This takes place in the whole House[25] giving all MPs a chance to debate amendments to the bill in committee. However, unlike the other stages there is no ideal timescale set for the report stage. There may well be attempts to undo changes previously secured at the

---

22 Through a feed called the 'annunciator service'.
23 A practice deemed core to the House through tradition.
24 Denison was Speaker of the House of Commons from 1857 to 1872.
25 In rare instances the committee stage can take place as a committee of the whole House.

committee stage. MPs can also forward new proposals for amendments. Debates can continue for several days or even weeks.

Third reading

This usually takes place on the same day as the report stage finishes, and it is the final debate on the contents of the bill. If clear agreement to the bill is ascertained before a debate there will usually be a motion[26] calling for the House to proceed to a vote without a debate. If the bill is approved it is tied with a green ribbon and sent to the House of Lords with a request from the House of Commons that it is approved.

Passage of a bill through the House of Lords

The procedure in the House of Lords basically mirrors that in the House of Commons: first reading, second reading, committee stage, report stage, third reading.

It is worth noting, however, that the Speaker of the House of Lords does not have a casting vote in the event of a tied vote of the House. Also when a vote takes place in the chamber rather than saying 'ayes' or 'noes' the phrases used are 'consent' and 'not consent'.

Amendment consideration

At the end of the third reading in the House of Lords the bill comes to rest, and it is returned to the originating House of Commons, so that they can consider amendments made by the House of Lords.

Before a bill can become an enacted statute *all* wording in it must be agreed by both Houses of Parliament. You can see now why it is most appropriate to state that legislation is law enacted in a 'fixed verbal form'. If the House of Commons disagrees with the amendments from the House of Lords and/or makes further amendments of its own, the bill has to go back to the Lords. A bill can be sent back to the Commons again after the Lords have considered the new amendments and agreed or disagreed.

This 'to and fro' process is referred to as 'ping pong', after the game of table tennis. If the House of Lords delay the bill due to disagreements then the Parliament Acts can be used as noted above to allow the final consent to come from the House of Commons only. The House of Lords has delayed and refused consent on several notable statutes in recent years including the Sexual Offences Amendment Act 2000 and the Hunting Act 2005.

It used to be the case that if a bill had not successfully completed all its stages through the two Houses by the end of the parliamentary session it was 'lost'. Those opposing it would deliberately try to delay it as long as possible in its passage through debates and committees so that the end of the parliamentary session was reached and the bill was lost. However, in 1998 the House of Commons Modernisation Committee proposed that it should be possible to carry over bills that have not completed their passage from

---

26 A motion is the technical term for an MP making a proposal to the House.

one session to the next and since 2004 this has been a Standing Order of the House of Commons.

Royal Assent

Even if the bill receives agreement from the House of Lords and the House of Commons it cannot become law until the monarch has assented to it. There is no legal rule that states the monarch must assent but by convention the monarch does always assent. The last time the monarch refused to assent to an Act was in 1707. The Royal Assent Act 1967 provides for formal assent by notification and there just needs to be a formal reading in both Houses of the short title of the Act signifying assent. Once the Royal Assent process has been completed the Act is ordered to be printed by The Stationery Office.[27]

Date in force of the Act

Unless the statute states anything to the contrary, an Act becomes law on the day it receives Royal Assent, and for the avoidance of doubt the whole of that day is included.

It may be the case that the whole of a statute has a delayed 'in force' date (for example, the Equal Pay Act 1970 did not come into force until 1975).

More usually it is individual sections of an Act that have delayed and different dates for coming into legal force. The statute itself may just contain a general permissive section stating that various parts of the legislation come into force, if they come into force at all, on a day to be set by the relevant authorised minister by order.[28]

The date in force is an important aspect of legal method and you should carefully check in Halsbury, or the online official site for legislation (www.legislation.gov.uk) to ascertain the current position of individual sections of any statute that you are researching.

SECONDARY LEGISLATION

In addition to creating primary legislation, Parliament can, by Act of Parliament, delegate the power to create legislation to others such as a minster of the Crown and various professional, regulatory or statutory bodies. Such power is limited to the creation of binding laws relevant for that body. For example, local authorities have the power to enact secondary legislation, called bylaws, relating to matters within their geographical jurisdiction. Ministers enact secondary legislation in the form of statutory instruments when the right to make certain changes to primary legislation has been given to them in the primary legislation itself.

Secondary legislation can also occur as private and local but this is rarer and we will not be looking at these matters in detail.

Figure 1.3 below gives you a basic idea of the detail of the different types of secondary legislation. It is divided into a range of types but it is statutory instruments that form the bulk of what we generically refer to as delegated or subordinate legislation.

---

27 TSO are the officially sanctioned publishers for all UK legislation, command papers, House of Commons or Lords papers, select committee reports and of Hansard.
28 This is a classic situation of secondary legislative law making.

1. BYLAWS

2. ORDERS BY COUNCIL

- These are orders made by the Privy Council exercising powers of their own usually concerning the regulation of professions. Can be used to transfer powers: The Scotland Act 1998 (Transfer of Functions to the Scottish Ministers etc.) Order 2006, SI 2006/304

3. STATUTORY INSTRUMENT: LOCAL

- SIs can be local, personal or private. Very few such SIs are subject to parliamentary scrutiny. Quite a few private and public Acts delegate powers for a local SI

4. STATUTORY INSTRUMENT PUBLIC: ORDER

- **Commencement Order:** also known as an 'appointed day order', this order brings primary legislation into force that was not in force on its day of enactment. It is not subject to a parliamentary procedure; it just needs to be laid before Parliament
- **Orders in Council** : Made by statutory authority they allow government to go through the Privy Council to make law and are used for standard and emergency measures. They have a very broad scope and are used under s2(2) of the European Communities Act 1972 to give effect to European Union (EU) law which does not automatically become part of the English legal system when enacted in the EU
- **Regulatory Reform Orders:** Under Regulatory Reform Act 2006 s1 government ministers can amend or repeal sections of primary legislation – this has been a controversial power
- **Remedial Orders:** If a UK court declares that legislation is incompatible with the UK's obligations under the European Convention on Human Rights it issues a certificate of incompatibility. The government can propose that it remedies the situation by a draft order. The draft proposal is laid before Parliament for 60 days. The Joint Committee on Human Rights reports as to whether there should be an order and then a draft order is laid. After a further 60 days there is a motion to approve by both houses and if approved the order is made and becomes law
- **Special Procedure Orders:** Certain orders because of their interference with rights have to allow those affected to petition Parliament. An example would be the compulsory purchase of land

5. STATUTORY INSTRUMENTS: HYBRID

- Whilst applying to all, these affect some persons/groups more than others and they go through special procedures in the House of Lords to ensure there has been consultation and consideration of any public objections
- **Example:** The Legislative Reform (Epping Forest) Order 2011: The Metropolitan Police wanted a base during the Olympics and Paralympics. Local residents and wildlife organisations raised objections. The order was approved by the House of Lords having gone through a special procedure

6. CHURCH MEASURES

- These relate to the Church of England where most changes even to the services require legal rules to be authorised by secondary legislation because of its status as the church established by law in England

7. REGULATIONS

Figure 1.3 Types of secondary legislation

Parliamentary control over secondary legislation

Secondary legislation does not need to go through the full parliamentary procedure used for primary legislation. This makes it quick to create and saves precious parliamentary time. It also provides flexibility in law making, and often allows those most involved with an area to create the rules. For example, professional bodies are better placed to enact rules regulating their own professions.

This process does raise questions about the adequacy of parliamentary scrutiny of secondary legislation. This is particularly important in relation to powers given to government ministers to amend and repeal primary legislation under the Regulatory Reform Order mechanism. Slapper and Kelly refer to this as the growing trend of '(dis)empowering Acts of Parliament'[29] in the pursuit of economic and business development, a trend that began with the Deregulation and Contracting Out Act (DCOA) 1994, and that is continued by the Regulatory Reform Act 2006, Business Enterprise and Regulatory Act 2013 and the Public Bodies Act 2011.

While much secondary legislation is delegated under the authority of primary legislation there is an exception in relation to Orders by Council. These have authority by virtue of the royal prerogative (command of the monarch) transferred to the government, and are powers exercisable by the government alone.

Generally secondary legislation is subject to one of two generalised parliamentary procedures. It needs to either go through:

An affirmative resolution procedure
OR
A negative resolution procedure
OR
A super-affirmative resolution procedure

None of the resolutions allow Parliament to amend the secondary legislation, only to approve it or object to it becoming law.

A combined House of Lords and House of Commons Joint Select Committee on Statutory Instruments was set up in 1973. Additionally the House of Commons has its own Select Committee on Statutory Instruments. Secondary legislation relating to the EU goes to a special committee, as do local authority bylaws.

Statutory instruments, the largest group of secondary legislation are drafted by the legal officers in the relevant government department after consultation with interested parties.

They have different terminology to that used in primary legislation and instead of being enacted they are 'made'. They can, however, be 'laid' before Parliament as a draft for approval or 'made' for a motion for annulment or rejection within a set timescale. If there

---

29 G Slapper and D Kelly *The English Legal System 2012–2013* (13th edn, Routledge, 2012) 112.

is no motion at the expiry of the set time they are then 'in force'. It is important that you understand these terms, which are set out for you below in Figure 1.4.

LAID

- Laying before Parliament means that a copy of the unsigned statutory instrument is laid on the table of the House of Commons (in the chamber). In the House of Lords a copy of it with the Votes and Proceedings Desk in the Journal Office, and for the House of Lords.

MADE

- When a statutory instrument has been signed by the relevant minister or person with authority. 'Made' is the final legally binding statutory instrument: it is NOT a draft.

IN FORCE

- The statutory instrument becomes law when signed
- But note the procedure under the negative resolution discussed below which requires a signed SI to await the elapse of a set period of days.

Figure 1.4 Statutory instruments: meaning of terms of art: laid, made, in force

Procedure for making statutory instruments

As the majority of secondary legislation is made under a delegated power to make a statutory instrument (SI) we will concentrate on this to give you a good foundation for understanding the procedure.

Most SIs are subject to a parliamentary procedure, either the affirmative resolution or the negative resolution referred to below, and follow the procedures for both as set out in the Statutory Instruments Act 1946, ss 4 and 5. The enabling (or parent) Act will prescribe the procedure that is to be used in relation to specific statutory instruments.

All SIs that have to go through the parliamentary procedure must contain explanatory notes setting out their scope. The procedures are relatively simple as set out below.

It is worth noting that the Parliament Acts of 1911 and 1949 which allow primary legislation to become law without the agreement of the House of Lords do not apply to secondary legislation. If the House of Lords object then the SI cannot proceed. A few SIs are limited by the parent legislation to obtaining only the approval of the House of Commons.

The negative resolution procedure

The SI is laid before Parliament in draft format and left for 40 days to see if there is any objection (which is in fact quite rare). If there is an objection then the SI is lost.

Alternatively, the SI is laid as made and there is a 40 day period to see if there is a motion called a 'prayer to annul' during those 40 days. If not, it becomes legally binding.

The affirmative resolution procedure

Both Houses of Parliament must approve the SI. The SI can initially be laid as a draft order, then later printed and placed into the numerical run of SIs. It cannot be 'made' unless both Houses approve it. Or it can be laid after making but it cannot come into force until it is approved. Another option is that it can be laid after making but cannot remain in force unless it has approval from the House of Commons and Lords within a statutory period of days (which is usually somewhere between 28 and 40 days).

The super-affirmative procedure

The powers delegated to ministers by the parent Act may require proposals for SIs to be subject to the super-affirmative procedure which requires them to lay before Parliament for a set period of days. They are then drafted with notes taken of any comments made. Other delegated legislation can also require this procedure.

Debates to affirm or annul SIs

It is difficult to find parliamentary time to debate these matters. Usually motions are heard late in the parliamentary day on the floor of the House or in one of the committees dealing with delegated legislation.

Other parliamentary procedures

There is provision for some SIs to be laid for a set period but they do not require any scrutiny and some SIs do not have to be laid at all.

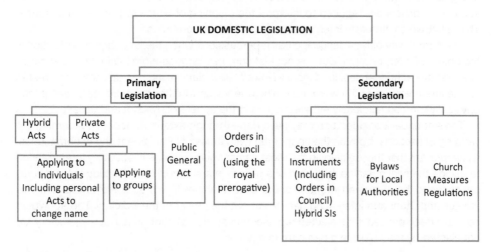

Figure 1.5 Types of UK domestic legislation

Lists of statutory instruments laid before Parliament

Lists of statutory instruments laid, approved and going through parliamentary procedures are published regularly by the parliamentary publications office so that members of the two Houses know where a SI is in its cycle of days. Figure 1.5 'Types of UK domestic legislation' sets out primary and secondary forms for your quick reference. Note that Orders in Council can manifest themselves as primary legislation (in relation to the royal prerogative) but in all other areas Orders in Council are secondary legislation in the form of statutory instruments.

USING LEGISLATION AND UNDERSTANDING JUDICIAL STATUTORY INTERPRETATION

It is particularly important to note that legislative language can be complex in its format and has the following characteristics:

- unusual grammatical forms;
- complex structure;
- tediously literal, dense text;
- scant punctuation;
- peppered with hierarchical alphabetical and numerical dividers.

Legislation as enacted will have inbuilt definitions of new terms, as well as a change in definitions of old terms for the purposes of a new area. It will contain defences (if applicable), and guidance with regard to interpretation of certain specified terms or procedures. Inevitably the judiciary are required to interpret the meaning of words or phrases in a statute. This is known as statutory interpretation or judicial interpretation.

The complexity of legal language has repercussions when the language of legislation is the object of interpretation. But it is not just complex language: ordinary words can cause interpretational headaches. In *Mandla v Dowell Lee* a claim of indirect discrimination rested on the interpretation of the word 'can'. The query was whether the word 'can' meant 'can physically' or 'can religiously – therefore can in the sphere of thought and belief'.

The Act under consideration may have gone through extensive debate concerning the wording of sections, both on the floor of the two Houses of Parliament and in committees. It is important that the judiciary in the most senior courts engage in statutory interpretation to decide the final meaning of a word of a phrase in a statute. However, judges have actually changed the presumed intention of Parliament by their interpretation of legislation. This creates important and interesting debates about the power of the judiciary. The Act would not have been passed if the elected representatives did not support it. But the judiciary are not elected by the public in a democratic manner.

CONCLUSION

It is essential to know and understand the processes for the creation of primary and secondary legislation and the structure of Parliament, the ultimate creators of legislation. But this information is only the background to being able to find and understand primary and secondary legislation so that you can competently construct legal arguments or critique aspects of them. Chapter 6 considers in detail how to find legislation in both its enacted and draft forms. Chapter 11 looks at issues of understanding it. Chapter 11 also includes a deeper consideration of statutory interpretation by the judiciary and an explanation of the relationship between cases and legislation.

CHAPTER SUMMARY

- Legislation is of two main types: domestic, enacted by the UK Parliament, and European Union legislation impacting UK law enacted by the EU.
- Legislation can be primary or secondary.
- Primary legislation is enacted by Parliament.
- Secondary legislation is enacted by others using powers given by primary legislation.
- Legislation is law in a fixed verbal form.
- Domestic legislation is the dominant form of law making in the English legal system. Parliament is split into two main 'Houses' or 'chambers'.
- The House of Commons is composed of 650 elected Members of Parliament.
- The House of Lords is composed of 760 Lords created by government.
- There is only one online official site for UK legislation which can be located at www. legislation.gov.uk.
- MPs and Lords have means by which they can present a private member's bill.
- Drafting of a government bill is by parliamentary counsel in the Office of Parliamentary Counsel.
- The passage of a public bill through Parliament is the same in both Houses as follows: first reading, second reading, committee stage, report stage, third reading.
- Drafting of statutory instruments varies. Generally, however, it is the civil servants in the government department covering the area of the parent Act who draft SIs.

DOMESTIC CASE LAW

2

After reading this chapter you should be able to:

- Appreciate the development of common law and equity.
- Understand the relationship between common law and equity.
- Have a firm grasp of the hierarchy of courts.
- Begin to understand the role and importance of the doctrine of precedent.
- Have an understanding of the basic jurisdiction of domestic courts.

INTRODUCTION

Case law is the law created by the senior judges deciding disputes in the law courts. The law that is created in this way is called the 'common law', a phrase used here in its narrower sense of judge-made law rather than in its wider sense of all of the law (legislative and judge-made) common to the English legal system.

During your legal education, you will be required to read many cases. They are often the legal authority pointed to for the presentation of legal arguments. It is important that you understand the law produced by these cases. Today, legislation is the main form of law making, but the judiciary have a major role to play in relation to statutory interpretation.

This chapter briefly describes the development of common law and equity, outlines the role of custom, and considers the structure, jurisdiction and judicial personnel of the courts. It also introduces the tribunal system, often a source of misunderstanding for students, and explains how in some circumstances it can interlink with the court system.

Key to the understanding of case law is the ability to appreciate the doctrine of precedent. This doctrine is briefly explained in this chapter, but an in-depth consideration of it is reserved for Chapter 10, 'Reading and understanding case law'. Equally important is to ensure you can competently locate the most up to date cases expressing legal principles or statutory definitions. Chapter 7, 'How to find domestic and European cases', deals with these issues.

THE DEVELOPMENT OF THE COMMON LAW

English law is described as being a common law system. Its initial creation and development was a by-product of the Norman invasion in 1066, as the conquerors required a law that would apply to everyone, 'royal law'. Yet despite knowing when it began to develop there is a lot that is unknown about the development of the common law. Historical sources show a lack of clarity with regard to a proper accounting of its development, the level of influence exerted by Roman law[1] and the precise nature of the range of local legal rules and differing legal systems operating in England prior to the Norman conquest. Much of the development of the common law and the institutions supporting it between the eleventh and thirteenth centuries remains uncertain.

Before 1066 there is evidence of separate systems of law operating in different areas of England controlled by different tribes (e.g., Danelaw, Wessex law, Mercian law). It is known that Roman law was influential in Europe generally between the first and fourth centuries; and that it was through Roman law that Christianity first exerted an influence on the English legal system. Despite this, Roman law was not popular in England (although some of our concepts in commercial law can be traced back to Roman law origins).

---

1   In England, Roman law was only used in the church courts of the Roman Catholic Church, still at that time under the political and religious power of Rome. The courts of the monarch never used Roman law.

What is clear is that as the Norman conquerors sought over successive centuries to centralise their power in the fragmented political and legal landscape of England, they centralised the law. The Normans developed a flexible system of political control covering the whole of England and Wales, giving power to the aristocracy in return for their loyalty to the monarch. The Normans were content to combine the legal rules and legal systems of local communities with a mix of their own rules. In this way no one community felt that the new legal rules were completely alien. However, because these rules were nationalised, ultimately all legal disputes were heard by the Norman monarchs. So while differing localised rules and laws operated in selected areas, it was the monarch who offered the 'common law', the new royal justice for all. The development of the common law usurped the authority of the local landowners and tribal leaders to resolve disputes.

It could be said that flexibility was the supreme act of political diplomacy of the Normans. Initially, they maintained that it was not necessary for the English common law to claim *exclusive* jurisdiction. This allowed space for the range of localised legal systems to shape English common law. As long as political loyalty locally was intact then local laws were tolerated as part of the nationalised system, with common law, the royal justice, offering dispute resolution in the courts. Over time, however, the Crown claimed exclusive jurisdiction for the common law over all other forms of law.

One of the first needs of the Normans was to have a judiciary capable of effectively and efficiently dispensing and developing their unified laws. They were initially restricted by their language ability and local hostility. The judiciary needed to be highly literate, but the obvious choice, the aristocracy, was hostile towards them. In their need they turned to the literate, ordained clerics of the Roman Catholic Church and trained them to be judges in the royal courts. Inevitably Christian influence and ethics became instilled in the developing common law.

These newly appointed 'judge-clerics' travelled the country on the monarch's authority hearing major criminal disputes, reading evidence, hearing witnesses and delivering judgment. These journeys and records formed a travelling, localised justice that was centralised administratively. It was this innovation that was to develop ultimately into the unified 'common law' legal system nationalised in terms of administration, jurisdiction, adjudication and law creation. This construction of a law that was common to all came to be referred to as the common law of England – a common law built up from judges' decisions as well as the commands of the sovereign.

In the early centuries after the Norman invasion a number of methods of dispute resolution existed locally alongside the royal, court-based common law. Most of these methods, such as the blood feud,[2] trial by battle[3] and trial by ordeal[4] had their origins in dispute resolution within tribal settings. Defendants at criminal law, and litigants at civil law, could initially choose between royal justice and other methods to resolve their legal dispute.

---

2 When the family of a victim sought to exact revenge by killing members of the aggressor's family.
3 When two sides to a dispute resolved it by engaging each other in battle, or by sponsoring a champion to fight on their behalf.
4 Trial by ordeal was a pagan ritual but was taken over by politics and Christianity. The accused person was subjected to an ordeal. There were several recognised ordeals such as the 'ordeal of water', the 'hot water ordeal', the 'ordeal of the cursed morsel' and the 'fire ordeals'. The support of the Church to trial by ordeal was forbidden in 1215.

The drawback associated with royal justice was its cost, and the fact that if a person was found guilty of breaking the King's peace – that is, acting against the Crown – his lands and monies would be forfeited to the Crown, leaving his family destitute. Many people elected to die under torture so that local justice would take effect and land and possessions would pass to the family, not the Crown. However, in time litigants began to accept using royal justice for dispute resolution.

As law professionalised during the eleventh and twelfth centuries, the teaching of English law took place via apprenticeships. Judges needed clerks, and litigants needed those who understood the law to advise them of the procedures and arguments that the law required.

Legal education took place in specialist Inns of Court, the only places which taught the common law necessary for the education of the legal professionals who worked in the royal courts. They were known as 'inns' of court because living and working space for lawyers and their students was merged into one area. The development of the role of barrister was made possible through the creation of the Inns of Court. The earliest Inns of Court were attached to churches because of the close connection between the clerics and the judges.

The Universities of Oxford and Cambridge limited the legal instruction they offered to Roman law, ignoring the development of the common law. Roman law was considered to be more academically demanding with its links to the idea of a classical education. It was not until the seventeenth century that the first law schools at Oxford and Cambridge began to turn their attention to the common law.

As the common law system evolved and judicial reasoning became more expansive, many justifications for law were grounded in Christian morality and illustrated with reference to the Christian sacred text, the Holy Bible. When Henry VIII instigated the split from the Roman Catholic Church in the sixteenth century he changed the nature of the relationship between the Christian religion and the state by retaining Christianity in its Roman Catholic form but removing it from the authority of Rome, and replacing that authority with his own. So he anglicised it, and assumed the role of the Defender of the Faith – the head and protector of the religion. Another consequence of the split was that the church courts (those which dealt with matters relating to religion) which had formerly been under the authority of Rome, became Courts Christian, or the Ecclesiastical Courts, functioning as part of the English legal system. These courts are still operating today but with a more limited jurisdiction.

Religion was used for many centuries as the litmus test of loyalty to the Crown, and religious oaths were required before people were allowed to engage in many senior public jobs. Increasingly in the common law courts, judges maintained that Christian law and ethics were an integral part of the law of England, a view that continued to be held until the twentieth century.

The characteristics of common law became its communality, its inclusivity, and its preference for providing supplementary legal rules rather than fixed absolutes. The common law remained flexible, making it capable of intricate adaptations to situations. These adaptations eventually produced the judge-made common law we work with today, along with the methods of argument preferred by the English legal system, methods that allow permutations and interpretations of those existing rules.

Eventually after several centuries the common law as a whole developed serious problems. Its valued inherent flexibility was lost and it became a rigid system of legal rules. Much of the problem lay in the procedure for bringing a case in the royal courts. A litigant had to buy a special form, called a writ, from the Chancellor's office. But it was not an open general form where a grievance could be stated. It was highly specific and a prospective litigant had to find the right one from hundreds of writs to cover the details of their case. Otherwise they risked their case being thrown out.

The writ system meant that bringing a legal case in the royal courts was extremely expensive. Court cases were also subject to heavy delays that could run into years. Another potential problem for a claimant was that they could only ask for financial compensation (monetary damages) even though money alone may not have constituted adequate recompense. A claimant may have needed certain possessions to be restored or returned, or for someone to stop doing something (or do something they were required to do). Common law therefore became unable to meet the demands of claimants.

DEVELOPMENT OF EQUITY

Rules that came to be known as 'equitable rules' began to develop as individual claimants petitioned the Crown for relief from the deficiencies of the common law. Although the monarch originally heard these cases in person, they were eventually delegated to the Lord Chancellor. The Lord Chancellor was a senior cleric in the politically and legally established Christian denomination, the Church of England. Because of his senior office and his role in the Church the Lord Chancellor was known as 'the keeper of the King's conscience.'

The word equity is derived from the idea of fairness. The Chancellor was able to consider matters from the perspective of fairness, rather than keep to the rigid forms of the common law. He would ask questions such as 'what would constitute a reasonable outcome?', or 'what is natural justice in the situation?' From the decisions of the Chancellor, equitable rules were developed to assist decision making. As petitions to the Lord Chancellor grew in the fifteenth century, the Court of Chancery was established to hear cases.

Rivalries developed between the Lord Chancellors' Court of Chancery and the common law courts. This rivalry came to a head in 1614 in several cases. In the case of *Courtney v Glanvil*[5] the head of the common law courts, the Lord Chief Justice, declared that the chancery courts, which he called a court of equity, could not interfere with any decision of the common law courts. The response from the Lord Chancellor was to declare in the *Earl of Oxford's case*[6] that, on the contrary, the Court of Chancery had the required jurisdiction to set aside any decision of the common law courts. Ultimately, after a period of acrimony, the supremacy of equity over common law was established after the matter was referred to King James I and his attorney general, Sir Francis Bacon. As the source of equity lay in

5   (1614) Cro Jac 343, 79 ER 294.
6   (1615) Rep Ch.

the King's residual power to be petitioned on any matter as the fountain of justice, and in his conscience, as kept by the Lord Chancellor, it was not a surprise that such a decision should have been reached.

The equitable rules that guided decision making in the chancery courts dealing with equity and remedies were broader than just the monetary damages of the common law. In

TABLE 2.1 AN ILLUSTRATIVE LIST OF EQUITABLE MAXIMS, REMEDIES AND RIGHTS

Equitable maxims	Equitable remedies	Equitable rights
'He who comes to equity must come with clean hands' A litigant wanting a remedy from equity must have behaved reasonably themselves	**Specific performance** A party to a contract is ordered to perform their contractual obligations. This will only be granted by the court if money damages would be inadequate in the circumstances	**The equity of redemption** The right to redeem (pay off) a mortgage
'Delay defeats equity' If a person has unreasonably delayed a matter, equity will not give them a remedy	**Injunction** A court order making someone do something or refrain from doing something. Examples would be:	**Rights of beneficiaries** of a trust to obtain their benefit
'Equity is a shield not a sword' Equity is not a claim that is demanded by the litigant, but equity will protect the litigant	• Freezing orders: to stop defendants taking assets out of the jurisdiction of the court • Search order: prevents documents being hidden from the courts and can lead to the searching of premises	
'Equity will not suffer a wrong to be without a remedy'	**Rectification** Allows contractual documents to be altered because as drafted they do not represent the actual agreement between the parties	
'Equality is equity' If a trust does not state how property or money is to be divided up then equal shares to each will be the operative rule	**Rescission** Allows contractual terms to be set aside returning the parties to where they were before the terms came into being	

equity defendants could be ordered to 'stop doing' something or 'to do' something and/ or return possessions belonging to the claimant. But to obtain full compensation, often a litigant was put in the position of having to pay to bring a case in the court of equity for non-monetary remedies after having paid to go to a common law court to obtain monetary recompense.

This state of affairs continued well into the nineteenth century when the Supreme Court of Judicature Acts of 1873 and 1875 declared that courts could dispense both common law and equitable rules using only one procedure. These Acts also gave statutory authority to the rule that should there be conflict between a common law rule or an equitable rule then equity would prevail (a rule that is now found in the Senior Courts Act 1981, s 49).

You will come across equitable doctrines (or maxims), remedies and rights throughout your study of law as they remain an important source of law. It is therefore important that you understand their origins and effect. Table 2.1 above sets out a range of equitable maxims, remedies and rights that equity brings. But do note that this is an illustrative, not an exhaustive, list.[7]

CUSTOM

As the common law developed it incorporated many local, unwritten, customary rules. A customary law or rule is a practice that communities agree is the only right way to act in that matter, because it is the 'customary way'. Customs can change from generation to generation and between geographic areas. But these customs came to determine how a legal dispute would be dealt with and by whom. Smith and Keenan define local custom in the following way: 'local customs consist in the main of customary rights vested in the inhabitants of a particular place to use, for various purposes, land held in the private own- ership of another'.[8]

Over time these oral customary rules held in the memory of communities were reduced to writing and became part of the common law. Slapper and Kelly note 'From this point of view, law may be seen as the redefinition of custom for the purposes of clarity and enforce- ment by legal institutions.'[9] However, some schools of thought maintain that common law legal rules and custom represent two completely different species of rules and that law often replaced custom rather than incorporating custom into itself.

Today, if a person wishes to maintain that a local customary rule that conflicts with a common law rule should be enforced they need to prove that the custom is reasonable, can be clearly set out, and has existed peacefully without any interruptions from 'time immemorial' (agreed to be 1189). The normal situation now is that it is sufficient to show the custom has existed within 'living memory' rather than 'time immemorial'. Furthermore, they must prove that there has been no clandestine aspect to the custom, and that it had been enjoyed without the use of force, or permission or underhandedness. Those who are raising the custom must demonstrate that they consider themselves to be bound by it and that the custom does not conflict with other local customs.

---

7   For further reading on equity see G Slapper and D Kelly *The English Legal System* (15th edn, Routledge, 2014–2015), 217–19.

8   C Wild and S Weinstein *Smith and Keenan's English Law* (13th edn, Longman, 2013).

9   See fn 7 p 13.

It is difficult, but by no means impossible, to prove a local custom. Customs are, however, proved in court and are a source of case law. The criteria by which customs can be proved are also broad enough to allow the judiciary to refuse the validity of a local custom should they so wish. But if the judiciary consider the custom to be established and that it fits the above criteria then it will take priority over a conflicting common law rule.[10]

ENGLISH LAW AND THE DOCTRINE OF PRECEDENT

The decisions of judges in those courts considered to be senior courts must generally be followed by judges in the same or lower court: if the facts of the legal dispute are similar and the same legal rule is involved. This practice is known as the doctrine of precedent. The doctrine of precedent is reliant upon the existence of a court hierarchy and a good system of law reporting (or courts keeping a reliable accessible transcript of the judgment). Otherwise no one will know what was said in an earlier case.[11]

It is often said by judges in their judgments that the doctrine of precedent has been observed for centuries. But, like the history of the common law itself, the truth of such statements is unclear. There is evidence of such practice in some cases recorded over the centuries.

Only two things can be stated with some certainty. First, that the judiciary have maintained a relatively strict adherence to the doctrine of precedent from the nineteenth century onwards and this coincided with a regularisation of law reporting. Secondly, that whilst all legal systems have some concept of precedent, the English legal system is exceptional because of its strict adherence to the doctrine of precedent.[12] Law reporting is considered in detail in Chapter 8, and the doctrine of precedent is considered in detail in Chapter 10.

THE COURTS

As you will have realised by now, courts of law are the institutions that hear and determine legal disputes based on the infringements of legal rules. Legal rules serve no purpose if there is not a system of officially sanctioned institutions for the adjudication of legal disputes with powers, as appropriate, to:

- punish the defendant in a criminal case or award damages and/or an equitable remedy to the complainant in a civil case;
- ensure enforcement of its criminal law punishments or award of civil law remedies;
- hear appeals from the outcome of trials.

The courts have developed over centuries, and very few were created by statute. At one time, the royal courts were part of the monarch's own household; however, as adjudication became a full time job it could not be conducted by the monarch alone.

---

10 *Egerton v Harding* [1974] 3 WLR 437, LA 150 is an example of a customary rule being proved in court in relatively modern times.
11 Law reporting is considered in some detail in Chapter 8 'How to find domestic and European law cases'.
12 Precedent will be discussed in more detail in Chapter 10.

As the powers of English monarchs were successively usurped or transferred to Parliament, changes to the structure and administration of the courts have increasingly been made by legislation. New courts have also been created by legislation. But change was slow in coming.

The first major overhaul of the structure (as well as the administration) of English civil courts occurred in the nineteenth century through the Judicature Acts of 1873 and 1875.

The Judicature Acts led, among other things, to the setting up of a unified system of appeal and the establishment of the Court of Appeal. The Court of Criminal Appeals was established by the Criminal Appeals Act 1907, and merged with the civil Court of Appeal in 1966. From that time onwards the Court of Appeal had a civil and a criminal division. Historically the House of Lords had a judicial function to hear appeals which, technically, were appeals to the Crown-in-Parliament.

The first major overhaul of the criminal court structure did not happen until the Courts Act 1975 which led to the establishment of the Crown Court to hear criminal trials.

There have been various major changes to civil and criminal court structure and administration since 1975. The Courts Act 2003 introduced far-reaching administrative changes to the organisation of English courts, unifying the administration of the English courts through a new institution, Her Majesty's Courts Service (HMCS), which was set up in 2005. This was the result of government support for the findings of a review of the criminal courts conducted by Sir Robert Auld and published in 2001.[13] In 2011 the tribunal system was merged into HMCS creating Her Majesty's Courts and Tribunals Service (HMCTS), finally streamlining the organisation of courts and tribunals.[14]

The HMCTS is part of the Justice Ministry; however, it is a completely separate agency. It can currently be accessed via http://www.justice.gov.uk/about/hmcts/. It encompasses all trial courts and the Court of Appeal (criminal and civil divisions) but does not include the Supreme Court. The Constitutional Reform Act 2005 established the Supreme Court of the United Kingdom as the final court of appeal, or court of last resort.

English law is today divided into many distinct areas with the main areas being civil and criminal. Civil law can be further subdivided into a range of distinct specialisms, for example contract, family and employment. Civil and criminal cases are heard in different courts, although often in practice a court will predominantly deal with one area, for example criminal matters, and that court may (or may not) have a limited jurisdiction to deal with civil matters, and vice versa.

Courts also specialise in the type of hearing they are predominantly engaged with, trials, judicial reviews or appeals. Trials (also known as first instance hearings) involve the presentation of evidence with witnesses usually being called and examined in open court (unless special arrangements have been made to have a live video link for such an examination). Parties to cases in trial courts can appeal through the appeals procedure within the court system.

Appeal hearings involve hearing a dispute about the outcome of a trial, either in relation to remedies awarded (civil actions) or sentence imposed (criminal trials). The technical phrase is that such courts have 'an appellate function'. Certain criteria have to be met

---

13 The Right Honourable Sir Robert Auld *A Review of the Criminal Courts of England and Wales*.
14 Tribunals are briefly discussed later in this chapter.

otherwise there can be no appeal and leave to appeal must be sought from the courts, again with criteria determining which court must be approached. Again in practice, whilst a court may predominately hear trials it may have a limited jurisdiction in relation to appeals, and vice versa.

Generic terms applied to courts

There are a range of different terms used to refer to courts and one court can qualify for several such descriptions: they are not mutually exclusive. It can be most confusing at first but you will soon get used to the different labels attaching to descriptions of the courts. To assist you Table 2.2 sets these terms out with a brief explanation.

Description of the main domestic courts

The courts described below do not form an exhaustive list but contain the main courts that you are required to be aware of. Courts are either predominantly superior (senior) or inferior (subordinate) courts, and will mainly exercise appellate or trial functions.

Appellate courts

The judges in the appeal courts are the most senior judges in the UK. The appeals in the senior appellate courts are conducted by legal argument and the submission of documentary

TABLE 2.2 RANGE OF REFERENCES TO ROLE/HIERARCHY OF COURT

Reference to court	Explanation of reference
Inferior court	These courts have limited jurisdiction, either geographic or financial
Superior court	These courts have unlimited jurisdiction, both geographic and financial
Trial court	The court where a dispute is heard for the first time; these are also known as first instance courts (because logically it is the first time the matter has gone to the court)
Appellate court	Hearing an appeal from a trial court or a subordinate appeal court. Some courts combine a trial and an appellate function
Civil court	Dealing with disputes between private legal persons awarding remedies. The court of appeal has a civil division
Criminal court	Dealing with actions by the state against individuals/groups imposing punishment. The court of appeal has a criminal division
A court of record	The proceedings of that court are kept at the public record office for the public to look at

evidence. No witnesses are called. Appeals are not automatically allowed and a party wishing to appeal the decision of a court usually has to seek 'leave to appeal'. A brief description of the senior appellate courts is given below. At the end of these descriptions Table 2.3 briefly sets out the main features of each court for your quick reference.

The Supreme Court of the United Kingdom (SCUK)

The Supreme Court is the final court of appeal for all criminal and civil cases in the English legal system (England, Wales and Northern Ireland). It also has limited jurisdiction in relation to the Scottish legal system where it is the final court of appeal for the inner court of session. Its jurisdiction covers the United Kingdom.

It was established by the Constitutional Reform Act 2005 and commenced hearing cases on 1 October 2009. It inherited the jurisdiction of the House of Lords which was the former final court of appeal.

Currently there are twelve 'Justices of the Supreme Court'. These include the President of the Supreme Court and the Deputy President of the Supreme Court. The court sits in its own dedicated building in Parliament Square, London.

The Court of Appeal (EWCA)

The Court of Appeal is divided into two divisions, the criminal appeal division and the civil appeals division. Its jurisdiction extends to England and Wales, but not to the entire United Kingdom in the way that the jurisdiction of the Supreme Court extends.

It is staffed by Lord/Lady Justices of Appeal. Normally three Justices of Appeal sit in court. For important cases it is possible for five or seven Justices of Appeal to sit in court. In rare circumstances the court can sit with one judge.

Appeal Court: criminal division

The head of the criminal appeals division is the Lord Chief Justice.

The criminal appeals division hears appeals against conviction and sentence from defendants in the Crown Court. It also hears references from the Attorney General on a point of law or on the grounds of an unduly lenient sentence being given. In cases where there has been an acquittal the acquittal will stand (Criminal Justice Act 1972, s 36) but a ruling can be given by the court supporting the appeal and this must be taken into account in further similar cases. Finally, it has jurisdiction to hear references by the Criminal Cases Review Commission concerning a potential miscarriage of justice.[15]

As noted above there is not an automatic right to appeal and the Court of Appeal also hears applications for leave to appeal to the Supreme Court.

Appeal Court: civil division

The Master of the Rolls is the head of the civil division which deals with appeals from the High Court and the county court. It also has jurisdiction to hear appeals from the upper

---

15 s. 9 Criminal Appeal Act 1995.

tribunal, Employment Appeal Tribunal, Immigration Appeal Tribunal, Lands Tribunal and the Social Security Commissioners. Tribunals are discussed in more detail later in this chapter. Table 2.3 sets out the appellate courts in a quick access table form.

Superior courts

A superior court is one whose decisions are not subject to any other court except an appellate court. These courts deal with trials and are also called courts of first instance. Some of these courts are more closely identified with criminal law and some with civil law cases. Most courts will major in one area of jurisdiction, but exercise limited jurisdiction in the other. At the end of the descriptions Table 2.5 briefly sets out the main features of each court for your quick reference.

The High Court

The High Court is split into three divisions for administrative purposes: Queen's Bench Division, Chancery Division, Family Division, and each of these three divisions is further subdivided. Its primary jurisdiction is civil at first instance but it also has an appellate juris-diction in a limited range of criminal and civil matters.

The judges sitting in the High Court are referred to as 'puisne' judges, a word derived from the old French for 'inferior'.

Queen's Bench Division

The head of the division is the Lord Chief Justice. Its jurisdiction is primarily civil. However, alongside its civil jurisdiction it exercises an appellate jurisdiction to hear criminal appeals from the magistrates' court by way of 'case stated'. No witnesses are called, and the appeal is conducted by legal argument and the submission of documentary evidence. It also has jurisdiction to hear criminal appeals from the Crown Court which has sat without a jury.

The Queen's Bench Division mainly deals with civil actions in contract and tort (acci-dent) claims, fraud, malicious prosecution, claims against the police and contentious pro-bate cases. Additionally it has the jurisdiction to hear civil appeals from the county courts.

The sub-divisional courts of the Queen's Bench Division

To more efficiently carry out its range of functions it also has three specialist sub-divi-sional courts, the Administrative Court, the Admiralty Court and the Commercial Court. The Administrative Court deals with applications for judicial review. This is an application to review the action of a public or a private body (e.g. a local authority or a sports club), mostly on the grounds that in exercising its public duties and making a determination that body has exceeded its lawful authority. As you may suspect the Admiralty Court deals exclusively with matters relating to shipping, although it also deals with issues relating to aircraft. Finally, the Commercial Court deals with actions arising in the fields of banking, insurance and finance.

TABLE 2.3 SUPREME COURT, AND THE COURT OF APPEAL: FUNCTION, JUDGES AND JURISDICTION

Court	Function	Judges sitting in court	Inferior court	Superior court	Criminal jurisdiction	Civil jurisdiction	Trial court (first instance)	Appellate court
The Supreme Court	Final court of appeal for all United Kingdom criminal and civil cases in England, Wales and Northern Ireland. No witnesses are called; all argument paper based. Sits in the Supreme Court building	12 Justices of the Supreme Court	X	√	√	√	X	√
Court of Appeal (Contains criminal and civil divisions)	**Criminal Division:** Deals with appeals from Crown Court (sentence, conviction or both) References on a point of law or grounds of an unduly lenient sentence from the Attorney General when there has been an acquittal (Criminal Justice Act 1972, s 36). Acquittal will stand References by the Criminal Cases Review Commission if the possibility of a miscarriage of justice (Criminal Appeal Act 1995, s 9) Application for leave to appeal to the Supreme Court **Civil Division:** Deals with appeals from the High Court, county court, Upper Tribunal, Employment Appeal Tribunal, Immigration Appeal Tribunal, Lands Tribunal, Social Security Commissioners Only hears legal argument and documentary evidence	Head of criminal division: Lord Chief Justice	X	√	√	X	X	√

The Chancery Division of the High Court

The head of the Chancery Division is the Lord Chancellor, although in practice it is the Vice-Chancellor that functions as the divisional head on a day-to-day basis. Its jurisdiction is exclusively civil. It is mostly concerned with civil trials in the areas of wills, estates, contentious probate, land and mortgage actions, trusts, company law, intellectual property and partnerships. It also hears appeals from the county court concerning issues such as bankruptcy. Like the Queen's Bench Division the Chancery Division has specialist sub-divisional courts. The Patents Court deals with ownership of products and the Court of Protection is concerned with the rights of persons with a disability.

The Family Division of the High Court

The head of division is the President of the Family Division. Its main jurisdiction is civil hearing trials relating to defended divorce, adoption and wardship. It exercises limited criminal jurisdiction. If a domestic violence issue is clearly connected to the issue of the settlement of family property, wills and probate, it has jurisdiction to hear the domestic violence issue. It also has a criminal appellate jurisdiction to hear appeals from magistrates' courts and the Crown Court in family issues.

The Crown Court

The jurisdiction of the Crown Court is mainly criminal. It hears criminal trials on indictment heard by jury, trials where the magistrates declined jurisdiction and trials of offences that can be heard by either the magistrates' court or Crown Court by the defendant's choice.

It also deals with referrals for sentencing from magistrates' courts where the statutory limit is considered inadequate and they seek a higher sentence.

The Crown Court exercises an appellate jurisdiction in the area of appeals against sentences imposed in the magistrates' court and appeals against conviction in the magistrates' court. It also exercises a very limited civil jurisdiction in relation to highways repair and other small matters.

It is staffed by High Court judges, circuit judges, deputy circuit judges (part time), recorders (part time) and assistant recorders (part time).

Inferior courts

This term basically means that the decisions of these courts are prone to being overturned by the superior courts.

The county court

Currently there are 169 county courts which deal with the majority of civil disputes in the areas of debt, personal injuries compensation, breach of contract relating to goods/property, divorce, adoption, wills, bankruptcy, housing disputes including mortgages, arrears of rent and repossessions.

Court		Description of court	Judges	Inferior court	Superior court	Criminal jurisdiction	Civil jurisdiction	Trial court	Appellate court
The High Court	**Queen's Bench Division**	First instance jurisdiction: Appellate jurisdiction: criminal appeals from magistrates' court, Crown Court sitting without a jury. Civil appeals from county court. **Specialist subdivisions:** Administrative Court: judicial review. Admiralty Court: shipping, aircraft. Commercial Court: banking, insurance, finance	Head: Lord Chief Justice. High court judges referred to as puisne judges (meaning inferior)	X	√	√ Appellate only	√	√ Civil only	√ Criminal and civil
	Chancery Division	First instance jurisdiction: Appellate jurisdiction: some civil appeals from the county court. **Specialist subdivisions:** Patents Court and the Court of Protection (care of persons with a disability)	Head: Lord Chancellor in name, Vice-Chancellor in practice. Puisne judges	X	√	X	√	√	√ limited
	Family Division	Civil trial but if domestic violence connected to settlement of family matters this can be heard. Hears appeals from magistrates' courts and Crown Court in family issues.	Head: President of the Family Division. puisne judges	X	√	√ Appellate	√	√	√ Criminal and civil
Crown Court		Jurisdiction mainly criminal: criminal cases on indictment heard by a jury; or where the magistrates declined jurisdiction; offences that can be heard by magistrate or Crown Court on defendant election. Also hears referrals for sentencing from magistrates' court. Hears criminal appeals against sentence and conviction in magistrates' court. Its civil jurisdiction is limited, e.g. highways repair.	Judges: High Court judges, circuit judges, deputy circuit judges (part time), recorders (part time), assistance recorders (part time)	X	√	√	√ limited	√	√

TABLE 2.5 INFERIOR COURTS: COUNTY COURT AND MAGISTRATES' COURT: ROLE, JUDGES AND JURISDICTION

	Description		Inferior court	Superior court	Criminal jurisdiction	Civil jurisdiction	Trial court (first instance)	Appellate court
County court	First instance jurisdiction: debt, personal injuries compensation, breach of contract relating to goods/property, divorce, adoption, wills, bankruptcy, housing disputes including mortgages, arrears of rent, repossessions There are geographical as well as financial limits on its jurisdiction Track system: Small claims, fast track, multi-track 169 county courts	Judges: circuit judges, deputy circuit judges, district judges, part time deputy district judges	√	X	√	√	√	X
Magistrates' court	Deals with majority of all criminal matters (90 per cent); all start in the court: bail applications, warrants for arrest or search, Youth courts, trial criminal: summary offences Trial civil recovery of civil debt, highways issues, family matters excluding divorce, care proceedings linked to children in Youth court	Heard by Justices of the Peace who are lay magistrates, sitting as three or a single district judge working full time salaried	√	X	√	√	√	X

There are geographical as well as financial limits on its jurisdiction. For the purposes of administrative efficiency the court operates a track system. The normal track deals with small claims mostly under £5,000, although there are a few exceptions. The fast track deals with claims that are under £25,000. The multi-track system deals with complex claims over £25,000.

The judges in the county court are circuit judges, deputy circuit judges, district judges and part time deputy district judges.

The magistrates' court

This court deals with nearly all criminal matters as the majority of criminal prosecutions must start in the magistrates' court. A number are then sent on to the Crown Court for trial. The magistrates' court also exercises criminal jurisdiction to hear bail applications, warrants for arrest or search, and summary offences. It also runs 'Youth courts' dealing with young offenders.

It also has civil jurisdiction in the area of recovery of civil debt, highways issues, family matters (excluding divorce) and care proceedings linked to children in Youth court.

Its primary judges are the Justices of the Peace who are lay magistrates, sitting on a bench of three, who are unpaid and part time. There is provision for some to be appointed as stipendiary magistrates and then a modest payment is received. The court is also staffed by salaried district judges working full time.

Tribunals

Tribunals were created by legislation in the twentieth century to primarily deal with disputes by individuals against the state (including government agencies) in particular in areas such as employment, rents, immigration, mental health and taxations. They are part of the administrative justice stream of the English legal system as their role is to review decision making. The tribunal system developed piecemeal from the 1950s and was restructured by the Tribunals, Courts and Enforcement Act 2007 (TCEA 2007).[16]

The TCEA 2007 creates a two tier system to include most tribunals and is geared only to appeals against decision making by state officials. The First-tier Tribunal is divided into chambers similar to the idea of courts in the courts system, each one hearing cases in particular areas. The Act also creates an Upper Tier Tribunal which mainly exercises review and appellate functions but has a limited first instance hearing role in other areas. It is a superior court of record. Its decisions are therefore binding on First-tier Tribunals.

In 2011 the administration of the tribunals was merged with the administration of the courts, creating Her Majesty's Courts and Tribunal Service (HMCTS). Some tribunals are noticeably left out of the restructuring, for example the Employment Tribunal and the Employment Appeals Tribunal.

---

16 This followed on from the Leggatt Report *Tribunals for Users: One System, One Service* (2001) www.tribunals-review.org.uk, accessed 20 June 2014.

Panels of members decide the outcome of cases in the upper and first tiers and for tribunals outside the tier system. These 'members' can be legally qualified in which case they are called a judge; additionally judges in the high court and other courts can sit as a member. Panel members also include experts in the area, for example doctors or surveyors. A judge may sit alone when deciding a case. Each panel has a tribunal chairman or, if a judge is sitting, a tribunal judge responsible for communicating the decision in writing. The senior president of tribunals heads up the tier system.

It is possible to appeal to the Court of Appeal and on to the Supreme Court from the Upper Tribunal, which can also refer some cases to the High Court.

A notable example of an important tribunal outside the tier system is the Employment Tribunal and the Employment Appeals Tribunal. Appeals can also go to the Court of Appeal and Supreme Court from Appeals Tribunals outside the tier system. This is illustrated in Figure 2.1. Table 2.6 gives information in a checklist format for your use.

Courts outside the hierarchical system of the English legal system

Several courts exert an impact on the English legal system because their decisions can form persuasive precedents or because statute has provided that their decisions should be taken into account in areas of relevance. There are three courts falling into this category:

- The Judicial Committee of the Privy Council (PC).
- The European Court of Human Rights (ECtHR).
- The Court of Justice of the European Union (CJEU, often just referred to as the CJ).

The Judicial Committee of the Privy Council

The Privy Council is composed of around 500 privy counsellors whose duty is to give advice to the monarch concerning the discharge of their state duties. Councellors have attained high public office. All past cabinet members, party leaders, archbishops, and current or past speakers of the House of Commons are automatically privy counsellors. The ministerial head of the Privy Council is its senior president. Several committees operate in the council and one of them is the Judicial Committee.

This is the final court of appeal for UK overseas territories, Crown dependencies, military sovereign bases overseas, ancient courts (prize courts, Court of Admiralty of the Cinque Ports) and ecclesiastical courts (Arches Court of Canterbury, the Chancery Court of York, Church Commissioners) and for those Commonwealth countries who have retained the court. A court normally consists of three or five judges. It shares the Supreme Court building in London. Table 2.7 below sets out checklist information.

Justices of the UK Supreme Court can sit (as can former Lords of Appeal in Ordinary) as well as Privy Councellors who are judges in superior courts in the Commonwealth.

The decisions of the Judicial Committee are considered to be persuasive precedents within the English legal system, but they do not have to be followed.

TABLE 2.6 TRIBUNALS TIER SYSTEM: ROLE, ADJUDICATORS AND JURISDICTION

	Description	Panel	First instance hearing	Appeal hearings	Superior court of record
First-tier Tribunal[17]	The First-tier Tribunal is divided into specialist chambers and chambers can be added as required. Current chambers include: • Social Entitlement Chamber (asylum, social security, child support, criminal injuries compensation) • Health, Education and Social Care Chamber (care standards, mental health, special educational needs, disability, primary health lists) • War Pensions and Armed Forces compensation • General Regulatory Chamber (charity, claims management, consumer credit, environment, estate agents, gambling appeals, immigration services, information rights, local government standards, transport) • Immigration and Asylum Chamber • Tax Chamber	Members may be a judge or legally qualified	√	X	X
Upper Tribunal	The Upper Tribunal is appellate and is divided into four chambers: • Administrative Appeals Chamber • Tax and Chancery Chamber • Lands Chamber • Immigration and Asylum Chamber Appeals on a point of law go to the Court of Appeal Civil division	Members may be a judge or legally qualified	X	√	√

17 Created by the Tribunals, Courts and Enforcement Act 2007, s 3.

TABLE 2.7 PRIVY COUNCIL: FUNCTION, ROLE, JUDGES AND JURISDICTION

Court	Function	Judges sitting in court	Superior court	Criminal jurisdiction	Civil jurisdiction	Appellate court
Judicial Committee of the Privy Council	Final court of appeal for a range of UK overseas territories and dependencies, some Commonwealth jurisdictions as well as for a range of UK ancient and ecclesiastical courts No witnesses are called, all argument paper based Sits in the Supreme Court building Three or five judges sit to hear a case	Current judges in the Supreme Court and Court of Appeal can sit Former Lords of Appeal in Ordinary, and privy councellors who are judges of the Court of Appeal or of some superior courts in the Commonwealth	√	√	√	√

THE EUROPEAN COURT OF HUMAN RIGHTS

ECtHR

This is a court established by the Council of Europe (CoE) in 1959 as a court to hear claims by individuals who had exhausted all of the avenues of complaint nationally available in relation to the European Convention on Human Rights 1950. Revisions to the structure of the CoE in 1998 led to the abolition of the existing ECtHR and the European Commission on Human Rights and the establishing of a new Court of Human Rights.

In 1996 UK citizens were given the right to petition the ECtHR. The enactment of the Human Rights Act by Parliament in 1998 changed the judges' relationship with the ECtHR. This Act allowed nationals to bring claims relating to alleged breaches of the European Convention on Human Rights (ECHR) in domestic courts. Individuals must have exhausted all of the avenues of complaint nationally available in relation to the European Convention on Human Rights 1950 before being able to take their case to the European Court of Human Rights. Section 2 of the Act places a duty on all English judges to take into account the case law of the European Court of Human Rights when deciding cases where they have been given jurisdiction by the Act. Table 2.8 contrasts this court with the Court of Justice of the European Union.

THE COURT OF JUSTICE OF THE EUROPEAN UNION

CJEU

Originally established in 1951 by the Treaty of Paris, its jurisdiction increased as the EU developed and it is now the main Court of the EU. Its powers can be found in the consolidated Treaty on the Foundation of the European Union 2012.

It is a grouping of courts but its primary courts are the Court of Justice and the General Court. The Court of Justice has the important role of ensuring the harmonious interpretation of the founding treaties of the EU and its secondary law through preliminary references. This is the situation where a domestic court in any of the member states of the EU is uncertain about the interpretation of an aspect of the EU treaties or EU secondary law. Its objective is also to ensure that conflicting law in member states is dis-applied. Case law of the CJ must be taken into account in member states when dealing with issues of EU law.

Since 2007 the General Court can hear preliminary references in certain areas. There is a limited right of appeal, within two months of a decision of the General Court, to the Court of Justice on matters of law only.

The hierarchy of the domestic courts (with reference to tribunals and European courts)

In the English legal system all courts have a determined place in a hierarchy of courts. It is extremely important to know and understand the basic framework for the hierarchy of

TABLE 2.8 EUROPEAN COURTS IMPACTING THE ENGLISH LEGAL SYSTEM: ROLE AND JURISDICTION

Court	Description	Inferior court	Superior court	Criminal jurisdiction	Civil jurisdiction	First instance	Appellate
The European Court of Human Rights[18] **The creation of the Council of Europe**	A court of the Council of Europe, not a court within the English legal system Hears claims by individuals who have exhausted all of the avenues of complaint nationally available in relation to the European Convention on Human Rights 1950 UK citizens were given the right to petition the ECtHR in 1996 In 1998 the Human Rights Act, s 2 placed a duty on all English judges to take into account case law of the European Court of Human Rights when deciding cases under certain articles of the ECHR	X	√	X	√	√	√
The Court of Justice of the EU[19] **The creation of the European Union**	It is the Court of the EU. It contains several courts but its primary courts are the Court of Justice and the General Court The jurisdiction of the Court of Justice is to ensure the harmonious interpretation of the founding treaties of the EU and secondary law of the EU, to ensure conflicting law in member states is dis-applied. Also, to deal with conflicts between member states relating to the EU, and to hear disputes between the EU institutions and member states Case law of the Court of Justice must be taken into account in member states when dealing with issues of EU law The General Court, since 2007, can hear preliminary references in certain areas. There is a limited appeal to the Court of Justice	X	√	X	√	√	√

18 See Chapter 4 for full details.
19 See Chapter 5 for full details.

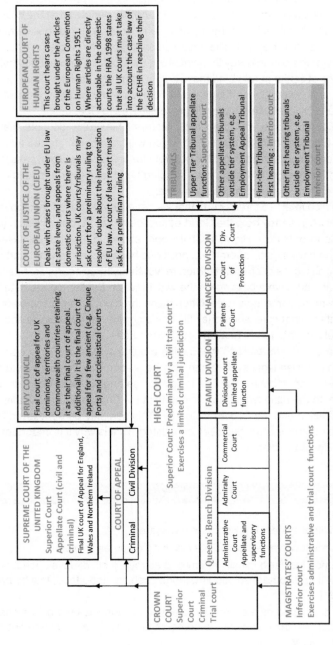

SUPREME COURT OF THE UNITED KINGDOM
Superior Court
Appellate Court (civil and criminal)
Final UK court of Appeal for England, Wales and Northern Ireland

COURT OF APPEAL

Criminal	Civil Division

HIGH COURT
Superior Court: Predominantly a civil trial court
Exercises a limited criminal jurisdiction

FAMILY DIVISION
Divisional court
Limited appellate function

CHANCERY DIVISION

Patents Court	Court of Protection	Div. Court

Queen's Bench Division

Administrative Court Appellate and supervisory functions	Admiralty Court	Commercial Court

CROWN COURT
Superior Court
Criminal
Trial court

MAGISTRATES' COURTS
Inferior court
Exercises administrative and trial court functions

PRIVY COUNCIL
Final court of appeal for UK dominions, territories and Commonwealth countries retaining it as their final court of appeal. Additionally it is the final court of appeal for a few ancient (e.g. Cinque Ports) and ecclesiastical courts

COURT OF JUSTICE OF THE EUROPEAN UNION (CJEU)
Deals with cases brought under EU law at state level, and appeals from domestic courts where there is jurisdiction. UK courts/tribunals may ask court for a preliminary ruling to resolve doubt about the interpretation of EU law. A court of last resort must ask for a preliminary ruling

EUROPEAN COURT OF HUMAN RIGHTS
This court hears cases brought under the Articles of the European Convention on Human Rights 1951. Where articles are directly actionable in the domestic courts the HRA 1998 states that all UK courts must take into account the case law of the ECHR in reaching their decision

TRIBUNALS

Upper Tier Tribunal appellate function: Superior Court

Other appellate tribunals outside tier system, e.g. Employment Appeal Tribunal

First-tier Tribunals
First hearing : Inferior court

Other first hearing tribunals outside tier system, e.g. Employment Tribunal
Inferior court

Figure 2.1 UK court structure: also showing its relationship with the tribunals, the Privy Council and two key European courts

courts as it provides a framework for understanding the doctrine of precedent. Figure 2.1 sets out a diagram of the court structure of the English legal system indicating the hierarchy of courts. An arrow pointing from one court to another denotes that the court the arrow points to holds a higher position in the hierarchy and exercises an appellate function over the decisions of the court below it. The most senior court is the Supreme Court.

The hierarchy of the courts is key in maintaining the doctrine of precedent which states that the decisions of senior courts bind those below it and themselves in similar cases. The Supreme Court is an exception in that it is not bound by any court in terms of precedent and it is not bound by itself. This issue will be considered in Chapter 11.

Whilst the diagram deals with the simple issue of hierarchy, do note that there are small appellate functions held by trial courts which will have been referred to above in the descriptions of each court. In addition it is possible for an appellant to bypass the Court of Appeal (through a process known as 'leap-frogging') and take their appeal directly to the Supreme Court if the appeal fulfils certain criteria.

The diagram also refers to three courts that we have already described above, the Privy Council (PC) shown in a grey box, the Court of Justice of the European Union (CJEU) and the European Court of Human Rights (ECtHR) both shown in blue boxes. Taken together these three courts have slightly anomalous positions because they are not part of the hierarchy of the English legal system court structure, yet these three courts are relevant courts, and their decisions do have a bearing on the way in which English courts determine legal issues dealing with the same legal rules. Often these three courts are a source of confusion because students are not sure where they fit. This diagram clearly explains and shows the nature of their relationship to the English court structure.[20]

Additionally the diagram refers to the English tribunal system in a grey box. The place of tribunals in the English legal system can also be a source of confusion; students want to know how and where tribunals 'fit'. The legislation setting up many tribunals, but not all, allows an appeal to the main two appellate courts in the English court structure (the Court of Appeal civil division and the Supreme Court).[21] This can only be done after the appeals process with the tribunal system has been exhausted. That is why it is important to include tribunals in the Figure 2.1 diagram.

CHAPTER SUMMARY

- The English legal system is a common law system.
- Case law is the law created by judges deciding disputes in court.
- As the common law (also initially referred to as royal justice) developed it got rid of other competing dispute resolution methods such as blood feud, trial by battle and trial by ordeal.
- Equity was developed as a separate system of law administered by the chancery courts to deal with the rigidity of the common law and its lack of remedies beyond monetary damages.

---

20 The CJEU and the ECtHR are considered in more detail in Chapters 5 and 4 respectively.
21 The Privy Council is considered in more detail in Chapter 7.

- The Supreme Court of Judicature Acts of 1873 and 1875 declared that courts could dispense both common law and equitable principles and that equity prevailed over common law.
- A customary rule is a practice that communities agree is the only right way to act in that matter; they can change from generation to generation and between geographic areas.
- Over time customary rules became part of the common law.
- The English common law system relies on a strict following of the doctrine of precedent.
- Courts of law are the institutions that that hear and determine legal disputes.
- English courts are in a hierarchical relationship which is pivotal to the operation of the doctrine of precedent.
- Criminal courts hear cases brought by the state against an individual and they dispense punishment.
- The first major overhaul of the structure (as well as the administration) of English civil courts occurred in the nineteenth century through the Judicature Acts of 1873 and 1875.
- The first major overhaul of criminal courts occurred in the Courts Act 1975 which also established the Crown Court.
- The Constitutional Reform Act 2005 established the Supreme Court of the United Kingdom.
- The Courts Act 2003 unified the administration of the English courts and set up a new institution, Her Majesty's Courts Service (HMCS).
- In 2011 the tribunal system was merged into HMCS creating Her Majesty's Courts and Tribunals Service (HMCTS). HMCTS does not include the Supreme Court.
- Tribunals are created by statute, only have statutory jurisdiction and have only been in existence since the mid-twentieth century. Tribunals were administratively reorganised by the Tribunals, Courts and Enforcement Act 2007 and merged with HMC Service in 2011 to form Her Majesty's Courts and Tribunals Service.
- The Privy Council (PC) is the highest appeal court for UK dominions and territories.

EUROPEAN AND INTERNATIONAL TREATIES

3

LEARNING OUTCOMES

After reading this chapter you should be able to:

- Understand what a treaty is.
- Appreciate that a treaty operates at the level of international law with no legal effect within the English legal system, unless domestic legislation gives it legal effect.
- Understand how some or all obligations in a treaty can also become part of English law.
- Be able to competently read, use and understand treaties.

INTRODUCTION

This chapter lays a foundation for you to acquire a basic understanding of treaties – agreements between states operative at the level of international law. Many students of law encounter difficulties with the vast number of unfamiliar terms used when they turn to a consideration of the influence of European treaties on English law. Often, this difficulty occurs simply because the nature of treaties in general is not understood. A step by step approach to treaties is taken. They are defined, their legal effect considered, and their standard format explained. This chapter also looks at the mechanisms for minimising dissent during treaty negotiations. It also considers methods for changing or being released from a treaty. The general matters about treaties discussed in this chapter hold true whether you are dealing with European treaties or treaties concerning continents outside Europe.

DEFINITION OF A TREATY

A treaty is a formal agreement between two or more states or international organisations. It can be in writing or purely oral. If a treaty is in writing it can be made up of a series of documents or just one document. It is governed by public international law and takes effect at the level of international law. A bilateral treaty is made between two parties and a multilateral treaty is concluded between more than two parties. This chapter focuses on written treaties between states recognised by the Vienna Convention on the Law of Treaties 1969 (VCLT), Article 2 of which states:

> For the purposes of the present Convention:
> '. . . "treaty" means an international agreement concluded between States in written form and governed by international law, whether embodied in a single instrument or in two or more related instruments and whatever its particular designation'

THE LEGAL EFFECT OF TREATIES WHEN CONCLUDED BETWEEN STATES

A treaty between states is part of public international law and breaches of the treaty can become disputes in the International Court of Justice. Both of these will now be considered in a little more detail.

Public international law (PIL)

There are conflicting views about what public international law is. This chapter will keep to the general definition that public international law regulates relations between states. It is possible to seek legal redress for violations of international law, for example at the International Court of Justice or at specialised international law courts or tribunals. However, states usually prefer political solutions such as negotiation through diplomatic channels. A serious response from a state to breaches of a treaty could be the recalling of their ambassador to show displeasure.

The International Court of Justice (ICJ)

International law is regulated by its own court, the International Court of Justice (ICJ) set up in 1945, replacing the earlier Permanent Court of International Justice. It is located in The Hague in the Netherlands, and is the primary place for adjudication on matters of public international law. Its judiciary are elected by the UN General Assembly and the UN Security Council. It only has jurisdiction in disputes when the parties are states, and all states involved agree that it can have jurisdiction. When making determinations in relation to treaties the ICJ uses the VCLT as a statement of legal principle even for those states that did not sign or ratify it. This is because the VCLT is considered to be a codification of existing public international rules.

The Vienna Convention on the Law of Treaties 1969 (VCLT)

The VCLT was signed in 1969 but did not come into force until 1980.[1] It is an important treaty because it sets out standard understandings relating to the international law of treaties. Currently 113 nation states have signed and ratified the VCLT (a notable exception being the United States of America). Although treaties are only binding on the states that have signed and ratified them, the VCLT is seen as a 'codification of customary international law', which means it is only confirming already existing law applicable to all states.

The VCLT 1969[2] provides that states who have agreed to be bound by a treaty should keep it in good faith, and not break its terms even if domestic law is in conflict. But this is somewhat aspirational particularly in relation to states, such as the UK, who only see international law as operating between states with no connection to national legal systems.

The contractual approach to treaties adopted by the states under the Vienna Convention

Whilst there are theoretical differences of opinion about the way in which states relate through treaties, the most popular view is that treaties can be seen as operating like contracts. Indeed the parties to a treaty are called the high contracting parties. The VCLT takes this contractual perspective.

A key feature of the contractual approach to treaties is the assumption that contracting states enter into treaties with the free consent to agree. There must be no evidence that a state is being forced into an agreement.

---

1 We will discuss delays between signature and date in force of a treaty later in this chapter.
2 Article 27.

SYNONYMS[3] FOR A TREATY

Treaties have a range of differing names. They can be referred to as a 'statute' or an 'act' which can be most confusing for the student of English law. More commonly they are referred to as 'conventions', 'charters', 'codes' and 'agreements'.

Although this chapter concentrates on treaties concluded between European states a treaty can be concluded between states in differing continents.

THE SUBJECT MATTER OF TREATIES

The potential subject matter of treaties is unlimited; they can relate to anything over which the signatory states have authority. Political reality however constrains what is, and is not, agreed to by governments.

Generally treaties tend to include aspirational statements and specific obligations. Aspirational statements can be generally described as those concerning ideals and expression of joint hopes, standing as statements of good intention. Treaties will usually contain specific obligations that states have undertaken to be bound by and if necessary they will set up required institutions, or make changes to previous arrangements.

THE FORM TAKEN BY WRITTEN TREATIES

There is no one special written form that is privileged as a treaty. A treaty can be legally concluded through a series of documents or letters, or by one document that may be subsequently amended in some way.[4] This chapter will, however, describe a treaty that is created in the first place as a single written document, which is the characteristic form of the majority of twentieth and twenty-first century treaties.

STANDARD ISSUES TO BEAR IN MIND WHEN DEALING WITH TREATIES

There are a range of standard issues that you will need to simultaneously bear in mind when dealing with a treaty. These are set out in Figure 3.1. Some of these have already been referred to and the other issues will now be discussed separately.

The standard layout of a treaty

Over time treaties have developed a mostly standardised layout, although there are variations. Figure 3.2 sets out the standard layout of a treaty in visual form before turning to a discussion of each aspect of the standard layout below.

---

3   Synonyms are words and phrases that are interchangeable when describing something as they all mean the same thing.

4   Jan Klabbers notes that archaeologists discovered a series of 'letters' inscribed in stone dating back to 1400 BCE concluding agreements between Syria, Palestine and Egypt. We know from a variety of sources that agreements between states date back to the beginning of historical records, and from this we can infer that they were also used in pre-history. Jan Klabbers *An introduction to international Law* Cambridge University Press (2nd edn 2009) 15.

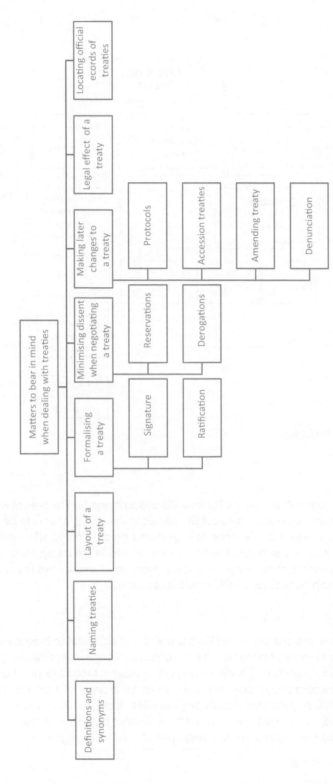

Figure 3.1 Standard issues to bear in mind when dealing with treaties

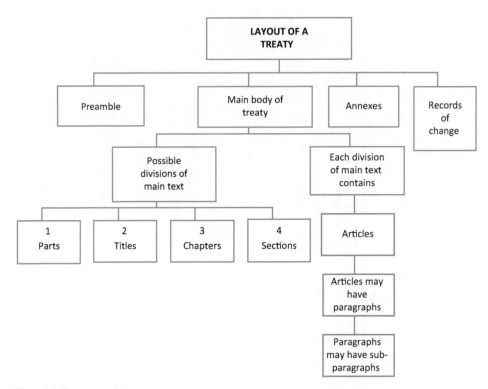

Figure 3.2 The layout of a treaty

The preamble

Before the treaty sets out its main obligations there is a preamble. The preamble serves a number of important purposes: it sets out the parties to the treaty, what is to be achieved by the treaty and it will contain a range of aspirational proposals and affirmations. If relevant it will also refer to the legal basis of the Acts agreed in the treaty. Customarily the entire preamble consists of one long sentence, composed of smaller two line paragraphs with each paragraph commencing with a capitalised word.

The main body of the treaty

This contains the obligations agreed and/or the creating of structural or organisational matters relating to the exercise of those obligations. At this point the layout of the treaty depends upon whether it is long or short. If one is dealing with a treaty of modest length, it is generally subdivided into successively smaller divisions referred to, in order of their occurrences, as parts, titles, chapters, and sections. A treaty may not utilise all of these organisational divisions.

Each part, title, chapter and section contains smaller passages of text called 'articles' which can be further divided into paragraphs and sub-paragraphs. You should note however that 'articles' run consecutively throughout the treaty regardless of the division of the treaty into parts, titles, chapters or sections.

An article is numbered using Arabic numerals. When referencing a treaty, you cannot refer just to the number but you need to refer to Article 1. Paragraphs are denoted by Arabic numerals in brackets, for example (1) and sub-paragraphs by lower case Roman numerals in brackets, for example (i). So Article 1(1)(i) would refer you to Article 1, paragraph (1) sub-paragraph (i).

As articles run consecutively you do not have to know which title, part, chapter or section they are in, it is enough to say Article 1. But if you are referring to Article 200 it is speedier to know which particular division it is in.

Treaties can also have documents attached, or annexed, to them which are formally known as 'written records of change'. These occur over time after the conclusion of the original treaty. Some can be purely administrative to fulfil the purposes of the treaty. Others can be protocols that can add or subtract articles from the treaty. These are discussed in more detail below.

Parties to a treaty

A treaty is first and foremost a political document. Signatories must have the authority to sign from the state and normally the signatories are the head of state or head of government or a government's foreign minister. If necessary another person can be authorised to sign a treaty. If this is the case the relevant head of state, head of government or foreign minister will issue a document called a 'full powers' document in favour of that other authorised signatory. It will normally only be a person who is of ambassadorial or ministerial status.[5]

The process of formalising an agreement of states to be bound by a treaty

There are normally two main stages to be undertaken in order to formalise a treaty – 'signature' and 'ratification'.

Signature

Once the matters to be included in a treaty are settled, the text is drafted, approved by all prospective high contracting states and then officially 'opened for signature'. Signature will be by the head of government, or another authorised person who is referred to as the 'signatory'.

If a treaty does not contain within it the requirement for ratification (which most do) then the customary rule under international law is that the signature alone suffices for the agreement to be in force.

Signature of a treaty requiring ratification should express more than just interest in the treaty; it should express a serious intention to ratify. It is not acceptable therefore at a moral or political level in international law to sign a treaty that requires ratification and whilst doing so make clear that the state is not going to even seek ratification.

---

5 The word formally used to denote those who hold the power to sign the treaty is plenipotentiary (Pl. Plenipotentiaries).

Ratification

The political structure of a state may require that it is not sufficient for the government to sign a treaty on their behalf. The whole government, or legislature, or people of each signatory state may need to approve the action taken by government in the usual manner for that state. This process of approval of treaties is referred to as 'ratification'. Ratification procedures vary among states; in some states it is sufficient for just the government to agree; in others a national Parliament must agree to the treaty for it to be ratified. In yet others a public vote, called a referendum, has to be held to see if a majority of those voting are in favour. If that is the case the state is bound by the outcome of the referendum.

Referendums are rarely used in the UK, mostly in connection to the European Union, or in relation to nation states, such as the relatively recent referendum on Scottish devolution. But it is worth noting that a UK Parliament is not bound by the outcome of a referendum. This is because the UK Parliament has supreme, sovereign authority within the state, and if acting legitimately it is not subservient to the will of the public or of the government.

The methods to minimise dissent in the negotiation process of a treaty

When a treaty is being negotiated by a group of nation states it may well be the case that whilst one state may be in favour of most of the treaty there are matters under discussion which they find unsatisfactory and cannot at that time agree to. Rather than risk the failure of the whole treaty, which could be an international political disaster, a method has been devised to get round these potential serious problems: reservation and derogation. It is important to note, however, that sometimes a certain article in a treaty under negotiation will expressly state that it cannot be the object of reservation. States also know that if necessary it may also be possible to negotiate a derogation after the signature and ratification of the treaty. Sometimes treaties forbid derogation from certain articles. These matters are regulated under Articles 19 and 20 of the VCLT.

Reservations: occur during negotiation of the treaty

If the nation state agrees with the core of the treaty but does not wish to be bound by certain aspects of the treaty they can make this clear by entering what is called a 'reservation'. They agree the treaty with the unsatisfactory item 'taken away': the state opts out of that aspect of the treaty. It may be the case that at a future date the state may agree the reserved articles. This mechanism allows states who may otherwise not be able to sign and ratify the treaty to go ahead and do so. The reservation is concluded by the signatory formally stating that they wish to reserve their right to consider aspects of the treaty. The state's 'reservation' is written and signed by the state in relation to the operation of that part of the treaty. It is possible to have several different types of reservations among multilateral treaties. An example of a reservation found in Article 57 of the European Convention on Human Rights (ECHR) demonstrates this point.

Article 57 – Reservations

1. Any State may, when signing this Convention or when depositing its instrument of ratification, make a reservation in respect of any particular provision of the Convention to the extent that any law then in force in its territory is not in conformity with the provision. Reservations of a general character shall not be permitted under this article.
2. Any reservation made under this article shall contain a brief statement of the law concerned.

A written record of the reservation is drawn up, signed by the state concerned, and attached to the treaty.

However, VCLT Art 19(c) provides that a state cannot make a reservation that is 'incompatible with the object and purpose' of the treaty that is the subject of the reservation.

Derogation: occurs after the treaty is in force

A derogation is something that happens after the treaty has been signed and ratified. It is a procedure that acts as an exception allowing states to restrict some rights in a treaty under certain conditions, for example in times of emergency. Sometimes certain articles in treaties specifically state that they cannot be the subject of a derogation. An example of this can be seen in Article 15 of the ECHR.

Article 15 – Derogation in time of emergency

1. In time of war or other public emergency threatening the life of the nation any High Contracting Party may take measures derogating from its obligations under this Convention to the extent strictly required by the exigencies of the situation, provided that such measures are not inconsistent with its other obligations under international law.
2. No derogation from Article 2, except in respect of deaths resulting from lawful acts of war, or from Articles 3, 4 (paragraph 1) and 7 shall be made under this provision.
3. Any High Contracting Party availing itself of this right of derogation shall keep the Secretary General of the Council of Europe fully informed of the measures which it has taken and the reasons therefor. It shall also inform the Secretary General of the Council of Europe when such measures have ceased to operate and the provisions of the Convention are again being fully executed.

Once a derogation is drawn up it is attached to the treaty.

When is a treaty actually 'in force'?

'In force' refers to the moment that the treaty is legally binding under international law and thus binding on the parties. In many instances a treaty can only come into force after it has been ratified by either all or a high number of signatory states. Usually an article towards the end of the treaty specifies how long after formal ratification the treaty is deemed to be in force. When a treaty is signed there is no way of knowing how long full ratification will take; it could take months or years. So there has to be a calculation for the 'in force date' that is based on days after the last signatory has ratified.

The legal effect of a treaty

Treaties may be wholly or partially enforceable against the high contracting parties under public international law.[6] They may also be enforceable within the domestic legal systems of those parties signing the treaty. Whether this is the case, and the nature of the mechanisms for enforceability, vary from state to state.

As agreements between states multiplied and issues arose over the relationship between national law and international law it gradually became apparent that in practice states adopted one of two possible stances with regard to international law and its relationship to national law – either a monist position or a dualist position.

Monist position

The monist position states that international treaties that have been signed and ratified by the state also immediately become part of that state's national legal system. The treaty therefore has a legal effect both in international law and domestic law. An example of a monist state would be the Netherlands.

Dualist position

The dualist position states that international treaties signed and if required ratified by the state do not immediately become part of that state's national legal system. These states categorise international law as a separate entity from national law with no legal effect upon it. Such a state would need to transform international law into national law via legislation.

This is the position adopted in the English legal system. Parliament must enact legislation, making provision for a treaty signed by the UK Government to have a legal effect in the English legal system. It is then said to be 'incorporated' into English law and to have effect as part of the national legal system. This legislation also usually makes provision for any later changes made necessary by the relevant treaty obligations to occur through the use of secondary legislation.[7]

The differences between the monist and the dualist positions and the processes by which treaties can become part of national law are set out in Figure 3.3.

---

6   The definition of international law is the regulation of relations between states.
7   See Chapter 1 for a general explanation of secondary legislation and fast track procedures.

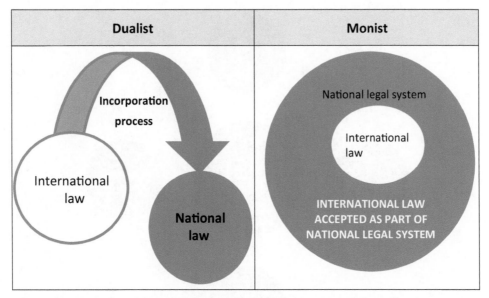

Figure 3.3 Dualist and monist legal traditions

Treaty names

Individual treaties are rather confusingly known by several different names. Every treaty has a formal name (which is usually abbreviated). In addition many treaties are by custom referred to by the place where the treaty was signed. This can lead to confusion and to students believing they are reading about two or even three treaties when they are in fact dealing with only one! Sometimes, relatively rarely, a treaty can also be renamed! Just be aware of this when you are reading about treaties in your textbooks, or in law cases or academic articles. This matter is discussed in more detail when discussing the European Union in Chapter 5.

General procedures for changing (amending) treaties

Treaties can be amended in several ways. The original signatory states can sign a new updating treaty to allow for major amendments. Or they can draft (draw up) a protocol which amends part of the treaty and is attached to the original. This section will go through general-ised procedures for change. However, some treaties may set up unique or different methods. These methods of changing a treaty can be seen in Figure 3.4, and are discussed below.

Protocols

A protocol is a formal document (that is usually a treaty by itself) which can introduce sub-stantial changes to an existing treaty. It is subject to the same processes of formalisation:

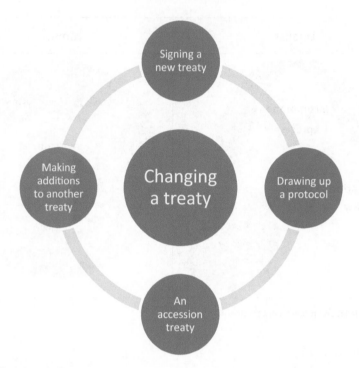

Figure 3.4 Changing a treaty

it must be signed and ratified, if ratification is required. It will come into force at a set date noted in the protocol. It is open to all the signatory states of the original treaty, but they are not bound to accept it. Different original contracting parties may agree to it or refuse to agree to it, in which case the protocol either totally fails if it is required to get the agreement of all, or it comes into effect in relation to those states agreeing to it. You will hear much more about protocols in relation to discussion of the European Convention on Human Rights.

New treaties

Sometimes a new treaty on a separate matter can be used to make amendments to existing treaties. You will be familiar with this idea from the discussion on UK legislation and the way in which sometimes new legislation can contain a few sections making changes to other, quite unrelated, legislation.

Accession treaties

It is possible for new states to become signatories of treaties that they were not originally party to by signing an accession treaty. When new states join as signatories to an existing treaty this constitutes a change to the original. In 1973 the UK joined the European Union by signing an accession treaty. Sometimes the opportunity is also taken to amend the original treaty in an accession treaty.

Procedures for a state to cease to be bound by a treaty: abrogation/denunciation

If a state wishes to cease to be bound by a treaty, it may sign an instrument cancelling its agreement. This is generally known as a denunciation or abrogation and it is attached to the original treaty. The treaty itself will normally specify how a party can leave.

Whilst individual signatories can cancel their obligation it is also possible for treaties to be denounced in their entirety and an article within the treaty may state that if the number of signatories reaches a certain low figure the entire treaty is automatically terminated.

Article 42 of the Vienna Convention allows for two methods of terminating a treaty:

- through a treaty itself making provision for denunciation of it; or
- if the treaty makes no provision itself then through the use of VCLT, Article 56.

Article 56 states that whilst the normal rule is that if the treaty is silent then denunciation or withdrawal of a party is not possible, denunciation can be implied into the treaty. Art 56 also states that if the parties can be shown to have intended to have made provision for denunciation then it may be possible to denounce it.

If the treaty can be denounced and there are grounds for the use of Article 56 there is a twelve month notice period.

Article 58 of the ECHR states the following within it as the terms for denunciation.

Article 58

Denunciation

1. A High Contracting Party may denounce the present Convention only after the expiry of five years from the date on which it became a party to it and after six months' notice contained in a notification addressed to the Secretary General of the Council of Europe, who shall inform the other High Contracting Parties.

OFFICIAL RECORDS OF TREATIES – ORIGINALS AND CERTIFIED COPIES

Differing groups of treaties will tend to have different places for formally keeping – technically 'depositing' – the original treaty. Usually the treaty itself will state where it is deposited. The treaties of the European Union for example are deposited with the Government of Italy. All treaties entered into by another European organisation, the Council of Europe, must be lodged with the CoE's Treaties Office. The European Convention on Human Rights is an example of a treaty concluded by the CoE. Furthermore, all member states of the United Nations by Article 102 of the Charter of the United Nations, must lodge a certified copy of all treaties they have entered into. This is to ensure that there are no secret treaties between nations who are members of the United Nations.

CONCLUSION

You have now been given a firm understanding of the ways in which a treaty can be created and changed, and should be able to find your way around the general layout and structure of a treaty. This will enable you to have a foundation for understanding the legal effect of treaties from the Council of Europe[8] and the European Union.[9]

CHAPTER SUMMARY

- A treaty is a political agreement between states regulated by international law.
- A treaty can have an effect at the level of national law if a state also makes official arrangements for this to occur.
- The layout of a treaty has a standard form and most treaties tend to have a formal name, an abbreviation, and a name referring to the place where it was signed.
- All treaties are formalised in two stages, signature and ratification, although ratification is not always required.
- Nation states either have a monist or a dualist position regarding international law.
- The UK is an example of a dualist legal system.
- To minimise dissent, signatories can enter a derogation or a reservation, but treaties can prohibit derogations and/or reservations in relation to certain articles.
- A protocol can be drawn up changing a treaty; this too is signed and ratified by all relevant states and attached to the treaty.
- There is no prior obligation on a signatory state of a treaty to sign and ratify protocols.
- If a protocol requires all original signatories to agree to it the change cannot be made if one signatory refuses.
- A treaty can also be changed in part or in total by a new updating treaty.
- New states can join as signatories to an existing treaty by means of an accession treaty.
- If a state wishes to cease to be bound by a treaty, it may sign an instrument cancelling its agreement; this is known as a denunciation or abrogation.

---

8   Established in 1949 by the Treaty of London.
9   Established in 1957 by the Treaty of Rome.

EUROPEAN CONVENTION ON HUMAN RIGHTS

4

LEARNING OUTCOMES

After reading this chapter you should be able to:

- Understand the basic background, structure and functions of the Council of Europe.
- Understand the European Convention on Human Rights.
- Appreciate the work of the European Court of Human Rights.
- Develop an understanding of the basic structure and operation of the UK Human Rights Act 1998.
- Understand the relationship between the European Convention on Human Rights and the UK Human Rights Act.

INTRODUCTION

The goal of this chapter is to help you understand the Council of Europe (CoE), focusing on its most important treaty, The European Convention on Human Rights 1951 (ECHR) and one of its most important institutions, the European Court of Human Rights. Finally, the chapter focuses on laying a firm foundation for your understanding of the Human Rights Act 1998 (HRA), an Act which introduces into English law the ability for citizens to bring claims under certain articles of the ECHR in domestic courts. The HRA also lays down statutory duties relating to Parliament, the courts and public authorities in the areas covered by the Act.

UNDERSTANDING THE COUNCIL OF EUROPE

The 'Council of Europe' is an organisation set up by the Treaty of London 1949[1] to actively monitor and support three main areas of European interest: human rights, democracy and respect for the rule of law.

Initially there were only ten founding states; Belgium, Denmark, France, Ireland, Italy, Luxembourg, Netherlands, UK, Norway and Sweden. Over the past 60 years a further 37 states have joined the original ten founding states bringing the current membership of the Council of Europe to 47 nations which together cover an estimated 800 million people. Any European state can be a member of the Council of Europe if certain basic minimum standards of conduct, particularly in relation to the observation of human rights and fundamental freedoms, are observed. Additionally the CoE will enter into partnership agreements with states outside Europe.

Special arrangements were made in 2010 to make it possible for the European Union to be a signatory to the Treaty of London although it is not by itself a European state. Prior to that the CoE had a good working relationship with the EU. Indeed, one of the conditions for membership of the EU has always been that a prospective member state is a member of the Council of Europe and a signatory of the ECHR. This was designed to ensure that a state's policies on human rights are acceptable. For many states, membership of the CoE is seen as a first step towards being in a position to accept the greater obligations involved with EU membership. However, the CoE is a completely separate institution from the EU and should never be confused with it.

The Council of Europe is composed of the heads of states of all signatory states of the Treaty of London. The organisation works through meetings of the council to discuss issues raised by their three main spheres of interest: democracy, maintenance of the rule of law, and the protection of human rights.

The scope of the activities undertaken by the Council of Europe is broad. Currently the CoE is engaged in a range of campaigns, working towards better representation and the upholding of human rights in relation to issues such as the Roma, protection of children

---

1   Also called the Statute of the Council of Europe – another example of a confusion of terms.

and discrimination. It has a Commissioner for Human Rights, an independent office elected by the parliamentary assembly for six years at a time.[2] The CoE is responsible for numerous conventions between states to agree on ways of dealing with issues such as cybercrime, torture, human trafficking, and violence against women, and has 'standing bodies' that monitor compliance with various CoE treaties in different areas. Two of the most well-known standing bodies are the European Commission against Racism and Intolerance (ECRI)[3] and the Group of Experts on Action against Trafficking in Human Beings (GRETA).[4]

Background to the establishment of the Council of Europe

Immediately after the Second World War (1939–1945) many states sought to establish organisations to ensure better co-operation between them with a view to avoiding future violent conflicts. A similar desire after the First World War (1914–1918) had previously led to the establishment of the League of Nations by the Treaty of Versailles in 1919. That treaty had as its primary functions promoting peace and security and protecting human rights. However the Second World War was in itself a clear indication of failure of the League of Nations. In 1945 50 nation states met in the US to consider and then sign the 'United Nations Charter' on 26 June. This established the United Nations and ultimately came into force on 24 October 1945 after ratification was completed.[5] A few years later, in 1948, after several years of discussions, the General Assembly of the United Nations adopted the Universal Declaration of Human Rights, a treaty aimed at ensuring that a range of basic human rights were accorded to all citizens of all signatory states. But it is important to be aware that this treaty does not have any enforcement mechanisms to use against states who breach it.

At the same time there was a concurrent desire to set up an organisation at the European level to exclusively concentrate on issues relating to human rights. Serious discussions about the establishment of a European-wide organisation can be traced back to the period 1943–1948 which spanned the last few years of the war and the first few years of peace. The UK prime minister, Sir Winston Churchill, in various speeches forwarded the view that there should be some grouping that he referred to as a '. . . kind of United States of Europe'. At the Hague Congress in 1948,[6] which he chaired, he also forwarded the idea that an institution called a 'Council of Europe' should be formed.[7]

While there were major differences of opinion about what sort of European organisation should be established and what its powers should be, two main options emerged from the congress:

(1) a loose-knit arrangement operating through representatives of the various governments meeting a few times a year in various forums or institutions;

---

2   See www.coe.int/commissioner, accessed 25 April 2013.
3   See www.coe.int/ecri.
4   www.coe.int/t/dghl/monitoring/trafficking/Docs/Monitoring/GRETA_en.asp.
5   www.un.org.
6   The Hague Congress 7–11 May 1948 was a large gathering of scholars, politicians, lawyers and other interested parties: see www.europeanmovement.eu/index.php?id=6788.
7   Sir Winston Churchill's Speech at the University of Zurich 19 September 1946 full text: http://assembly.coe.int/Main.asp?link=/AboutUs/zurich_e.htm.

(2)   the creation of a body that was to be a political and legal union of sovereign states with its own institutions, legal personality and law. Such a body would require states to give away some of their sovereignty in certain areas.

The first option was ultimately preferred by the Hague Congress and led to the Council of Europe being set up in 1949. As the second option would inevitably have resulted in each member state losing aspects of their national sovereignty, this option was not popular amongst all states, including the UK.

The Council of Europe flag and anthem for Europe

In 1955 the CoE adopted the symbol of twelve golden stars in a circle as a Flag to symbolise Europe. This flag was also adopted by the European Union in the 1980s. As both the CoE and the EU are separate European organisations, since the adoption of the flag by the EU, the Council of Europe tends to wrap a lower case 'e' around the stars to differentiate CoE use of it from that of the EU. However, as the idea behind the flag is that it is supposed to be used to signify Europe generally and not any one organisation this seems a rather contradictory move towards signifying difference!

In 1972 the CoE also adopted 'Ode to Joy'[8] as the European anthem. Again the idea was to have an anthem signifying Europe not any one organisation within it. The Council of Europe has always maintained that 'Ode to Joy' should be seen as 'the' anthem of Europe, not of any particular organisation. This rationale was behind the EU's adoption of it in the mid-1980s.

Whilst these moves to present a unified face for Europe are good, they can present problems for students who muddle the two different organisations. The CoE is distinct from the EU. The media are often at fault as they themselves muddle the two organisations!

THE INSTITUTIONS OF THE COUNCIL OF EUROPE

The Council of Europe has seven main institutions, as set out in Figure 4.1.

All of these are discussed on the CoE website http://www.coe.in. This chapter will only focus on one of the CoE's most important institutions, the European Court of Human Rights.

EUROPEAN COURT OF HUMAN RIGHTS (ECTHR)

The European Court of Human Rights was established in 1959 by powers contained in the European Convention on Human Rights (ECHR). It operated part-time under international law hearing cases concerned with violations of the ECHR. It did not sit as a full-time court until 1998.

---

8   This is the final movement of Beethoven's 9th Symphony.

Figure 4.1 The institutions of the Council of Europe

Table 4.1 sets out the main facts concerning sittings, appointment to the court, jurisdiction, judgments and enforcement procedures.

In 1998 for the first time applicants were able to bring claims directly to the court without going through another agency first. Then, in 2010, in an effort to deal with the large increases in applications to the court, Protocol 16 was introduced, allowing senior domestic courts and tribunals the option of asking the European Court of Human Rights for 'advisory opinions' on matters relating to the application and/or interpretation of the rights and freedoms defined in the ECHR and its protocols. This, it is hoped, will develop more of a sense of responsibility towards human rights in domestic courts.

TABLE 4.1 EUROPEAN COURT OF HUMAN RIGHTS: SITTINGS, APPOINTMENT OF JUDGES, JURISDICTION, PROCEDURE, JUDGMENTS AND ENFORCEMENT: ECHR REQUIRES ALL HEARINGS TO BE IN PUBLIC

Sittings: Court can hear claims as full court, or be divided into smaller chambers, as indicated below

Plenary	The court deals with administrative matters sometimes by sitting as a full court. It never adjudicates as a plenary, or full court, of 47. It does however elect its important office holders in plenary (court's president, vice-president, registrar and deputy)
Committee	3 judges
A chamber of the court	7 judges
Full chamber	17 judges

Standard appointment, jurisdiction and procedure

Appointment	Judges are elected for a non-renewal term of 9 years Each member state of the CoE nominates 3 of its judges for 1 to be elected when the current judge is nearing the end of office
Jurisdiction	Individual applications on breach of the ECHR (majority of actions) Actions between member states Requests for opinions

Judgments

Article 46 of ECHR states member states should be prepared to be bound by a final judgment

A final judgment gives a rationale for the decision

A declaration is issued to note the violation by the relevant member state. Court may order party in violation to pay legal expenses of claimant and it can award moral or material damages

Enforcement

The Committee of Ministers deals with the enforcement of judgments

UNDERSTANDING THE EUROPEAN CONVENTION ON HUMAN RIGHTS 1950

Shortly after the signature and subsequent ratification of the Treaty of London in 1949 the parliamentary assembly of the Council of Europe issued a report on human rights. This led directly to the European Convention on Human Rights (ECHR). It was opened for signature on 4 November 1950, and ratified by the UK Parliament in 1951. Ratification by all states took several years to complete and the ECHR did not come into force until 3 September 1953. Only two languages are considered official languages of the ECHR – French and English.

The rationale behind the ECHR is the protection of an agreed core of human rights, such as the right to life, to a family, to privacy, and to freedom from slavery. Later protocols have extended the rights protected by the ECHR, to include amongst other rights economic, social, educational and cultural rights and the right to economic and political determinism for states and indigenous peoples. The text used in discussions in this chapter is from the official version published by the European Court of Human Rights '. . . as amended by the provisions of Protocol No. 14 (CETS no. 194) as from its entry into force on 1 June 2010.'

It operates under international law and contains the right for individuals to bring actions against states in Article 34. This provision really does make it a unique feature, different from any other human rights treaty in the world.

Article 34: Individual applications

The Court may receive applications from any person, non-governmental organisation or group of individuals claiming to be the victim of a violation by one of the High Contracting Parties of the rights set forth in the Convention or the Protocols thereto.

However, Article 34 only takes effect when all domestic remedies are exhausted. Unfortunately the sad reality is that, despite continuing attempts to reform the European Court of Human Rights, a case before the court can take years to be heard and is extremely expensive.

Pilot judgments of the ECtHR

During efforts to reform the ECtHR and improve its efficiency it was decided to introduce a new procedure for applications against states concerning repetitive breaches of the same article in the ECHR or a protocol to it. It was noted further that the number of pending repetitive cases was in the region of 150,000 per year. The procedure is called the pilot judgment as it guides other interpretations in the same type of cases to allow the identification of a group of applications against a state involving the same issue. One case is chosen for hearing and resolution. But in addition to dealing with the applicant, the pilot judgment is concerned with identifying a standard problem with a state's adherence to the ECHR in relation to a specific article or articles. It then imposes an obligation on the state to deal with the problem. Other applications dealing with the same matter are frozen on the strict understanding that the state will deal with the judgment promptly and in a satisfactory manner.

Leaving the ECHR

A party can leave the ECHR if they comply with the provision of denunciation which is laid out in Article 58. Member states can only apply to leave after the expiry of five years as a member and the further expiry of a six month notice period. Additionally Article 58(2) makes clear that denouncing the ECHR does not release the member state from responsibility for any violation occurring before the date of denunciation.

Protocols to the ECHR

Currently there are 16 protocols in force. Each new protocol must be signed and ratified by those member states who agree to it. But many of the signatories of the ECHR have not signed and ratified later protocols. Many parties to the ECHR, including the UK, using allowances made in the ECHR, have refused to sign and ratify a protocol. It is most important to ensure that you always make clear whether you are discussing an article in the ECHR or an article in one of its protocols.

One main reason for using protocols rather than amending the ECHR is that a state can remain a party to the core human rights in the ECHR, even if it disagrees with something the other states would like to add. For example, Protocol 13 to the ECHR abolishes the death penalty but one signatory, Russia, will not accept this protocol. Because it is a protocol to the ECHR Russian citizens do not lose their ECHR rights.

Sometimes a particular protocol intends certain articles in it to additionally be seen as new convention rights. The protocol will require the signature and ratification of all members of the CoE before it can come into force. Sometimes it can take years to obtain the consents. If all member states will not sign or ratify it then the protocol will fail.

Protocols are used to:

- add rights to the ECHR and limit the capacity to derogate or make a reservation;
- make amendments to the ECHR to effect administrative or structural changes to the enforcement of the treaty or deal with derogations/reservations and other matters.

Derogations and reservations

Articles and paragraphs in a protocol may be the subject of derogations and/or reservations in certain circumstances.

THE ECHR, ITS PROTOCOLS AND THEIR LEGAL IMPACT ON ENGLISH LAW[9]

While the UK signed and ratified the ECHR in 1951, it entered a reservation with respect to some of the articles in the subsequent protocols that it has signed and ratified. In addition, the UK has not signed protocols 4, 6 and 13. When dealing with protocols it is particularly important to know which member states of the Council of Europe have signed and ratified protocols and where exactly there are derogations and reservations, as this affects the legal influence of the ECHR on those states.

The UK adopts a dualist position with regard to treaties under international law, therefore the ECHR and decisions of the ECtHR have had no automatic impact on English law. If a case goes to the court and is successful against the UK the Court has no power to force the UK to take any remedial action.

---

9   See the Equality and Human Rights Commission Research Report 83 'The UK and the European Court of Human Rights', Alice Donald, Jane Gordon and Philip Leach, Human Rights and Social Justice Research Institute. London Metropolitan University Spring 2012 www.equalityhumanrights.com/uploaded_files/research/83._european_court_of_human_rights.pdf.

In 1965 the UK Government gave UK citizens the right to take their grievances directly to the European Court of Human Rights. As time passed several judgments occurred that were highly embarrassing for the UK Government. Despite their lack of legal effect in the UK the government does have an obligation under international law to comply and it has done so, with the notable exception of claims that the government refusal to allow prisoners voting rights in public elections was a breach of the ECHR.

However, although the ECHR and the decisions of the ECtHR had no force in the English legal system, they were not ignored. The English courts were indeed influenced by them. Judges in the UK's Supreme Court have stated that they would presume that Parliament did not intend to legislate contrary to the ECHR. Therefore, when judges in court needed to choose between two possible interpretations of the law in a situation, one conforming to the ECHR and one not conforming, then the interpretation in conformity with the ECHR is generally preferred. Lord Bridge of Harwich gave a clear indication of this in the *Brind* case 1991[10] stating:

> '. . . it is already well settled that, in construing any provision in domestic legislation which is ambiguous in the sense that it is capable of a meaning which either conforms to or conflicts with the Convention, the courts will presume that Parliament intended to legislate in conformity with the Convention, not in conflict with it'.[11]

Despite the general view expressed above, Lord Bridge was careful to stress that it should not be assumed that such an interpretation *must* be applied, as judicial discretion remained.[12] He observed however that in the current case the discretion used by the Secretary of State had no limit attached to it and therefore when Parliament does this it means just that. There are no limits and:

> '. . . to presume that it must be exercised within Convention limits would be to go far beyond the resolution of an ambiguity. It would be to impute to Parliament an intention not only that the executive should exercise the discretion in conformity with the Convention, but also that the domestic courts should enforce that conformity by the importation into domestic administrative law of the text of the Convention and the jurisprudence of the European Court of Human Rights in the interpretation and application of it'.[13]

The UK and violations of the ECHR and its protocols

As a signatory of the ECHR and a range of its protocols, the UK has been the subject of applications to the European Court of Human Rights for violation of the treaty on many occasions, as have other signatory states.

---

10 See *R v Secretary of State for the Home Office, ex p Brind* (1991) 1 AC 696. *Brind* was a case concerning an alleged violation of Article 10, the right to freedom of expression, and Article 13, the right to an effective national remedy. It was raised in connection with the Secretary of State's statutory powers to prohibit certain broadcasts by the Independent Broadcasting Authority (IBA) and the British Broadcasting Corporation (BBC).

11 Ibid at 697.

12 See generally Equality and Human Rights Commission Research report 83: fn 23.

13 Ibid at 698.

Between 1975 and 1990, 30 cases were brought against the UK. In 21 of these the European Court found that the government had violated the ECHR or its protocols. Just seven years later in 1997, the total of successful cases against the UK Government was in the region of 50.[14] In total between 1959 and 2012 it was the object of 21,000 applications; 17,000 of these were declared inadmissible or struck out. Of the 4,000 proceeding, 489 reached court and in 289 cases a violation of the ECHR was found.[15]

The UK has imposed a blanket ban on convicted prisoners in detention being allowed to vote in public elections. This was held to be a violation of Article 3 of Protocol No. 1 to the Convention in the *Hirst (No 2)* judgment of 6 October 2005. The UK is a signatory of Protocol 1 and had 2,500 applications before the ECtHR on this point. The Court chose one of them, *Greens and MT v the United Kingdom* to be the pilot judgment.[16] The problem it identified as requiring remedy was the blanket ban. The court adjourned all applications and its final judgment that they had been a was breach. The court gave the UK six months from the final judgment to bring its national law in line with the protocol.

This is a still a major issue for the UK, which does not wish to make a change. A draft bill, the Voting Eligibility (Prisoners) draft bill, was sent for pre-legislative scrutiny and after about a year in December 2013 the committee reported that a bill should go forward to give prisoners serving sentences of twelve months or less the right to vote in European, general and local elections. But the bill was not referred to in the Queen's speech in 2014 and currently has not been forwarded. This draft bill is also being scrutinised by the Committee of Minsters of the CoE as it has enforcement functions for ECtHR judgments.

It should however be noted that around 90 per cent of the several thousand applications made against the UK generally in relation to treaty violations under the ECHR and its protocols are declared inadmissible in the ECtHR.

A useful illustration of the way in which an applicant can use the ECHR occurred in *Reynolds v the UK*[17] which came to a final judgment on 13 March 2012. The applicant's son, a schizophrenic, was a short-term, voluntary inpatient in a local authority-run mental health unit and had fallen to his death from their building in 2005. The applicant's argument was that although he was clearly on the receiving end of negligent care she had no effective remedy allowed in UK civil law whereby liability for his death could be allocated. The ECtHR found that there had been a violation of Article 13 (right to an effective remedy) read together with Article 2 (right to life).

The treaties office of the Council of Europe

The treaties office of the Council of Europe shows in a clear, tabular format, the protocols that have not been signed, or ratified, by various states, including the UK.[18]

---

14 For a source of statistics and critical commentary see the details of the law report in fn 24.
15 Violations 1959–2012 UK www.echr.coe.int/Documents/Overview_19592012_ENG.pdf accessed 26 July 2013. Overview 1959–2012 ECHR, June 2013, European Court of Human Rights, Public Relations, Council of Europe, F-67075 Strasbourg cedex.
16 23 November 2010.
17 *Reynolds v the UK* [2012] ECHR 437 accessible from Bailii (www.bailii.org/ECHR/2012/437.html) official citation 55 EHRR 35.

THE UK HUMAN RIGHTS ACT 1998 (HRA)

In 1998 the Human Rights Act gave UK citizens the right to bring cases in the UK's domestic courts against a public authority for the breach of most, but not all, of the articles protecting human rights in the ECHR and selected articles in protocols ratified by the UK. It also gives an overriding power for the Crown to intervene in any proceedings brought by individuals against a public authority.

The Act further stipulates that the UK Parliament when enacting public general legislation, as well as the courts of the English legal system. Courts are subject to certain procedures and obligations with dealing with certain articles in the ECHR.

Background to the Human Rights Act 1998 and current concerns

The Labour Government that came to power in 1997 had, as one of their major election manifesto promises, improving the protection of human rights in the UK. They quickly published a White Paper, 'Rights brought home: the Human Rights Bill',[19] with an attached draft bill. It gave UK citizens the right to bring claims against public authorities (governments, local authorities, large utility companies exercising state-like functions, etc.) in domestic courts. It also set out plans to make UK public authorities more accountable for their actions with regard to human rights violations. Individuals could also raise the issue of human rights violations under the ECHR and relevant protocols in any proceedings brought against them by a public authority. For the purposes of this Act courts are seen as public bodies that can be the object of a claim.

Relatively quickly the Human Rights Act 1998 was enacted, and it came into force in October 2000. It has had a turbulent reception and since it came into force there have been numerous suggestions that it should be repealed and replaced with a bill of rights that is specifically UK orientated. The latest offering was from the 'bill of rights commission' which issued its report 'A UK Bill of Rights? – The Choice Before Us' in December 2012.[20] There was no real agreement on the way forward and no doubt this issue will also arise in the courses you are studying throughout your degree programme.

We began this section noting that there is currently a debate amongst lawyers and politicians as to whether the HRA should indeed be repealed. In June 2012 a private member's bill, the Human Rights Act 1998 (Repeal and Substitution) Bill 2012–13, was laid before Parliament for a first reading by Charlie Elphicke MP. It had a second reading on 1 March 2013 but was withdrawn after the debate.

The key sections of the Human Rights Act 1998

The next part of the chapter sets out key sections that taken together make clear the overall function of the HRA.

---

18 http://conventions.coe.int/Treaty/Commun/QueVoulezVous.asp?NT=046&CM=7&DF=02/05/2013& CL=ENG, accessed 1 May 2013.

19 CM 3782, London: HMSO.

20 Vol 1 accessible as a pdf from www.justice.gov.uk/about/cbr.

The HRA is designed to make it easier, cheaper and quicker for individuals to take action against public authorities for violations of the ECHR and its protocols when carrying out their public functions.

It does this by listing the articles that are covered by the Act in s 1 and naming them 'convention rights'. It is immediately apparent from s 1 that key articles in the ECHR, notably Articles 1 and 13, are not to be included. Therefore a claim for their breach cannot be heard in our domestic courts. The full text of all 'convention rights' is set out in Schedule 1.

In relation to these convention rights the HRA sets up a statutory duty to be imposed on all public authorities (including the courts and Parliament in its law making capacity) to ensure they function in a manner that is compatible with the ECHR.[21]

Courts have a statutory duty to interpret primary and secondary domestic legislation in a manner compliant with the Convention rights.[22] Should the court consider that primary legislation breaches convention rights it can issue a statement of incompatibility.[23] They have no rights to declare the primary legislation invalid. It is left to the government to decide whether it will begin the process of amending incompatible legislation.

What is clear from court cases is that the power in s 4 to issue a statement of incompatibility is considered to be the exceptional course of action. Lord Hutton in *R v Attorney General* [2003] made this point quite clear when discussing the appropriate role of the court:

'. . . it is not the function of the courts to keep the statute book up to date . . . ss 3 and 4 of the Human Rights Act 1998 are not intended to be an instrument by which the courts can chivvy Parliament into spring-cleaning the statute book.'[24]

Nor does the legislation allow the judiciary to invalidate an Act of Parliament and Parliament can just as easily repeal the HRA.

The requirement for courts to take into account the case law of the ECtHR has exerted an impact on the way that English judges interpret both legislation and case law. The English judiciary have had to make changes to their standard methods of interpretation of statutes.[25] In those areas where the courts have a duty to consider the case law from the European courts they confront a major difference. In English court cases it is customary for dissenting judgments to be published. These are judgments expressing a particular judge's disagreement with the majority decision of the court. Even where several judges agree on an outcome they can disagree on the detailed route they took to their agreement. Each judge can choose to issue a judgment, therefore in English courts judges are used to dealing with several judgments in previously decided cases that they may be considering. However, it is customary for the ECtHR to give one decision and the reasons given for their decision are usually less detailed than in English courts.

---

21 Section 6.
22 Section 3.
23 Section 4.
24 *R v Attorney General* [2003] UKHL 38, 36, Lord Hutton.
25 We will be considering statutory interpretation in Chapter 11.

This does not mean that English courts do not themselves give reasons in cases dealing with the ECHR but the cases it receives from the European level have to be incorporated into their decisions and these cases come from a different tradition where the detailed rationale for the decision is not expected or required.[26] However, it is accepted that these cases do in fact lay down firm guidelines that need to be followed.

Figure 4.2 sets out the various sections dealing with the statutory duties imposed on English courts and tribunals, the UK Parliament and UK public authorities.

Several high profile cases in UK courts applying the HRA have led to clashes between government ministers and the decisions of judges in court cases. After the high profile case of *Omar Othman v the UK*[27] (Omar Othman is known in the UK as Abu Qatada) the Home Secretary, Teresa May and the prime minister, David Cameron said they would review the question of whether the UK should even remain party to the European Convention on Human Rights.

The facts of the case revolved around the government's attempts to have Omar Othman deported to Jordan. The government had lost court cases on several occasions; Othman pleaded that deportation would be a breach of his right to a family life as his family were in England. Eventually, when he left the UK of his own accord, the government were quick to point out that the taxpayers' bill for the fight to deport Abu Qatada was over £1.7 million including a legal aid bill of £687,658, and more than £1 million in Home Office legal fees. No mention was made of the fact that it was the government who had forced the issue to court again and again.

Teresa May said that she wanted to put reforms into a pending immigration bill at the end of 2013 restricting appeals based on a right to a family life.

'The problems caused by the Human Rights Act and the European Court in Strasbourg remain and we should remember that Qatada would have been deported long ago had the European Court not moved the goalposts by establishing new, unprecedented legal grounds on which it blocked his deportation. I have made clear my views that in the end the Human Rights Act must be scrapped. We must also consider our relationship with the European Court very carefully, and I believe that all options – including withdrawing from the convention altogether – should remain on the table.'[28]

Both Teresa May and David Cameron seem to have forgotten that membership of the EU depends on being a signatory state of the ECHR (but of course they are also constantly querying whether the UK should be in the EU). These debates show the nexus between the political and the legal aspects of our European relationships.

---

26 That is deciding current cases on the same basis as previous similar cases in the Court of Appeal or Supreme Court depending on where the case is currently being heard – there is more discussion on these matters in the chapters covering case law. Equally as you will have noted from discussion in Chapter 4, the same issues arise in cases relating to the European Union. Nor are EU cases from the Court of Justice of the European Union (CJEU) based on the English system of rigid adherence to precedent.

27 http://hudoc.echr.coe.int/sites/eng/pages/search.aspx?i=001-108629.

28 Teresa May, speaking in the House of Commons on 7 July 2013.

Duties of English Courts and Tribunals Sections 2–4

- **HRA s2**: A statutory duty is imposed; courts MUST take account of decisions of the ECtHR and the Committee of Ministers.
- **HRA s3**: A positive statutory duty is imposed when interpreting primary and secondary legislation to do so in a manner that is compatible with 'convention rights' set out in Schedule 1.
- **HRA s4**: Courts can issue a declaration of incompatibility if they consider primary or secondary legislation is not convention right compliant.
- Court cannot declare primary legislation invalid
- Court can under certain circumstances declare secondary legislation invalid.

Duties of UK Parliament dealing with legislation Section 19

- **HRA s19**: Public General Bills entering Parliament must contain before its second reading a memorandum of compatibility issued by the minister responsible for the bill stating it complies with the Convention rights.
- If Parliament wishes it may remedy problems of incompatibility noted by the courts and tribunal by issuing a Remedial Order (a form of secondary legislation) on a fast track to deal with it.
- A minister can issue a memorandum of incompatibility which must state why it is incompatible and that despite this the government wishes to proceed.

Duties of Public Authorities Section 6

- **HRA s6**: Public bodies have a statutory duty imposed on them to act in compliance with convention rights.
- The definition of public body expressly **includes** courts and tribunals.
- The definition of public body expressly **excludes** Parliament.
- The definition of a public body **includes** hybrid private/public organisations which have a clear public function, such as utility companies.

Figure 4.2 Statutory duties imposed by ss 2–4, 6 and 19 of the HRA 1998

CONCLUSION

You have now a firm, basic understanding of the Council of Europe, the background to its creation and its institutions. You will also understand the origins of the ECHR as a treaty emanating from the CoE, and how, over time changes have been made to the ECHR by protocols. We have also discussed the interrelationship between the UK's HRA 1998 and the ECHR, and looked at some of the potential challenges that this relationship introduces. You should therefore be in a good position to understand how to read the ECHR, its protocols and cases concerning the interpretation of the rights protected. Additionally you should be able to understand the relationship between the HRA and the ECHR. You should have picked up from your reading of this chapter that there are current heated debates in the UK as to whether the UK should denounce the ECHR. You will also have noted the important fact that the European Union is an entirely separate organisation from the Council of Europe, placing you in a good position to turn to Chapter 5 on European Union law.

CHAPTER SUMMARY

Understanding the Council of Europe:

- The Council of Europe was established by the Treaty of London 1949 by Belgium, Denmark, France, Ireland, Italy, Luxembourg, Netherlands, UK, Norway and Sweden. It has a current membership of 47.
- The Council of Europe originally set up three institutions: the Committee of Ministers, the Commission on Human Rights (EComHR) and the European Court of Human Rights (the ECtHR). The EComHR and ECtHR were merged in 1998.
- The Council of Europe has a working relationship with the EU but it is not an institution of the EU. It is a completely distinct organisation with its own institutions.

Understanding the European Convention on Human Rights:

- The ECHR was signed in 1950 and ratified by the UK Parliament in 1951. It came into force in 1953.
- In 1965 the UK Government eventually gave UK citizens the right to take their grievances to the European Court of Human Rights to be heard under European law. Their decisions had no legal impact in the UK.
- The rationale behind the ECHR is the protection of a series of agreed rights considered core to life.

Understanding the Human Rights Act 1998:

- The Human Rights Act 1998 allows British citizens to bring cases alleging breach of most of the articles in the European Convention (ECHR) in UK courts.
- Major omissions are Articles 1 and 13 of the ECHR.
- All bills introduced into Parliament must have a declaration that the proposed legislation is compatible with the UK's obligations under the ECHR (s 19).
- The HRA does not prohibit the enactment of legislation that is incompatible, but Parliament will have to be convinced that such legislation is for a good reason.
- The judiciary must interpret all UK legislation in a manner that is compatible with the ECHR unless it is impossible to do so and judges will strain to do this (s 3).
- Judges in domestic courts can issue a declaration that legislation before it is incompatible with the ECHR but such a declaration cannot invalidate primary legislation (s 4).
- Article 35 of the ECHR states that individuals can only bring an action if all domestic remedies have been exhausted.

EUROPEAN UNION LAW

5

LEARNING OUTCOMES

After reading this chapter you should be able to:

- Acquire a basic understanding of the development of the EU through its treaties.
- Be aware of the law making functions of the Court of Justice of the European Union, the Council of the European Union, the Commission and the European Parliament.
- Distinguish between, and understand, the sources of primary EU law (treaties) and the source and types of secondary EU law (regulations, directives, decisions, opinions and recommendations).
- Appreciate the different legal effects of each type of EU law.
- Appreciate the relationship between the English legal system and EU law particularly in relation to the issue of the supremacy of EU law.

INTRODUCTION

As a student of English law you need to acquire a firm understanding of EU law and its impact on the English legal system. This also involves having a basic understanding of the European Union (EU) and its institutions. This chapter is divided into the following four main sections to allow you to gain competency in these areas:

(1)   Understanding the EU.
(2)   Understanding EU institutions.
(3)   Understanding the EU legal order and European Union law (EU law).
(4)   Understanding the supremacy of EU law and its impact on the English legal system.

These areas are set out in Figure 5.1 which details the various issues to be considered under each of these four main headings. Do be patient with the information you are about to read and ensure that you take the time to understand it at your own pace.

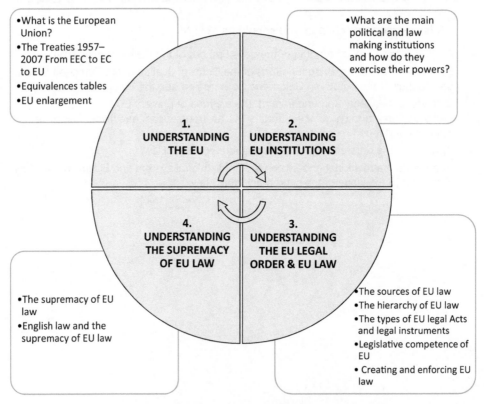

Figure 5.1 **Areas you need to understand when dealing with European Union law**

UNDERSTANDING THE EUROPEAN UNION (EU)

Throughout this chapter there will only be a reference to the EU. The founding treaties in the 1950s refer to the European Economic Community (EEC), and the Treaty of European Union refers to the European Community (EC). The Treaty of Lisbon in 2007 made provision for all references to the EEC and EC to be replaced throughout all documentation by 'EU'.

What is the EU?

The European Union (EU) is a supranational organisation created by treaties. Those signing the treaties are known as member states of the EU. The EU is able to act in its own right through powers given to it through its founding treaties. By signing the treaties each member state has given some of its sovereign power to the EU in areas where the EU has been given 'legislative competency' to create law. In practice this has also meant that member states are required to ensure that EU law becomes part of their own domestic legal system.

The EU's current areas of legislative competency are set out in Figure 5.2 below but they are continually expanding. Current major areas would include agriculture, environment, research and technology, as well as free movement of goods, labour and capital.

The founding treaties of the EU

The EU is now regulated by two updated and consolidated founding treaties[1] concluded between member states of the EU.

The first founding treaty is the Treaty of Rome 1957 (No 2), which is now known as the Treaty on the Functioning of the European Union (TFEU) as published in 2012 in a consolidated updated version. The second founding treaty is the Treaty of Maastricht 1992, known as The Treaty on European Union (TEU) and again published in 2012 in a consolidated updated version. Through these treaties the EU has its own legal order, its own laws and its own legal personality.

European citizens

Since 1992 all citizens of member states are also European citizens. This extends the rights previously granted to workers (the right to reside in another member state, or access medical services and benefits) to economically self-sufficient citizens as well.

Core functions of the EU

Essentially the EU has established an area for free trading in which European Union citizens (that is the citizens of member states of the EU) have the right to work, or seek work, in other member states of the EU. The EU expects free movement of goods and workers between member states, and has legislative powers to ensure it. Recently the EU has

---

1   Which are now more often referred to as the 'constituent treaties' of the EU.

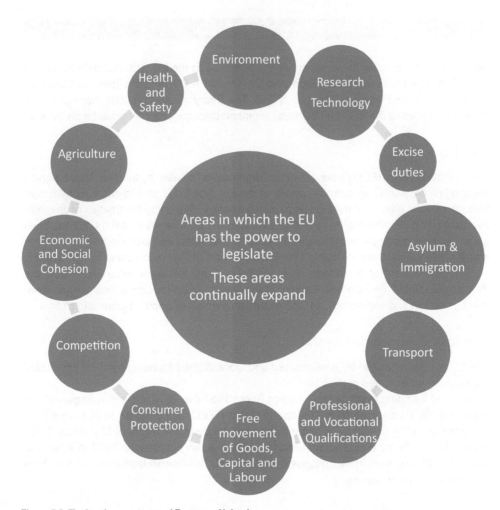

Figure 5.2 The legal competency of European Union law

acquired powers to legislate in relation to the asylum and immigration policies of member states in so far as these may affect the free movement of workers.

UNDERSTANDING THE DEVELOPMENT OF THE EU THROUGH ITS TREATIES 1957–2007

The Hague conference in 1949 discussed the future of Europe.[2] Two views of the future relationships amongst European states came out of the conference. One led to the setting

2   See Chapter 4 for a more detailed discussion of the Hague conference.

up of the Council of Europe, and was a vision of a Europe bound together by agreements encouraging co-operative action. The other was a vision for a sovereign, federal Europe. Sir Winston Churchill coined the phrase a 'united states of Europe'. This vision was the beginning of the development of the EU.

In the period 1951–1957, France, Belgium, Italy, Luxembourg, Netherlands and West Germany signed three treaties setting up three distinct European Communities.

(1)   The Treaty of Paris 1951, establishing the European Coal and Steel Community (ECSC).[3]
(2)   The Treaty of Rome No 1 1957, establishing the European Atomic Community (EURATOM).[4]
(3)   The Treaty of Rome No 2 1957, establishing the European Economic Community (EEC).[5]

The EU today has evolved out of the three communities over the last 60 years (although currently EURATOM still has its own legal personality).

To assist your understanding of the EU so that you may better understand EU law as it impacts the English legal system we will consider its development through the main treaties signed between 1975–2014. Please take time to properly consider Figure 5.3 which will enable you to see the relationship between the treaties to be discussed.

The Treaty of Rome (No 2) 1957, date in force 1 January 1958

This treaty is the founding treaty of the EU. Its formal title was the 'treaty establishing the European Economic Community' (informally the EEC Treaty). This treaty places the obligation on member states to give away some aspects of their own sovereignty to allow EU law to be part of the law of member states. It also set up the main EU institutions that we have today and determined their law-making powers and the types of law they could create.

Although subject to revisions and name changes, the Treaty of Rome 1957 No 2 remains central to the EU. In 1992[6] it was renamed the Treaty Establishing the European Community (abbreviated to 'EC Treaty').Then in 2007[7] it was extensively revised and renamed the Treaty on the Functioning of the European Union (TFEU). The current up to date version of this treaty is the consolidated version of TFEU 2012. It is essential to refer to the latest consolidated version.

The Brussels Treaty 1965 (The Merger Treaty),[8] date in force 1 July 1967

This treaty merged the institutions of all three communities referred to above, although each community, at this time, remained distinct.

3   Set up by the Treaty of Paris, the Treaty Establishing the European Coal and Steel Community signed on 18 April 1951 and in force on 23 July 1952. The European Coal and Steel Community was set up for a limited time of 50 years which expired on 23 July 2002 at which time the ECSC was subsumed into the EU.
4   Set up by the Treaty of Rome No 1, signed on 25 March 1957 and in force on 1 January 1958.
5   Set up by the Treaty of Rome No 2 in 1957, signed on 25 March 1957 and in force on 1 January 1958.
6   By the Treaty of Maastricht.
7   By the Treaty of Lisbon.
8   Brussels Treaty signed 8 April 1965 and in force 1 July 1967.

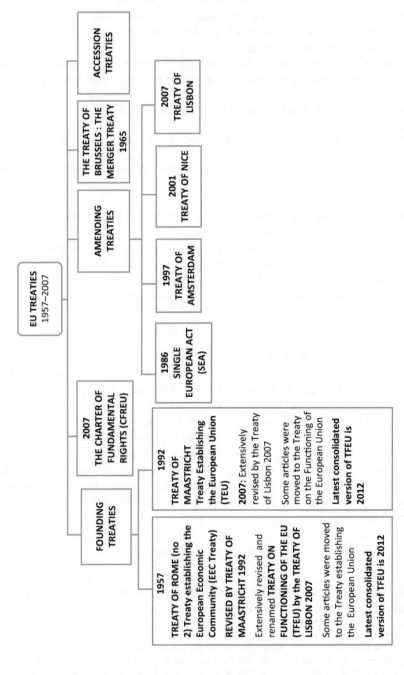

Figure 5.3 EU treaties 1957–2007

EU TREATIES
1957–2007

FOUNDING TREATIES

THE CHARTER OF FUNDAMENTAL RIGHTS (CFREU)
2007

AMENDING TREATIES

THE TREATY OF BRUSSELS : THE MERGER TREATY 1965

ACCESSION TREATIES

1957
TREATY OF ROME (no 2) Treaty establishing the European Economic Community (EEC Treaty)
REVISED BY TREATY OF MAASTRICHT 1992
Extensively revised and renamed **TREATY ON FUNCTIONING OF THE EU (TFEU) by the TREATY OF LISBON 2007**
Some articles were moved to the Treaty establishing the European Union
Latest consolidated version of TFEU is 2012

1992
TREATY OF MAASTRICHT Treaty Establishing the European Union (TEU)
2007: Extensively revised by the Treaty of Lisbon 2007
Some articles were moved to the Treaty on the Functioning of the European Union
Latest consolidated version of TFEU is 2012

1986
SINGLE EUROPEAN ACT (SEA)

1997
TREATY OF AMSTERDAM

2001
TREATY OF NICE

2007
TREATY OF LISBON

The Single European Act 1986 (SEA),[9] date in force 1 July 1987

The aim of the Single European Act, which was a treaty, was to finally reach the initial goal of the EU – the completion of the single market. For this, the founding treaty was reformed and the institutions of the EEC were reformed to give more powers to the European Parliament (EP) and introducing majority decisions for the Council of the European Union.[10]

It seemed to many that the vision for closer unity and European federalism might be attainable.

The Treaty of Maastricht 1992 (TEU), date in force 1 November 1993

Debates on expansion and greater co-operation between member states resulted in the Treaty of Maastricht, formally named the Treaty on European Union (TEU), referred to as the second founding treaty of the EU.[11] It made fundamental changes to the structure of the then European Community and created the EU as a political and social, but not legal, entity. The establishing of the EU itself gave the desire among the member states for greater union a more formal basis.

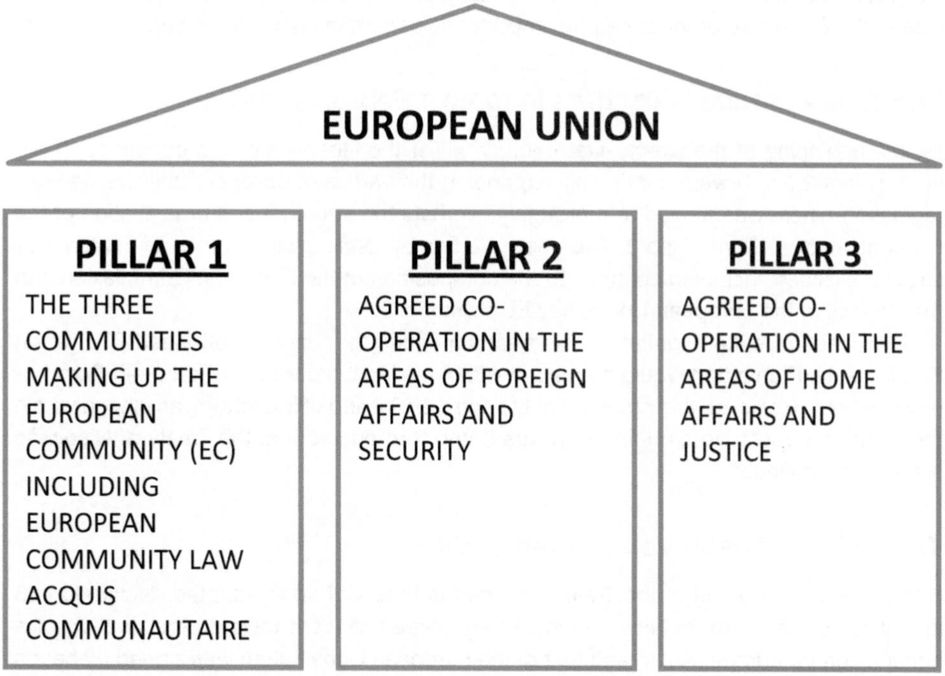

EUROPEAN UNION

PILLAR 1	PILLAR 2	PILLAR 3
THE THREE COMMUNITIES MAKING UP THE EUROPEAN COMMUNITY (EC) INCLUDING EUROPEAN COMMUNITY LAW ACQUIS COMMUNAUTAIRE	AGREED CO-OPERATION IN THE AREAS OF FOREIGN AFFAIRS AND SECURITY	AGREED CO-OPERATION IN THE AREAS OF HOME AFFAIRS AND JUSTICE

Figure 5.4 The three pillars of the European Union

---

9 Signed on 17 February 1986 in Luxembourg and 28 February at The Hague and in force 1 July 1987.
10 We will be considering the EP in more detail later in this chapter.
11 Signed 7 February 1992, in force 1 November 1993.

The TEU formalised greater co-operation between states and renamed the Treaty of Rome No 2 the Treaty Establishing the European Community (EC Treaty). It set up three main areas of collaboration and co-operation within the newly established EU, which were referred to as the 'three pillars of the EU' and these are set out below in Figure 5.4.

The treaty added more areas in which the EU, through its first pillar 'legal order' had the competency to engage in legal regulation. It also increased the powers of the European Parliament, allowing it a greater role in the process of creating legislation. The Maastricht Treaty also referred for the first time to the concept of the European Citizen.[12]

An important benefit of the EU's existence in the second and third pillars only at this time was its introduction of a co-operative element, free of legal regulation, that it allowed potential policies relating to legal regulation to be considered among member states before decisions needed to be made to make them legal obligations under the legal order of the EC.

A number of changes have been made to this treaty, particularly in 2007 necessitating the publication of a consolidated version in 2012 incorporating all later amendments.

The Treaty of Amsterdam 1997, date in force 1 May 1999

The Treaty of Amsterdam[13] can be described as a 'housekeeping' treaty. It renumbered the EC Treaty, continued the reform of the key institutions and added further legal competencies to the EU. It also emphasised the importance of human rights to the European Union.

The Treaty of Nice 2001, date in force 1 February 2003

By the beginning of the twenty-first century whilst the legal order was contained in pillar 1, pillars 2 and 3 were continually expanding their areas of co-operation outside legal regulation. There was a need to thoroughly overhaul the structure and organisation of the EU contained in pillars 2 and 3. The treaty did this by dealing with a range of contentious structural issues, including changes to the composition of the European Commission and the Council of the European Union, key EU institutions.

The heads of state negotiating this treaty intended to launch an attached Charter on Fundamental Rights that would be placed within the legal order of the European Community in pillar 1. However, this proved highly controversial and ultimately it was placed within the looser co-operative grouping of pillars 2 and 3 to ensure that the Treaty of Nice was signed and ratified.[14]

The 'failed' Constitutional Treaty 2004

Shortly after the signing of the Treaty of Nice the heads of state adopted declaration 23 (attached to the Treaty of Nice) in which they agreed to work towards the drafting of a constitution for Europe. An agreed text of the European Constitution was signed by heads of state in July 2004. However, after the treaty failed to be accepted in two referendums (in the Netherlands and in France), the ratification process in the other countries was brought to a halt.

---

12 Articles 17–21.
13 Signed 2 October 1997.
14 Signed on 26 February 2001 and ratified and in force on 1 February 2003.

The Treaty of Lisbon 2007

This Treaty was a major reforming treaty to implement the essential structural changes that had been proposed in the failed constitution. It amends the Treaty on European Union (TEU). Additionally it renames the EC treaty the Treaty on the Functioning of the EU (TFEU). The Treaty of Lisbon also makes clear that the EU is founded on both of these treaties as amended. It also clarifies which powers belong to the EU acting alone, and which powers are shared with EU member states.

The Treaty made provision for the European Union to supersede the European Community as a single legal, political, social and economic entity. The three pillars established in TEU were merged and provision made for the word 'Community' to be replaced by the word 'Union' in all treaties, secondary EU law and documentation.

The treaty also incorporated the Charter of Fundamental Rights into the law of the European Union stating the Charter has equal value with the two founding treaties (TFEU and TEU). Additionally, the treaty made provision for the EU to accede to the European Convention on Human Rights.

The powers of the European Parliament were again increased, and changes were made to voting procedures in the Council of the European Union (to be discussed below). Democratic representation was extended by setting up the European Citizens' Initiative. This is the right for European citizens to request the European Commission to propose a law if one million European citizens, from at least 25 per cent of the member states, sign a representation for a law in an area covered by the competency of the EU.

The Treaty of Lisbon also establishes two important new posts: the office of the permanent President of the European Council; and the new High Representative for Foreign Affairs.

The main treaties

Table 5.1 lays out the main treaties with their relevant dates, date in force and main purpose and classifies them as founding treaties, amending treaties and accession treaties. It also includes the various formal and informal names by which the treaties are known. Following on from Table 5.1, Table 5.2 sets out the treaties that are currently in force. Post 2012 there are five current treaties.

The consolidated version of the two founding treaties 2010

In 2010 the EU published consolidated and updated versions of the two founding treaties which were extensively reorganised and the Treaty of Rome was renamed the Treaty on the Functioning of the EU (TFEU), the Treaty on European Union (TEU) was retained in name but extensively reorganised. Some articles were moved between the two founding treaties. The Charter of Fundamental Rights of the EU (CFREU) was attached, and part of the law of the EU. These have now been superseded by a consolidated version published in 2012.[15]

It is essential to refer to the most up to date consolidation of important treaties which can easily be done by accessing the EU treaties database on the official EU website[16] and checking the official latest version.

---

15 2012/C/326/01   http://eur-lex.europa.eu/LexUriServ/LexUriServ.do?uri=OJ:C:2012:326:0001:0012:EN:PDF accessed 22 October 2013.
16 http://eur-lex.europa.eu.

TABLE 5.1 CHRONOLOGICAL LIST OF TREATIES DEVELOPING THE EU				
Place	Date signed	Date in force	Formal title	Common abbreviation
LISBON	13.12.2007	1.12.2009	Treaty of Lisbon amending the Treaty on European Union and the Treaty establishing the European Community	Treaty of Lisbon
NICE	27.2.2001	1.2.2003	Treaty of Nice amending the Treaty on European Union, the Treaties establishing the European Communities and certain related Acts	Treaty of Nice
AMSTERDAM	2.10.1997	1.5.1999	Treaty of Amsterdam amending the Treaty of the European Union, the Treaties establishing the European Communities and certain related Acts	Treaty of Amsterdam
MAASTRICHT	7.2.1992	1.11.1993	Treaty on European Union	Treaty of Maastricht, or Maastricht or TEU
LUXEMBOURG	1986	1.7.1987	Single European Act	Single European Act or SEA
BRUSSELS	8.4.1965	1.7.1967	Merger Treaty	The merger treaty
ROME no1	25.3.1957	1.1.1958	Treaty establishing the European Atomic Energy Community	EURATOM
ROME no 2	25.3.1957	1.1.1958	Treaty Establishing the European Economic Community	The Treaty of Rome (EEC treaty) BUT: Treaty renamed in 1992 (EC treaty) AND renamed in 2007 (TFEU)
PARIS	18.4.1951	23.7.1952	Treaty establishing the European Coal and Steel Community	Treaty of Paris

TABLE 5.2 CURRENT TREATIES OF THE EU IN FORCE

NB: How to understand the references to the official journal and CELEX numbers given below will be explained in Chapter 8.

Treaty	Official journal reference	EUR-Lex (CELEX number)
Treaty of Lisbon 2007	OJ C 306, 17.12.2007	12007L/TXT
Treaty on the Functioning of the European Union Consolidated version 2012	OJ C 326, 26.10.2012	12012E/TXT
Treaty on the European Union Consolidated version 2012	OJ C 326, 26.10.2012	12012M/TXT
Treaty establishing the European Atomic Energy Community (consolidated version 2012)	OJ C 327, 26.10.2012	12012A/TXT
Charter of Fundamental Rights of the European Union 2012	OJ C 326, 26.10.2012, pp. 391–407	12012P/TXT

Additionally the European Atomic Community 1957 (EURATOM) was also republished as an official consolidated treaty in 2012.

Table of equivalences

As a result of all of the changes to treaty articles, it became hard to know where articles in previous treaties had ended up during the updating and consolidating! Some articles had been through more than one change. As the founding treaties (now TFEU and TEU) have been changed so often the EU has published a table of equivalences online so that you can find the new location of treaty articles![17]

EU enlargement

The membership of the EU is not closed:[18] any European state meeting the appropriate criteria for membership can apply to join. Enlargement first occurred in 1973 which was when the UK joined; currently there are 28 member states.

UNDERSTANDING THE INSTITUTIONS OF THE EU

The functions of the EU are carried out by institutions created in the treaties. As far as possible the powers given to the institutions ensure national and EU interests are balanced.

---

17 www.eur-lex.europa.eu/LexUriServ/LexUriServ.do?uri=OJ:C:2010:083:0361:EN:PDF.
18 Expansion will next consider states in south-eastern Europe and there are several official accession candidate countries.

Article 13 of TEU lists seven institutions of the EU, and five of these are key for understanding policy and law making in the EU. They are:

(1)   The European Council which is the politically most powerful institution.
(2)   The Commission, the only institution with the power to propose legislation.
(3)   The Council of the European Union which has the power to adopt legislation in partnership with the European Parliament.
(4)   The European Parliament.
(5)   The Court of Justice of the EU (CJEU), charged with ensuring EU law is harmoniously interpreted and enforced.

Each of these are set out in Figure 5.5 and they will now be discussed in turn.

The European Council: the key policy/political institution

When the heads of state of the governments of each of the member states meet together this was always informally referred to as the European Council. However, since the Treaty of Lisbon 2007 this gathering has been given the status of an institution of the EU with its own president. It is the most powerful political gathering within the EU and is responsible for the vision and policy direction of the EU though it does not have law making power. It has a President established by the Treaty of Lisbon.

The three key institutions for law making

Figure 5.6 gives you an immediate idea of the role of each of these institutions and it is followed by a more detailed description of their functions and powers.

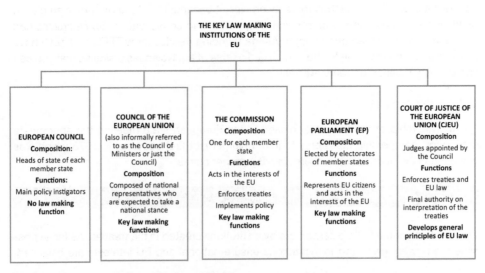

Figure 5.5 The key law making institutions of the EU

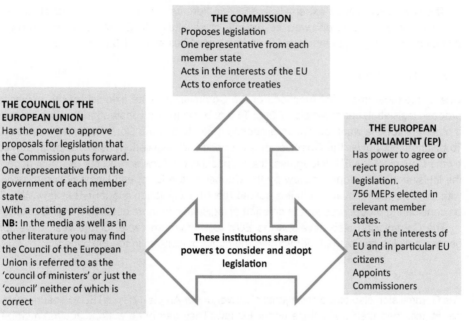

THE COMMISSION
Proposes legislation
One representative from each member state
Acts in the interests of the EU
Acts to enforce treaties

THE COUNCIL OF THE EUROPEAN UNION
Has the power to approve proposals for legislation that the Commission puts forward.
One representative from the government of each member state
With a rotating presidency
NB: In the media as well as in other literature you may find the Council of the European Union is referred to as the 'council of ministers' or just the 'council' neither of which is correct

THE EUROPEAN PARLIAMENT (EP)
Has power to agree or reject proposed legislation.
756 MEPs elected in relevant member states.
Acts in the interests of EU and in particular EU citizens
Appoints Commissioners

These institutions share powers to consider and adopt legislation

Figure 5.6 The three key institutions for law making

The European Commission (the Commission)

The Commission, the Council of the European Union and the European Parliament are the key institutions for law making.

The Commission is composed of one representative from each member state, called commissioners. They are expected to make decisions to further the interests of the EU and not privilege their own national interests. They have the power to propose draft legislation to the Council and to the European Parliament. Additionally, other institutions, including the Council and the European Parliament, can ask the Commission to propose legislation in certain areas. It has its own permanent secretariat in Brussels.

The president of the Commission is proposed by the European Council, and the Parliament has to confirm the candidate by a majority, otherwise the European Council has to find someone else.

The president, commissioners and their personal and general administrative and managerial staff are collectively referred to as the College of Commissioners. It is now mandatory for the college to include the High Representative for Foreign Affairs of the EU.

The work of the Commission is broken down into specific subject areas relating to external or internal matters, such as economics or foreign affairs, or split according to generalised areas such as legal services or the European Anti-Fraud Office.

The Commission is an extremely large institution. Its human resources statistics published annually on the Europa website (the official website of the European Union)[19] showed that it had 32,666 people employed in various capacities as at 31 March 2013.[20]

Law making powers

One of the most important functions of the Commission is its exercise of the power to propose legislation under Article 17(2) of TEU and it is the only institution that can do this. If other institutions want legislation proposed it has to ask the Commission to propose it. To balance this power the Commission's proposals for legislation must first be approved by the Council of the EU. If it agrees, the proposal is put forward and the EU must accept the legislation and adopt it as law by the Council of the European Union acting together with the European Parliament. If it is agreed then the legislation is adopted as law. We will be considering procedures for the creation of legislation in more detail later in this chapter.

The Commission also develops the EU's legislative timetable for the year, develops general policies, for example forwarding the rights of workers in the EU generally.

Judicial powers

The Commission also exercises a judicial power under Article 17(1) of TEU to ensure member states keep their obligations under EU law. They can bring actions against member states in the Court of Justice of the EU (CJEU) using powers in Article 258 of TFEU.

The Council of the European Union (also referred to as the 'council of ministers' or the 'council')

Each member state has one representative on the Council. There has been a president of the Council since 2007. S/he determines when the Council should meet which is normally bi-monthly. The presidency of the Council is held by a country on a rotating basis.

Powers of the Council

The members of the Council each represent their national interest and its powers are set out in Article 16 of TEU. Their role is to approve Commission proposals for law, as well as to be proactive in setting out legislation under Article 241 of TFEU. The Council can suggest that the Commission consider proposing legislation in a particular area and it can delegate powers to the Commission. The recent amendments to the treaties since Lisbon have required the Council to share more power with the European Parliament and the Commission.

Warning: potential naming confusions concerning institutions

It is easy to confuse the EU institutions of the European Council and the Council of the European Union. Furthermore it is unfortunately all too easy to confuse either of these with a completely separate organisation called the Council of Europe (CoE). The CoE also has an institution, 'the Committee of Ministers', which can be confused with the EU institutions. It is

---

19 http://ec.europa.eu.
20 See http://ec.europa.eu/civil_service/about/figures/index_en.htm for a full breakdown of figures.

most important that you do not muddle the institutions of the CoE with any of the institutions of the EU, or confuse the two EU institutions of the European council and the Council of the EU. You just need to be aware of this potential for confusion and make sure you understand the different names and what they each refer to. Table 5.3 assists you to keep them separate.

The European Parliament (EP)

The EP is currently composed of 756 Members of the European Parliament (MEPs). Each member state elects its own MEP who cannot also be a Member of Parliament (MP) in their own national legislature. The EP is the institution that represents the populations of the member states. It is organised along political affiliations, but at the European level of political organisation. The EP exercises important powers of co-decision with the Council of the EU. If the EP does not agree to the proposed legislation it cannot be adopted and become EU law.

Court of Justice of the European Union (CJEU)

The main function of the CJEU is to ensure that the Treaties of the Union are consistently applied and interpreted across EU institutions and in the legal systems of member states. The CJEU includes several courts.

The Treaty of Paris 1951 initially established the European Court of Justice (ECJ) which became the court of all three original communities. Its jurisdiction increased as the EU developed and it had courts added to it to assist it. Finally the Treaty of Lisbon made various structural changes, changing the names of courts to end up with the Court of Justice of the European Union (CJEU). Its current powers are set out in the TFEU.

TABLE 5.3 TRYING TO AVOID NAMING CONFUSIONS!		
Institution	**Organisation**	**Description**
European Council	EU	Heads of state or government of EU member states
The Council of the European Union **NB:** This institution is also quite often referred to as the council of ministers or the council by media and politicians so look out for that!	EU	An important part of the arrangements for law making within the EU
The Council of Europe (CoE)	CoE	Organisation set up in 1949 with a primary role to protect human rights, the rule of law and democratic governance
The Committee of Ministers	CoE	The Committee of Ministers is one of the institutions of the CoE

Its primary courts are the Court of Justice (CJ) which was formerly the European Court of Justice (ECJ) referred to above,[21] the General court (GC)[22] which was formerly the Court of First Instance prior to 2007, and the civil service tribunals.[23] Those who are part of the judiciary in member states as well as academics can be appointed as judges to the CJEU. We will be considering the court in more detail later in this chapter.

UNDERSTANDING THE EU LEGAL ORDER AND EU LAW

The EU legal order: the acquis communautaire

The founding treaties of the EU have never stated that the EU has its own legal order; however, the CJ has held that it does. In 1962 in the leading case of *van Gend en Loos* the court stated:

'. . . the Community constitutes a new legal order in international law, for whose benefit the States have limited their sovereign rights, albeit within limited fields, and the subjects of which comprise not only the member states but also their nationals. Community law, therefore, apart from legislation by the member states, not only imposes obligations on individuals but also confers on them legal rights. The latter arise not only when an explicit grant is made by the Treaty, but also through obligations imposed, in a clearly defined manner, by the Treaty on individuals as well as on member states and the Community institutions.[24]

Two years later the CJ heard the case of *Costa v ENEL*[25] and held:

'. . . As opposed to other international treaties, the Treaty instituting the EEC has created its own order which was integrated with the national order of the member-States the moment the Treaty came into force; as such, it is binding upon them. In fact, by creating a Community of unlimited duration, having its own institutions, its own personality and its own capacity in law, apart from having international standing and more particularly, real powers resulting from a limitation of competence or a transfer of powers from the States to the Community, the member states, albeit within limited spheres, have restricted their sovereign rights and created a body of law applicable both to their nationals and to themselves. The reception, within the laws of each member state, of provisions having a Community source, and more particularly of the terms and of the spirit of the Treaty, has as a corollary the impossibility, for the member state, to give preference to a unilateral and subsequent measure against a legal order accepted by them on a basis of reciprocity.'[26]

The sources of EU law

There are several core sources of EU law: primary law as set out in the treaties, and secondary law created by the institutions of the EU. The law created by the institutions is

---

21 Jurisdiction and its important actions found in Articles 19, and 251–281 of TFEU.
22 Jurisdiction in Articles 251–281 of TFEU.
23 Jurisdiction and its important actions found in Article 257 of TFEU.
24 *NV Algemene Transport-en Expeditie Onderneming van Gend en Loos v Nederlandse Tariefcommissie* [1963] CMLR 105, 129.
25 (Case 14/1964) *Costa v Ente Nazionale per l'Energia Elettrica (ENEL)* [1964] CMLR 425.
26 Ibid at 456.

secondary because they gain their power to create law from the treaties. Secondary law comes in several types. The Court of Justice of the EU also has the power to establish general principles of EU law. The primary and secondary sources and legal principles are set out below in Table 5.4.

TABLE 5.4 CORE SOURCES OF EU LAW		
1	Primary law	**The treaties** Various articles in EU treaties are capable of creating law if they conform to the conditions for this to happen which are now laid out in the Treaty of Lisbon
2	Secondary law	Laws created by the EU institutions by powers given in Article 288 TFEU and are: • regulations • directives • decisions • recommendations • opinions
3	General principles of EU law	These are developed by the CJEU

Each of these three sources will be discussed in a little more detail before turning to consider the hierarchy that operates between the differing types of EU law.

PRIMARY LAW OF THE EU

The EU's primary law is created by the founding treaties (TFEU AND TEU)[27] which are considered to be the supreme source of primary law in the EU. They also authorise and facilitate secondary forms of law making. The Court of Justice of the European Union (CJEU) has stated that TFEU and TEU can be likened to a constitution.

Individual articles in other treaties can be recognised as creating primary EU law and the CJEU has laid down guidelines to be followed to determine whether a treaty article is enforceable primary law. Moreover, the Treaty of Lisbon 2007 lays out procedures to be adopted to determine when a treaty article can be deemed to be primary law.

Secondary law of the EU

All EU law proposed and adopted by the institutions of the EU is secondary law, and these make up the major source of EU law. Such law is considered to be secondary because the primary sources of law, the treaties, created the institutions and determined the types of law they could 'adopt'. In the EU law is 'adopted' rather than 'enacted'.

---

27 When you study EU law in your second or third year of law studies you will hear of a few other more minor sources of primary law of the EU.

Article 288 TFEU states:

'to exercise the Union's competences, the institutions shall adopt regulations, directives, decisions, recommendations and opinions'.

Of the five types of 'adoption' listed, only three: regulations, directives and decisions
are legally binding legal instruments. Regulations, directives and decisions adopted under
Article 288 of TFEU must be signed by the Presidents of the European Parliament and the
Council of the EU.

Figure 5.7 The general principles of EU law

TABLE 5.5 HIERARCHY OF LEGAL NORMS
1. Treaty articles
2. General principles of law
3. Secondary EU law (regulations, directives, decisions)

The two final categories, recommendations and opinions, enable the Union institutions to express a view to individual or groups of member states. They are not binding and do not place any legal obligation on those addressed. Sometimes opinions can be followed by legally binding Acts, or opinions can even be required to be issued before proceedings can be commenced by the institutions against a member state in the CJEU.

General principles of EU law (developed by the Court of Justice)

Like all legal systems, the legal order of the EU through the CJEU has developed certain principles that inform the interpretation and, to a certain extent, the creation of law. These principles cover a range of issues and are not closed. They are set out in in Figure 5.7.

These general principles include the idea that all are equal before the law and that the law of the EU will maintain due process.

Hierarchy of legal norms

The Treaty of Lisbon 2009 makes clear that EU legal norms should be seen in a particular hierarchy. Some forms of law are able to change others because they have a higher place in the hierarchy of legal norms in the EU. This can be likened to the way in which in the English legal system the legislation of the Westminster Parliament can change English case law because it is of higher authority than case law.

For now it is only necessary for you to be aware of the hierarchy between treaty articles, general principles of law and EU secondary law (regulations and directives) and these are set out in Table 5.5 in order of hierarchy.

THE LEGAL EFFECT OF EU PRIMARY AND SECONDARY EU LAW

It is essential that you understand the legal effect of the different types of primary and secondary EU law. Initially in 1957 it was assumed that EU law only gave legal rights and obligations to member states and to EU institutions. However, in the 1960s the CJEU held that individuals and private companies could make a claim under EU law in certain circumstances. The right to bring any such action varies according to the type of EU law infringed. We will now consider the effect of EU law on member states and then on individuals and/or private companies.

Effect of EU law on member states

Member states must keep their obligations under EU law; if they do not then other member states or institutions of the EU can bring legal action against them for violation of EU law. The Commission has an obligation to enforce the treaties and EU law and will take legal action against member states for breach of the law.

Much of EU law is directly applicable in the legal system of member states as soon as it is in force in the EU (some treaty articles, regulations and decisions) and binding in its entirety. Other forms of EU law are binding only as to 'their outcome' (directives). EU law that is 'directly applicable' and EU law 'binding as to outcome' are explained in more detail below.

EU law that is 'directly applicable'

EU law that is directly applicable becomes part of the legal system of all member states as soon as it comes into force in the EU legal system. The CJEU has determined that primary law (treaty articles) is directly applicable and binding in its entirety on member states if certain criteria are met.

Article 288 of TFEU, when setting out the different types of secondary law, makes clear that 'regulations', the main form of secondary EU law, are directly applicable if certain criteria are met and are binding in their entirety. It also provides that another form of secondary law, decisions of EU institutions, are directly applicable and legally binding in their entirety to those addressed. Decisions are only addressed to one or more member states but not to all.

EU law that is binding 'as to outcome': directives

Law that is binding as to outcome specifically applies to another form of secondary legislation, directives. These are specific requests to member states to ensure a particular goal is achieved within a set timescale (usually several years). Directives leave it up to the state to determine how that goal should be achieved. The state can choose to use non-legal means to achieve the goal if they so wish. Directives therefore are said to be legally binding as to 'outcome'. They are a good way of allowing flexibility to member states as they acknowledge that there are different ways of doing things. They have been used extensively to formulate and implement policies within the EU, for example for ensuring equal pay for workers.

The effect of EU law on private organisations and individuals: direct effect

As noted above, as soon as treaty articles meeting the required criteria, regulations and decisions are in force they become part of the national legal system of each member state. Where the CJEU has accepted that individuals can claim under EU law it is said that the relevant EU law has 'direct effect'.

Direct effect has two dimensions, horizontal and vertical, because legal systems operate at two levels, the public and the private.

Vertical direct effect

'Vertical direct effect' is the phrase used to describe the situation where EU legal rules are enforceable in the public realm against the state or other recognised public body by individuals and private bodies (private companies). These legal rules can be described as having 'vertical direct effect' because the state is in a superior, hierarchical position with regard to both private individuals and non-state organisations.

Horizontal direct effect

Horizontal direct effect is the phrase used to describe the situation where EU legal rules are enforceable in the private realm between individuals or private companies against other individuals and/or private companies. At this level legal rules are referred to as having a 'horizontal direct effect': 'horizontal' because both parties in the legal dispute are on the same hierarchical level with regard to each other.

Both horizontal and direct effect are illustrated in Figure 5.8.

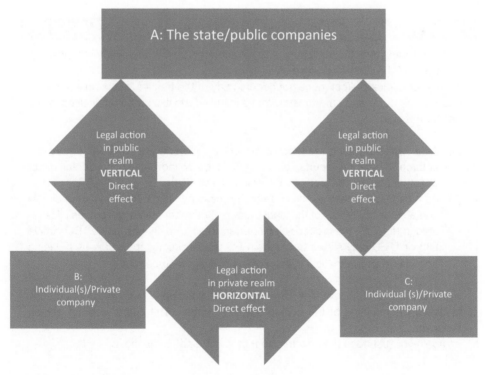

Figure 5.8 Possible horizontal and vertical legal direct effect

Direct effect and directives

The CJEU has held that in special circumstances directives can have vertical direct effect against the state or public authorities. However, they can never have horizontal direct effect. This is because they are addressed to the state for the state to deal with.

Criteria for determining whether direct effect can apply to an EU law

The collective case law from the CJEU indicates that before any primary or secondary rule of EU law can be held to have 'direct effect' it must conform to the following criteria:

- the legal rule that is the source of the claim must not require any action from the relevant member state that is the object of the complaint. (And of course directives do); and
- the legal right to be enforced must be clear and precise;
- the legal rule must be capable of activation without recourse to the state (which is not the automatic case in relation to articles in a treaty concluded at state level or a directive issued to the state demanding certain outcomes within a timescale).

Alert: Confusion of terms!

The two terms 'directly applicable' and 'direct effect' can be used interchangeably, even in the CJ, which is not correct.

The term 'direct effect' does not occur in any of the treaties. It is a phrase developed by the CJEU and unfortunately for us in the courts it is consistently used in two different senses.

(1) As a term describing the process by which individuals acquire rights they can enforce in national courts, either against other individuals (horizontal direct effect) or against the state itself (vertical direct effect).

(2) As a descriptive term to describe the process by which EU law is immediately and automatically part of the legal system of member states as soon as it is created in the EU – the process also referred to as 'directly applicable'. But Article 288 of TFEU only states that certain EU law is directly applicable as meaning becomes part of the legal system of the relevant member state.

From a pragmatic point of view there is a need to accept this confusion, and seek to derive the meaning of the phrase from its context. The courts use the phrase synonymously.

Again you just need to know this so that you are not confused.

ENFORCEMENT OF EU LAW

Whilst the treaties set up a situation in which EU law is supreme over national law there are inevitably conflicts and incompatibilities that occur between EU and national law. These conflicts have to be resolved in the best interests of the EU and the furtherance of its goals. When this happens the founding treaties make provision for the Commission to take action against a member state, or a member state to take action against another member state. The CJ can impose sanctions and has enforcement powers.

The role of the Commission

The Commission is charged with ensuring the enforcement of EU law, and it has powers to enforce it. Article 58 of TFEU states that if the Commission believes there has been a violation of EU law by a member state it can take action. This includes the power to take action against a member state that has failed to implement a directive in the timescale given. Although the Commission has a great deal of discretion concerning whether it will seek to obtain observance of the law through court action, the majority of actions in the CJEU are from the Commission bringing action against member states.

Article 259 of TFEU also allows actions by member states against other member states for breach of EU law, although it is worth noting that such actions rarely reach the CJEU for a hearing. Member states must bring the matter to the attention of the Commission. If the Commission does not respond, or if their issued reasoned opinion does not resolve the matter, the state can bring an action in the CJEU. If the matter reaches the CJEU member states will normally accept its ruling.

Article 260 of TFEU does make provision for enforcement procedures but these rarely need to be invoked. In such circumstances the Commission is called upon to deliver a second reasoned opinion, followed by a second action by the Commission in the CJEU to determine the fine.

The role of the CJEU in enforcing EU law

The CJEU is the adjudication forum for disputes relating to treaty articles and secondary law between:

- Member states and the institutions of the EU.
- Member states and other member states.
- Claims by individuals and private organisations.

Most cases are dealt with in the CJEU and we will concentrate on that court.

Preliminary rulings

The founding treaties state that if there is a case in a national court raising a question about the interpretation of a treaty article a domestic court can refer the query to the CJEU for a 'preliminary ruling' as to the correct interpretation of the relevant article. If the domestic

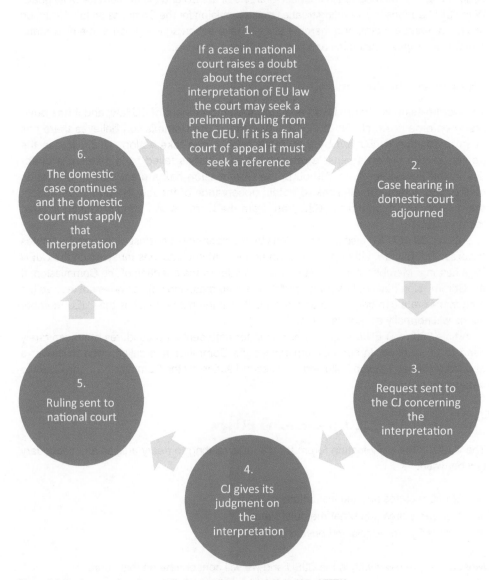

Figure 5.9 Basic procedure for a preliminary ruling under Article 267 of TFEU

court is a court of last resort for example the Supreme Court in the UK, then the court must refer the matter to the CJ for a preliminary ruling on the correct interpretation. The case is stopped in the national court while the reference is sought. That interpretation is sent back to the national court who must apply it to the case before it.[28] This area is now regulated by Article 267 of TFEU.

This is an extremely important process for developing EU law. The concept of 'direct effect' discussed above was only made possible because of preliminary rulings by the CJ.

It is maintained that the relationship between the EU courts and the national courts is one of equals determining issues in differing but complementary areas. The national court has discretion whether to refer, unless it is a final appeal court (such as the UK Supreme Court) in which case they must refer. Preliminary rulings given to one national court need to be taken into account by the courts of other member states dealing with the same EU law.

Figure 5.9 briefly indicates the procedure in national and EU courts relating to preliminary references.

Institutions acting in excess of their powers (ultra vires)

The CJEU has powers under Articles 263 and 265 to consider the acts of the institutions and to determine by a judicial review if they have acted within the powers given to them by the treaties. If they exceed their powers the court can declare that their actions do not have legal validity.

UNDERSTANDING THE SUPREMACY OF EU LAW AND THE IMPACT OF EU LAW ON THE ENGLISH LEGAL SYSTEM

EU law claims supremacy over the national law of member states of the EU in areas of its legislative competency. Supremacy of EU law has two dimensions: what does the EU understand by the supremacy of EU law, and what is the member states' interpretation of the supremacy of EU law. We will consider both dimensions.

What does the EU understand by the supremacy of EU law?

It was the CJEU that developed the doctrine of the legal supremacy of EU law over domestic law of the member states in cases coming before it in the 1960s. In *Costa v ENEL*,[29] it held that the supremacy of EU law was the cornerstone of the EU legal order.

The failed constitutional treaty in 2004 contained an explicit reference to the supremacy of EU law in a 'primacy article'. But when the Lisbon Treaty was being negotiated the insertion of such a primacy article proved to be a highly contentious matter and it was dropped from the treaty to ensure the treaty itself was ratified. However, Declaration 17, 'Concerning Primacy', attached to the Treaty of Lisbon affirmed the place of the case law of the EU in establishing the supremacy of EU law, noting:

---

28 In limited areas there is now provision, yet to be activated, to delegate preliminary references to the general court.

29 See fn 25.

'The conference recalls that, in accordance with well settled case law of the Court of Justice of the European Union, the Treaties and the law adopted by the Union on the basis of the Treaties have supremacy over the law of member states, under the conditions laid down by the said case law.'

The European Council's legal service was also asked to attach its opinion on supremacy to this declaration. They affirmed that supremacy is a 'cornerstone principle' established by the cases of *van Gend en Loos* and *Costa*.[30]

The assertion by the EU of the supremacy of EU law over national law only has meaning, of course, if member states 'buy in' to this principle of supremacy and support it in practice as well as in theory. Member state disagreement tends to be theoretical rather than practical.

Member states are expected to positively work to assist the EU in its tasks and Article 4(3) of TFEU provides:

'The member states shall take any appropriate measures, whether general or particular to ensure fulfilment of the obligations arising out of this treaty or resulting from action taken by the institutions of the Union. The member states shall facilitate the achievement of the Union's tasks and refrain from any measure which could jeopardise the attainment of the union's objectives'.[31]

English law and the supremacy of EU law

By signing the Accession Treaty of 1973 the UK Parliament agreed to be bound by the founding treaties of the EU and accept the case law developed by the CJEU. Inevitably therefore it also recognised the judicial development of the acquis communautaire, and the supremacy principle established in *Costa* and developed further in later cases. The CJ stated in *Costa*:

'. . . the law stemming from the Treaty'. . . [is] 'an independent source of law'. . . [which cannot], 'because of its special and original nature, be overridden by domestic legal provisions, however framed, without being deprived of its character as community law and without the legal basis of the community being called into question . . .'

Because of the UK's dualist position with regard to international law it was necessary for UK legislation to be enacted making provision (among other things) for the supremacy of EU law.

The constitutional theory of the UK, expressed in the doctrine of the absolute sovereignty of any one Parliament to legislate as it wishes, presents an immediate difficulty with regard to the acceptance of the supremacy of EU law. Only a current Parliament retains

---

30 See fns 24, 25, 26.
31 This provision was originally found in Article 5 of the EEC Treaty, which became Article 10(5) of the EC Treaty and ultimately has now settled as Article 4(3) of TFEU.

the ultimate legal sovereignty to enact or repeal any law. As it is sovereign no other law could be imposed upon it without permission. It is not bound by previously agreed law, and can repeal it. The UK has no procedure for specially protecting law that may be said to go to the heart of the constitution. Joining the EU therefore marked a tremendous shift of thinking in relation to parliamentary sovereignty.

These arguments can become highly theoretical, but for the purposes of practical law and politics the UK enacted the European Communities Act 1972 (ECA 1972) which contained provisions to ensure that appropriate EU law becomes part of the body of English law as soon as it is in force in the EU. The subordination of English law to EU law is therefore based on a legal footing. ECA 1972, s 2(1) as amended now states:

> 'All such rights, powers, liabilities, obligations and restrictions from time to time created or arising by or under the Treaties, and all such remedies and procedures from time to time provided for by or under the Treaties, as in accordance with the Treaties are without further enactment to be given legal effect or used in the United Kingdom shall be recognised and available in law, and be enforced, allowed and followed accordingly; and the expression "enforceable EU[32] right" and similar expressions shall be read as referring to one to which this subsection applies.'

So as you can see from reading s 2(1), all directly applicable EU law is immediately part of the legal system and enforceable; additionally a range of rights and powers as well as remedies shall be recognised and/or used in the UK.

In the context of UK constitutional theory on the sovereignty of Parliament, the ECA 1972 was controversial as undoubtedly this legislation resulted in Parliament voluntarily ceding sovereignty in those areas where the EU has been given law making competency. Although theoretically, 'ceding' implies the possibility of 'taking back' sovereignty, the inevitable consequence of this would be to leave the EU. If there was the political will and a clear mandate to leave then, in principle, there is nothing to stand in the way of such action.

In *The Coalition: Our Programme for Government*[33] the government made the commitment that they would:

> '. . . ensure that there is no further transfer of sovereignty or powers [from the UK to the EU] over the course of the next Parliament . . . Any proposed future treaty that transferred areas of power, or competences, would be subject to a referendum on that treaty – a "referendum lock" . . .
>
> We will examine the case for a United Kingdom Sovereignty Bill to make it clear that ultimate authority remains with Parliament.'

Due to changes brought about by the Lisbon Treaty, The European Community Act 1972 was amended by the European Union Act 2011 to allow a series of changes flowing

---

32 'EU' substituted for word 'Community' in s 2(1), substituted (1.12.2009) by European Union (Amendment) Act 2008 (c. 7), ss 3, 8, Sch Pt 1; SI 2009/3143, Art 2.

33 www.cabinetoffice.gov.uk/media/409088/pfg_coalition.pdf.

from the Treaty of Lisbon 2009 to be incorporated into the English legal system. It also pro-vided the opportunity that in certain circumstances a referendum would be needed before changes required by the EU would be enacted in the UK.

When EU law, in the form of a directive, requires legal implementation in the English legal system this is usually done by using fast track secondary legislation procedures already referred to in Chapter 1. The ECA 1972 specifies some areas, such as taxation, cannot be subject to change by secondary legislation. These are fully listed in the Sched-ule to the Act and in these areas implementation of the directive must be accomplished by a primary Act of Parliament.

The provisions of s 2(1) of the ECA 1972 also places the decisions of the CJEU within the UK doctrine of precedent; s 3 of the ECA 1972 makes clear that if any question arises as to the interpretation of EU law this is a question of law to be dealt with by either an EU court using a preliminary reference or the domestic court taking into account the principles of CJEU case law.

Yet it was not until the case of *Factortame v UK*[34] that the precise nature of the relation-ship between EU law and UK law settled. Before *Factortame* the English judiciary took two main approaches to the interpretation of EU law and the cases of the CJEU. One approach relied exclusively on rules of statutory interpretation.[35] The judges assumed that by enact-ing the ECA 1972 it was the intention of Parliament that any ambiguities between EU law and UK law were to be resolved in favour of the interpretation according supremacy to EU law. However, the other view was that should it seem clear from the Act that Parliament intended to deviate from EU law, the court would follow the Act of Parliament, an approach which gives no guarantee of the supremacy of EU Law. But the judgment of Lord Bridge in *Factortame* explicitly accepted the supremacy of EU law and that in the provisions of the ECA 1972 Parliament had voluntarily limited their sovereignty. Lord Bridge succinctly summed up the position by stating:

> '. . . whatever limitation of its sovereignty Parliament accepted when it enacted the European Communities Act 1972 was entirely voluntary. Under the terms of the Act of 1972 it has always been clear that it was the duty of a United Kingdom court, when delivering final judgment, to override any rule of national law found to be in conflict with any directly enforceable rule of Community law. Similarly, when decisions of the European Court of Justice have exposed areas of United Kingdom statute law which failed to implement Council directives, Parliament has always loyally accepted the obligation to make appropriate and prompt amendments. Thus there is nothing in any way novel in according supremacy to rules of Community law in those areas to which they apply and to insist that, in the protection of rights under Community law, national courts must not be inhibited by rules of national law from granting interim relief in appropriate cases is no more than a logical recognition of that supremacy.'[36]

In *Thoburn v Sunderland*[37] Laws LJ stated that English legislation falls into two main sections: 'ordinary' statutes that can easily be assumed to be repealed by later legislation

---

34 *Regina v Secretary of State for Transport, Ex parte Factortame Ltd and Others (No 2)* Case C 213/89 [1991] 1 AC 603 House of Lords and before European Court of Justice 11 October 1990.
35 See Chapter 2 for information on statutory interpretation in UK cases.
36 Case C 213/89 [1991] 1 AC 603, 659.
37 2002 EWCA HC 195.

in the absence of any words to the contrary, and 'constitutional' statutes which cannot be impliedly repealed; these can only be repealed using express words stating that it is repealed. He used as his illustration of a 'constitutional statute' the European Community Act 1972, although he did not of course just mean EU related Acts, but also Acts such as the Magna Carta, the Acts of Union and the Human Rights Act.

Whilst undoubtedly at present Parliament has chosen to cede sovereignty, and English courts uphold this, there is no real barrier to any Parliament revoking the ECA 1972.

CONCLUSION

This chapter attempts to give you a snapshot of EU, its institutions, its sources of law and the differential impact of differing types of EU law. Taken together this gives you a firm foundation for understanding the EU, its institutions and its law.

CHAPTER SUMMARY

- The EU is a supranational organisation created by treaty and composed of member states who have ceded it their sovereignty in certain areas.
- European states can join the EU by signing an accession treaty providing that all existing member states agree.
- There are two founding treaties: TFEU and TEU.
- The Charter of Fundamental Rights 2007 has equal value with the two founding treaties.
- The European Council is the main political body determining policy, drafting and signing treaties which normally require ratification.
- The Commission proposes secondary EU law and also has the power to take member states to court for breach of law.
- The Council of the European Union has the power to agree and adopt EU secondary law.
- The European Parliament, together with the Council of the European Union, has the power to agree and adopt EU secondary law.
- The Court of Justice of the European Union (CJEU) hears claims relating to breach of EU law and also issues preliminary rulings on the correct interpretation of EU law when requested to do so.
- A national court of final appeal must refer to the CJ for a preliminary ruling if there is a query concerning the correct interpretation of EU law.
- The EU has its own legal order, the acquis communautaire (translated as Community law).
- EU law is supreme over the national law of member state.
- Primary EU law is derived from articles in EU treaties.

- Secondary law is created by EU institutions using powers given in the founding treaties.
- Secondary law are regulations, directives, decisions, recommendations and opinions.
- EU law can be 'directly applicable': that is, it becomes law in member states as soon as it is in force in the EU.
- Primary and secondary law may have direct effect, and can found a claim by a private person.
- Direct effect can be 'vertical' (e.g. the individual against the state or vice versa) or horizontal (e.g. the individual against an individual).
- The UK enacted the European Communities Act 1972 to ensure EU law is supreme.

PART 2

FINDING LAW – EFFECTIVE LEGAL RESEARCH

Your success in your legal studies depends upon your competent understanding of the law, primary texts of law as well as the contexts of law, which involves consideration of secondary texts, texts about law. Part 2 therefore focuses exclusively on the sets of skills revolving around 'how to' find both primary law and secondary legal materials about law. In order to do this you need to understand how to use your university law library and how to efficiently access their print and electronic sources. Additionally, while many of the electronic sites that you will access through your university library will be subscription only sites, you will also need to, or desire to, access electronic sites outside your university's e-library and it is important that you understand how to navigate, as well as critically evaluate, these free, open access internet resources.

Part 2 contains four chapters as follows:

Chapter 6 *How to get the most out of your university print and e-library* begins from the view that your ability to competently use the law library is essential for your success in the study of law. It ensures that you can understand the structure and layout of the library as a whole and the law collection within it, and develops your competency in searching and accessing its materials.

Chapter 7 *How to find domestic and European legislation* focuses attention on familiarising yourself with the print and internet sites for accessing legislation, and the range of citations used to enable it to be located. Time is spent discussing ways to ensure that you retrieve the most up to date version of the relevant law. The chapter also considers accessing primary and secondary law and accessing primary and secondary draft law.

Chapter 8 *How to find domestic and European cases* concentrates on the location of hard copy reports of cases (law reports) and e-copy law versions of cases. It also considers the distinctions between reported and unreported cases, and court transcripts and reports. In terms of law reports it discusses the hierarchy of the law reports in terms of their evaluation by the senior judiciary, as you do not want to work from a law report that is considered to be an inferior report. The citations of a law case are also considered. Sometimes you may wish to locate cases for historical purposes, but you will usually want to locate the most up to date legal rule and the chapter discusses how to ensure that you have done this in relation to your use of cases.

Chapter 9 *How to find secondary material: texts about law* discusses the skills required for the competent location of texts about law. There are an enormous range of such materials and part of the rationale for this chapter is to make you aware of them and their pros and cons: a range that includes reference texts such as dictionaries and encyclopaedias, academic books and journal articles, professional articles, parliamentary papers and debates, reports by parliamentary committees; reports by non-governmental agencies such as charities or independent think tanks; as well as web pages by leading academics, media reports and blogs by individuals or pressure groups. You need to understand the authority (if any) and the limits of the usefulness of any secondary material that you use. Many students often do not go much further than the textbook in their research and as a consequence their understanding of law remains relatively unsophisticated; certainly not of a standard to achieve the highest grades (and in some cases even lower pass grades). Students must keep up to date with academic thought about the area of law they are studying as well as keep up to date with the actual law itself. It also takes the time to consider how to check the authenticity, reliability and authority of free access internet resources.

HOW TO GET THE MOST OUT OF YOUR UNIVERSITY PRINT AND E-LIBRARY

LEARNING OUTCOMES

After reading this chapter you should be able to:

- Understand the structure and layout of the standard university library and the context of the law library within it.
- Understand the difference between primary and secondary sources of legal information.
- Develop a competent approach to locating, accessing and searching electronic resources.
- Develop strategies to ascertain the authority and validity of retrieved materials.

INTRODUCTION

The key tools of the trade of the law student are initially found in the university library. Here you will find the law itself, in texts *of* the law. You will also find texts *about* the law, describing and critiquing the law and its institutions. The acquisition of excellent library research skills is an essential task undertaken in the first term. But you will find that you continually need to develop them throughout your studies. If you become a research student after your degree you may, in time, be able to access the prestigious research only, reference only libraries such as the British Library in London.

Before looking in detail at the location of the law as well as texts about the law it is important to ensure that you understand and appreciate the indispensable role of the university library in your degree studies.

This chapter concentrates on mapping the overall structure of the library, the range of available resources for the study of law and their storage formats (whether in print or electronic formats). It covers the location of print and electronic law resources and discusses the need to quickly develop competent library IT skills. You need to understand how to search the library's online catalogue and the nature of online databases, research gateways and other e-resources.

There are several excellent detailed texts on the market that talk students through the use of the library. It is not the intention of this chapter to repeat that information. These texts are necessary reference texts in their own right and are referred to in the further reading section. In addition, each university library will have a selection of guides to its resources.

Walking into the university library can be a daunting experience. New students of all ages often report a feeling of inadequacy when first confronted with the scenes of a typical library lobby. There are lots of people (all of whom seem to know what they are doing); there are issue desks, banks of computers, banks of photocopiers, unfamiliar signage, student study support staff and private study rooms. There may be coffee bars, and some may have imposing atriums built to a scale which dwarfs individual users; there are cloakrooms and rules about bags. Entrance to the library is often through security checks and the scanning of your library card. Some libraries have not taken on the dimensions of huge factory buildings or implemented security measures, but even these can feel extremely alien to the new student.

Librarians and lecturers do realise, however, that students need to be orientated to the library and the structure of its resources so that they can use it competently. You will find that all libraries arrange a general induction to the layout and range of resources for new students. Additionally the law department, usually in liaison with library staff, will arrange for a series of specialist training sessions to introduce new law students to the print and electronic collections. Often there are opportunities for updates and more advanced training throughout the first year and one to one assistance may be offered to students who lack confidence. It is important to be aware of what support and training is on offer in your library so that you can make best use of it. Many libraries and departments also provide links to in-house and external online tutorials concerned with using the library. You should check for these in your university's departmental, library, study support and induction web-pages as well as on your department's preferred virtual learning environment (VLE).

In the past, university libraries, with their large print collections, were referred to as storehouses of knowledge. Today the volume of the printed resources becomes insignificant in relation to the volume of academic and official, non-subscription and subscription,

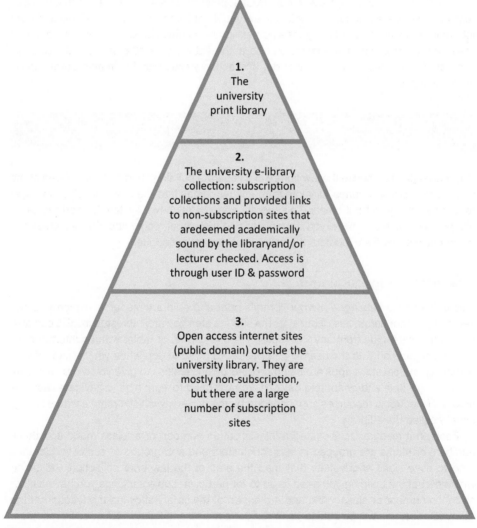

1.
The
university
print library

2.
The university e-library
collection: subscription
collections and provided links
to non-subscription sites that
aredeemed academically
sound by the libraryand/or
lecturer checked. Access is
through user ID & password

3.
Open access internet sites
(public domain) outside the
university library. They are
mostly non-subscription,
but there are a large
number of subscription
sites

Figure 6.1 How the volume of different types of legal resources compare

electronic resources on offer through the standard university library. The library electronic resources are dwarfed by the freely available electronic resources generally available, the constant supply of which seems inexhaustible. There will also be large numbers of subscription sites outside your library's e-resources. Only a few are chosen by universities. Figure 6.1 illustrates the proportions of different formats in which materials can be accessed, and roughly indicates their proportions in relation to each other. When using the library it is important to use the best of the full range of available sources for the task in hand.

In year 1 of a law degree you need to acquire the basic skills of searching, and you will then work hard to build on these to construct sophisticated search strategies that you can rely on. If you are researching a particular law you do not want to overlook reliable and valid information because your library research skills are patchy. Nor do you wish to base an essay for an important assessment on non-authoritative, unreliable, non-academic open internet site sources. Many students do, and achieve extremely low marks bordering on fail for doing so.

THE GENERAL STRUCTURE AND LAYOUT OF UNIVERSITY LAW HOLDINGS

Your university may house the law library in a separate building, or in a separate area of the main library. Some libraries fully integrate law resources into the main classification system of the library without creating a separate space. Whichever system is used the same signpost is required to allow you to begin to find the actual rooms and shelves where the resources you need are located: the online main library catalogue.

The main library catalogue

This is the online catalogue of your library's print and e-library resources which you can search by author name, title of book, or the subject area you are interested in. You can also search this catalogue from any PC, laptop, mobile phone, or tablet with an internet connection, signing on with the user ID and password given to you when you registered with the library. Increasingly, apps are being created by universities to give you more versatility when using Apple and/or android devices. You will need to learn how to navigate vast reservoirs of electronic resources subscribed to by the university which create a virtual library, usually called the e-library.[1]

Each print resource is allocated a 'classification number' or a 'class mark' and these numbers or marks are grouped in subject clusters and sub-groups of subjects. Libraries tend to have signs and leaflets that map the area of the law print collection, indicating which part of the building you need to go to for particular subjects. Once you have a classification number or class mark, and a diagram of the library showing the location of the law resources, you will be able to go to the correct area and locate your specific resource.

---

1   The invention of printing was revolutionary in the spread of knowledge; a revolutionary innovation of similar dimensions has occurred through the electronic communication of knowledge.

The classification number is located by searching the main online library catalogue. Many libraries, but not all, have banks of computers around the library and in the reception area, which you can use to access the catalogue.[2]

You will also find access to the cataloguing system of the e-library. Often you can locate these in a number of ways by scrolling down a menu of the various resources and databases, or using a quick search to locate a particular database, or journals, or gateway by alpha order. For example, if you are in the databases areas and click on 'find databases' you will get an alpha bar. If you wanted to locate Westlaw, clicking on 'W' will bring up all the databases starting with W and you can choose Westlaw. All university e-library and print collections are not exact replicas of each other. There will be deviations from the standard. Do make use of library guides which are usually free in the library or available online.

TYPES OF PRINT MATERIALS AND THEIR STANDARD LOCATIONS

Print material comes in a range of types and sizes. All law material is not laid out in one integrated sequence but, for reasons of ease of use and rationality of layout, it is segregated into different spaces.

Many lecturers find it useful to put important books, or multiple copies of set text books on the 'short loan' system. This means that the book is loaned for only a few hours at a time. Short loan books can be placed behind the issue desks and requested or they can be placed on open shelving. Most short loan books are only for use in the library and cannot be removed, although some short loan books can be taken out overnight just prior to the library closing, or for the weekend. Lecturers may also put in short loan a photocopy of an article from a journal not in the print collection or the electronic subscription collection of the library.[3] Fines for such books can be by the hour.

Now that so much is available online the types of resources that need to go to short loan are those that are not readily available online, such as law books.

The main types of printed resource are:

- Reference texts, digests, encyclopaedias, indexes, dictionaries.
- Thin resources (pamphlets).
- Parliamentary papers.
- Journals (academic and professional).
- Law reports.
- Legislation.
- Books about the law (textbooks, scholarly or research works).

The nature of each of the above print resources will be briefly described and examples of leading publications in the areas of reference and primary law will be given.

---

2   If you sign in at the login prompt screen with your user ID and password you will find you are in your own section where you can check which books, if any, you have borrowed, when they are due back, and reserve books.

3   Some lecturers may also post a digital version of material from a popular library book on their VLE.

Reference

There are always some books that tend to be abnormally large. These are usually reference books and it is standard practice for them to be placed together in a reference section of the main library, as it is recognised they only tend to be dipped into for limited and highly specific information. You need to find out where they are, whether they are in the law area, in the general reference section or divided between the two areas. Examples of reference books include dictionaries, encyclopaedias, digests, indexes, and bibliographies.

The sets of reference texts which are the most authoritative source of law are *Halsbury's* published by Butterworths and available in hard copy and online, through LexisNexis which is also Butterworths. *Halsbury's* include the following publications:

- *Halsbury's Laws of England and Wales*: First published in 1907 to give a full statement of all of the laws of England and Wales, case law, legislation, and now, more recently European law. It uses an alphabetic system to track law composed of several complementary cross referenced publications. It has main volumes (organised by subject and re-published around every 20 years), a table of contents and a consolidated index published yearly which will either reference the main volumes or the cumulative supplement. The cumulative supplement is published yearly to update the main volumes. Additionally, monthly digests give updates to allow a subject search for the appropriate volume. As it is concerned with individual laws classified by subject one statute could be divided up among several volumes as often different law concerning different subjects can be contained in the one statute.
- *Halsbury's Statutes of England and Wales*: First published in 1929 it is considered to be the most authoritative source for primary and secondary legislation in England and Wales. It also refers to cases affecting or prompting legislation. The schema used is the same as for the laws, main volumes, tables of contents, indexes, cumulative supplements and monthly digests. Volumes are published when it is considered necessary. Fuller details of all publications linked to *Halsbury's Statutes* will be considered in Chapter 7.
- *Is it in force?* Gives a full listing of all statutes or parts of a statute in force and not in force.

Thin resources (pamphlets)

There are also some print resources that are very thin (pamphlets) and these will tend to be stored together generally in the main library, with law related ones placed in the law library if it is in a separate area.

Parliamentary papers

There is a vast array of materials generated by Parliament, including verbatim reports of proceedings of the two Houses of Parliament, details of committee meetings, reports and material produced by government departments (reports, statistics, recommendations, and policy reviews). Not all libraries will keep a print collection of parliamentary papers.[4] They are useful for research purposes as secondary texts that shed light on the reasons for legislation, and for changes to bills as they go through the parliamentary law making process.

Journals

Journals are collections of articles about the law published throughout the year. Academic journals (also called periodicals) are written by academics and are an important resource for the development of your understanding of law and are vital for competent performance in seminars and assessed work.

There are also a range of professional journals that are written by practising lawyers and intended for the profession. These can be of use as long as you remember they are not academic but professional.

Journals are published two, three or four times a year, with some professional journals being published more frequently. Because of their publication throughout the year journals contain the most up to date information and analysis. We will consider them more fully in Chapter 9.

The law journals may be grouped together in the law library; however, some libraries do like to keep all their periodicals together in one place regardless of discipline and here science rubs shoulders with art. It is important to be aware that many disciplines in their own specialist journals contain professional and academic articles about the law and you are therefore likely to find relevant articles about law in other disciplines such as psychology, sociology, anthropology, medicine, politics or history.

Law reports

These are primary texts of law, reports of important cases decided by senior judges in the courts. They are published in several series by private publishers but the most respected collection is published by a charity, the Incorporated Council of Law Reporters. The courts have established a hierarchy of law reports by publisher and the ICLR are at the top. Law reports are usually stored in the law library area and are classified within a particular series of law report by year date, although there can be other ways of referencing such as by volume number. They cannot be removed from the library and are for reference only. We will be considering how to find law reports in Chapter 8.

Legislation

Legislation enacted by Parliament constitutes a primary text of law. It is divided into collections of primary and secondary legislation by a range of publishers and as noted above, the most authoritative is *Halsbury's Statutes* which is mainly a reference text. We will consider locating legislation in detail in Chapter 7.

---

4   The most extensive collection is housed in the London School of Economics and Political Science Library.

Books

These secondary texts tend to be divided into topics and sub-topics, for example criminal law or the law of contract. It is worth remembering that the date of publication of a book is likely to be 6–24 months after the completion of the manuscript of the book, due to the time needed for the publication process. This means that the law described in books may be out of date. You must always check the publication date of the book, and you should double check the status of the law to be careful. Also, as with journals, it is important to be aware that many other disciplines interact with the law and you are therefore likely to find relevant books in other subject areas.

THE STRUCTURE AND LAYOUT OF THE ELECTRONIC COLLECTION

The competent location and search of the range of electronic materials is an essential skill for the law student. You need to learn how to navigate vast reservoirs of electronic resources in the e-library, which will include subscription sites used by the university as well as links to free sites considered to be useful.[5]

Initially you may find the array of internet sources overwhelming. But in fact they can be reduced to a few overarching categories within which you can research. These will be set out below. Electronic resources mirror in many ways the materials contained in print collections. The best electronic materials are developed by commercial organisations, with annual subscription fees. However, there is a wide range of additional databases and internet gateways which open a huge array of electronic resources.

An internet gateway, which can be referred to as a portal, is a single website that collects together a range of internet links on related topics. Search engines are powerful tools that have indexed a large number of webpages, and allow you to retrieve data through simple keyword searches. Some gateways and databases are free, whilst others are commercial and require username and password information. Many will be accessible through the electronic library (e-library) of your institution.

The standard university law library will have subscriptions to many electronic resources that retrieve materials from the UK, the EU and a range of world collections of legal rules. They will also keep lists of free electronic materials available on the internet. There is a great difference between subscription sites, with accurate presentation of legal rules and academic commentaries, and non-subscription, open access, sites which may not be accurate. That said, you should explore the full range of available data. Some free sites are of great importance. For example, the only official site for revised statutes (that is the most up to date online version of a statute) is the new government UK Statutes Database,[6] which is free to access.

Accessing the e-library collection

When you sign in to the main library catalogue, click on the icon for the e-library and you will be taken into the sources. Your library will often group access by subject. You can

---

5   As already noted, the invention of printing was revolutionary in the spread of knowledge; a revolutionary innovation of similar dimensions has occurred through the electronic communication of knowledge.

6   www.legislation.gov.uk.

therefore click on 'law' and be sent to another listing of sources. Some of these will be subscription sites and some free sites. There will be different access conventions for each of the electronic materials. The majority require an internationally recognised login and password, referred to as an Athens password. Today most university library students' login and password details are also automatically accredited as Athens logins and passwords. At induction you will be told your own library's conventions. Whilst the majority of the electronic collection can be accessed from anywhere, including your home if you have internet access, a few resources can only be accessed from computers based in the library itself. The catalogue will make clear which resources can only be accessed on campus.

Whilst the majority of your electronic resources will come to you via the internet, your library may also have a range of CD-ROMs and microfiche (texts on film viewed through specialised machines). Whilst both are older forms of technology they can still hold valuable data.

When you have your library access sorted out, take time to explore the e-library at your leisure. It will not be time wasted as you need to acquire the skills to access a range of databases quickly and easily, in order to locate materials for seminar and assessment purposes. You would not just walk into a large university library and wander around until you accidentally found the law section and then luckily stumble across a relevant law book. You would locate the catalogue and engage in a methodical search. Many students approaching a database, however, do the equivalent of just aimlessly wandering around. If they do not haphazardly locate any sources from inadequate searches they erroneously conclude no such sources exist. Map the terrain of the electronic sources as well as you would the library print collection. Your lecturers will be only too pleased to guide you generally, as will library staff.

TYPES OF ELECTRONIC MATERIALS AND THEIR STANDARD LOCATIONS

The same types of material available in the print collection are available through electronic sources in the e-library, but, with the exception of books, there are also many more materials available in electronic form. Figure 6.2 shows the type of resources generally available.

These resources are located in a range of different places as illustrated in Figure 6.3. The government open site UK Statutes Database contains only legislation. Subscription databases such as Westlaw, LexisNexis can each contain a large range of resources such as law reports, legislation, journals, and more. You will learn more about the contents of these databases in Chapters 7–9.

The resources on the internet include nearly all of those that we have listed above for print collections but the following additional resources are available:

■   Reference (most notably Halsbury online via Butterworths LexisNexis).
■   UK parliamentary papers from www.parliament.uk, as well as individual government departments.
■   Journals (academic and professional).

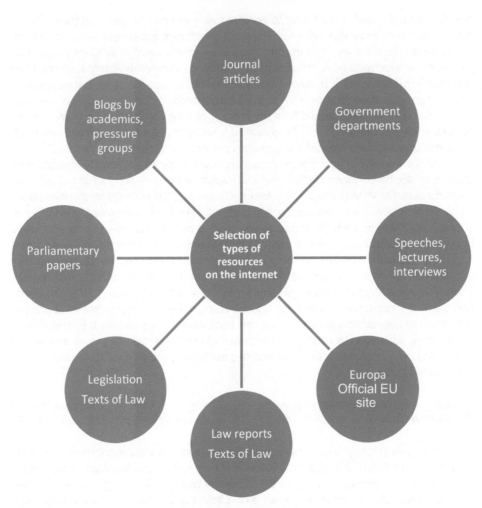

Figure 6.2 A selection of legal resources available on the internet

- Law reports.
- Legislation.
- Books about the law (textbooks, scholarly or research works).
- Blogs by noted academics and practitioners.
- Websites of pressure groups (e.g. Amnesty International).
- Websites containing articles and lectures by noted academics.
- Media sites containing news reports and much more.

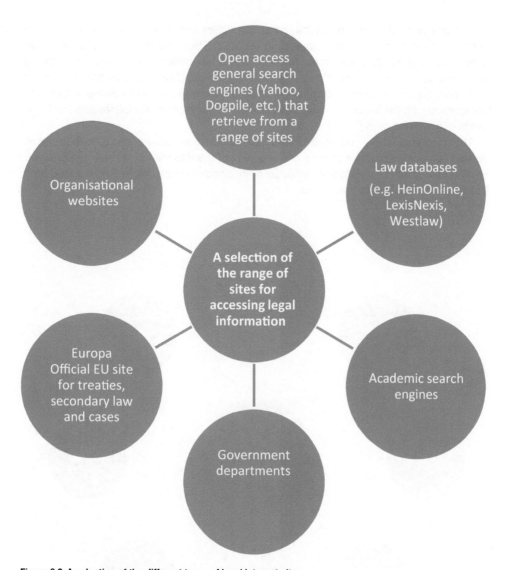

Figure 6.3 A selection of the different types of legal internet sites

Your university e-library will give you access to the databases and internet gateways that allow you to access reliable reference sites, texts of the law and texts about the law or connected to the law. You will be taught how to use them to most efficiently access the material they contain.

The one area where the electronic collection differs enormously (at present) from the print collection is in the area of academic e-books. There are not many academic law books available as yet in electronic formats. The small collection of e-books is growing but these, as yet, are nowhere near approaching the capacity of the books in the print collection. There is a particularly poor selection of law books currently available online in comparison with the larger numbers of academic books in other disciplines and the thousands of fiction e-books.[7]

The main area where you need to exercise caution is accessing the open, free public domain sites as you cannot be sure of the quality of the information you will retrieve. You could easily obtain out of date information or incorrect analysis. We will now spend time looking at the issues with these sites.

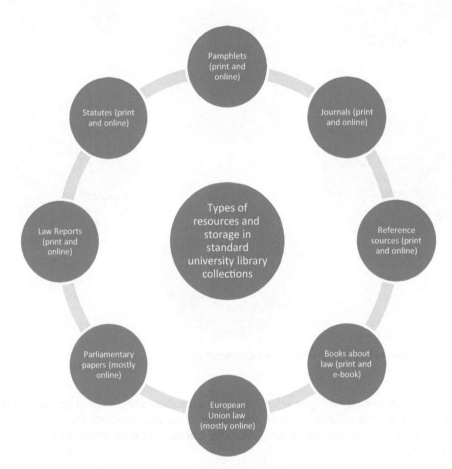

Figure 6.4 Types of resources in standard university library collections

---

7   Many lecturers may put e-versions of chapters from books and journal articles that they use for a specific course onto the VLE. There are strict copyright rules about what can be posted and you may find that there are not any on your VLE, or of course your department or particular lecturers may not use the VLE. Lecturers may also put links to websites on their VLE for you to explore.

Public domain sites: open access free internet electronic sources located outside the e-library

Here we properly enter the third level of the triangle shown in Figure 6.1 above. In this category the electronic resources are unlimited and extremely varied. They are often updated daily.[8] They may include student sites, propaganda sites, news sites, organisational sites, individual sites, university sites, government department sites, and thousands of other types of sites. Some of these may be of use to you, but you need to be very clear what you are dealing with and have a good strategy for ascertaining the authority and reliability of retrieved data.

A large number of organisations, such as charities and pressure groups, have extensive literature on their sites. Many universities around the world make some aspects of their electronic materials available free on the internet. Some individual academics in university departments make their speeches, lectures and articles available. Some university professors have their own websites, often accessible through their university departments' websites. All these types of sites open another world of electronic source material and many will have links enabling you to go to other sites with similar material.

Figure 6.4 sets out the main types of resource in the library and their common forms of storage and access.

PRIMARY TEXTS OF LAW (WHETHER PRINT OR ONLINE)

Primary legal materials – texts of the law

Texts of law, or primary legal materials, are documents containing the law itself, such as law reports, statutes, regulations, bylaws, international treaties, European treaties and law from other jurisdictions. Primary law can be found in resources in print or electronic formats, on a subscription or non-subscription basis.

These resources can be official versions, sanctioned in some way by Parliament, the EU or the courts, or they may be unofficial versions reproduced from official versions by other publishers and organisations. You need to know the authority of the version you are reading and whether it can be trusted for reliability.

The text of statutory legal rules can be obtained in full text form, summary form, or revised form (where amendments to statutes have been put into the text of the original statute).[9] Law reports of law cases can also be retrieved in full text or summary versions.[10] You need to know whether you have the verbatim text or a summary, and legal analysis should only be carried out on the full text versions. You also need to know if the case you are considering has been changed by later cases. For statutory legal rules you also need to have confidence that you are using the most up to date and correct wording. You also need to know which law reports may have dealt with the interpretation of legislation.

No one print or electronic resource will contain all of the law. Many databases start at differing dates and some of the oldest law is in print form only.

---

8 This is why the OSCOLA referencing system states proper practice requires you to put the date of access when using an internet address in circumstances where there is no other print reference to use.
9 See Chapter 1 for detail about UK and EU legislation.
10 See Chapters 2 and 3 respectively for detail about UK and EU case law.

> **Intellectual health warning!**
>
> Primary texts of legal rules located in law reports and legislation are **not** academic materials – they are **legal** materials.

SECONDARY TEXTS ABOUT LAW (WHETHER PRINT OR ONLINE)

Secondary texts of law are texts dealing with the explanation, description or analysis of legal issues, or of the primary texts of law and we will be considering how to find them in Chapter 9.

Your library will subscribe to journals and other important secondary material and in many cases these will be available in both print and electronic formats. You will find that many materials, particularly law reports, statutes, and journal articles are stored in both electronic and print formats. There is a lot of cross referencing between print and electronic versions, for although the strategies for access differ between them, the nature of the two main types of storage, and the functions for their ultimate use, remain the same. They both offer collections of information, explanation, description, innovation and argument as well as records of legal rules from the courts and Parliament.[11]

CONCLUSION

This chapter has concentrated on the university library and set out the range of material you are liable to have access to in its law collections both in print and online to enable you to appreciate their extent. It is important not to view your institution's e-library as an optional extra, but to treat it as an essential and integrated aspect of your university's provision for the study of law. Each type of resource has been generally discussed to assist you to have a view of the whole before we discuss how to find particular types of resources in the next three chapters. There is no shortcut to competency in the law library: you will need to put the time in.

CHAPTER SUMMARY

- The study of law is exclusively the study of documents containing the law (primary sources) and books and other resources about the law (secondary sources).
- The law library functions as a major gateway to help you find your source materials, in both print and electronic form.
- There are particular conventions for citing primary law, and for the hierarchy of law reports, that should be observed.

---

11 Finding secondary sources will be considered in Chapter 9.

- Electronic databases can be particularly useful tools if you do not know the citation of a specific case.
- You should take care to consider the credibility, version and currency of any source you use.
- Open access internet sources should be questioned in terms of who posted the material, why and when.

HOW TO FIND DOMESTIC AND EUROPEAN LEGISLATION

7

LEARNING OUTCOMES

After reading this chapter you should be able to:

- Be familiar with the terminology used to locate legislation.
- Understand citations for domestic and European Union treaties and legislation.
- Locate domestic and EU legislation in print versions and online.
- Locate EU legislation and treaties in print versions and online.
- Locate Council of Europe treaties relating to and including the European Convention on Human Rights in print versions and online.
- Appreciate how to find draft primary and secondary legislation and know when it is or is not available.

INTRODUCTION

Legislation is the most important primary source of law in the English legal system.[1] This chapter explains how to locate print and online versions of domestic legislation from the English legal system, EU legislation and treaties, and Council of Europe treaties concerning the ECHR.

Efficiently locating the most up to date legislation or treaty on any topic you require is a key skill. It involves becoming familiar with the standard methods for referencing legislation and where to find the legislation. These are tasks that can initially seem overwhelming to the new law student.

You will find that most legislation can be located in print and electronic formats in your university library often through the use of subscription sites. However, university libraries are increasingly turning to online versions to decrease costs and physical storage requirements that are needed for their hard copy collections. Many online providers offer a pdf of the print version. Legislation can also be located on open access sites outside the library provision or through subscription sites. Legislation can be retrieved in an official version or unofficial version produced from official versions by other publishers and organisations. You need to be aware of the status of any legislation you are reading.

The text of legislation retrieved can be in full text, summary or revised forms. A revised form has amendments to a statute incorporated into the text of the original statute.[2] You need to know whether you have the verbatim text or a summary or a revised form of the legislation. You need to know the authority of the version you are accessing and reading and whether it can be trusted for reliability; and also most importantly you need to be confident that it is the most up to date version.

This chapter gives a step by step approach to location of legislation and is divided into the following sections:

- How to locate domestic legislation in the English legal system:
  - Terminology, primary and secondary legislation and the range of terms used to refer to it.
  - How to understand citations for locating legislation.
  - How to locate legislation in print collections.
  - How to locate legislation online.
  - How to locate draft legislation.
- How to locate European Union legislation and treaties:
  - Terminology.
  - How to locate treaties and legislation in print collections (official and unofficial).
  - How to locate treaties and legislation and cases online (official and unofficial).
  - How to understand citations in the official journal relating to legislation.
  - How to locate draft legislation.

---

1 For a detailed consideration of English, and EU and Council of Europe treaties and legislation see Part 1–5.
2 See Chapters 1 and 5 respectively for detail about domestic and European Union legislation.

- How to locate treaties of the Council of Europe:
  - ☐ Terminology.
  - ☐ How to locate treaties in print and online collections (official and unofficial).
  - ☐ How to understand official citations.

HOW TO LOCATE PRIMARY DOMESTIC LEGISLATION

There are a number of different types of primary legislation, as discussed in detail in Chapter 1. However, this chapter will only refer to the location of the main form of primary legislation, Public General Acts; and to the main form of secondary legislation, statutory instruments. We will consider how to find print and online primary legislation first and then print and online secondary legislation. Once you have understood the methodology you will be able to transfer that knowledge if you wish to find other primary or secondary legislation.

There are many print and online resources that enable you to find out if there is a Public General Act (a statute) covering a particular subject, or to locate a statute by name, or to locate a statutory instrument.

It is important however that you know how to find the up to date version of any statute. Often the resources will only have the full text of the statute as originally published. Many sources only give summaries of the legislation. This can be useful but must never be confused with the up to date full text version of the legislation. So you need to become familiar with what each print and online version can offer.

Before we consider the available print and online resources it is important to look at the terminology used when referring to primary and secondary legislation, as it can be confusing. We will then consider issues of the citation of legislation which is key to understanding how it is catalogued and stored.

Terminology

Similar words and phrases meaning legislation tend to be used interchangeably in textbooks, lectures, seminars and the media. Many of these are synonyms (words meaning the same thing). Additionally, certain phrases about legislation are also used that may be unfamiliar, for example 'date in force'. Therefore it is a good idea to start with some basic definitions of terms you will come across.

Primary legislation

The following words are used interchangeably and all mean the same thing – primary legislation:

- Legislation.
- Act of Parliament.

- Act.
- Legislative act.
- Statute (which means a decree).

Types of primary legislation

- A Public General Act.
- A private Act.
- A private member's Act.
- A hybrid Act.
- Orders **in** Council.

Secondary legislation

The following words have the same meaning as secondary legislation:

- Delegated legislation.
- Subordinate legislation.

Types of secondary legislation

- Bylaws.
- Orders **by** Council (the Privy Council).
- Statutory instruments.
- Court Rules Committees.

Year of enactment

This is the date that the Act received Royal Assent and was placed in the statute book.

Date in force

The date in force is the date that either the entire primary or secondary legislation comes into force as law, or parts or a part of it comes into force. A major issue when engaged in the task of considering the meaning and application of legislation is whether specific legal rules contained in the legislation are currently in force as law. When you are engaged in research it is essential to know if the law you have retrieved is the most up to date version. Amendments may have been made, or the entire statute repealed, or repealed and its provisions partly placed in other legislation. Changes can occur by:

- Parliamentary authority, through primary legislation amending it (adding to or subtracting from it) or by repeal (abolishing it).
- Others exercising their rights to make changes by secondary legislation to a primary Act.

■ The Supreme Court or the Court of Appeal determining the meaning of words and
   phrases in the legislation. Although English courts have no power to amend or
   abolish legislation their power to interpret legislation can have a major impact on its
   application.

How to understand citations for domestic legislation

It is essential that you understand the way in which the legislation you are locating is cited.

Citation of primary legislation: Public General Acts

Every statute has a long title and usually a short title. The short title if there is one is
stated in one of the sections within the statute itself. For example, the Human Rights
Act 1998, s 22(1) states 'This Act may be cited as the Human Rights Act'. It is the short
title that is used for citation purposes. Since 1963 the statute is cited with the year of
enactment of the legislation, a year running from 1 January to 31 December. Please
make sure you understand that the year of enactment, however, is not the same as the
date in force.

Every statute also has its own number in the year identifying it chronologically. This is
its 'chapter' number in the 'statute' book for the relevant year. The Human Rights Act was
the 42nd Act of 1998 and its chapter number is therefore 42. The number is preceded by
a lower case 'c' to indicate chapter.

The order of the full citation for an Act is:

■ Short title: The Human Rights Act.
■ Year: 1998.
■ Chapter: c.
■ Chapter number: 42.

   e.g. Human Rights Act 1998 c42

Prior to 1963 statutes were not cited by the chronological year, but by their number in the
years of reign of the monarch at the time of the Act (called the regnal year). The chapter number was still used with regnal years. A regnal year starts from the date of the monarch's accession to the throne. But there is a little complication as parliamentary years run
from autumn to summer, so it may be possible for there to have been two Parliaments in
one regnal year depending on when in the year the monarch succeeded. Then both years
need to be referred to. The order of the full statutory citation for regnal years was:

■ Short title.
■ Regnal year(s).

- Monarch abbreviated.
- Chapter number.

Citation of secondary legislation: statutory instruments

Statutory instruments are the largest grouping of secondary legislation. They are cited by their name, followed by the date, and then the abbreviation SI, the year they were 'made'[3] and the date is repeated followed by a slash and the noting of the serial number, for example:

The Export Control (Russia, Crimea and Sevastopol Sanctions) (Amendment) Order 2014, SI 2014/2932

Like chapter numbers the serial number is consecutive indicating its order in the SIs for the relevant year.

The citation given to the SI by Parliament is used in print copies and online versions of the legislation.

Citations and referencing your work

The citation for primary or secondary legislation must be used in your written work; however, you are additionally required to give your source, and if it is online, the date of access. The official print version is the Queen's Printer's copy. The only official site for legislation is the official government website www.legislation.gov.uk.

If you are using another site or print version this must be referenced. These matters are dealt with in Chapter 19.

How to locate statutes in print form in the university library

There are a number of hard copy reference texts that allow you to locate statutes by their name or by topic. Sometimes you will want to find out if there has been any legislation on a certain topic, rather than looking for a specific statute and we will show you how to do this. Usually any reference text you access to locate legislation will have a linked series of publications that cross reference each other. Usually you will be able to search through subjects and sub-topics to locate lists of statutes by name, or you can search by name. Each entry will direct you to the location of the full text.

We will consider the following print resources for legislation:

- Chronological table of statutes.
- Current law legislation citators (containing current law statutes citatory).

---

3   SIs are 'made' not 'enacted', see Chapter 1 for full details.

- Current law statutes annotated.
- *Halsbury's Laws of England*.
- Index to statutes 1235–1990.
- Law reports: statutes.
- Public General Acts and measures.

Each reference source tends to provide differing information and most notably you should not assume the legislation you have retrieved is up to date as many sources just give the original text of the legislation without indicating any amendment or other change to it. There is no substitute for exploring these sources yourself and you will be given ample opportunity to do so in the first few weeks of your study.

Chronological table of statutes

These tables are printed by The Stationery Office (TSO). The Stationery Office was created when Her Majesty's Stationery Office (HMSO) was privatised in 1996. The TSO prints most UK public documentation including Hansard,[4] and have partnered with the National Archives to produce the official online database for UK legislation, www.legislation.gov.uk.

The chronological table details all statutes since 1235 by year and chapter number. There is also a chronological table of statutory instruments (which is also online). The tables are a fascinating and essential place for historical research.

A drawback with the table is that it is always several years out of date. The table indicates when statutes have been changed in any way. It uses standard abbreviations to indicate whether a statute has been applied (appl) amended (am), or repealed (rep). Any statute in the list that is in italics is either not in force or only partially in force.

Current law legislation citators (containing current law statutes citator)

Current law is published by Sweet and Maxwell in three series, a case citator, a legislation citator and yearbooks. We are only concerned here with the legislation citator.

The current law citator is a source of summary information only about legislation in a series of volumes listing legislation by year and chapter number. Nonetheless it is extremely useful in that it indicates repeals, amendments and commencement dates of statutes as well as giving lists of cases in which the legislation has been applied. You can access the following:

- Current law statute citator 1947–1971, lists statutes cited in court between 1947 and 1971.
- Current law legislation citator 1972–1988.
- Current law legislation citator 1989–1995.

---

4 Hansard among other things publishes edited records of debates in Parliament (edited because repetitions and mistakes are taken out of the record). It is published daily: www.parliament.uk/business/publications/hansard/commons/ or www.parliament.uk/business/publications/hansard/commons/lords and debates from 1803 can be accessed online at Historic Hansard (http://hansard.millbanksystems.com/).

- Current law legislation citator 1996–1999.
- Current law legislation citator 2000–2001.
- Current law citator by annual volumes since 2001.

Additionally there is also the *Monthly Digest* which is a looseleaf publication that gives the most up to date legislation in the current calendar year and notes legislation in force. Found in the current law statutes annotated service file.

Using the printed citator to check on amendments is quite cumbersome as you will need to check every volume since the statute you are checking was enacted to find out if there have been any amendments to the original text. You will also have to look at the annual looseleaf publications since 2002 and the monthly publications for the year you are in.

Current Law Statutes annotated (from 1994 to 2000 it was called Current Law Statutes)

This is also published by Sweet and Maxwell and is a list of statutes from 1947 in alphabetical order. There is no online version of this resource. It is annotated and lists public and local Acts which have been amended or repealed by primary or secondary legislation, or considered in court. It also lists all enabling legislation for statutory instruments during the period of the volume.

It contains the full text of Public General Acts as they were originally enacted. It gives the legislative history of each provision, quoting as relevant from Hansard debates, concurrently with the full text of the relevant provision. It also refers to bills, Green and White Papers and to leading cases relating to the legislation including cases leading to legislation. They are just in pamphlet form. TSO will ultimately incorporate these into public Acts and measures. The legislative history is particularly useful for research purposes.

When using this publication in order to ensure that the legislation you use is up to date you should check the current law legislation citator.

Halsbury's Statutes

Published by Butterworths and available in hard copy and online (through LexisNexis which is also Butterworths). While it gives the full text of statutes with amendments and repeals, it is also a summary reference text detailing relevant debates in Hansard, explanatory notes with the bill, and cases applying the legislation and interpreting it.

The hard copy version is divided into law reports and statutes. It has a cumulative digest of legal rules and an index.

Halsbury's Statutes of England identifies legislation that has been corrected and/or repealed. *Halsbury's Statutory Instruments* gives a classification of statutes 'in force', as well as giving the text of a selection of rules, orders and regulations.

Halsbury's Statutes is divided into a series of volumes and updates as follows:

The main volumes: These contain the full text of statutes organised by topic and annotated with changes incorporated into the text. There is a table of contents listing all Acts and also a subject index.

Current Statutes service: Six looseleaf volumes are published each year updating the main volumes with Acts passed since their publication.

The Cumulative Supplement: This summarises the effect of new legislation on the legislation in the main volumes, so it updates previous volumes with references to repeals and amendments of case references. Each Act is updated until the end of the year previous to the date of publication of the supplement. Therefore reading it in 2015 you will have up to date information up until, and including, 31 December 2014.

The Noter-up Service: This gives information concerning changes to the legislation in the main volumes and the Current Statutes service since the publication of the cumulative supplement.

Consolidated index: This is the annual index of the main volume and the Current Statutes service, which also contains an alphabetical list of statutes (the table of statutes). A search by name of Act will retrieve a number in bold (the volume number) followed by the page number. The abbreviation '(S)' indicates that the Act is in the Current Statutes service. It is useful as it has alphabetical, chronological and subject indexes to the legislation.

Halsbury's *'Is it in force?'*

This is an annual publication giving commencement dates of all Public General Acts from 1961 and lists all Public General Acts not yet in force. For statutes predating 1961 you need to use the Chronological Table of Statutes. It is also available online from LexisNexis.

You can use this publication to find out if a section of a statute has come into force. You will find you are given the date it came in force and information concerning the legislation bringing it into force. It may have been brought into force by a statute or a statutory instrument, or by other means, according to details laid out in the relevant statute.

The expected date in force of any legislation listed is also given.

Destination tables

Use this to track provisions of consolidating legislation back to earlier provisions.

If you know the name of the Act, search for it in the consolidated index in the alphabetical list of statutes. You will find the statute followed by a number in bold and then a second number. The bold number is the volume number and the second number is the page reference in the volume. One difficulty with Halsbury's is that the main volumes are arranged by subject matter. As statutes tend to deal with a range of subjects, one statute may appear in many different sections of Halsbury's. You will not find the full text of the statute. When you have all of the information you wish you will need to check that it is still 'in force' or if it is a very new statute if all of it or only part of it is 'in force'. This facility only goes back to 1961 so you would need to consult another source for pre-1961 statutes. The noter-up will update 'in force' changes.

If you want to see if there is any existing legislation on a subject area. Again a bold number indicates a volume number and the following number is a page in that volume. Halsbury's allows you to do this initially through the Table of Statutes and general index, which is a large consolidated index arranged by subject.

Do not let the sheer size of this publication daunt you. It is reasonably easy to navigate and you can completely rely on its contents. But do make sure that when you use it to locate any statute you use the main volumes in conjunction with the cumulative supplement and the noter-up service.

How to use Halsbury's Statutes

The way in which *Halsbury's Statutes* is organised means that you need to consult not only the main volumes but the cumulative supplement and the 'noter-up' to check the most up to date position of the legislation you are concerned with. A good method to use to locate a specific Act is as follows:

■ To find out which volume has the full text of the Act you need to look at the Table of Statutes and Consolidated Index which gives you the volume number of the statute in bold, as well as the page number, or if it predates the main volumes you are given the reference (S) after the volume number so that you know to consult the Current Statutes Service.

■ When you locate the main volume you will find the full text of the statute with the text of amendments in square brackets. You will be alerted to the removal of text by three dots, . . . (ellipses). Footnotes give you more details about interpretation, relevant cases etc.

■ To ensure you have up to date legislation check the 'Cumulative Supplement' for any updating. You will note that it is subdivided into 50 so you can access the exact volume number that you want and you can then scan it for the page number. If you cannot find any entry this means that you can be certain that up until the date of the supplement there have not been any changes.

■ Then to be absolutely sure check the noter-up which contains information after the publication for the Cumulative Supplement, which is divided in the same way as the supplement.

You can also search by subject which requires the same steps, but you need to consult the subject indexes in the Table of Statutes and Consolidated Index.

Halsbury's Statutes Citator

This is an annual publication that just gives information concerning all amendments and repeals relating to statutes. This gives you fast access if you want to know if a section has been repealed since the last volume was published, but no text is given. The noter-up will give you the most detailed information.

You will need to know the year of enactment as it is organised by year, and then the name is given. To assist you the citator includes an alpha list of statutes with date of Royal Assent. The Statutes Citator is organised by year and then within each year alphabetically.

Index to the Statutes (1235–1990)

Published by The Stationery Office (TSO) this gives a full cross reference by subject plus a chronological list of Acts in force, with a good cross referencing system.

Law Reports: Statutes

The *Law Reports: Statutes* are published by the Incorporated Council of Law Reporting (ICLR) in annual volumes with parts published several times a year which means it is only ever a few months out of date.

Public General Acts and measures

Published by The Stationery Office (TSO) this contains the full original text of the statute. It does not direct you to amendments or repeals in relation to a statute. They also publish *Local and Personal Acts* from 1968; however, this does not contain the full original text of the statute, and the list gives no indication of amendments or repeals to the legislation listed.

It has two indexes containing an alphabetical listing of all statutes enacted in the year and a chronological list of statutes enacted in the year. The statutes and measures[5] are set out in full text. Secondary legislation is kept in lists, and some parts of it are in text format. All secondary legislation in force is classified to aid location but not all is replicated in the full text.

How to locate statutes online

The easiest way to access legislation online is through your university's e-library search facility. As already noted many university libraries are moving away from print to e-copy in relation to primary legal material. There is a vast array of online access both subscription based and in the public domain (free). Subscription databases tend to offer useful searchable extras in addition to the full text of legislation. For example you can search for cases dealing with your legislation, as well as locate journal articles, or even e-books discussing the legislation, (although there are currently very few e-books).

---

5   These are created by the General Synod of the Church of England which must be enacted by Parliament.

The main subscription sites

■ Westlaw: published by Sweet and Maxwell www.westlaw.com containing UK, Irish, EU legislation, a large range of academic and professional journals.

■ LexisNexis: published by Butterworths www.lexisnexis.co.uk covers UK legislation and also provides *Halsbury's Statutes* online.

■ Justis: www.justis.com containing a growing collection of UK, Irish and EU case reports. UK case records go back to the earliest year books in 1163 and it refers to legislation from 1235.

Public domain 'free' sites

By far the largest set of free resources can be found in the public domain, but these do vary in reliability from site to site. The following sites are the more reliable and include legislation made available by government and Parliament. They will all have differing cut-off dates for the start of the collections and will vary in the information on offer.

The following sites are in the public domain:

■ **Official government site** for all UK legislation: www.legislation.gov.uk.

■ **British and Irish Legal Information Institute** (BAILII) http://www.bailii.org contains British and Irish legislation. It takes its statutory data from the Office of Public Sector Information (OPSI) and is a free searchable site.

■ **Office of Public Sector Information** www.opsi.gov.uk. This site contains the full text of Public General Acts, since 1988, and local Acts, since 1991, and reproduces the statute in the form in which it was originally enacted. It contains statutory instruments going back to 1987. This site does its utmost to get a copy of a statute online within a day of its publication.

■ **Parliament www.parliament.uk** here you can locate current legislation.

Each site will have its own particular navigation. Which sites you access and what you understand about the site will determine whether you retrieve the most up to date legislation.

To give you a more detailed explanation of access and searching online sites to familiarise you with online searching we will look at searching on the following sites:

■ Public domain site: legislation.gov.uk (as it is the official site for domestic legislation).

■ Subscription site: Westlaw: www.westlaw.com.

Public domain site: www.legislation.gov.uk

This is the only official record of all statutes (and statutory instruments) from 1297. It was launched as a free public service in December 2006 and is extremely 'user friendly'. A caveat with the site is that it is still in the process of updating statutes with many alterations pending. However, you are always given details of those pending alterations in a drop down menu. So you would not make a mistake unless you failed to check the 'changes' areas of the site.

When you access the database you will be presented with the home page illustrated in Figure 7.1 which contains a number of tabs which allow you to browse, access new legislation or look at changes to legislation. You will also find a quick 'search all legislation' box. If you know the details of the legislation you want you can search for it here.

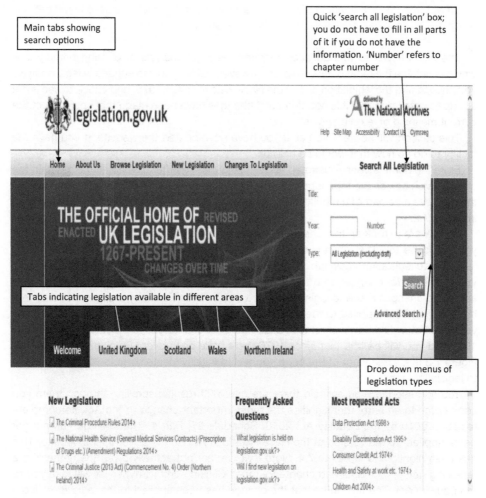

Figure 7.1 Annotated screenshot of home page

To indicate methods of searching the site guided exercises are used and it would be useful if you could go through this exercise, either now or later, having retrieved the website so that you can follow through the guided exercise locating the various web pages.

Guided exercise: Race Relations Act 1976

We will use the following research question to illustrate search techniques for a legislation search.

What is the current meaning of the phrase 'ethnic origins' originally used in the definition of 'racial grounds' in s 3 of the Race Relations Act 1976?

The final answer to this question requires the legal analysis of existing primary law, which is outside the remit of this chapter. However, before you can engage in legal analysis you have to find the legislation, s 3 of the Race Relations Act 1976, and check to see if it is still up to date law and if it is not, find out if changes have been made that could affect the current meaning of 'ethnic origins'.

This section will address you as if you have now located the website. If you have the facility to do so now that would be helpful.

From the home screen (illustrated above in Figure 7.1) enter 'Race Relations Act' in the quick search box on the top, right hand side of the home page, and enter the date. You will then retrieve it as part of a tabulated list. This list also alerts you to 'changes' as illustrated in Figure 7.2.

If you were to click on the 'changes to legislation' box as noted in the table of contents you would be told that changes dealing with the entire Act could be accessed via the 'changes to legislation' main tab. Clicking on this you would retrieve a search box allowing you to search for changes to a specific Act within a specific timescale. The search only applies to changes made to legislation since 2002. There are many changes pending that have not yet been applied to the text of the legislation on the site and the site is dealing with this. You would however retrieve a tabulated list of changes to the Race Relations Act 1976 and you will be told that since 1976 there have been over 600 changes to the Act. Figure 7.3 is a screenshot of the page you would initially locate by going to the 'changes to legislation' tab.

You can see that you are told there are over 600 results; scrolling through them you soon come to an entry that signifies the most important change to the Act, its complete repeal in 2010 by the Equality Act 2010, Schedule 27, Part 1. That change has not yet been 'applied' to the version of the Race Relations Act on the government website. This has been highlighted in Figure 7.4. Note that you are not actually given the name of the repealing Act, just its date and chapter number. Clicking on this hyperlink will take you to the Equality Act. The tick notes that the change has been applied to the legislation. Note as you scroll down that changes to the legislation have been made by both statutes and statutory instruments (identifiable in the listing by the reference to 'order').

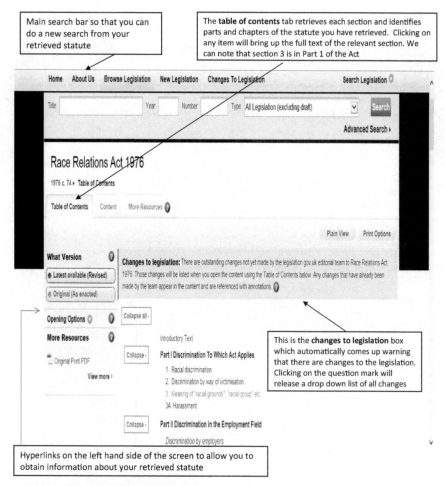

Main search bar so that you can do a new search from your retrieved statute

The **table of contents** tab retrieves each section and identifies parts and chapters of the statute you have retrieved. Clicking on any item will bring up the full text of the relevant section. We can note that section 3 is in Part 1 of the Act

This is the **changes to legislation** box which automatically comes up warning that there are changes to the legislation. Clicking on the question mark will release a drop down list of all changes

Hyperlinks on the left hand side of the screen to allow you to obtain information about your retrieved statute

Figure 7.2 Screenshot of retrieved Race Relations Act

Summary of our search so far

We have executed the following four steps:

(1) Accessed the home page http//www.legislation.gov.uk (see Figure 7.1).
(2) Used the quick search box in the top left hand corner of the home page where we gave details of the statute we wanted (see Figure 7.2).
    (a) Title: (Name of the legislation): Race Relations Act.
    (b) Date: Year of enactment of the legislation: 1976.
    (c) Number: This refers to the chapter number. We left it blank as we did not have it.

Figure 7.3 Screenshot of changes to legislation results for the Race Relations Act 1976

Act 1976	1976 c. 74	Act	saved (6.5.1999)	Scotland Act 1998	1998 c. 46	s. L2(a)-(d)	✔		
Race Relations Act 1976	1976 c. 74	Act	amended (prosp.)	Immigration and Asylum Act 1999	1999 c. 33	s. 22 (adding 1996 c. 49 s. 8A (10))	✔		
Race Relations Act 1976	1976 c. 74	Act	transfer of powers in part (W)	The National Assembly for Wales (Transfer of Functions) Order 1999	1999 No. 672	art. 2 Sch. 1	✔		
Race Relations Act 1976	1976 c. 74	Act		The Channel Tunnel (International Arrangements) (Amendment No. 4) Order 2001	2001 No. 3707	art. 4	✔		
Race Relations Act 1976	1976 c. 74	Act	construed as one	Nationality, Immigration and Asylum Act 2002	2002 c. 41	s. 66(4)	✔		
Race Relations Act 1976	1976 c. 74	Act	applied by SI 1994/1405 art. 4(1A) (as inserted)	The Channel Tunnel (Miscellaneous Provisions) (Amendment) Order 2007	2007 No. 2908	art. 2(3)	✔		
Race Relations Act 1976	1976 c. 74	Act	transfer of functions in part	The Transfer of Functions (Equality) Order 2007	2007 No. 2914	art. 3(2)(c)	✔		
Race Relations Act 1976	1976 c. 74	Act	repealed	Equality Act 2010	2010 c. 15	Sch. 27 Pt. 1			
Race Relations Act 1976	1976 c. 74	Act	transfer of functions	The Transfer of Functions (Equality) Order 2010	2010 No. 1839	art. 3(1)(c)			

Figure 7.4 Screenshot of changes to the Race Relations Act 1976, with entry noting its repeal highlighted

    (d)   Type: This refers to whether it is a Public General Act, or a private Act etc. The Race Relations Act is primary legislation, and a Public General Act. If you did not know the classification of the legislation you could click on 'All legislation'.

(3)   Clicked on the hyperlink for the retrieved Act obtaining a screen page showing the statute's 'Table of Contents' tab which lists the parts and sections in the legislation, and shows an alert for changes to the legislation (see Figure 7.3).

(4)   Clicked on changes to legislation in the table of contents; we were led to the main menu bar at the top of the screen and the 'changes to legislation' tab. Filling

that in we retrieved a table noting changes that contained 600 entries, screen page 3 (see Figure 7.4) eventually noted the Act has been repealed by 2010 c. 15 Schedule 27, Part 1, and further told that a statutory instrument no 2279 in 2010 replaced Sch 27 (SI 2010/2279, Article 13, Schedule 2). That entry is set out below.

'Act repealed by 2010 c. 15 Sch. 27 **Pt. 1** (Sch. 27 Pt. 1 was substituted by SI 2010/2279, art. 13, Sch. 2)'

Having completed steps 1–4 and located the Act we now need to find the text of s 3 of the Race Relations Act 1976 as originally enacted, locate the phrase 'ethnic origins' and consider changes. Whilst we know from step 4 that the entire Act has been repealed we do not know if the text of s 3 has been kept and put into another statute, and if so whether it remains the same or has been edited by the deletion of words or the addition of words. This is not the end of the matter either as 'ethnic origins' may have been the object of judicial interpretation in cases.

Next steps: locating and considering changes to s 3 of the Race Relations Act 1976

We will now continue and locate the original text of s 3 and any changes to it on replacing the Act.

1. Access the full text of s 3 from the contents tab by clicking the hyperlink to s 3. Then click the 'Changes alerted to' box to the top of the right hand side of the text. It will drop down to reveal the following: s. 9 coming into force by SI 2010/2317 art. 2(2)(c) s. 9(5) power to repeal or amend conferred by 2013 c. 24 s. 97(7)–(10)s. 9(5) words omitted by 2013 c. 24 s. 97(2) s. 9(5)(a) words inserted by 2013 c. 24 s. 97(3) s. 9(5)(b) words inserted by 2013 c. 24 s. 97(4) The caste power.
2. Return to the table of contents for the Equality Act 2010, you now know you need to look at s 9 of the Equality Act, to see if all of it or part of it contains s 3, and in particular if it refers to 'ethnic origins',
3. If no changes are alerted for s 9 of the Equality Act you have now located the most up to date version of what was s 3 of the Race Relations Act 1976.

Of course you have only found out that s 3 of the Race Relations Act has been repealed by s 9. Equality Act. You do not know the answer to the research question yet. Read it again.

Now you will have located some of the basic information to begin to answer it! You have found the legislation and started your research investigation. We will return to this research question to explore cases and secondary texts later in this part of the book.

Finding legislation in print and electronic formats

We have now completed the section dealing with accessing primary legislation in print and electronic formats. To give you a quick reference to access the following, Table 7.1 indicates how to use the main print or electronic resources to locate primary legislation.

TABLE 7.1 QUICK REFERENCE: ACCESSING PRIMARY LEGISLATION USING PRINT AND ELECTRONIC SOURCES			
PRINT SOURCE		**ONLINE SOURCE**	
PRINT RESOURCE	**DESCRIPTION OF PRINT RESOURCE**	**NAME OF WEBSITE**	**FACILITIES**
N/A	N/A	**BAILII:** FREE SERVICE British and Irish Legal Information Institute	Can browse, search full text
CHRONOLOGICAL TABLE OF STATUTES: Published by TSO. Details repeals (rep) or amendments (am). Usually 2 years out of date.	List commences in 1235 Statutes 'not in force' are in *italics and* Statutes in force are in **bold** Good for historical research.	N/A	N/A
CURRENT LAW LEGISLATION CITATORS Lists legislation by year and chapter number in several series. Within the series of *current law legislation citators* is the *Current law statute citator* listing public & local Acts for the same period that have been amended, repealed or considered in court	1. Current law statute citator 1947–1971 2. Current law legislation citator 1972–1988 3. Current law legislation citator 1989–1995 (SI from 1993) 4. Current law legislation citator 1996–1999 5. Current law legislation citator 2000–2001 6. Annual Volumes from 2002 7. Monthly Digest from 2002 (also notes legislation in force)	**LEXIS LIBRARY** SUBSCRIPTION ONLY SERVICE This usefully cross references to *Halsbury's*	Can browse, search full text

PRINT SOURCE		ONLINE SOURCE	
PRINT RESOURCE	**DESCRIPTION OF PRINT RESOURCE**	**NAME OF WEBSITE**	**FACILITIES**
CURRENT LAW STATUTES ANNOTATED Contains a table of legislation *not* yet in force	Full text of Public General Acts (published close to the publication of the hard copy) Gives legislative history of provisions	**LAWTEL** SUBSCRIPTION ONLY	Can browse, search full text
INCORPORATED COUNCIL OF LAW REPORTING STATUTES (ICLR)	Annual volumes Parts issues over the year		
HALSBURY'S STATUTES OF ENGLAND **Published by Butterworths** One of the aims of this publication is to give an up to date version of all Public General Acts. A range of cross referenced publications throughout the year aim to do this. Look at the main volumes to locate your law, then the cumulative supplement and then the noter-up. It is organised by subject area so you may find that the statute you are researching is split among several volumes according to subject matter	1. **The Main volumes**: the full text of the statutes organised by topic. 2. **Current Statutes service:** Loose leaf volumes (6) updating main volumes 3. **The Cumulative Supplement:** summarises effect of new legislation on the legislation in the main volumes 4. **The Noter-up service** note changes to the above three publications 5. **Consolidated index** annual index of the main volumes & Current Statutes service with an alpha list of statutes, search by name of Act 6. **Is it in force?** Annual publication giving commencement dates of all Public General Acts from 1961 and lists all Public General Acts not yet in force. For statutes predating 1961 you should use the Chronological Table of Statutes	LexisNexis produced by Butterworths	

TABLE 7.1—continued			
PRINT SOURCE		**ONLINE SOURCE**	
PRINT RESOURCE	**DESCRIPTION OF PRINT RESOURCE**	**NAME OF WEBSITE**	**FACILITIES**
	7. Destination tables: Tracks consolidating legislation back to earlier versions		
		HeinOnline <http://www.heinonline.org> (Subscription only)	Full set of UK statutes from 1215–1713 under Statutes of the Realm
PUBLIC GENERAL ACTS AND MEASURES Published by The Stationery Office (TSO)	Alphabetical index & Chronological index to all legislation by chapter number to locate full text of all Public General Acts and measures, General Synod Measures, Church of England, list of all local and personal Acts	**LEGISLATION. GOV.UK** FREE SERVICE This is the official site for legislation	Can browse, search full text legislation with revisions incorporated into the text
N/A	**N/A**	**WESTLAW** SUBSCRIPTION ONLY	All Acts since 1927

HOW TO LOCATE SECONDARY LEGISLATION

We will stay with legislation.gov.uk but turn our attention to finding statutory instruments (SI) as the main form of secondary legislation.

Figure 7.5 is a screenshot of UK statutory instruments, which can be obtained by clicking on the 'all legislation' drop down menu on the home page (see Figure 7.1) and clicking on statutory instruments. As you can see, Figure 7.5 gives a chart of the number of statutory instruments published 2000–2009 and 2010–2014. You can use the navigation bar under the chart to look at earlier years. Under the chart is a list of statutory instruments. In the left hand panel under 'legislation by type' you can choose whether to look at all UK SIs or those of Wales, Scotland and Northern Ireland.

Once you have located your statutory instruments a drop down changes alert will allow you to ascertain the most up to date version.

Figure 7.5 Screenshot of UK Statutory Instruments

If you know the name of your SI you can use the quick search box on the legislation home page. Or if you come across an SI mentioned in a search for changes in primary legislation you can just click on it and locate the full text.

How to locate draft primary and secondary legislation

There will be times in your studies when it is useful to be able to locate the bills currently going through Parliament. A bill is the draft form of an Act and it can change considerably as it goes through the Houses of Parliament. Or you may wish to locate former versions of bills (draft bills). The official online site www.legislation.gov.uk does not keep records of draft primary legislation, although it does have the full text draft secondary legislation.

Locating draft primary legislation

Extensive information on draft primary legislation can be located on the UK parliamentary website, www.parliament.uk. Here you can also look at draft bills, which are copies of bills *before* they have been formally introduced in Parliament and have begun their way through the procedures for enactment. You can also find out where any bill is in its passage through Parliament.

Figure 7.6 Screenshot of the whereabouts of the Affordable Homes Bill 2014–2015

Using the Parliament website (www.parliament.uk)

Having accessed the site, navigate to primary legislation and then to bills. Icons denote whether a particular bill has its introduction pending, and whether it is currently in the House of Commons or House of Lords. If you click on any bill in your retrieved list you will be told where it is in its passage through the house and what the next stage is. This is illustrated in Figure 7.6, a screenshot of the Affordable Homes Bill.

You can see from Figure 7.6 that it gives a general diagram of the full procedures of a bill with the current stage of the bill you are considering highlighted in black. When shown online, the procedures in the House of Commons box are green and those in the House of Lords are in red, with the amendments stage showing as an 'A' in a half green and half red circle.

Clicking on the 'last event' box (lower left hand corner of the screen in Figure 7.6) shows this bill was last debated in the public bills committee. You can then explore the retrieved full text debate. Committee on 29 October 2014. Clicking on the 'next event' will inform you that it is to be a continuation of the committee debate.

If you wish to know what has happened before click on 'all previous stages of the Affordable Homes Bill 2014–2015'. You can then see that the committee stage started on 22 October, at its first sitting. The dates when the first and second readings took place are also given. Clicking on any of these hyperlinks will take you to the full text of the bill, debates concerning the bill, committee proceedings and other matters connected to the bill.

Locating draft secondary legislation

It may be important to locate draft secondary legislation. This will not be in the hard copy and online collections of current law. Again, the most extensive record can be found on the parliamentary website as here you can find the text of debates if any, about the proposed draft SI as 'Laid', and the progress of the SI.

It is worth knowing that www.legislation.gov.uk will give you the text of all draft secondary legislation under headers. By way of example the list of types of secondary legislation awaiting approval on 7 November is set out below showing the numbers of each type.[6] There are a large number of SIs awaiting approval. Clicking on any will give you access to the full text of the awaiting secondary legislation.

- UK Statutory Instruments (73,713).
- Northern Ireland Statutory Rules (7,553).
- Scottish Statutory Instruments (6,361).
- Wales Statutory Instruments (3,443).
- Northern Ireland Orders in Council (622).
- UK Statutory Rules and Orders (306).
- Church Instruments (57).
- UK Ministerial Orders (28).

The lists are in a standard format and state which SIs have been laid before Parliament and where each one is in its cycle of days if it is using the normal negative resolution.[7] If you want to find out where any of the above are in the process of being approved you will need to leave the legislation.gov.uk site and go to the lists of draft secondary legislation on the parliamentary website. It also lists SIs, separating them into several areas as demonstrated in Figure 7.7, a screenshot of the parliamentary publications list in its online version.[8]

A further screenshot, Figure 7.8, shows the range of SIs and other types of secondary legislation on LIST NO. 14: Friday 7 November 2014, that are subject to the affirmative resolution procedure.

In its totality the above list contains 56 SIs subject to the affirmative resolution procedure laid between 4 June and 4 November that must receive the approval of both Houses of Parliament or be lost. As the Parliamentary Acts 1911 and 1949 do not apply to secondary legislation the House of Lords can veto prospective secondary legislation where its approval is required under the affirmative resolution procedure. The list of SIs subject to the negative resolution procedure for the same period is shown in Figure 7.9. SIs in this classification must await the passing of 40 days and then they automatically become 'made'.[9]

Searching for legislation on a subscription site: Westlaw

Westlaw is a subscription only site. You can access all legislation on Westlaw. It is an extensive database dealing with legislation and cases from the UK, the EU and a range of

6   http://www.legislation.gov.uk/secondary accessed 7 November 2014.
7   See Chapter 1 for details of the negative resolution.
8   www.publications.parliament.uk/pa/cm/cmsilist/cmsilist.htm.
9   See Chapter 1 for details.

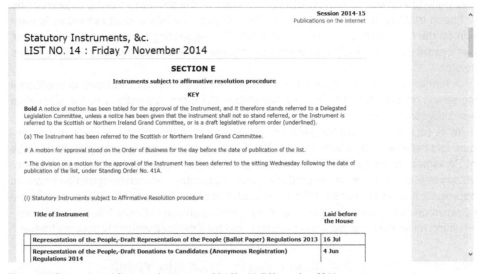

Statutory Instruments, &c.
LIST NO. 14 : Friday 7 November 2014

A. Bills and Acts of the Northern Ireland Assembly
   (laid before Parliament under section 15 of the Northern Ireland Act 1998)

B. Treaties subject to negative resolution procedure
   (laid under section 20 of the Constitutional Reform and Government Act 2010)

C. Instruments subject to negative resolution procedure:

   i   Statutory Instruments

       Statutory Instruments which have not previously appeared in section C

   ii Other rules, statutes, &c

D. Special Procedure Orders

E. Instruments subject to affirmative resolution procedure:

   i   Statutory Instruments

       Statutory Instruments approved by the House since the previous list

   ii Statutory Instruments subject to affirmative resolution within a statutory period

       Statutory Instruments approved by the House since the previous list

   iii Miscellaneous instruments, Church of England Measures, &c

F. Instruments subject to no Parliamentary procedure
   (laid since the previous list)

G. Proposals for instruments subject to super-affirmative procedure

Figure 7.7 Screenshot of SIs subdivided by methods for approval

Session 2014-15
Publications on the Internet

Statutory Instruments, &c.
LIST NO. 14 : Friday 7 November 2014

SECTION E

Instruments subject to affirmative resolution procedure

KEY

Bold A notice of motion has been tabled for the approval of the instrument, and it therefore stands referred to a Delegated Legislation Committee, unless a notice has been given that the instrument shall not so stand referred, or the instrument is referred to the Scottish or Northern Ireland Grand Committee, or is a draft legislative reform order (underlined).

(a) The instrument has been referred to the Scottish or Northern Ireland Grand Committee.

\# A motion for approval stood on the Order of Business for the day before the date of publication of the list.

* The division on a motion for the approval of the instrument has been deferred to the sitting Wednesday following the date of publication of the list, under Standing Order No. 41A.

(i) Statutory Instruments subject to Affirmative Resolution procedure

Title of Instrument	Laid before the House
Representation of the People,-Draft Representation of the People (Ballot Paper) Regulations 2013	16 Jul
Representation of the People,-Draft Donations to Candidates (Anonymous Registration) Regulations 2014	4 Jun

Figure 7.8 Screenshot of Statutory Instruments List No 14, 7 November 2014

(i) Statutory Instruments

Instruments and draft Instruments laid before the House under the Statutory Instruments Act 1946 (sections 5 and 6) are subject to negative resolution for a period of forty days, beginning with the day on which copies of them are laid. In reckoning this period, no account is taken of any time during which Parliament is dissolved or prorogued, or during which both Houses are adjourned for more than four days. Draft Legislative Reform Orders subject to negative resolution (underlined in this list) are subject to the same timetable except that adjournments are discounted if either House (rather than both Houses) is adjourned for more than four days.

S.I., 2014/14, No.	Title of Instrument	Laid before the House	No. of days unexpired on date of issue
2007	Merchant Shipping,-Port Security (Port of Rosyth) Designation Order 2014	30 Jul	1
2038	Immigration,-Immigration and Nationality (Fees) (Consequential Amendments) Order 2014	31 Jul	2
2040	Judicial Appointments and Discipline,-Judicial Appointments and Discipline (Addition of Office) Order 2014	31 Jul	2
2059	County Court,-Civil Proceedings Fees (Amendment No. 3) Order 2014	1 Aug	2
2054	Criminal Law,-Ukraine (European Union Financial Sanctions) (No.3) Regulations 2014	1 Aug	2
2044	Senior Courts of England and Wales,-Civil Procedure (Amendment No. 5) Rules 2014	1 Aug	2
2068	Education,-(1) Prospects College of Advanced Technology (Government) Regulations 2014	5 Aug	2
2067	(2) Prospects College of Advanced Technology (Incorporation) Order 2014	5 Aug	2
2077	Ecclesiastical Law,-(1) Church of England (Miscellaneous Provisions) Measure 2014 (Appointed Day No. 2 and Transitional and Saving	6 Aug	2

Figure 7.9 Screenshot of the list of statutory instruments subject to the negative resolution

other jurisdictions. It also contains thousands of full text articles both academic and professional as well as containing the abstract only of thousands more. All primary legislation is annotated with changes. Westlaw is extensively used in UK law schools, and the site also has a range of excellent training tutorials for the efficient use of Westlaw.

Your access to Westlaw will be through your university e-library. When you have clicked on Westlaw in your institution's list of subscription databases available, you will arrive at its front search screen, set out in Figure 7.10.

You will note that there are several tabs at the top of the screen that can be accessed as needed (e.g. training tutorials and help). The next set of tabs contains access to the collections of materials on Westlaw. Here you will note there is a tab for legislation.

Primary legislation search

Also on the front page is a quick 'search Westlaw UK' which is very useful if you know the name of the legislation you wish to access. You can also search by subject here using keywords. The quick search only searches UK legislation currently in force. If we again use our search for the Race Relations Act 1976 we will retrieve a list of references and scrolling through them you will find a list set out in Figure 7.11 of references to the Act.

The letter 'R' in a box (red online) beside any retrieved reference denotes it has been repealed. From entry 10 in Figure 7.11 you know the preamble is repealed, and searching through all of the others you note all the parts are too. The date of repeal is given, and after each reference you will find a reference in brackets to a 'version'. All previous versions of a section from the original onwards can be retrieved in full text. In this way you get a record

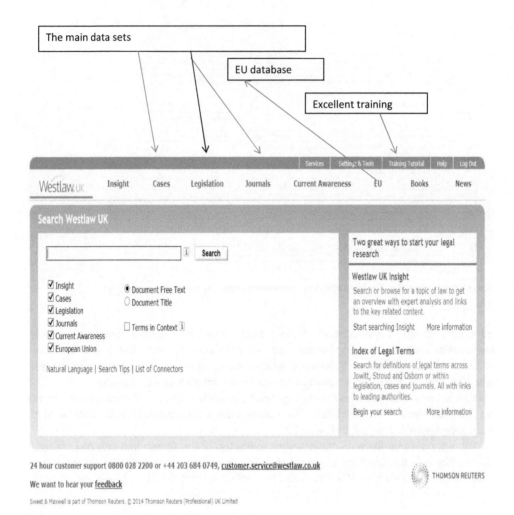

Figure 7.10 Annotated front page of Westlaw showing quick search boxes

of the changes to the section which is particularly valuable for researching legal development, and perhaps as required linking it to political necessity or policy.

Clicking on 9 in the list in Figure 7.11, 'Arrangement of Provisions', you will get the table of contents of the Race Relations Act 1976 with the repeal icon beside each section. However, you can also still access the repealed section (s 3) that we are interested in. Clicking on s 3 we are only told the detail of the amendments and do not have access to the original text of s 3. But you can obtain this by going to 'advanced search' and giving the name of the Act and selecting a point in time; you will be asked to select whether you want

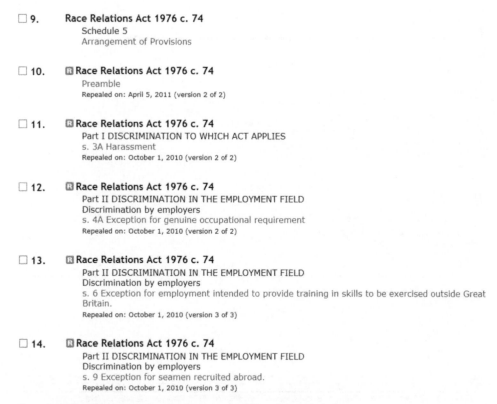

☐ 9.   **Race Relations Act 1976 c. 74**
          Schedule 5
          Arrangement of Provisions

☐ 10.   ▣ **Race Relations Act 1976 c. 74**
          Preamble
          Repealed on: April 5, 2011 (version 2 of 2)

☐ 11.   ▣ **Race Relations Act 1976 c. 74**
          Part I DISCRIMINATION TO WHICH ACT APPLIES
          s. 3A Harassment
          Repealed on: October 1, 2010 (version 2 of 2)

☐ 12.   ▣ **Race Relations Act 1976 c. 74**
          Part II DISCRIMINATION IN THE EMPLOYMENT FIELD
          Discrimination by employers
          s. 4A Exception for genuine occupational requirement
          Repealed on: October 1, 2010 (version 2 of 2)

☐ 13.   ▣ **Race Relations Act 1976 c. 74**
          Part II DISCRIMINATION IN THE EMPLOYMENT FIELD
          Discrimination by employers
          s. 6 Exception for employment intended to provide training in skills to be exercised outside Great
          Britain.
          Repealed on: October 1, 2010 (version 3 of 3)

☐ 14.   ▣ **Race Relations Act 1976 c. 74**
          Part II DISCRIMINATION IN THE EMPLOYMENT FIELD
          Discrimination by employers
          s. 9 Exception for seamen recruited abroad.
          Repealed on: October 1, 2010 (version 3 of 3)

Figure 7.11 Westlaw: retrieved results for a search of 'Race Relations Act'

'law in force' or 'historic law' and you need to select 'historic law'. Figure 7.12 shows the advanced search page having entered 'Race Relations Act 1976' and 's 3'.

Figure 7.13 is the result of a search for s 3 of the Race Relations Act 1976 and the point in time chosen was 01/01/2000. The site will go back to legislation in force from January 1991. I chose 1976–2010. The cut-off date of 2010 is chosen as this was the date of the repealing statute as we now know.

Figure 7.13 notes that the version of s 3 retrieved was in force from 13 June 1977 to 18 July 2003. If you click on the version tab (which tells you there are three) you will find out that version 2 was in force July 2003–1 October 2010, and finally version 3 will tell you the current situation that it was repealed by 2010 c.15 Sch. 27(1). You are not however directed to s 9 of the Equality Act which we know amended s 3 of the Race Relations Act so you will need to access it and search through to find 'racial grounds'. This can be done from the table of contents.

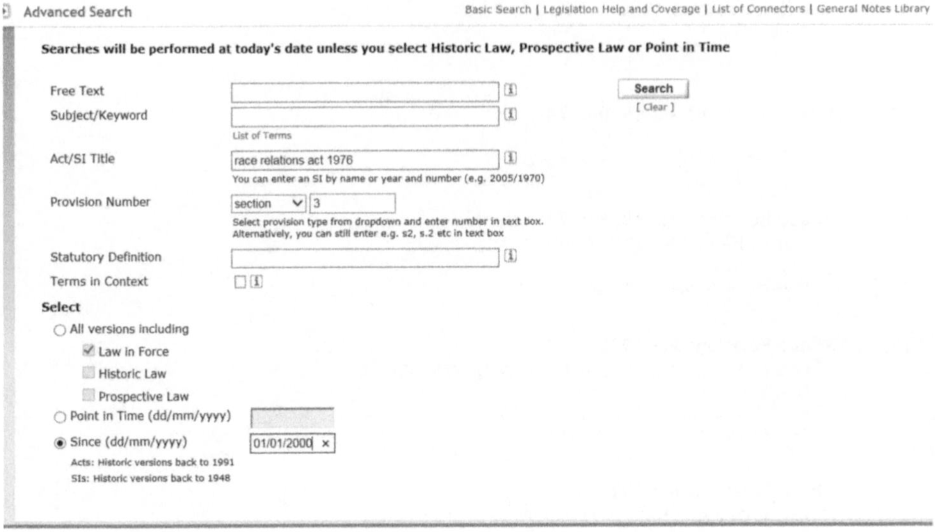

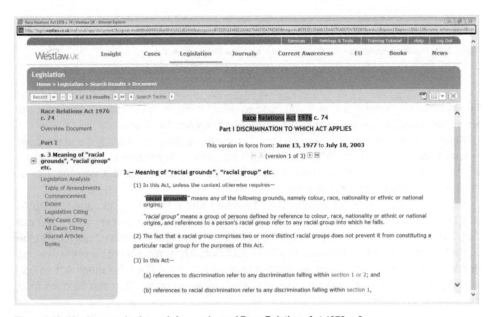

Figure 7.12 Westlaw: advanced search page

Figure 7.13 Westlaw: result of search for versions of Race Relations Act 1976, s 3

Secondary legislation

To search for statutory instruments in legislation search you can again search by title or subject. If you want to know the text of repealed SIs you need to use the historic option on the advanced search. Table 7.2 below is a quick access table for locating secondary legislation.

TABLE 7.2 QUICK ACCESS: HOW TO LOCATE DOMESTIC SECONDARY LEGISLATION (SI) IN PRINT AND ONLINE

PRINT		ONLINE	
NAME OF PUBLICATION	**FACILITIES**	**NAME OF WEBSITE**	**FACILITIES**
DAILY LIST OF GOVERNMENT PUBLICATIONS Printed by The Stationery Office	Gives a list of the SIs published each day	**THE STATIONERY OFFICE (TSO)** www.tsoshop. co.uk>	Daily list
LIST OF STATUTORY PUBLICATIONS Hard copy by The Stationery Office	This is the monthly copy of the daily list above	**www.legislation. gov.uk** FREE SERVICE Managed by the National Archives this site is the *official place* for online publication for new legislation	Can browse, search full text. But does not keep revised text versions of statutory instruments,
LIST OF STATUTORY INSTRUMENTS This is just the list, there is no full text. by The Stationery Office (TSO)	This is the yearly publishing of the monthly list above. SI indexed by subject, and also using numbers	**BAILII : www. bailii.org** FREE SERVICE: The British and Irish Legal Information Institute	Can browse, search full text
HALSBURY'S STATUTORY INSTRUMENTS	1. Main volumes (arranged alphabetically by subject) 2. Main service binder (no 1). This gives changes to instruments already in the main volumes	**WESTLAW** www.westlaw.com SUBSCRIPTION ONLY SERVICE	Can browse, search full text and obtain text of repealed

TABLE 7.2—continued			
PRINT		**ONLINE**	
NAME OF PUBLICATION	**FACILITIES**	**NAME OF WEBSITE**	**FACILITIES**
You need to check the latest updates for any change Same protocols for updating as *Halsbury's Statutes*. If you know name & number of the SI use the alphabetical list of instruments	3. Additional Texts Service Binder (no 2). This is the full text service of SIs not yet in the main volumes 4. Consolidated Index and alphabetical list of statutory instruments Annual volume giving the consolidated index by subject and alpha listing of SI according to title		acts by using the historic option in the advanced search box.
CURRENT LAW LEGISLATION CITATOR	This includes alpha list of SIs and the Statutory Instrument Citator. Details repeals, amendments or modifications	**LEXIS LIBRARY** www.lexisnexis. com Cross references to *Halsbury's*	Can browse, search full text
		LAWTEL	Can browse, search full text

EUROPEAN TREATIES AND SECONDARY LEGISLATION

EU primary law is located in EU treaties and protocols; secondary law is derived from the law making of the EU's institutions, the main forms being regulations, directives and opinions.

Print

Since 1 July 2013 print formats of EU law in all but a few cases do not constitute an authentic, official copy of the law; the only official copy is the online version. Another more forceful way of stating this is to say the hard copy/print copy has no legal value and is not deemed the legal document. That said there is a useful print publication in English that is updated each year: Blackstone's *EU Treaties and Legislation*.[10]

---

10 N Foster *Blackstone's EU Treaties and Legislation* (Oxford University Press, Oxford, 2014–2015).

Online

EUR-Lex is the major resource for EU law. The EU site, EUR-Lex: www.eur-lex.europa.eu contains information and the full text of all EU law. It is also the host for the official journal of the EU.

The official journal has all EU treaties (between the EU and member states as well as between the EU and external organisations), adopted legislation (secondary legislation by the institutions of the EU) and decisions in cases in the CJEU. It is organised into different series; the ones relating to primary legislation and treaties are as follows:

L Series: contains all EU legislation including recommendations and opinions. Here you can find the original text and amendments to it.

CE Series: this has preparatory Acts (drafts) currently going through the legislative process.

Special edition: This has the official translation of all EU legislation in the language of each member state since it joined the EU. This includes English translations since the UK joined in 1973.

The problem with the official journal is that it is rather off-putting to navigate. Because of this many use the EU law and related documents on the home page of EUR-Lex which gives the official journal reference.

The top tabs allow you to search, amongst other things, the official journal, or EU law and related documents, where you will find treaties as well as secondary legislation and

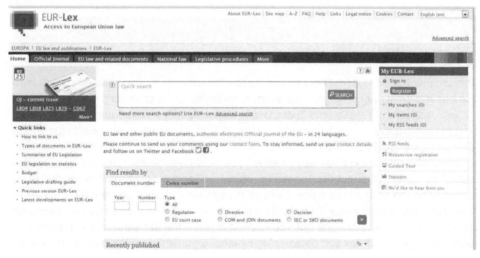

Figure 7.14 Screenshot of Eur-lex home page

preparatory Acts. If you know what you are looking for you can use the quick search box at the bottom of the front page. Additionally you can use the tab 'national' to retrieve all the national law of all member states relating to the implementation of treaties and secondary legislation.

Take time to navigate this site and find out the range of information you can obtain from it.

Online Subscription sites also deal with EU law. Westlaw has a tab for it on its home page and the search mechanisms are the same as those already referred to. There is a separate main tab. You can also use the general quick search tab on the home page. Other subscription sites such as LexisNexis and Lawtel also cover the EU.

LOCATING THE EUROPEAN CONVENTION ON HUMAN RIGHTS (ECHR) AND ITS PROTOCOLS

When you are researching the ECHR (and any other treaty) you must ensure that you have up to date knowledge of treaties/protocols, their signature and whether all or only some signatory states ratified them. It is not enough just to check derogations and reservations from the original treaties, and later treaties whether new or accession.

With regard to the Council of Europe (CoE) you can locate this treaty and its subsequent protocols on the Council of Europe Treaty Office website www.conventions.coe.int.

You can get a full list or search for specific items and changes or narrow it to the ECHR. As at July 2014 the CoE had entered into 219 treaties called conventions or protocols. You may be surprised that there is so much activity as you may have limited your understanding of the CoE to just the European Convention on Human Rights. Do explore the site and understand the type of information and primary law it contains.

HOW CAN A STUDENT RETRIEVE OUT OF DATE LAW AND GET THEIR ANSWERS TO QUESTIONS ABOUT LEGISLATION WRONG?

This chapter has considered how to find up to date legislation. How then is it possible to use out of date legislation in your research for seminars or assessment?

Your lecturers will make clear that there is no excuse for a law student making errors over the basic issue of accessing up to date legislation. Many will expect you to get it right after just a few weeks of study in your first year.

This section considers the way in which you could accidentally use out of date legislation by using out of date textbooks or articles or using older cases that are still good authority but do not reference any changes in legislation as they are reports of cases in court predating any changes. Out of date journal articles and books can be very useful for issues of analysis and critique but you have to acquire the expertise in transferring this to any changes to the law and determining whether arguments constructed remain valid.

Secondary texts: out of date textbooks, articles, etc.

One basic error concerning retrieving current legislation is the use of out of date textbooks, books, and articles. If you thoughtlessly fail to check publication dates of books and articles, or fail to note the website is no longer updated, it is highly likely that you will learn out of date law, as the law changes relatively quickly in the legislative area. A text book is usually at least six months out of date if not more.

Earlier we used the research question based on finding out if there have been changes to s 3 of the Race Relations Act. It is easy enough to go to the library and retrieve potentially relevant secondary texts.[11] However if they are pre-2010 they will only refer to the Race Relations Act 1976, s 3, which as you know was repealed by the Equality Act 2010. Furthermore if you did this the text would discuss the leading case of *Mandla v Dowell Lee* (decided in 1979 by the House of Lords). Part of this case revolved around the important issue of the meaning of the phrase 'ethnic origins'. The textbook notes that s 1 of the Race Relations Act 1976 gives a right to bring a claim of direct or indirect discrimination under the Act if you have been discriminated against on racial grounds. 'Racial grounds' is a typically general term and drafters of legislation do need to be as general as possible. Section 3 defines 'racial grounds' by referring to a list of words/phrases that fall within the meaning of racial grounds. This list includes the phrase 'ethnic origins'.

You would further learn that the courts have had to define 'ethnic origin' because the Race Relations Act does not define 'ethnic origins' as used in s 3. *Mandla v Dowell Lee* is the leading case on the meaning of 'ethnic origin'.

However hopefully you now know that if you referred to s 3 of the Race Relations Act 1976 you would be in trouble. Section 3 of the Race Relations Act 1976 was replaced by s 9 of the Equality Act 2010. Does this mean that case law decided on s 3 is now invalid? The law on equality has changed in numerous ways since 2010. So before you begin accessing secondary texts you need to find out if the law you have been reading about in the case is still current and in force.

Primary texts: law reports

Law cases can be a source of error as they will refer to the legislation in force at the time of the legal dispute. However the law may have changed or those legal rules may have been placed in another statute. Reliance on cases without checking whether the statutes they refer to are still in force is a problem. Some case law databases will let you know there have been changes. The print version will not.

It is possible to get in a muddle with case law as just reading the case will not necessarily alert you to the fact that the location of the statutory rule has changed, or it has been amended or repealed. You would therefore be wise to check that s 3 of the Race Relations Act 1976 is still good law. You will then find that the references to racial grounds in the Race Relations Act 1976 are now located in the Equality Act 2010, s 9.

11 We will be considering finding secondary text in Chapter 9.

Legislation databases

If you use public domain sites you may think that whatever you retrieve is correct and up to date. There is a general view that the internet is up to date. But in fact some sites do not update regularly, or at all. You may consider a general internet search a good idea. But if you pick a site that is not updated then you will get the law wrong. Always check the date that the site was last updated. It could have been several months or in some cases a few years ago. However, if you checked it two months ago the law may have changed. Also a general search can retrieve long lists of sites to access including those in other jurisdictions. You do not want to talk about a Race Relations Act from another jurisdiction.

It is safest to refer to the official government site which is online only, to be sure you have the correct legislation. You can use this in tandem with other database resource sites that your university library has subscribed to, such as Westlaw. Again there are many online learning materials that tell you how to use these databases, and you will need to take time to learn how each of these operates.

QUESTIONS TO TEST YOUR UNDERSTANDING OF FINDING LEGISLATION

Please answer these using the official government website http://legislation.gov.uk.
All questions relate to s 9 of the Equality Act 2014:

(1)   Has s 9(5) been amended in accordance with s 9(5)(a)?
(2)   What is the power under s 207(4)(b) referred to in s 9(6)?
(3)   What is the meaning of ethnic origin referred to in s 9(1)(c)?

Answers are located at the end of this chapter after 'further reading'.

CONCLUSION

Nearly all research for legislation is now conducted online, through the university e-library. But that does not absolve you from the need to locate it in hard copy format in your library. Sometimes historical research has to be conducted using archived hard copy. Most of our online sources go back to the thirteenth century, and for older law you will need a print version; however, some pre-thirteenth-century legislation may be in facsimile on a specialist website.

Take time to look at print encyclopaedias, and look at the hard copy legislation your library holds, taking the time to understand how it is set out and how it self-references. Do make use of any free information your library has prepared to assist you to navigate legislation. Also take the time to look at the online private subscription sites and the public domain sites. If you put the time in you will develop highly efficient online search strategies. There are many online learning materials that tell you how to use these databases. Go through any of the training tutorials provided by subscription sites such as Westlaw.

Domestic legislation

- Domestic legislation can be located in hard copy and online.
- Online sources of legislation are split into free public domain sites as well as subscription sites. The subscription sites can offer a broader range of tools and search facilities.
- The public domain sites are:
  - ☐ Official government site for all UK legislation : www.legislation.gov.uk.
  - ☐ British and Irish Legal Information Institute (BAILII) http://www.bailii.org.
  - ☐ Office of Public Sector Information: www.opsi.gov.uk.
  - ☐ Parliament www.parliament.uk.
- The subscription sites are:
  - ☐ Westlaw: published by Sweet and Maxwell www.westlaw.com.
  - ☐ LexisNexis: published by Butterworths www.lexisnexis.co.uk.
  - ☐ Justis: www.justis.com.
- The official site for all UK legislation is the public domain site, www.legislation.gov.uk.
- It is vital to know if legislation is in force, which can be done quickly through print and online sources. www.legislation.gov.uk.
- Changes to legislation are automatically incorporated into www.legislation.gov.uk.
- Parliament keeps hard copy and extensive online records of all legislation.
- Draft primary and secondary legislation can be fully accessed on the Parliament website.
- Draft statutory instruments are accessible on the www.legislation.gov.uk site but it does not contain draft primary legislation.

EU treaties and legislation

Hard copy

- Since 1 July 2013 print editions of EU law are not the authentic official copy; the only official copy is the online version.
- A useful publication in English updated each year is Blackstone's *EU Treaties and Legislation*.
- There are also a range of student statute books.

Online

- EUR-Lex: www.eur-lex.europa.eu: contains information and the full text of all EU law. It is also the host for the official journal of the EU.

■ The official journal is located on the EUR-Lex site and since 1 July 2013 the online version has been the authentic version superseding the print version in all but a few cases.

European Convention on Human Rights

■ The Treaty and its subsequent protocols can be located on the Council of Europe Treaty Office website www.conventions.coe.int which is a free access public domain site.

■ Westlaw, LexisNexis and Lawtel all provide easy to use subscription based search for EU law.

ANSWERS TO QUESTIONS

1. Has s 9(5) been amended in accordance with s 9(5)(a)?

Yes; if you search 'changes to legislation' you will find that s 9 has been amended by the Enterprise and Regulatory Reform Act 2013, s 97 to include 'caste' as a protected characteristic under 'race'.

2. What is the power under s 207(4)(b) referred to in s 9(6)?

Locate the section through the table of contents. Generally s 207 provides power for the minister of state to make an order or regulations (which by virtue of s 207(2) must be by statutory instrument) unless there is an express prohibition contained in a section. These are both forms of subordinate or secondary legislation produced as statutory instruments. Subsection 4(b) provides that orders and regulations under the section '(b) may include consequential, incidental, supplementary, transitional, transitory or saving provision'.

3. What is the meaning of ethnic origin referred to in s 9(1)(c)?

A quick check of the general interpretation s 212 reveals it does not define 'ethnic origin'. Section 214, index of defined expressions informs you of that.

Schedule 28 lists the places where expressions used in this Act are defined or otherwise explained. It does not refer to 'ethnic origin'. From this you can conclude that in the absence of a statutory definition there will be a need to rely on case law and as you know the leading case is *Mandla v Dowell Lee*.

HOW TO FIND DOMESTIC AND EUROPEAN CASES

8

LEARNING OUTCOMES

After reading this chapter you should be able to:

- Locate domestic cases in hard copy and online.
- Understand the difference between domestic court transcripts and law reports.
- Understand the range and types of law reports available.
- Be aware of the hierarchy of law reports.
- Understand domestic and EU case citations.
- Locate EU cases from the Court of Justice of the European Union in hard copy and online.
- Locate cases from the European Court of Human Rights in hard copy and online.
- Deal with the issue of unreported domestic cases.

INTRODUCTION

This chapter explains how to locate printed and online law reports from the English legal system, the European Union and the European Court of Human Rights. It will also consider how to locate court transcripts of cases. Law reports are an important, primary source of law in the English legal system,[1] as well as key in determining the meaning of words and phrases used in legislation.[2] It is essential to be able to efficiently locate them. Since the advent of digital archives of the transcripts of many court cases a vast mass of unreported case are available. These may be used in court, but there are strict rules concerning their use.

This chapter gives a step by step approach and is divided into the following sections:

- Locating domestic cases in the English legal system:
  - ☐ Terminology: law cases, case law, legal authority, law reports, court transcripts.
  - ☐ The development of law reporting.
  - ☐ The hierarchy of law reporting.
  - ☐ How to understand case citations.
  - ☐ How to understand neutral citations.
  - ☐ How to locate cases in print collections.
  - ☐ How to locate cases online.
- Locating European Union law cases:
  - ☐ How to locate cases in print collections (official and unofficial).
  - ☐ How to locate cases online (official and unofficial).
  - ☐ How to understand case citations.
- Locating ECHR law reports from the ECtHR part of the Council of Europe:
  - ☐ How to locate cases in print collections (official and unofficial).
  - ☐ How to locate cases online (official and unofficial).
  - ☐ How to understand case citations.

LOCATING CASES IN THE ENGLISH LEGAL SYSTEM

Records of law cases are produced in various ways, and not all are available outside the archives of the courts. Since 2000 many courts have made their verbatim transcript of the judgment in cases freely available online via the relevant court's website. Additionally charitable and commercial companies publish general and specialist series of reports of important cases.[3] The reports vary in the information given. Some will give a summary of the case and/or include the arguments of the barristers for the parties as well as the full text of the judgments. They usually list cases referred to in the judgments, noting whether a case has been distinguished or applied. Keywords or catchwords may also be provided noting the main issues the case is concerned with. These reports are in print series and/or online and often found in both formats.

Your university library will provide you with access to a wide range of these reports both in print formats and online though the e-library.

---

1 For a detailed discussion of English case law see Chapter 2
2 For details of statutory interpretation see Chapters 1 and 2.
3 See Chapter 2 for detail.

Terminology

The words or phrases 'law cases', 'case law', 'cases', 'legal authority', 'authority', 'law reports', 'court transcripts' or just 'transcript' are often used interchangeably in textbooks, lectures, seminars, and in the media. However, they each have a different and precise meaning. Therefore it is a good idea to start with some basic definitions so that you are at least aware of the technically correct meaning of key words and phrases. Table 8.1 sets these out.

TABLE 8.1 TECHNICAL MEANING OF KEY WORDS/PHRASES USED IN RELATION TO COURT CASES AND THEIR REPORTING	
Term	**Explanation**
Law case:	A law case refers to a court hearing of a legal dispute. This can be a trial, in which case it is the first time that the legal dispute has been heard in court. The correct terminology is to call this a 'first instance' hearing. Or a court hearing can be an appeal, against the trial outcome, the award of damages in a civil case, or against the outcome of a previous appeal.
Court transcripts:	A court transcript is the verbatim written record of the judgments delivered in court compiled by an employee of the court, the court stenographer, although digital technology is increasingly being used in the courts. The transcript is archived by the court. Many English courts make their transcripts freely available online, and these can be accessed through Her Majesty's Courts and Tribunals Service www.hmcourts-service.gov.uk. Additionally many subscription databases which publish law reports also publish the transcript alongside the law report as a pdf
Case law:	This is the term used to refer to law cases in which there has been the creation of, or amendment to, a common law rule by senior judges in their judgments in the Court of Appeal or the Supreme Court. When a law case creates or extends a legal rule it creates a legal precedent, and becomes a legal authority[4]
Legal authority	A law case that, in its written form (which can be a court transcript or a privately published report) creates a precedent that can be used in legal argument; and can bind a court in the hierarchy of courts (they must abide by the legal rule created in the law case)[5]
Law report	A law report is a written record of a law case produced by a private law report publisher. There are no official English legal system law reports. Law publishers will publish a case when it is considered that it establishes a precedent, or it resolves an uncertainty in law. Some law reports are considered more reliable than others and the courts have acknowledged, through practice directions, a hierarchy of private law reports with the 'Law Reports' series by the Incorporated Council of Law Reporting (ICLR) at the top

4   Ibid.
5   In Chapter 2.

The development of law reporting in the English legal system

The English legal system is a common law legal system with a relatively strict adherence to the doctrine of precedent which states that judges in court must follow the decisions of the senior judiciary in the higher courts when determining cases before them.[6] As we only know what judges say because of the written reports of proceedings it is essential to have a system of accurate reporting of legal cases. If you cannot trust the reporting upon which the precedent is based, then you cannot trust the law.

Surprisingly, there are no *official* series of law reports in England to equate with the Queen's Printer's copy of an Act of Parliament. The Stationery Office (TSO) is responsible for publishing revenue, immigration and social security law cases. However, traditionally, law reports remain in the hands of private publishers. It is a long-established, but conventional rule that a law report, if it is to be accepted by the relevant court as a legal authority, must have been prepared by, and published under, the name of a fully qualified barrister.

Because the publishers of law reports are private organisations, each publisher will tend to structure their reports differently, perhaps adding footnotes or summaries, perhaps including or excluding the arguments put by counsel. However, what remains constant across all reports is that words attributed to the judge in his or her judgment have to remain a true and accurate record of the words that were actually spoken by the judge. As the editors of each series of law reports can choose which cases to publish, some cases can appear in more than one law report series.

Parties to a legal dispute being heard in court have to accept the decision of the court at the time it is given. This is the court's determination of the decision between the parties. The detail of any precedent developing from the case is noted after the case has been reported and more widely read and discussed. Editors of law report collections, academics and judges may all publish articles and commentaries on a particular case. But it is only in the reasoning of judges in later cases in the senior courts that the precedent value of a law case can be tested, and affirmed or distinguished.

Whilst the competent production of reliable law cases is indispensable to the operation of the doctrine of precedent, such law reports have actually only been available in England since 1865, but[7] the reference to the use of the doctrine of precedent has been made for hundreds of years.

There were law reports before 1865 but they are not considered completely reliable. There are a range of fragmentary law reports covering the period 1272–1535 known as *Yearbooks*. The Yearbooks begin with Edmund Plowden's Commentaries, but it was not until the eighteenth century that three law reporters, Burrow, Cowper and Douglas began to work towards standardising how the reports appeared.

Towards the end of the eighteenth century judges got involved in the appointment of reporters to the courts and either reviewed reports of their judgments or made written versions of their judgments available to the reporters. The Yearbooks were

---

6   See Chapter 10 for more detail on the operation of the doctrine of precedent.
7   Ibid.

handwritten for hundreds of years in legal French, with some being printed from the fifteenth century onwards.

However, it is not always possible to discover if the report in the Yearbook is of an actual case or a moot (a fictional legal argument staged as a competition between lawyers). The detail given in these reports varies. Some reports record outcome, but not facts; others record facts and outcome, but give no reasoning process. Quite often no judgment is recorded, only the pleadings. The quality of the report also varies considerably. These facts contribute to their unreliability as a source. Consequently they are rarely cited in court. There is a modern reprint of the Yearbooks by the Selsdon Society and by the Ames Foundation with an English translation. The Bodleian Library, Oxford University has a full print collection of the Yearbooks.

There is also another set of law reports dating from the late fifteenth century to 1865 that exist in a series of reports called 'the nominate reports' meaning (named reports). These are reports classified according to the name of the reporter, such as Coke's Reports. They too suffer from unreliability relating to the information found in them. There are even concerns that some reports are written by partisan lawyers in such a way as to be slanted towards a particular reading of the reasoning of the case to ensure the same reading in later cases coming before the court.

By the nineteenth century, a court-authorised reporter was attached to all higher courts and their reports were published in collected volumes catalogued by the name of the relevant

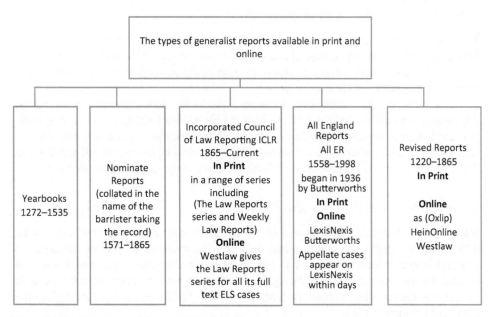

Figure 8.1 The types of generalist reports available in print and online

reporter. In 1865, there were 16 reporters compiling and publishing authorised reports and in that year these reports were amalgamated into the Incorporated Council of Law Reporting (ICLR) which became a charitable organisation in 1970. As a general rule, law reports pre-dating the ICLR's creation in 1865 are considered to be of doubtful accuracy and reliability as legal authorities. While these reports can be referred to in legal argument in court, they rarely are.

Today, there are numerous, often competitive, private publishers of law reports. The range of types of available law reports is shown in Figure 8.1 which additionally includes sources that are pre-1865, indicating whether they are also available online.

There are a number of publishers of law reports and the editors of each will apply different criteria for determining which law cases to report. Measured against the vast numbers of cases that are not reported the percentage of cases that are reported is very small. It has been estimated that the cases in the ICLR's *Law Reports* only cover 7 per cent of the cases in the higher courts in any given year.

Some published law reports are annotated, particularly for the use of practitioners; others are left without annotations or introductions. There are generalist law report series reporting important cases in a range of areas of law. But private law publishers have also introduced a specialist series of reports dealing with only one area of law such as employment law, criminal law and company law.

Note on unreported cases generally

The vast majority of cases are unreported but many of these are published online as court transcripts. An increasing number of cases in transcript format in the archives of the court and the Supreme Court Library, contains thousands of files of unreported cases. These record witness statement and judgments.

Court transcripts have been free online since 1996 with more and more courts making this service available. An archive of House of Lords cases from 1996 can be located at www.publications.parliamen.uk/pa/ld/ldjudgmt.htm under the parliamentary business tab. You can locate Privy Council decisions from 1999 to 2009 at privy-council.org.uk; you will also find that there are a few pre-1999 decisions. Post 2009 you can find decisions at www.jcpc.gov.uk.

Case summaries and full text cases

Many of the online databases, as well as the digests in print form, give case summaries. Whilst there is nothing wrong with a case summary you must realise that a summary is an interpretation of the case by someone else. It is not the actual law case, and it does not contain the law, nor is it a legal authority. The author may have misinterpreted the case. To access the law you need to read the judgments in the full text in the law report. Only the judgment contains the law.

The development of digital technology has allowed the development of a vast range of electronic retrieval systems for accessing the details of thousands of unreported cases.

This has caused its own problems and there has been a legitimate concern that courts would be inundated with cases that did not really contain any new law. As a consequence of this concern the House of Lords, in the case of *Roberts Petroleum Ltd v Bernard Kenny Ltd*,[8] took the step of forbidding the citation of unreported cases of the Civil Division of the Court of Appeal without special leave.

THE HIERARCHY OF THE LAW REPORTS

Although there are no official series of law reports an accepted hierarchy of law reports has been established by the senior courts through their practice directions. The most reliable reporting is considered to be found in the *Law Reports* series published by the ICLR. This series reports the most important cases heard in the Supreme Court (and previously the House of Lords), the Privy Council, the Court of Appeal, the High Court (Chancery, Family and Queen's Bench divisions), the Employment Appeals Tribunal and the European Court of Justice. They are bound in differing series of law reports, the Appeal cases (AC), and then the High Court decisions in Queen's Bench Division, Chancery, Family and Probate. These are checked by the judges sitting in the relevant case prior to publication.

The ICLR *Law Reports* series reports all cases:

- Where new rules or principles are introduced into the legal system.
- Which modify existing rules of principles of the legal system.
- Which resolve doubt in relation to a question of law.
- Which the Council considers important in terms of instructiveness.

The *Law Reports* series contains the argument of counsel for the parties and each report is checked before publication by the judges' bench hearing the case. The courts have made clear that these are the most authoritative reports and must be cited over and above any other series of reports that may have published the same case.

The *Law Reports* are published monthly in four sections and bound annually:

(1)   Queen's Bench (QB), and the Court of Appeal.
(2)   Chancery (Ch) and the Court of Appeal.
(3)   Family (Fam) Divisions of the High Court and the Court of Appeal.
(4)   Appeal Cases (AC) heard in the UK Supreme Court and Judicial Committee of the Privy Council.

The reports are available in subscription form in print or online only formats, or both, by the ICLR.

In 2012 the Lord Chief Justice, Lord Judge, issued a 'Practice Direction: Citation of Authorities (2012)'[9] which in effect sets out the hierarchy for citation of authorities in court

---

8   [1983] 2 AC 192.
9   Practice Direction: Citation of Authorities (2012) 1 WLR 780 – ICLR.

as it determines the following practice when an authority is cited in court, in written or oral submissions:

(1)   When a judgment is reported in the Law Reports series of the ICLR (AC, QB, Ch and FAM) that report must be cited and no other.

(2)   If the judgment is not in the law reports series at the time of the case and it is in the ICLR's Weekly Law Reports (WLR) or the All England Law Reports (All ER) then either of these reports can be cited.

(3)   If a judgment is not in the Law Reports, WLR or the All ER a report in any authoritative specialist series can be used provided it 'contain[s] a headnote and [is] made by individuals holding a Senior Courts qualification (for the purposes of s 115 of the Courts and Legal Services Act 1990)'.[10] The ICLR also publishes another set of law reports known as the Weekly Law Reports (WLR); these are published prior to any checking by the judiciary in small pamphlet format. Ultimately they are bound in volumes for the year. Those in Volumes 1 and 2 can be found checked by the judges in the Law Reports series. Those in Volume 3 have not found their way into the Law Reports. While the Law Reports take 10–14 months to be published the Weekly Law Reports, because they are not checked, take five months.

(4)   If a judgment is not reported in 1–3 above then any report it is cited in can be used.

(5)   Reference can be made to the official transcript of a court case if there is no report.[11] A judgment can have two stages, as 'handed down in court' which may then be subject to later changes and the final version filed as the official transcript. The handed down version cannot be cited in court. (You can get these from the courts or BAILII (http://www.bailii.org/). But unreported cases should only be cited if they contain a relevant legal principle that is not available in a reported case.

(6)   If counsel considers that the case that is the correct one to cite in the hierarchy does not for some reason give the 'full picture' then he or she is at liberty to explain this to the court and use another law report. Occasions do arise when one report is fuller than another, or when there are discrepancies between reports. On such occasions, the practice outlined above need not be followed, but the court should be given a brief explanation why this course is being taken, and the alternative references should be given.

It is good to get into the habit of automatically adopting the rule that you will only use the most authoritative version of the report in your written work. Similarly, should you decide to engage in mooting, a competitive form of formal legal argument between two teams of students role playing counsel, you will lose vital marks if you do not cite the most authoritative law report of the case you are using.

What is the relationship of electronic forms to print forms of law cases?

The electronic collections of unreported as well as reported law cases are huge, far in excess of those printed. It was the huge array of electronic cases that led to the introduction

---

10 Ibid 8.
11 A judgment can have two stages, as 'handed down in court' which may then be subject to later changes and the final version filed as the official transcript. The handed down version cannot be cited in court.

of neutral citations by the courts to bring an order to the reference system used in relation to unreported cases. As use of the internet spirals and more law reports of cases are converted into electronic form this raises an issue for the legal system. What is the relationship of electronic forms of cases to print formats, particularly in relation to the hierarchy of law reporting? When should a court seriously consider cases that are unreported in print version, but are reported electronically? The electronic source does not displace the hierarchy of the print series.

CHOOSING YOUR LEGAL AUTHORITIES

When reading any law report you should ask whether it is the most authoritative version available. Or are there more authoritative versions? You should also consider whether there is any other case that is only recorded electronically that may be of authority.

You could also ask yourself if there might be any unreported case that could be more authoritative than the law report you have located. This would only be a task you would undertake for research or professional purposes. As you now know the courts have strict rules about admitting as authoritative, cases where only electronic versions are available.

Just because a case has not been reported, or if it is only reported in electronic format, it does not mean it *cannot* be an important case or be used. You would need to access court transcripts yourself to determine these matters, and keep to the established rules for using them in court.

HOW TO UNDERSTAND CITATIONS

Neutral citations

Since 2001 every approved judgment in the Supreme Court, Privy Council, Court of Appeal, the Administrative Court, and latterly the divisions of the High Court (Chancery, Queen's Bench, Commercial, Admiralty, Family, etc.) has been given a neutral citation by the court as shown in Figure 8.2. It is a very simple citation. The names of the parties are given followed by the year of the case in square brackets (indicating this is the year that the case was heard), the jurisdiction (e.g. UK for United Kingdom or EW for England and Wales).[12] This is followed by the court (e.g. SC, CA, HC), the jurisdiction of the court, whether civil (Civ) or criminal (Crim). Finally a sequence or serial number assigned to the case is given.

To assist you with learning the court abbreviations and to reinforce court structure Figure 8.3 below sets out some of the most used abbreviations in neutral citations.

The neutral citation is completely independent of any private law report citations. If you are dealing with a case that has a neutral citation, the neutral citation must be given before any citation of a law report of that case.

---

12 The Supreme Court has UK wide jurisdiction whilst the Court of Appeal and the High Court only have jurisdiction within the English and Welsh legal systems.

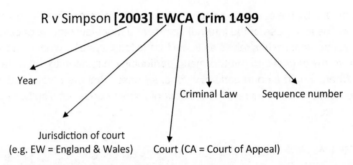

Figure 8.2 Constituent parts of a neutral citation

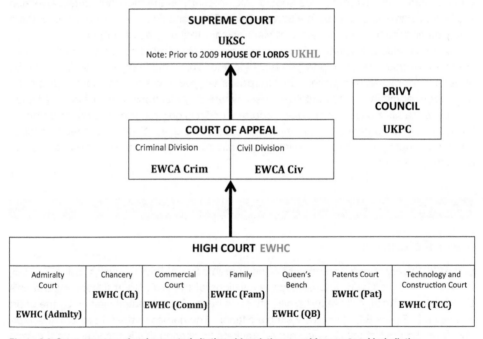

Figure 8.3 Court structure showing neutral citation abbreviations used for court and jurisdiction

The neutral citation must be given immediately after the names of the parties and this is then followed by any report of the case (given in order of hierarchy). The citation for *R v Simpson* is set out to demonstrate this.

R v Simpson [2003] EWCA Crim 1499, [2004] QB 118, [2003] 3 All ER 531

UNDERSTANDING LAW REPORT CITATIONS OF THE PRIVATE PUBLISHERS

When a case is reported by a private publisher it will have a citation which is the abbreviated reference to the case. Any e-copy of the reported case will also give the citation of the printed report. The citation gives slightly differing information depending upon the print or exclusively online location of the case, and whether the case is reported by a private publisher or is unreported (in which case the only written record would be the court transcript).

If the report of the case is only online then the full web address must be given to pinpoint the case. Additionally, if you are using this citation you must give the date you accessed the site.

Whilst there may seem at first to be far too many citations for you to remember you will find that understanding the broad logic of citations means that you know how to read new citations.

The size and numbers of important cases cannot be predicted each year and therefore publications of law reports must have room to expand. They are therefore published in series. The standard format adopted by many publishers is to issue small looseleaf publications of selected law reports weekly, monthly, quarterly, or half yearly which will eventually be bound into annual volumes. These pamphlet-sized publications usually have the publisher, date run and prospective volume number and page numbers running along the spine.

They are then bound yearly into a book or books, called a volume. The year, the series and the volume number for the year are printed on the spine of the book, along with an abbreviated form of the publication's name. When there is a particularly busy year there will be more than one volume for the year and each volume will be numbered consecutively, 1, 2, and 3, and so on. Each volume will run chronologically from January to December, with volume 1 containing cases from January onwards.

Each publisher of private reports will have different abbreviations, but what remains static is the fact that normally a citation includes the year of the case, an abbreviation of the full name of the private report, the volume number if applicable and the page number in the print version of the report.

Some publishers will separate out cases heard in the Court of Appeal and the Supreme Court. Some series of reports only deal with specialist areas of law, such as company law, or employment law; other series are generalists dealing with all areas.

As you are asked to locate law cases you will become familiar with the range of reports and forms of citation. You will start to internalise the different abbreviations without effort. In your early days of study it may be useful to keep a modest list of abbreviations handy as a quick translation.

The citation provides all of the information you need to give the proper reference in your written work – with the caveat that there are a few differences in referencing systems used in UK Law schools.[13] If you do not recognise the abbreviation in your citation then it is quick

---

13 See the section on referencing and plagiarism.

TABLE 8.2 ABBREVIATIONS FOR LAW REPORTS PUBLISHED IN PRINT	
AC	Appeal Cases (Law Reports series)
All ER	All England Law Reports
All ER (EC)	All England Reports European Cases
BCLC	Butterworths Company Law Cases
Ch	Chancery (Law Reports series)
CLR	Commonwealth Law Reports
CMLR	Common Market Law Reports
Cox CC	Cox's Criminal Cases (Law Reports)
Cr App R	Criminal Appeal Reports
ECC	European Commercial Cases
ECHR	European Commission on Human Rights Decisions and Reports 1976–1998
ECR	European Court Reports 1954 (Court of Justice of the European Community)
ECR 1-	European Court of First Instances/General court report
ER	English Reports
Fam	Law Reports Series Family
HRLR	Human Rights Law Reports
ICR	Industrial Cases Reports
IRLR	Industrial Relations Law Reports
KB	King's Bench (Law Reports series)
QB	Queen's Bench (Law Reports series)
TLR	Times Law Reports

and easy to refer to the Cardiff Index to Legal Abbreviations which is locatable online at www.legalabbrevs.cardiff.ac.uk.

You will find over 100 law report abbreviations on the database. Table 8.2 above lists the most popular abbreviations you are likely to come across in your first year of study.

It is useful at this point to give some detailed consideration of year dates (both of the case and publication) and party names as used in law report citations.

Year dates and law reports

Prior to 1890 year dates were not put on volumes of law reports – other conventions were used to locate the case, and the year was not part of the citation. Most usually an abbreviated version of the author's name, often just an initial of the surname was used to locate the case, with volume number and page numbers being indicated, for example *Heydon's Case* (1584) 3 Co Rep 7a 101.

The above report abbreviation 'Co' refers to Sir Edward Coke, an influential figure in sixteenth-century law. His reports are in seven volumes, and are a collection of writings. They concerned cases where he had been counsel, cases he had been in court for, and cases he had heard of! He began them while still a law student. Of variable quality in the early years from 1572, they stabilised from 1579. Note the round brackets indicating you need to know the date to find the case in Coke's Reports.

Today, the dates of pre-1890 cases are placed in round brackets ( ) in the law report citation. This indicates the fact that you do not need the date in order to find the case, though it may be helpful. You will need a name of a publication or an author, and a volume number. Law reports post-1890 place the date in square brackets [ ] to indicate that the year the case was published is necessary to locate it. You may wonder why it is necessary to mention cases pre-1890. However in the English common law system it is quite possible that some of the leading cases you will need to refer to were reported pre-1890.

Date of reporting a case contrasted with date of hearing a case

The year date given in the citation is the year in which the case was reported. You need to be aware that it is possible that the case itself may not have been heard in that year. For example, a case may be heard in late December and not reported until January when the year date will have changed. Also sometimes an editor is slow to realise the importance of a case, or its importance is not realised until another case has referred to it. Then the case can only be published at the earliest opportunity but it may already be several years after the case was heard. It is therefore important to check the date of hearing in the actual report itself so that you do not make an error concerning when the case was heard.

Case names

Case names are cited in different ways according to whether they are criminal, civil or judicial review cases, family law cases,[14] probate cases or shipping cases.[15] You will learn these differences slowly but initially you are most likely to come across criminal cases and civil cases in your first year of study. Therefore only these two will be considered.

Criminal cases

R v Camplin [1978] AC 705 is the citation for a criminal case. You can see that the first name is a capital letter, R. This is an abbreviation of the Latin for King (Rex) and Queen (Regina). A criminal case is brought in the name of the Crown, for the monarch is the head of state. The defendant's name in criminal proceedings comes second as the monarch is bringing a case against the defendant for an alleged breach of the criminal law. The notation signifying the prosecution is the italicised letter *v*, which stands for the Latin 'versus', meaning 'against'. However, if you are speaking and refer to the citation the reference to

---

14 Which are usually anonymised.
15 Usually the name of the ship is used.

'v' is always 'and' not 'versus'. Figure 8.4 gives a breakdown of the elements making up the full citation

Initially you can go to the section of the library where the law reports are kept, and locate the volume you need by searching chronologically through the spines of the Appeal Cases series. Once located you turn to page 705. Or you can access it online.

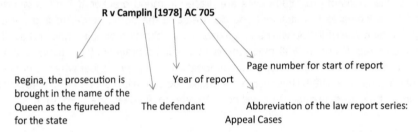

R v Camplin [1978] AC 705

Regina, the prosecution is brought in the name of the Queen as the figurehead for the state

Year of report

The defendant

Page number for start of report

Abbreviation of the law report series: Appeal Cases

Figure 8.4 Constituent parts of citation for a criminal case published in the ICLR Law Reports series

Civil cases

The names of both parties are given in civil trial law report citations with the complainant's name given first and the defendant's second. The notation 'v' is used and the citation rules are the same, as shown in Figure 8.5 where the breakdown is given for *George Mitchell v Finney Lock Seeds* [1983] 2 AC 803. This is a civil appeal so the complainant's name is given first: this is the party bringing the action. The second name is that of the party defending the action. In an appeal case the party bringing the appeal is the first name given. When the case is located you will note that it was finally heard in the House of Lords.

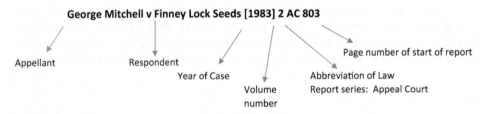

George Mitchell v Finney Lock Seeds [1983] 2 AC 803

Appellant

Respondent

Year of Case

Volume number

Page number of start of report

Abbreviation of Law Report series: Appeal Court

Figure 8.5 Constituent parts of citation for a civil case published in the ICLR Law Reports series

Correctly citing law cases before and after 2001

There are a few general rules concerning what information goes into citations before and after the introduction of neutral citations by the courts in 2001 and these are set out in Table 8.3.

TABLE 8.3 CORRECTLY CITING LAW CASES BEFORE AND AFTER 2001		
Type of Report	Cases before 2001	Cases after 2001
Reported cases	• Party names • Law report citation In order of the hierarchy of law reporting if more than one e.g. *George Mitchell v Finney Lock Seeds Ltd* [1983] 2 A.C. 803; [1983] 3 W.L.R. 163; [1983] 2 All E.R. 737; [1983] 2 Lloyd's Rep. 272; [1983] Com. L.R. 209	• Party names • Neutral citation • Law report citations in order of the hierarchy of law reporting if more than one e.g. *Regus (UK) Ltd v Epcot Solutions Ltd* [2008] EWCA Civ 361; [2009] 1 All E.R. (Comm) 586
Unreported cases	• Party names • Date of hearing • Court	• Party names • Neutral citation

How to locate cases in the print collections when you do not know the citation

Sometimes you may not have a full citation and in this situation the following publications, regularly updated throughout the year, can assist in the location of the full citation. They also give you a summary of the facts of the case and its outcome. This is useful when you are engaging in research as they have a subject search and will list cases relevant to topics. You can then read summaries of located cases to decide their relevance before locating them. Table 8.4 considers search strategies for locating law reports in three publications:

(1) The current law case citatory.
(2) The law reports consolidated index.
(3) The Digest.

How to locate cases online

Law cases are collected together in databases which work by linking words, so that you can do a keyword search to retrieve resources according to the keywords you use. You can think of a database as a cross referenced address book, where each word has an 'address': the computer links and cross references until it finds the address or potential addresses called up by your search terms.

If you do not retrieve a case with your keyword search, this does not mean that there is no case; it could simply mean that the keywords you selected did not find it. You can

TABLE 8.4 HOW TO LOCATE LAW REPORTS IN PRINT COLLECTIONS

NAME OF PUBLICATION	DESCRIPTION	
CURRENT LAW CASE CITATOR In three date sets 1947–1976 1977–1988 1989–2002 NB: Current law is also online on Westlaw as the case and legislation locators	• Each case is given a case number • Lists parties in alphabetical order by first party and criminal cases are listed by R and then alphabetical • Gives a case summary of the facts and judgment as well as useful information about the procedural history of a case • At end of citations for a particular case location indicated by word *Digested* followed by a numbers e.g. *10/70*. The first number is the year and the second the number of the case in the volume for that year. You can then find it and obtain a summary of the facts and the judgment **QUESTIONS: Q:** What if I don't know the date of the case? **A:** You will have to look through every volume	• An italicised word *Applied* followed by numbers e.g. *Applied 12/45* would indicate where we could find a case that applied the case we are looking for. Entries can be made concerning when the case was *Considered, Distinguished or Followed* • Annual bound volumes • Monthly updates in the *Current Law Monthly* updates
LAW REPORTS CONSOLIDATED INDEX Bound in red they are also called the red book or the red indices. Spine states Law Reports Index; each volume covers 10 years from 1951 1951–60 1961–70 1971–80 1981–90 1991–2000 2001–2009	In addition to the 10 yearly red books there are pink books, the 3 monthly supplements for the current year. Law cases indexed are from • Law Reports • Weekly Law Reports • All England Law Reports • Industrial Cases Reports • Lloyds Law Reports • Local Government reports • Road Traffic Reports • Tax Cases	The index lists cases by • Names of first party • Subject matter • Indicates which cases were considered

THE DIGEST	Main Volumes/Continuation Volumes	Consolidated table of cases 3 Volumes	When you find the entry you will see that they give other cases that are noted as Apld (Applied)
This is a massive source of information on cases commencing in 1919 with its publisher ambitiously intending to give a digest of the whole of the law of England (plus a large body of law from other jurisdictions). It was previously known as the English and Empire Digest and carries cases from 1500. Currently in its third edition which is colloquially referred to as the Green Band because it has a green band on the spine of its volumes. This is usually a few months out of date	These have digests of cases and each volume deals with a particular subject matter. There can be more than one volume for a subject and there may therefore be one or more sub volumes e.g. 3(2) is Volume 3 sub volume 2 **Cumulative Supplement 2 Volumes** This is the annual update **Quarterly Survey** contains cases digested since the last cumulative supplement so you can see if a case that you are interested in has been considered since being heard	This is the alpha listing of cases **Consolidated index 2 Volumes** This is the subject list in alpha order for those subjects covered by the digest and gives a volume number and reference numbers. Cases dealing with more than one subject can appear in two volumes **When you use the digest to locate cases** if you know the name look in the consolidated table of cases; you may find there are two volumes or more referred to if more than one subject is dealt with. When you go to the relevant volume, consulting the table of cases at the front which is again in alpha order, it gives you the case number of the digest.	Colns (Considered) Dist. (Distinguished) When you locate the digest to find cases about certain subjects you locate the subject volume you are interested in and then look at the table of contents at the front of the volume (or use the consolidated index)

always search by the name of the party as well but of course if that is a common name such as Jones you would need to think of other search terms you can use.

There are a large number of databases relating to the location of cases and many duplicate the holdings of others and each will have slightly different search functionality. However, if you are searching for cases by subject it is a good idea to ensure that your search is as wide as possible. Alternatively if you are searching by a case name you want a thorough search to ensure the law in that case has not been changed by subsequent cases.

The range of databases give access to differing law report series over different timescales, and they may give access to the official transcript of the court as well as reports. It will take time for you to learn which report series can be located on which database.

Make yourself familiar with each of the sites as soon as you can. Some subscription sites may not be available in your institution. You are likely to find that your institution's library provides guides to the databases that it subscribes to. Additionally, most sites have help tabs as well as tutorials for those who are new to the database. Westlaw for example offers printed training material.

Most universities have access to subscription databases such as Westlaw, Justis or LexisNexis. None of these carry the full range of law reports and you will find that you will need to access all of them if possible. An important free access database to be aware of is BAILII www.bailii.org which covers England and Wales, Scotland, Northern Ireland and the EU. Table 8.5 gives you basic information on the holdings of the database and its search facilities.

The particular value of databases such as Westlaw or LexisNexis is that in addition to the law report you will find a case summary provided, and where relevant a list of case notes or articles written about the case, and later cases referring to it. Westlaw also provides access to the court transcript of the judgment. Table 8.5 gives you more detailed

TABLE 8.5 HOW TO LOCATE LAW REPORTS: ONLINE DATABASES

DATABASES AND STANDARD INFORMATION	CONTENTS:	SEARCH FACILITIES (e.g. Keyword, first party search etc.)
BAILII FREE SERVICE <www.bailii.org>	**Contents:** Contain case law from England, Wales, Scotland and the European Union	Keyword, first party, topic search etc.
CASETRACK SUBSCRIPTION SERVICE <www.casetrack.com> Provider: Merrill Legal Solutions	**Contents:** Contain judgments from the last 14 years in excess of 80,000 judgments [variable start dates for each court however]: Court of	Keyword, first party, search

DATABASES AND STANDARD INFORMATION	CONTENTS:	SEARCH FACILITIES (e.g. Keyword, first party search etc.)
[they are the only official transcribers for the Court of Appeal and Administrative Court and one of the official transcribers for the High Court which means that judgments can appear therefore in a matter of hours]	Appeal Criminal and Civil divisions 4/96 – current. Administrative Courts 4/96 – current, Divisional court of the High Court, Chancery, Queen's Bench, Admiralty, Mercantile, Technology and Construction courts, Employment Appeal Tribunal from 7/98 – current, VAT Tribunal form 1/2002 – current and some judgments from the European Court of Human Rights and the European Court of Justice	
JUSTIS SUBSCRIPTION SERVICE <www.justis.com> Provides a pdf of the reported case which has the original pagination and layout Justis also offers Justcite: SUBSCRIPTION SERVICE enabling the search of multiple jurisdictions to find leading cases	**Contents:** Contain case law from England, Wales, Scotland, Ireland, and the European Union and international law. Contains among others the Law Reports, English Reports, Industrial Cases Reports and Family Law Reports Law goes back to 1163	Keyword, first party, search
LAWTEL SUBSCRIPTION SERVICE <www.lawtel.com> Provider Thomson Reuters	**Contents:** Covers a range of courts including The Supreme Court, Privy Council, Court of Appeal (Civil), Court of Appeal (Criminal), High Court, Selected tribunals, Crown Court, County court. Covers unofficial transcripts available the same day and official transcripts and covers hundreds of cases that are not reported elsewhere	Keyword, first party, search Can search by judge or particular statutory provisions discussed in a case
LEXISLIBRARY SUBSCRIPTION SERVICE Provider Butterworths	**Contents:** Contain case law from England, Wales, Scotland and the European Union	Keyword, first party, search Can search by judge or particular statutory

TABLE 8.5—continued

DATABASES AND STANDARD INFORMATION	CONTENTS:	SEARCH FACILITIES (e.g. Keyword, first party search etc.)
		provisions discussed in a case
WESTLAW SUBSCRIPTION SERVICE Uses the Law Report Series in preference to others if one exists. It also provides a pdf of the print version of the law reported case which has the original pagination and layout	**Contents:** Contain case law from England, Wales, Scotland and the European Union. Where a case is not on the database links given to where the case may be located	Keyword, first party, search. Can search by judge or particular statutory provisions discussed in a case

information on accessing cases on several databases. The following pages also show you screenshots of several of the main law case databases. Her Majesty's Courts Service (HMCS) publishes Court of Appeal and Supreme Court judgments within one day; with other courts and tribunals they are published as soon as possible. It is an important database because it also allows you to search for cases coming to court, and notes which cases have applied for leave to appeal.

SEARCHING FOR CASES USING ONLINE DATABASES

Now it is useful for you to familiarise yourself with these databases by considering some screenshots. We will look at two subscription sites, Westlaw and Lexis®Library, and then a free site, Bailii.

Subscription sites

The value of these is that they offer 'extras' such as journals that contain articles that can be cross referenced to cases (indexes and abstracts as well as many full text). You can retrieve all judgments by a given judge as well.

Westlaw

When you first access Westlaw via your university library you will be taken to the login page which gives you the option to do a quick search. The login page screenshot can be seen in

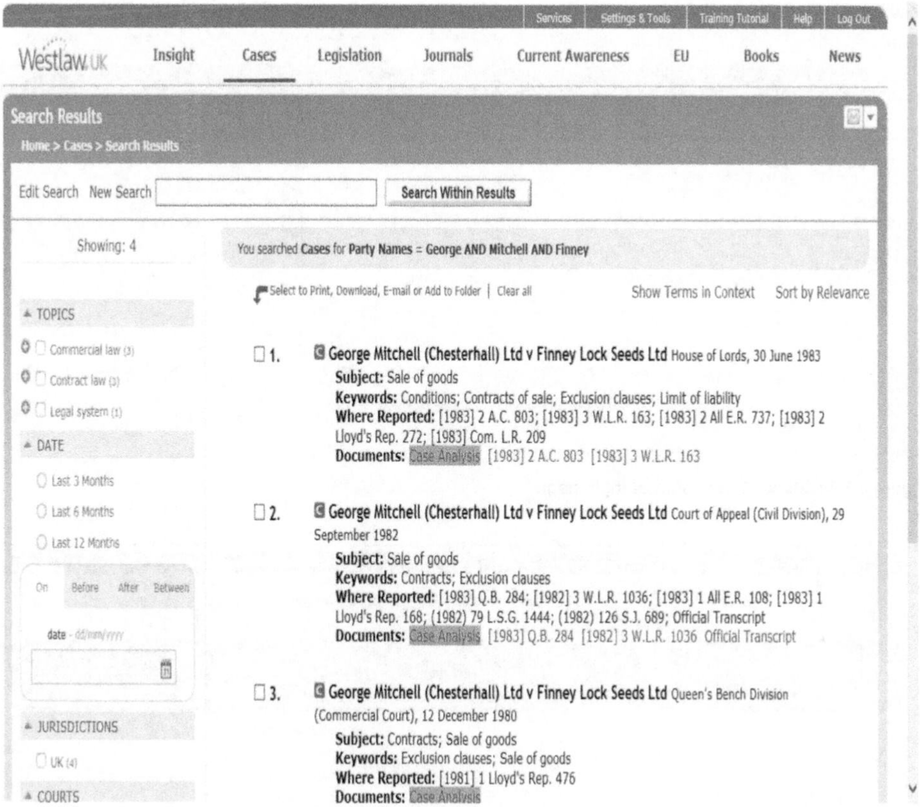

Figure 8.6 Retrieved results 1–3

Figure 8.7. Note that one of the tabs at the top of the screen is the 'Training tutorial' which is beside 'Help' if you just get stuck on one point rather than require full training. We have entered the party names *George Mitchell v Finney* and pressed search.

If this is not sufficient you can click the 'Cases' tab and do a more detailed search.

Both searches, which only asked for 'George Mitchell Finney', making no distinctions between parties, retrieved the same information and the cases of relevance as set out in Figure 8.6. As you can see from the first retrieved case in Figure 8.6, hyperlinks give access to two ICLR reports from the 'Law Report' series and the 'Weekly Law' series.

As you can see from the retrieved sources 1–3 all have 'case analysis' highlighted at the end of the entry. Beside the case analysis are the hyperlinks to the full online reports, listed in order of their hierarchy. Note that entry 2 has an official transcript. All three entries read from 3–1 suggest that entry 1 is the report of the House of Lords appeal hearing, and was probably an appeal from a Court of Appeal hearing cited in entry 2. This leaves entry 3 to

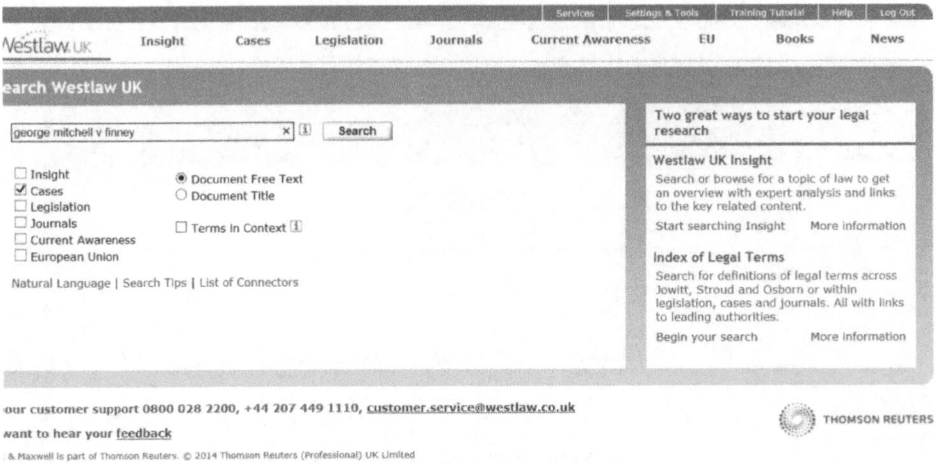

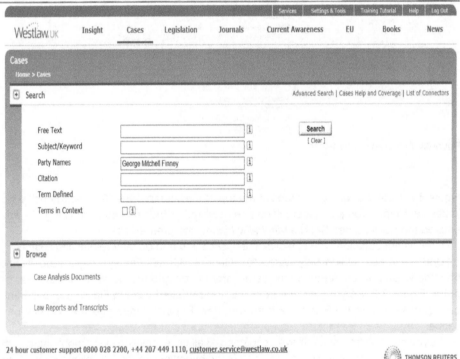

Figure 8.7 Westlaw: Screenshot of login page

Figure 8.8 Westlaw: screenshot of detailed search in cases

be the report of the trial in the High Court. It is important that you can understand and read citations together to give yourself a view of what the procedural history of the case may be.

It is essential to use the most up to date version of a case, and cases can change dramatically on appeal. Online databases allow this to be ascertained in minutes.

Lexis®Library

Lexis®Library is another subscription database. When you sign on you are again presented with a quick search facility as shown in the screenshot for Figure 8.9.

If you wish to do a more detailed search you can move to that page shown in Figure 8.10; note the scroll down in advanced search which enables you to search by court.

Both the 'quick search' and the search in cases retrieve the relevant cases; as you can see from the Figure 8.11 screenshot there are two reports for the House of Lords appeal shown separately: in Westlaw the list of citations is given after one entry for the House

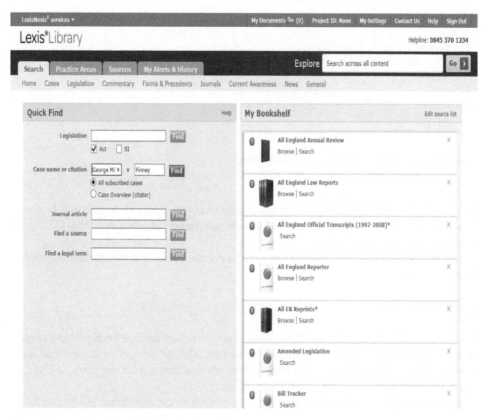

Figure 8.9 Lexis®Library screenshot of quick find page

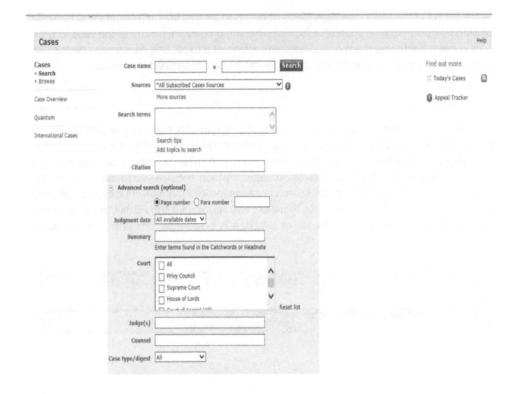

Figure 8.10 Lexis®Library screenshot of cases web page

of Lords. Again, the reports relating to the House of Lords, Court of Appeal and Queen's Bench have been located. Both reports can be accessed, whereas only the AC report could be accessed on Westlaw.

The left hand side screen menu allows you to narrow the search results to area, name, court, jurisdiction.

BAILII

The next set of screenshots are from Bailii which is a free service unlike Westlaw and Lexis®Library which are subscription only. When you sign on you arrive at the initial web page (see Figure 8.12) and you can immediately choose cases from the menu in the top right hand corner.

You can access case law search and you are given a range of options, see Figure 8.13.

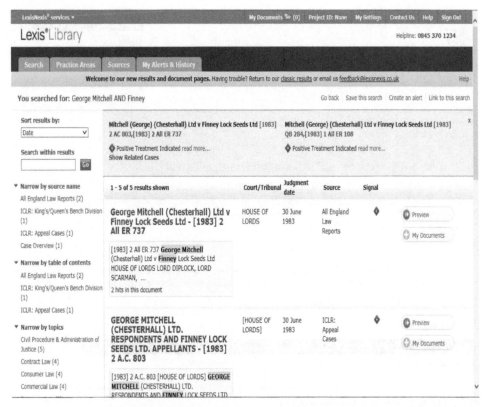

Figure 8.11 Lexis®Library screenshot of retrieved cases

However, from the result of this search, again for *George Mitchell v Finney Lock Seeds*, we note that the database only shows the appeal in the Court of Appeal. This is a good demonstration of the error of assuming that the case you have retrieved is the most recent. It is often a good idea to look in more than one database to cross check your findings. This can be seen from Figure 8.14.

You are directed to one case, the Court of Appeal decision in 1983, but as we know from the Westlaw cases there is a later House of Lords appeal.

EUROPEAN CASES

You will be referred to cases relating to the law of the EU and the decisions of the ECtHR (the Council of Europe institution dealing with disputes concerning the ECHR) in many of your modules. This section gives you basic information to help you to locate these cases.

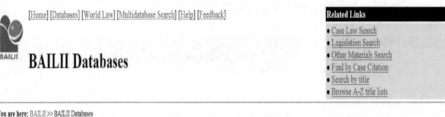

[Home] [Databases] [World Law] [Multidatabase Search] [Help] [Feedback]

Related Links
- Case Law Search
- Legislation Search
- Other Materials Search
- Find by Case Citation
- Search by title
- Browse A-Z title lists

BAILII Databases

You are here: BAILII >> BAILII Databases
URL: *http://www.bailii.org/databases.html*

[England and Wales] [Scotland] [Northern Ireland] [Jersey] [United Kingdom] [Ireland] [Europe] [Other Documents]

The following is a list of the databases that BAILII holds arranged by jurisdiction and type of material: case law, legislation and other material. You can search each database by keyword or browse each database by date or A-Z title list. Click on the database link to access the search screen.
To access material that is not on BAILII, see the World Law service.

Scope:

- BAILII databases contain British and Irish case law, legislation and other materials (e.g. Law Commission Reports), and European case law.
- Most of the databases contain predominantly recent material, but the coverage varies and both old and new content is being added on an ongoing basis.

Refer to the database listings below to view the current scope of coverage for each database.

England and Wales

England and Wales Case Law   Welsh Legislation
Courts
                                                                     • Acts of Wales

Figure 8.12 Bailii: Screenshot of sign in page

Locating European Union law cases

Locating cases in print collections

Unlike the English legal system the EU legal system does have an official set of law reports – the 'Law reports before the Court' which since 1991 are organised in two parts. Part I reports cases heard in the Court of Justice of the EU (CJEU), and Part II reports cases of the Court of First Instance. In the English legal system publication of appellate courts and trial court judgments is relatively quick, as discussed. Unfortunately there is not a quick turnaround of the official reports for EU courts. Part of this is due to the need to translate judgments into the official languages of the EU, and this can take in the region of 18–24 months. This means that the official reports are not a useful source for up to date law. Researchers and lawyers needing up to date information on cases must consult private publishers, and as you know now these collections will not be comprehensive but will only cover cases considered important by the editors.

[Home] [Databases] [World Law] [Multidatabase Search] [Help] [Feedback]

Case Law Search

Related Links
• Find by Case Citation
• Search by title
• LawCite Search
• Browse A-Z title lists

You are here: BAILII >> Case Law Search
URL: *http://www.bailii.org/form/search_cases.html*

Basic Search | Legislation Search | Other Materials Search | Advanced Search | Multidatabase Search

Citation:		e.g. [2000] 1 AC 360
Case name:	George Mitchell v Finney	e.g. barber v somerset
All of these words:		e.g. breach fiduciary duty
Exact phrase:		e.g. parliamentary sovereignty
Any of these words:		e.g. waste pollution radiation
Advanced query: [Help]		e.g. pollut* and (nuclear or radioactiv*)
Optional dates:	From To	Enter as yyyy, yyyymm, or yyyymmdd
Sort results by:	○ Date ○ Jurisdiction ○ Title ⦿ Relevance	
Highlight search terms in result:	⦿ Yes ○ No	

[Search]

To limit jurisdictions, use tick-boxes below:

☐ **United Kingdom: Courts**   ☐ **England and Wales: Courts**   ☐ **Scotland: Courts**

☐ House of Lords   ☐ House of Lords   ☐ House of Lords

☐ Supreme Court   ☐ Supreme Court   ☐ Supreme Court

Figure 8.13 Case law search options

[Home] [Databases] [World Law] [Multidatabase Search] [Help] [Feedback]

Search results

Related Links
• Case Law Search
• Legislation Search
• Other Materials Search
• Find by case citation
• Search by Title
• Browse A-Z title lists

You are here: BAILII >> Search results

Repeat search over: WorldLII databases : WorldLII web search : Google

Searching for: **title (George) and title (Mitchell) and title (v) and title (Finney)** (boolean query) [Edit search] [RSS feed for this search]

Sort results by: ○ Title ○ Jurisdiction ⦿ **Relevance** ○ Date ○ Date (oldest first) [Re-sort]

Total documents found in BAILII databases: 1

1. George Mitchell (Chesterhall) Ltd. v Finney Lock Seeds Ltd. [1982] EWCA Civ 5 (29 September 1982) *(View without highlighting)* [100%]
   ([1982] EWCA Civ 5, [1983] 1 All ER 108, [1983] QB 284; From England and Wales Court of Appeal (Civil Division) Decisions; 76 KB)

Repeat search over: WorldLII databases : WorldLII web search : Google

BAILII: Copyright Policy | Disclaimers | Privacy Policy | Feedback | Sponsors | Donate to BAILII

Figure 8.14 Bailii screenshot of retrieved case of *George Mitchell v Finney Lock Seeds*

There are two main sources of reliable but unofficial private publications: the *Common Market Law Reports* which have been published since 1962 by Sweet and Maxwell and the *All England Law Reports* (European cases) which have been published since 1995.

Locating cases online

There are a range of databases that give details of EU cases. The most important is accessed via EUROPA, the website of the EU which has a link to the European Legal Portal published in all the languages of the EU. The case law section is updated on a daily basis and carries reports of the CJEU and the Court of First Instance, and contains judgments as well as the opinion of the Advocate General.

The official reports are also available online in full text on CELEX. This is a subscription service which can be accessed via EUROPA (the official site of the EU), through subscriptions to JUSTIS and Eurolaw or directly from CELEX. The other databases we have already discussed above in relation to the English legal system, Westlaw, LexisNexis and Lawtel, also contain EU cases.

Understanding EU case citations

Cases in the CJEU and Court of First Instance (previously the General Court and renamed by the Treaty of Lisbon) are reported as two different series: the CJEU as series C and the CFI (GC) as series T. The first aspect of the citation therefore is stating the series classification as either C or T. This is followed by the year of hearing separated by a forward slash from the serial number of the case which indicates which case of the hearing year it was. This is similar to the idea of sequence numbers used in neutral citations for domestic cases referred to above. Next the names of the parties to the case are given. After the party names the year recorded in square brackets indicates the year of publication of the official record; this is followed by the abbreviated reference ECR to the official reports noting in capitalised Roman numerals whether the case is in Part I (CJEU cases) or Part II (CFI/GC). Knowing the part numbers enables you to tell at a glance which court heard the case reported. A hyphen then separates the part number from the page number. This information is set out in Figure 8.15 below.

Locating ECHR law reports from the ECtHR part of the Council of Europe

There exist both official and unofficial reports of cases, and it is important to remember that in addition to the ECtHR, the European Commission on Human rights had jurisdiction to hear cases until its abolition in 1998.

Print collection

There is an official print series of reports for the European Court of Human Rights (ECtHR) which is located in the 'Reports of Judgments and Decisions'. Most recently there has

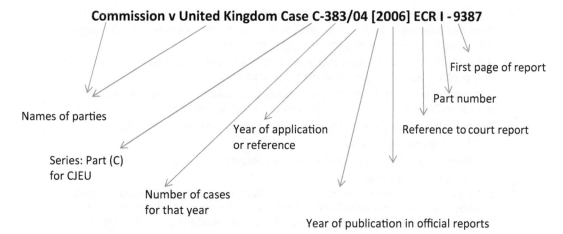

Commission v United Kingdom Case C-383/04 [2006] ECR I - 9387

First page of report

Part number

Names of parties

Year of application
or reference

Reference to court report

Series: Part (C)
for CJEU

Number of cases
for that year

Year of publication in official reports

Figure 8.15 The constituent parts of a European law report citation

been a move towards the publication of selected cases only. In common with the EU official reports there is a delay of at least a year before publication.

Researchers, lawyers and students therefore are again reliant on private publishers for up to date information on cases, using the European Human Rights Reports (EHRR). They are acceptable in the English and Welsh courts.

If you need access to decisions of the European Commission on Human Rights pre-1998, these can be located in two reports series that are split by date. The collection of decisions of the European Commission on Human Rights (citation is CD) contains reports from 1955 to 1973 in volumes 1–46. From 1974 to 1998, reports can be found in the Decisions and Reports (citation DR) in volume 46 onwards.

E-collections

HUDOC is an official site, containing full judgments which are free to access (hudoc.echr. coe.int/). However you can also access selected cases through the subscription services of Westlaw, Justis, Lawtel and Casetrack.

CHAPTER SUMMARY

Domestic cases

- A law case is a court hearing of a legal dispute.
- A court transcript is the written record of the judgments delivered in court compiled by an employee of the court.

- Case law is the term used to refer to decided legal disputes in the courts in which there has been the creation of, or an amendment to, a common law rule by judges in their judicial decisions during the hearing of the case.
- A legal authority is a law case that in its written form (which can be a court transcript or a privately published report) creates a precedent.
- A law report is a written record of a law case produced by a private law report publisher. There are no official English legal system law reports.
- The following hierarchy of law reports emerges from practice directions:
  - ☐ *Law Reports* series (ICLR).
  - ☐ *Weekly Law Reports* or *All England Law Reports*.
  - ☐ An authoritative specialist series.
- Since 2001 every approved judgment in the Supreme Court, Privy Council, Court of Appeal, the Administrative Court, and latterly the divisions of the High Court (Chancery, Queen's Bench, Commercial, Admiralty, Family, etc.) has been given a neutral citation by the court.
- The neutral citation is completely independent of any private law report citations.
- The year date given in a citation is the year in which the case was reported. You need to be aware that it is possible that the case itself may not have been *heard* in that year.
- Case names are cited in different ways according to whether they are criminal, civil or judicial review cases, family law cases, probate cases or shipping cases.
- When citing reported cases before 2001 you must give party names and the law report citation (in order of the hierarchy of law reporting if more than one).
- If citing reported cases after 2001 you must give party names, neutral citation and law report citations (in order of the hierarchy of law reporting if more than one).
- If citing unreported cases before 2001 you must give party names, date of hearing and court.
- If citing unreported cases after 2001 you must give party names and neutral citation.
- Justis is a particularly useful database for research as it contains case law going back to 1163 and legislation back to 1235 for not only the UK but also Ireland and the EU.
- Her Majesty's Courts Service (HMCS) publishes Court of Appeal and Supreme Court judgments within one day, with other courts and tribunals as soon as possible.

European Union cases

- The official law reports of the EU are the 'Law reports before the Court'.
- It can take up to two years for the official reports for EU courts to be published.
- European Legal Portal (now known as New EUR-Lex) is updated on a daily basis.
- The official reports are also available online in full text on CELEX, a free service which can be accessed via EUROPA, or through subscriptions to third parties such as Justis and Eurolaw.

European Convention cases from the European Court of Human Rights

- The official series of reports for the European Court of Human Rights (ECtHR) are located in the 'Reports of Judgments and Decisions'. There is a delay of up to a year before publication.
- There is an official site, containing full judgments, which is a free access site, HUDOC (hudoc.echr.coe.int/).

Unreported cases

- The vast majority of cases are unreported and many of these are published online, usually as court transcripts which have been free online since 1996.
- An archive of House of Lords cases from 1996 can be located at www.publications. parliament.uk/pa/ld/ldjudgmt.htm.
- Privy Council decisions from 1999 to 2009 can be located at http://privycouncil. independent.gov.uk/; you will also find that there are few pre-1999 decisions. Post-2009 you can find decisions at www.jcpc.uk.

HOW TO FIND SECONDARY MATERIAL: TEXTS ABOUT LAW

9

LEARNING OUTCOMES

After reading this chapter you should be able to:

- Locate a range of relevant secondary texts (texts about law).
- Develop strategies to ascertain the authority and validity of secondary materials retrieved from the internet.

INTRODUCTION

Reading secondary texts (books about law) is essential for the development of your understanding of law. There are many types of secondary texts available from the print and e-collections in your university library as well as on open access internet sites. An example of the type of texts available would include:

- Reference texts: dictionaries, encyclopaedias, digests, indexes, bibliographies.
- Books/research monographs.
- Academic and professional journal articles.
- Official documents (command papers, proceedings in Parliament, debates in Parliament, parliamentary research papers, government presentations to Parliament in the form of policies, briefings, information and minutes of committees.
- Reports by charitable organisations in the field.
- Reports by independent 'think tanks'.
- A large number of organisations, such as charities, universities and pressure groups have extensive literature online.
- Many universities around the world make some aspects of their electronic materials available free on the internet.
- Some individual academics in university departments make their speeches, lectures and articles available and often have their own websites.
- Media reporting.
- Blogs.

As students of law studying for a law degree you are engaged in the academic stage of a legal education. Among other things in your learning you are required to keep up to date with some of the latest academic thought in your area. Academic journals and books critique an area of law, explain the emergence of a new idea or area of law, or offer an academic commentary on an area of law. These materials can bring exceptional scholarship to a reader. Where they are concerned with actual legal rules you will need to check that the commentary and the rule given in the book are up to date.

Your library will subscribe to journals and reference material and in many cases these will be available in both print and electronic formats. Many journals will provide electronic access to current and back issues if your library has a print subscription. Journal articles are never more than two to four months out of date at the date of publication.

Just as you can search texts of law by topic, print indexes and digests, electronic databases allow you to search for secondary texts. When you are engaging in research for seminars and assessment it is particularly useful to be able to search databases of journals. For example JSTOR allows you to search by title, author, or keywords. JSTOR[1] is a large archive collection of out of date journal articles, whilst Blackwell Synergy allows a search of all of its publications including current journals. But to avoid disappointment get

---

1 www.jstor.org.

a list from the library catalogue of the range of journals to which your library subscribes. Make yourself familiar with your library's print collection of law journals and also with their electronic collection of law journals. Print collections of journals are reference only and must be read in the library; if an electronic version is available you can read it anywhere with internet access using your library ID and password.

As you move through the first year of your studies you will gain an appreciation of the importance of secondary law texts both from textbooks that explain the general area of law, through to scholarly books which carefully explore one area of law from a complex set of perspectives. As with primary sources, you should also assess whether the author of a secondary text has appropriate credentials.

Books written as student textbooks, such as this one for example, are not books of any legal authority. Some by longevity and respect for their views do get mentioned in court but it is not common practice. Books can be out of date before they are published so you do need to consult academic journals for up to date legal commentary.

The majority of the journals that you will read will be academic. This means all articles placed in a particular edition of the journal will have been read before publication by two other academics working in the same area, who must agree that the article is academically sound and adds to the current debates. This process is called peer review, or peer refereeing, and the journals which undertake this checking prior to publication are called refereed journals. The peer review process ensures that the article and the journal are reliable. This does not mean that what is said should be believed or should not be questioned, but it does mean that you can read it and trust it to be of an authoritative nature.

Other journals are professional and not intended in any way to be academic but practical. Some of these can be extremely useful for law students at the academic stage of their training.

GENERAL ISSUES RELATING TO SEARCHING FOR SECONDARY TEXTS

There is an excellent overall online training tutorial originally devised by a law librarian, Sue Pettit, to introduce students to the range of material on the internet, and how to use it.[2] This training tutorial has been updated and further developed and contains invaluable information concerning legal research, navigating sites and assessing the reliability of the information you retrieve. It has excellent information on secondary texts about law.

William Twining, a well-known professor of philosophy, once issued a text that he called the *Law Cookbook*, a series of 'recipes' for success in legal method and reasoning.[3] This developed into a popular text, co-authored with Professor David Miers, *How To Do Things With Rules*.[4]

---

2   Virtual Training Suite for law students to help them get the most out of internet search. Designed by a range of UK academics. The training site on the library is part of it. Stephen Whittle is the current author of the material, his predecessor was Sue Pettit. www.vts.intute.ac.uk/he/tutorial/lawyers accessed 14 August 2014. Hosted by tutorpro.

3   W Twining and D Miers *How to Do Things with Rules: A Primer of Interpretation* (4th edn, CUP, Cambridge, 1999) Appendix 111, 421–33.

4   W Twining and D Miers *How to Do Things with Rules: A Primer of Interpretation* (4th edn, CUP, Cambridge, 1999).

The 'cookbook' is an excellent metaphor,[5] especially related to electronic and complex print texts. You may not wish to cook, but if you did, you would not start off by cooking the most complex recipe or by simply reading recipes. You would learn the basics of cooking and then add on more complex variants to your simple starting recipes. This is the underlying approach of this section, to lay out some basic research strategies, or recipes, for searching print and electronic collections, to acquire secondary material about the law.

It will allow you to experiment and provide the tools you need to gain an understanding of law library research. You will learn best by going into the print collections, or logging into the electronic collections, and browsing the sources.

Academic study involves the application of proper and rigorous research for materials, followed by your selection of the most appropriate resources, which are then subjected to competent and rigorous interpretation.[6] The effort taken to locate material is only the beginning of academic work, but it is an essential task because you need to locate the most authoritative and correct texts.

As you practise locating secondary material you will find that your skills increase and improve. In addition to the face-to-face training that your department and/or library will provide, there are excellent training guides produced by most university libraries to assist in locating and searching particular print and electronic resources. In addition, many databases such as Westlaw contain detailed instructions both in print format, and online. All databases will contain either help tutorials or 'hints' in a drop down menu. These can be useful if you have a problem. But it is better to also know how to properly navigate the site.

SEARCH STRATEGIES

Search strategies for print and electronic materials both start in the same place, with your research question and an idea of the type of information you are looking for. You need to assess whether the material you have located is reliable and in the case of journal articles that it is the most current, scholarly material. You may find that you retrieve articles by leading scholars that are opposed to each other in their views. You need to deal with this difference of opinion and synthesise these views in your writing and research for tutorials. However first things first – before you can engage in this type of critique you need to know how to locate the best, and most relevant, materials you need with a carefully thought out strategy based on:

- **what** you are looking for; and
- **why** you are looking for it.

For the following discussion on searching for resources we will assume that you are researching for the following essay question:

---

5   A metaphor can be defined as the act of describing something unknown by reference to something known.
6   Analysis and interpretation of retrieved material will be dealt with later in the book.

Is it correct to maintain that in *R v Secretary of State ex. P. Factortame (No 1) and (No 2)* the English courts and the Court of Justice of the European Union (CJEU) made it clear that English courts have the power to suspend Acts of Parliament conflicting with the European Union (EU) and that the CJEU can determine what national remedies should be available? Critically discuss.

This is an essay based on the reading of law reports and from Chapter 8 you know how to locate these cases. However, your ultimate task is to decide whether the description given in the quote is correct. To do this you will need to search for relevant secondary material which must be mainly from academics. The views of legal professionals as well as politicians can sometimes give your research some extra avenues to explore and views to consider. But at university you are primarily responding from an academic legal perspective not a professional legal and/or political perspective. We will look at only three types of secondary text, journals, books and official documents.

Journal articles

What are journals?

A journal is a collection of articles (and book reviews and case comments) by a range of different writers. Law journals can cover the area of law generally or consider law from a specific disciplinary perspective (such as anthropology, sociology) or from one specific area of law (e.g. contract, criminal law). The main focus of a journal can be academic or non-academic (e.g. a professional journal for barristers, or solicitors). Law students are always expected to use several academic articles in written work and for tutorial work which may be supplemented by non-academic professional journal articles if relevant. Academic articles are scholarly pieces written about a particular topic or issue within a subject and often constitute the most up to date thinking in an area.

The following Table 9.1 gives a practical illustration of areas covered by a journal, their abbreviation and whether they are academic or professional.

JOURNAL TITLE ABBREVIATIONS

All journals have an abbreviation of the journal title (e.g. in Table 9.1 the *Cambridge Law Review* becomes CLR.) and you will come to know the main abbreviations. Table 9.2 gives a list of a few commonly accessed journals together with their abbreviation. A full listing can be obtained online from the Cardiff Index to Legal Abbreviations.[7] There is also a print only alternative, Index to Legal Citations and Abbreviations;[8] however, do be aware that this will always be slightly out of date.

---

7   www.legalabbrevs.cardiff.ac.uk.
8   D Raistrick *Index to Legal Citations and Abbreviations* (4th edn, Sweet and Maxwell, 2013).

TABLE 9.1 ILLUSTRATIVE EXAMPLES OF JOURNAL, TYPE, AREAS AND ABBREVIATIONS

AREA	EXAMPLE JOURNAL	Abbreviation	Academic	Professional
General Journal	The Cambridge Law Review	CLR	√	X
Particular area of law	Immigration, Asylum and Nationality Law	IANL	√	X
Disciplinary perspective	Sociology of Crime, Law and Deviance	SCLD	√	X
Professional journal	New Law Journal	NLJ	X	√

JOURNAL ARTICLE CITATIONS

Publishers of journals need a recognised system of organising their journals so that they can be easily accessed by readers in their printed formats as well as online. This is essentially done by date order of publication. Each year will have its own volume; however, some journals will re-number volumes at the start of each year, and others use volume numbering going back to the beginning of the journal. The majority of academic journals are published more than once a year in 'issues'. Therefore each volume number will be followed by a number in brackets; this indicates which issue of the year the article is in (e.g. 72(1) refers to volume 72 and issue no 1 for the year).

The citation for a journal article is ordered as follows: author name, article title, abbreviation of journal name, year of publication, volume number, issue number in brackets and page reference, followed by the reference as set out in Table 9.3 below.

Finding online journals using Westlaw

While print runs of certain journals are currently kept by many university libraries, as a general trend universities are moving to online access only. The value to students is that if they have their own means of accessing the internet these journals are available 24/7 to suit the students' study habits.

We have already considered Westlaw in relation to cases and legislation. With regard to journals the search facility allows you to search journals for relevant articles by:

- using keywords;
- subject;

TABLE 9.2 JOURNAL ABBREVIATIONS

The following list of journal abbreviations indicates those you may be required to access at the start of your studies and throughout your studies. There are hundreds of journals however and if you are unfamiliar with the abbreviation given to you then you will need to search for the full titles of the journal using one of the systems referred to above. Always be clear whether the journal article you are reading is in an academic or professional journal. The table also indicates where the relevant journal may be obtained online through subscription sites. It is worth noting that different sites may hold differing date runs of journals.

Abbreviation of journal title	Full title of journal	Academic	Professional	Online?
CJQ	Civil Justice Quarterly		√	Westlaw
CLJ	Cambridge Law Journal	√		Cambridge Journals online, HeinOnline
Crim LR	Criminal Law Review	√		Westlaw, lawtel,
JCL	Journal of Criminal Law	√		Lexis®Library
JLS	Journal of Law and Society	√		Wiley online library
LQR	Law Quarterly Review	√		Westlaw, HeinOnline
LS	Legal Studies	√		Wiley online library, HeinOnline
MLR	Modern Law Review	√		Lawtel, Wiley online library, HeinOnline
NLJ	New Law Journal		√	Lawtel, Lexis®Library
OJLS	Oxford Journal of Legal Studies	√		Westlaw, Lexis®Library
PL	Public Law	√		Westlaw, Lawtel
PLJ	Property Law Journal	√		Lawtel
SJ	Solicitors Journal		√	Lawtel
SLR	Statute Law Review	√		Westlaw
WebJCLI	Web Journal of Current Legal Issues	√		Lawtel

TABLE 9.3 FULL CITATION OF JOURNAL ARTICLES

All university libraries will have online access to the majority of journals that you will need. The library's computerised indexing system will allow you to locate journals by browsing journal titles or indicating a specific name. All systems vary slightly so you must identify the systems used by your library. Once located the journal name will be a hyperlink to the database that stores it.

Author	Munday R
Title	*Fisher v Bell* revisited: misjudging the legislative craft
Abbreviation of journal name	CLR
Year date of publication	2013
Volume number	72
Issue number	(1)
Page numbers	50–64 Note: Do not just give the start number
Full citation:	Munday R, Fisher v Bell revisited: misjudging the legislative craft, CLJ 2013, 72(1), 50–64 If you know your library has the print copy the citation will allow you to go directly to the area storing the print version and take it off the shelf.

NB: Do not confuse the general citation used by each journal with the requirements of academic referencing systems for use in the written work method of placing such references into essays etc. There are several different academic referencing systems used in universities (e.g. Harvard or the Oxford System for the Citation of Legal Authorities (OSCOLA)). These may require you to use slightly differing punctuation, fonts, or presentation of author name and journal details

See Chapter 19 for fuller details on academic referencing.

- general terms;
- cases cited in the journal article;
- journal title;
- article title;
- author.

It is relatively straightforward to use the quick search box to locate a specific journal article by name or by author name. But you may well find that often you are searching to see if an article has been written on a particular topic. The keyword search allows you to do this. But do not assume that there are no articles if you do not retrieve any. Your keywords may not have retrieved articles that exist; changing your keywords may allow you to locate the articles you want. When you retrieve your search results you will find that either the title is clearly relevant or you may need to read the abstract. If you have not used an advanced search to narrow the publication dates of articles you wish to retrieve do keep a careful eye on dates as you do not want to locate out of date information. Westlaw is useful in that it keeps a list of journals in full text on the site and additionally refers to journals in abstract where it does not have full text. It is not an exhaustive site but currently states that it has 110 full text journals available.[9] These include journals published outside the Sweet and Maxwell group, for example Cambridge University Press and Oxford University Press. Helpfully Westlaw also has a link allowing access to abstracts of articles on the legal journals index database. This database carries over 500,000 titles.

Finding journals on Lawtel

This site is also a Sweet and Maxwell site so it will contain some material that is also found on Westlaw. However, it tends to specialise more in the area of professional legal journals which can be particularly useful in ensuring you know the lawyers' views of up to date law as well as reading academic views. It too can be searched by using keywords, by subject, general text (free text) or by journal title or author, and your searches can be date limited.

Finding journals on Lexis®Library

This database contains the full text of around 100 journals and the abstracts of many more; it also contains practitioner journals. You can search within one specific journal which is particularly useful and is a facility that is not available on Westlaw. But do not get into the habit of just using one journal. Even if your preferred journal is excellent it cannot give you the wide ranging understanding obtained by looking at good academic articles from a range of journals. Many generalist journals contain in-depth articles on a range of topics. If you were researching criminal law and limited yourself to just the criminal law review you may miss an important article in one of the generalist journals such as the journal of legal studies.

Finding journals on HeinOnline (www.heinonline.org)

This is a database from Hein and Co, a leading American publisher; however, it contains a large number of UK and European journals. It will retrieve your journal as a page image so you see the article as it appeared in the print version.

There is a good source of archived academic journal articles held on JSTOR which is a subscription database that you will be able to access through your university library.

---

9   Accessed 5 January 2015.

However these are out of date and so you must decide if you need up to date information on an area of law. If you are interested in various academic views relating to a topic then these may be of use, as long as you also use them with updated articles as well.

If you decide to engage in a public domain search for journals outside the provision of your library you need to be extremely careful about what you may find. You could find a student journal from a university in another legal jurisdiction; this is not going to be an academic journal. Or you may locate Q and As put on the web by leading law firms or individual lawyers. Or you may find out of date articles. These will generally be professional rather than academic.

BOOKS

In addition to journal articles you will also be required to read all or part of a number of books for each of your modules. You need to know how to access them efficiently, either by title, or by researching to see if there are any books of authority on the topic you are concerned with.

The library catalogue

The print collection of your university library is going to be your main source of books for borrowing or reading and therefore your first port of call will again be the online library cataloguing system. There are very few law e-books.

It is possible with a note from your university library to have reading rights in other university libraries. This is most useful if you are studying some distance from your home address: you may be able, out of term time, to read books in any good university law library near your home. Additionally if your library does not stock the book you need you can fill in an interlibrary loan form, but it can take weeks before your book arrives in your university library.

The university online library catalogue will allow you to access books by title, author, or the use of keywords. Each university catalogue system will work differently; however all will contain print or online guides to the system. Again this is an area where you should experiment accessing books on topics early on in the academic year so that you know how to find books when told to read a chapter.

A valuable online resource for accessing books is COPAC (www.copac.ac.uk) which is an amalgamation of the online catalogues of major UK as well as Ireland, specialist, university and national libraries (e.g. The British Library). You can find some interesting material on this catalogue, including small specialist monographs that are not in your university's library.

Using print only materials

You can also locate books using printed materials by accessing a legal bibliography, which can be general or specialist, and when you have a book in front of you, you can consult its bibliography and may well obtain leads for further reading from it. Or check out the references in footnotes or endnotes in your set text or other book. You might find that the textbook may only give a basic outline of an area but if you look at footnotes you will often find that they direct you to further, more detailed, reading.

General note on module 'set textbooks'

Some lecturers will advise you to buy a particular book, a set text. If this is the case, do seriously considering buying the book if your finances will allow you to do so. This textbook will have been carefully chosen by your lecturer as the best and most up to date book to accompany the course. You will find that you will often be expected to read a section or a chapter before a tutorial or a lecture. You may think it will be enough to read the library copy of the set text. While this may be sensible, if many students decide to do this you may find that you cannot get your hands on the book to read it for assessments or tutorials.

If you decide you want to use a different textbook do check with your lecturer that it is appropriate. Your lecturer may have decided not to use that book for very specific reasons. For example, it may not cover all of the topics on the course. Alternatively you may feel that the set textbook is too difficult, or you cannot follow it. Do ask your lecturer for advice as they may be able to recommend another text to use instead, or to read first before going back to the set text you have a problem with.

Even if you do buy the recommended textbook this does not mean that you will not have to locate and read other books when researching for tutorials or assessments.

LOCATING OFFICIAL DOCUMENTS

The use of the term 'official document' refers to publications by the two Houses of Parliament (command papers, parliamentary papers, debates, committee proceedings), the government and government departments, local authorities, etc. If you are researching legislation the parliamentary website[10] or relevant government or government department website[11] can offer an invaluable insight into the rationale for proposed legislation. This has been referred to in Chapter 7.

For the purposes of this discussion we will only consider accessing a few official documents:

Command papers.

Parliamentary papers.

Parliamentary debates.

But the information given can be transferable and act as a standard guide to access other types of official documents.

---

10 www.parliament.uk.
11 www.gov.uk.

COMMAND PAPERS

When the government presents publications to Parliament they are known as command papers, so called because of the following formula of words at the beginning of them:

'Presented to Parliament by the Secretary of State for . . . by Command of Her Majesty'.

There are many different types of command paper. You have already come across two, White Papers and Green Papers, in Chapters 1 and 7. White Papers present the government's proposals for legislation, or policy initiatives. Green Papers tend to be purely consultation documents. In addition to these command papers also include:

- State papers.
- Government responses to select committee reports.
- Reports of Royal Commissions as well as other committees of inquiry.
- Statistics and annual reports of government bodies (but not all).

The majority of command papers are kept in series identifiable by numbers. In addition to numbered series there are some command papers that are not in numbered series.

The numbered series of command papers began in 1833; the sixth series which began in November 1986, is the current series.

The full range of dates and references for the six series are as follows:

Series 1: 1833–1869 which is numbered [1]–[4222].

Series 2: 1870–1899 which starts with prefix C. and is numbered [1]–[9550].

Series 3: 1900–1918 which starts with the prefix Cd. and is numbered [1]–[9329].

Series 4: 1919–1956 which starts with the prefix Cmd and is numbered [1]–[9889].
    (Square brackets around numbers was abolished in 1922.)

Series 5: 1956–1986 which starts with the prefix Cmnd and is numbered [1]–[9927].

Series 6: 1986–to date.

Note after the first series prefixes are added to differentiate the series so that numbers do not become confused. If you refer to a command paper by the number 2500 it will not mean anything unless you know the prefix. If it is Cmd 2500 you know that the prefix Cmd was used for series 4. Therefore it can be located in series 4.

You may find that your library organises its collection of command papers according to the parliamentary session. This is a problem if you do not know the date of the command paper you are looking for.

Online access to command papers

As command papers are official government publications, most of them can be located in full text on the www.gov.uk website. You can also locate some in the National Archives www.webarchive.nationalarchives.gov.uk/20140210084229/http:/www.official-docu ments.gov.uk.

This is the only official documents website hosted by TSO. It can be searched and documents located can be printed. It contains a full list of command papers and House of Commons Papers (HCP) from 17 May 2005 onwards. Only a few papers predating 2005 can be found on this site from 1994.

If you want to see the government's response to any select committee reports these are accessible by consulting the relevant committee pages, or through links on the relevant government department websites.

Locating parliamentary papers

House of Commons papers and House of Lords papers detail the work of the two Houses, for example details of voting procedures, minutes, select committee reports.

The Parliament website[12] gives the dates and online access for a range of parliamentary papers. Some are not available online and where this is the case it is stated. This information is set out in Figure 9.1. From the parliament.uk site you can click on each link to immediately access papers.

Finding reports of parliamentary debates

Whilst many reports may be given of debates in Parliament the only official reports of parliamentary debates are provided by Hansard, and generally the shorthand reference for official reports of debates is just 'Hansard'. It is printed on a daily basis and reprinted each week in 'weekly Hansard' and an index is published fortnightly. At the end of each parliamentary session all debates are issued as a bound volume; these volumes run into the hundreds. Hansard reports are in a column (two to a page) format with each column numbered consecutively throughout the year so that passages can be precisely and quickly pinpointed. For referencing purposes the volume number and column number is given.

They are published online at www.parliament.uk/business/publications/hansard under Hansard Commons or Lords. You can search by dates, but the current online record only goes back to 1988/9 (House of Commons) and 1994/94 (House of Lords). For online

---

12 Accessed 5 January 2015.

Parliamentary Papers (Sessional Papers, Blue Books) – House of Commons

Commons Sessional Papers, 1714–1800

- Lambert edition at the subscription service House of Commons Parliamentary Papers, widely available in universities and other large reference libraries

Commons Parliamentary Papers, 1801–2004

- Subscription service House of Commons Parliamentary Papers (http://parlipapers.chadwyck.co.uk/home.do) widely available in universities and other large reference libraries.

House of Commons Committee reports, 1997 to present All Select Committee publications

- (http://parliament.uk/business/publications/committees/select-committee-publications/)
- Command papers and other government papers, 2005 to present : http://www.gov.uk

Parliamentary Papers (Sessional Papers, Blue Books) – House of Lords

Lords Sessional papers, 1714–1805

- Torrington edition at the subscription service House of Commons Parliamentary Papers, widely available in universities and other large reference libraries

Lords Parliamentary Papers, 1805–2001: No electronic versions available.

House of Lords Committee reports, 2001 to present

- online Lords Select Committee publications (http://parliament.uk/business/publications/committees/select-committee-publications/lords-select)

Deposited Papers – House of Commons and House of Lords

Deposited Papers, House of Commons, pre January 2007:

- Not available electronically or online. Contact Parliamentary Archives (www.archives@parliament.uk) for hard copies.

Deposited Papers, House of Commons, post January 2007:

- Parliament website

Deposited Papers, House of Lords, pre January 2007:

- Not available electronically or online. Contact the Parliamentary Archives for hard copies.

Deposited Papers, House of Lords, post January 2007:

- Parliament website

Figure 9.1 Accessing Parliamentary Papers

records before that you would need to use the parliamentary archives and access historic Hansard going back to 1803 at hansard.millbanksystems/com.

Using TSO official documents online

Official Publications Online is a subscription service from TSO enabling a search of a huge range of official publications which also includes command papers (as well as legislation, bills, parliamentary debates from Hansard) and offers instant, searchable access. A pdf of the relevant official publication is posted on the date of its print publication. It also has RSS feeds which are of great value to professionals, alerting them to upcoming issues. It is also valuable because it has all the official documents in one place, so you do not have to look at a number of different sites. It covers UK Scottish, Welsh and Northern Irish legislation and parliamentary papers. However, your institution may not have a subscription.

> ### GOOD PRACTICE WITH INTERNET RETRIEVAL AND EVALUATION OF OPEN ACCESS MATERIAL

When you are not using subscription materials, or free official documents online but using public domain free access material it is important to ensure you apply your mind as to whether what you have retrieved is of use. How can you work within good academic criteria to ensure the authority and reliability of your retrieved sources? You will be severely penalised for drawing on non-academic sources and you could end up learning wrong law. It is even possible to retrieve erroneously repealed legal rules, or school essays!

If you draw on your institution's electronic collection of subscribed materials, these will again have gone through the same type of academic quality control discussed above. They will have been filtered by your lecturers and your law librarian. However, your e-library may well be linked to databases and search engines that can retrieve less reliable material. It is possible to jump from one link to another and reach a site that is not academically sound. This section provides some guidance on being able to assess the reliability of retrieved electronic material, with the aim of locating relevant good quality academic information.

Obviously staying close to your e-library resources is one way of keeping to good quality material but there will be times when you wish to use material on the internet and it is wise to have some quality control strategies in place, particularly as anyone can put anything on the internet.

Previously you were referred to the Virtual Training Suite for Lawyers,[13] a resource that provides an excellent tutorial on ascertaining the reliability of retrieved internet sources. It suggests you ask yourself three important questions:

- **Who** has posted this?
- **Why** have they posted it?
- **When** was this information posted?

We will now consider each of these questions in more detail.

---

13 Fn 2.

Who has posted this?

Initially look for the name of the author, or the organisation issuing the information. Many websites will have a 'contact us' or 'about us' page. Check it to see how forthcoming the individual or organisation is about their aims and qualifications. You can also gain a lot of information from the website's address or URL (the uniform resource locator). Consider the web address for Canterbury Christ Church University's student induction pages.[14] Figure 9.2 shows how you can deconstruct this to learn about the organisation, the type of institution and its location.

If you have a good habit of searching for electronic academic information within your e-library you should be able to rely on your sources. But you should not take anything for granted.

Why have they posted it?

Consider what you can find out about the standpoint of the author. The information that you have accessed could be prejudiced towards one point of view. The importance of academic work is that it is able to sum up evidence on both sides of an argument and move to conclusions based on the weight of evidence. You may have retrieved highly emotive or persuasive material that is not academic. You need to look at any information given to the author, and the business they may be involved in. Is it a government site, a pressure group site, a lone writer with no credentials tied into an organisation? Is it a media or a news site? Is the source a journalist?

When was this information posted?

Information on the internet may have been correct when it was posted but, especially in law, it can easily become out of date. Always try to find the date when the webpage was last updated.

As you become more familiar with internet search techniques you will gain more knowledge of the types of sites that are reliable and those that should not be trusted. Open access internet sites rarely have academic content, so they may be of limited use for your work. However, material from news media and sites belonging to non-governmental organisations or important pressure groups can sometimes be valuable. If you know the source of the information, and understand what type it is (e.g., non-academic or academic, propagandist, and so on) you will be able to use it properly. For example, you may wish to subject standard news reporting to academic scrutiny and access a site to retrieve suitable data to interrogate.

Do not use open access sites for obtaining an overview of an area of study or research. It is highly likely that if you do so you will not obtain an overview that is reliable.

---

14 www.canterbury.ac.uk/induction/students accessed 24 April 2009.

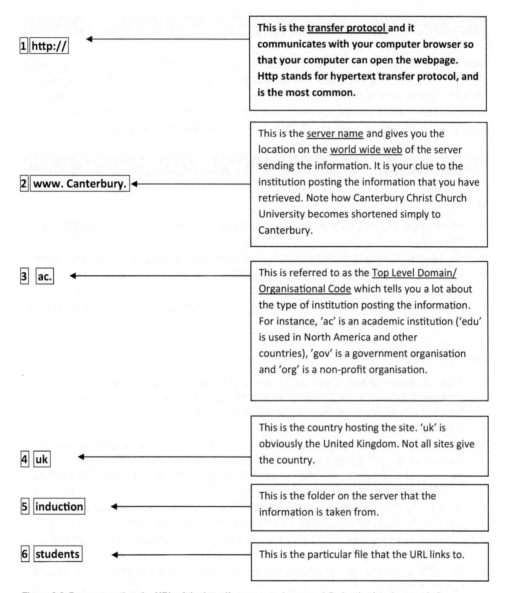

1 | http://

This is the <u>transfer protocol</u> and it communicates with your computer browser so that your computer can open the webpage. Http stands for hypertext transfer protocol, and is the most common.

2 | www. Canterbury.

This is the <u>server name</u> and gives you the location on the <u>world wide web</u> of the server sending the information. It is your clue to the institution posting the information that you have retrieved. Note how Canterbury Christ Church University becomes shortened simply to Canterbury.

3 | ac.

This is referred to as the <u>Top Level Domain/ Organisational Code</u> which tells you a lot about the type of institution posting the information. For instance, 'ac' is an academic institution ('edu' is used in North America and other countries), 'gov' is a government organisation and 'org' is a non-profit organisation.

4 | uk

This is the country hosting the site. 'uk' is obviously the United Kingdom. Not all sites give the country.

5 | induction

This is the folder on the server that the information is taken from.

6 | students

This is the particular file that the URL links to.

Figure 9.2 Deconstructing the URL of the http://www.canterbury.ac.uk/induction/students website

CONCLUSION

Now you are in a good position to competently access secondary texts for use in developing your understanding of the law you are studying. Do take the time to practise accessing print and online secondary material outside of being told to do so. The more familiar you become, the easier it will be to obtain your information; be aware of the range of online sites you can look at, and develop your methods of evaluation of sources.

CHAPTER SUMMARY

General

- An essential aspect of the study of law is the location and use of secondary texts about law.
- You need to develop efficient and competent research strategies for secondary texts.
- You should take care to consider the credibility, version and currency of any source you use.
- You need to be particularly careful to assess the reliability of open access secondary texts.

Journal articles

- A journal is a collection of articles (and book reviews and case comments) by a range of different writers. Law journals can cover the area of law generally or consider law from a specific disciplinary perspective.
- A journal can be academic or professional.
- All journals titles are abbreviated. If you do not know the abbreviation for a journal the online Cardiff Index to Legal Abbreviations gives a full listing (www.legalabbrevs. cardiff.ac.uk). The print only alternative is *Index to Legal Citations and Abbreviations* by D Raistrick (4th edn, Sweet and Maxwell, 2013).
- Westlaw, Lawtel, Lexis®Library and HeinOnline are all good sources for journals. Many full text articles are carried as well as abstract only articles.
- Blackwell Synergy allows online searches of all its own journals but you need to check what holdings your library has subscribed to.
- JSTOR is a good source of articles but it is an archive database and does not carry current articles.

Books

- Begin with your university catalogue.
- COPAC is an online amalgamated catalogue of important university, private and national libraries in the UK.

■ Print resources can give you access to new titles of books, see *Current Law Monthly Digest* and *Current Law Yearbook*.

Official documents

■ You will find that some official documents will be in print version in your library.
■ You can access them in print formats.
■ You can access them online in various date runs. The only official site is free, the national archives official documents. But this only contains full listings from 2005.
■ TSO has a subscription service, government publications online.

PART 3

READING AND UNDERSTANDING LAW

As students of law it is important you can competently read and understand legislation, case law, the law of the European Union and the mix of European civil law and English domestic law involved in the law relating to human rights. The three chapters in this part are designed to assist you with the task of understanding and using the primary texts of law.

Chapter 10 *How to read and understand domestic cases* focuses on how to understand the language of the judgments. It begins with an initial discussion of the doctrine of precedent, which is key to understanding the particular system judges adopt for reaching decisions in English cases. The doctrine maintains that if a similar case to one before a court has already been decided by the senior judiciary (in the Court of Appeal or the Supreme Court) then the case must be decided the same way by all courts (although the Supreme Court allows itself the limited practical ability to ignore an earlier similar decision of its own). This chapter also considers how to read a judgment, what to look out for, how to break into complex judicial language and how to write a good case note of a law report, and how to deal with a series of linked cases.

Chapter 11 *How to read and understand domestic legislation* focuses exclusively on legislation, discussing the layout of legislation, and how to make sense of the format and language of statutory provisions. It also discusses the role of statutory interpretation in the development of ideas about the meaning of words and phrases used in legislation. It contains a survey which includes presumptions, linguistic aids to interpretation, the role of headings, margin notes within the statute and the use of external documentation (extrinsic aids) to discern the intention of the statute (e.g. explanatory notes, Hansard and other allowed policy documentation).

Chapter 12 *How to read and understand ECHR and EU law* considers how to read and understand the treaties, secondary legislation and cases of EU law. Exercises allow students to work through the language of each area of law and develop skills for breaking into texts. Time is taken to discuss how to understand the language of the judgments of the respective courts, and how to read a judgment. With regard to human rights the focus is on how to understand the case law of the European Court of Human Rights, and the relationship between the ECHR and the Human Rights Act 1998.

By the end of Part 3 you should feel confident in your approach to handling and using primary law sources, because you have developed in your understanding of its construction, methods of interpretation and its language, an understanding you will continue to develop throughout your law studies.

HOW TO READ AND UNDERSTAND DOMESTIC CASES

10

'In almost every case except the very plainest, it would be possible to decide the issue either way with reasonable legal justification.'

Lord Hugh Macmillan

LEARNING OUTCOMES

After reading this chapter you should be able to:

- Understand the rationale and theory behind the doctrine of precedent.
- Explain the doctrine of precedent.
- Appreciate the difference between theoretical and practical considerations of precedent.
- Competently read a case and prepare a case note.
- Identify the constituent parts of the *ratio* of a case.

INTRODUCTION

An understanding of the doctrine of precedent is essential for the successful study of law. In this chapter we will briefly consider the theory of precedent before focusing on practical advice for reading a judgment by a judge or judges determining cases in a court of law. This chapter will also explain how to read both individual and related cases and look for the links between them. Finally, strategies will be suggested to help you break down the language and argument of a judgment.

LEGAL DISPUTE RESOLUTION IN COURT

The few legal disputes that cannot be resolved by negotiation or last minute settlements outside the court are determined by judges in the trial courts and, in an even smaller number of cases, by the senior judiciary in the appellate courts. The word 'few' must be stressed here: only about 4 per cent of all formally commenced disputes reach a hearing in court and many of these settle at the doors of the courtroom.

The decisions of judges are delivered orally in court, when the judge may read a pre-written judgment or speak from notes. These words spoken and recorded constitute the text that contains any legally binding rules. At the time of delivery, the judge's words are usually recorded verbatim by the court stenographer. In addition, law reporters, employed by publishers, may be in court taking shorthand notes. The record of all judgments will be kept by the court. But some decisions, thought to be important to the development or understanding of the law, will also be published commercially. A case that is chosen for publication in this way is called a law report. Each publisher will structure their reports differently, perhaps adding footnotes or summaries, but the words attributed to the judge have to remain a true and accurate record of the words actually spoken. The reports given the highest regard are those that allow the judge concerned to check the accuracy of the written record before publication.

Usually, judges in the civil courts and the appellate courts (both criminal and civil) will reflect upon the case before reaching a final decision – holding back, or reserving, judgment until a later date. In criminal cases the judge may sentence immediately after the jury has reached a verdict in the trial court, or call for reports and sentence at a later date. What judges say in their judgments is of immense importance, not only for the litigants, but for the development of the law.

The phrase 'common law' has different meanings according to the context in which it is used. One of its meanings relates to the legal rules developed by senior judges when deciding cases in the appeal courts (the Court of Appeal and the Supreme Court). Common law when used in this sense relates to legal rules that are not created by the authorisation of Parliament but through the act of the most senior judges in the English legal system.[1]

---

1 There has been, and continues to be, much argument among legal philosophers as to whether judges actually *make* or *create* law 'out of nothing' through their reasoning, or merely *declare* what the law has always been. Many judges state that they do not make the law, they discover it and thus *declare* what it has always been. This latter viewpoint is referred to as the *declaratory theory* of law making.

INTRODUCING PRECEDENT

In the English legal system if a judge knows that the case before the court is similar to an earlier decided case then the current case must be decided in keeping with the reasoning process used in that previous case. There are certain criteria that must be followed in determining not only whether the current case is similar to a previous case, but whether the court is bound, which depends on the court's position in the hierarchy of courts.[2] This process is known as the 'doctrine of precedent'. The doctrine is referred to by the use of a Latin phrase:

Stare decisis et non quieta movere: 'to stand by decisions and not disturb the undisturbed'.

In practice this phrase is shortened to:

Stare decisis: 'to let the decision stand'.

The practice of precedent is not a legally imposed requirement but one that has been developed as a matter of custom and practice in the higher courts since the nineteenth century. Although most legal systems have some notion of previous decisions being taken into account when new cases are decided, in the English legal system it is a practice enforced by the senior judiciary with an unparalleled rigour which makes the English legal system unique among *all* others.

A key part of a lawyer's job is to research previous cases meticulously in order to help them predict the outcome of the current case – after all, there is no point in going to court if the exact point the client wishes to make has already come before a court and been determined to his detriment. The doctrine of precedent as it stands is therefore a useful tool although the possibility of a different interpretation being placed, for example, on the meanings of words that were previously thought to be settled can never be ruled out.

Persuasive precedents

In addition to those precedents that are binding there are also a group of precedents that are persuasive only. That means that they are of sufficient standing to be taken seriously but are not binding because they are from another common law legal system, or from the Judicial Committee of the Privy Council. For example the case of *Attorney General of Jersey v Holley*[3] was a Privy Council case. However, it had a bench of seven judges, all of whom were also senior judges in the House of Lords at that time. Because of this the case dealt with identical law to the English, but took a different approach and clarified doubts.

---

2   See Chapter 2 for a discussion of the hierarchy of courts.
3   [2005] UKPC 23; [2005] 2 AC 580 (PC)

That case was subsequently referred to in the English senior courts and precedents were set using it as a persuasive precedent.

Relationship between legislation and precedent

If the law created by the authority of Parliament (legislation) is in conflict with a common law principle developed by judges, it will *always* overrule common law.[4] Judges therefore must implement statutory law even if it is in conflict with existing applicable common law rules.

Requirements for an effective system of precedent

The doctrine of precedent requires:

- An effective system of law reporting and/or an effective system of accessing court transcripts of judgments.
- A clear hierarchical court structure.
- Clear rules of practice setting out the duties of and responsibilities of judges in each court with regard to the doctrine of precedent.

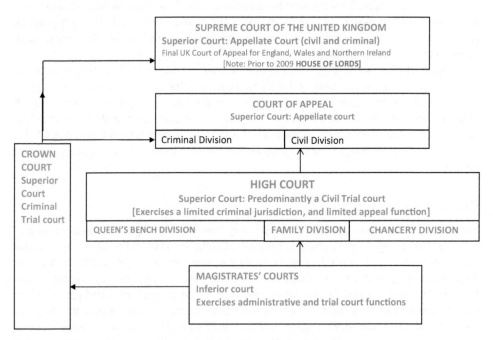

Figure 10.1 UK court structure: with arrows showing hierarchical relationships

---

4   See Chapter 1 on the sovereignty of Parliament.

Hierarchy of the courts

The hierarchy makes clear which courts can overrule the decisions of other courts in appeals[5] and is fundamental to an understanding of when a given court is bound by a previous case.

Generally a court is bound by precedents of those courts that are above it in the hierarchy, and by precedents previously established in the same court, though there are some exceptions. Each court is responsible for drawing up its own practices. Changes are made by 'practice statements' which are published in the law reports.

Understanding the theory of the doctrine of precedent

Many legal theorists and practitioners have attempted, over the years, to give precise definitions of the English doctrine of precedent. No one is completely right or wrong and the definitions vary. However, a few theoretical ground rules can be established, which at least place the operation of the doctrine of precedent within a context we have already discussed. For instance:

- judges at all levels of the court hierarchy *must follow* similar decisions of the higher courts;
- judges in the Supreme Court have the freedom to decline to follow their own previous decisions.

From a theoretical as well as a practical point of view, this strict adherence to precedent brings the following benefits to the legal system:

- certainty of the law;
- curbs arbitrary decisions;
- maintenance of equality;
- provides a rational base for decision making.

Some argue that the doctrine also brings disadvantages. It can:

- make the law inflexible;
- force legal change to be slow and convoluted;
- encourage tedious hair-splitting tendencies in legal argument.

Key to the operation of the doctrine is the meaning of 'similar' which we will now consider in light of differing academic views.

What does 'similar' mean?

How similar must a previous case be before it becomes a precedent? The facts of cases usually vary in some way and the doctrine does not specify that the case must be identical.

---

5   See Chapter 2.

Sometimes, counsel for the litigants will strenuously argue that previous cases are not precedents because they can be distinguished on their facts. In other words, they are not similar.

There is no single definition of the word, 'similar', and this is where the judge can bring subjective influences into the decision making processes. He or she can determine what 'similarity' is in the current case weighed against the precedent; in this way, extremely subtle 'differences' can be found between two cases.

Law is about life and life rarely replicates itself exactly, but trends and degrees of similarity can be noted. Figure 10.2 sets out some questions that are important to the issue of similarity:

Q: Must the law in the binding case be similar to the law now?	Q: What happens if there are small differences in the facts of each case?	Q: What if there are small differences in the law?
•A: Yes	•A: It depends. If these small differences are material facts, the binding case will possibly be applicable	•A: It depends on the differences. The same legal rule although perhaps in another place may constitute 'similar'

Figure 10.2 Q & As on similarities

Dealing with the slippery issues of similarity is a difficult and interpretative exercise. But once you are able to determine that a previous case is similar, then next one must consider 'how can the reasoning in the case be extracted?'

Finding, understanding and using the reasoning in a case

Cases defined as similar must also be decided in accordance with the same *reasoning* process, since the actual doctrine of precedent refers to adherence to the *reasons* for deciding past cases. But how does one find that reasoning?

Wambaugh,[6] a theorist working in America in the late nineteenth century, suggests that one way of ascertaining the reason for the decision (the *ratio decidendi*) is to look for a general rule of law in the judgments and test whether it is foundational for deciding the case by translating it into the negative form. You can then see if the case would have been decided differently. This negative method of finding the *ratio* or rule is illustrated in Figure 10.3.

Another respected legal theorist, Goodhart, wrote an influential article 'Determining the ratio decidendi of a case' which refers far more to the *principle* in the case than the *ratio*.[7] Goodhart emphasises the consideration of facts:

- What are the material facts, as found by the judge?
- What is the judge's decision?
- Unless there is a new material fact (or there are some missing material facts) a future court, depending upon its place in the court hierarchy, and thus its obligations under the doctrine of precedent, must follow it.

---

6   E Wambough, 'The study of cases 1894' cited in R Cross and JW Harris *Precedent in English Law* (Clarendon Press, Oxford, 1991), 52–53.

7   A Goodhart, 'Determining the ratio decidendi of a case' 22 *MLR* 117.

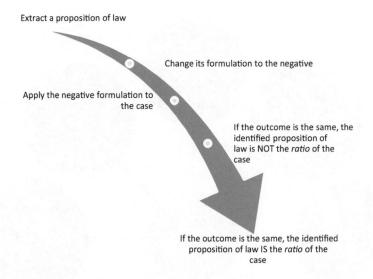

Extract a proposition of law

Change its formulation to the negative

Apply the negative formulation to the case

If the outcome is the same, the identified proposition of law is NOT the *ratio* of the case

If the outcome is the same, the identified proposition of law IS the *ratio* of the case

Problem: this method is designed to work only with one proposition of law

There can be more than one proposition in a case.

Figure 10.3 Wambaugh's method for location of the precedent

A major problem with Goodhart's suggested method is his emphasis upon the facts. Although it can be said that reading a judgment in the light of the facts of the case is a core requirement of the doctrine, attention also needs to be given to the way that the case is:

- argued;
- pleaded (exactly how have the lawyers formally lodged the complaint?);
- reasoned,

in relation to other precedents.

Wambaugh, Cross and Goodhart's methods are summarised in Figure 10.4.

Even when considered together, there are still problems. In particular:

- What should an interpreter do when there is a decision without reasons? Can the *ratio* be inferred?
- What can be done with the diversity of forms of judgments?

These are matters you need to think about theoretically.

Figure 10.4 Differing methods of finding the *ratio*

The differing strengths of a precedent

While it is true to say that the *ratio decidendi* of a previous case comes from the language of the judgment, as an interpreter, the judge in a later case can bring new meanings to the law.

In the senior appellate courts three, five or seven judges can sit in a given appeal. Each can give judgment, although often a judge will simply concur. Often in an appeal case there will be a clear majority in agreement with regard to both the outcome of the case and the reasoning that supports that outcome. A majority judgment by the senior judiciary in agreement on outcome and reasoning creates a strong precedent as it represents the *ratio* of the majority of the court.

At times there may be one or more minority judgments. In such cases, there will be agreement with the majority view that a particular party should win the case – that is they agree on outcome. However, there may be disagreement with the majority view of the legal reasoning process leading to that decision. Each of these minority judgments represents a reasoned judgment with a *ratio*. Unless all of those in the minority agree with each other it is possible to have several different *ratios*. If several respected senior judges agree in their minority judgment then it is possible to argue in certain circumstances in a later case that the precedent of the majority should be overridden in favour of the minority view. An appreciation and understanding of such complexities of precedent could help you to achieve top marks in your assessments.

The implementation of the doctrine of precedent is difficult in those cases where there is no clear preferred *ratio*. But what if the different judges in a case agree on outcome and disagree on the reasons for that outcome?

Judges may also dissent on outcome but either agree or disagree with the majority *ratio*. Dissenting judgments do not form precedents. But it is possible with the passage of time that the dissenting view comes to be considered the prevailing view and later courts may be able to privilege that dissenting judgment.

A lack of agreement among judges about the reasoning process can weaken the precedent value of the case.

Consider, for example, these two different scenarios:

- The majority of judges agree to dismiss/allow the appeal on one ground. A minority of judges agree with the majority as to outcome, but base their decision on a different ground. In this situation, the *ratio* of the majority is binding and strong. The *ratio* of the minority may become the object of weighty consideration in a future case.
- The majority agree to dismiss/allow the appeal but there is no common ground as to why the appeal has been dismissed or allowed. In this situation, there is no clear majority in favour of any *ratio*. The case, therefore, lacks authority for the narrowest interpretation of the *ratio*. It is impossible to state clearly how such a case is viewed other than to treat it as a weak authority.

It is difficult if not impossible to come up with a clear formula that will always work for ascertaining the *ratio* of a case. Law is organic, about life, not mechanics. But a reasonable idea of the difficulties in ascertaining the *ratio* is a necessary and revealing step for any interpreter. Ignoring these difficulties will ultimately lead to simplistic and inadequate construction of legal arguments. If an argument is being made on weak, tenuous or stretched grounds, it is better to know that it is. Deciding whether a case is a precedent involves consulting a wide range of sources and using a broad range of skills. Figure 10.5 outlines a simplified version of the process outlining the questions you should ask.

Handling precedent in a series of cases

In your studies, you will be expected to read cases both in isolation and as a series of cases which over a course of years develop a principle of law or which demonstrate how a principle of law has been retained or changed.

Imagine that you are sitting as a judge in the Court of Appeal civil division and you are dealing with an appeal court case, Case E. Counsel for both parties have referred to Case A. Counsel for the appellant has argued that Case A is a precedent binding on you in your

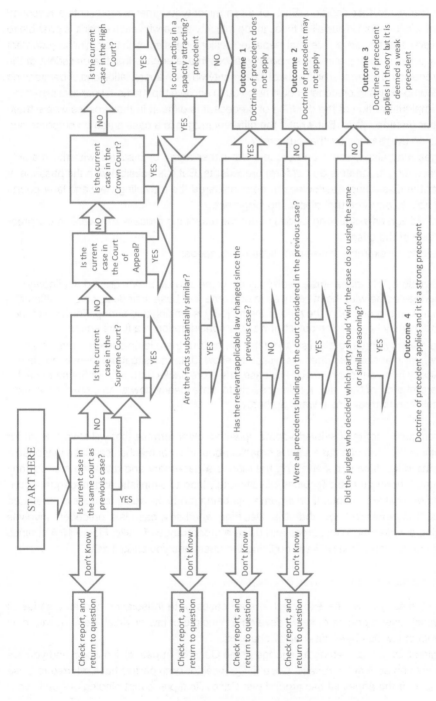

Figure 10.5 A flow chart to determine whether a previous reported law case (previous case) is a precedent for the case you are considering currently (current case)

determination of the dispute. Counsel for the respondent argues that it is not binding on you. Both have also referred you to cases B, C and that have followed Case A. Cases in the Court of Appeal and Supreme Court.

You will need to ascertain from an objective, neutral perspective which, if any, of these cases are binding on you. As you will know from your understanding of the court hierarchy, the Court of Appeal binds, and is bound by the Supreme Court.

You should then look at the facts of the cases and the legal rules applicable as well as the grounds of appeal in each case to determine at a basic level whether the case is similar and therefore potentially binding on you.

Your method might look like this:

- Ascertain the material facts of Case A and consider whether they are similar to the facts in Case E.
- Ascertain the legal rules applicable in Case A and consider whether they are similar to the legal rules to be applied in Case E.
- If you are dealing with similar facts and legal rules the Case could well be binding.
- Ascertain the *ratio* (or *ratios*) applicable in Case A and consider whether you agree with the formulation as given by counsel. They may have given conflicting formulations and you will have to ultimately agree with one not the other.
- Consider the judgments in the Cases B, C and D and their discussion concerning the *ratio* in Case A and the reasons for finding themselves bound by it.
- Finally, formulate a rule of law based on your interpretation of Cases A, B, C, D and apply this to your reasoning in Case E.

Interpreting precedent in practice

Part of the lawyer's particular expertise is in knowing how to quickly look through past cases to find relevant decisions which either support or oppose a client's case. Searches can be made, first, to pinpoint cases dealing with specific legal rules. A range of cases with similar facts can then be pulled from this first trawl of data. After careful reading, the lawyer must then construct detailed arguments drawing on those similarities with other cases that will support the client's position, or negate the potential precedent value of cases that would not help the client. This latter skill is called *distinguishing*, and it is particularly important for those who wish to argue that a precedent should not be followed.

A lawyer may need to argue convincingly that the part of the previous judgment that the opposing counsel is relying upon is not part of the reasoning process leading to judgment; that it was an 'aside' comment, based on a hypothetical situation (technically referred to as an *obiter dictum* comment). On the other hand, this may be the only argument that a lawyer has to support the client's position. If an *obiter dictum* comment was made by a senior judge in the Court of Appeal or the Supreme Court, and it is of direct relevance to the exact circumstances of the present case, then it could be argued that this is an important indicator of what that court would do if such a case came before it.

Where there is more than one judgment, the lawyer's task in ascertaining the strength of a precedent may be more difficult. It is possible that a dissenting judgment could eventually come to represent the majority view of an area of law. If the judge who is dissenting has a particular reputation for excellence, then the dissenting judgment will be seriously considered by those coming to read the case for the precedential value of the majority judgments.

An understanding of the doctrine of precedent and the ability to locate the reasoning in a case or series of cases is vital if the lawyer is to succeed in any of these tasks.

The practical implementation of the doctrine of precedent

Unfortunately for law students there are no simple shortcuts to understanding the practical everyday working of the doctrine of precedent in the courts. You will need to read, make notes on, interpret and think about the judgments you are reading and be confident in your ability to handle and use law reports.

Handling law reports

Figure 10.6 sets out the issues to be considered when handling law reports.

Engaging with the language of judgments

Law reports can present a challenge to students in terms of their legal content but also in terms of their usage of sophisticated and complex language. It is useful to consider the law report not just as an official public document but also as a literary text.[8] The examples and illustrations used may be drawn from many spheres, including politics, history, art, religion, or literature. They may include quotations from different languages or be liberally peppered with Latin legal maxims (such as *stare decisis*).

The new law student will need to engage with the sophisticated evaluation of the English legal system's most senior judges, whose judgments are not spoken for the lay person. These judges will have combined years of successful practice of the law with excellent language skills, in-depth knowledge of technical substantive law, and finely honed advocacy skills. They may discuss several complex issues simultaneously, applying and interpreting the law to the facts of specific disputes.

You will need to develop your skills in reading, language and writing in order to be able to obtain:

- a good grasp of the relevant area of substantive law;
- an appreciation of issues relating to language usage;
- an understanding of the doctrine of precedent in practice;
- a familiarity with legislation and its interpretation;
- a sound foundation in the mechanics of argument construction to make initial sense of the text.

---

8   In the past decade a growing number of scholars have become interested in exploring law as a literary text and in exploring literary texts as mirrors of the law (see Chapter 3). A particularly fascinating text is T Ziolkowski, *The Mirror of Justice: Literary reflections of legal crisis* (Princeton University Press, Princeton, 2003). For a classic work of fiction exploring the ideology of law you may be interested to read K Kafka, *The Trial* (Random House Press, New York, 1956). It is also available as an e-book free according to licensing conditions from Project Gutenberg, www.gutenberg.org.

1. COURT
- Name of the Court
- e.g. Supreme Court

2. CASE NAME
- Case Name:
- e.g. *George Mitchell v Finney Lock Seeds*

3. CITATIONS
- Citations
- Neutral citation post 2001. At the top of the printed page you will see the law report citation (e.g. [1983] 2 AC 803)

4. DATES
- The date of hearing is given, and the date of judgment.
- When judges reserve judgment to provide a written judgment then this date is indicated
- Remember not to assume that the date of the report is the date of the hearing

5. JUDGES
- The judges hearing the case are given
- It is important that you become familiar with the senior judges

6. CATCH WORDS
- These words are chosen by the reporter as important key issues dealt with in the case. They are used to categorise the case in law citators and databases. They refer to subject matter and to legislation (if any) considered in the case

7. HEADNOTE
- The overall summary of the dispute and outcome by reporter. The reporter sometimes can make a mistake and those who only read the summary will have an erroneous view of the law. So do not just read headnotes. You can find here information concerning the effect of the case on the law; it may indicate what case law was affirmed or overruled

8. CASES REFERRED
- A list of cases referred to in the course of judgment

9. HISTORY
- **Procedural history:** This sets out any previous hearings that have taken place in the course of the case reported e.g. previous appeals and the detail of the trial at first instance

COUNSEL
- Names of counsel are given

JUDGMENT(S)
- The judgment will give the relevant (material) facts of the case and reasoning

Figure 10.6 Issues to be considered when handling law reports

Law reports at appellate level

Law reports at appellate level fall into two broad categories:

(1)   Those cases where the judge(s) have extracted a 'new' legal rule from close considera-tion of previous cases in order to give a legal claim that had not previously been known or certain. There may have been a general agreement that such a rule existed but no such rule had been specifically created by an institution with the power to do so (the court or, of course, Parliament). These can be described as cases that are **sources of law**. They are strictly binding on courts according to their place in the hierarchy.

(2)   Those cases where the judge(s) are grappling with the meaning of legislative words and phrases in order to determine the case. These are cases involving **statutory interpretation**, that is, the judicial determination of the meaning of words and/or phrases in a statute. Here the decision of a senior court concerning the meaning of those words is treated as binding in subsequent cases until challenged.

From the mid-twentieth century the majority of cases have fallen into category 2: statu-tory interpretation. Often this application will be purely a matter of routine but sometimes doubts will arise about the meaning of words in the relevant legislation. The rules of statu-tory interpretation will be discussed in more detail in Chapter 11.

Reading a law report: a series of guided exercises on George Mitchell (Chesterhall) Ltd v Finney Lock Seeds *[1983] 2 AC (*George Mitchell *case)*

We will now turn to a range of practical demonstrations concerning how to read a law report using the *George Mitchell* case. We will approach it using a range of detailed exer-cises and studies which, taken together, are designed to demonstrate a methodology for the competent reading of law reports, taking case notes, evaluating the case, and using it to construct legal arguments.

   We will deal with:

■   The anatomy of a law report, being comfortable with print and online formats.
■   Obtaining a general overview of the case.
■   Best practice when writing case notes.
■   Breaking into text generally and specifically.
■   How to engage in a detailed reading of the judgment in this case to assist with understanding and summarising. This is also designed to help you follow the analysis in the case of a complex issue of the relationship between the common law limiting liability for loss and protective statutory rules that run alongside them prohibiting use of the common law rules if certain statutory criteria apply.
■   Evaluation of the case to use it in the construction of legal argument.

   To best use these studies and exercises for the development of your understanding of read-ing law reports and the law it would be ideal if you have the Westlaw database version of the case open as well as the Westlaw pdf of the print version. While you will effectively have two win-dows with seemingly identical text, the print version layout is different and this should be noted.

The anatomy of a law report

Before you can read a law report with confidence it is essential to understand the layout of standard law reports. Indeed it is crucial to understand how a law report is compiled and to distinguish between the notes by the barrister who is reporting the case, earlier hearings prior to the appeal you may be reading and the judgments in the case you are reading.

Only the judgments given by the judges are the legal part of the report, capable of making common law or interpreting the existing common law and statutory law with legal authority.

Figure 10.7 shows you the differing parts of a law report, although you will not find these headings in the report itself. This is followed by Figure 10.8 which is a snapshot of the first two pages of the print version of the report of *George Mitchell v Finney Lock Seeds* as found in the ICLR Law Reports, Appeal Cases series. Follow the pdf version on Westlaw of original print version. Figure 10.8 is annotated with the headings in Figure 10.7.

The next few pages of the law report deal with the arguments of counsel which are followed by judgments beginning with Lord Diplock on page 809; he agrees with the judgment of Lord Bridge but wished to make a few salient points. Lords Scarman and Rothwell state on page 810 in two or three lines that they too agree with the judgment of Lord Bridge. It is Lord Bridge's judgment that we will dissect later in this series of exercises.

It is far more likely that you will use a database to read cases. It can give greater information. A quick search of the Westlaw database retrieves the reports of the three hearings in the case (in the High Court, the Court of Appeal and the House of Lords) as indicated by the screenshot in Figure 10.9.

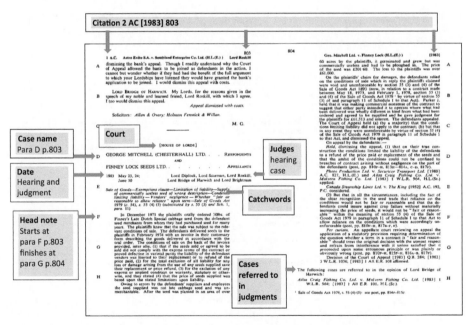

Figure 10.7 The anatomy of a standard law report (using the *George Mitchell* case)

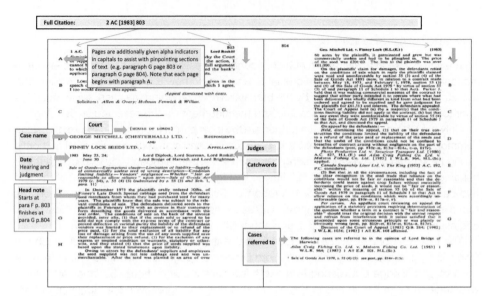

Figure 10.8 Anatomy of a law report: first two pages of ICLR Appeal Court law report of *George Mitchell v Finney Lock Seeds* [1983] 2 AC 803

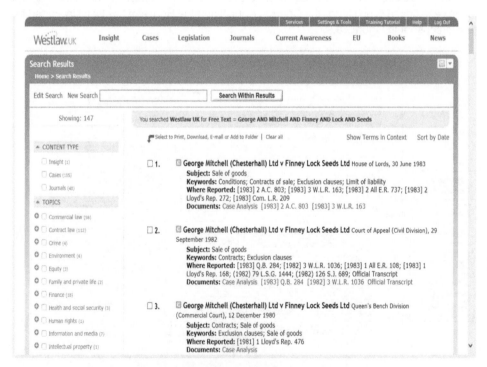

Figure 10.9 Screenshot of *George Mitchell v Finney Lock Seeds*

You will note that the first entry is the report of the case heard by the House of Lords on 30 June 1983. The second is the report of the Court of Appeal (civil division) hearing and the third is the report of the hearing in the Queen's Bench Division (commercial court). If you are in a rush it can be easy to access the wrong hearing of the case. Use the citation to check which one is the right one to read.

The first source contains two blue hyperlinks [1983] AC 803 and [1983] 3 WLR 163. You want to read the version that is highest in the hierarchy of law reporting – in this instance [1983] AC 803. When you first locate the case on Westlaw, it will appear on screen as illustrated in Figure 10.10. Note the arrow to the pdf version. Figure 10.7 shows the beginning of the pdf version.

Obtaining a general overview of the case

Initially you should approach the case as though you are engaging in it as an English comprehension exercise. This will show how far you can get by close and careful reading without a detailed knowledge of the law (in this case, the law of contract).

This exercise requires your *active* engagement. You will be given the context of the case, so that you are not working completely in the dark, before being guided through several stages of reading.

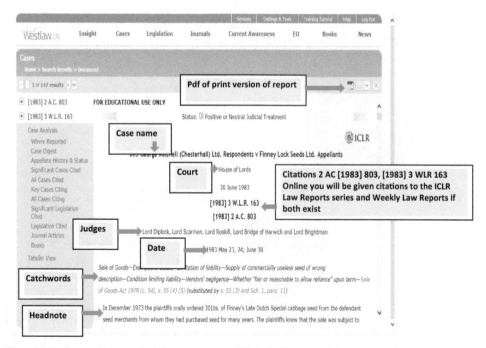

Figure 10.10 Screenshot of retrieved case of *George Mitchell v Finney Lock Seeds* indicating anatomy of the report as shown

The context of the case

Whilst you do not need any pre-knowledge for this exercise it is, of course, useful if you understand the legal context of the dispute in a case. For this reason, the basic framework of the law of contract is set out in Figure 10.11. The triangles denote the basic stages of making a contract, living or keeping it, and ending it.

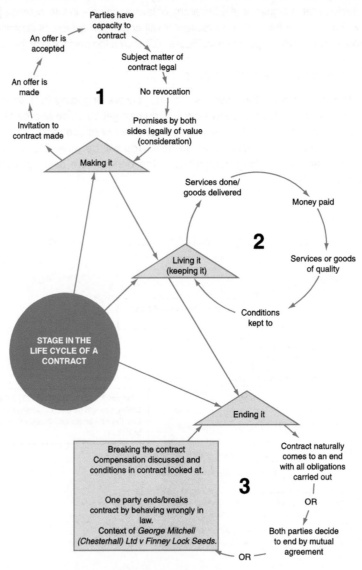

Figure 10.11 The basic framework of the law of contract

A contract is a legally binding agreement between two or more parties. Usually a contract will contain provisions that outline the compensation payable to one party should the other break the contract by not fulfilling their obligations under the terms of that contract.

The events which occur in *George Mitchell* are summarised in the square by the triangle labelled 'Ending it'. Look at the circular flow of reasons for ending the contract and note what each one is. This case does not concern a mutual agreement to end the contract, or it coming naturally to an end. This case is set in the text box dealing with one of the parties being accused of breaking the contract and as a consequence compensation is requested.

The facts of the case

The contract in this case concerned the purchase of cabbage seed by George Mitchell, the plaintiff company (today we would refer to them as the 'complainant') from Finney Lock Seeds, the defendant company. The contract contained a clause stating that damages for breaking the contract (breach of contract) were subject to a damages limitation clause. This clause provided that if the seeds were defective any damages payable would be limited to the replacement of the seeds purchased. The buyer would not be compensated for any other loss, for example loss of profits due to having defective seeds. The plaintiff company engaged in industrial farming and purchased the cabbage seeds to grow for the next year.

The seeds proved defective and the crop failed leading to large profit losses.

This case is particularly interesting because it is an example of a situation in which common law rules, created by the judges in previous cases, can operate alongside statutory rules dealing with the same subject.

The basic reading of the case

To identify the main issues in the case requires some determination. If you are able to master the methodology used here, you will be able to apply it to other cases.

Stage 1 has been divided into four tasks for you to engage with:

(1)   Locate the case online or in print, and turn to the judgment of Lord Bridge. Read it as quickly as you can but ensure you understand what you are reading, and time yourself. Do not take notes. If this reading takes you more than 60 minutes you need to work on your reading strategies generally.

(2)   Now read the entire law report, being aware of the different types of information given:
    (a)   names of the judges;
    (b)   court and dates of appeal;
    (c)   catchwords added by the publisher;
    (d)   summaries of the finding in previous courts dealing; with this case, constructed by the reporter;
    (e)   summaries of the arguments of counsel for both parties;
    (f)   all judgments will be reported as near to verbatim as possible;
    (g)   the outcome of the appeal you are reading.

(3)   The judgments that you read are the part of the law report that contains the law. As you read the judgment note how each paragraph begins and ends. You will often find signposts to meaning at the beginning and end of paragraphs, and they may contain indicators of the progression of a discussion or argument. Note any technical language. Look up words you do not understand in a good English dictionary or law dictionary. Try and extract the issue that is the ground of appeal and the reasoning that has led to the outcome in the case. Write notes as you go along to help your understanding. But try to avoid just writing it all out in your words!

(4)   Finally summarise in writing, in no more than 200 words, what this case is about:
   (a)   identifying the court, facts and legal issues relevant to the appeal;
   (b)   indicating the reasons for the decision in this case.
      (i) You will find that knowledge of facts or of the applicable rules taken alone will not help you identify the reasoning in the case. You need to look for passages in the text that discuss the reasons why those rules applied to those facts which led to a particular outcome being decided by the court.

DO NOT PROCEED ANY FURTHER UNTIL YOU HAVE QUICKLY READ THE CASE AND COMPLETED THE ABOVE TASKS 1–4.

Consideration of your summary for task 4

Look at your summary and see which of the following summaries, 1 or 2, is the closest match for your own.

Summary 1: Summary of *George Mitchell v Finney Lock Seeds* [1983] 2 AC 803

This is an appeal case in which the appellant, a commercial agricultural company, placed an order for a specific type of seed. The supplier sent the wrong seeds and the crop failed leading to a large loss of profits. The contract between the appellants and respondents for the supply of seed contained a limitation clause limiting compensation payable to the cost of replacement seeds. The major financial loss incurred by the buyer due to the wrong seeds being sent was far in excess of the cost of the seeds.

Summary 2: Summary of *George Mitchell v Finney Lock Seeds* [1983] 2 AC 803

This is an appeal case in the House of Lords. The appellant, a commercial agricultural company placed an order for a specific type of seed. The supplier sent the wrong seeds and the crop failed leading to a large loss of profits.

The contract between the appellants and respondents for the supply of seed contained a limitation clause limiting compensation payable to the cost of replacement seeds. The major financial loss incurred by the buyer due to the wrong seeds being sent was far in excess of the cost of the seeds.

The trial court said that the seller was liable to pay full compensation. The seller appealed to the Court of Appeal and lost. He then appealed to the House of Lords and again lost on the grounds that the Unfair Contract Terms Act 1977 took priority over the operation of the common law rule allowing such limitation clauses.

A particular complicating issue concerned whether the contract was made within a range of dates specified in the legislation.

At trial, and on appeal to the Court of Appeal and on appeal to the House of Lords, the buyer won the case. The court held that although at common law the limitation clause was operative, it was rendered inoperative by the application of the Unfair Contracts Act 1977. Therefore the buyer was entitled to receive compensation from the seller for loss of profits as well as the replacement of seeds.

How useful is summary 1?

The main problem with this summary is the lack of essential detail given, a list of specific issues are set out below:

- This summary is too general. It sets out the facts and the issue in the case, which is whether the limitation clause is operative.
- However, the actual dispute at trial and the actual ground of appeal in the Court of Appeal was not referred to, it just says there is an appeal and it is correct to say the buyer wants the seller to pay compensation. There is always a specific ground of appeal. What was it here?
- We do not know the court as it is not mentioned in the summary.
- We do not know why the court decided as it did.
- There is no basic information on dates, or applicable rules. In its present state the summary is unhelpful and could not be applied to a legal solution.

If your summary only referred to the matters in summary 1, or did not refer to all of the matters in summary 2, you need to revise your approach to reading for sense.

Always consider what a reader of your summary needs to know to make sense of the case, and apply it to other situations.

What is useful in summary 2

It gives a much fuller summary of the facts, and details the reasons for the dispute and makes clear the issue at stake is whether a common law rule on limitation clauses should

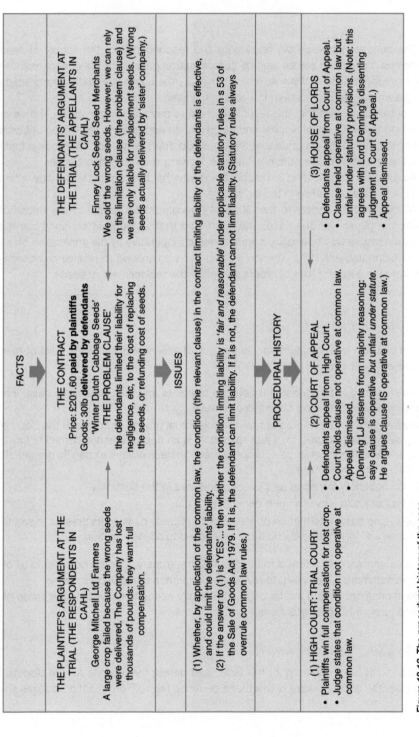

FACTS

THE PLAINTIFF'S ARGUMENT AT THE TRIAL (THE RESPONDENTS IN CA/HL)

George Mitchell Ltd Farmers
A large crop failed because the wrong seeds were delivered. The Company has lost thousands of pounds: they want full compensation.

THE CONTRACT
Price: £201.60 **paid by plaintiffs**
Goods: 30lb **delivered by defendants**
'Winter Dutch Cabbage Seeds'
'THE PROBLEM CLAUSE'
the defendants limited their liability for negligence, etc, to the cost of replacing the seeds, or refunding cost of seeds.

THE DEFENDANTS' ARGUMENT AT THE TRIAL (THE APPELLANTS IN CA/HL)

Finney Lock Seeds Seed Merchants
We sold the wrong seeds. However, we can rely on the limitation clause (the problem clause) and we are only liable for replacement seeds. (Wrong seeds actually delivered by 'sister' company.)

ISSUES

(1) Whether, by application of the common law, the condition (the relevant clause) in the contract limiting liability of the defendants is effective, and could limit the defendants' liability.
(2) If the answer to (1) is 'YES'... then whether the condition limiting liability is '*fair and reasonable*' under applicable statutory rules in s 53 of the Sale of Goods Act 1979. If it is, the defendant can limit liability. If it is not, the defendant cannot limit liability. (Statutory rules always overrule common law rules.)

PROCEDURAL HISTORY

(1) HIGH COURT: TRIAL COURT
- Plaintiffs win full compensation for lost crop.
- Judge states that condition not operative at common law.

(2) COURT OF APPEAL
- Defendants appeal from High Court.
- Court holds clause not operative at common law.
- Appeal dismissed.
(Denning LJ dissents from majority reasoning: says clause is operative *but unfair under statute*. He argues clause IS operative at common law.)

(3) HOUSE OF LORDS
- Defendants appeal from Court of Appeal.
- Clause held operative at common law but unfair under statutory provisions. (Note: this agrees with Lord Denning's dissenting judgment in Court of Appeal.)
- Appeal dismissed.

Figure 10.12 The procedural history of the case

apply or whether the common law here is inoperative due to the application of the Unfair Contract Terms Act. However it still has problems:

- We do not have precise information on the grounds of appeal, just generalised grounds. You must always give the specific grounds of appeal.
- We still do not know **why** the Court of Appeal decided the case as it did. We are just told that the court noted the common law provision was inoperative because of the Unfair Contracts Terms Act 1977. We do not have the reasoning in the case. Yet the reasoning is key for an understanding of the operation of the doctrine of precedent.
- We do not know the case law establishing the common law rules.
- We do not have precise information on applicable statutory rules.
- We do not have the basic information on the judges sitting and the dates of hearing.

If your summary contained all of the information in summary 2 you are certainly on the right track. If not, do take the time to consider why you did not pick up on the points in the summary. Did you read too quickly, or did you not fully understand what you were reading, or did you fail to take notes to help you? Were you confused by the language of the judgment? Are you a slow reader? It is particularly important to know the procedural history of the case. Look at Figure 10.12 which gives information on this point gained from a reading of the headnote and confirmed in reading of the judgments. Remember, details in the headnote could be wrong so do check in the judgments.

We will return to these summaries at the end of this chapter in the section 'writing a usable case note'. Constructing a competent case note of a law report is the core skill for all students and practitioners.

How to break into difficult text

You will no doubt have felt during your construction of your case note that it was difficult to identify and understand the main issues in the case; even at the level of basic comprehension this is not an easy task. Whilst it may not be too difficult to locate the specific sentences where the judge says what the issues are, you may have to work hard to reach a place of understanding, as the judgment will inevitably include unfamiliar vocabulary, unfamiliar legal references, complex grammatical structures and dense, perhaps dry, text.

In his judgment Lord Bridge gave a particular label to the limitation clause at the centre of the case. He called it 'the relevant condition' and identified two issues in the case on page 811 at paragraphs G–H of his judgment.

> **G** The first issue is whether the relevant condition, on its true construction in the context of the contract as a whole, is effective to limit the appellant's liability to a refund of the price of the seeds ('the *common law issue*'). The second issue is whether, if the common law issue is decided in the appellant's favour,

> they should nevertheless be precluded from reliance on this limitation of lia-
> bility pursuant to the
> **H** provisions of the modified s 55 of the Sale of Goods Act 1979 which is set
> out in para 11 of Schedule 1 to the Act and which applies to contracts made
> between 18 May 1973 and 1 February 1978 (the *statutory issue*).

Lord Bridge at page 811 (print or pdf Westlaw version).

Although at first sight this text is difficult to follow, note that Lord Bridge gives the two issues in the case shorthand labels, as set out below. (Both labels are *underlined* in the blue text box above.)

(1)   The first issue concerns whether the limitation clause is effective and limits the liability of Finney Lock Seeds. He calls this the 'common law issue'.

(2)   The second issue only needs discussion if the answer to (1) is that the limitation clause is effective. The question then is whether statutory protection should override the common law rule and prohibit the seller from relying on the limitation clause. This is the 'statutory issue'.

The entire text is difficult so how do you break into it? The following section gives some strategies for breaking down text into manageable sections using the text in the blue text box above.

A first strategy for breaking into the text is to remember that each paragraph is connected to the paragraphs above and below it. If you are ever stuck with your reading, stopping and re-reading the paragraphs above and below the one you are struggling with may be enough to resolve your difficulty. Each paragraph usually contains a main topic sentence which is then elaborated upon in the remaining sentences.

STRATEGY 1

One way of trying to understand a paragraph that is causing you problems is to set it out with divisions and spaces. The text above in the blue text box has been set out in such a manner in Figure 10.13 below annotated. Figures 10.14 and 10.15 demonstrate the annotation of the language of paragraph G and H. Figure 10.14 deals with the first issue, and Figure 10.15 deals with the second issue.

This activity will reveal where you lack understanding, highlight the areas of interconnection and help you to identify words and phrases that need clarification. Remember that where a statute is concerned the actual words are *fixed* in law by the statute. When dealing with a judgment, any common rules contained and constructed in the judgment do not fix rules with specific words. It is said that the decisions of judges state rules in an *unfixed* verbal format.

G The first issue **is-**:

whether the relevant condition,
[on its true construction in the context of the contract as a whole]

is effective
[to limit the appellant's liability to a refund of the price of the seeds
('the-common law issue').]

H The second issue **is-**:

whether,
if the common law issue is decided in the appellant's favour,

they should nevertheless

be precluded from reliance
on this limitation of liability

pursuant to the

provisions of the modified s 55 of the Sale of Goods Act 1979
which is set out in para 11 of Schedule 1 to the Act

and which applies to contracts
made between 18 May 1973 and 1 February 1978
('the statutory issue').

Figure 10.13 Verbatim text of G & H of Lord Bridge's judgment on p 811 set out in different text layout to aid understanding

STRATEGY 2

The text could be set out as a diagram, and this is illustrated by Figure 10.14 which deals with the first issue referred to in para G of the judgment. Additionally Figure 10.14 has been annotated using three 'Understanding check' boxes in white. These pose questions or give information. They could also be used in conjunction with the text layout in Figure 10.13. The white boxes test your understanding of the text you are reading and its context. It is essential to relate what you are reading back to information you already possess and view it in light of that information. Context is everything in the process of reading law reports.

STRATEGY 3

Figure 10.15 deals with paragraphs G and H in Lord Bridge's judgment, dealing only with the second issue. It takes the whole text approach without reformatting its layout as in

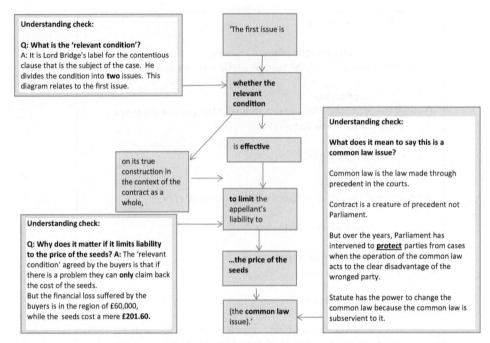

Figure 10.14 Verbatim text of Lord Bridge from page 811, with annotations to check for understanding

Figure 10.13 and gives annotations that purely relate to the relationship of one part of the text to another. We could more formally call it a diagram giving only internal annotation. No external information beyond the words of the text is given (unlike the annotations in Figure 10.14 which deal with external matters to aid understanding).

You can use any method you like that works for you to break into difficult text and ascertain its meaning in context.

How to engage in a detailed reading of the judgment in this case to assist with understanding and summarising

Preliminary matter: the procedural history of the case

Before moving on to explore Lord Bridge's opinion in detail, it is useful to ensure that you understand the procedural history of this case. You may find it useful to glance back to Figure 10.12 and note the basic procedural history outlined there. This will enable you to obtain an appreciation of the differences in opinion by the various judges who have considered the case before its arrival in the House of Lords.

Initially the case was won by the buyers of the seed, in the trial court (the High Court). The buyers were the original claimants,[9] George Mitchell (Chesterhall) Ltd. The sellers of the seed, Finney Lock Seeds, (the defendants) in the High Court immediately appealed to the Court of Appeal, where they become the appellants, and they again lost. This did not deter

---

9   Although at the time of this case in 1983 they would have been called plaintiffs.

them and they appealed to the House of Lords, where they also lost. There was a lot of money at stake: the difference between the £201.60 that the seeds cost or the £90,000+ that the trial judge awarded for loss of profits.

Having read and considered the wording of the two issues in the case, we can see that if the appellants succeed in issue 1 they may still fail overall if they fail over issue 2. Can you understand why? (The answer is in the first sentence setting out 'the second issue', see Figure 10.15.) Logically, one would expect Lord Bridge to commence with the arguments over issue 1, the common law issue, as this is the gateway to an argument over issue 2 which would only take place if issue 1 is decided in the appellant's favour. Until all of these matters are linked and understood it is not possible to fully comprehend the reasoning in the case.

By now you will have read Lord Bridge's speech several times and you should appreciate that the arguments in this case are quite complex.

Very early on in his judgment, Lord Bridge organises the disputed limitation by saying that 'the issues in the appeal arise from three sentences in the conditions of sale' and are

Understanding check of the internal language of the text: The second issue only has to be determined if the court decides that at common law the limitation clause applies in the appellant's favour. If they decided that it does the court will then look at the statutory provision to see if it prohibits the appellants from relying on the common law limitation

G ...

The **second issue** is whether, if the common law issue is decided in

the **appellant's favour**, they should nevertheless be precluded from

H reliance on this **limitation of liability** pursuant to the provisions of

the **modified s55** of the Sale of Goods Act 1979 which is set out in

para 11 of Schedule 1 to **the Act** and which applies to contracts made

between 18 May 1973 and 1 February 1978 (the statutory issue).

Understanding check of the internal language of the text: This is the second issue, and is the decision as to whether the statute

Understanding check of the internal language of the text: The Sale of Goods Act 1979

Understanding check of the internal language of the text: The common law condition limits the liability of the appellants

Figure 10.15 Annotation of Lord Bridge's paragraphs G & H p 811 of his judgment

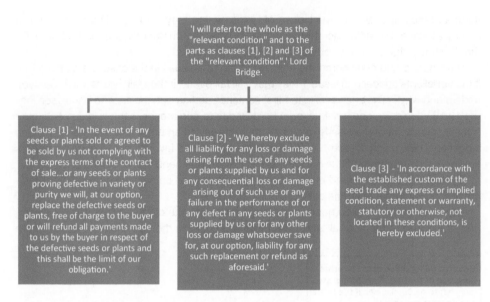

Figure 10.16 The imposition of relabelling on the relevant condition

part of the terms of the contract. To make things easy he numbers these as 1, 2 and 3. He then states that he will call each sentence a clause as shown in Figure 10.16. You will recall that we have already discussed the meaning of 'relevant condition', and the two issues Lord Bridge splits the case into.

It is important that you do not miss such relabelling; if you do you would not be able follow the discussion about it! The structure he imposes is set out below using his verbatim words.

In order to break into the whole judgment of Lord Bridge, it has been set out in a three column table. Column 1 allocates numbers to sections of verbatim text. Column 2 contains the verbatim text of Lord Bridge. Where it is considered useful each numbered section of verbatim text is summarised in column 3. As far as possible each numbered section relates to a paragraph.

Writing a précis of each paragraph helps you to understand each of the different ideas.

Once you have achieved mastery at reading law texts you will no longer need to write down your précis, but will automatically take in the contexts and signals in the text, only occasionally writing down an idea or proposition in an argument.

Each paragraph is a stepping stone, leading the reader to the end of the text and the conclusion of the argument. As paragraphs relate to one another you should not skip any in your reading. If you do not understand something in a paragraph, read the paragraphs before and after it to help clarify the issues. If you find references you do not understand cast your eyes back to see if this has already been clarified.

Lord Bridge's judgment has been split into 22 sections of text which are set out in Table 10.1.

Activity

(1)   Read Lord Bridge's judgment from numbered text [1]–[22].

(2)   As you read, without reading the summary in column 3, consider whether you understood the original text. If not, why not?

(3)   Try to classify the function of each paragraph under headings such as:

- descriptive;
- setting out facts;
- procedural;
- conclusion;
- proposition or point in an argument;
- inference;
- evidence.

Identifying the function of individual paragraphs and clusters of paragraphs is one way to organise a text in terms of its arguments and its proofs. Paragraphs build argument by laying out propositions and evidence (proofs). This will help you to identify the arguments and see how the text builds up to a final decision.

(4)   Summarise only the essential detail of each paragraph. If you do not understand what the paragraph is saying remember the strategy of looking at paragraphs above as well as immediately below to search for understanding and sense.

Check each of your paragraph summaries against those provided in Table 10.1, asking yourself whether:

- your summary contains ALL of the same information;
- you missed anything;
- the summary paragraphs in Table 10.1 are easier to understand and, if so, consider why this might be.

A quick review of the paragraph summaries in Table 10.1 begins to reveal the patterns in the argument that Lord Bridge is constructing. Re-reading the paragraphs while looking at the statutory diagrams in Figures 10.17 and 10.18 (in Table 10.1) allows the argument to be reviewed whilst looking at the entire provision in s 55 of the Sale of Goods Act 1979.

The paragraph approach has also isolated the common law issue and the statutory issue. Reviewing Figure 10.12 above, dealing with the facts, issues and procedural history enables you to appreciate the differences between the reasoning in the Court of Appeal and the House of Lords, even though both courts reached the same decision.

At this stage, it should be possible to identify the precise rationale behind the court's view of the common law issue and the statutory issue. It should also be possible to pinpoint precisely the statutory areas of relevance and how the court dealt with the issue. Figure 10.19 provides a summary of this information in diagrammatic form.

As your proficiency in reading cases develops, you may find you are able to move straight to a diagrammatic representation, although, ultimately, a brief conventional textual note should be made to supplement the diagram.

TABLE 10.1 COMPARING VERBATIM TEXT OF LORD BRIDGE'S JUDGMENT IN *GEORGE MITCHELL V FINNEY LOCK SEEDS* ILLUSTRATING ACCURATE SUMMARISING OF THE RANGE OF LEGAL ISSUES AND THE ARGUMENT AS IT IS BUILT BY LORD BRIDGE

Para	Lord Bridge: Judgment (divided into numbered paragraphs). *George Mitchell v Finney Lock Seeds* 1983 2 AC 803: VERBATIM TEXT	Summary of paragraph
[1]	My Lords, the appellants are seed merchants. The respondents are farmers in East Lothian. In December 1973 the respondents ordered from the appellants 30 lb of Dutch winter white cabbage seeds. The seeds supplied were invoiced as Finney's 'Late Dutch Special'. The price was £201.60. Finney's Late Dutch Special was the variety required by the respondents. It is a Dutch winter white cabbage which grows particularly well in the acres of East Lothian where the respondents farm, and can be harvested and sold at a favourable price in the spring. The respondents planted some 63 acres of their land with seedlings grown from the seeds supplied by the appellants to produce their cabbage crop for the spring of 1975. In the event, the crop proved to be worthless and had to be ploughed in. This was for two reasons. First, the seeds supplied were not Finney's Late Dutch Special or any other variety of Dutch winter white cabbage, but a variety of autumn cabbage. Second, even as autumn cabbage the seeds were of very inferior quality	Facts set out. The seller delivered the wrong cabbage seed and inferior seed to the buyer who, as a consequence, had a failed crop with grave financial consequences. The contract of sale limited the seller's liability to a refund of the price of the seeds
[2]	The issues in the appeal arise from three sentences in the conditions of sale indorsed on the appellants' invoice and admittedly embodied in the terms on which the appellants contracted. For ease of reference it will be convenient to number the sentences. Omitting immaterial words they read as follows: (1) In the event of any seeds or plants sold or agreed to be sold by us not complying with the express terms of the contract of sale . . . or any seeds or plants proving defective in varietal purity we will, at our option, replace the defective seeds or plants, free of charge to the buyer or will refund all payments made to us by the buyer in respect of the defective seeds or plants and this shall be the limit of our obligation. (2) We hereby exclude all liability for any loss or damage arising from the use of any seeds or plants supplied by us and for any consequential loss or damage arising out of such use or any failure in the performance	Issues arise from three sentences in the conditions of sale. These are set out and identified. Lord Bridge states he will call the contentious limitation clause 'the relevant condition', and will refer to each sentence as a clause, so clauses 1, 2, 3. If a student reads carelessly this important explanation will be overlooked then the phrase 'relevant condition' and 'clauses 1, 2, 3' will

	of or any defect in any seeds or plants supplied by us or for any other loss or damage whatsoever save for, at our option, liability for any such replacement or refund as aforesaid. (3) In accordance with the established custom of the seed trade any express or implied condition, statement or warranty, statutory or otherwise, not stated in these Conditions is hereby excluded. I will refer to the whole as 'the relevant condition' and to the parts as 'cll 1, 2, and 3' of the relevant condition	cause confusion when they are used later in the text to refer to his divisions of the contentious limitation clause
[3]	The first issue is whether the relevant condition, on its true construction in the context of the contract as a whole, is effective to limit the appellants' liability to a refund of £201.60, the price of the seeds (the common law issue). The second issue is whether, if the common law issue is decided in the appellants' favour, they should nevertheless be precluded from reliance on this limitation of liability pursuant to the provisions of the modified s 55 of the Sale of Goods Act 1979 which is set out in para 11 of Sch 1 to the Act and which applies to contracts made between 18 May 1973 and 1 February 1978 (the statutory issue)	Sets out the two issues as the common law and the statutory issues. Gives details of relevant legislation
[4]	The trial judge, Parker J, on the basis of evidence that the seeds supplied were incapable of producing a commercially saleable crop, decided the common law issue against the appellants on the ground that: ... what was supplied ... was in no commercial sense vegetable seed at all [but was] the delivery of something wholly different in kind from that which was ordered and which the defendants had agreed to supply. He accordingly found it unnecessary to decide the statutory issue, but helpfully made some important findings of fact, which are very relevant if that issue falls to be decided. He gave judgment in favour of the respondents for £61,513.78 damages and £30,756 interest. Nothing now turns on these figures, but it is perhaps significant to point out that the damages awarded do not represent merely 'loss of anticipated profit', as was erroneously suggested in the appellants' printed case. The figure includes, as counsel for the appellants very properly accepted, all the costs incurred by the respondents in the cultivation of the worthless crop as well as the profit they would have expected to make from a successful crop if the proper seeds had been supplied	Discusses the finding of the trial judge that under the common law the 'relevant condition' could not be relied upon by the sellers. The reason being the seed delivered was 'wholly different'. (As we have already noted, issue 2, the statutory issue, need only be dealt with if issue 1 is decided in favour of the sellers.)

TABLE 10.1—continued

Para	Lord Bridge: Judgment (divided into numbered paragraphs). *George Mitchell v Finney Lock Seeds* 1983 2 AC 803: VERBATIM TEXT	Summary of paragraph
[5]	In the Court of Appeal, the common law issue was decided in favour of the appellants by Lord Denning MR, who said ([1983] 1 All ER 108, p 113; [1983] QB 284, p 296): On the natural interpretation, I think the condition is sufficient to limit the seed merchants to a refund of the price paid or replacement of the seeds. Oliver LJ decided the common law issue against the appellants primarily on a ground akin to that of Parker J, albeit somewhat differently expressed. Fastening on the words 'agreed to be sold' in cl 1 of the relevant condition, he held that the clause could not be construed to mean 'in the event of the seeds sold or agreed to be sold by us not being the seed agreed to be sold by us'. Clause 2 of the relevant condition he held to be 'merely a supplement' to cl 1. He thus arrived at the conclusion that the appellants had only succeeded in limiting their liability arising from the supply of seeds which were correctly described as Finney's Late Dutch Special but were defective in quality. As the seeds supplied were not Finney's Late Dutch Special, the relevant condition gave them no protection. Kerr LJ, in whose reasoning Oliver LJ also concurred, decided the common law issue against the appellants on the ground that the relevant condition was ineffective to limit the appellants' liability for a breach of contract which could not have occurred without negligence on the appellants' part, and that the supply of the wrong variety of seeds was such a breach	Discusses the finding of Denning LJ in the Court of Appeal. Denning LJ thought the common law issue should be decided in favour of the sellers. He said that the wording of the condition was sufficient to cover the situation. Kerr and Oliver LJ decided the common law issue against the sellers. Kerr LJ's reasoning was that the condition would only cover them for *defects* in the *'correct'* named seeds. Not for delivery of the wrong seeds. Oliver LJ's reasoning was that the condition did not cover the breach because it only happened through the negligence of the seller
[6]	The Court of Appeal, however, was unanimous in deciding the statutory issue against the appellants	The Court of Appeal, however, was unanimous in deciding the statutory issue against the sellers
[7]	In his judgment, Lord Denning MR traces, in his uniquely colourful and graphic style, the history of the courts' approach to contractual clauses excluding or limiting liability, culminating in the intervention of the legislature, first, by the Supply of Goods (Implied	Refers to Denning LJ in Court of Appeal, tracing the history of the court's approach to limitation or

	Terms) Act 1973, and second, by the Unfair Contract Terms Act 1977. My Lords, in considering the common law issue, I will resist the temptation to follow that fascinating trail, but will content myself with references to the two recent decisions of your Lordship's House commonly called the two Securicor cases: *Photo Production Ltd v Securicor Transport Ltd* [1980] 1 All ER 996; [1980] AC 827 and *Ailsa Craig Fishing Co Ltd v Malvern Fishing Co Ltd* [1983] 1 All ER 101	exclusion conditions. Lord Bridge picks out two relevant cases (*Photo Production Ltd v Securicor Transport Ltd* [1980] 1 All ER 101 and *Ailsa Craig Fishing Co Ltd v Malvern Fishing Co Ltd* [1983] 1 All ER 101) and uses these to explore the common law issue. Note that the judge is beginning to deal with cases decided previously and commenting upon them in relation to whether he is bound by the doctrine of precedent
[8]	The *Photo Production* case gave the final quietus to the doctrine that a 'fundamental breach' of contract deprived the party in breach of the benefit of clauses in the contract excluding or limiting his liability. The *Ailsa Craig* case drew an important distinction between exclusion and limitation clauses This is clearly stated by Lord Fraser ([1983] 1 All ER 101, p 105): There are later authorities which lay down very strict principles to be applied when considering the effect of clauses of exclusion or of indemnity: see particularly the Privy Council case of *Canada Steamship Lines Ltd v R* [1952] 1 All ER 305 at 310 [1952] AC 192, 208, where Lord Morton, delivering the advice of the Board, summarised the principles in terms which have recently been applied by this House in *Smith v UMB Chrysler (Scotland) Ltd* 1978 SC (HL) 1. In my opinion these principles are not applicable in their full rigour when considering the effect of conditions merely limiting liability. Such conditions will of course be read *contra proferentem* and must be clearly expressed, but there is no reason why they should be judged by the specially exacting standards which are applied to exclusion and indemnity clauses	Lord Bridge brings up the phrase 'fundamental breach'. The word 'fundamental' suggests an important breach or break of the contract. The essence of the points made are that: – the *Photo Production* case made it clear that, even if there is a finding of fundamental breach of contract by one party, like the seller here, this finding does not stop a party, the seller, relying on limiting or excluding conditions in the contract; – the *Ailsa Craig* case drew distinctions between:

TABLE 10.1—continued

Para	Lord Bridge: Judgment (divided into numbered paragraphs). *George Mitchell v Finney Lock Seeds* 1983 2 AC 803: VERBATIM TEXT	Summary of paragraph
		limiting clauses and exclusion clauses Basically, limitation clauses should not be judged according to the strict principles applied to exclusion clauses, although they remain to be construed *contra proferentem* against the party claiming their protection (*contra proferentem* means construed strictly/against the party relying on it)
[9]	My Lords, it seems to me, with all due deference, that the judgments of the trial judge and of Oliver LJ on the common law issue come dangerously near to reintroducing by the back door the doctrine of 'fundamental breach' which this House in the *Photo Production* case had so forcibly evicted by the front. The judge discusses what I may call the 'peas and beans' or 'chalk and cheese' cases, i.e., those in which it has been held that exemption clauses do not apply where there has been a contract to sell one thing, e.g., a motor car, and the seller has supplied quite another thing, e.g., a bicycle. I hasten to add that the judge can in no way be criticised for adopting this approach since counsel appearing for the appellants at the trial had conceded 'that, if what had been delivered had been beetroot seed or carrot seed, he would not be able to rely on the clause'. Different counsel appeared for the appellants in the Court of Appeal, where that concession was withdrawn	Lord Bridge criticises the trial judge, Parker J, and the Court of Appeal judge, Oliver LJ, for trying to go back to the position before the *Photo Production* case. Lord Bridge said a fundamental breach *does not* stop a party relying on exclusions or limitation clauses
[10]	In my opinion, this is not a 'peas and beans' case at all. The relevant condition applies to 'seeds'. Clause 1 refers to 'seeds sold' and 'seeds agreed to be sold.' Clause 2	Lord Bridge points out that the condition applies to seeds

refers to 'seeds supplied'. As I have pointed out, Oliver LJ concentrated his attention on the phrase 'seeds agreed to be sold'. I can see no justification, with respect, for allowing this phrase alone to dictate the interpretation of the relevant condition, still less for treating cl 2 as 'merely a supplement' to cl 1. Clause 2 is perfectly clear and unambiguous. The reference to 'seeds agreed to be sold' as well as to 'seeds sold' in cl 1 reflects the same dichotomy as the definition of 'sale' in the Sale of Goods Act 1979 as including a bargain and sale as well as a sale and delivery. The defective seeds in this case were seeds sold and delivered, just as clearly as they were seeds supplied, by the appellants to the respondents. The relevant condition, read as a whole, unambiguously limits the appellants' liability to a replacement of the seeds or refund of the price. It is only possible to read an ambiguity into it by the process of strained construction which was deprecated by Lord Diplock in the *Photo Production* case [1980] 1 All ER 556, p 568; [1980] AC 82, p 851 and by Lord Wilberforce in the *Ailsa Craig* case [1983] 1 All ER 101, p 102	sold and indeed seeds were sold! Lord Bridge says that the condition unambiguously applies to the present situation
[11] In holding that the relevant condition was ineffective to limit the appellants' liability for a breach of contract caused by their negligence, Kerr LJ applied the principles stated by Lord Morton giving the judgment of the Privy Council in *Canada Steamship Lines Ltd v R* [1952] 1 All ER 303, p 310; [1952] AC 192, p 208. Kerr LJ stated correctly that this case was also referred to by Lord Fraser in the *Ailsa Craig* case [1983] 1 All ER 101, p 105. He omitted, however, to notice that, as appears from the passage from Lord Fraser's speech which I have already cited, the whole point of Lord Fraser's reference was to express his opinion that the very strict principles laid down in the *Canada Steamship Lines* case as applicable to exclusion and indemnity clauses cannot be applied in their full rigour to limitation clauses. Lord Wilberforce's speech contains a passage to the like effect, and Lord Elwyn Jones, Lord Salmon and Lord Lowry agreed with both speeches. Having once reached a conclusion in the instant case that the relevant condition unambiguously limited the appellants' liability, I know of no principle of construction which can properly be applied to confine the effect of the limitation to breaches of contract arising without negligence on the part of the appellants. In agreement with Lord Denning MR, I would decide the common law issue in the appellants' favour	Lord Bridge says that Kerr LJ (in the Court of Appeal) in finding for the seller had in fact misinterpreted what Lord Fraser had said about *The Canada Steamship v R* [1952] 1 All ER 303 in the *Ailsa Craig* case! This is an excellent paragraph for demonstrating the way in which judges argue about other cases, following, distinguishing, overruling or stating the precedent of a case erroneously. Lord Bridge decides the common law point in favour of the sellers in agreement with Lord Denning in the Court of Appeal

TABLE 10.1—continued		
Para	**Lord Bridge: Judgment (divided into numbered paragraphs).** *George Mitchell v Finney Lock Seeds* **1983 2 AC 803: VERBATIM TEXT**	**Summary of paragraph**
[12]	The statutory issue turns, as already indicated, on the application of the provisions of the modified s 55 of the Sale of Goods Act 1979, as set out in para 11 of Sch 1 to the Act. The 1979 Act is a pure consolidation. The purpose of the modified s 55 is to preserve the law as it stood from 18 May 1973 to 1 February 1978 in relation to contracts made between those two dates. The significance of the dates is that the first was the date when the Supply of Goods (Implied Terms) Act 1973 came into force containing the provision now re-enacted by the modified s 55, the second was the date when the Unfair Contract Terms Act 1977 came into force and superseded the relevant provisions of the Act of 1973 by more radical and far-reaching provisions in relation to contracts made thereafter	Lord Bridge turns to discuss the 'statutory' issue. We now begin to understand the reference to 'the Act' in issue 2 as set out by Lord Bridge at para 2. The modified s 55 of the Sale of Goods Act 1979 is set out. The Sale of Goods Act 1979 was a statute that was pure consolidation. (This means that it merely collected together the existing law and put it in one place.) Modified s 55 preserves the law between 18 May 1973 (the date that the Supply of Goods (Implied Terms) Act came into force) and 1 February 1977 (the date that the Unfair Contract Terms Act 1977 came into force)

[13] The relevant subsections of the modified s 55 provide as follows:

(1) Where a right, duty or liability would arise under a contract of sale of goods by implication of law, it may be negatived or varied by express agreement . . ., but the preceding provision has effect subject to the following provisions of this section. . . .

(4) In the case of a contract of sale of goods, any term of that or any other contract exempting from all or any of the provisions of s 13, 14 or 15 above is void in the case of a consumer sale and is, in any other case, not enforceable to the extent that it is shown that it would not be fair or reasonable to allow reliance on the term.

(5) In determining for the purposes of sub-s (4) above whether or not reliance on any such term would be fair or reasonable regard shall be had to all the circumstances of the case and in particular to the following matters – (a) the strength of the bargaining positions of the seller and buyer relative to each other, taking into account, among other things, the availability of suitable alternative products and sources of supply; (b) whether the buyer received an inducement to agree to the term or in accepting it had an opportunity of buying the goods or suitable alternatives without it from any source of supply; (c) whether the buyer knew or ought reasonably to have known of the existence and extent of the term (having regard, among other things, to any previous course of dealing between the parties); (d) where the term exempts from all or any of the provisions of s 13, 14 or 15 above if any condition is not complied with, whether it was reasonable at the time of the contract to expect that compliance with that condition would be practicable; (e) whether the goods were manufactured, processed, or adapted to the special order of the buyer . . .

(9) Any reference in this section to a term exempting from all or any of the provisions of any section of this Act is a reference to a term which purports to exclude or restrict, or has the effect of excluding or restricting, the operation of all or any of the provisions of that section, or the exercise of a right conferred by any provision of that section, or any liability of the seller for breach of a condition or warranty implied by any provision of that section . . .

Section 55, sub-ss (1), (4), (5) and (9) are set out. Students need to study s 55 carefully to ensure that they understand what it is providing for and that they can follow the discussion of it by Lord Bridge. To assist there follows an 'aside' dealing with understanding s 55.

TABLE 10.1 — continued

An aside: a consideration for the statutory rule of the modified s 55 of the Sale of Goods Act 1979

This is an appropriate moment to look in more detail at s 55 of the Sale of Goods Act 1979. To understand properly the development of the reasoning of the court on the statutory issue, it is vital to get to grips with the basic layout, interconnections and effect of the provisions. Often, students do not pay sufficient attention to such matters and then wonder why they cannot understand discussions!

The purely textual explanation is complicated and needs to be read in conjunction with the statutory provision. Two diagrams will follow:

(1)   Figure 10.17 sets out s 55 in its entirety. This enables the relationship between differing sub-sections and paragraphs to be seen. It will be annotated.

(2)   Figure 10.18 is a précis version of s 55, identifying the most relevant sections according to the facts of the case. The figure indicates whether the relevant section applies to this case, does not apply or whether it is unknown whether it applies.

Section 55 is highly complex and you should consider it in detail before we return to the rest of Table 10.1 and the judge's deliberation. It is often helpful for readers to stop and check their understanding, or to check their view against that of the judge. This reflection begins the process of evaluation. Please carefully study both diagrams and understand them.

Hopefully you now have a clearer picture of s 55. Often, students continue reading text when it is clear to them that they do not understand what they are reading. You should never go on reading when you know that you do not understand what you are reading. You should instead stop and return to that last point in the text when you did understand and re-read – slowly and carefully until you do understand, or at least have a partial understanding that stands a chance of growing as you read on. It may be helpful to try to create a diagram like Figure 10.18 to help you to understand.

In texts discussing complex issues, tiny connectors, if missed, rob the reader of understanding. A paragraph by paragraph reconsideration will often restore comprehension.

We can now return to the paragraph by paragraph summary where Lord Bridge is about to discuss s 55.

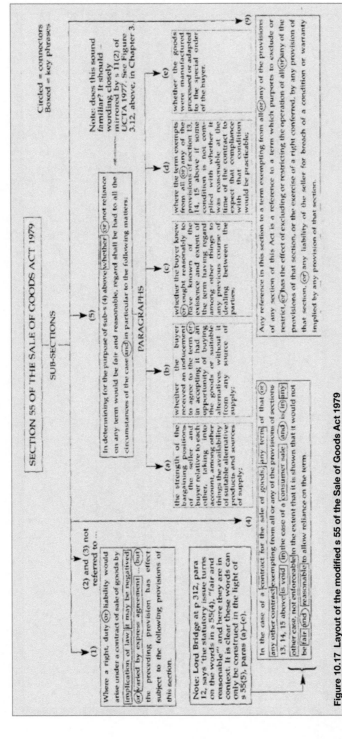

Figure 10.17 Layout of the modified s 55 of the Sale of Goods Act 1979

TABLE 10.1—continued

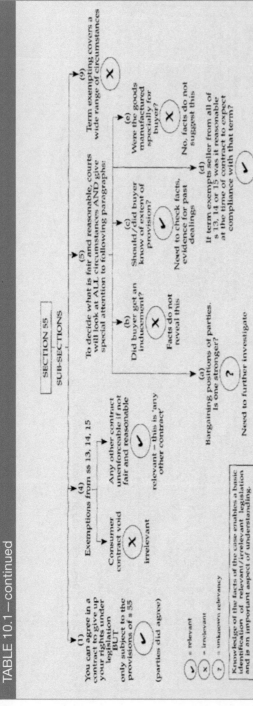

Figure 10.18 Revised diagram of section 55

| [14] | The contract between the appellants and the respondents was not a 'consumer sale', as defined for the purpose of these provisions. The effect of cl 3 of the relevant condition is to exclude, *inter alia*, the terms implied by ss 13 and 14 of the Act that the seeds sold by description should correspond to the description and be of merchantable quality and to substitute therefor the express but limited obligations undertaken by the appellants under cll 1 and 2. The statutory issue, therefore, turns on the words in s 55(4) 'to the extent that it is shown that it would not be fair or reasonable to allow reliance on this restriction of the appellants' liabilities, having regard to the matters referred to in sub-s (5). | Lord Bridge observes that the contract in question is not a consumer contract but 'any other contract': This information is obtained by a careful reading of s 55(4) plus knowledge of what a consumer sale is; look back at Figure 10.17 and re-read s 55(4). This contract is not a consumer contract and therefore falls under the second heading in s 55(4).

Lord Bridge further observes that cl 3 of the relevant condition exempts the seller from liability for breach of ss 13 and 14 of the Sale of Goods Act.

– This is a good example of the need to have an active dialogue with the text. Clause 3 is the third sentence of the relevant condition and the relevant condition is the condition limiting liability.

– How is this known? Because in paragraph 2 of his opinion Lord Bridge states (see précis above): issues arise from three sentences |

TABLE 10.1 – continued

Para	Lord Bridge: Judgment (divided into numbered paragraphs). *George Mitchell v Finney Lock Seeds* 1983 2 AC 803: VERBATIM TEXT	Summary of paragraph
		in the conditions of sale. These are set out and identified. He states he will call this the relevant condition, and will call each sentence a clause, so cll 1, 2, 3. Lord Bridge goes on to say that ss 13 and 14 provide that: items sold by description should correspond to the description; items sold should be of merchantable quality, and that cll 1 and 2 substitute for the full protection of the legislation the limited obligation to replace seeds or refund price of seeds. Lord Bridge sums up that the statutory issue depends on whether cll 1 and 2 are 'fair and reasonable' according to the criteria as set out in s 55(4) and (5).
[15]	This is the first time your Lordships' House has had to consider a modern statutory provision giving the court power to override contractual terms excluding or restricting liability, which depends on the court's view of what is 'fair and reasonable'. The particular provision of the modified s 55 of the 1979 Act which applies in the instant case is of limited and diminishing importance. But the several provisions of the Unfair Contract Terms Act 1977 which depend on 'the requirement of reasonableness', defined in s 11 by reference to what is 'fair and reasonable', albeit in a different context, are likely to come before the courts with increasing frequency. It may, therefore, be appropriate to consider how an original decision what is 'fair and reasonable' made	This is the first time that the court has considered the statutory power to interfere with the limiting or excluding liability that has been agreed between the parties at common law. This is a far reaching power to interfere with the freedom of individuals to contract. The court can say 'no', you cannot freely agree this, because, in our opinion, it is not fair and reasonable. The actual decision in this case

in the application of any of these provisions should be approached by an appellate court. It would not be accurate to describe such a decision as an exercise of discretion. But a decision under any of the provisions referred to will have this in common with the exercise of a discretion, that, in having regard to the various matters to which the modified s 55(5) of the 1979 Act, or s 11 of the 1977 Act direct attention, the court must entertain a whole range of considerations, put there in the scales on one side or the other and decide at the end of the day on which side the balance comes down. There will sometimes be room for a legitimate difference of judicial opinion as to what the answer should be, where it will be impossible to say that one view is demonstrably wrong and the other demonstrably right. It must follow, in my view, that, when asked to review such a decision on appeal, the appellate court should treat the original decision with the utmost respect and refrain from interference with it unless satisfied that it proceeded on some erroneous principle or was plainly and obviously wrong.	specifically regarding s 55 is of limited importance (as we are told s 55 is protecting the contracts made between 18 May 1973 and 1 February 1978) and, as such, would soon outlive its usefulness. He discusses the fact that the exercise of any power to decide what is fair or reasonable will involve legitimate judicial differences and that the courts should refrain from interfering with the decision of the previous court unless they feel that there was a clearly wrong decision or that the case was decided on some clearly erroneous principle.
[16] Turning back to the modified s 55 of the 1979 Act, it is common ground that the onus was on the respondents to show that it would not be fair or reasonable to allow the appellants to rely on the relevant condition as limiting their liability. It was argued for the appellants that the court must have regard to the circumstances as at the date of the contract, not after the breach. The basis of the argument was that this was the effect of s 11 of the 1977 Act and that it would be wrong to construe the modified s 55 of the Act as having a different effect. Assuming the premise is correct, the conclusion does not follow. The provisions of the 1977 Act cannot be considered in construing the prior enactments now embodied in the modified s 55 of the 1979 Act. But, in any	Lord Bridge turns to a question of construction, the meaning of words used in the statute. The onus is on the respondents to show that it would not be fair or reasonable to allow the appellant to rely on the relevant condition. Appellants said the court must look at the situation at the date of the

TABLE 10.1—continued

Para	Lord Bridge: Judgment (divided into numbered paragraphs). *George Mitchell v Finney Lock Seeds* 1983 2 AC 803: **VERBATIM TEXT**	Summary of paragraph
	event, the language of subss (4) and (9) of that section is clear and unambiguous. The question whether it is fair or reasonable to allow reliance on a term excluding or limiting liability for breach of contract can only arise after the breach. The nature of the breach and the circumstances in which it occurred cannot possibly be excluded from 'all the circumstances of the case' to which regard must be had.	contract, but Lord Bridge said that the true meaning of the phrase in s 55(5) 'regard shall be had to all the circumstances of the case' must mean that the situation at the time of breach *and* after breach must be taken into account.
[17]	The only other question of construction debated in the course of the argument was the meaning to be attached to the words 'to the extent that' in sub-s (4) and, in particular, whether they permit the court to hold that it would be fair and reasonable to allow partial reliance on a limitation clause and, for example, to decide in the instant case that the respondents should recover, say, half their consequential damage. I incline to the view that, in their context, the words are equivalent to 'in so far as' or 'in circumstances in which' and do not permit the kind of judgment of Solomon illustrated by the example.	Lord Bridge discusses another issue of the meaning of words used in the statute. The meaning of the words 'to the extent' in s 55(4). Lord Bridge asks: 'Is it fair and reasonable to allow partial reliance on a limitation clause, to decide . . . that the respondents should recover say, half their consequential damage?' Lord Bridge goes on to say that he considers that the meaning of the phrase 'to the extent' is 'in so far as or in circumstances in which'. He suggests that the phrase does not 'permit the kind of judgment of Solomon illustrated by the example'. The reference to Solomon is typical of the literary/religious referencing that one often finds in cases. Solomon was an Old Testament king accredited with much wisdom in

		his judging. When confronted with a baby claimed by two mothers he suggested cutting it in half so each could have half. The false mother agreed, the real mother said no, the other mother could have the baby. Thus, he located the real mother.
[18]	But for the purpose of deciding this appeal I find it unnecessary to express a concluded view on this question.	Lord Bridge goes on to say that his answer in relation to the question is not necessary for the outcome of this case and declines to answer one way or the other! It is interesting to note that if he *had* categorically answered the question, yes or no, it would be a clear example of an *obiter dictum* statement in a strong case by a senior judge and may well have been used in argument in a later case where this issue is at the core of the case.
[19]	My Lords, at long last I turn to the application of the statutory language to the circumstances of the case. Of the particular matters to which attention is directed by paras (a) to (e) of s 55(5) only those in paras (a) to (c) are relevant. As to para (c), the respondents admittedly knew of the relevant condition (they had dealt with the appellants for many years) and, if they had read it, particularly cl 2, they would, I think, as laymen rather than lawyers, have had no difficulty in understanding what it said. This and the magnitude of the damages claimed in proportion to the price of the seeds sold are factors which weigh in the scales in the appellants' favour.	Eventually, Lord Bridge turns to the 'application of the statutory language' to the case. He states that only s 55(5) (a) and (c) are relevant. (This is the moment to re-read s 55(5) (a) and (c) above, if you do not remember the provisions. Otherwise, one loses sight of the argument!) As to s 55(5) (c), he says of course the buyer knew of the condition as it was standard throughout the trade.

TABLE 10.1 — continued

Para	Lord Bridge: Judgment (divided into numbered paragraphs). *George Mitchell v Finney Lock Seeds 1983 2 AC 803: VERBATIM TEXT*	Summary of paragraph
[20]	The question of relative bargaining strength under para (a) and of the opportunity to buy seeds without a limitation of the seedsman's liability under para (b) were interrelated. The evidence was that a similar limitation of liability was universally embodied in the terms of trade between seedsmen and farmers and had been so for very many years. The limitation had never been the subject of any protest by the National Farmers' Union. These factors, if considered in isolation, might have been equivocal. The decisive factor, however, appears from the evidence of four witnesses called for the appellants, independent seedsmen, the chairman of the appellant company, and a director of a sister company (both being wholly-owned subsidiaries of the same parent). They said that it had always been their practice, unsuccessfully attempted in the instant case, to negotiate settlements of farmers' claims for damages in excess of the price of the seeds, if they thought that the claims were 'genuine' and 'justified'. This evidence indicated a clear recognition by seedsmen in general, and the appellants in particular, that reliance on the limitation of liability imposed by the relevant condition would not be fair or reasonable.	As to s 55(5) (a), he states that there was evidence that similar limitations had never been negotiated with representative bodies. Witnesses for the appellant said that it had always been their practice in genuine justified claims to settle above the price of the seeds but that, in this case, settlement had not been possible. Lord Bridge said 'this evidence indicated a clear recognition . . . that reliance on the limitation of liability imposed by the relevant condition would not be fair or reasonable'.
[21]	Two further factors, if more were needed, weigh the scales in favour of the respondent. The supply of autumn, instead of winter cabbage seed was due to the negligence of the appellants' sister company. Irrespective of its quality, the autumn variety supplied could not, according to the appellants' own evidence, be grown commercially in East Lothian. Finally, as the trial judge found, seedsmen could insure against the risk of crop	Lord Bridge concluded, therefore, that wrong seed was supplied due to the negligence of the applicant's sister company. Seedsmen could insure against the risk of crop failure

		caused by the wrong supply without materially increasing the cost of seeds.
	failure caused by supply of the wrong variety of seeds without materially increasing the price of seeds.	
[22]	My Lords, even if I felt doubts about the statutory issue, I should not, for the reasons explained earlier, think it right to interfere with the unanimous original decision of that issue by the Court of Appeal. As it is, I feel no such doubts. If I were making the original decision, I should conclude without hesitation that it would not be fair or reasonable to allow the appellants to rely on the contractual limitation of their liability. I would dismiss the appeal.	Lord Bridge felt no doubts about the decision of the Court of Appeal over statute. Lord Bridge refers to an earlier point in para 15 that it is wise to 'refrain from interference' in matters of legitimate judicial difference.

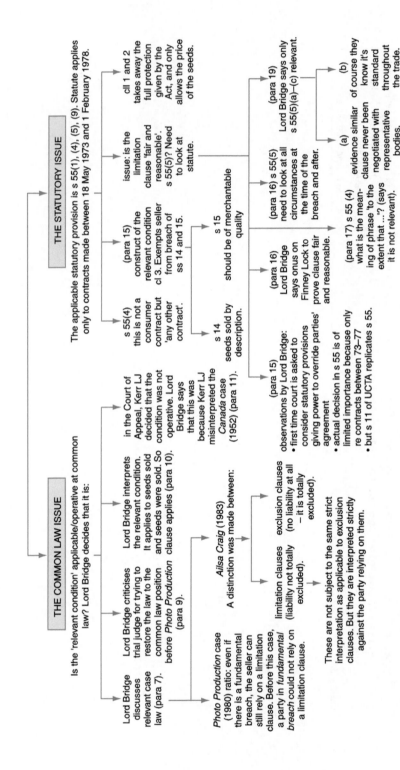

THE COMMON LAW ISSUE

Is the 'relevant condition' applicable/operative at common law? Lord Bridge decides that it is:

Lord Bridge discusses relevant case law (para 7).

Lord Bridge criticises trial judge for trying to restore the law to the common law position before *Photo Production* clause applies (para 10).

Lord Bridge interprets the relevant condition. It applies to seeds sold and seeds were sold. So *Photo Production* clause applies (para 10).

in the Court of Appeal, Kerr LJ decided that the condition was not operative. Lord Bridge says that this was because Kerr LJ misinterpreted the *Canada* case (1952) (para 11).

Photo Production case (1980) ratio: even if there is a fundamental breach, the seller can still rely on a limitation clause. Before this case, a party in *fundamental breach* could not rely on a limitation clause.

Ailsa Craig (1983)
A distinction was made between:

limitation clauses (liability not totally excluded).

exclusion clauses (no liability at all – it is totally excluded).

These are not subject to the same strict interpretation as applicable to exclusion clauses. But they are interpreted strictly against the party relying on them.

THE STATUTORY ISSUE

The applicable statutory provision is s 55(1), (4), (5), (9). Statute applies only to contracts made between 18 May 1973 and 1 February 1978.

s 55(4)
this is not a consumer contract but 'any other contract'.

(para 15) construct of the relevant condition cl 3. Exempts seller from breach of ss 14 and 15.

issue: is the limitation clause 'fair and reasonable'. s 55(5)? Need to look at statute.

cll 1 and 2 takes away the full protection given by the Act, and only allows the price of the seeds.

s 14 seeds sold by description.

s 15 should be of merchantable quality

(para 15) observations by Lord Bridge:
• first time court is asked to consider statutory provisions giving power to override parties' agreement
• actual decision in s 55 is of limited importance because only re contracts between 73–77
• but s 11 of UCTA replicates s 55.

(para 16) Lord Bridge says onus on Finney Lock to prove clause fair and reasonable.

(para 16) s 55(5) need to look at all circumstances at the time of the breach and after.

(para 19) Lord Bridge says only s 55(5)(a)–(c) relevant.

(para 17) s 55 (4) what is the meaning of phrase 'to the extent that ...'? (says it is not relevant).

(a) evidence similar clause never been negotiated with representative bodies.

(b) of course they know it's standard throughout the trade.

Figure 10.19 Summary: court's rationale for decision

Constructing a usable case note

One of the most important skills in the toolkit of a law student or legal professional is the ability to read a case and make a usable record of it. This is called a 'case note'. The purpose of a case note is to record, in a quick and accessible form, all of the important issues for the later use of the case (for example, deciding whether to apply the case to the facts of another legal problem). Ideally the case note will contain all necessary specific information and reasoning to allow its author to use it in subsequent problem scenarios for solving legal problem questions.

A case note can only be made once you have read and re-read the case under con-sideration and obtained a thorough understanding of the case and the interrelationships between the legal rules discussed, the facts of the case, and the reasoning of the court. You have certainly done this in relation to the *George Mitchell* case.

There are different ways of listing the information that should be included in a case note. A case note must be sufficiently thorough and reliable in order that you do not have to re-read the case again.

A usable case note must record all of the above items in Table 10.2. If it does not it is of limited or no use to you. If it merely records the facts, the issues before the court and the outcome between the parties but does not record the judicial reasoning it cannot be applied to other similar fact situations, as you do not know the reasoning. A case note that only records the judicial reasoning and not the facts cannot be applied because the very idea of 'similarity' rests upon similar facts as well as similar legal rules.

By the time a case reaches the appellate court the dispute will be quite narrow and in many ways may be very different from the dispute on the facts between the parties in the previous trial or appellate court. For example, in a discrimination case the original argu-ment between the parties may concern the discrimination against one party by the other in their workplace, contrary to the Equality Act 2010. The point on appeal could however be concerned simply with the appropriate meaning of a word or a phrase in a section, sub-section, paragraph or sub-paragraph of the legislation. This demonstrates why it is

TABLE 10.2 INFORMATION REQUIRED FOR A CASE NOTE	
1. Formal citation of law report being noted.	9. Procedural history of the case which should indicate original claim, outcome of trial and the grounds of appeal and outcome of case in any previous appeal court.
2. Name of court.	
3. Names of judges.	
4. Date of court hearing of the case.	
5. Facts.	
6. Specific ground of appeal in the law report you are reading.	10. The record of judicial reasoning as to why those rules applied to those facts in that way. Each judge's reasoning should be indicated separately.
7. Identification of applicable legal rules and cases referred to.	
8. Brief reference to what was held by the court hearing the case in the law report.	11. Decision of the court on the appeal (the outcome between the parties).

essential to have information on facts, rules, issues and grounds of appeal, reason for the outcome of the case. Several important cases under the Equality Act 2010 have turned on the meaning of the word 'can'. You can only properly use your case note in legal argument when you know and understand the reasoning of the court and are able to state briefly, but correctly in your note together with the relevant facts, the legal issues before the court and the applicable legal rules considered.

Activity: Writing a usable case note

(1) Using the list in Table 10.2 as headings write a case note of the case of *George Mitchell v Finney Lock Seeds* [1983] 2 AC 803. There were three other judges besides Lord Bridge sitting in the court, Lord Diplock, Lord Scarman and Lord Roskill. What they say or do not say must be recorded in your final case note.

(2) Taking into account all of the judgments in this case do you consider that this case is a strong or a weak precedent?

Once you have written your own case note, you can check your version with the specimen case note of *George Mitchell v Finney Lock Seeds* after the chapter summary, as well as the answer to questions 2 above. If you carefully complete this exercise and find that your answers are similar in most respects to the model answers you have the basic skill of reading law reports in place. Now all you have to do is . . .

practise, practise. . . . Practise . . . reading cases!

CONCLUSION

This chapter has been concerned with introducing, in some depth, common law/case law, the second major source of English legal rules discussed in this book. The role of the judiciary in the development of English law has become apparent as the chapter has progressed and the doctrine of precedent has been laid out. This chapter has also indicated the central importance of a careful dissection of the law reports to ensure that the correct aspects of the case are correctly summarised for a case note and further use. It must be understood in relation to domestic legislation and European law as together they lay a firm, indispensable foundation for understanding 'how to' handle and understand legal rules, and how to understand the relationship between case law, legislation and European Union law.

The major case study in this chapter, *George Mitchell v Finney Lock Seeds* is important for a demonstration of reading and handling case law and understanding judge-made common law rules and their relationship to judge-made equitable legal rules. But it is also important because it is a case that is concerned with the relationship of judge-made law to statutory rules; for the senior judiciary are the final interpreters of the meaning, extent and limits of domestic legislation. This issue is explored in greater detail towards the end of Chapter 11.

CHAPTER SUMMARY

- The doctrine of precedent means English judges, when deciding cases in court, must refer to similar prior decisions of the higher courts, and keep to the *reasoning* in those cases.
- Much depends on the definition of the word 'similar', and this is determined by the judges in the court.
- Locating the *ratio* or principle of a case can be difficult and there may be dissenting views among the judges hearing the trial or the appeal.
- The practice of the doctrine of precedent in the English legal system requires a system of accurate reporting of legal cases.
- Law reports are reports of important cases (e.g. cases where the judge has extracted a 'new' legal rule and/or cases involving statutory interpretation).
- A paragraph by paragraph reading approach is the best way to gain an in-depth understanding of the law report of a case.
- A case note must include date of hearing, citation, court, procedural history, the facts of the case, the legal issues before the court, legal rules discussed, the judicial reasoning of each judge for the decision reached and the outcome between the parties.

ACTIVITY WRITING A USABLE CASE NOTE
QUESTION 1

SPECIMEN CASE NOTE OF GEORGE MITCHELL V FINNEY LOCK SEEDS

CITATION: [1983] 2 AC 803
COURT: House of Lords
JUDGES: LJJ: Diplock, Scarman, Roskill, Brightman, Bridge
DATE: May 23, 24 June 30
FACTS

The respondents (George Mitchell) purchased 30 lb seeds from the appellants for £201.60 in December 1973. The invoice contained a standard limitation clause stating that the only liability of the appellants for breach of contract by them was replacement of the seeds or a refund of the cost of the seeds. All other liability was excluded. The respondent's crop failed because the wrong seed and seed of an inferior quality had been delivered due to the negligence of the appellant's sister company. This caused them excessive damage that could not be covered by the cost of replacement seed.

The appellants argued that the standard limitation clause applied and is not negated by negligence, and furthermore that it was unaffected by s 55 of the Sale of Goods Act.

The respondents argued the reverse maintaining the limitation clause was unenforceable.

The House of Lords held:

(1) The common law condition was not negated by negligence, agreeing with the minority argument of Lord Denning in the Court of Appeal.

(2) However it was not a fair and reasonable limitation clause and was therefore rendered unenforceable by s 55 of the Sale of Goods Act 1979.

Cases referred to:

Ailsa Craig Fishing Co Ltd v Malvern Fishing Co Ltd [1983] 1 H WLR 964; [1983] 1 All ER 101, HL (Sc).

   Canada Steamship Lines Ltd v The King [1952] AC 192; [1952] 1 All ER 305, PC
Considered

   Photo Production Ltd v Securicor Transport Ltd [1980] AC 827; [1980] 2 WLR 283; [1980] 1 All ER 556, HL(E).

Applied

Statutory rules referred to
   Sale of Goods Act 1979, s 55 (4) (5).

PROCEDURAL HISTORY

Trial

The plaintiffs (George Mitchell) claimed damages and argued that the standard common law on the limitation clause did not apply because it was not a fair and reasonable requirement imposed on limitation clauses by s 55 of the Sale of Goods Act 1979.

   The defendants (Finney Lock Seeds) argued that the limitation clause was valid.

   Parker J held: The limitation clause was not operative at common law because of the defendant's negligence in delivering the wrong seed.

   Court of Appeal: Denning, Kerr, Oliver LJJ

   The defendants appealed to the Court of Appeal on the grounds that the limitation clause was valid. The plaintiffs, now the respondents, argued the limitation clause was invalid due to negligence and if it was not invalid due to negligence it was unenforceable due to the operation of s 55 of the Sale of Goods Act 1979.

Kerr and Oliver LJJ held the limitation clause could not be relied upon because:

(1) on its true construction the condition did not apply at common law because loss due to the negligence of sister company and the seed was wholly different than delivery of the wrong seed (Kerr and Oliver LJJ). Therefore the condition did not apply due to negligence, but they also applied s 55 of the Sale of Goods Act 1979 holding that the clause was not fair and reasonable. (**Note**: having said the clause did not apply at common law because of negligence, s 55 of the Sale of Goods Act was irrelevant as it is only operative if the clause is deemed to apply at common law!)

(2) **Denning LJ** held, in the minority, that the limitation clause could apply at common law. However, it was not enforceable because it was not a fair and reasonable clause under s 55 of the Sale of Goods Act 1979.

House of Lords

The appellants (Finney Lock Seeds) appealed to the House of Lords. Held:

Lord Diplock: He made clear that he agreed with the minority reasoning of Lord Denning in the Court of Appeal. He notes that he has read and agrees completely with the reasoning of Lord Bridge in this case in the House of Lords which dismisses this appeal following Lord Denning's reasoning.

Scarman, Roskill, Brightman LJJ: note their agreement with the reasoning of Lord Bridge which was the majority judgment in the case.

Lord Bridge

He agreed with the reasoning of Denning LJ in the Court of Appeal on:

(1) The common law issue

That the limitation clause was operative and could effectively limit liability. The wording of the condition was unambiguous in this regard. Limitation clauses do not have to adhere to the strict principles laid down for complete exclusion clauses (see *Ailsa Craig* (1983) which are negated by negligence). These must be clearly expressed and must be strictly interpreted against the party relying on them (*contra proferentem*). The limitation clause does not have to be so strictly interpreted and was still capable of enforcement.

Decision partly supported by the following precedents

Photo Production Ltd (1980).

Even in cases of fundamental breach, (core) limitation clauses are available to be relied upon by one party. *Ailsa Craig* (1983). There is a difference of approach appropriate between limitation and exclusion clauses. Limitation clauses do not have to be so strictly interpreted.

He also agreed with Lord Denning on the matter of:

(2) The statutory issue

However, even though the clause was enforceable at common law, after considering s 55(4), (5)(a) and (c), Lord Bridge decided that the common law provision was overridden by the statutory obligation in s 55(4) for such clauses to be fair and reasonable otherwise. The clause was therefore unenforceable.

The grounds for deciding clause unfair and unreasonable were that:

(a)   in applying s 55(5) (a), it was clear that in the past appellants had sought to negotiate a settlement that was higher than the price of seeds and had not relied on the limitation clause;

(b)   the supply of seed was due to the negligence of appellant's sister company;

(c)   the appellant could easily have insured against loss due to negligence.

Ratio

Common law limitation clauses are not negated by negligence, however s 55 of the Sale of Goods Act requires such clauses to be fair and reasonable.

Obiter dicta

(a)   The phrase 'to the extent that' discussed and said to mean 'in so far as' or 'in the circumstances which'. Section 54(4). Although this is not relevant to this case it is possibly an important *obiter dictum*.

(b)   There may be some mileage in discussions concerning whether there can be partial reliance on limitation clauses again. Although this is not relevant to this case, possible important *obiter dicta*.

(c)   The phrase 'in all the circumstances' in s 55(5) means one should take account of circumstances at and after the time of the breach.

(d)   Appellate courts in a case like this, where there is room for legitimate judicial difference, should refrain from interfering unless it is considered that the decision reached was based on the application of wrong principles or the case is clearly wrongly decided.

Outcome: Appeal dismissed.

Precedent value: This is always determined after the case during the reasoning in a similar case, however the prediction would be that due to the unanimity in the House of Lords this is a majority judgment and therefore creates a strong binding precedent.

HOW TO READ AND UNDERSTAND DOMESTIC LEGISLATION

LEARNING OUTCOMES

After reading this chapter you should be able to:

- Read, use and understand domestic legislation and the language used in statutes.
- Understand the relationship between different parts of a statute.
- Understand how judges approach statutory interpretation.
- Demonstrate an awareness of the rules of statutory interpretation, and other practices used when interpreting statutes.
- Understand how to use unofficial and official databases to efficiently and quickly obtain an overview of a statute.

INTRODUCTION

This chapter introduces techniques and skills for using and handling domestic legislation. When used broadly the word legislation includes domestic UK legislation, delegated legislation, and EU legislation. This chapter will deal with domestic legislation[1] and mainly focuses on primary legislation, the 'Public General Act' which will be referred to as a 'statute'. However, the skills you will learn are transferable to secondary legislation and to other types of primary legislation.[2]

The standard layout of domestic legislation will be briefly noted,[3] before turning to consider the range of techniques and skills needed to competently handle legislation. You will be introduced to various techniques for breaking into the language of legislation and understanding the statute as a whole. Finally the role of statutory interpretation will be explored.

Your skills in all areas will be tested and developed through guided exercises and questions related to specific legislation. Practice will allow you to steadily increase your intellectual awareness, language appreciation, and skills of prediction concerning interpretation difficulties. These skills will allow you to develop the ability to evaluate and critique legislation and use it to construct legal arguments.

There are a number of skills that need to be utilised together to properly understand and handle legislation. These are set out below in Figure 11.1.

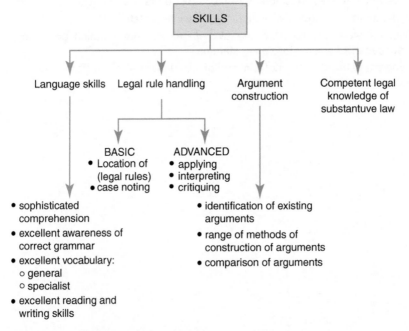

Figure 11.1 **Skills required for understanding legislation**

---

1 Chapter 12 deals with European Union legislation.
2 See Chapter 1 for a detailed consideration of primary and secondary legislation.
3 See Chapter 1 for a detailed consideration of layout of legislation.

THE LAYOUT OF A STATUTE

Central to the analysis of statutes is the ability to understand how the statute is structured as a whole, and what the relationship is between the different areas of the statute. As discussed in detail in Chapter 1 there is a standard method of laying out statutes which, when recognised and understood, becomes a great help for analysis.

A statute is generally divided into a preamble, parts, sections and schedules. In smaller statutes parts may not be used. Also schedules may not be used either.

Each part will deal with different aspects of the overall collection of legal rules and their meanings contained in the statute. These parts can be subdivided into several Chapters. Each part and any chapters are divided into sections (often abbreviated as 's' (singular) or 'ss' (plural)) which give more details in each area.

As appropriate, sections will set out legal rules, and deal with definitions and administrative matters. Sections can be further divided with the use of Arabic numerals into subsections (abbreviated as 'sub-s' (singular) or 'sub-ss' (plural)). Sub-sections are capable of further division, with the use of Roman numerals, into paragraphs (abbreviated as 'para' (singular) or 'paras' (plural)). Paragraphs can be further divided with alphabetical ordering into sub-paragraphs (abbreviated as 'sub-para' (singular) or 'sub-paras' (plural)).

Sections are used to simplify navigation through the statute, and section numbering runs consecutively across any divisions into 'parts' or 'chapters'. They are not used in Schedules.

At the end of the statute, there will often be Schedules (a capital 'S' is always used) and these are numerically divided as well. These deal with matters raised in the various parts, perhaps setting out administrative procedures to be observed, or definitions to be applied. But note that Schedules can also contain definitions. Schedules only relate in some manner to previous sections in the Act. They cannot create anything new.

Statutes also contain marginal notes, headings and sub-headings. These are organising devices and are not part of the law. You will recall that the words in a statute setting out legal rules are referred to as 'rules in a fixed legal format'. Only those words carry the law.

Correct understanding of the relationship between parts, chapters, sections, subsections, paragraphs, sub-paragraphs, marginal notes, headings and schedules enables the general layout of the Act to be ascertained. Assistance is also obtained from the 'long title' of the Act (which looks more like a long sentence describing the area covered by the Act). Figure 11.2 shows the differing elements of a statute with a brief explanation of each one.

USING AND HANDLING A STATUTE

Usually you will only need to deal with a few sections in a statute. It is always useful however to be aware of the general purpose of the statute. The sections you are analysing and

STATUTE
- Law in fixed verbal form enacted by UK Parliament
- Referred to by short title

PREAMBLE
- First name of monarch
- Long title of Act
- Date of royal assent
- Words of enactment

PARTS
- A statute will usually be divided into a series of Parts (not all are, particularly if they are short statutes)
- Each Part will tend to refer to a different topic area
- Parts may come with Margins and Headers; these do not form part of the law

SECTIONS
- Each part is divided into smaller numbered sections using Arabic numerals.
- Sometimes, when a statute is amended and sections are inserted, capitalised alpha markers are used e.g. A
- Sections may come with Margins and Headers; these do not form part of the law

SUB-SECTIONS
- Each section may be divided into smaller numbered sub-sections using Arabic numerals enclosed with brackets e.g. (1)
- Sub-sections may come with Margins and Headers; these do not form part of the law

PARAGRAPHS
- Each sub-section may be divided into smaller paragraphs using Roman numerals enclosed within brackets e.g. (ii)
- Paragraphs may come with Margins and Headers; these do not form part of the law

SUB PARAGRAPHS
- Each paragraph may be divided into smaller sub-paragraphs using lower case alphabetical markers enclosed within brackets e.g. (a)
- Sub-paragraphs may come with Margin and Headers; these do not form part of the law

SCHEDULES
- Makes further arrangements, or gives further information concerning matters already mentioned in sections. No new topic matter can be introduced in a schedule, they can only refer to issues raised in parts and sections
- They use Roman numerals in capitals e.g. IV

Figure 11.2 Summary: Courts rationale for decision

applying can then be seen as part of a whole. It is also important to know how the parts of a statute fit together, and understand when sections are connected to each other and should be read together and when they are not.

The Equality Act 2010 (EA 2010) will be used to assist you to understand:

- the overall structure of legislation;
- the importance of careful research to ensure that the legislation you have is the latest version; and
- the importance of understanding the layout of individual sections and links between sections.

Exercises will be used to further your understanding.

The overall structure of legislation

Those who draft legislation decide whether it should be divided into parts and/or schedules. They also make decisions about choice of language. Drafters try to ensure that as far as possible the language used in the statute is clear and general; making it both understandable and capable of being applied to new, but connected, situations.

Often it is the generality of statutory language that can cause interpretational issues.

Legislation can be described as legal rules created in a 'fixed verbal form'. The phrase 'fixed verbal form' means that only *those* exact words in that order, as enacted by Parliament, form the legal rule. We will come back to this point when we discuss statutory interpretation by the judiciary.[4]

When you are dealing with sections in a statute it is important to be aware that these sections are part of a collection of rules in the statute and they are linked by the fact that they deal with similar issues. You will need to find out which words or phrases used in sections have attached definitions or defences and if there are any guidelines given in the statute affecting the application of a particular section. These can be set out in a sub-section of the section you are dealing with, in other sections of the Act. Definition, for example, can be in schedules attached to the Act. So it is never enough just to assume that the section or sections you have been referred to are the only sections you need to be aware of.

You should initially read the section carefully for clues as to definitions elsewhere, and read the table of contents of the statute to see if there are any sections clearly referring to interpretational matters. This also assists you in gaining a more context based idea of the statute which is useful to have when considering your sections.

The screenshot in Figure 11.3 shows you the first entries in the online arrangement of the Equality Act 2010 from the Westlaw database. As Westlaw contains academic journal articles and cases as well as legislation it is also ideal for locating cases, and academic articles that relate to the section(s) you are dealing with.

We will consider the information that is given in the Figure 11.3 screenshot, which shows Parts 1 and 2 of the Act; there are more but these are not on the screenshot. Furthermore

---

4   Although, as you will see when considering statutory interpretation in this chapter, judges interpreting words and phrases in court will often deal in the substitution of words for those in the statute in an attempt to clarify meaning and this can give rise to more problems.

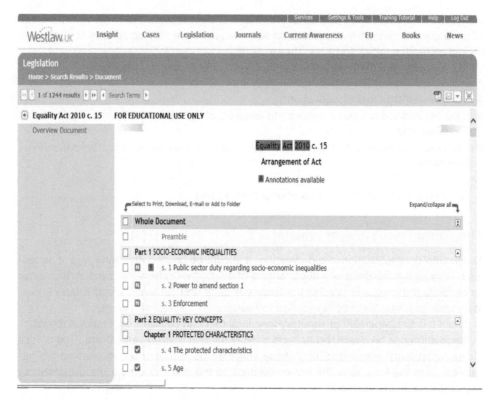

Figure 11.3 Screenshot of arrangement of Equality Act 2010

we can see that Part 2 is divided into chapters, as Chapter 1 Protected Characteristics is on screen. Sections 1–5 are on screen.

You will note three box icons containing 'N', '!' or '√' are used as annotations in front of sections 1–5 on the left side of the screenshot.

- N: indicates sections not yet in force on the date that Westlaw was accessed (this is relevant to ss 1–3).[5]
- !: indicates that an amendment to section 1 is pending.
- √: indicates that the section was in force on the date of access.
- If you were to scan down the retrieved page you would find a further box icon with an 'R' in it indicating that a section has been repealed.

The second tab at the top of the screen shot on the fr left indicates that this Act was one of 1,244 search results. This is because of the number of statutory instruments that have been published under the Act.

---

5   Accessed 29 October 2014.

You should further note the icon for a pdf in the top right hand corner of the screen. This takes you to an annotated copy of the print version of the statute published by The Stationery Office.

The Figure 11.4 screenshot shows you the opened pdf at the table of contents. This is the same as the 'arrangement of Act' found online, but is in its print version. However in this online version by Westlaw the same icons are inserted into the pdf by the editors of Westlaw and all areas of the Act are hyperlinked for easy movement around it.

You will recall that the official version of legislation is found on the government website, www.legislation.gov.uk. You should always check this to ensure the information retrieved from any other source is correct.

Figure 11.5 shows the first entries for the 'table of contents' from www.legislation.gov. uk and which are accessed by the table of contents tab. It is annotated; an automated box is on screen stating that there are outstanding changes to the table of contents not yet made by the editorial team.

Note that on the left hand side of the screenshot you have two choices: to view the legislation as originally enacted and the latest revised version. It can be extremely useful when you are engaged in research to be able to view the original version of the Act. But for ascertaining current law you need to access the revised version.

Figure 11.5 shows that the website indicates that there are changes to s 1 and clicking on the relevant section you will find a box stating there are changes and you are offered the opportunity to 'view outstanding changes'. Click on the s 1 alert: you will find out how s 1 is affected by other legislation.

The Figure 11.6 screenshot gives you the screenshot revealing the changes to s 1 and effects yet to be applied. Also note that the tab entitled 'prospective' gives the new section wording.

Equality Act 2010   *Page 596*

Table of Contents

Equality Act 2010 c. 15.. 1

    Preamble 1

Part 1 SOCIO-ECONOMIC INEQUALITIES.. 1

    ⬚ ⬛ s. 1 Public sector duty regarding socio-economic inequalities...................... 1

    ⬚   s. 2 Power to amend section 1... 3

    ⬚   s. 3 Enforcement... 4

Part 2 EQUALITY: KEY CONCEPTS.. 5

    Chapter 1 PROTECTED CHARACTERISTICS...................................... 5

        ☑   s. 4 The protected characteristics.. 5

        ☑   s. 5 Age.. 5

Figure 11.4 pdf from Westlaw of original print version open at table of contents

Figure 11.5 Screenshot of the Equality Act 2010 showing part of the table of contents from www.legislation. gov.uk (accessed 29/10/14)

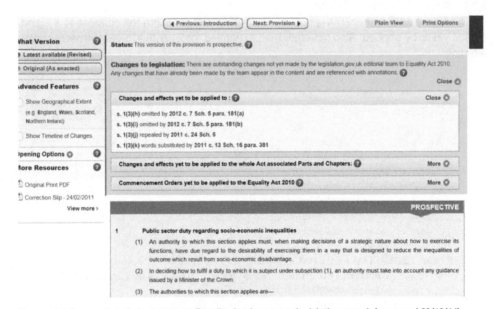

Figure 11.6 Screenshot of changes to s1 Equality Act from www.legislation.gov.uk (accessed 29/10/14)

From a quick survey of the table of contents or arrangement of the Equality Act 2010 on either of the two databases we have considered, you can get an overview of how the Act is divided as well as what it is concerned with and changes to the Act both made and prospective.

This basic information is set out in Figure 11.7.

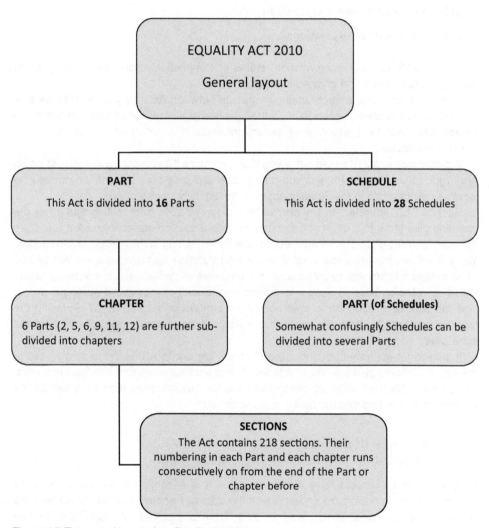

Figure 11.7 The general layout of the Equality Act 2010

Figure 11.7 indicates that the Equality Act has 16 parts, 218 sections (many of which are further divided into sub-sections, paragraphs and sub-paragraphs) and 28 schedules.[6]

Earlier, the importance of checking for definitions was referred to. A search of the table of contents reveals that Part 16 of the Act is headed 'interpretation'[7] and contains three sections relating to issues of interpretation:

212. General interpretation.

213. References to maternity leave, etc.

214. Index of defined expressions.

Section 212 'General interpretation' states in alphabetical order the meaning to be given to certain words and phrases in the Act.

Definitions of words and phrases can change between Acts so you need to be sure you are using the correct definitions. In the absence of any guidance you can check the Interpretation Act 1978 which gives general information on interpretation of words and phrases in statutes.

A closer look at s 212 would show you that it contains 13 sub-sections, many of which are divided into paragraphs and sub-paragraphs and give core information concerning what key expressions in the Equality Act such as 'equality clause' mean.

Section 212(1)(d) refers to the phrase 'non-discrimination rule' stating that it has the meaning given to it in s 61. If you are dealing with a section earlier in the Act that uses the term 'equality clause' it is important to check its meaning in the interpretation section. You will not necessarily know what is in the interpretation section of a given Act so you need to read it in any Act to make sure you are aware of definitions. Do not be someone who only relies on second hand information from books or lectures: it could be wrong! You can acquire a quick comprehension of the content of the statute by skimming the table of contents for both the body of the Act, the parts and/or sections and for the schedules.

In addition, peppered throughout the Act there are sections that define terms used in the Act. You should also remember that words and phrases, even those defined in an Act, can be the subject of statutory interpretation. Case law therefore may have settled the meaning of words and that too needs to be searched.[8]

The importance of careful research to ensure that the legislation you have is the latest version

Chapters 1 and 7 should have made clear that it is essential to retrieve up to date information on legislation. You must check the dates of books, articles, cases and the last update of any website you are browsing. They may predate the legislation or discuss sections that have been repealed or changed. This issue is discussed in detail in Chapter 7.

---

6   If you need to remind yourself what sections, parts, chapters and schedules are please refer to Chapter 1.
7   www.legislation.gov.uk accessed 29 October 2014.
8   Detailed search techniques for cases and legislation can be found in Chapters 6 and 7 respectively.

The importance of understanding the layout of individual sections and links between sections

A basic skill that must be developed if you are to successfully understand and handle statutes is being able to competently navigate sections with confidence, understanding the standard layout of a section. Section 9 of the Equality Act 2010 will be used to demonstrate how to begin to understand links between parts of a section. The section will be set out, and initial questions asked leading into a guided exercise based on s 9.

There are a number of phrases and words in this section that you may not be familiar with, for example:

- 'protected characteristic';
- 'racial group';
- 'ethnicity or national origins';
- 'caste'.

Some words or phrases you may understand at an everyday level; however, it is possible that they have been given a different legal meaning. Here you might have included 'racial group', 'race'. The key skill is being able to find out from the text what the aim of the section is, and what meaning, if any, has been given to words in it.

Table 11.1 sets out the text of s 9 together with a brief summary of it and each of its sub-sections. This is a strategy to try and increase your ability to read statutory language. Ask yourself if you would have been able to summarise the relevant text.

One method for understanding the links in a section is to reduce it to a simple tree diagram showing which 'bits' of the section are linked to other 'bits', and which are freestanding. You have to understand the section before you can use it. This visual link will help you to see a section as a diagram enabling a visual link between parts of the section to be seen.

Figure 11.8 shows a diagram of the current version of s 9. The two websites we have referred to in this chapter both show that s 9 as originally enacted has been the object of changes, and the revised text is set out in the diagram in blue text.

The diagram with text shows the links clearly. However, you can reduce your schematic diagram to just links between sub-sections. Here you can see in Figure 11.9 below that only three sub-sections have paragraphs and that there are no sub-paragraphs. As you can see there are no linking words such as 'if', 'and', 'or' to be particularly careful of. But we now know s 9 has been amended.

Locating the purpose of the section you are considering: exploring s 9 of the Equality Act 2010

Locating the purpose of legislation you are reading can be a difficult matter and takes patience as well as skills application. You cannot apply law you do not properly understand. You have spent time considering the structure of s 9 of the Equality Act 2010. To allow yourself to be satisfied that you have a correct view of what the section is aiming to do, it is useful

TABLE 11.1 S 9 EA ANNOTATED

Equality Act 2010: s 9	Brief summary
(1) Race includes – (a) colour; (b) nationality; (c) Ethnic or national origins.	The language here is so sparse the best summary is the text as it stands.
(2) In relation to the protected characteristic of race – (a) a reference to a person who has a particular protected characteristic is a reference to a person of a particular racial group. (b) A reference to persons who share a protected characteristic is a reference to persons of the same racial group.	The sub-section is making clear the extent of the phrase 'protected characteristic' of race. Paragraph (a) refers to a person *who has a particular protected characteristic* and paragraph (b) refers to persons *who share a protected characteristic*. Two situations are referred to here, a particular protected characteristic and those sharing a particular characteristic.
(3) A racial group is a group of persons defined by reference to race; and a reference to a person's racial group is a reference to a racial group into which the person falls.	This defines the meaning of race and racial group; persons defined by reference to race. Reference to the person's racial group is to make a reference to the racial group into which the person falls.
(4) The fact that a racial group comprises two or more distinct racial groups does not prevent it from constituting a particular racial group.	Two or more distinct racial groups may be considered to comprise a racial group.
(5) A Minister of the Crown may by order – (a) amend this section so as to provide for caste to be an aspect of race; (b) amend this Act so as to provide for an exception to a provision of this Act to apply, or not to apply, to caste or to apply, or not to apply, to caste in specified circumstances.	This section makes provision for a statutory instrument to be made by the Minister. The clue that this is allowed is found in the phrase 'by order'. She may order amendments to s 9 allowing 'caste' to be an aspect of race. She can also amend the section asking for any exception to a provision of this Act to apply or not to apply to caste. You need to check for changes.
(6) The power under s 207(4)(b), in its application to subs (5), includes power to amend this Act.	Here reference is made to another section of the Act. You will need to look this up.

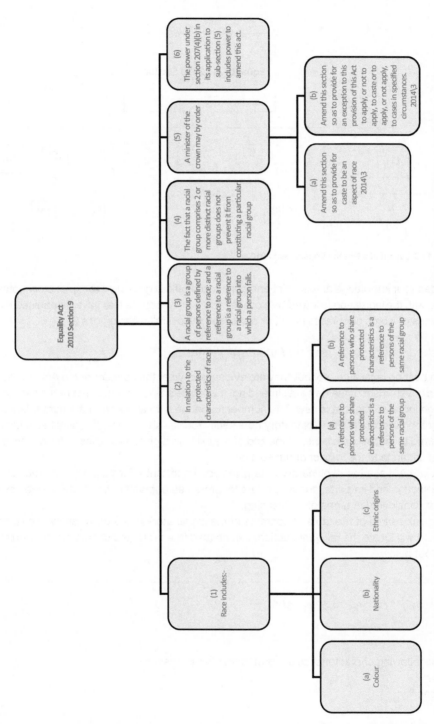

Equality Act 2010 Section 9

(1)
Race includes:-

(a)
Colour

(b)
Nationality

(c)
Ethnic origins

(2)
In relation to the protected characteristics of race

(a)
A reference to persons who share protected characteristics is a reference to persons of the same racial group

(b)
A reference to persons who share protected characteristics is a reference to persons of the same racial group

(3)
A racial group is a group of persons defined by reference to race; and a reference to a racial group is a reference to a racial group into which a person falls.

(4)
The fact that a racial group comprises 2 or more distinct racial groups does not prevent it from constituting a particular racial group

(5)
A minister of the crown may by order

(a)
Amend this section so as to provide for caste to be an aspect of race 2014\3

(b)
Amend this section so as to provide for an exception to this provision of this Act to apply, or not to apply, to caste or to apply, or not apply, to cases in specified circumstances. 2014\3

(6)
The power under section 207/(4)(b) in its application to sub-section (5) includes power to amend this act.

Figure 11.8 Tree diagram of s 9 of the Equality Act 2010 as originally enacted. Blue text indicates that a sub-section has subsequently been amended.

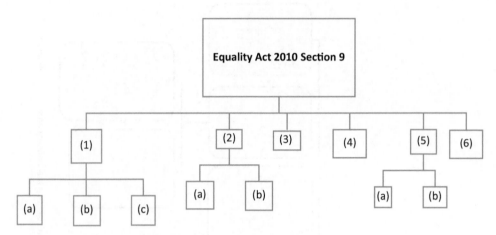

Figure 11.9 Layout of s 9 of the Equality Act 2010

to widen your knowledge at this point and consult the official government explanatory notes issued with the legislation followed by a cases search for any cases that have determined the meanings of words or phrases in s 9, or discussed the overall meaning of s 9.

The explanatory notes re: s 9 of the Equality Act 2010

These bear no legal authority but they are evidence of what the sponsor of the Act, invariably the government of the day, was intending. It will give an idea of the effect of the section, highlighting anything that is new. The numbering on the left hand side of the note refers to paragraph numbers in the explanatory note itself. You will also notice that only the section is referred to, not sub-sections. At the end of these notes it gives examples to further assist you to understand the impact of the section.

As you will see the explanatory note gives you important information on the meaning of the section and its parts, and also refers to 'protected characteristic', a phrase we have not yet considered in terms of its meaning.

A quick search of the table of contents of the explanatory notes on Westlaw accessed 29.10.14 will locate the relevant section, s 4, headed 'the protected characteristics' which is set out below.

Section 4 of the Equality Act 2010

4 The protected characteristics

The following characteristics are protected characteristics –
age;
disability;

gender reassignment;
marriage and civil partnership;
pregnancy and maternity;
race;
religion or belief;
sex;
sexual orientation.

The list of protected characteristics referred to in s 4 is not exhaustive in the sense the legislature could add to it. But at the time of accessing this section only these characteristics were protected. They cover a range of attributes that people may have, and the characteristics listed are protected by the Act. So if a person is discriminated against because of their race this would be illegal under the Act as race is a protected characteristic. We can also see that s 9 is necessary because it defines what is meant by the term 'race'. The term 'race' includes colour, nationality and ethnicity. Other sections in the Act define each of the protected characteristics in the list in s 4.

The explanatory notes state that all of the protected characteristics were protected by legislation in force when the Equality Act was going through Parliament. However, it is noted that caste, as an aspect of race, was not protected. It is to be included in s 9 as an area that the Minister may wish to add. Read s 9(5) again: note it is giving power for the future, and s 9(4) refers to 'caste'.

Understanding the impact of changes to statutes

It is important to know if the law you have is current. The original s 9(5) gives the Minister the right to add 'caste' to the list of protected characteristics, and for any use of s 9 generally or s 9(5) specifically you would need to check if this had occurred. It is easy to use the drop down menu on the official government website to look for changes to legislation. In relation to s 9 of the Equality Act the 'change to legislation' box on that site notes the following changes:

s **9** coming into force by SI 2010/2317, art 2(2)(c)
s **9(5)** power to repeal or amend conferred by 2013 c.24, s 97(7)–(10)
s 9(5) words omitted by 2013 c.24, s 97(2)
s 9(5)(a) words inserted by 2013 c.24, s 97(3)
s 9(5)(b) words inserted by 2013 c.24, s 97(4)

You should have been able to identify that 2013 c.24 is a citation to legislation. This website only refers to a statute making changes by its citation. Equally you should have already identified that SI relates to statutory instrument and again only its citation is used.

A quick search for 2013 c.24 will retrieve the Enterprise and Regulatory Reform Act and we can note the text of s 97. Online you can just click on the hyper-link in the changes box.

---

s 97 Equality Act 2010: caste as an aspect of race

(1) Section 9(5) of the Equality Act 2010 is amended in accordance with subsections (2) to (4).

(2) Omit 'may by order'.

(3) In paragraph (a) (power to provide for caste to be an aspect of race) at the beginning insert 'must by order'.

(4) In paragraph (b) (power to provide for exceptions to apply or not to apply to caste) at the beginning insert 'may by order'.

(5) A Minister of the Crown –

    (a) may carry out a review of the effect of s 9(5) of the Equality Act 2010 (and orders made under it) and whether it remains appropriate, and

    (b) must publish a report on the outcome of any such review.

(6) The power under subs (5)(a) may not be exercised before the end of the period of 5 years beginning with the day on which this Act is passed (but may be exercised on more than one occasion after that).

(7) If a Minister of the Crown considers it appropriate in the light of the outcome of a review under subs (5), the Minister may by order repeal or otherwise amend s 9(5) of the Equality Act 2010.

TABLE 11.2	
Revised version of s 9(5) due to the operation of s 97 2013 c.24 s 97	**Note of changes and comment**

(5) A Minister of the Crown – . . .
  (a) must amend this section so as to provide for caste to be an aspect of race;
  (b) may by order amend this Act so as to provide for an exception to a provision of this Act to apply, or not to apply, to caste or to apply, or not to apply, to caste in specified circumstances.
	1. 'May by order' has been deleted from the first line and replaced by the word 'must'.
	Note
	This change has a great impact because it opens up the protection of the Equality Act to those covered by the caste system, adding therefore to the list of protected characteristics. The addition of one word 'must' has changed everything.
	    The phrase 'may by order' is inserted into the beginning of the first line of paragraph (b)

(6) The power under section 207(4)(b), in its application to subsection (5), includes power to amend this Act.	**Comment:** Sub-sections 5, 6 and 7 relate to the Minister being given the power to respectively • review the appropriateness of amendments to s 9(5) • after the expiry of five years. • and repeal s 9(5) if deemed appropriate Sub-sections (8)–(10) relate to the boundaries of the power (8), and the fact that the power is exercisable by statutory instrument only (9) laid in draft form before Parliament (10).

Section 97 only applies to s 9 of the Equality Act 2010 and gives you a good example of the use of non-textual amendment. You are told what words to omit and/or add. Note too that only s 97 ss (2)–(4) amend s 9(5). The rest of the sub-sections in s 97 relate to the exercise of the Minister's powers.

You need to compare and contrast before and after change to determine what has changed and what this means. Table 11.2 above sets out s 9(5) as revised by s 97 of the Enterprise and Regulatory Reform Act.

This change has a great impact because it opens up the protection of the Equality Act to those covered by the caste system. The addition of one word 'must' has changed everything.

Armed with this information you are in a position to describe the changes and then consider the impact of these changes, although at that point you will need to locate secondary sources to give you the views of academics and professional lawyers on these changes.

Activity: Questions on section 9

The following questions on s 9 of the Equality Act 2010 are designed to test the consolidation of the skills you are learning and to ensure that you have a firm foundation. Answers can be found at the end of this chapter. If you go online please only use www.legislation.gov.uk.

Consolidation exercise questions on s 9	
1	Is the phrase 'protected characteristic' a special term of art as used in s 9(2)?
2	How can one racial group (defined in s 9(3)) be composed of two racial groups as stated in s 9(4)?
3	Has s 9(5) been amended in accordance with s 9(5)(a)?
4	What is the power under s 207(4)(b) referred to in s 9(6)?
5	What is the meaning of ethnic origin referred to in s 9(1)(c)?

Do remember when you have a query concerning changes to legislation and wording of legislation this is the only **official** site that can answer your queries. Other databases[9] such as Westlaw, LexisNexis and Bailii also retrieve the statutory information you need and give invaluable extra information relating to journal articles. But they are not the official site.

---

9   Further information on the range of databases is given in Chapter 7.

Linking a series of sections due to their interconnections

Above the links *between* statutes have been discussed with regard to changes to legislation. It is also vital to understand how several sections are linked together within a statute to obtain a full picture of what the Act is providing. We will now do a guided exercise.

Guided exercise

Locate the Equality Act 2010 online in the www.legislation.gov.uk website and click on the table of contents tab. Scan down the contents and try and get an overview of Part 1, Chapter 2 of the statute which has the heading 'Prohibited conduct'. Make a note of what you think it is concerned with before reading on.

Chapter 2 of the contents outlines the three ways in which the Act is infringed, by discriminatory behaviour taken because a person has a protected characteristic and/or by harassing or victimising a person because they have a protected characteristic

Reading s 13 of the Equality Act 2010

This section deals with direct discrimination, one of the behaviours that is illegal if it is done because of a protected characteristic. Read the section carefully and after you have done so consider the following questions:

(1) Using your own words describe what behaviour is directly discriminatory.
(2) Write an explanation of the relationship between s 13(1) and sub-sections (2)–(6).
(3) Does s 13 contain within it a defence to direct discrimination or indicate that there is one elsewhere in the statute?

From reading s 13 it can be seen that sub-s (1) defines direct discrimination in general terms as treating someone less favourably than another because they have a protected characteristic. To know if a person had been discriminated against you would have to check an up to date list of protected characteristics in s 4 along with the specific definitions of each of those protected characteristics. Remember how the protected characteristic of race in s 4 is further defined in s 9 including the giving of examples.

Section 13 in sub-sections (2)–(6) then sets out specific details concerning when direct discrimination applies in slightly differing ways to certain protected characteristics. There is no general defence for direct discrimination. Each sub-section in s 13 makes clear the extent of protection within various protected characteristics.

Some sub-sections are highly specific, for example s 13(6) states that breastfeeding is included in the protected characteristic of sex, but, however, when a discrimination claim based on breastfeeding occurs in the workplace this is not included in the definition of sex.

It is also important to note in terms of linking sections together that s 13(7) states that s 13 is subject to ss 17(6) and 18(7). This means that s 13 must be read in terms of the provisions in ss 17(6) and 18(7). Equally clear is the absence of any allowed excuse or defence in relation to a claim for direct discrimination.

In order to obtain a full and understandable reading of s 13 it has been necessary to refer to s 4 listing the protected characteristics; and to note that in any given case the sections dealing with the definition of each protected characteristic contained in other sections (e.g. 'race' in section 9) may need to be considered. Furthermore we learn the entire section is subject to ss 17(6) and 18(7).

Reading s 19 of the Equality Act 2010

This section prohibits indirect discrimination. It is set out in a tree diagram below to assist with the identification of links between the section and its sub-sections.

Note that s 19 of the Equality Act 2010 contains smaller linking words (e.g. 'if', 'and') which have been highlighted in bold for your ease of reference. These are important connectors (words that link one set of words to another) such as 'if', 'and' and 'or', small words that can be easily overlooked. But their function is to enable you to see which sub-sections and paragraphs or sub-paragraphs are connected and which, if any, are not connected.

The connectors between the sections, sub-sections, paragraphs and sub-paragraphs reveal the type and function of the connection. For example, if the connector between two sub-sections, or paragraphs within that sub-section is 'or' the connector is indicating that *two* things are in the *alternative*. 'Or' indicates an either/or situation. The connector 'and', indicates that things on both sides of it have to be present. There is a major difference between saying '1 or 2', and saying '1 and 2'. This distinction is important to bear in mind when reading a legal rule in a fixed verbal format.

Before reading on answer, the following questions based on your reading of s 19:

ACTIVITY

Consolidation questions: s 19 EA 2010	
1	What is 'indirect discrimination'?
2	What conditions have to be met before the behaviour identified as indirect discrimination is actionable?
3	Does s 19 provide for a defence?

From your reading of s 19, particularly its header, you will have noted that it is about indirect discrimination. It occurs when a 'provision, criterion or practice' relating to all persons in an environment covered by the Act, places a heavier burden on certain people due to their possession of one or more protected characteristics.

A concrete example would be a business that listed its criteria for promotion: 'attendance at evening in-house training'. It is statistically proven that more women than men have childcare responsibilities in the evening, so less woman are able to attend. Therefore such a rule is potentially indirect discrimination because it affects women more than men.

Sub-section 19(2)(d) allows a limited defence: if A can show that the provision, criterion or practice is a 'proportionate means of achieving a legitimate aim' then it is not indirect discrimination. Everything depends on what a legitimate aim might be.

The phrase 'legitimate aim' is not defined in the legislation and therefore what it might mean will be a question for the judiciary to decide in cases. As precedents on its meaning

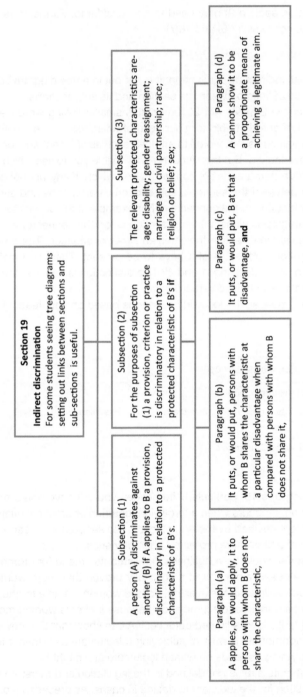

Section 19

Indirect discrimination

For some students seeing tree diagrams setting out links between sections and sub-sections is useful.

Subsection (1)

A person (A) discriminates against another (B) if A applies to B a provision, criterion or practice which is discriminatory in relation to a protected characteristic of B's.

Subsection (2)

For the purposes of subsection (1) a provision, criterion or practice is discriminatory in relation to a protected characteristic of B's **if**

Subsection (3)

The relevant protected characteristics are-
age; disability; gender reassignment; marriage and civil partnership; race; religion or belief; sex;

Paragraph (a)

A applies, or would apply, it to persons with whom B does not share the characteristic,

Paragraph (b)

It puts, or would put, persons with whom B shares the characteristic at a particular disadvantage when compared with persons with whom B does not share it,

Paragraph (c)

It puts, or would put, B at that disadvantage, **and**

Paragraph (d)

A cannot show it to be a proportionate means of achieving a legitimate aim.

Figure 11.10 Layout of s 19

are decided by the senior courts any precedents will be read into the Act by courts deter-mining whether a defendant has a 'legitimate aim'.

Consolidation exercise

Before moving on to consider statutory interpretation, the following exercise is designed to test whether you have a basic understanding of using legislation. It is also designed to further develop your competency in handling statutes.

Exercise 1: reading and comparing changes, a look at s 3 of the Race Relations Act 1976 and s 9 of the Equality Act 2010 (both sections are set out)

Section 3 of the Race Relations Act 1976 (RRA 1976) defined racial grounds for the purposes of bringing a discrimination action. It was replaced by s 9 of the Equality Act. Read the two versions (s 3 and then s 9) which are set out side by side in Figure 11.11 and answer the following questions.

Comparison of S3 RRA 1976 and s9 EA 2010	
Race relations Act 1976 Section 3	**Equality Act 2010 section 9**

3. Meaning of "racial grounds", "racial group" etc.E+W+S
(1) In this Act, unless the context otherwise requires—
• "racial grounds" means any of the following grounds, namely colour,
• race, nationality or ethnic or national origins;
• a person's racial group refer to any racial group into which he falls.
(2) The fact that a racial group comprises two or more distinct racial groups does not prevent it from constituting a particular racial group for the purposes of this Act.
(3) In this Act—
  (a) references to discrimination refer to any discrimination falling within section 1 or 2; and
	9. Race
	This sectionnoteType = Explanatory Notes has no associated
	(1) Race includes—
	  (a) colour;
	  (b) nationality;
	  (c) ethnic or national origins.
	(2) In relation to the protected characteristic of race—
	  (a) a reference to a person who has a particular protected characteristic is a reference to a person of a particular racial group;
	  (b) a reference to persons who share a protected characteristic is a reference to persons of the same racial group.
	(3) A racial group is a group of persons defined by reference to race; and a reference to a person's racial group is a reference to a racial group into which the person falls.

Race relations Act 1976 Section 3	Equality Act 2010 section 9

(b) references to racial discrimination refer to any discrimination falling within section 1, and related expressions shall be construed accordingly.
 	
(4) A comparison of the case of a person of a particular racial group with that of a person not of that group under section 1(1) [F1or (1A)] must be such that the relevant circumstances in the one case are the same, or not materially different, in the other.
	(4) The fact that a racial group comprises two or more distinct racial groups does not prevent it from constituting a particular racial group.
	
	(5) A Minister of the Crown may by order—
	  (a) amend this section so as to provide for caste to be an aspect of race;
	  (b) amend this Act so as to provide for an exception to a provision of this Act to apply, or not to apply, to caste or to apply, or not to apply, to caste in specified circumstances.
	
	(6) The power under section 207(4)(b), in its application to subsection (5), includes power to amend this Act.

Figure 11.11 Comparison of S3 RRA 1976 and s9 EA 2010

Questions
    (i) What general language differences occur between the two sections: s 3 of the RRA 1976 and s 9 of the EA 2010?

    (ii) Which of the two sections is the easier, if any, to understand?

    (iii) What major differences are there between the two sections?

ANSWERS AT THE END OF THE CHAPTER.

We will now turn to consider statutory interpretation.

STATUTORY INTERPRETATION

It is essential to recognise and analyse the strategies used by the judiciary when they engage in the interpretation of legislation. Judges are called upon to interpret words in many types of legal document. We are only considering legislation. We will start by considering interpretation from a general perspective.

The general idea of interpretation

It can be argued that an interpreter creates something new when they engage in interpretation. It could be the case that an interpretation which is triggered by an article for example bears no resemblance to the writer's intention.

Judicial interpretation

The majority of law cases deal with the interpretation of legislation. Senior (unelected) judges effectively have the final 'say' when they engage in statutory interpretation. This gives them an unprecedented power to determine the meaning of words in legislation enacted by the democratically elected Parliament.[10] Issues of tremendous importance can be raised when a problem about the meaning of a statutory provision goes before a court.
    Important questions need to be answered such as:

- What does this section provide for?
- How do these legal rules apply to this factual situation?
- What is the general social impact of this legislation as a whole?
- Does this legislation effectively deal with the matters it was intended to deal with?

    Judges must bring an interpretation in court; they cannot say 'I do not know the meaning of this legislation' and decline to adjudicate a dispute. Additionally, when judges give their interpretation of legislation in the senior courts they can change the entire meaning of a statutory provision. The power of their authority ensures that their interpretation is the given meaning, until another judge, or the legislature, changes that meaning.

THE NEUTRALITY AND OBJECTIVITY OF LAW

It is often claimed that the law is objective and neutral. Given the fluidity of law and its vulnerability to a range of external and internal factors, claims that it is neutral and objective can often seem compromised. How plausible is it to maintain the neutrality of English law when considering disputes between litigants as well as the state and the individual?
    A first question should be 'What do we mean by the term "neutrality"?'. Academics take different positions in relation to this question, depending upon their overall philosophical or theoretical positions concerning the development and function of law. Certainly it cannot be denied that the bulk of modern English law is a political creation of Parliament. This politically constructed law is then interpreted by judges in the court, who continue to mould it as they have done for centuries. Can we ever be certain that judges do not 'tinker' with the meanings of words or phrases in legislation to achieve an outcome that represents their partisan view?

---

10 It is also worth noting here that if a given Parliament has a substantial government majority (that is, there are a large number of government MPs compared with representatives from other parties) then it is the government of the day that gets through the legislation that it wants, which may not be a democratic representation of the will of the majority of the people.

Judges are social actors with their own preferences who we credit with the attempt to act fairly in judgment, despite themselves and their natural inclinations. However, at root a judgment is a subjective text and a student's or a lawyer's interpretation of that text is also subjective. Any interpretation should be tested against the text and evaluated to see if it is a plausible reading.

If we are seduced by the view that the law is the creation of scientific objectivity, and its language easily dissected we will flounder when we become aware of the inevitable imprecision of language.

If we consider law to be like a field, we could say that politicians determine the broad landscape while judges determine where the gateways in and out of that field might be. They do this by their chosen definitions of rules or words which are then applied to the facts of a particular legal dispute. Their reasoning is powerful as it can narrow or broaden the effect of law.

The rules of statutory interpretation

How do judges set about deciding the meaning of words? Words can change their meaning over time, and courts will disagree over the meaning of words in differing time periods.

Meanings, not perceived by those drafting the legislation, may lie latent in the words of that legislation. These can then be drawn out in court in a manner potentially defeating the supposed intention of the law, making the rule unfit for purpose. Or interpretation may narrow or extend the meaning of the rule. Below, the three rules of statutory interpretation (the literal, the mischief and the golden rules) are discussed as well as the more recent approaches of the purposive rule and the teleological[11] approach to interpretation. These rules are, however, rules of practice not rules of law. Therefore a question to pose to yourself is 'Do judges really use the rules of statutory interpretation? If so, which rule do they use first?'

Judges rarely, if ever, state that they are applying a certain rule of interpretation. Often, judges look to see if there can be a literal meaning to the words used in the disputed statutory rule. However, there is no rule that states that they must use the literal rule first. Holland and Webb[12] quite correctly assert that perhaps the better question relates to what style of interpretation judges use. Interpretation is more a question of judicial style than the use of interpretational rules. Indeed, should you attempt to use the rules of statutory interpretation as a guide in the interpretation of a statutory word or phrase, the uselessness of the rules as an interpretational tool will become immediately apparent. However, as a justificatory label they may have a function. As you gain experience in reading judgments you will notice vast differences in judicial styles. Some judgments seem to be based on a blow-by-blow analysis of precedents and earlier usage of words; others seem to be based on tenuous common sense rationales.

Judicial decisions based on the *external* context of the statute will be identified by the judge, or should be. Sometimes this is the result of decision making that appears to be based on issues of public policy (a particularly favoured device in the 1960s and 1970s). Reliance on public policy rationale can be referred to as the 'grand style' or the 'teleological' approach.

---

11 An approach that looks at the purpose of the law and interprets it accordingly. This can involve looking at external documentation rather than just staying with the internal dimensions of the statute.

12 J Holland and J Webb, *Learning Legal Rules* (6th edn, 2006) p 257.

The meaning of a rule and words used to construct the rule can also turn on the *form of* the statute itself, that is, its *internal* context. Judges who rigidly adopt the internal approach are often referred to as *formalists*. Such judges say that they do not create law, they find it. They find it by following the pathways of the rules of statutory interpretation, by moving *within* the statute.

A closer consideration of the simplest definitions of the rules of statutory interpretation enables the classification of the literal rule as the *formalist* approach and the mischief rule as the *teleological* approach. The golden rule, of course, allows one to ignore the formalist approach of the literal rule. It is most likely to result in a teleological approach as the judge, through the golden rule, is released from formalism!

It is therefore essential to have some appreciation of the approaches that the judges take to the issue of interpretation. Without this appreciation you will struggle to fully understanding the shifts in the meaning of legislation that can occur as it goes through the courts.

Many court cases require senior judges to interpret domestic legislation (as well as European legislation and treaties) in order to determine the outcome of the case before them. Also many appeals centre on doubt about the meaning of rules.

When judges engage in statutory interpretation they have to:

- apply legislative rules to various fact situations;
- decide the meaning of words and phrases used in the statute (of course words can mean many things, and that meaning can change over time);
- deal with judicial disagreement over the meaning of words.

The senior judiciary have developed a range of rules of interpretation (although they are not rules in a legal sense and are more like conventions); however, they are strictly followed. These rules are the:

- literal rule;
- golden rule;
- mischief rule.

The mischief rule has developed into the purposive rule and more generally into a teleological approach to interpretation influenced by the approach of European judges working within a civil law legal system. This last approach is unsurprising as in cases dealing with EU law and also the law relating to human rights (which is embedded in the European Convention on Human Rights) judges are now required by English legislation to keep to the decisions of the CJEU and the ECtHR.

In addition, over time, presumptions have also been established. These are pre-assumptions by the judiciary concerning certain matters. For example that Parliament would not intend to repeal a statute without expressly providing for this in later legislation.

General rules for approaching the language of statutes, which we call linguistic rules, have also been established and they still tend to be expressed in Latin. Additionally there are identifiable aids to interpretation both from within the statute (intrinsic aids) and permissible aids to interpretation from sources outside the statute (extrinsic aids).

We will now look at each of these groups, rules of statutory interpretation, presumptions, linguistic rules and aids to interpretation in turn.

The three main rules of statutory interpretation

There are three main rules of statutory interpretation which are set out below in Figure 11.12.

The mischief rule as already noted also developed into the teleological approach and instead of just finding the mischief that the statute was intended to remedy, the judge looks for the 'spirit' of the Act.

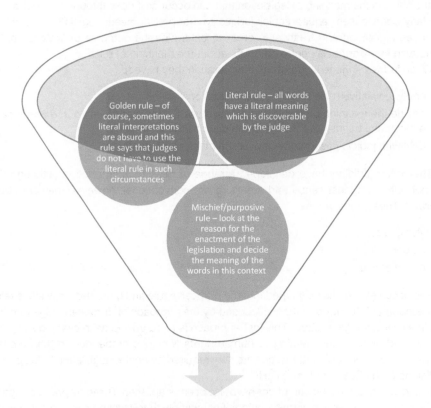

The three main rules of statutory interpretation

Figure 11.12 The three main official rules of statutory interpretation

The literal rule

Essentially this rule states that words should always be given their ordinary, plain and literal meaning. If the words are clear those words state Parliament's intention. Judicial decisions going back over a century agree that this rule is important for preserving the intention of Parliament and ensuring that the democratic parliamentary will is imposed by judges in courts.

One of the more interesting cases to demonstrate the literal rule is the criminal case of *Whiteley v Chappell* (1868).[13] Whiteley was charged with impersonating a 'person entitled to vote', as he had pretended to be a dead person using that name when he voted. The defence argument in court was that a dead person could not vote; or more strictly according to the wording of the legislation was not 'entitled to vote'. Therefore as the defendant had impersonated someone who was not entitled to vote he had not committed the offence. At the trial the judges agreed with this argument.

Now, on a literal interpretation of the words of the offence of impersonating a 'person entitled to vote' this result causes no problems. Yet from the perspective of the law there is no doubt that had Parliament been asked if they had intended the offence to cover the circumstances of the case against Whiteley they would have said 'Yes'.

This case demonstrates the ways in which it is possible for a literal interpretation to undermine the intention of Parliament. You may of course think that the legislators in Parliament should have been more careful with their use of words in the legislation, to ensure that it covered all possibilities. Should the judges, in deciding cases to their satisfaction in court, fill in gaps in legislation or is that the job of the legislator? Which is the correct path for justice and for interpretation?

Drafting legislation is not a scientific art and there will always be mistakes when the generalised words of a section in a statute do not cover all the specific instances it should cover. In *Whiteley*, the statute was designed to stop fraudulent voting at elections by people pretending they were someone else. Parliament only wished those entitled to vote to do so. Whiteley was not entitled to vote. But, as the statute did not list the specific scenario of his case, he was acquitted.[14] What do you consider to be the best way out of this situation if it arose in court? Keep the facts of *Whiteley* in your mind, and consider whether it would have been useful to apply the second rule of statutory interpretation: the golden rule to the case.

You may think that the decision in *Whiteley* was in keeping with the section stating the offence. As there was no other section covering the situation it is right that Whiteley should have been acquitted. Maybe you take the view that Parliament can always amend the legislation to cover the situation in *Whiteley*. But another argument is that using the literal rule led to absurdity and it should not have been applied. It is worth remembering that one person's 'absurdity' may be another person's 'correct' interpretation.

The golden rule

This rule states that the literal rule should be followed except on those occasions when to apply the literal rule would lead to absurd results or go against public policy. We can argue that the decision in *Whiteley* led to absurdity, allowing a defendant to be acquitted on a technicality.

---

13 *Whiteley v Chappell* (1868) LR 4 QB 147.
14 The Law Commission 21 stated very forcefully that the main problem with the literal rule was that it places 'undue emphasis on the literal meaning of the words of a provision' and this in turn 'assumes an unattainable perfection in draftmanship'.

Another classic criminal case illustrates the golden rule in operation: *R v Sigsworth* [1953] Ch 89. Sigsworth had murdered his mother who had died intestate (that is without making a will). The Administration of Estates Act 1925 provided that in such cases the possessions and lands of the deceased go to the next of kin, who was the son, Sigsworth. The court ruled that in a case such as this it would be absurd to allow the son to profit from her death and refused to allow him to inherit; operating a principle of equity that 'a person cannot benefit from his own wrong'.

The mischief rule

Think of the *Whiteley* case again, as we move on to discuss the last of the three main rules of statutory interpretation: the mischief rule. This rule in fact predates the previous two, finding its source in *Heydon's* case (1584) 3 Co Rep 7a.

The mischief rule states that if conditions of doubt arise in a specific statute the judge can look to the purpose of the Act and the mischief (the wrong) that it was supposed to remedy or prevent. Indeed the initial rationale for legislation was to correct weaknesses in the existing common law. So if a problem with interpretation arose in the court the judge chose the interpretation that best remedied the weakness in the common law. However, it was also extended to cover later legislation and new legislation dealing with mischiefs.

In 1980 Lord Diplock, in the case *Jones v Wrotham Park Settled Estates* (1980),[15] made clear the usefulness and current status of the mischief rule. In his judgment he took the opportunity to state that the court should be able to say 'yes' to three questions before they can operate the mischief rule.

(1)   Can the court precisely ascertain the mischief the Act was intended to remedy?
(2)   Is it apparent that the Act failed to deal with it?
(3)   Is it possible just to state what additional words read into the Act would rectify the situation?

Would these questions have been of use in *Whiteley v Chappell*? The court could have answered 'Yes' to questions (1) and (2) above. And no doubt a few words aptly inserted into the relevant section would have resolved the situation. Why do you think they did not themselves think of applying the mischief rule?

The purposive rule

The mischief rule has been developed into the 'purposive approach', which locates a suitable interpretation that gives effect to the general purpose of the legislation. It is an approach of increasing importance and was recognised by Lord Steyn relatively recently in the House of Lords case of *R (Quintavalle) v SS Health*.[16] During the course of his judgment, Steyn stated:

> The pendulum has swung towards purposive methods of construction. This change . . . has been accelerated by European ideas . . . the shift towards purposive interpretation is not in doubt.[17]

---

15   *Jones v Wrotham Park Settled Estates* (1980) AC 74.
16   [2003] 2 AC 687.
17   At para 21.

The case of the *Royal College of Nursing (RCN) v DHSS*[18] provides a good illustration of the use of the purposive rule. The issue in the case concerned the correct interpretation of the phrase 'registered medical professional', a phrase used in a number of statutes. The Royal College of Nursing required a definitive answer due to its use in abortion legislation. There were conflicting interpretations. Does the phrase 'registered medical professional' just refer to doctors or could it apply to nurses?

The RCN took the Department of Health and Social Security to court over the issue. The court held by a three to two majority that abortions by nurses alone were lawful as the purpose of the Act was to stop back street abortions by medically unqualified persons,[19] and therefore for the purposes of the Abortion Act 1967 as amended a nurse was a 'registered medical professional'.

The teleological approach

One can also refer to a fourth possible rule, described as the teleological approach. This asks for a further leap in interpretation from the narrower constraints of locating the mischief the Act is designed to remedy, or locating its purpose, to looking at the *spirit* of the Act. This approach takes a much broader view of the legislation and is useful when considering European Union law, which presents particular problems for the English courts as it is drafted by the legislator in much broader terms than English legislative drafting. European law refers to broad principles, leaving the courts a great deal of leeway relating to interpretation. Indeed, the courts must make use of this leeway as they cannot find the information they need in the detail of the words in the law.

When Parliament enacted the European Communities Act 1972, s 2(4) it bound UK courts to take into account all legal rules arising from treaties or other forms of European law and to interpret cases in court (within the areas under the jurisdiction of our membership of the Union) in accordance with EU law. Often it is necessary for courts to take into account issues such as socio-economic policy. There are many examples of this happening particularly in relation to sex discrimination, racial discrimination and more recently age and religious discrimination, in the workplace. It is also used in domestic courts when dealing with claims under the Human Rights Act which require the court to take into account cases in the ECtHR.

Other aids to statutory interpretation

Presumptions

Presumptions represent the accepted judicial view of the way in which manifestations of particular circumstances will be treated and understood, at least until tangible evidence to the contrary is produced. They tend to arise from theoretical and practical principles of the law. Examples of presumptions are:

■ legislation does not intend to change the common law unless this is clearly expressed;

---

18 *The Royal College of Nursing v DHSS* [1981] 1 All ER 545.
19 Ibid.

- legislation does not have retrospective effect (it cannot make unlawful lawful behaviour that occurred prior to the legislation being enacted) unless clearly expressed;
- Parliament does not intend to bind the Crown by law if this is not clearly expressed;
- legislation does not intend to prohibit judicial review unless this is clearly expressed.

Linguistic rules

Linguistic rules apply to the way in which judges will approach the language of legislation in certain circumstances. These rules are known by their Latin tags, for example:

ejusdem generis (the same type);

If general words follow on from a list of specified things the general words only apply to things of the same nature on the list. A word therefore cannot be dealt with in isolation.

noscitur a sociis: A word is known by the company it keeps.

expressio unius est exclusio alterius: to state one thing is to exclude another.

ignorantia leges non excusat: ignorance of the law is no excuse.

Intrinsic aids to interpretation

Intrinsic aids to interpretation are the signposts *within* a particular piece of legislation to assist the reader to make sense of it (often referred to as aids that are 'within the four corners of the legislation'). Taken to its logical conclusion this suggests that the whole of the statute needs to be referred to for meaning.

If you think back to the layout of statutes shown at the beginning of this chapter directed to short and long titles, marginal notes, headers, the preamble and of course punctuation. Additionally any examples in the statute are considered to be intrinsic aids to interpretation.

All of these devices are *not* part of the actual law contained in the statute but they point to divisions of the statute and its words, and to issues of formatting. They are, as such, aids to interpretation. You will also see that schedules are referred to as well as parts. Not all statutes have these but when they are present there may be a separate interpretation section, or such a section may be included in the main body of the statute. All of these devices should be included. Schedules are part of the statute and are extremely important in determining the meaning of words or phrases.

Extrinsic aids to interpretation

Extrinsic aids to interpretation are the signposts *outside* a particular piece of legislation which assist the judge to make sense of it. These are of several types. There is a generic interpretation statute, the Interpretation Act 1978 that gives a definition of words commonly found in statutes. For example it states in s 6 that words referring to the masculine gender include the feminine (and vice versa). But be warned: any statute can give a different interpretation to these words. Additional extrinsic aids are described below.

Reference to earlier statutes using the same word

Courts are able to look at the use of some words in earlier statutes for guidance on the meaning of a word, as long as it is clear that the use of the word is about the same matter. The Latin term *in pari materia* is used to denote this action.

Dictionaries

If a word has no recognisable legal meaning the court is permitted to consult a dictionary.[20] However, since words can change their meaning over time, different editions of dictionaries may include different definitions. Obvious words whose meanings have changed would include, for example, 'gay'. Each dictionary could also give a different perspective on a word. Which is the 'right' one?

Travaux préparatoires

In many European legal systems working from variants of Roman law within civil code systems, courts are able to study public materials produced during the course of the journey from a draft to finalised legislation. These documents are referred to as preparatory works or *travaux préparatoires*.

Hansard

Traditionally UK judges were not permitted to look at documents produced before the Act was drafted (e.g., government reports, recommendations or other policy documents), or at any proceedings in Parliament as the bill was going through its journey to becoming an Act. These latter documents are recorded verbatim by Hansard. The underlying rationale for not allowing access to this material is the fact that Article [IX] of the Bill of Rights 1689[21] allows MPs to say what they wish within Parliament, stipulating that 'Parliament ought not to be . . . questioned in any court of law or place outside Parliament'. This had been widely interpreted to mean that it was not even permissible to look at Hansard, the verbatim record of the debates and committees in Parliament.

However, a change was signalled in the case of *Pepper v Hart* [1993].[22] The judges in the House of Lords were of the opinion that Hansard could be referred to if:

- the legislation that is the object of the statutory interpretation is ambiguous, obscure or leads to absurdity;
- the document relied on relates to statements by the minister or promoter of the legislation, together with any other parliamentary documents as necessary to understand such statements;
- the statements relied upon are clear.

The House said that this should only happen in rare cases, not as a matter of course. Six judges were in agreement with this course of action but one, Lord Mackay, dissented. He argued that the practicalities involved would be tremendously expensive. Lord Bridge

---

20 We have in other chapters referred to the case of *Mandla v Dowell Lee* [1983] 2 AC 803 which concerned ascertaining the meaning of the word 'ethnic', and the case is a good demonstration of the problems of using dictionaries to find the meaning of the word. See judgment of Lord Denning in the Court of Appeal.

21 1688 c. 2 (Regnal. 1 Will & Mar Sess 2).

22 *Pepper v Hart* [1993] 1 All ER 42 (HL).

considered that the court would not use its power very much, although he was initially proved wrong (concurrent with the greater use of this freedom, drawbacks became apparent). Exactly how much ambiguity suffices to open Hansard, and how clear must the minister's statement be?

By 1996 the House of Lords was voicing concern about the freedom given by *Pepper v Hart*.[23] Lord Steyn[24] has even severely criticised *Pepper v Hart* in non-judicial situations such as after-dinner speeches or public lectures. The main issue is that, of course, any word in a statute can in certain contexts be thought ambiguous. Opening up Hansard for discussion and determination by the judges raised the possibility that understanding concerning the meaning of words and phrases could be completely overturned.

In 1995 a practice direction had been issued relating to the usage of Hansard material for the purposes of statutory interpretation.[25] This was repeated in a later consolidating practice statement in 1999 covering the Court of Appeal (Civil Division)[26] and then later the criminal courts.[27] Now if a party to a case wishes to rely on Hansard, they must serve copies of the extract and a short précis of their argument on the other party or parties at least five working days before the hearing.

So, the decision in *Pepper v Hart* has had a mixed reception from the judiciary, and judges speaking extra-judicially have been highly critical of it.[28] Doubtless it marks an important paradigm shift with regard to judicial interpretation.

Explanatory notes

The department of state sponsoring bills now issues explanatory notes in important areas of law to guide the reader. They do not form part of the statute, are not authorised, and have no legal effect. But such notes do have their uses, particularly as an aid to understanding the aim and intent of the drafter of the legislation. Those aims and intentions, however, can of course change during the act of interpretation in court. If you read the explanatory notes of legislation you need to be aware that case law may have changed the interpretation laid upon a certain section, etc., by the explanatory notes.

Interpretation Act 1978

This Act sets out a range of issues relating to interpretation. The Act provides general meanings for words (e.g. that the masculine always includes the feminine and vice versa unless it is specifically stated this is not to be the case).

Which rules of interpretation should be used, when, and in what order?

The rules of interpretation that have been so far identified are not, themselves, legal rules but guidance rules. And you will not be surprised to learn that no legal rules exist that state which

---

23 Brown Wilkinson LJ was one of the majority judges in *Pepper v Hart*, but in *Melliush (Inspector of Taxes) v BMI (No 3)* [1996] AC 454 he said that the ministerial statement had to be directed to the very point that is the subject of doubt in the current case.

24 J Steyn 'Pepper v Hart A Re-examination' (2001) 21 *Oxford Journal of Legal Studies* 59.

25 Practice Direction (Reference to Extracts from Hansard) [1995] 1 WLR 192; 20 December 1994.

26 [1999] 1 WLR 1059.

27 [2002] 1 WLR 2870.

28 K Llewellyn *The Common Law Tradition* (Little Brown, Boston Mass, 1960).

rules of interpretation can be used; nor their order of use. What we should consider, however, is how judges choose the appropriate rules of interpretation applicable to the job in hand, and how they explain that choice. Some might say judges merely want to be seen to have a method so that they are not accused of just creating law, but you would be better off thinking of statutory interpretation as allowing the use of a range of styles of interpretation. Everyone is different and individual judges prefer and use different styles of interpretation.

Nearly 50 years ago, long before the development of cases such as *Pepper v Hart*, Karl Llewellyn[29] noted that judges in fact have two styles of interpretation: the grand style and the formal style. The formal style is quite rigid in its deference to tradition, doctrine and the view that judges should not and do not create law. The grand style is used by judges who are more creative and flexible in their use of interpretation.[30]

Statutory interpretation and the European Convention on Human Rights

The Human Rights Act 1998 (HRA 1998) gives claimants the right to go to a domestic court to bring an action for infringement of the European Convention on Human rights (ECHR). This requires the judiciary to interpret the Convention.

The HRA 1998 states that in doing so they must recognise the decisions of the European Court of Human Rights. Section 2 of the HRA imposes a statutory duty on courts; they must take account of decisions of the ECtHR and the Committee of Ministers.

Section 3 imposes a positive statutory duty on courts when interpreting primary and secondary domestic legislation to do so in a manner that is compatible with 'convention rights' set out in Schedule 1.

The requirement for courts to take into account the case law of the ECtHR has exerted an impact on to the way that English judges interpret both legislation and case law. The English judiciary have had to make changes to their standard methods of interpretation of statutes.[31] In those areas where the courts have a duty to consider the case law from the European courts they confront a major difference. In English court cases it is customary for dissenting judgments to be published. These are judgments expressing a particular judge's disagreement with the majority decision of the court. Even where several judges agree on outcome they can disagree on the detailed route they took to their agreement. Each judge can choose to issue a judgment, therefore in English courts judges are used to dealing with several judgments in previous decided cases that they may be considering. However, it is customary for the ECtHR to give one decision and the reasons given for their decision are usually less detailed than in English courts, although at times a dissenting judgment may be published.[32]

This does not mean that English courts do not give reasons in cases dealing with the ECHR but the cases it receives from the European level have to be incorporated into their decisions and these cases come from a different legal tradition where the detailed rationale

---

29 An excellent case study of Llewellyn's observation can be found in the case of *Davis v Johnson* [1978] 1 All ER 841 (CA) affd [1978] 1 All ER 1132 (HL). It is also the subject of an excellent case study by Twining and Miers *How to Do Things with Rules* (2013). An informative and interesting summary of this area is also contained in Holland and Webb *Learning Legal Rules* (6th edn, OUP, Oxford, 2006).

30 Is this not another description of the teleological approach?

31 We will be considering this more in Chapter 12.

32 This was done in the case of *Al-Skeini and others v The United Kingdom* (Application no. 55721/07; Reported: (2011) 53 EHRR 18; 30 BHRC 561; [2011] Inquest LR 73; *Times*, July 13, 2011 and available on HUDOC www.hudoc.echr.coe.int/sites/eng/pages/search.aspx?i=001–105606#{"itemid":["001–105606"].

for the decision is not expected or required.[33] Although it is accepted that these cases do in fact lay down firm guidelines that need to be followed.

Statutory interpretation and secondary legislation

It is not just primary legislation that calls for statutory interpretation. There are thousands of pages of secondary legislation published each year, and these too can become central to legal disputes prompting a need for interpretation. More or less the same rules apply as those that we have already briefly noted, but with secondary legislation there are also extra tasks and issues that require consideration.

Secondary legislation has to be read in conjunction with the parent Act. The Interpretation Act 1978 states in s 11 that words used in the secondary legislation must be interpreted to have the same meaning as words used in the parent Act. But, if the parent Act itself is vague, the court will probably have to consider the meaning of both.

Whilst primary legislation has hierarchical standing over common law, secondary legislation does not. The courts, therefore, will not wish to apply an interpretation that dislodges established common law. While courts cannot declare a primary Act invalid they can declare secondary legislation invalid if the powers delegated have been overstepped.

Summary to statutory interpretation

This brief discussion reveals the different approaches to statutory interpretation that can occur as one case travels through the judicial system. It is worth noting that the rules of statutory interpretation that a judge is applying are not generally referred to in the course of the judgment. Context and judicial attitudes or preferences determine the rules used. Only careful analysis of the judgment will indicate the 'styles' of interpretation that seem to be represented.

Interpretational problems can never be solved by the neat application of interpretational rules. Even worse, perhaps, the rules do little or nothing to solve problems. Perhaps all they do is justify solutions. There is rarely one right answer, only a range of more plausible and less plausible outcomes, varying according to interpretational styles. Judges use their creativity in working out a solution according to criteria which must be rational either in reality or in argument. They invariably go beyond the text when constructing answers. Lord Denning, for example, moved from dictionary definitions to subjective assertion. Often, judges say no more than 'this is the answer because I say so'.

Judges, as previously noted, can be classified as formalists or contextualists. Knowing this it may sometimes be possible to guess which rules the judges are using, though sometimes you may not understand what they are arguing. At times, judges themselves are wrong and not too sure themselves of the appropriate outcome. This is what makes comprehension of the methods of statutory interpretation, and the use of precedents, so difficult. It is essential to realise the limits of a supposed scientific approach and the limitless possibilities that open up when the illogical bridges from one set of rationales to the next are located.

---

33 That is, deciding current cases on the same basis as previous similar cases in the Court of Appeal or Supreme Court depending on where the case is currently being heard – there is more discussion on these matters in the chapters covering case law. Equally as you will have noted from discussion in Chapter 3, the same issues arise in cases relating to the European Union. Nor are EU cases from the Court of Justice of the European Union (CJEU) based on the English system of rigid adherence to precedent.

As judges engage more with the European dimensions of interpretation they are being forced to engage more often with the teleological approach used in European cases. As discussed in Chapter 4, the Human Rights Act 1998 states that judges deciding cases on the enforcement of European Convention rights *must* have regard to the case law and jurisprudence of the European Court of Human Rights. In addition, by virtue of the European Communities Act 1972 (as amended) English courts are required to take notice of the decisions of the Court of Justice of the European Union. It is highly likely that this consistent engagement will result, over time, in a profound change to the tradition of statutory interpretation within the English legal system.

CONCLUSION

The majority of English law is in the form of legislation. Understanding statutory provisions context is a core skill for the competent critical evaluation of the rationale for a particular statute. It is also core for the competent legal analysis and application of statutory provisions when engaging in legal problem solving.

Being able to understand the layout of statutes, and of sections within them, as well as appreciating the links between sections in a statute, and between several statutes, ensures that you are in a good position to begin the task of understanding the detail of any legislation you are dealing with.

Competent analysis of legislation also involves the equally important skill of reading case law. It is essential to also be aware of any leading cases determining the meaning of words and phrases in the legislation you are considering, and understand the process of statutory interpretation.

Whilst many databases can assist you with finding a statute and then searching within, it is essential to appreciate that there is only one official source of legislation, the government's online database, www.legislation.gov.uk which is hosted by the National Archives.

CHAPTER SUMMARY

- A range of skills need to be used to understand legislation: language skills, substantive knowledge skills, argumentative skills and rule handling skills.
- Correct understanding of the relationship between parts, chapters, sections, subsections, paragraphs, sub-paragraphs, marginal notes, headings and Schedules enables the general layout of the Act to be ascertained.
- Always use up to date, reliable academic or professional sources to ascertain whether legislation is current.
- The only official source of information on statutes and changes to them is the government's online database at www.legislation.gov.uk.
- When statutes do not define the meaning of words in them and a legal dispute is before the courts the judiciary engage in statutory interpretation.

- There are three conventional 'rules' of statutory interpretation developed by the judiciary: the literal, golden and mischief rules.
- The mischief rule has given rise to the purposive rule and the teleological approach.
- Judges also use presumptions, linguistic rules and intrinsic and extrinsic aids to interpretation.
- When secondary legislation is the object of statutory interpretation it must be read in conjunction with the parent Act.

CONSOLIDATION TO EXERCISE (COMPARISON BETWEEN S 9 OF THE EQUALITY ACT 2010 AND S 3 OF THE RACE RELATIONS ACT 1976)

(1) What general language differences occur between the two sections?

The language in s 3 of the RRA 1976 retains the old format of 'he' meaning 'she' in general terms. Provision for this is made under the Interpretation Act 1978. Section 6 provides
'In any Act, unless the contrary intention appears,—

(a)   words importing the masculine gender include the feminine;
(b)   words importing the feminine gender include the masculine;
(c)   words in the singular include the plural and words in the plural include the singular.'

However s 9 moves away from masculine and feminine and adopts the more neutral words 'person' and 'persons' instead.

(2) Which section is the easier, if any, to understand?

I would suggest that s 9 of the EA 2010 is easier in terms of using a much more straightforward layout. It is more logically set out, particularly in terms of distinguishing between race and racial grounds.

(3) What major differences are there between the two sections?

Section 9 of the EA 2010 introduces the concept of 'caste' into the definition of race, and racial grounds.

Section 9 does not include the reference to comparison set out in s 3(4) of the Race Relations Act 1976. In fact this is found in s 23 of the EA 2010 and is now applied generally (unless expressly excluded in relation to any protected characteristic). This was ascertained by looking down the sections in part 2 of chapter 2 and noting one was sub-headed 'comparison by reference to circumstances'.

HOW TO READ AND UNDERSTAND ECHR AND EU LAW

12

LEARNING OUTCOMES

After reading this chapter, you should be able to:

- Give a basic description of a civil law legal system.
- Appreciate the main differences between a civil law and a common law legal system.
- Read and understand EU treaties and secondary law (in particular legislation made by the institutions of the EU and judgments of the EU Court of Justice).
- Appreciate the way in which articles in EU treaties have been renumbered and at times placed into other treaties.
- Appreciate how the renumbering and where applicable the relocation of articles can be checked.
- Appreciate the need to be aware of changes when reading cases from the ECtHR prior to certain changes taking place.
- Understand the difference between EU law and the law relating to the ECHR.
- Understand the nature of links between the EU and the ECHR.
- Understand the relationship between the ECHR and the Human Rights Act 1998.
- Be able to competently read and understand law reports and court reports of cases in the European Court of Human Rights (ECtHR).

INTRODUCTION

This chapter is divided into three sections. Section 1 briefly considers the nature of a civil law legal system and the differences between it and a common law legal system. Section 2 deals with the legal system of the EU, the acquis communautaire. It outlines the system, and discusses the meaning of key terms that are essential for understanding EU law. This provides a basis for a discussion of the different types of EU law (EU treaties, secondary legislation and cases in the Court of Justice, the CJEU) and how to understand and read them.

Section 3 deals with the European Convention on Human Rights and its impact on the human rights law of the English legal system. It deals with reading and understanding the ECHR and cases in the European Court of Human Rights (ECtHR). This court's procedures and principles are also drawn from concepts of civil law. In addition this section deals with the relationship between the ECHR, the Human Rights Act 1998 and decisions of the English and UK domestic courts.

SECTION 1: CIVIL LAW[1] LEGAL SYSTEMS

The vast majority of the legal systems of the world, and nearly all European legal systems are based on a civil law legal system. Among the member states of the EU only the English legal system and the Irish legal system are common law systems; all other states have civil law systems.

At its most generalised level a civil law legal system contains a clearly identifiable set of core legal rules and principles that are viewed as the primary law of the state. There are, however, several differing types of civil law systems, or civilian law systems. Many of them codify the primary law in a code.

Whilst there are several types of civil law system all of them, to a greater or lesser extent, have their roots in the Roman law of the city state of Rome codified in the Code of Justinian, the 'corpus juris civilis' in the sixth century CE.

In Europe Roman civil law has also been mixed with Napoleonic law. This was developed by Napoleon as a break with the past, and was aimed at introducing a system of law untainted by its development and use by overthrown royal regimes. Roman civil law has also been mixed with Germanic law and canonical (or ecclesiastical) law. The law of the Roman Catholic Church was always based on Roman law; even in England much of current ecclesiastical law is civilian in orientation and procedure.

Staying with the concept of a legal code, in a civilian system the code is viewed as the only primary law. This means that the decisions of the courts relating to the law are not seen as capable of constituting primary law. They are viewed as secondary and subordinate to the primary law. Courts make case by case decisions based on the code and

---

1   The word civil law is used within the common law legal system. However, it has an entirely different meaning relating to actions between private legal persons (e.g. actions in contract, tort, employment law). Here its meaning is used in a different sense to describe an entire legal system.

in doing so they do not have to concern themselves at all with the concept of precedent. Although sometimes, if the court wishes, there can be reference to past cases and this could be viewed as drawing upon a diluted form of precedent.

It is important for you to understand that the code in a civilian legal system cannot be likened to a statute in the English legal system. The code is a broad sweep generalised and abstracted set of laws and principles rather than the detailed specific provisions found in English legislation.

Differences between civil law systems and the English common law legal system

A civil legal system usually has a code of all laws that are the primary law of the state, and judgments in law cases do not create law. The case is always subordinate to the code. A particular difference between the common law and civil law system is the operation of the idea of precedent in the courts. English common law courts are bound by previous precedents as we have already discussed in Chapter 10. Civil law courts allow themselves to be persuaded by precedent, but can ignore any relevant previous cases. Civil law systems therefore have cases where rules are applied to situations to resolve disputes. But the same answer does not have to be given each time a similar case comes to court. While in the English common law system a judge can 'declare' law (and is declaring what it always was) in the civil law system there is a much heavier reliance on codes enacted by government. Whilst the common law concentrates on the application of law to the material facts of individual disputes, the civil system concentrates on issues at stake in cases, and adherence to the code. It is the issue now before the court that is of concern and there is no desire to unpick the facts of earlier cases.

Another, noticeable difference relates to trial procedure. While the English trial is adversarial with a relatively passive role being undertaken by the judge, the European civil law legal systems are inquisitorial. Judges are pro active and engage in investigating the case. Additionally there are differences with the way in which the courts prefer to be given evidence and legal argument for the trial. The English legal system requires oral proceedings while civil legal systems have primarily written proceedings. Oral investigations and submissions as part of the court case can occur over a period of months.

SECTION 2: UNDERSTANDING AND READING EU LAW

There are a number of issues that are important for a solid understanding of EU law which in turn enables you to read EU law. You need to be aware of the EU legal system, the different types of law within the EU legal system and their differing legal effects. Some of these matters are discussed in detail in Chapter 5 but for your ease of reference the main features of the legal system of the EU are briefly set out below.

THE LEGAL SYSTEM OF THE EU: THE ACQUIS COMMUNAUTAIRE

The EU has its own civil law based legal system, the acquis communautaire (sometimes just referred to as the 'EU acquis', or even just 'acquis') which is a recognised part of the legal order of international law. It does not contain a code; however, the treaties establishing the EU have status as constitutional treaties, and they contain articles that are primary law, whilst a range of secondary laws are constantly being adopted by EU institutions. The acquis communautaire was not directly created by the founding EEC Treaty of 1957. However its existence was made clear by the Court of Justice of the European Union in two leading cases in 1962 and 1964 respectively, *Van Gen den Loos*[2] and *Costa v ENEL*[3].

This legal system is composed of a range of policy and law making institutions and sources of law. EU law itself is mainly sourced in:

- Primary law: treaty articles deemed to create legal obligations and duties.
- Secondary legislation created by the institutions of the EU as set out in Article 288 of the TFEU:[4]
  - ☐ Regulations/directives/decisions adopted by the institutions and legally binding.
  - ☐ Recommendations and opinions adopted by the institutions that just express their view on a matter. These are legal documents and part of the legal system but they are not legally binding.
- Legal principles: established by the CJEU in its court judgment. These principles[5] are not a closed list, in the future more could be added, currently they are:
  - ☐ Due Process.
  - ☐ Equality.
  - ☐ Equity.
  - ☐ Fundamental rights.
  - ☐ Legitimate expectations.
  - ☐ Legal certainty.
  - ☐ Procedural propriety.
  - ☐ Proportionality.
  - ☐ Subsidiarity.

The different types of EU law have the following differing legal effects:

- Law that is 'directly applicable:' law considered to be directly applicable becomes part of the domestic legal system of all member states as soon as it comes into force in the EU legal system. These laws are:
  - ☐ Treaty articles if certain criteria are met (as developed and determined by the Court of Justice of the EU).

---

2   *N.V. Algemene Transport-en Expeditie Onderneming van Gend en Loos v Nederlandse Tariefcommissie* [1963] CMLR 105, 129.
3   (Case 14/1964) *Costa v Ente Nazionale per l'Energia Elettrica (ENEL)* [1964] CMLR 425.
4   Treaty on the Functioning of the European Union consolidated version 2012.
5   For a fuller explanation of general principles please see Chapter 5 and particularly Figure 5.7.

☐   Regulations in their entirety (as determined by Article 288 of the TFEU).

☐   Additionally, decisions, which are addressed to one or more member states, are directly applicable in their entirety on those member states addressed (as determined by Article 288 of the TFEU).

■ Law that is binding 'as to outcome': directives. These laws are specific requests for member states to achieve a goal within a specified timescale, but the state can decide how to do this. Therefore they are said to be legally binding as to '*outcome*'. Directives have been used extensively to formulate and implement policies within the EU.

■ Law that has 'direct effect': This is mainly EU law treaty articles or regulations that the Court of Justice has deemed capable of giving individual citizens rights that they claim in their national courts. If certain conditions are met the court has also determined that directives can also have direct effect.

☐   Vertical direct effect: Rights and obligations can be the subject of a legal action by individuals or non-state companies against the member state.

☐   Horizontal direct effect: Rights and obligations can be the subject of legal action between individuals or non-state companies.

The two terms 'directly applicable' and 'direct effect' are often erroneously used as interchangeable even in the CJEU. You will have to take the context into account to determine what the court means. The term direct effect does not appear in any of the treaties as it was an approach developed by the court. Directly applicable does occur in the treaties. A detailed discussion of these issues can be found in Chapter 5.

The nature of the trial process in the EU civil law legal system: the acquis communautaire

The trial is characterised by the civil law system's preference for an inquisitorial method of dispute resolution. The inquisitorial method of judicial investigation expects evidence and legal argument to be primarily submitted to the court in writing, and does not usually require any oral evidence or legal argument to be presented.

What type of case gets to the CJEU?

The CJEU hears the following types of case:

(1)   Action between member states and the institutions of the EU, usually the Commission, brings action against member states breaching EU law.

(2)   Actions between member states relating to breach of EU law.

(3)   Actions by individuals or private organisations in their national courts against their own member state.

(4)   Requests for a preliminary ruling concerning the correct interpretation of EU law, including whether a law has direct effect.

Requesting a preliminary ruling

The preliminary ruling is the most important action in terms of its impact on the English legal system. We will therefore concentrate on this type of case, using it to explore the relationship between cases and treaties or secondary legislation (regulations, directives etc). One of the most important duties and powers of the Court of Justice is to be the final arbiter of the correct interpretation of EU primary and secondary law. It is the only court with the power to interpret EU law and hear requests by states relating to claims challenging the validity of EU law. Most often this power to interpret finds expression in the request for a preliminary ruling.

Article 267 of the TFEU[6] states that a national court may ask the CJEU a question arising in a case before it about the correct interpretation of Community law, or the validity of law under EU law. The case is paused, and once the CJEU has given its preliminary ruling the case restarts but that ruling must be applied.

When should a state court seek a preliminary reference?

The most important role of the Court of Justice is in ensuring the harmonious interpretation and application of the two Founding Treaties of the EU (TFEU and TEU) through its power to hear a 'preliminary reference' as set out in Article 267 of the TFEU.

Article 267 Treaty on the functioning of the European Union (TFEU) (ex Article 234 of the TEC)

The Court of Justice of the European Union shall have jurisdiction to give preliminary rulings concerning:

(a) the interpretation of the treaties;

(b) the validity and interpretation of acts of the institutions, bodies, offices or agencies of the Union.

Where such a question is raised before any court or tribunal of a member state, that court or tribunal may, if it considers that a decision on the question is necessary to enable it to give judgment, request the court to give a ruling thereon.

Where any such question is raised in a case pending before a court or tribunal of a member state against whose decisions there is no judicial remedy under national law, that court or tribunal shall bring the matter before the court.

If such a question is raised in a case pending before a court or tribunal of a member state with regard to a person in custody, the Court of Justice of the European Union shall act with the minimum of delay.

---

6   Formerly Article 234 of the TEU, and prior to that Article 177 of the EEC Treaty.

A preliminary reference is a request for guidance on the meaning of any aspect of an article or articles in the founding treaties or any secondary legislation created by EU institutions. Where national courts are applying EU law they either have a discretion or an obligation to request a preliminary ruling on a matter of the interpretation of EU law or a review of legality of EU law before continuing with the case. If the national court is a final appellate court then they must request a preliminary ruling. If the court is not a final appellate court the relevant court may refer. The national court must implement the ruling of the Court of Justice.

Article 267 makes clear that only the CJEU has the power to determine a matter of interpretation or validity of EU law. Their determination is immediately applicable to all member states. Most of the preliminary references made relate to matters of a financial nature, for example imposing duty taxes on imports and exports.

Later in this chapter we will be considering the case of *van Gend en Loos* 1962. This was a preliminary reference concerning whether an import tax by Dutch authorities was valid under EU law. To give you an idea of what a preliminary reference question looks like the question in *van Gend en Loos* is set out below:

'(1) Is Article 12[7] of the EEC treaty[8] directly applicable[9] and can individuals make a claim in their own domestic courts under Article 12?

(2) If the answer to (1) is 'yes', was the application of an import duty in breach of Article 12 or was it a reasonable alteration as allowed by Article 12?'

Look at the text below extracted from Article 267.

Where such a question is raised before any court or tribunal of a member state, that court or tribunal may, if it considers that a decision on the question is necessary to enable it to give judgment, request the court to give a ruling thereon.

Can you predict any issues of interpretation that may occur with this text? Consider the phrase 'if it considers that a decision on the question is necessary to enable it to give judgment.' What is the meaning of 'necessary' in this context? Case law in the CJEU, *Costa v ENEL*,[10] determined that the decision that it was necessary to refer is one purely for the member state's court. Further case law, *CILFIT Srl v Ministro della Sanit*[11] makes clear when such a request for a preliminary ruling is not necessary. These are situations where the question raised about EU law is irrelevant to resolving the case before the national

---

7 Now Article 30 of the TFEU.
8 Provisions of the EEC Treaty after its amendment to TEU now split between the TEU consolidated version 2010 and the Treaty on the Functioning of the EU consolidated version 2010. You can track changes to numbering using the table of equivalences.
   www.eur-lex.europa.eu/LexUriServ/LexUriServ.do?uri=OJ:C:2010:083:0361:EN:PDF accessed 13 October 2014.
9 Directly applicable EU law becomes part of the English legal system when it comes into force in the EU legal system. Article 288 of the TFEU sets out the different types of EU law and whether they are directly applicable. See also Chapter 5.
10 Case 6/64 *Costa v ENEL* [1964] ECR 585.
11 Case 283/81 *CILFIT Srl v Ministro della Sanit* [1982] ECR 3415; [1983] 1 CMLR 472.

court, or the CJEU has already given a preliminary ruling on the same matter or where in fact there is no real interpretational issue, the right interpretation is clear.[12]

How do we know there is a clear meaning however, when one person's clarity may be another person's obscurity? There have been differences of opinion in the English courts on whether the meaning is clear and no preliminary reference need be requested. There is leeway in this notion of 'clear meaning' for national courts to do what they want, but this has not been the case.

Procedure to be followed by a domestic court in the English legal system when making a preliminary reference

The Court of Appeal and the High Court in the English legal system, and the UK Supreme Court, have all issued virtually identical practice directions setting out the procedure to be adopted when a relevant court is making a request for a preliminary ruling. The Court of Appeal and High Court are covered by *Practice Direction (ECJ references: procedure) Supreme Court [1999]*.[13] The UK Supreme Court is covered by *The Supreme Court of the United Kingdom Practice Direction 11 The Court of Justice of the European Union*.[14]

The practice directions state that the case must be stopped if a matter covered by Article 267 arises, its determination is required to dispose of the case, and the court wishes to make a reference to the Court of Justice requesting a preliminary ruling. Although, as you know, according to Article 267 if the court concerned is the final appeal court, as the UK Supreme Court is, it must make a reference to the Court of Justice.

The relevant national court must draft the question that is the subject of the request for a preliminary ruling. And when doing so it must bear in mind when drafting the question that it must be capable of easy translation as it will be translated into all of the languages of the member states. In addition to sending the request the national court must send a summary containing details of the procedural history of the case, relevant facts of the case, outline of legal arguments presented, applicable national law, names of the parties, rationale for making the reference and the EU law that is affected. The request is sent by the senior master of the Queen's Bench Division to be lodged with the registry of the CJEU.

It is the Court of Justice that determines how the reference should be heard, either in a full plenary or in chambers. It must sit in a Grand Chamber when a member state or an institution which is a party to the proceedings so requests, and in particularly complex or important cases. Since 2007 the EU general court can hear preliminary references in areas where it has been given jurisdiction to do so.

As soon as the registry of the CJEU receives the request for a preliminary ruling it is translated into the official languages of the EU and sent to interested parties which include all member states. Any interested party then has two months in which to make a submission in relation to the request. The case is assigned to a judge rapporteur and to an Advocate General.

---

12 This is similar to the French law doctrine of 'acte clair' when if the meaning is clear there is no question of needing an interpretation.
13 1 WLR 260.
14 UKSC Practice Direction 11.

The judge will issue an initial report on the request and gives advice as to the appropriate legal forum for the case to be dealt with. This can be in chambers (courts of three–five judges) or in Grand Chamber, or in a plenary of the whole court. Important requests are conducted in plenary. The judge will also determine whether there are any matters of fact or law upon which further information is required. He then summarises the legal issues and observations of interested parties who submit during the two month period.

The role of the Advocate General is to present a range of legal arguments relating to the application and to advise the court as to the most appropriate outcome. The court does not have to follow the advice of the Advocate General. But it is taken into account.

When the judge reaches a view a draft preliminary ruling is sent to the other members of the court for observations. The court will issue only one final opinion, giving their judgment on the request and giving their ruling, and this will be under the name of one judge. There are no dissenting or majority opinions in the CJEU as these are not customary in civil law systems. The opinion will not normally contain reasons for the decision, but if the opinion disagrees with the Attorney General's advice reasons may be given.

GUIDED EXERCISE: READING AND UNDERSTANDING THE CASE OF
VAN GEND EN LOOS V NEDERLANDSE TARIEFCOMMISSIE **(CASE 26/62)**
[1963] ECR 3 (VAN GEND EN LOOS) PAGE 00095 (AGO PAGE 00001)

The purpose of this task is to enable the development of your confidence in reading official EU judgments, and consolidate your understanding of preliminary references. A relatively short judgment concerning a request for a preliminary ruling has been chosen. Decided over 50 years ago, it remains a leading case on the legal effect of Article 12 of the European Economic Treaty (EEC Treaty) 1957, the founding treaty of the EU. Because of its age the judgment allows you to see in action the issue of needing to know how the numbering and location of treaty articles have changed. For example, the judgment from 1963 uses the old names and numbering of the EEC Treaty. Do you know where to find these articles with their current numbering? The founding treaties of the EU were extensively rearranged after the Lisbon Treaty in 2009. You need to know how to find out if an article has also changed its treaty location. The judgment also gives you a chance to see the terms 'directly applicable', and 'direct effect' being used, and for you to consider if you understand what they mean and can follow the judgment.

You will be reading a copy of the official online European Court Report of the judgment in this case. The text is here in the chapter in Table 12.1. However, it is locatable online from the official journal on EUR-Lex. With a few exceptions the online version of the judgment in the official journal is the legally accepted judgment. A print form of the judgment is not considered legally acceptable. This online version is available in all of the languages of the member states in the EU.

The opinion of the Advocate General (AGO) is not included in the judgment and does not form part of the legally accepted judgment. It is, however, placed online in the same ECR, with a different page number referenced. Reading the judgment without having read the AGO's opinion presents quite starkly the limited information that is put into the judgment. If you wish, after you have read the judgment you should access the AGO for the case online and consider it.[15]

Reading this case will demonstrate the need to be aware of, and sensitive to, a number of pieces of information:

- The status of the CJEU and its jurisdiction.
- The authority of the CJEU within the English legal system.
- Understanding the terminology used to describe differing EU law (articles, regulations, directives, etc.).
- The relationship between differing EU rights and obligations.
- Being able to determine the impact of the case, if any, on the English legal system.

This guided reading gives you an opportunity develop an understanding of the above issues.

This case is also reported in the UK Common Market Law Reports[16] as well. The CMLR[17] report is of course unofficial, but we will be referring to some differences between the official ECR report of judgments and the law report in the CMLR.

The initial reading of the judgment in van Gend en Loos

It is always a good idea to quickly read documents before a more considered reading, as long as you know why you are reading them. Ideally locate the report of the judgment on the EUR-Lex website.[18] When you have located the site go to the Official Journal[19] of the EU. The report can also be accessed from the EU section of Westlaw. Read the judgment carefully. Once you have read the case quickly and have a general idea of what it is about, read it a second time, more slowly, and then answer the following questions. In no more than 50 words, state the facts of the case (the fewer words the better).

- What does van Gend en Loos want the court to allow?
- What has to be decided before van Gend en Loos can get what they want?
- What is the rationale behind the decision?
- What are the legal issues in the case?
- Do you find the language of the case difficult, or the case itself difficult to read? Give reasons for your answer.

The second reading: the tabulated micro-analysis of the case

What you may have noticed in your reading of the case and subsequent answering of the questions is that the language of the law report is very different in style to that of an

---

15 *NV Algemene Transport-en Expeditie Onderneming van Gend en Loos v Nederlandse Tariefcommissie* [1963] ECR 3, p 00001.
16 Published by Sweet and Maxwell since 1962.
17 (1963) CMLR 105.
18 http://www.eur-lex.europa.eu.
19 http://eur-lex.europa.eu/oj/direct-access.html.

English law report. You are reading a translation of the working language of the EU, which is French not English, although all languages have equal status within the Community. What you will have immediately noticed is that the report reads as a series of descriptions and assertions. You will not find the reasoned, illustrative argumentative techniques that are the more familiar to the common law lawyer. Think, for example, of the case *George Mitchell (Chesterhall) Ltd v Finney Lock Seeds*.[20]

To assist you to engage with this case, it has been broken down into a table style format that takes you through each paragraph in Table 12.2. The table places the original text of the case (with paragraphs numbered) beside the summary of that paragraph. You may well find it extremely useful to see a steady demonstration of summarising dense or technical text. In addition, a classification of the function of each paragraph is given under headings such as:

- description;
- setting out facts;
- procedural;
- conclusion;
- proposition or point in an argument;
- inference.

The layout of the table is therefore as in Table 12.1.

TABLE 12.1 GUIDED READING (VAN GEND EN LOOS)

Column 1	Column 2	Column 3
Text Section Number, and Law Report or Guide Headers	Verbatim report divided into numbered text selections (column 1) and as required alpha paragraphs for illustration purposes	Summary of text selection and Guide comments as considered necessary
Text Section Number Law Report or Guide Headers	Verbatim report divided into numbered text selections (column 1) and as required alpha paragraphs for illustration purposes.	Summary of text selection and Guide comments as considered necessary
1. EU: Case 26/62 Celex No. 662CJ0026 European Union Cases Court of Justice	Judgment of the Court of 5 February 1963. *NV Algemene Transport-en Expeditie Onderneming van Gend & Loos v Netherlands Inland Revenue Administration*. Reference for a preliminary ruling: Tariefcommissie – Pays-Bas – Case 26–62	**SUMMARY** This states that this is the judgment of the court with regard to a request for a preliminary ruling from the Tariefcommissie. The parties to the national action are named

20 [1983] 2 All ER 732–44.

TABLE 12.2 GUIDED READING: ANNOTATED TABLE OF THE VERBATIM TEXT OF NV ALGEMENE TRANSPORT-EN EXPEDITIE ONDERNEMING VAN GEND & LOOS V NETHERLANDS INLAND REVENUE 1963 ECR ADMINISTRATION [1963] ECR 3

Column 1	Column 2	Column 3
Text Section Number Law Report or Guide Headers	Verbatim report divided into numbered text selections (column 1) and as required alpha paragraphs for illustration purposes.	Summary of text selection and Guide comments as considered necessary
EU: Case 26/62 Celex No. 662CJ0026 European Union Cases Court of Justice	Judgment of the Court of 5 February 1963. *NV Algemene Transport-en Expeditie Onderneming van Gend & Loos v Netherlands Inland Revenue Administration.* Reference for a preliminary ruling: Tariefcommissie – Pays-Bas – Case 26–62 *European Court reports* *French edition Page 00003* *Dutch edition Page 00003* *German edition Page 00003* *Italian edition Page 00003* *English special edition Page 00001* *Danish special edition Page 00375* *Greek special edition Page 00863* *Portuguese special edition Page 00205* *Spanish special edition Page 00333* *Swedish special edition Page 00161* *Finnish special edition Page 00161* European Court reports 1963 Page 00095 © European Commission © ELLIS Publications	**SUMMARY** This states that this is the judgment of the court with regard to a request for a preliminary ruling from the Tariefcommissie. The parties to the national action are named.
Keywords		
2.	1. PROCEDURE – PRELIMINARY RULING – JURISDICTION OF THE COURT – FOUNDATION – INTERPRETATION OF THE TREATY (EEC TREATY, SUBPARAGRAPH (A) OF THE FIRST PARAGRAPH OF ARTICLE 177) 2. PROCEDURE – PRELIMINARY RULING – QUESTION – CHOICE – RELEVANCE (EEC TREATY, SUBPARAGRAPH (A) OF THE FIRST PARAGRAPH OF ARTICLE 177)	**SUMMARY** These seven items under TEXT are then discussed in summary form as set out in column 2 text selection number 3

3. SUMMARY		SUMMARY

| | 3. EEC COMMUNITY – NATURE – SUBJECTS HAVING RIGHTS AND OBLIGATIONS – INDIVIDUALS
4. MEMBER STATES OF THE EEC – OBLIGATIONS – FAILURE TO FULFIL OBLIGATION – NATIONAL COURTS OR TRIBUNALS – RIGHTS OF INDIVIDUALS (EEC TREATY, ARTICLES 169, 170)
5. CUSTOMS DUTIES – INCREASE – PROHIBITION – DIRECT EFFECTS – INDIVIDUAL RIGHTS – PROTECTION (EEC TREATY, ARTICLE 12)
6. CUSTOMS DUTIES – INCREASE – FINDING – DUTIES APPLIED – CONCEPTS (EEC TREATY, ARTICLE 12)
7. CUSTOMS DUTIES – INCREASE – CONCEPTS (EEC TREATY, ARTICLE 12) | **SUMMARY**
This is a summary of the text that follows in text selections 4–17. The numbering within this box is provided by the court report. It is set out in clear language.
GUIDE COMMENTS
Item 2 is interesting as it makes clear the reasons for the framing of the questions within a national action is of no interest to the court hearing the request for a ruling. |

3. SUMMARY

1. In order to confer jurisdiction on the court to give a preliminary ruling it is necessary only that the question raised should clearly be concerned with the interpretation of the Treaty.
2. The considerations which may have led a national court to its choice of questions as well as the relevance which it attributes to such questions in the context of a case before it are excluded from review by the court when hearing an application for a preliminary ruling.
3. The European Economic Community constitutes a new legal order of international law for the benefit of which the states have limited their sovereign rights, albeit within limited fields, and the subjects of which comprise not only the member states but also their nationals.

Independently of the legislation of member states, community law not only imposes obligations on individuals but is also intended to confer upon them rights which become part of their legal heritage. These rights arise not only where they are expressly granted by the Treaty but also by reason of obligations which the Treaty imposes in a clearly defined way upon individuals as well as upon the member states and upon the institutions of the community.

Item 3 was an exceptionally important ruling, that the EEC Treaty created a new legal order capable of imposing obligations and rights on member states and their individual nationals.

TABLE 12.2—continued

Column 1	Column 2	Column 3
	4. The fact that Articles 169 and 170 of the EEC Treaty enable the Commission and the member states to bring before the court a state which has not fulfilled its obligations does not deprive individuals of the right to plead the same obligations, should the occasion arise, before a national court.	Item 5 states that Article 12 creates direct effect (that is an individual can bring a claim under it against their government in their national courts).
	5. According to the spirit, the general scheme and the wording of the EEC Treaty, Article 12 must be interpreted as producing direct effects and creating individual rights which national courts must protect.	Item 7 gives the final ruling of the court. After the Treaty is in force higher customs duty levied against a product are illegal as infringing Article 12. This is the case whether there is
	6. It follows from the wording and the general scheme of Article 12 of the Treaty that, in order to ascertain whether customs duties and charges having equivalent effect have been increased contrary to the prohibition contained in the said Article, regard must be had to the customs duties and charges actually applied by member states at the date of the entry into force of the Treaty.	an obvious increase or it's caused by a re-classification of existing duties.
	7. Where, after the entry into force of the Treaty, the same product is charged with a higher rate of duty, irrespective of whether this increase arises from an actual increase of the rate of customs duty or from a rearrangement of the tariff resulting in the classification of the product under a more highly taxed heading, such increase is illegal under Article 12 of the EEC Treaty.	
4. Parties	In case 26/62 Reference to the court under sub-paragraph (a) of the first paragraph and under the third paragraph of Article 177 of the Treaty establishing the European Economic Community	Notes which national court has asked for a preliminary reference under Article 177 (3) of the EEC Treaty and

by the tariefcommissie, a Netherlands administrative tribunal having final jurisdiction in revenue cases, for a preliminary ruling in the action pending before that court between *N v Algemene transport – en expeditie onderneming van Gend & Loos*, having its registered office at Utrecht, represented by H.G. Stibbe and L.F.D Ter Kuile, both advocates of Amsterdam, with an address for service in Luxembourg at the consulate-general of the Kingdom of the Netherlands And Nederlandse administratie der belastingen (Netherlands inland revenue administration), represented by the Inspector of Customs and Excise at Zaandam, with an address for service in Luxembourg at the Netherlands embassy.	names the parties to the national action.

Subject of the Case

5.	On the following questions: 1. Whether Article 12 of the EEC Treaty has direct application within the territory of a Member State, in other words, whether nationals of such a state can, on the basis of the Article in question, lay claim to individual rights which the courts must protect. 2. In the event of an affirmative reply, whether the application of an import duty of 8 per cent to the import into the Netherlands by the applicant in the main action of ureaformaldehyde originating in the Federal Republic of Germany represented an unlawful increase within the meaning of Article 12 of the EEC Treaty or whether it was in this case a reasonable alteration of the duty applicable before 1 March 1960, an alteration which, although amounting to an increase from the arithmetical point of view, is nevertheless not to be regarded as prohibited under the terms of Article 12.	The full questions put by the national court to the Court of Justice are set out, 1. Does Article 12 have direct effect allowing individuals to bring an action in their national courts? 2. If it does allow individuals to bring a claim was the import duty of 8% (originally 3 per cent prior to new classification being set up) levied by the Netherlands illegal as an increase within the meaning of Article 12.

6. GROUNDS

7. I – procedure	No objection has been raised concerning the procedural validity of the reference to the court under Article 177 of the EEC Treaty by the tariefcommissie, a court or tribunal

TABLE 12.2—continued

Column 1	Column 2	Column 3
	within the meaning of that Article. Further, no grounds exist for the court to raise the matter of its own motion.	
8. II – the first question		
9. A – jurisdiction of the court	**a)** The government of the Netherlands and the Belgian government challenge the jurisdiction of the court on the ground that the reference relates not to the interpretation but to the application of the Treaty in the context of the constitutional law of the Netherlands, and that in particular the court has no jurisdiction to decide, should the occasion arise, whether the provisions of the EEC Treaty prevail over Netherlands legislation or over other agreements entered into by the Netherlands and incorporated into Dutch national law. The solution of such a problem, it is claimed, falls within the exclusive jurisdiction of the national courts, subject to an application in accordance with the provisions laid down by Articles 169 and 170 of the Treaty. However in this case the court is not asked to adjudicate upon the application of the Treaty according to the principles of the national law of the Netherlands, which remains the concern of the national courts, but is asked, in conformity with subparagraph (a) of the first paragraph of Article 177 of the Treaty, only to interpret the scope of Article 12 of the said Treaty within the context of Community law and with reference to its effect on individuals. This argument has therefore no legal foundation. **b)** The Belgian government further argues that the court has no jurisdiction on the ground that no answer which the court could give to the first question of the tariefcommissie would have any bearing on the result of the proceedings brought in that court. However, in order to confer jurisdiction on the court in the present case it is necessary only that the question raised should clearly be concerned with the	**SUMMARY** This selection makes clear that the Court has jurisdiction and rejects the following arguments put by the Netherlands and the Belgian governments maintaining that is has not. **a)** Both governments say the court has no jurisdiction because they require an answer to the question of whether the EEC Treaty or Netherlands legislation takes precedence. This argument is rejected. It is not about precedence but about the effect and scope of Article 12 within Community law on individuals. **b)** The Belgian government's argument that it has no jurisdiction because an answer to the first question would have no relevance to the

		SUMMARY
	interpretation of the Treaty. The considerations which may have led a national court or tribunal to its choice of questions as well as the relevance which it attributes to such questions in the context of a case before it are excluded from review by the Court of Justice. It appears from the wording of the questions referred that they relate to the interpretation of the Treaty. The court therefore has the jurisdiction to answer them. This argument, too, is therefore unfounded.	determination of the national action in the national court is rejected. This is because the question relates to the interpretation of the treaty which is within its jurisdiction.
10. B – on the substance of the case	**a)** The first question of the tariefcommissie is whether Article 12 of the Treaty has direct application in national law in the sense that nationals of member states may on the basis of this Article lay claim to rights which the national court must protect. To ascertain whether the provisions of an international Treaty extend so far in their effects it is necessary to consider the spirit, the general scheme and the wording of those provisions. **b)** The objective of the EEC Treaty, which is to establish a common market, the functioning of which is of direct concern to interested parties in the Community, implies that this Treaty is more than an agreement which merely creates mutual obligations between the contracting states. This view is confirmed by the preamble to the Treaty which refers not only to governments but to peoples. It is also confirmed more specifically by the establishment of institutions endowed with sovereign rights, the exercise of which affects member states and also their citizens. Furthermore, it must be noted that the nationals of the states brought together in the community are called upon to cooperate in the functioning of this community through the intermediary of the European Parliament and the Economic and Social Committee. **c)** In addition the task assigned to the Court of Justice under Article 177, the object of which is to secure uniform interpretation of the Treaty by national courts and tribunals, confirms that the states have acknowledged that community law has an authority which can be invoked by their nationals before those courts and tribunals. The conclusion to be drawn from this is that the community constitutes a new legal order of international law for the benefit of which the states have limited their	**SUMMARY** This selection turns to a discussion of the issues raised by the first question. **a)** Does Article 12 have an effect on individual nationals of member states requiring protection by the national court? The interpretation of the article rests on the spirit of the article and its wording. **b)** The Court states that the EEC Treaty is different to other international treaties that only apply to signatory states. The preamble to the treaty refers to 'peoples' as well as governments. The institutions of the Community exercise rights affecting both states and their citizens. The member states are required to co-operate in its functioning and through institutions such as the European Parliament. **c)** The object of Art 177 is to obtain uniform interpretation across

TABLE 12.2—continued

Column 1	Column 2	Column 3
	sovereign rights, albeit within limited fields, and the subjects of which comprise not only member states but also their nationals. Independently of the legislation of member states, community law therefore not only imposes obligations on individuals but is also intended to confer upon them rights which become part of their legal heritage. These rights arise not only where they are expressly granted by the Treaty, but also by reason of obligations which the Treaty imposes in a clearly defined way upon individuals as well as upon the member states and upon the institutions of the community. **d)** With regard to the general scheme of the Treaty as it relates to customs duties and charges having equivalent effect it must be emphasized that Article 9, which bases the community upon a customs union, includes as an essential provision the prohibition of these customs duties and charges. This provision is found at the beginning of the part of the Treaty which defines the 'foundations of the community'. It is applied and explained by Article 12. **e)** The wording of Article 12 contains a clear and unconditional prohibition which is not a positive but a negative obligation. This obligation, moreover, is not qualified by any reservation on the part of states which would make its implementation conditional upon a positive legislative measure enacted under national law. The very nature of this prohibition makes it ideally adapted to produce direct effects in the legal relationship between member states and their subjects. The implementation of Article 12 does not require any legislative intervention on the part of the states. The fact that under this Article it is the member states who are made the subject of the negative obligation does not imply that their nationals cannot benefit from this obligation. **f)** In addition the argument based on Articles 169 and 170 of the Treaty put forward by the three governments which have submitted observations to the court in their	member states and acknowledges individual nationals can invoke it. The court states the treaty sets up a new legal order with rights and obligations that are part of national laws and applicable to states and their nationals. **d)** Article 9 of the treaty constitutes a customs union prohibiting increases, which is detailed in Article 12. **e)** Article 12 prohibits the increase and no state can make a reservation and refuse to abide by Article 12. This creates rights between individuals and member states, a relation referred to as 'Direct effect'. It does not need any legislation to be passed in the states. **f)** They reject the argument by the three governments submitting written observations that it is enough that Articles 169 and 170 allowing a member state infringes their obligations to be brought

before the court. This has no relevance to the fact that an individual can bring an action before their own national court when direct effect has been acknowledged as here.

g) The court considers Articles 169 and 170 would be ineffective to protect individuals after a conflicting national decision.

h) Individuals seeking to protect their rights would also constitute an effective extra form of supervision ensuring that those rights are maintained.

statements of case is misconceived. The fact that these Articles of the Treaty enable the Commission and the member states to bring before the court a state which has not fulfilled its obligations does not mean that individuals cannot plead these obligations, should the occasion arise, before a national court, any more than the fact that the Treaty places at the disposal of the Commission ways of ensuring that obligations imposed upon those subject to the Treaty are observed, precludes the possibility, in actions between individuals before a national court, of pleading infringements of these obligations.

g) A restriction of the guarantees against an infringement of Article 12 by member states to the procedures under Article 169 and 170 would remove all direct legal protection of the individual rights of their nationals. There is the risk that recourse to the procedure under these Articles would be ineffective if it were to occur after the implementation of a national decision taken contrary to the provisions of the Treaty.

h) The vigilance of individuals concerned to protect their rights amounts to an effective supervision in addition to the supervision entrusted by Articles 169 and 170 to the diligence of the Commission and of the member states.

It follows from the foregoing considerations that, according to the spirit, the general scheme and the wording of the Treaty, Article 12 must be interpreted as producing direct effects and creating individual rights which national courts must protect.

11. I – the second question

12. A – the jurisdiction of the court

SUMMARY

a) and b) set out the view of the Belgian and Dutch governments which is that the first question raised for the preliminary reference does not require any interpretation of the treaty but requires the tariff's classification to be examined, an examination that

a) According to the observations of the Belgian and Netherlands governments, the wording of this question appears to require, before it can be answered, an examination by the court of the tariff classification of ureaformaldehyde imported into the Netherlands, a classification on which *van Gend & Loos* and the inspector of customs and excise at Zaandam hold different opinions with regard to the 'tariefbesluit' of 1947.

b) The question clearly does not call for an interpretation of the Treaty but concerns the application of Netherlands customs legislation to the classification of aminoplasts,

TABLE 12.2—continued

Column 1	Column 2	Column 3
	which is outside the jurisdiction conferred upon the Court of Justice of the European Communities by subparagraph (a) of the first paragraph of Article 177. The court has therefore no jurisdiction to consider the reference made by the tariefcommissie. c) However, the real meaning of the question put by the tariefcommissie is whether, in law, an effective increase in customs duties charged on a given product as a result not of an increase in the rate but of a new classification of the product arising from a change of its tariff description contravenes the prohibition in Article 12 of the Treaty. d) Viewed in this way the question put is concerned with an interpretation of this provision of the Treaty and more particularly of the meaning which should be given to the concept of duties applied before the Treaty entered into force. Therefore the court has jurisdiction to give a ruling on this question.	is outside the jurisdiction of the Court of Justice. c) and d) make clear that they do have jurisdiction because the question is about the interpretation of Article 12 of the treaty. It concerns whether an increase resulting from a new classification of the product by the tariff is prohibited by Article 12, and a consideration of the concept of duties applied before the treaty in force.
13. **B – on the substance**	It follows from the wording and the general scheme of Article 12 of the Treaty that, in order to ascertain whether customs duties or charges having equivalent effect have been increased contrary to the prohibition contained in the said Article, regard must be had to the customs duties and charges actually applied at the date of the entry into force of the Treaty. Further, with regard to the prohibition in Article 12 of the Treaty, such an illegal increase may arise from a re-arrangement of the tariff resulting in the classification of the product under a more highly taxed heading and from an actual increase in the rate of customs duty. It is of little importance how the increase in customs duties occurred when, after the Treaty entered into force, the same product in the same member state was subjected to a higher rate of duty. The application of Article 12, in accordance with the interpretation given above, comes within the jurisdiction of the national court which must enquire whether the dutiable	**SUMMARY** When applying Article 12 it is necessary to look at duties charged on the date treaty entered into force so that it can be determined if there has been an increase. When considering the case one can look at re-classifications or actual increases. The application of Article 12 to the national case of *van Gend en Loos* is a matter for the national court. The Court of Justice has no jurisdiction to determine between the conflicting views in the written submissions; that

product, in this case ureaformaldehyde originating in the Federal Republic of Germany, is charged under the customs measures brought into force in the Netherlands with an import duty higher than that with which it was charged on 1 January 1958.

The court has no jurisdiction to check the validity of the conflicting views on this subject which have been submitted to it during the proceedings but must leave them to be determined by the national courts.

is a matter for the national court to determine.

SUMMARY

Based on the pleadings, initial reports, hearing the parties, hearing the opinion of the Advocate-General, and referring to relevant articles of the EEC Treaty and the procedure of the court the court determines as follows.

14. RECITALS	On those grounds upon reading the pleadings; upon hearing the report of the judge – rapporteur; upon hearing the parties; upon hearing the opinion of the advocate-general; having regard to Articles 9, 12, 14, 169, 170 and 177 of the Treaty establishing the European Economic Community; having regard to the protocol on the statute of the Court of Justice of the European Economic Community; having regard to the rules of procedure of the Court of Justice of the European Communities.	**GUIDE COMMENT** These are an extremely brief setting out of the grounds for the decision. Note it refers to several documents and hearings not set out as part of this report.
15. COSTS	The costs incurred by the Commission of the EEC and the member states which have submitted their observations to the court are not recoverable, and as these proceedings are, in so far as the parties to the main action are concerned, a step in the action pending before the tariefcommissie, the decision as to costs is a matter for that court.	**SUMMARY** No costs recoverable by those submitting written observations. Costs in relation to the parties to the action are to be determined by the national court (in this case the tariefcommissie).

TABLE 12.2—continued

Column 1	Column 2	Column 3
16. **Operative part** **RULING**	The court in answer to the questions referred to it for a preliminary ruling by the tariefcommissie by decision of 16 August 1962, hereby rules: 1. Article 12 of the Treaty establishing the European Economic Community produces direct effects and creates individual rights which national courts must protect. 2. In order to ascertain whether customs duties or charges having equivalent effect have been increased contrary to the prohibition contained in Article 12 of the Treaty, regard must be had to the duties and charges actually applied by the member state in question at the date of the entry into force of the Treaty. Such an increase can arise both from a re-arrangement of the tariff resulting in the classification of the product under a more highly taxed heading and from an increase in the rate of customs duty applied. 3. The decision as to costs in these proceedings is a matter for the tariefcommissie.	**SUMMARY** The court accepts that Article 12 has direct effect and gives rights to individual citizens against their member state. Furthermore these rights must be protected in the national courts. To find out whether there has been an unlawful increase under Article 12 of the duties charged at time of entry into force of the EEC Treaty. An increase can result from a re arrangement of a tariff.
17. **Index**	Subject Free movement of goods; customs union	**GUIDE COMMENT** These are the keywords of the case and would be inserted into databases etc.
18. **Dates**	**Date of judgment:** 1963/02/05 **Date lodged:** 1962/08/16 **Date overview of document:** 05/02/1963 **Date of application:** 16/08/1962	**GUIDE COMMENT** This gives you a chronology and you can see that the application was made to the court (lodged) in August 1962. Judgment was given in February 1963.

		GUIDE COMMENT
19. **References**	**Celex number:** 662CJ0026 Case citations 11957E000 11957E012 11957E169 11957E170 11957E177 11957E177- L1LA P 21 22 25 **Concerns:** Interprets 11957E012	**GUIDE COMMENT** The Celex number is the identifying number for this case in the official journal. The case citations relate to cases considered. These are not mentioned in the text.
20. **Bibliographic Information**	**Authoring institution:** Court of Justice **Basic treaty:** European Economic Community **Legal instrument:** Judgment, Case law, ECJ **Document type:** Judgment **Type of procedure:** Reference for a preliminary ruling **Authentic language:** Dutch **Observations (from)** Commission, Netherlands, Belgium, Federal Republic of Germany, member states, institutions **Judge:** Hammes **Advocate General:** Roemer **National Court:** *A9* Tariefcommissie, uitspraak van 14/08/1962 (8847/48 T) **Nationality:** Netherlands **Books: Numerous books consulted are then listed. (50+)** **Publication reference:** European Court reports	**GUIDE COMMENT** The bibliography information has been given a different layout for ease of reference and edited in relation to books. The only judge mentioned is Hammes. However, there were seven judges in court. The report is issued in the name of one judge and no dissenting or minority view referred to.

You will be able to see how the text builds up to a final decision. You should be able to clearly see how this is done and also come to view yourself on the outcome.

Work through this text slowly. You will find the task gives you a foundation for reading EU law reports. You should be checking the original paragraph to see if you would have made a correct précis.

If you are able to understand law reports and legislation you then have a firm foundation for essay writing and legal problem solution. It is important to realise that your evaluation and critique of a topic in law is only as good as your initial comprehension of the issues, rules, facts and arguments in the text (in other words, you cannot run before you can walk).

COMMENT ON VAN GEND EN LOOS

The Common Market Law Reports (CMLR) which are published by Sweet and Maxwell contain the written submitted opinion of the Advocate General (AGO). This will contain the agreed facts, procedure history, and analyse the arguments submitted by the parties and others. The AGO will give an opinion on the correct determination of the matter. The opinion does not have to be followed by the courts. You can also locate the Advocate General's opinion from EUR-Lex; it will come up automatically when you have searched for a case.

Having persevered with the reading of the case and the notations, the differences between this EU and common law reports is stark. The judges in the ECJ (now CJEU) do not use analogy, poetic language, asides, stories, counter arguments. They do not set out their rationale for decision making.

There is a veneer of scientific detachment in the language of the court. The style is unadorned description, technical language without explanation, assertion, the summarising without comment of a wide range of arguments by the parties, the Advocate General, and the governments wishing to make observations. Arguments in other cases, or arguments given by the parties, are dismissed without explanation with phrases such as, 'this is misconceived', 'No, this is not right' and states 'this is the case' without giving reasons why.

The court argues deductively without making any attempts to refer to policy. Yet it must surely be aware of the policy dimensions of its decisions. If it had decided against *van Gend en Loos*, then the power of the fledgling EU would have been severely diminished. In the view of the Advocate General, companies would follow the national customs tariffs and not be guided by the provisions of the treaty. The court may well have been taking the opportunity to assert the power of the EU over the individual member state, although this is conjecture in the absence of any comment on policy from the court itself.

Potentially powerful and persuasive arguments were put forward that the ECJ did not have the jurisdiction to hear the case; the court merely replied that they did have jurisdiction. This was based on the grounds that the meaning behind the question raised an issue of interpretation within its jurisdiction.

The court's simplistic decision that any arithmetical change, even if it resulted from a re-classification within the existing order rather than a deliberate increase, would constitute an infringement of the treaty – is severe and open to question. In the face of arguments that would concentrate upon the intention of member states concerning infringement, the ECJ says any arithmetical increase constitutes an infringement irrespective of intention.

Indeed, much policy has to be read into all judgments of the ECJ and this judgment is no exception. Perhaps given the tensions between member states and their creation, the EU, this is a wise and deliberate policy. The member states gave birth to something that, in many respects, is more powerful and can dictate terms to an individual member state.

There is little usage of what may be described as the forensic skill of the English judge. The major part of the report concerns summaries of the arguments put forward by both parties, the Advocate General, other interested member states, and the governments of affected member states.

Given the detail of the summarised arguments, and the range of arguments presented, it is interesting to note that it is acceptable for the court to dismiss arguments without reasons. Theoretically, of course, an English judge could do the same, but the entrenched method of reasoning by analogy based on precedent makes such a course of action unlikely.

The founding treaties of the EU have never stated that the EU has its own legal order; however the cases of *van Gend en Loos* and *Costa* made clear that there was indeed an EU legal system. In this way, potentially boring cases about tax and import duties can create fundamental changes. At no time has the CJEU changed its mind and said that the EU does not have its own legal system: it follows the earlier cases on this point.

READING AND UNDERSTANDING THE PRIMARY AND SECONDARY LAW OF THE EU

In Chapter 3 general issues relating to treaties were considered in detail and in Chapter 5 the primary law of the EU (its treaties) and the major secondary law of the EU (regulations and directives) were described and their relationship explained. In Chapters 8 and 7 respectively you were told how to locate cases and primary and secondary legislation.

The anatomy of EU primary and secondary law

Now we turn to the practical consideration of the standard anatomy of EU primary and secondary law in the form of treaties, regulations and directives.

Primary law of the EU: treaties

You can find detail on the standard layout of a treaty in Chapter 3. To refresh your memory however, Table 12.3 breaks down the standard layout of a treaty.

Aspirational sentiments sit alongside legal requirements in the EU founding treaties (and indeed in all other treaties of the EU). The preamble's aspirational words will set the scene for the treaty and what follows and a section of the preamble to the TEU consolidated version 2012 is set out below to demonstrate this.

> **Preamble to 2012 Consolidated Treaty on European Union (TEU)**
>
> *PREAMBLE. . .*
>
> **[Member states are listed and the treaty continues with the preamble stating that they are]**
>
> **RESOLVED** to mark a new stage in the process of European integration undertaken with the establishment of the European Communities,
>
> **DRAWING INSPIRATION** from the cultural, religious and humanist inheritance of Europe, from which have developed the universal values of the inviolable and inalienable rights of the human person, freedom, democracy, equality and the rule of law,
>
> **RECALLING** the historic importance of the ending of the division of the European continent and the need to create firm bases for the construction of the future Europe. . .

TABLE 12.3 THE LAYOUT OF A TREATY: STANDARD LAYOUT

PREAMBLE	The 'preamble' to a treaty precedes the detailed provisions and will indicate the purposes to be achieved by the treaty and will contain a range of aspirational proposals and affirmations. Covers everything until reaching the specific enactments in the treaty	
DIVISIONS	**Explanation**	**Example**
PARTS	A treaty can be subdivided into PARTS. Only capitalised text is used	PART SEVEN
TITLES	Parts can be subdivided into 'TITLES' using text that is always capitalised and numbered with Roman numerals	TITLE V.
CHAPTERS	Titles can be subdivided into CHAPTERS using text that is always capitalised and numbered with Roman numerals	CHAPTER IV
SECTIONS	Chapters can be subdivided into SECTIONS using text that is always capitalised and numbered with Roman numerals	SECTION III
ARTICLES	Each Part, Title, Chapter, or Section (depending on the divisions used for the treaty) is further divided into smaller numbered 'articles' using Arabic numbers. The designated reference is always to lower case text and number, not just 1	Article 1
PARAGRAPHS	Each article may be divided into smaller numbered 'paragraphs.' Text is not used but Arabic numerals continue to be used but they are placed in brackets	
SUB PARAGRAPH	Each paragraph may be divided into smaller numbered 'sub-paragraphs' and now there is a resort again to lower case alphabetical markers in brackets	

ADDITIONS TO TREATY		
RECORDS OF CHANGE	Written record of amendments/changes: (protocol). Written records of different arrangements with signatories: (derogations, reservations) Written record of signatory cancelling signature: (abrogations) Written records of change are attached to the original treaty	
ANNEXES	The additions to the end of the treaty	

Because the founding treaties establish the EU as a legal personality the EU can enter into treaties with organisations and states outside the EU.

When you read a treaty it is particularly important to check that you are reading the most current revised or consolidated version. Treaties are often changed in part by later ones; the Treaty on European Union for example was the object of major changes in the Lisbon Treaty 2009.

Sometimes important treaties are consolidated with versions published that bring together all changes to the treaty at the time of the consolidation. Therefore in 2010 all previous changes to the Treaty on European Union were put into a consolidated version of it. An updated consolidated version was published in 2012. So you need to check that you have access to the latest consolidated version.

Not only can treaties be changed by articles in other treaties, they can also be changed by protocols attached to them. When changes are made, some member states may not wish to agree them or abide by them; others may wish to do so. Protocols on many occasions, although there are exceptions, allow some member states to sign and be bound and others not to sign and be bound. If you have a specific enquiry about the UK and a protocol you must find out if it is a signatory. Chapters 3 and 4 consider these matters in detail.

It is a simple matter to check on the Europa website to find out changes to the treaties, and obtain information about signatories to protocols.

SECONDARY LAW OF THE EU: REGULATIONS, DIRECTIVES, DECISIONS, RECOMMENDATIONS, OPINIONS AND GENERAL PRINCIPLES OF LAW ESTABLISHED BY THE COURT OF JUSTICE OF THE EU

The treaties setting up the EU made provision for it to exercise its functions through the ability to 'adopt' a range of different mechanisms. Article 288 TFEU states:

> to exercise the Union's competences, the institutions shall adopt regulations, directives, decisions, recommendations and opinions.

The two most important forms of secondary legislation are regulations and directives.[21]

---

21 Chapter 5 gives details on the way in which each of these types of law are created and by whom.

Regulations

Regulations are addressed to all member states and become law as soon as they are enacted in the EU. Like treaties they are prefaced by aspirational clauses. The legally binding content is only contained in the articles of the regulation. The standard layout of a regulation is set out in Table 12.4.

Figure 12.1 sets out an edited version of a regulation from 1992, when the EU was still referred to as the EEC; an older version is given to again instil in you the importance of being aware of changes to treaties and names. The figure indicates the layout and use of text to signal differing divisions of the regulation. The main text has been left out because the figure is for layout demonstration purposes only. The blue arrow shows that the legal standing clauses and the aspirational clauses punctuate the simple sentence of authority that 'the Council of the European Communities[22] . . . has adopted this regulation'.

TABLE 12.4 THE STANDARD LAYOUT OF A REGULATION	
Citation	Abbreviation of community EU (older regulations due to name changes will be EEC or EC) Followed by a number indicating its chronological order in the year of its adoption, followed by a slash with a two number year date
Title of regulation	
Institution adopting the regulation	
Legal standing	Immediately after the heading the words 'Having regard' appear several times as each institution consulted is listed
The 'whereas' aspirational clauses	Unlike treaties the aspirational clauses in a regulation are not prefaced by any header. They are only identifiable by the fact that the paragraphs containing the aspirations are not numbered and titled, and they are all prefaced by the word 'Whereas'. See Figure 12.1 below for an example. These clauses are not in any manner legally binding
Articles	As noted in Article 288 of the TFEU these are legally binding 'in their entirety'
Annexes	These can contain important definitions and clarifications, as Figure 12.1 below illustrates

---

22 In 1992 the EU was composed of three communities; this has now merged into the EU and references are to Union rather than Community.

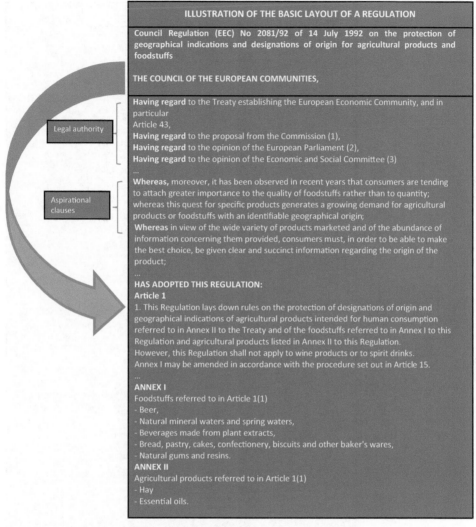

Figure 12.1 Illustration of the basic layout of a regulation

Directives

Directives are secondary legislation specifying that member states must achieve a particular goal by a specific date. A member state can choose to achieve that goal by non-legal as well as legal means. Directives therefore are binding as to their stated outcome.

The layout of a directive can vary slightly but most follow the structure indicated in Table 12.5.

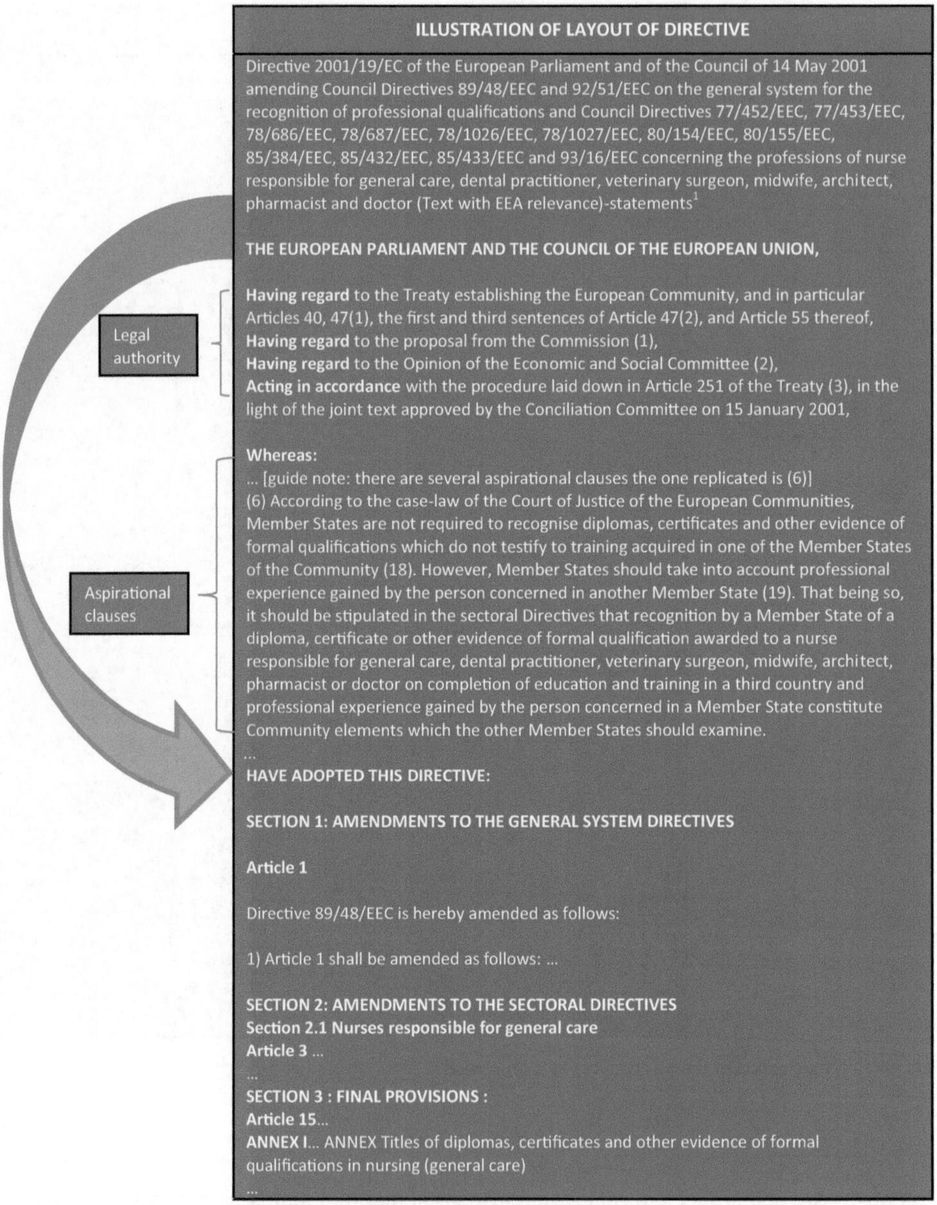

ILLUSTRATION OF LAYOUT OF DIRECTIVE

Directive 2001/19/EC of the European Parliament and of the Council of 14 May 2001 amending Council Directives 89/48/EEC and 92/51/EEC on the general system for the recognition of professional qualifications and Council Directives 77/452/EEC, 77/453/EEC, 78/686/EEC, 78/687/EEC, 78/1026/EEC, 78/1027/EEC, 80/154/EEC, 80/155/EEC, 85/384/EEC, 85/432/EEC, 85/433/EEC and 93/16/EEC concerning the professions of nurse responsible for general care, dental practitioner, veterinary surgeon, midwife, architect, pharmacist and doctor (Text with EEA relevance)-statements[1]

THE EUROPEAN PARLIAMENT AND THE COUNCIL OF THE EUROPEAN UNION,

Legal authority

Having regard to the Treaty establishing the European Community, and in particular Articles 40, 47(1), the first and third sentences of Article 47(2), and Article 55 thereof,
Having regard to the proposal from the Commission (1),
Having regard to the Opinion of the Economic and Social Committee (2),
Acting in accordance with the procedure laid down in Article 251 of the Treaty (3), in the light of the joint text approved by the Conciliation Committee on 15 January 2001,

Aspirational clauses

Whereas:
... [guide note: there are several aspirational clauses the one replicated is (6)]
(6) According to the case-law of the Court of Justice of the European Communities, Member States are not required to recognise diplomas, certificates and other evidence of formal qualifications which do not testify to training acquired in one of the Member States of the Community (18). However, Member States should take into account professional experience gained by the person concerned in another Member State (19). That being so, it should be stipulated in the sectoral Directives that recognition by a Member State of a diploma, certificate or other evidence of formal qualification awarded to a nurse responsible for general care, dental practitioner, veterinary surgeon, midwife, architect, pharmacist or doctor on completion of education and training in a third country and professional experience gained by the person concerned in a Member State constitute Community elements which the other Member States should examine.
...

HAVE ADOPTED THIS DIRECTIVE:

SECTION 1: AMENDMENTS TO THE GENERAL SYSTEM DIRECTIVES

Article 1

Directive 89/48/EEC is hereby amended as follows:

1) Article 1 shall be amended as follows: ...

SECTION 2: AMENDMENTS TO THE SECTORAL DIRECTIVES
Section 2.1 Nurses responsible for general care
Article 3 ...
...
SECTION 3 : FINAL PROVISIONS :
Article 15...
ANNEX I... ANNEX Titles of diplomas, certificates and other evidence of formal qualifications in nursing (general care)
...

[1] *Official Journal L 206 , 31/07/2001 P. 0001 - 0051*

Figure 12.2 Illustration of the basic layout of a directive

TABLE 12.5 THE STANDARD LAYOUT OF A DIRECTIVE

Legal standing	Immediately after the heading the words 'Having regard' appear several times as each institution consulted is listed
The 'whereas' aspirational and/or purpose clauses	As with regulations these are not headed but they are identified as in regulations by the first word of each section of text, 'Whereas'
Articles	As noted in Article 288 of the TFEU, these are legally binding as to their 'outcome'. If a directive is divided into different sections the numbering of the articles will run across all sections without interruption
Annexes	These are attached to the directive and can contain important definitions and clarifications, as Figure 12.2 above illustrates
Statements	Institutions of the EU who have collaborated for the directive can attach a statement to the directive

Figure 12.2 illustrates you will find an extract from a directive with the articles split up into three sections which allows for the grouping of like topics together. It amends two previous directives on the general system for recognition of professional qualifications and amends 13 directives relating to regulation of a range of professions. In the annexes there are references to the titles of recognised professional qualifications. As you will see its layout is similar to a regulation. It differs in that it is not binding in its entirety, but only binding as to outcome. The directive states that the Commission will report back on its actions in pursuit of the goals of the objective in two years' time (2003).

Law cases concerning the meaning of words in directives and regulations are regularly brought to court. The CJEU determines all such cases and exercises considerable power to state the meaning of words in the documents presented. The Court of Justice is charged with being the final arbiter of the meaning of words and phrases, and also has a duty to maintain harmonisation of application of EU law throughout the EU and its member states.

READING AND UNDERSTANDING THE LAW RELATING TO THE EUROPEAN CONVENTION ON HUMAN RIGHTS (ECHR)

Understanding the structure and layout of the ECHR

The European Convention on Human Rights is divided into three sections, each numbered using upper case Roman numerals. It does not contain Parts or Titles or Chapters.

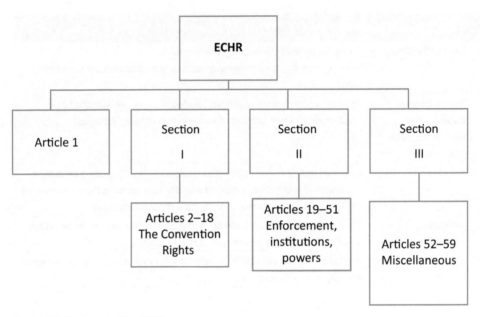

Figure 12.3 The layout of the ECHR

Figure 12.3 gives you an overview of this structure and which issues are dealt with in its various sections.

As you can see from Figure 12.3, Article 1 sits outside the three main sections. It contains the key 'Obligation to respect human rights' stating that:

> 'The High Contracting Parties shall secure to everyone within their jurisdiction the rights and freedoms defined in Section[23] I of this Convention'.

Article 1 ensures that the rights contained in Section I of the ECHR are not just confined to citizens of signatory states but are given to 'everyone within' the 'jurisdiction' of a signatory state. The word 'everyone' is key. Article 1 is supported by Article 34 which allows individuals to make claims.

The rights contained in the ECHR

Section 1 contains Articles 2–18 setting out the rights that are available to 'everyone'. The list of rights is set out below in Table 12.6.

As you will notice, Articles 15–18 begin discussion of limits. All of the above rights are conferred with differing types of criteria relating to enforcement. Rights in the Convention

---

23 Again be aware that treaties can be divided into titles, sections, chapters, each of which contains articles. 'Section' as used here should not be confused with a section in UK legislation.

TABLE 12.6 ECHR SECTION I: ARTICLE 1 THE GENERAL OBLIGATION AND ARTICLES 2–18 THE CONVENTION RIGHTS CONSOLIDATED VERSION 2010 INCLUDING PROTOCOL 14

Article	Right	Additional comment
Article 1	Obligation to respect human rights	Rights given to **everyone** within the borders of the State
Article 2	Right to life	
Article 3	Prohibition of torture	
Article 4	Prohibition of slavery and forced labour	
Article 5	Right to liberty and security	Covers both arrest and trial
Article 6	Right to a fair trial in an unbiased and independent forum	
Article 7	No punishment without law	Creating a crime with a punishment operative when act done
Article 8	Right to respect for private and family life	Which includes correspondence
Article 9	Freedom of thought, conscience and religion	Right to practise religion at home and change religion if desired
Article 10	Freedom of expression	Covers responsible press and personal expression orally or in writing
Article 11	Freedom of assembly and association	For peaceful meetings, or to join trade unions
Article 12	Right to marry	Which includes having a family
Article 13	Right to an effective remedy	Covers complaint to court and others in order to be heard if rights are violated
Article 14	Prohibition of discrimination	Rights in the Convention and its protocols are read regardless of discrimination
Article	**Limits**	**Comment**
Article 15	Derogation in time of emergency	Rights can be breached but arbitrary killing/torture is prohibited
Article 16	Restrictions on political activity of aliens	Possible even if it conflicts with Articles 3, 10, 11 and 14
Article 17	Prohibition of abuse of rights	Nothing in the ECHR can be used to damage rights in ECHR
Article 18	Limitation on use of restrictions of rights	General law can be used to restrict rights if necessary

are given in one of three ways, as absolute, limited or qualified rights. Table 12.7 indicates the main differences between these types of right.

Section II of the Convention contains Articles 19–51 dealing with issues relating to the enforcement of rights and the powers of adjudicators. Section III contains Articles 52–59 listed as dealing with miscellaneous issues. It makes provision for derogation, reservation, signature, ratification and denunciation. Amendments to Article 59 in 2012 now make provision to allow the EU to become a signatory of the ECHR. So the importance of any section labelled 'miscellaneous' should not be underestimated!

TABLE 12.7 ABSOLUTE RIGHTS OR UNQUALIFIED RIGHTS, LIMITED RIGHTS AND QUALIFIED RIGHTS (NOTE THIS DIVISION ALSO APPLIES TO RIGHTS GIVEN IN PROTOCOLS TO BE DISCUSSED LATER)

Absolute or unqualified rights	Limited	Qualified[24]
The member states of the ECHR can never withhold or take away these rights, e.g. Article 3	These rights may be limited by the member states of the ECHR under explicit and finite circumstances, e.g. Article 5	They can be interfered with by member states of the ECHR but a balance is between individual rights and the needs of the wider Community or state interest, e.g. Articles 9–11

Adding new rights to the ECHR via protocols

Some protocols add rights that are to be regarded as additional articles to the ECHR, with the provisions of the ECHR applying to them. An example can be given by referring to Article 5 of Protocol 1. Protocol 1 conferred rights to protection of property (Article 1), education (Article 2) and to free elections (Article 3). Article 5 provides the following:

Article 5

Relationship to the Convention

As between the High Contracting Parties the provisions of Articles 1, 2, 3 and 4 of this Protocol shall be regarded as additional Articles to the Convention and all the provisions of the Convention shall apply accordingly.

---

24 The law must underpin interference with qualified rights and interference must be to achieve one of the legitimate aims set out in the relevant article. These can vary but often include national security, the prevention of disorder or crime, and public safety. Interference must also be required in a democratic society, be a response to 'a pressing social need', and be a proportionate way of dealing with social need.

This is not the case with all rights given in protocols to the ECHR and you need to carefully check any protocol to see what it says concerning this matter.

Protocol 7 continued to add rights to the ECHR. Article 4 makes it clear that everyone has the right not to be tried twice for the same offence. Customarily this is called the 'double jeopardy law'. This article, by paragraph 3 also makes quite clear that there can be no derogation from Article 4.

Part 10 of the Criminal Justice Act 2003 removes the 'double jeopardy law' in exceptional circumstances. It was a law that had been operative in the English legal system since the time of the Norman Conquest in 1066. Now in the UK if certain circumstances apply a person can be tried twice for the same offence. The UK is not a signatory to this protocol.

Making amendments and repeals to articles in the ECHR

Some protocols make amendments to the ECHR relating to structural and organisational change. Protocol 14 was signed in Strasbourg on 13.5.2004 (in force until 1 June 2010) and states that its purpose is to engage in 'amending the control system of the Convention'. It made a number of changes to the European Court of Human Rights and the number of judges staffing it. Obviously any changes to the ECHR can result in the renumbering of articles in the original convention. Protocol 14 removes an article in the ECHR so its numbering inevitably changed. It also added paragraphs to articles in the ECHR. In addition, it made a major change to Article 59(2) of the ECHR allowing the EU to accede to the ECHR.

Article 17 of Protocol 14 made provision for the EU to accede to the ECHR. It was considered strange for some time that whilst every member state of the EU had to be a party to the ECHR the EU itself could not be a party as the ECHR was only open to European states, and the EU was not a European state. Therefore the EU was not obligated to protect human rights in pursuance of its law and policy making. During 2000–2004 the EU was working on an EU constitution. The constitution was intended to require accession to the ECHR, but amendments to the ECHR were required in order for this to happen. Protocol 14 made provision for this to occur as follows:

Article 17 Protocol 14

Article 59 of the Convention shall be amended as follows:

1. A new paragraph 2 shall be inserted which shall read as follows: '2. The European Union may accede to this Convention.'
2. Paragraphs 2, 3 and 4 shall become paragraphs 3, 4 and 5 respectively.

This was an exceptionally important change.

The importance of up to date knowledge of the ECHR and its protocols

It must now be clear to you that when you are researching the ECHR (and any other treaty) you must ensure that you have up to date knowledge of protocols, their signature and ratification. It is not enough just to check derogations and reservations from the original treaties, and later treaties whether new or accession. With regard to the CoE you can do this by checking the original of the treaty on the Council of Europe Treaty Office website and locate the most recent copy as amended by current protocols.[25] Then you can note whether the member state you are considering has signed and ratified all aspects of the ECHR and all protocols in full.

CJEU AND CONVENTION

The CJEU discusses the Convention in terms that are binding and to be taken into account in their decision making. Adherence to it is one of the principles of law of the EU and changes to the Convention have now allowed the way for the EU to sign it in its own right. At present this has not occurred. When it does, decisions of the ECtHR will be binding on the CJEU.[26]

Understanding ECtHR cases

Procedure in court

> **Language:** the official language of the ECtHR/Convention is English and French.
>> Court will accept claims in any officially recognised language of a contracting state.
> **Who can claim:**
> Individuals against contracting states infringing their rights
> **Inter-state claims for breach: rare**
> The Committee of Ministers of the Council of Europe may ask the court for an advisory opinion concerning an issue of interpretation of the ECHR if a majority of ministers agree.
> **Procedure**
> **An application is lodged with the registry of the ECtHR**
> Application allocated to a judge rapporteur who determines if a case should proceed to court. If it can, it is determined in the appropriate forum (chamber, Grand Chamber, plenary).

The government of the state in which the claim made is then asked if they have any observations to bring.

The court can make any investigations it wishes to examine the claims and expects contracting states to be compliant and assist in all information required.

---

25 www.conventions.coe.int/ At the time of writing (May 2013) the most current copy of the ECHR (updated with protocols 1–14) published by the Council of Europe as a pdf can be located at www.echr.coe.int/NR/rdonlyres/D5CC24A7-DC13–4318-B457–5C9014916D7A/0/Convention_ENG.pdf.

26 See Chapter 4 for specific details.

Interested persons or groups who are not a party to the action may submit written observations to the court; they are called third party interveners.

There may not be a hearing in the ECtHR; a decision can be made by the chamber, and that decision becomes final after three months have elapsed without a request for referral to the Grand Chamber. If the Grand Chamber refuses a decision to refer to them their decision is final.

The authority of the court is provided by Article 46 by virtue of which the signatory states to the ECHR agree to accept the decision of the court in their judgments. But the ECtHR has made clear that it does not consider it has any powers to order a contracting state's law invalid, or its administrative procedures invalid.

Where the court has been asked to make an advisory opinion, however, signatories do not have to agree to accept it.

It is the Committee of Ministers that is charged to enforce the decision of the court ensuring that contracting states do in fact change their law to ensure compatibility with the Convention. It is important to note the decisions of the ECtHR are only binding on the relevant contracting state not all contracting states, although it would be unwise for any contracting state to completely ignore rulings of the court in their day-to-day actions as they too may be taken to the court and be unable to successfully defend their position given the previous ruling of the ECtHR.

Reports of cases

The official reports of the Council of Europe are *The Reports of Judgments and Decisions*. These contain the most important leading judgments, decisions or advisory opinions of the ECtHR since 1998, which is the date on which the new court of human rights commenced its jurisdiction.[27] These reports are available online on HUDOC under the classification of importance level 'Case Reports'. Only cases in certain classifications are reported in full. Others remain as a summary. HUDOC also contains an enormous number of unreported cases. There are also a series of private reports that cover decisions of the court, the best being *European Human Rights Reports* published by Sweet and Maxwell since 1962 to report leading cases.

Understanding and reading cases in the ECtHR

The majority of reported cases (whether official or unofficial) are, of necessity, quite long. Usually more than one article of the ECHR is involved, and often more than one applicant. The jurisdiction of the court and the determination of actions in relation to each article and each application must be established. Also summaries of actions by each of the applicants in national courts will need to be given. An applicant must have exhausted all available remedies nationally before lodging an application with the ECtHR. This means that the outcome of cases in several national court actions may need to be summarised.

The law of the defendant state in relation to the claim needs to be carefully examined against the facts of the cases and the existing case law from the ECtHR concerning the ECHR.

Usually the facts of such cases tend to be complicated.

27　Details can be located in Chapter 4.

Because of the length of these cases we do not take the same approach to an ECtHR case as we have for the EU and English legal system cases, replicating the text. We will use the following case to assist reading and understanding cases and procedures before the court:

AL-SKEINI AND OTHERS v THE UNITED KINGDOM (Application no. 55721/07; Reported: (2011) 53 EHRR 18; 30 BHRC 561; [2011] Inquest LR 73; *Times*, 13 July, 2011 and available at *http://www.bailli.org/eu/cases/ECHR/2011/1093.html.*

Case to be referred to as *Al-Skeini*.

As you can see from the references that have been given to you this case was reported in four private reports (EHRR, BHRC, Inquest LR and Times LR). It is also in the official print report from the *Reports and Decisions of the Court* and an e-copy can also be found, free, on HUDOC (the reference is given above).

It is important when dealing with ECtHR reports to ensure you carefully read the dates of the procedures. For example the judgment in the above case was delivered on 7 November 2011 but it was lodged with the ECtHR in 2007. The facts relate to deaths of Iraqi citizens in 2003/4. The full procedural history contained in the reports of the case of *Al-Skeini* show that the case took seven years to move from first application in the UK national courts to the judgment of the Grand Chamber of the ECtHR in 2011. It will also show that the nature of the complaints had to change in light of the decisions reached by the UK courts. From a close consideration of dates it can be seen that to achieve a ruling in the ECtHR takes many years, not least because there is a requirement that all national remedies must be exhausted before an application can be made to the court. Careful reading of the procedural history and outcomes gives you a good grip on the case and allows you to read the entire report, if you need to, in context. Often as a new student to law you would not be required to read the entire case! The *Al-Skeini* case in the EHRR is 84 pages long and comprises over 43,000 words.

However, utilising various reading techniques that are discussed in the academic skills section of this book, you can scan for the procedural history using headings to guide you. There are headings directing you to the facts from which you can ascertain the case concerned various actions flowing from the death of 13 Iraqi citizens at the hands of the British military. Headings direct you to a decision by the Secretary of State and headings direct you to the actions in the national courts and finally the lodging of an application with the ECtHR and the final determination of the Grand Chamber of the ECtHR. Of course, this just gives you what amounts to a chronological chart of actions and results. To be able to apply the findings of the court, as the English courts are obliged to do under the Convention and the Human Rights Act, the reasoning of the court needs to be given.

The judgment is issued under the name of one judge, although 17 judges sat in the Grand Chamber to hear the case. The judgment contains clear reasoning supporting the decision. A dissenting judgment has also been published in relation to *Al-Skeini*, a situation that does not arise in the CJEU. Also there is no concept of the Advocate-General's opinion.

Table 12.8 sets out the procedural history of the case as found in the judgment.

Access the full EHRR report of the case of *Al-Skeini* on Westlaw (via cases) and guided by the procedure above read it through slowly, checking that you understand what section you are reading, for example a summary of the domestic case, or the reasoning of the ECtHR. Note too the dissenting judgment. Can you follow where the arguments diverge?

Handling just one ECtHR case in your own time will enable you to be confident with reading and understanding these cases.

The Human Rights Act 1998

Although there is no requirement for contracting states to the ECHR to incorporate it into their domestic law, many have done so, usually at the time of signing the ECHR. The UK Government has not done this, although the UK was a founding contracting party signing the Convention in 1950. However, the Human Rights Acts 1998 (HRA) gave UK citizens the right to bring an action in their domestic courts. It did not allow actions relating to all articles in the ECHR and its protocols. Therefore it is important to note that it is erroneous to state that the HRA incorporated the ECHR into English law. English law now allows actions relating to certain rights to be heard in domestic courts.

The HRA, s 1 allows citizens to bring actions alleging breach of their rights under:

- Articles 2–12 and 13 of the ECHR.
- Articles 1–3 of the First Protocol.
- Article 1 of the Thirteenth Protocol.

These articles in the ECHR and its protocols were designated 'convention rights' by the HRA.

So a new category was created by the Act, actions by citizens alleging breach of 'convention rights'.

Section 1 of the HRA provided additionally that all claims under allowed articles in the HRA, s 1 were to be interpreted by the court in the light of the limitations on rights found in Articles 16–18 of the ECHR.

The HRA does however introduce a duty imposed on all public institutions to ensure that it acted in compliance with the ECHR.[28] English courts are covered by this duty and are additionally required to take into account judgments of the ECtHR in relation to the Convention rights in the HRA.

The Act also makes provision for the minister of state to add or withdraw articles in treaties or protocols from s 1. The minister must also issue a statement of compatibility with the ECHR for all legislation, and if it is not compatible state that Parliament went ahead anyway. English courts can determine if legislation is compatible with the Convention and if it is not they can issue a statement of incompatibility.

---

28 Section 6.

TABLE 12.8 PROCEDURAL HISTORY OF *AL-SKEINI AND OTHERS V THE UNITED KINGDOM* (APPLICATION NO. 55721/07) TAKEN FROM NON-OFFICIAL PRIVATE REPORT (2011) 53 EHRR 18

Date	Decision making body/court and reason for application by applicants	Decision
26 March 2004	UK SECRETARY OF STATE FOR DEFENCE: regarding the death of 13 Iraqi civilians (including the applicants to the case we are considering): • to determine if there should be an inquiry	Decides that there will be no inquiries into their deaths, no acceptance of liability for their deaths and no payment to relatives
11 May 2004	DIVISIONAL COURT OF THE HIGH COURT (UK) consider application for judicial review of the Secretary of State for Defence's decisions • The claimants had sought review and declarations that there had been infringements of the procedural and the substantive obligations of Articles 1 and 2 (and, in the case of the sixth applicant, Article 3) of the ECHR	Judge of the Divisional Court directs that six test cases from the 13 cases lodged for judicial review should proceed to a hearing. With others stopped pending the outcome of the test case
14 December 2004	DIVISIONAL COURT hears application for judicial review	Court rejects the claims of the first four applicants, accepts the claim of the sixth
21 December 2005	COURT OF APPEAL hears appeals by the first four applicants	Court dismisses the appeals by the first four applicants, on the grounds that the Iraqi relatives did not fall within UK legal jurisdiction. Court did recognise an Iraqi in custody in a military detention centre within UK jurisdiction. They also dismissed a cross-appeal by the Secretary of State concerning the sixth applicant
13 June 2007	HOUSE OF LORDS hears the appeal by the first four applicants that the UK did have jurisdiction over the Iraqi claimants, and a cross-appeal by the Secretary of State that the UK did not have jurisdiction	Court held UK jurisdiction did not cover the first four applicants, there was no need to investigate or make compensation payments. The UK conceded it did have jurisdiction over the fifth applicant; Secretary of State commences an investigation.

Date	Decision making body/court and reason for application by applicants	Decision
12 November 2007	The six applicants lodged their application for an action in the ECtHR against the British Government's refusal to accept jurisdiction covered the Iraqi claimants. They argued their Iraqi relatives were within the jurisdiction of Article 1 (right to life) when they died and that in five of the applicant's cases they had failed to investigate under their duty to do so under Article 2	
16 December 2008	Application allocated to the fourth section of the court and notice of application given to the UK Government.	Parties filed submissions
16 Jan 2010	Fourth section court relinquished the case to the Grand Chamber	UK Government and parties filed further submissions re merits of the application and case. Third party interveners filed submissions: Bar Human Rights Committee, the European Human Rights Advocacy Centre, Human Rights Watch, Interights, the International Federation for Human Rights, the Law Society, and Liberty
9 June 2010	Grand Chamber: public hearing	9, 15 June 2010 and 15 June 2011: three days of private deliberations by court. Judgment adopted on 15 June 2011
7 November 2011	Grand Chamber: delivery of judgment	Applicants 1–5 were within the jurisdiction of the UK at the time of death under Article 1 and that the UK Government had failed to investigate as required by Article 2, furthermore compensation was payable to them. Although the applicants' claims for just satisfaction were not accepted

The structure of the Human Rights Act

Take time to consider Figure 12.4[29] which gives the layout of the HRA 1998.

As you can see the Act is set out as a series of 22 sections (containing no parts) and four schedules, two of which do contain parts. Schedule 1 of the Act sets out the full text of the ECHR articles and protocol articles referred to in s 1.

Section 1 of the Act currently covers most of the articles in the ECHR but not all, and a few articles in protocols. Holland and Webb[30] discussing the HRA say that it has rather selectively given elements of the Convention a special legal status as 'convention rights' under HRA, s 1. It therefore maintains UK dualism regarding obligations in international law'.[31]

Article 1 of the ECHR is omitted from the HRA because it imposes a general duty on all signatories of the ECHR to makes rights available to 'everyone' in a state. Parliament however chooses to give the right to bring an action to UK citizens only, a very specific and narrow category of person. The word 'everyone' in Article 1 ECHR is a much broader label and can apply to tourists, workers from other states outside the EU as well as illegal immigrants. The UK can of course be taken to the ECtHR by a non-citizen but such a person does not have the right under the HRA to bring an action in a UK court for breach of the rights referred to in the HRA.

The Convention rights

These are set out in s 1.

---

1. — The Convention Rights

(1)   In this Act 'the Convention rights' means the rights and fundamental freedoms set out in –
   (a)   Articles 2 to 12 and 14 of the Convention,
   (b)   Articles 1 to 3 of the First Protocol, and
   (c)   Article 1 of the Thirteenth Protocol, as read with Articles 16 to 18 of the Convention.

(2)   Those Articles are to have effect for the purposes of this Act subject to any designated derogation or reservation (as to which see sections 14 and 15).

(3)   The Articles are set out in Schedule 1.

(4)   The [Secretary of State] may by order make such amendments to this Act as he considers appropriate to reflect the effect, in relation to the United Kingdom, of a protocol.

---

29   www.legislation.gov.uk/ukpga/1998 on 27 July 2013. The information for this diagram was accessed on the official government online site. It therefore includes changes to the Act since enactment in 1998 and 27 July 2013.
30   J Holland and J Webb *Learning Legal Skills* (7th edn, OUP, Oxford).
31   Ibid, 310.

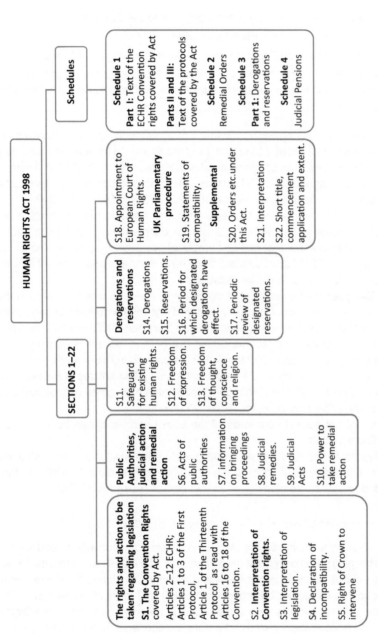

HUMAN RIGHTS ACT 1998

SECTIONS 1-22

Schedules

The rights and action to be taken regarding legislation
S1. The Convention Rights covered by Act.

Articles 2–12 ECHR;
Articles 1 to 3 of the First Protocol,
Article 1 of the Thirteenth Protocol as read with Articles 16 to 18 of the Convention.

S2. Interpretation of Convention rights.

S3. Interpretation of legislation.

S4. Declaration of incompatibility.

S5. Right of Crown to intervene

Public Authorities, judicial action and remedial action

S6. Acts of public authorities

S7. information on bringing proceedings

S8. Judicial remedies.

S9. Judicial Acts

S10. Power to take remedial action

S11. Safeguard for existing human rights.

S12. Freedom of expression.

S13. Freedom of thought, conscience and religion.

Derogations and reservations

S14. Derogations

S15. Reservations.

S16. Period for which designated derogations have effect.

S17. Periodic review of designated reservations.

S18. Appointment to European Court of Human Rights.

UK Parliamentary procedure

S19. Statements of compatibility.

Supplemental

S20. Orders etc.under this Act.

S21. Interpretation

S22. Short title, commencement application and extent.

Schedule 1
Part 1: Text of the ECHR Convention rights covered by Act

Parts II and III:
Text of the protocols covered by the Act

Schedule 2
Remedial Orders

Schedule 3
Part 1: Derogations and reservations

Schedule 4
Judicial Pensions

Figure 12.4 The layout of the Human Rights Act 1998

> (5) In subsection (4) 'protocol' means a protocol to the Convention –
>
>   (a) which the United Kingdom has ratified; or
>
>   (b) which the United Kingdom has signed with a view to ratification.
>
> (6) No amendment may be made by an order under subsection (4) so as to come into force before the protocol concerned is in force in relation to the United Kingdom.

Consider the text of s 1 again. Notice that s 1(1) introduces the term 'convention right' to specifically refer to (a) Articles 2–12 and 14 of the ECHR, to (b) specified articles in Protocol 1 to the ECHR and to (c) specified articles in Protocol 13 to the ECHR. These are the subject of the legislation. Section 1(1) further notes that the Convention rights listed in s 1(1)(a)(b)(c) are to be read in conjunction with Articles 16 and 18 of the ECHR.

Have you noticed however that this legislation only refers to two protocols, 1 and 13? Not all protocols relate to new rights and this Act concerns rights imposing public duty. However, you will now know that quite a number of protocols give rights. The UK is not a signatory of all of the ECHR protocols and there is no mandatory requirement for contracting states to the ECHR to sign all later protocols.

Section 1(4) gives the Secretary of State power to make an order[32] amending the HRA as may be required by protocols yet to be entered into by the government and ratified by Parliament. Section 1(5)(b) even provides that the Secretary of State could include in the Act by delegated legislation protocols signed but not yet ratified. A reading of s 1(1)(a) makes clear that Articles 1 and 13 of the ECHR are omitted from the rights covered by this Act. Furthermore, we note that in s 1(1)(b) and (c) only a few articles in the two protocols are referred to. Section 1(2) states that only those rights highlighted as 'convention rights' are included where there are no derogations or reservations.

Schedule 1 of the Act sets out in detail the ECHR rights that can be the subject of a claim in an English court.

If you have accessed the most up to date version of the Act from the official site then you should not have any worry that you are missing protocols recently adding to the rights to be included under 'convention rights' as that phrase is used in the Act.

Illustrative examples of issues raised by the ECHR in relation to UK cases

The case of *Al-Skeini and Others v the UK*[33] already referred to above is a good illustration of non-citizens bringing an action against the government. The ECtHR found that the British Government had violated Article 5 (right to liberty and security) and Articles 1 and 2 respectively. In *Al-Skeini* the applicants claimed breaches of the ECHR right to life when there was a failure to investigate the death of relatives killed in the course of security operations by the British Army in Basrah. If you recall Article 1 states that a state is responsible for 'everyone', and the court found that as the UK has assumed the authority to be responsible for the security in South East Iraq it was consequently liable for the safety of the civilian population harmed by its activity. This action could not have been brought in the domestic courts under the HRA 1998 as the

---

32 An order is a species of secondary or delegated legislation, which have been discussed in Chapter 1.

33 (Application no. 55721/07; Reported: (2011) 53 EHRR 18; 30 BHRC 561; [2011] Inquest LR 73; *Times*, 13 July 2011.

claimants were not citizens, but that fact does not free the government of responsibilities under Article 1. This case caused a furore in the British press, and in the government, who began to heighten their call for the UK to remove itself from the ECHR and the jurisdiction of the court.

Another decision relating to national security and terrorism, *Omar Othman v the UK*[34] in July 2012, was the object of much criticism in the UK. The UK wished to deport Omar Othman (known in the UK primarily by the name Abu Qatada) to Jordan, where he had been convicted in his absence on various terrorism charges. The government were keen for him to be deported. The UK had obtained a range of diplomatic promises from Jordan that Abu Qatada would not be subjected to ill treatment. Abu Qatada claimed these were false. The ECtHR ultimately found a breach of Article 6 'right to a fair trial' in that they considered there would be a risk that previously obtained evidence based on torture would be used against him at a planned retrial in Jordan. They ruled therefore that deportation would be contrary to Article 6. This was a tremendous upset for the UK, made worse by the fact that this was the first time ever that that such a finding had been made by the Court. It was an important ruling for the European Court of Human rights in that it was meant to convey the strong message that it adhered to international consensus that information extracted by torture made a fair trial impossible. Later applications made by Abu Qatada as the UK endeavoured to deport him related to allegations that his rights to a family life under the ECHR had been violated. Eventually he chose to leave in July 2013.

CONCLUSION

This chapter has explained how to read and understand the law of the EU and under the ECHR. The status of EU law as a legal system operating as part of the order of international law has been discussed and the types and effects of EU primary and secondary law, including the incorporation of directly applicable EU law have been explored. The important role of the CJEU has also been explored. It has the power to be the final arbiter of the interpretation of EU law and a core power it possesses is to give a preliminary ruling on the interpretation of a particular law at the request of a national court needing an answer to determine the case before it. A leading EU case, *van Gend en Loos*, where a preliminary ruling was requested, has been dissected and related to the treaties and secondary law of the EU, including the issue of article renumbering and relocation. English judges hearing cases in the domestic courts must apply the rulings of the CJEU.

The EU is a distinct body from the Council of Europe who were the authors of the ECHR. However the CJEU considers the ECHR binding upon it when engaged in decision making. Also there are current plans to incorporate the ECHR into the EU legal system.

The ECHR is part of the order of international law and is enforced by the ECtHR. It gives rights to everyone living within a contracting state. While the UK Human Rights Act only gives citizens the right to bring actions in domestic courts alleging breach of 'convention rights', which are rights given by specified articles of the ECHR and its protocols, not all articles.

All of these important interconnections need to be understood when dealing with both the law of the EU and the law relating to the ECHR.

---

34. http://hudoc.echr.coe.int/sites/eng/pages/search.aspx?i=001-108629.

EU law

- The EU has its own legal system, the acquis communautaire or acquis, founded on civil law.
- A civil law system operates quite differently to a common law system particularly in relation to drafting of laws, trial procedures, role of the judges, and the role of judgments in court.
- The CJEU has developed, and continues to develop, general principles of law (e.g. legal certainty, equality).
- EU law in the form of treaties and regulations can be 'directly applicable' in the legal systems of member states and enforceable in the courts of the member states. If criteria are met EU law that is 'directly applicable' can have 'direct effect' in member states' legal systems.
- 'Horizontal direct effect' allows a citizen or private organisation of a member state to take action against another citizen or private organisation.
- 'Vertical direct effect' allows a citizen or private organisation of a member state to take action against the member state.
- It is possible but rare for directives to be deemed to have vertical direct effect if conditions are met. They can never have horizontal direct effect.
- The CJEU is the final arbiter on matters of the interpretation of EU law. Preliminary ruling procedure allows national courts to request a ruling on the correct interpretation of EU law if it is needed to determine a case before it.

Understanding the law relating to the ECHR

- The ECHR is the creation of the Council of Europe. It gives rights to everyone within a contracting state to bring an action for infringement of the ECHR to the ECtHR.
- The ECHR has been amended by a series of protocols, some of which also give rights.
- The CJEU views the ECHR as binding upon it when deliberating.

Understanding the Human Rights Act 1998

- The HRA allows citizens of the UK to bring actions in domestic courts under certain articles of the ECHR and its protocols, which are referred to as 'convention rights' in s 1.
- The Act imposes a duty on all public bodies to act in accordance with the ECHR, s 6. The public duty extends to the courts.
- The minister of state has the power to add to or withdraw rights in the HRA, s 1.
- The minister of state must either declare legislation compatible with the ECHR or explain why Parliament will go ahead with that legislation anyway.
- The courts may decide legislation is incompatible with the ECHR and issue a formal declaration of incompatibility.
- The decision of the ECtHR only has effect at the level of international law. The decisions of domestic courts have effect within the English legal system.

PART 4
LEGAL REASONING SKILLS

'Imagination is more important than knowledge.'

Albert Einstein

This section of the book is concerned with your competency in identifying, constructing and critiquing arguments. The ability to construct an argument is a key skill in all disciplines and many professions. The lawyer is not just a wordsmith as mentioned earlier in this book; the lawyer is also an argument-smith, the skilled producer of arguments. You may also be surprised to be informed that it takes imagination and creativity as well as knowledge to build an elegant argument. That is why the quotation from Albert Einstein has been chosen to hover over this Part of the book. It is challenging you to take time to consider the comment and decide if it is right, and if it is, in what way imagination is important. There is of course a dramatic exaggeration in the quotation but does it hold any grain of truth do you think?

Chapter 13 *How to construct an argument* introduces the general characteristics and structure of arguments, and the basic building blocks of argument (propositions, evidence, conclusions). It also explores inductive and deductive forms of arguments. Once students have understood the basics they can go on learning about the nature of arguments throughout their academic, vocational and professional lives. The chapter also spends time considering the nature of rules and problems. This consideration is necessary; law students spend much of their time identifying problems and applying rules to resolve problems. Therefore it is important to understand something about their intrinsic character.

Legal education requires legal and/or academic arguments to be deployed – it is important to know what each looks like.

Chapter 14 *English legal reasoning: theory and practice* considers legal reasoning methods in the English common law system and looks in detail at how to break down problem scenarios and apply law to facts. It concentrates on fact management as well as legal analysis. The management and understanding of the facts of problems is essential for the appropriate application of law. This chapter provides the basic material for legal problem solution, because in order to engage in legal analysis you need to be able to work at the basic level of matching facts to the elements making up a legal rule. If you cannot do this you will not understand how to apply law reports to problem questions to reach a solution. You will be unlikely to be able to apply a range of secondary academic texts and law reports to construct essay arguments either.

Chapter 15 *European legal reasoning* looks at the differences between English common law reasoning and civilian legal reasoning and it is important that you are aware of these differences, otherwise you will not properly understand EU cases in the CJEU, or EU written law, or cases heard in the ECtHR. It is the methodology of the civilian system that determines the method of drafting legislation and treaties as well as the methods for dealing with legal disputes before the courts. The chapter also considers the way in which decisions in the European Court of Human Rights slightly deviate from the approaches in the Court of Justice of the European Union but nonetheless remain civilian.

Taken together chapters in this part introduce you to reasoning techniques that are core to the enterprise of legal study. If you take the time to read them, and complete guided exercises where they are given, you will be rewarded with an increase in your competency to construct arguments which will increase your understanding of law.

HOW TO CONSTRUCT AN ARGUMENT

13

'Logic is the anatomy of thought.'

John Locke

LEARNING OUTCOMES

After reading this chapter you should be able to:

- Define 'argument' and explain its general characteristics.
- Distinguish between inductive and deductive argument.
- Appreciate the importance of analogous reasoning in the English legal system.
- Appreciate the process of argument construction and the skills required to complete them effectively.
- Understand the relationship between the diagnosis of problems and the construction of rules to solve problems.
- Understand the relationship between facts, evidence and legal rules.
- Appreciate the limitations of logical reasoning and the necessity of legal judgments.
- Define and differentiate between inductive, deductive and abductive reasoning.
- Be aware of the need to develop critical thinking.

INTRODUCTION

Everyone argues at some point in their everyday life, with family, friends, employers, work colleagues, fellow students and teachers. The tools used for arguments like this are usually not precise and are often driven by emotional responses to other people's behaviour, such as anger, frustration, anxiety, and even love. Despite their seriousness in terms of the potential consequences to relationships and status, these arguments are informal and non-academic. Argument in universities, where it is manifested as academic argument, and in the courtroom or negotiator's office, where it has a professional and punitive form, has a more formal definition.

This chapter introduces the concept of formal, academic argument, and outlines the basic characteristics of argument and argumentative terms in order to enhance your ability to use properly the legal and academic source material that you will research for seminar work, assessments and exams.

This chapter considers the definition of argument, and the general characteristics of an argument. It will also look at three types of argument necessary for success in law; inductive, deductive and analogic argument, and considers the relationship between facts, evidence and legal rules in the construction of legal argument. The chapter also explores the important relationships between problem diagnosis, development of rules to resolve the problem and subsequent application of those rules to similar situations.

After reading this chapter you should be able to understand and develop the skills required to identify, construct and attack an argument.

Time is spent at the beginning of the chapter looking at the relationship between diagnosis of problems and the construction of rules to solve problems. If you wrongly diagnose a problem no solutions will work!

WHAT IS AN ARGUMENT?

Formal and informal arguments all comprise a range of assertions and counter assertions that lead to a resolution of the argument to the satisfaction of one of the parties, if not both. It is useful to remember that 'to argue' is a verb and therefore 'argument' is an action. There are always two sides to an argument even if one side seems passive.

The word 'argument' has a range of meanings, all of which revolve around proving the validity of an assertion. Take a careful look at Figure 13.1 which illustrates the various meanings of 'argue' and 'argument'. It gives three meanings of the verb 'to argue' (in Latin, French and English) and highlights the meaning now commonly used.

In this book we will use the following definition of argument:

An argument is a series of statements, some backed by evidence, some not, which are purposely presented in order to prove, or disprove, a given position.

Latin root - Arutari:	French root - Arguere:	English root - to Argue. The root that acquired ascendancy in English is the French. English meaning is now:
• to prattle, prate/frequent	• to make clear, convict • to assert, prove • to accuse	• to bring reasons to support or deny a proposition • to maintain that something is the case by the bringing of reasons to prove that it is so

Figure 13.1 The Latin, French and English meanings of 'to argue'

Figure 13.2 demonstrates that law is not alone in having argument as a core activity. It shows how various academic disciplines use the English meaning of argue, each with slightly differing meanings but all coming under the main idea of argument, as supporting or denying propositions or maintaining that something is the case by bringing reasons.

As noted in the blue text box above our preferred definition of argument refers to supporting 'a given position'. Such 'given position' in a legal context could be:

(1)   Anna is guilty of theft contrary to the Theft Act 1968.
(2)   Anna is not guilty of theft contrary to the Theft Act 1968.
(3)   The European Union does not belong to its citizens.
(4)   The European Union does belong to its citizens.

Note that the given positions expressed as statements in (1) and (2) are different to those in (3) and (4). Whilst (3) and (4) could be the subject of a theoretical essay, or the topic of a debate, (1) and (2) are assertions that require the consideration of legal rules and facts to determine innocence or guilt, as in a court case. However, good arguments for all four positions would share similar structures and characteristics, and we will return to these positions later in the chapter.

Developing your skills of argument

Argument is both a process and an activity. To engage in the *process* of argument is to deploy methodically a *series* of arguments.

An argument can be viewed as a journey *from* problem *to* solution, or *from* an allegation *to* a conclusion denying or supporting that allegation. In the case of legal problems, this journey consists of interpretation and application of legal rules to legal problems. This journey cannot be undertaken without preparation and if the preparation is not properly carried out then the destination may not be reached. Many students hate the preparation and the journey but the challenges involved in argument construction will help refine your study, research, legal and language skills. If the preparation and the journey can be

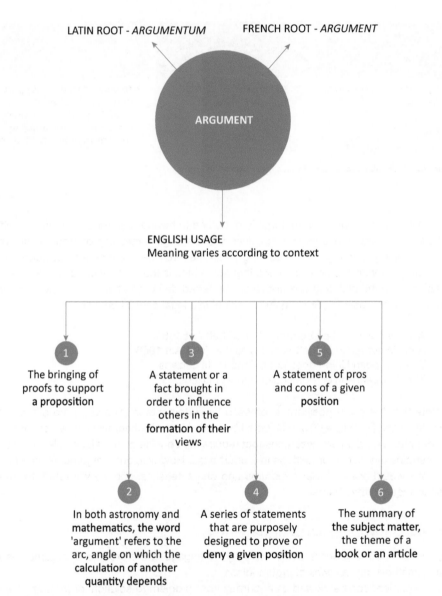

Figure 13.2 Different meanings of the word 'argument' as used in English

enjoyed, and not just endured, then the road is set for lifelong successful learning leading to good results.

The journey from problem to solution requires a map: a map others can follow, a map that allows the argument-crafter to take readers, or listeners, along with them to the desired destination. A map that eloquently explains why it is not a good idea to take this side-road or that alternative route, a map that also explains how, if matters were different, another route could have been taken. To create a good map, you need a good balance of skills, as illustrated in Figure 13.3.

An argument will only be as good as the ability of the person constructing it, to use this range of skills they have developed. As each skill develops so will the quality of your argument identification and construction,

Legal arguments take place through the mediating influence of oral and written language. As you will discover, language is a notoriously flexible and subjective medium of communication. We have already noted this flexibility when discussing statutory interpretation. Language and its interpretation mould the law and determine outcomes.

Critical thinking

Key to successful argument is the ability to engage in critical thinking. One important characteristic of highly competent people is that in many areas of their lives they have

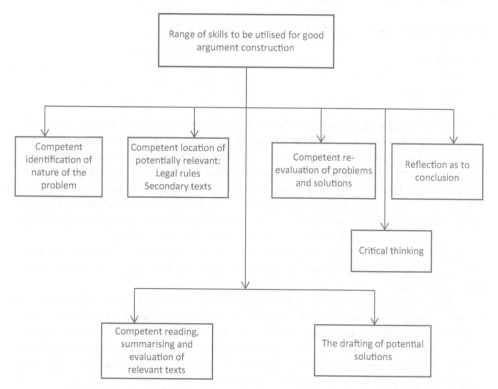

Figure 13.3 Skills required for good argument construction

developed *a critical approach* to what they do, see and think. Not critical in the sense of 'fault finding' but critical in the sense of exercising judgments based upon careful:

- observation;
- investigation;
- consideration,

of the issues relevant to the matter about which a judgment is to be made.

Most educators and senior managers would state that critical thinking, critical analysis and critical reflection are essential skills sought after in students and employees. Usually, these phrases are not defined but are left as vague attributes. However, the skills involved are not vague, for they are identified by others looking for them. Some people define critical thinking as a cluster of skills, which includes:

- reasoning logically;
- the ability to locate underlying assumptions;
- analytic and argumentative skills.

In terms of approaches to study, it can mean the ability to be:

- curious;
- flexible;
- sceptical.

Critical thinking is usually thought of as an academic or intellectual skill but it also has crucial practical applications in life. What should be clear is that it is not just a cerebral rational attribute and act. Critical thinking is equally informed by passion, emotion and imagination. Imagination can in fact be essential to leaps of creativity that are later identified as 'critical'. Being a critical thinker therefore is bigger than just cognitive acts of logical reasoning, and the careful consideration of argument. It also involves an ability to find assumptions behind beliefs, actions and behaviour, and bring creativity to the activity of thinking. Critical thinking involves the whole person and can be seen as a life-enhancing necessity.

The ability to think critically is crucial to understanding our personal relationships, envisioning alternative and more productive ways of organising the workplace, and becoming politically literate.[1]

Critical thinkers will be able to put forward justification for their ideas and actions and those of others. They can compare and contrast work through processes, subject justifications to a number of interpretations, and they can predict and test the accuracy of those predictions. They can work artificially by constructing models of the 'real' and recognise that is what has been constructed. Critical thinking also involves 'reflection', subjecting your learning to analysis by comparing it with practice.

---

1   S Brookfield *Developing Critical Thinkers: Challenging Adults to Explore Alternative Ways of Thinking and Acting* (Jossey-Bass, San Francisco, CA, 1987), 14.

Critical thinkers are always searching for the hidden assumptions behind what others just call 'common sense', or 'everyday' accepted ways of acting or thinking. They are aware of diversity in values and behaviour. When critical thinkers locate underlying assumptions they know they have to ask if they fit in with current notions of social reality. These assumptions are carefully dissected and their accuracy, as well as their validity, questioned. At this point these competent individuals consider alternative ways of acting and alternative assumptions to back them.

For critical thinkers nothing is closed, fixed, or certain. Everything is potentially flexible, open and possible. They are always questioning what lies behind the ideas, beliefs or actions that people hold or take. This is not to say that critical thinkers hold no strong views or cannot believe in anything. It is possible to hold the strongest convictions that something is right while accepting that all values, views and beliefs are open to question and that there may be alternative views. Critical thinkers can always imagine another plausible story, explanation, or value. They are not going to believe in universal truths without thorough investigation and indeed will probably always remain healthily sceptical of universal views, truths and explanations.

If a critical thinker holds a clear view, it is held lightly with scepticism. If strong evidence to the contrary occurs the view will be reconsidered. As Cottrell notes:

> 'Scepticism in critical thinking means bringing an element of polite doubt. In this context, scepticism does not mean you must go through life never believing anything you hear and see. This would not be helpful. It does mean holding open the possibility that what you know at the given time may be only part of the picture.'[2]

Critical thinkers are flexible thinkers, but not fickle thinkers and they are not afraid of alternatives. Constant questioning heightens the awareness of critical thinkers, as they always approach givens as if the view could be otherwise.

This takes us a long way beyond the discipline of law, legal method and studying law but the intellectual process involved in critical thinking is the basis of studying. Each discipline may require slightly differing approaches that accord to its accepted practices and procedures, but the foundational importance of critical thinking remains intact within every part of the academic community. Each discipline will have developed its own beliefs, practices and procedures, its own theory and methods and its own underlying assumptions. The study of law is no exception.

Competency in critical thinking develops over time and no doubt all readers of this book will have developed some critical thinking skills outside the study of law, although they may not have put a name to the process. This development can be transferred to your legal studies even if you have never really considered the issue of critical thinking before. In academic studies, critical thinking and a healthy scepticism of universality are demonstrated

---

2   S Cottrell *Critical Thinking Skills: Developing Effective Analysis and Argument* (Palgrave Macmillan, 2005), 3.

by approaches to reasoning. Critical thinkers, for example, are aware that often arguments contain contradictions and these contradictions have to be looked for. They are also able to distinguish between differing types of statement. For example, they can understand the difference between a statement of fact and a statement of opinion. This naturally affects the expertise of their reasoning processes as it makes a great deal of difference whether an argument is based on opinions or facts!

The core of critical thinking is the constant and considered identification and challenging of the accepted truth. It requires the evaluation of values and beliefs as well as competing truth explanations and, of course, texts. It involves both rationality/objectivity and emotions/subjectivity and the questioning of the very categories of thought that are accepted as proper ways of proceeding. If you think critically, you will:

- *search* for hidden assumptions;
- *justify* assumptions;
- *judge* the rationality of those assumptions;
- *test* the accuracy of those assumptions.

Texts will form the 'bare bones' of much of your studies. They are delivered in language that has to be read, interpreted, questioned and seen in its fragmented contexts, so it is vital to develop a critical approach. The critical thinker has to engage not only with micro-questions within a text, from both superficial and deep readings, but also with macro issues surrounding topics, courses and ultimately the legal system. Much of your degree study will involve working with legal primary or secondary texts, reconciling, distinguishing and/or following the arguments of others, as well as the tentative construction of your own arguments. You must be able to identify arguments set out in texts, offer your views on their weaknesses and strengths, and understand why an argument can be considered good or bad. Much of your time may be spent explaining alternative interpretations that may be very close to one another. When deciding what words mean in texts we make far-reaching decisions and often engage with morals, religion, justice and ethics. Critical thinkers look for hidden assumptions underlying the face value explanations of texts. They are not deceived by theorists, particularly those who make claims of neutrality, and are aware of the power of language and the value of argument. They know that all texts are not logical and do not necessarily feel that they have to be so.

Many students think it strange that in their first term of study they can be asked to critically evaluate an article written by a leading scholar. The rationale for this is that by reading the work of leading scholars students can see the ways in which a strong argument is deployed. Sometimes a theorist who has constructed a very elegant theory from quite normal information known to students is used to teach about theory construction. Students are also asked to read the work of scholars critiquing other scholars, and in this way students begin to understand how to critique themselves, and the work of others.

If you identify and carefully take apart the arguments of leading academics you will learn how they put together an excellent argument. You will begin to extract from an article, or a chapter in a book, the main and secondary arguments. You will identify the evidence that they have used to support their arguments. You will also see many ways of structuring arguments. You will of course come across some academics who argue most elegantly, interlinking the parts of their argument to create a highly persuasive conclusion.

When you read these academics or when you read any material you should be in the process of having a dialogue with that writer 'in your head' as you read, make notes and consider what you are reading. Academics, professionals and especially students cannot find out everything for themselves through the first-hand experience of doing research and evaluating it. They have to rely on the work of other people who have done the initial research. But that work should only be relied on after you have subjected it to careful consideration and critique. You should never accept the arguments of another without careful reflection and if possible double-checking the evidence supporting the arguments. In other words not just the argument but the evidence it is based on should be subjected to critical reflection and analysis.

It is also important for students to learn quickly that in actual fact theories, interpretation or arguments may only be partially correct. As you ask, and answer, some of your critical questions you will develop a better understanding of areas of study. This will allow you to competently discuss increasingly complex topics as your understanding of the topic develops. In academic life new questions constantly arise and cannot be resolved by an internet search. It is then the task of the astute student to apply known understandings to the new circumstances and questions. You are only expected to identify and understand the relevance of new questions in your area of study to engage with them. You are certainly not expected to resolve any new intellectual and academic dilemmas.

Critical thinking is a dynamic process involving a range of different mental processes, including attention to detail, focus, organisation and classification, and ultimately evaluative judgment of the arguments you are reading. For the first months of study, and even the first year, critical thinking will be somewhat of an artificial process that you need to keep remembering. Ultimately it will become a way of looking at the world so that you automatically question everything and evaluate it, and where necessary adjust your understanding. If you subject your own arguments to critical evaluation, in time the habit of employing critical thinking as you read and write will become ingrained.

In the academic life of the university it is normal to critically query the correctness of the reasoning of other academics and to state your doubts about their strength as long as you back this up with evidence. However, just as in real life, there is a level at which we must operate on trust despite all our questions as critical thinkers. We need to trust at times that the argument we read is based on information that is plausibly correct, but we need to make informed decisions about what we choose to take on trust. In academic study it is expected that our belief in certain academic points of view or positions are fully explored so that we more fully understand the basis of that belief. As you acquire better habits of critical thinking as a process you will more naturally become aware that your emotional standpoints, and your attitudes to the author, have to be placed to one side. You will realise that you need to take a neutral objective view as you approach a text and identify and evaluate the arguments to ascertain whether they are plausible or not. At that point you are ready to express your own view, your own argument and forward your own evidence to support it.

Always remember that an author must give you clear reasons for each of his or her arguments before you take a position agreeing or disagreeing with the argument. As you move through the levels of study over the years of your degree you should find that the quality of your reasoning improves substantially. Ultimately you will be able to evaluate quickly and efficiently the reasoning of others, spot internal contradictions in their work and 'read between the lines' and identify or hazard a guess at the underlying or hidden assumptions that the argument is based upon. You will far more easily engage in comparing and contrasting the opinions of the academic authors you read, and you too will be able to form categories and engage in the prediction of outcomes. Above all you will become competent in the skill of attention to detail.

Not only are critical thinking skills vital to your study but they will be of enormous value to you in the workplace. They are transferable skills which you can use in all settings to evaluate properly your courses of action. Not only will critical thinking help you save time, you may also be saved from making bad decisions!

PROBLEMS AND RULES

Before continuing to discuss the details of argument construction and the legal reasoning preferences of the English legal system it is useful to look briefly at the nature of problems and rules. Legal disputes are arenas in which legal rules are used to resolve problems. Therefore a proper understanding of the interpretation and deployment of legal rules is essential to constructing a good argument. However, choices can always be made about which rules to apply, and how to apply them to specific legal problems.

We will consider general matters about the idea of problems and rules. This will encourage you to take a broader view of legal rules and legal problems which will be of use in your legal analysis.

The nature of problems

Problems occur in a variety of different contexts, and include for example:

- a difficult question put forward for an answer in scholastic disputation;
- the question asked in the standard formal logic method of deductive reasoning;
- in mathematics and physics, a problem is an investigation or a question which, starting from our idea of a 'given position', investigates some fact, result or law.

Twining and Miers (2013)[3] writing in the context of handling legal rules give a more detailed description:

---

3   W Twining and D Miers *How To Do Things with Rules* (5th edn, CUP, Cambridge, 2013).

A problem arises for an individual when she is faced with a puzzling question to answer, or a difficult choice to make, or some obstacle in the way of achieving a particular objective. A person is faced with a theoretical problem when she is confronted by a question calling for an answer that dissolves the puzzlement or solves the problem, without necessarily calling for action. A person is faced with a practical problem when there is some doubt about what to do. It is unwise to draw too sharp a line between theoretical and practical problems.[4]

Of course it is not just individuals who have problems; problems can have a corporate or social impact requiring community or societal action. The real issue is how you move from problem to solution, something students often find difficult. If you can correctly identify, classify and interpret problems you will be able to begin the journey from problem to solution. But solving problems also requires imagination and solutions can even involve guessing and testing. Twining and Miers (2013)[5] point out that problems change their nature according to the perspective, or standpoint from which they are viewed.

Even a seemingly simple problem can be complex for those seeking a solution. Many problems come not as single units but as a series of interconnected issues and problems. Problems, like so many other issues, are *processes*, often *complex processes*. If you do not understand the nature of problems generally, it can be difficult to understand the nature of legal rules, and the complexity of using legal rules as solutions to problems.

Solving problems

Problem solving and problem management are parts of everyday life and the skills you have developed in these areas can help you turn your attention to more methodical approaches when dealing with complex legal problems. However, you may not always be aware of how you solve life problems, and some of the techniques you may use, like anger, fear, frustration or running away, would be most unsuitable in academic work.

Just as legal problems themselves can comprise a series of interconnected issues and problems, their solutions are the end product of a series of complicated interrelated operations.

Effective problem solving involves accurately:

- identifying that there is a problem;
- classifying what type of problem it is (this determines much about the eventual solution);
- presenting a solution to the problem.

Solutions can be aimed at *dealing* with the problem, or making the problem-solver *feel better*. Solutions aimed at making the problem-solver feel better could include doing

---

4   Ibid, 114.
5   Ibid.

Step 1: CLARIFICATION of individual's standpoint, role, objectives, general position.

Step 2: PERCEPTION by individual of the facts constituting the situation.

}   **Identification** of the problem

Step 3: EVALUATION of one or more of the elements making the situation undesirable, obstructive or bad (in other words, 'what's the problem?').

Step 4: IDENTIFICATION of a range of possible solutions to the perceived problem.

Step 5: PREDICTION of:
    (a) the cost of each option
    (b) obstacles associated with each option.

}   **Diagnosis** of the problem

Step 6: PRESCRIPTION: choosing a solution to the problem and the construction of an effective policy for solving the problem.

Step 7: IMPLEMENTATION of that policy.

}   **Prescription** for solution followed by **implementation** of solution

Figure 13.4 Twining and Miers' problem-solving model

nothing, removing themselves from the situation, or effecting a reconciliation and extraction of a promise not to repeat the behaviour.

In many disciplines, professionals use problem-solving models which enable users to check certain steps along the road to eventual solution. One of the best known and most useful problem-solving methods within legal education is the model set out in Twining and Miers (2013).[6] Their seven steps model for problem solution is set out in Figure 13.4. They identify issues of identification (steps 1–3), classification (step 3), prescription (steps 4–6) and implementation of the solution (step 7).

Many organisations and individuals can be too quick to jump to step 6 (prescription), before they have had an opportunity to correctly diagnose the problem. This error can often be seen in government's 'knee-jerk' reaction to a crisis, and can also be seen in students when confronted with an essay.

Even when you try to follow a model or imagine all eventualities, solutions to problems can often cause more problems. If you search deeper into a problem, it is usually found to be a cluster of problems with a range of causes, and a range of potential solutions, each with a different set of obstacles and costs. This means lawyers tend to solve problems in a range of ways, mostly revolving around the application and meaning of legal rules.

---

6   Ibid.

The nature of rules

There are many meanings of the word 'rule'. A rule can be a principle or a maxim governing individual or group conduct in life or in a game. It can be a system that creates a way of life, like the rule of St Benedict that prescribes the actions of a monastic group. Some rules only have force within religious or social settings; others have effect within legal settings. Some rules only have force within a given academic discipline, such as philosophy, law or indeed legal method. Even language is subject to rules such as the rules of grammar and punctuation. Students must obey rules, although literary luminaries like James Joyce have attempted to subvert these rules by simply refusing to obey them. Figure 13.5 sets out a definition of a rule highlighting its constituent parts.

Different rules share these general characteristics but vary in terms of who has the power to create or interpret them and what the consequences for breaking them might be.

A rule often represents the view of a group concerning lawful, moral or socially acceptable action. For example, the English legal system, like most legal systems, values human life and prohibits unlawful killing. The 'Do not kill' rule also has social and moral functions, backed by a range of religious or philosophical groups worldwide. To enable these functions to be enforced the rule has been given a legal base and infringement can lead to severe penalties. There will always be difficult situations even when a legal rule and its standard meanings seem to be fixed. For example is assisted dying out of love for the person concerned murder?

Figure 13.6 sets out the different classifications of rules that you might come across.

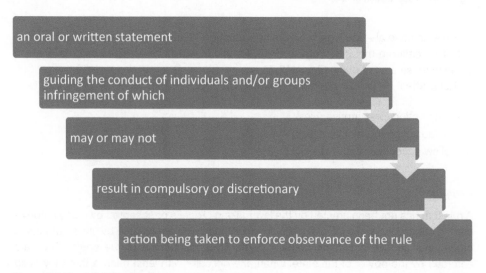

Figure 13.5 The definition of a rule

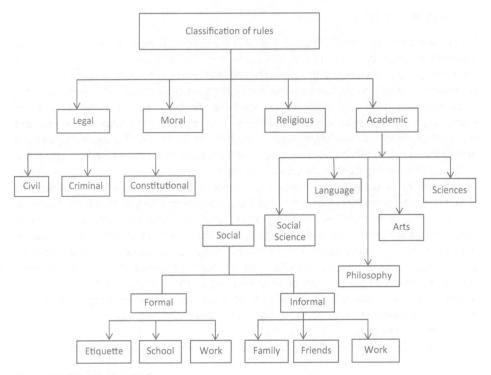

Figure 13.6 Classification of rules

Rules in general – and legal rules are no exception – relate to people engaging in certain activities, either in thought, word or deed. Particular words are used to enforce this and some of these are set out in Figure 13.7.

Rules affect behaviour in a range of ways. They can:

■ stop action (prescriptive rules);
■ guide action (normative rules);
■ allow action (facilitative rules).

Legal rules

A rule that has not been created by the law making process or accepted by those empowered to create law is a legal rule. In England, all legal rules are created by state-authorised procedures (judges are office holders in the state institutions of the court). They are enforced by the power of the state. Often, the difficulty with legal rules is that they need to be general and need to be applied to specific, particular situations. This means that the wording of legal rules needs to be carefully considered. But inevitably these words will

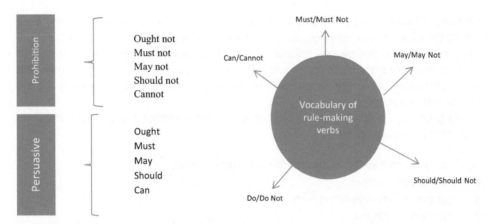

Figure 13.7 A vocabulary of rule-making verbs

be the object of *interpretation*. That a rule seems applicable may be clear but the precise meaning of an important word or phrase may not always be.

Statutory rules in our simple majority democracy often reflect the political values of the party in power. They can, therefore, be described as instruments of policy. Whatever the original intention of the political designers of the statutory rule, when users of these rules come to interpret them, defects in design are often apparent because words can, so often, be made to mean what the originator did not intend them to mean: another reminder that language is flexible.

CONSTRUCTING ARGUMENTS

Now that a little thought has been given to:

- the meaning of argument;
- critical thinking;
- the nature of problems and rules;
- the mediating power of language,

it is hoped that the complexity of any attempt to solve problems by recourse to rules is better appreciated. Now we are in a position to consider how to argue.

HOW TO ARGUE

It is essential that lawyers are able to construct arguments and use effective reasoning to resolve legal problems. Without that core skill, a lawyer lacks competence. One of the difficulties of legal argument is that the answer to a legal problem in court is rarely clear cut. All the evidence will not necessarily have the same degree of plausibility, or be of the same strength. The law may be unclear, and all of these issues need to be ordered into the best argument that can be constructed. This is why argument involves the deployment of imagination and creativity alongside an understanding of applicable legal rules and the problems they address.

The good news is that argument construction utilises a number of preparatory skills you have already engaged with:

- finding appropriate texts and choosing the most useful;
- summarising texts;
- researching and organising texts;
- critique and analysis;
- collecting appropriate materials in order to persuade the listener of the validity of the arguments presented.

Reasoning involves:

- preparation and collection of information;
- ordering and organisation of information;
- working through the information once the issues that it supports are clear.

When people set out on a journey, they normally have an idea of where they are going. If they do not know where they are going, this is usually a matter of deliberate choice. When you begin to consider argument construction, you need to know where you are going: 'to begin with the end in mind'. If you do not know where you are going you may become exhausted and frustrated and end up arbitrarily writing in your essay or problem solution, words which imply 'therefore, this is the end'. It is not possible to craft a good argument by accident. Having said that, useful information to include as evidence for an argument may be uncovered accidentally. However, the argument itself can *never* be accidentally or *mindlessly* constructed. It is a technical ability that must be understood and practised knowingly.

Evidence

Legal argument is a delicate balance of propositions backed by evidence. Such evidence will depend on the context of the argument and could involve facts, legal rules and theories. If the dispute is a legal problem, argument construction will be concerned with the application of existing rules connected by reasoned comments to persuade the listener of the validity of adopting the outcome suggested. In the courtroom, both parties put forward arguments and the judge chooses the argument that is either the most persuasive or the closest to the judge's own belief concerning the outcome of the case. Evidence substantially increases the persuasiveness of an argument. An argument that is a series of propositions not backed by evidence is unlikely to succeed in any area of study or dispute resolution. On your course you will need to engage with tasks that require you to apply legal rules to hypothetical fact scenarios in legal problem solution activities.

The role of judicial judgments in argument construction

So far, in this text, there have been opportunities to read judgments and you will have noted that the judges have presented their decisions in the form of reasoned responses to the questions posed by the case. The trial court is the place where conflicting claims are resolved by the judge(s). Much of your study will revolve around the decisions of the senior judiciary. Each case is based on particular grounds of appeal. One side succeeds because, in the opinion of the judges, theirs is the most persuasive argument in relation to the specific grounds of appeal.

The reasoning most valued within law demonstrates a consistency of approach and logic; consistency is highly valued. However, the law is not, and cannot be, a closed system. Analytically there are always other possibilities, which inevitably means that much legal decision making is contingent. There may be a better solution, and if one is located in another case then decision making may change according to the restraints of the doctrine of precedent.

No argument can ever be 100 per cent sound and our legal system requires less than perfect proof. In a civil court the contingent nature of legal decision making turns on proof based 'on a balance of probabilities'. This means that when the arguments of litigants are weighed against each other, one litigant's argument appears to be more probably correct. In the criminal trial courts the contingent nature of legal decision making is demonstrated by the requirement that the court finds that the prosecution, or the defence, has 'proved beyond all reasonable doubt' the correctness of their argument. So, accusing someone of not having a perfect argument is not in itself a good argument. No one has a cast-iron case. Does that surprise you?

Decisions as to correct action can only be made by people who are able to distinguish between competing arguments and determine that, in a given set of circumstances, one argument is more valid than another. Judges are, of course, the ultimate arbiters of the acceptable decision. Sometimes, this decision is quite subjective.

For the practising lawyer, a valid argument is of the utmost importance. In the classroom, you are constantly called upon to practise and refine your skills in legal problem solving by engaging in reasoning processes leading to full-scale argument construction.

It is now time to explore and apply the more formal aspects of general argument construction: logic, deduction and induction.

LOGIC

It is generally believed that academic and professional lawyers and, indeed, law students, are skilled in the art of legal reasoning which rests on logic. Furthermore, it is believed that they are people who argue 'logically'. To most, the term 'logical' indicates that a person can separate the relevant from the irrelevant and come to an objective view, based often on supposedly objective formulae. Colloquially, people sometimes accuse those who change their mind or who are emotional in their arguing, of allowing their emotions to get the better of them, of 'not being logical'.

The dictionary defines logic as the science of reasoning, thinking, proof or inference. Inference involves drawing a conclusion from something known or assumed using reasoning. Consider Figure 13.8 for a more visual description.

Logic can even be defined as a science in its own right, a sub-branch of philosophy which deals with scientific method in argument and the uses of inference. The German philosopher Georg Hegel described logic as the fundamental science of thought and its

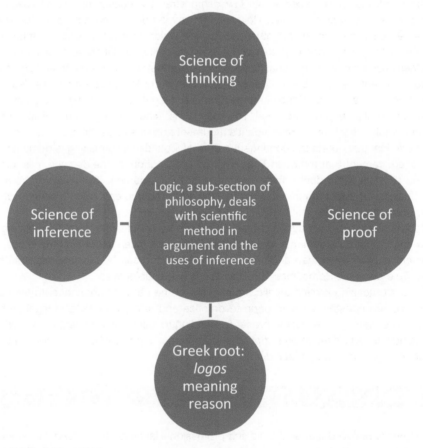

Figure 13.8 Definition of logic

categories. It can certainly claim to be an accurate form of reasoning: its root is found in the Greek word *logos* meaning reason.

Lawyers, like scientists, spend time supporting statements with evidence and considering how one might weigh evidence on a scale of weak to strong. What is it that is actually proved by the evidence? However, lawyers deal in words, reports and reconstructions. Unlike scientists, lawyers are not present observing the wrong, the accident or the incident. But as appropriate they can draw upon the reports of those witnesses who were there, formal statements by the parties, upon digital or DNA evidence, other forensic evidence, and other documentary evidence (such as copy correspondence, contracts). This evidence must be compiled properly and legally by those presenting it.

The logician, like the lawyer, deals in statements. Sometimes the more technical term 'proposition' is used. In the context of logic, the word 'proposition' can be most simply explained as a statement or assertion about something. More particularly it is a statement that is put forward as the basis of an argument that brings evidence for or against its validity. A proposition is expressed as a sentence. In the science of logic, the proposition takes on a more formal role as a particular type of sentence statement in which the topic of the sentence, *the predicate* is affirmed or denied concerning the *subject* of the sentence.

To put this more simply in English the predicate of a sentence is that part of the sentence in which you are told something about the subject. The subject is what the sentence is about (a person, a category, a class or concepts). In a formal argument it is expected that there is proof for the predicate in the proposition.

Essentially, logic is the study of propositions and how conclusions may be correctly obtained from them through the process of reasoned argument. There are two main types of logical reasoning: deduction and induction. Each of these will be discussed below.

Deduction

Deductive reasoning occurs in an extremely stylised manner and follows a standard procedure and structure. It is the process by which two statements (propositions) containing information are used to construct a third concluding statement. This draws out of the precise wording of the previous two propositions, new information to express by way of a concluding statement.

Statements are variously called 'premises' or 'propositions'.

There is no permission to conclude by way of plausibility or probabilities: the third statement conclusion can only be extracted from the linguistic forms making up the major and minor statements. Therefore the conclusion of a deductive argument is said to be *compelled*, and the reasoning system is *closed*. The formal model used for this argument is called a syllogism.

In deductive reasoning, the argument follows a prescribed form called a syllogism, as set out in Figure 13.9. The first statement in a deductive argument is known as the 'major premise' and it is a general or normative statement; the second statement is known as the minor premise and it is particular rather than general. The third statement is the

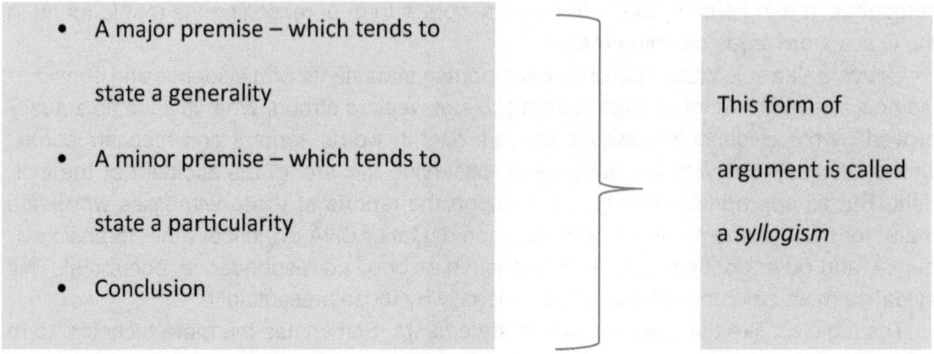

- A major premise – which tends to state a generality
- A minor premise – which tends to state a particularity
- Conclusion

This form of argument is called a *syllogism*

Figure 13.9 **The components of a deductive reasoning argument**

conclusion. Figure 13.9 sets these three statements out as the component parts of deductive reasoning.

To give a concrete illustration we will consider the fictional character of Anna who is accused of stealing a book from a book store, an act that is contrary to s 1 of the Theft Act 1968 which prohibits stealing. The argument against her can be set out as follows:

Major premise: Stealing is contrary to section 1 of the Theft Act 1968.
Minor premise: Anna has stolen a book.
Conclusion: Therefore Anna has committed theft under s 1 of the Theft Act.

You may already have noticed from this scheme of argument that deductive reasoning leaves no space for examining the truth or otherwise of the premises making it up. It is therefore of limited use within a legal context. This leads us to note that in fact whilst a deductive argument can be logically valid (that is it is expressed in the correct form) it cannot be assumed to be true. We can easily verify the truth of the major proposition (that stealing is against s 1 of the Theft Act) by checking the primary law. But we have no way of knowing if the minor proposition is true without a full trial. The proof or otherwise of the major and minor premises is outside the remit of deductive reasoning.

Analytically there are always other possibilities. A deductive syllogism can be useful when a precedent is being teased out for the first time and its logical consequences need to be tracked. It is also useful for pinpointing exactly what aspects of a legal rule have been infringed. We will explore this in the fictional case study of *R v Anna* in Chapter 14.

Induction

Inductive reasoning involves arguments that put forward a first particular proposition, or thesis, followed by a series of propositions relating to facts and evidences. The last proposition, or conclusion, is drawn out of the previous propositions. One of the most important differences from deductive reasoning is that the reasoning system is *open*, meaning it can be possible for more than one conclusion to be drawn. It is based on inferences. Then decision makers need to choose the conclusion they consider the most plausible in light of the arguments presented to them.

As with deductive reasoning, the conclusions are based on propositions. However, in inductive reasoning, the conclusion reached extends beyond the facts in the premise. It is not compelled; it is *drawn out*. The supporting propositions make the conclusion probable but there is no one absolutely clearly correct conclusion as there is for deductive argument.

An inductive argument can, for example, have as an inference a generalisation, such as 'innocent people do not run away'. Different types of generalisations are set out in Figure 13.10.

A generalisation can be quite easily challenged as it is usually constructed on flimsy arguments. Inductive argument is perhaps the closest to the everyday legal argument where decisions are made concerning which party to a legal dispute wins the case because their 'story', in terms of the law's authority about the way current law applies to their claim, is accepted by the court, a story that will have been made up of a range of main and subsidiary arguments.

Like deductive reasoning, from a purely scientific point of view, inductive reasoning has no interest in the actual truth of the propositions that lead to the conclusion. The court, on the contrary, is most concerned with establishing that the conclusion is correct and that the propositions are correct. Just because a logical form is correctly constructed, it does not mean that the conclusion expressed is true. The truth of a conclusion depends upon whether the major and minor premises express statements that are true. The statements may be false. Much time is spent by lawyers in court attempting to prove the truth of statements used as building blocks in the construction of arguments.

Think back to our one-line propositions above about Anna stealing a book. The prosecution may argue she stole the book because she was seen leaving the store with it. The

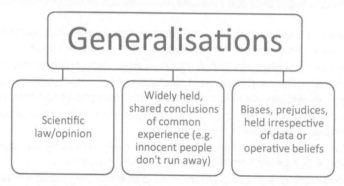

Figure 13.10 Types of standard generalisations which can find their way into inductive argument

defence will wish to argue she did not. Or the defence may argue, say, that she did not leave the store intending to take the book but intending to look at the quality of its colour plates in daylight. Both sides will have to support their argument with evidence. The side that the court decides has the stronger argument backed by evidences will win the case.

Analogous reasoning

A subdivision of inductive reasoning is reasoning by analogy or analogous reasoning. The Greek word 'analogy' means likeness, or similarity, and is used to describe the equality of ratios of proportions in mathematics. In logic it expresses the resemblance of attributes between two or more things.

Analogous reasoning is used in English legal reasoning. Lawyers in the courts argue from rules developed in previous cases on the grounds they are alike. As you may realise this is the reasoning required by the doctrine of judicial precedent. In doing this they reason from the general to the particular, applying abstract generalised rules from previous cases to the particular current case.

CONCLUSION

Students must be competent argument constructors and dismantlers. An ability to construct a good argument is the core of successful study in any area. The ability to identify someone else's argument, take it to pieces and cast doubt on its main propositions is part of this key skill. To be able to do this is to understand the nature of arguments and the effect that the correct diagnosis of problems and use of legal rules has on the ability to build a good argument. Learning formal methods of argument can assist you in the development of cohesive legal arguments.

CHAPTER SUMMARY

- An argument is a series of statements, some backed by evidence, some not, which are purposely presented in order to prove, or disprove, a given position.
- Problem-solving models can help you work in order through the key steps.
- A good model for law is Twining and Miers' Diagnostic model (clarification, perception, evaluation, identification, prediction, prescription and implementation).
- If a legal problem is wrongly diagnosed, any argument constructed will be as flawed as the erroneous diagnosis in the first place.
- Deductive reasoning is a closed system of logic in which the only possible conclusion is compelled from the major and minor propositions.
- Inductive reasoning is an open system of logic in which the probable conclusion is drawn out of the propositions. It can result in more than one conclusion.

- Analogous reasoning is a subspecies of inductive reasoning. It is the preferred method of argument in the English legal system. In analogous reasoning general rules from previous cases are applied to a particular case to seek a solution to the issue in hand.

- Reasoning itself cannot always prove or disprove the facts of a case.

- The civil courts resolve issues based on an argument being considered on a balance of probabilities to be correct.

- The criminal courts resolve issues based on an argument being considered to be correct beyond all reasonable doubt.

ENGLISH LEGAL REASONING: THEORY AND PRACTICE

14

'The life of the law has not been logic; it has been experience. The felt necessities of the time, the prevalent moral and political theories, intuitions of public policy, avowed or unconscious, even the prejudices which judges share with their fellow men, have had a good deal more to do than the syllogism in determining the rules by which men should be governed. The law embodies the story of a nation's development through many centuries, and it cannot be dealt with as if it contained only the axioms and corollaries of a book of mathematics.'

Oliver Wendell Holmes, Jr.

LEARNING OUTCOMES

After reading this chapter you should be able to:

- Understand the difference between fact analysis and legal analysis.
- Understand the way in which an argument relies on factual analysis, legal reasoning, persuasion and critical thinking.
- Construct a competent legal argument.
- Critique and deny the correctness of legal argument and give an opposing argument.

INTRODUCTION

Law students tend to be taught law through a method that emphasises law cases and relies heavily on the development of argumentative strategies to apply the law and facts to simulated legal problems. This chapter looks closely at the basics of legal reasoning and argument formation in English law. Building on Chapter 13 it concentrates on practical issues connected with argument construction. This chapter considers in detail the relationship between propositions used to construct an argument and the proofs supporting those propositions.

LEGAL REASONING THEORY

We can obtain a different perspective on law by considering it from the point of view of legal philosophy, customarily referred to as jurisprudence. Although there are many schools of legal philosophic debate, it can be crudely suggested that there are four main ways of considering law from a philosophical perspective. Each has developed chronologically but can operate side by side in modern legal thought.

The first view is to imagine law as *reason*. From this perspective it is argued that either man, or the cosmos, contains principles of rational and reasonable order. And this order can be seen to be replicated in rational beings. This is the perspective of the **natural law** schools of legal thought.

The second view imagines law as a matter of lawful enactment by authorised institutions of the state. This is the view of the **positivist** schools of legal thought. Law is in this sense about power and power discourse.

Both the positivist and the natural schools of jurisprudence were initially influenced by religious ideas and have room for notions of the divine.

A third view is that the law is no more than the translation of life experience into rules enforced by the state. This is the view of the school of legal realism.

The fourth view states that law reflects the power roles of those who control the state and is held by critical legal scholars.

As each view is now discussed briefly try to consider which view you prefer, and why you prefer that view.

Natural law

In natural law schemas, the ideology put forward is that of reason being ascertainable by each person through their own rational enquiry. The law discovered is the law of the natural order of things. Many religions where there is a view that men and women are fallen from the blessing of a God or Gods, can find this view a problem, as the law thus located by way of human reasoning is inevitably flawed. Some secular arguments critiquing natural law are also based on the logical grounds of the impossibility of human infallibility. If you are interested in exploring these areas you will find a range of arguments presented by religious professionals constructing differing frameworks to accommodate religious forms of natural law alongside its secular forms.

Positivism

Positivism argues that there is no higher order of things discernible by reason (secular or divine) and that law is created and maintained purely by power and will. Over time this creates habits of obedience to sovereign power. The only matter of importance is that law is properly created. In English law this would mean by the authority of judges or Parliament. In other words, law is law if it is validly enacted. The positivistic 'law-as-law' philosophy is the most popular view in English legal theory.

The leading English legal positivist HLA Hart champions this view.[1] For him all rules, including legal rules, have both an external and an internal dimension. By this he means that not only do they come from somewhere (the external dimension), but that those to whom the rules apply observe them or react to them (the internal dimension).

Both the value and the problem of this position lie in its potential for de-politicising legal analysis and de-unifying moral positions. Under a 'law-is-law' perspective, if a regime is stable and predictable and it has sanctioned institutions to create, adjudicate and enforce law then the law is to be deemed law, irrespective of its enactment and enforcement, and irrespective of whether it is lacking in democracy. Therefore a corrupt and immoral regime using its legal system and laws to impose appalling sanctions on some, or all, of its people would have the right to do so.

One of the major criticisms of Hart is by Dworkin[2] who argues that law is *more* than just rules, that it also includes principles. Dworkin identifies the existence of discretion as a core problem of law. As all interpretation is constructive, he argues, it imposes purpose on the object of interpretation. While interpreters can differ on the 'purpose and value' of assumed common interpretations the important decision occurs in the moment of choice, for choice remains at the point one decides what constitutes the 'best' interpretation. Dworkin argues that the law has an investment in the constancy of its power to ensure that all of the law's decisions and interpretations are the best they can be. Dworkin's problem is that he dislikes the idea of discretion, but where there is choice of interpretation there is always discretion. You will already have realised that the language of law is flexible having considered issues of the development and interpretation of law.

---

1   HLA Hart *The Concept of Law* (2nd edn, Oxford University Press, 1994).
2   Ronald Dworkin *Taking Rights Seriously* (Duckworth, London, 1978). Ronald Dworkin *Law's Empire* (Fontana, London, 1986).

'Western' and the Anglo-American legal traditions consistently claim that law is a specialist, scientific pursuit separated from other social phenomena. Whilst it can be said that the English legal tradition developed by way of its common law tradition, it is no different in its structure from the majority of Western legal systems (that are based on variants of Roman law), in its claims about the unitary and specialist nature of law. It is after all the product of the Normans' rationalisation of a range of localised law in its creation of common law.

It is important at the beginning of your studies to appreciate that the law can change in terms of its content and its form. This in turn allows it to be used to play different social, economic and political roles

Within this framework if one looks back centuries, considering English law as royal law, judge law, parliamentary law, or a mix of all three, it is argued that the law still retains the unity of an external and internal view of law. It comes from somewhere and those to whom it is addressed are required to obey it. The *external dimension* of law can always be pointed to whatever its ideational source might be (e.g. wizards, kings, judges, religion, politics, soldiers). It is this ideational core of law that is unchanging, and through it law can claim its unique role to maintain social order and notions of the desirability of communal order. While law's flexibility allows its content to change, legal institutions can also promote the unity and unchanging nature of law itself. The ideational core of law constitutes the unchanging 'presence' of law.

The internal dimension of law is its practical level of the content of law as applied to the world and where practitioners point to interim institutional sources, the legislature, the courts, the European Union and international treaties.

Legal realism

In the US, a movement known as *legal realism* developed (it is also popular with Swedish legal theorists). Legal realism maintains that law is what really happens-in-practice, at the level of the everyday.[3] To give a flavour of this movement there is no better example than Oliver Wendall Holmes' famous description of law as a magic mirror reflecting back the experience of life,

'. . . wherein, . . . we see reflected, not only our own lives, but the lives of all men that have been. . .'.[4]

On another occasion he specifically refers to the law using the genre of fairy tales, describing the law as likened to

'. . . a princess . . . eternally weaving into her web dim figures of the ever lengthening past. . .'[5]

This is an interesting allusion to Tennyson's poem *The Lady of Shallott*

'There she weaves by night and day, a magic web with colours gay', cursed to watch the world through a mirror on pain of death to look directly.

---

3   The theorists most associated with this stream are Karl Llewellyn, Jerome Frank and Oliver Wendell Holmes.
4   OW Holmes *The Common Law* (Cambridge, Mass, Belknap Press, 1963) 20–21.
5   Holmes, ibid, 22.

Here the illusion is of a seamless trail of history. In both these quotations, Holmes is referencing both the everyday level of law and its ideational core through his metaphoric references to magic, myth, story and royalty. Indeed the reference to stories is most appropriate in relation to law, and particularly English law. Each legal case revolves around the telling of stories. It can be overlooked that when these stories go to court it is the judge's final legitimation story – the authorised story of the court, patched together from the perceptions and evidence of the stories of the parties – that becomes the written record of the law. From this perspective law can be viewed as a collection of dynamic stories: stories whose texts yield information concerning the many contexts of law in action (e.g. political, social, institutional, and religious contexts).

The critical legal theory movement

As the discussion returns to stories and language, so we return to the view of law as a power-filled system of communication. The *critical legal theory* movement argues that legal scholarship fails if it does not look at the power dimensions of the law, through a careful interrogation of its hidden assumptions and figurative language.[6] Goodrich's (1986) analysis of law-talk shows that legal language is no more and no less than a social practice patterned by its background, contexts and officials, and that its texts therefore reflect and express:

'. . . the roles, purposes and ideologies of its participants or subjects, these implicit or unconsciously regulated operative meanings are accessible to study through their expression in the lexicon, syntax and semantics of the text.'

Goodrich (1986:76).

We could say here that its texts are again a mirror, although Goodrich argues the text is not a magic mirror but a mirror in which we can discover the true nature of law, its power and its motivations.

It has been cleverly argued by White[7] that:

'the greatest power of law lies not in particular rules or decisions but in its language . . . in the way it structures sensibility and vision . . . law offers opportunities to tell one's story and be heard. Thus law is a method of translation as well as integration'.[8]

White further argues that primary legal texts (legislation and cases) are designed to be applicable not only to the matter in hand but are a response expected to apply to unforeseen situations noting that the law:

'. . . creates as it were a new dimension of reality, running across time and space, in which it aims at, even claims, a consistency of result and significance that in the nature of things cannot wholly be allowed. The legal text thus stimulates and works by a desire not for the discovery of actual human intention but for a different sort of meaning: for the creation of a general language of justice that will govern a wide range of particular cases over time in a consistent and fair way.'[9]

---

6   Here mention could be made of critical legal scholars such as Peter Goodrich, Costas Douzinas, Peter Fitz-patrick and latterly Adam Geary.
7   JB White *The Legal Imagination* (abridged edition, Chicago University Press, Chicago, 1985).
8   Ibid, 114.
9   Ibid, 133–134.

ENGLISH LEGAL REASONING IN PRACTICE

Whatever theoretical view of law making you prefer, or is put forward by theorists, the law has to be able to be used on a daily basis by legal professionals and litigants. We now turn to consider in detail how English common law reasoning takes place in practice.

Legal argument

Legal argument concerns not only laying out facts and rules, it also involves aspects of persuasion, and the determination of where the weight of evidence favours one side of a dispute. Judges or jurors decide whether an argument is strong or weak, proved or unproved.

How does the court decide the criteria for the *evaluation* of an argument and assess whether it is more supported by the evidence than an opposing argument on the same matter? Evaluation cannot be solely guided by rules. Just as argument construction is in part a matter of personal preferences involving creativity and imagination, so evaluation is a personal enterprise too, as well as a professional or academic enterprise.

Different people will take different views of the evidence, and relate the evidence to the issues in different ways. Much depends upon an individual's ability both to imagine and reason; to imagine doubts, as well as links in proof; to imagine other arguments, particularly those of the 'other side'. Nothing exists in the realm of methods to tell anyone what a strong link may be. We may be excellent at the processes of transmitting, storing and retrieving facts and information but we may not have similarly developed skills of obtaining defensible conclusions from these facts and this information.

The law as an institution has a vested interest in demonstrating that its trial procedures are fair and its legal rules are neutrally applied. In this context not only are pseudo-scientific approaches to decision making applied to the production of evidence but they are applied to the accepted methods of legal reasoning and legal argument construction. Emotional and passionate language from lawyers is deemed unacceptable. It occurs and is censored, yet judges often refer to it in their judgments. Theory states legal argument must be a dispassionate appeal to reason, based on argument supported by evidence validly produced according to the rules of evidence and applicable legal rules as applied to a set of facts. The majority of trials involve competing versions of the facts or of the meaning of words in legal rules (otherwise there would not be a contested trial).

Constructing argument presupposes competency in a number of complex skills groupings, such as:

- the use of various methods of legal reasoning (deductive, inductive and abductive);
- understanding logic and its limits;
- handling language well;
- interpreting and applying rules;

- understanding the nature of problems, and the use of rules to solve them;
- appreciating the concept of problem solving, or problem analysis;
- distinguishing between fact analysis and legal analysis;
- appreciating various definitions of argument;
- engaging with the concept of argument as a process and as a structure;
- understanding discrete terms such as propositions, evidence and inference which make up the constituent parts of argument.

At the academic stage of education the standard framework around which teaching takes place is that of legal analysis. Legal education is orientated towards the case method: how cases in courts are described and analysed. Your skill in understanding cases, how they have been argued and how the law has been applied, is tested by asking you to solve a hypothetical problem based on hypothetical facts. Often students are asked to present advice for one fictional party to a case. You will need to use the library (virtual or real) to search in books, journals and law reports to find similar, analogous cases, noting how these have been decided and why. You can then infer how the hypothetical case you have to argue will be decided, basing your inferences on the way applicable legal rules were applied in real cases. The legal analysis that students are trained to carry out, of course, involves basic analysis of the facts of the case. Which are the material facts? How can the facts as given be organised to make it clear that earlier cases apply? In the standard university problem question, the facts do not need to be ascertained; they are given as a neat, logically ordered, story. In real life, these stories are messier, the relevant facts are more difficult to extract, and the solutions are not so clear.

At the vocational stage of legal training, students are taught to engage in factual analysis and this provides the framework for the course. Students are taught how to structure, organise and analyse a large amount of what is called 'raw data' such as witness statements. They learn how to draw out the probable story from clients, the inferences in the data and see how available evidence can support the argument on the case to be proved. Very few clients present with a neat story. Evidence is matched to the relevant facts, the facts in issue (e.g. 'Anna stole a book'). The legal principles are assumed. Indeed this aspect of legal education reverses the university-education process of drawing out legal analysis. The legal principles here are not in issue, but are a given. In our example, there is no doubt that theft is against the law. The test of development for the student is to see how skilled they are in deciding whether the available factual data can be put into a structure that makes it possible to construct a viable argument: for example, constructing an argument that proves Anna is guilty of theft because enough evidence exists to prove the elements of the unlawful act according to the relevant standard of proof. Or to argue the reverse, that she is not guilty of theft.

The common law model rests on assumptions that underlie both theory and practice and this will become clear as legal study is undertaken. It is said that in fact it rests on notions of the ideal type of rationalist tradition.[10] This model involves *the pursuit of 'truth'*

---

10 See generally W Twining and D Miers.

through rational means. Can you make accurate present judgments based on reasoning in cases occurring in the past on similar facts? This is certainly what the doctrine of precedent demands. The English legal system has developed principles designed to draw out that past reasoning and use it in the present and to obtain consistent decision making. Such a pursuit has as a high, but not overriding priority, the securing of justice under law. The model of adjudication is instrumentalist in that the pursuit of truth through reason is only a means to achieving a particular type of justice: the implementation of substantive law.

The mode of legal decision making is rational not irrational and, because it is highly aspirational, its practice is often critiqued. As discussed in Chapter 13, the mode of reasoning used in the English legal system is inductive, analogic reasoning. Although there is room for constructing deductive argument, proof always needs to be by inductive means.

A lawyer has to be competent in both legal analysis and factual analysis. Constructing argument requires careful attention to detail, planning and understanding. There is a close relationship between:

- facts of cases;
- legal rules;
- case law and legislation;
- language usage;
- logic and reasoning;
- planning;
- imagination;
- evidence.

All of the above need to be combined with excellent skills in critical thinking.

At this point it is worth restating the definition of argument used in this book:

> *An argument is a series of statements, some backed by evidence, some not, that are purposely presented in order to prove, or disprove, a given position.*

Argument can also be described as the process of maintaining that something is the case, for example, that Anna stole the book, and of bringing reasons to support that case. If Anna were charged with a crime, the charge would note that 'Anna stole a book contrary to s 1 of the Theft Act'. This charge is an assertion or proposition where the subject (Anna) committed the predicate (stealing the book) contrary to the Theft Act. Tangible evidence, such as witness testimony, forensic evidence or documentary evidence, could provide reasons to support this proposition.

The process and dynamic act of reasoning can be described as a careful journey through various propositions. Each of these propositions can found its own argument with reasons being brought to support or deny it depending on your standpoint in the argument. As noted in Chapter 13 problems tend not to arise singly; they come in clusters. Arguments similarly tend not to arise as a one-off, but in clusters.

Argument by analogy

As noted in Chapter 13, argument by analogy is a form of inductive reasoning and the most common form of argument in English law. Such an argument begins by stating that two objects are observed to be similar by a number of attributes. The conclusion then draws similarities between the two objects with respect to a third. The strength of the argument depends upon the degree of relationship between the objects.

Lawyers are advisors and they offer predictive advice based on how previous similar cases have been dealt with. All advice is based on the lawyer's perception of what would happen in court, based on that lawyer's experience of how judges reason. This is usually enough to ensure that, in the vast majority of civil cases, matters between disputants are settled.

The English legal system operates a relatively rigid adherence to the doctrine of precedent. Since argument by analogy looks for similarities between things it is ideally suited to the use of precedent in the English legal system. The lawyer confronted with a particular fact scenario and a doubt about the extent of a legal rule, or the meaning of words, will look at other previous cases in the senior courts for guidance.

The strength of the precedent in a previous case is carefully considered to find out what it is and whether it is binding or only a persuasive precedent.

The facts of previous cases setting precedents are also carefully scrutinised. Are they the same as the current case or different? If they are different, are they similar enough to be 'like' facts for the purposes of precedent? The legal rules in previous cases are also scrutinised to check whether they are about the application of similar, or 'like' rules, even if they have been placed in updating legislation for example.

In the vast majority of cases, the outcome of a case will simply be an application of existing law to the facts. Occasionally, the decision creates a new law which may or may not be stated as a proposition of law. Reasoning by analogy is a process of reasoning by comparing examples in order to reach a conclusion in a novel situation. It involves three key stages:

(1)   the similarity between the cases is observed;
(2)   the rule of law *(ratio decidendi)* inherent in the first case is stated. Reasoning is from the general to the particular (deductive reasoning);
(3)   the general rule in (2) is applied to the case for decision. At this point, reasoning is from the particular to the general (inductive reasoning).

Recall that in Chapter 13 we set out the deductive argument that Anna has stolen a book in the form of a syllogism as follows:

Major premise: Stealing is contrary to s 1 of the Theft Act 1968.
Minor premise: Anna has stolen a book.
Conclusion: Therefore Anna has committed theft under s 1 of the Theft Act.

We noted that the minor premise has to be proved, it cannot just be assumed to be the case. This is where inductive argument begins. There will be two conflicting views, Anna did steal the book or she did not. Both prosecution and defence will present arguments to the court supported by evidence to try and reach a situation of proof that is deemed to make their argument believed to be correct 'beyond all reasonable doubt'. To do this they will use inductive argument which begins with the theory (thesis) for the prosecution that Anna stole a book, and for the defence that Anna did not steal a book.

To assist you with your understanding of the process of creating inductive arguments we will use a fictitious case of *R v Anna*.

The building blocks of an inductive argument

The thesis

The first proposition in an inductive argument is the thesis (which, as you can see from the deductive argument in the blue text immediately above, is also the minor, particular premise of the deductive argument.

We will take the role of the prosecution as our main standpoint for illustration purposes. Our first proposition, the thesis, is:

Anna stole a book.

We then proceed to build our inductive argument looking first at the legal rule she is alleged to have infringed to see what it requires to be proved and then considering the facts of the case. At present of course we have not considered s 1(1) of the Theft Act 1968 or know any facts.

The thesis makes a reference to an illegal act by the word 'stole'. We know from the deductive argument that the legal rule alleged to have been infringed by Anna is s 1 of the Theft Act 1968 which is set out below:

Section 1 Basic definition of theft.

(1) A person is guilty of theft if he dishonestly appropriates property belonging to another with the intention of permanently depriving the other of it; and 'thief' and 'steal' shall be construed accordingly.

---

(2)   It is immaterial whether the appropriation is made with a view to gain, or is made for the thief's own benefit.

(3)   The five following sections of this Act shall have effect as regards the interpretation and operation of this section (and, except as otherwise provided by this Act, shall apply only for purposes of this section).

A criminal offence usually requires that the prosecution prove that the defendant actually carried out the guilty act (*actus reus*) and when doing so had a guilty mind (*mens rea*) that propelled them to do the guilty act. If the guilty mind cannot be proved then Anna cannot be found guilty. If the prosecution cannot prove all necessary aspects of the prohibited act were carried out by Anna then she cannot be found guilty. You will explore these matters in greater depth in criminal law modules; however, to follow this illustration of building an inductive argument in the case of *R v Anna* you need to be aware of the physical and mental components of criminal legal rules as s 1 of the Theft Act uses both.

Before looking at the next Figure (14.1) carefully read s 1(1) of the Theft Act and see if you can point to aspects of the rule that cover the mental element of a guilty mind as well as the aspects of the rule that specifically relate to the practicalities of carrying out the wrongful act. To assist you the legal rule contains five elements that must be proved for a conviction. Can you find them, and can you allocate them to either having a legally guilty mind (the *mens rea*) or carrying out the guilty act (the *actus reus*).

Looking at the elements in Figure 14.1 you will see that some of them relate to the *actus reus* (guilty act) and some to the *mens rea* (guilty mind).

An argument involving a dispute about any legal rule will be a balance of legal analysis, (matching the legal rule, and case law or legislation dealing with its interpretation to the facts) and factual analysis (organising the facts according to their evidential value and their relevance to the identified legal issues). But you need to split your legal rule into its constituent parts. Civil legal rules also at times involve aspects relating to the mental state of a respondent such as negligence.

Factual analysis

We can now consider the types of evidence that may be needed to prove the *actus reus* or *mens rea* elements.

For example, witness statements may show that a person was seen taking an item from a shop and that the item belonged to the shop (satisfying point 1. Appropriate) and that it constitutes property (satisfying point 3). It is necessary to read other sections in the Theft Act, s 3 (defining 'appropriates'), s 4 (defining 'property') and s 5 (defining 'belonging to another') to check you are correct. The property itself may also be put in evidence. You also need to be aware that cases may have interpreted words in the relevant sections.

The basic five elements requiring to be proved in a prosecution for theft
Text of s 1 of the Theft Act 1968 as amended
(1) A person is guilty of theft if he dishonestly appropriates property belonging to another with the intention of permanently depriving the other of it; and 'thief' and 'steal' shall be construed accordingly.   (2) It is immaterial whether the appropriation is made with a view to gain, or is made for the thief's own benefit.   (3) The five following sections of this Act shall have effect as regards the interpretation and operation of this section (and, except as otherwise provided by this Act, shall apply only for purposes of this section).
The table below deals with the definition of 'Theft Act 1968' as found in s 1(1). Section 1(1) can be split into five elements that need to be proved for a conviction. Four of these elements are defined by other sections in the Theft Act as noted in s 1(3) and these other sections are referred to in column 2 of the table below. But do not forget that case law decisions can still determine exact meanings of words and you will need to look at case law to see if any relevant aspects of s 1 have the object of statutory interpretation; even though the statute itself purports to define elements 1–3 and 5. Note that basically element 4 (column 3) is not defined by statute. Note too that s 1(3) states the definitions in the 'five following sections' only apply to the interpretation of s 1(1) unless expressly said to extend further.

COLUMN 1 ELEMENTS OF *ACTUS REUS*: THE GUILTY ACT	COLUMN 2 STATUTORY DEFINITION OF ELEMENTS OF ACTUS REUS	COLUMN 3 ELEMENTS OF *MENS REA*: THE GUILTY MIND	COLUMN 4 STATUTORY DEFINITION OF ELEMENTS OF MENS REA
1. Appropriates	s 3 This is an adverse dealing with property. Case law holds this includes touching the property of another or receiving it as a gift.	4. Dishonestly	*NOT defined* however s 2 lists situations that *are not* dishonest. Case law is important here where the standard test is whether the defendant considered what they had done was dishonest, and if not would the ordinary person in the street consider what the defendant had done was dishonest (*R v Ghosh*).
2. Property	s 4 This has been the subject of statutory interpretation.	5. Intention to permanently deprive	s 6 This has been the subject of statutory interpretation by the court.
3. Belonging to another	s 5 This has been the subject of statutory interpretation.		

Figure 14.1 Section 1 of the Theft Act and the five required elements in the definition of theft

The *mens rea* elements, the issues relating to the state of mind of the person, are more challenging. How does one prove dishonesty? Is it enough to say that the defendant walked out of the shop with an item? No, because there could have been a range of reasons for that action: she could have forgotten she had it with her, she could have been going to check it out in the light, she might have been borrowing it with the intention to bring it back. Some of these reasons may negate the suggestion of dishonesty, others might negate the intention of permanently depriving.

As you can see the simple allegation 'Anna stole a book' raises legal issues of some complexity.

Let us suppose the 'agreed facts' (that is facts that both the prosecution and the defence agree) of *R v Anna* are as follows:

---

(1) Anna visited Discount Gold book stores.

(2) She took a book, Herring's Criminal Law, from the shelf

(3) She put the book in her bag

(4) She left the book store without paying for the book.

(5) Anna is stopped by the security office and asked to empty her bag.

(6) Anna complies and the book is found to have been among the contents of her bag. Anna complies with the request.

(7) Anna complies with the request to go to the officer's office where she agrees to answer questions.

She was eventually taken to the police station where she made the following statement to the police saying that it was all a mistake and she had not intended to keep the book.

Anna's statement to the police: I went to the Discount Gold Bookstore on 7 February 2015 around 11am. I wanted to buy the new edition of Herring's Criminal Law to help me in my studies.

I was really shocked by how expensive it was and there was no way I could buy it. I felt stressed, I spent about 20 minutes or so looking through the book and realised that in fact there were only limited changes and I thought I could smuggle the book out of the shop, take it to the university and photocopy the pages I needed and take it back to the shop later the same day. So I put it in my bag.

As I was leaving the store I was stopped by this really officious security officer who made me empty the contents of my bag all over the pavement. I was really upset and embarrassed and was crying. He picked up the book I had smuggled out of the shop.

I agreed to go back to his office because people were staring at me. He gave me a drink of water and then when I had calmed down a bit he asked if he could ask me some questions. I said 'yes' because I wanted to get it sorted so that I wasn't late for lectures.

He asked me if I had paid for the book. I said I hadn't because I was just borrowing it and was intending to bring it back later. I really don't know why there is such a fuss. Of course I didn't steal it! I admit it must look odd that I took a book from the Discount Bookstore and left without paying for it. But surely anyone would understand why I did and wouldn't consider for one moment that what I did was theft. I'm no thief, although the security officer thought it was the wrong thing to do, I didn't think I was doing something illegal. It's not criminal to take a book to copy a bit of it and return it later. At no point did it ever occur to me to keep the book.

The police also took a statement from the security officer set out below.

Statement of the security officer:

I often saw Anna in the bookshop, and on 7 February she was in the law section of the store while I was doing my rounds. I noticed that she looked very agitated and kept looking at the shelves and looking around in a way I thought seemed suspicious.

I watched her for about 30 minutes making sure that she did not see me and then I saw her take a book from the shelf and put it into her bag. She then turned away from the shelf, and walked quite slowly out of the shop making no attempt to pay for it.

I followed her out of the shop and asked her to stop and empty her bag right there in the street and when she did so I saw one of the store's books 'Herring's Criminal Law' came out of her bag.

I asked her to come into my office in the store. She was very upset and I gave her a glass of water. When she was more composed I told her that I needed to ask her a few questions and that I would be writing down her answers. She shrugged and said 'OK then'. I asked her if she had bought the book. She replied 'No I am sorry but I haven't'. I then asked her if this meant that she had left the store without paying for it and she replied 'yes'. I asked her if it was an accident, and she had forgotten the book was in her bag and that she had really meant to pay for it. She replied that she hadn't forgotten she had an unpaid for book in her bag. She said that she was just borrowing it for a few hours to photocopy some pages to assist her studies. Then she was going to bring it back to the store and put it back on the shelf. I asked her if she thought that was a problem in any way for the store. She said she couldn't see why being without the book for a few hours could be a problem for the store.

I checked the computerised sales/stock system. This confirmed that the book belonged to the store, and that it had not been purchased that day.

I then called the police. By this time Anna was crying and saying it was all a mistake and she wanted to go home.

After consideration, the Crown Prosecution Service agreed she should be charged with theft under s 1(1) of the Theft Act 1968.

The prosecution has several pieces of important information gleaned from the statement of the security officer who is an eye witness:

(1) He saw Anna take a book from the shelf and leave the store.
(2) He stopped Anna outside the store and found a book in her bag.
(3) The store's computerised sales/stock system verifies that the book in Anna's bag belongs to the store.
(4) The computerised sales/stock system verifies that the book had not been logged out of the store due to purchase.
(5) When questioned by the security officer Anna said she had taken the book without paying for it because she was just borrowing it for photocopying before bringing it back.

From these statements we can infer that Anna took the book out of the store intending to steal it.

The agreed facts we have, together with eye witness evidence and Anna's statement to the police appear to contain enough evidence to prove all of the elements (both *actus reus* and *mens rea*) making up the s 1(1) definition of theft. For your assistance the various elements are set out below in column 1 of the table and linked to facts known in column 2.

COLUMN 1 ELEMENTS OF *ACTUS REUS*: THE GUILTY ACT	COLUMN 2 FACTS LINKED TO ELEMENTS IN THE *ACTUS REUS*
1. Appropriates	Anna admits taking the book, that is, to appropriating it
2. Property	The book is tangible property
3. Belonging to another	The book belongs to another – the store

However, the prosecution do have some concerns about obtaining a conviction because her statement raises a number of queries concerning whether she had the required guilty mind or *mens rea*. The following assertions by Anna could be accepted by a jury and negate the *mens rea* elements:

(1) She decided to smuggle the book out of the shop in her bag and photocopy it and she was going to return it to the store afterwards.

(2) At no point did she intend to keep the book.

(3) She is convinced that what she did was not dishonest and equally convinced most other people would agree with her.

The table below sets out the issues linked to the elements of the *mens rea*.

COLUMN 1 Elements of *mens rea*: guilty mind	COLUMN 2 Evidence that Anna did not have the required guilty mind
4. Dishonestly	Anna did not consider what she had done was dishonest, as she just borrowed it to photocopy it. What if the ordinary person in the street (according to the jury who would hear the case) considers what the defendant had done was not dishonest?
5. Intention to permanently deprive	s 6 This has been the subject of statutory interpretation.

If Anna alleges that she did not intend to permanently deprive the owner of the book, or if there is no dishonesty found then the *mens rea* remains unproved unless the prosecution can do so. If it cannot be proved Anna cannot be held guilty.

Legal analysis

The lawyer not only has to marshal all of the facts to prove the *actus reus* and the *mens rea*; he or she must also know what law cases may affect the way in which certain words making up the legal rule have been interpreted in the statute or the cases, as well as know if there is sufficient proof in relation to the *mens rea*. The lawyer ought to know that dishonesty has caused much concern in the law relating to theft and several cases deal with it. In addition the Theft Act makes clear that an intention to deprive permanently is not necessarily negated by saying that the item was only borrowed and the cases on this should also be considered. Similarly, whilst property has to 'belong to another' there are a range of difficult cases where you can steal your own property because of the way in which the law has been developed. We will now set out how we may go about building an argument for the prosecution based on the information we have. Figure 14.2 shows the relationship between deductive and inductive reasoning for the prosecution. Note carefully how you can see immediately that the minor premise of the inductive argument becomes the thesis of the inductive argument.

The use of 'inference' in argument construction

The use of inference and being aware of its pitfalls are an important part of building an argument. Consider the following definitions of to *infer* and *inference* and bear them in mind in the following discussion.

To infer: to draw a conclusion from something known, or assumed, or from evidence through the use of either deductive or inductive reasoning.
An inference: that which is inferred.

Inductive reasoning is always concerned with drawing out conclusions from known situations, facts, evidence and rules. Inference is used to connect parts of an argument. Those using inference, however, must be aware of a number of potential errors they could make. One of the most common errors is overlooking the possibility of a plurality of causes or alternative explanations to the one inferred.

For instance, each fact inferred by the prosecution as leading to an inference of Anna's guilt could provoke one of the following counter responses from the defence:

- an explanation as to why the assertion is misguided (it could be explained away);
- a straight denial (denying the validity or existence of the evidentiary fact backing your inference);
- the assertion of a rival inference.

Therefore when you are setting up an argument it is important to identify possible alternative conclusions and test them out. The question then becomes 'which are the stronger

Deductive reasoning

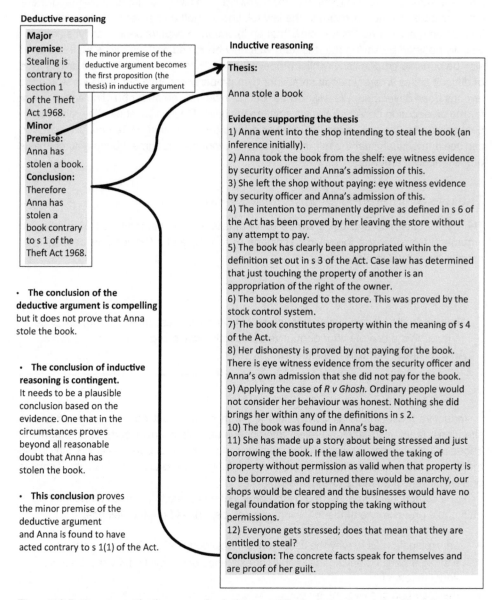

Major premise: Stealing is contrary to section 1 of the Theft Act 1968.	The minor premise of the deductive argument becomes the first proposition (the thesis) in inductive argument

Inductive reasoning

Major premise: Stealing is contrary to section 1 of the Theft Act 1968.

Minor Premise: Anna has stolen a book.

Conclusion: Therefore Anna has stolen a book contrary to s 1 of the Theft Act 1968.

- **The conclusion of the deductive argument is compelling** but it does not prove that Anna stole the book.

- **The conclusion of inductive reasoning is contingent.** It needs to be a plausible conclusion based on the evidence. One that in the circumstances proves beyond all reasonable doubt that Anna has stolen the book.

- **This conclusion** proves the minor premise of the deductive argument and Anna is found to have acted contrary to s 1(1) of the Act.

Thesis:

Anna stole a book

Evidence supporting the thesis
1) Anna went into the shop intending to steal the book (an inference initially).
2) Anna took the book from the shelf: eye witness evidence by security officer and Anna's admission of this.
3) She left the shop without paying: eye witness evidence by security officer and Anna's admission of this.
4) The intention to permanently deprive as defined in s 6 of the Act has been proved by her leaving the store without any attempt to pay.
5) The book has clearly been appropriated within the definition set out in s 3 of the Act. Case law has determined that just touching the property of another is an appropriation of the right of the owner.
6) The book belonged to the store. This was proved by the stock control system.
7) The book constitutes property within the meaning of s 4 of the Act.
8) Her dishonesty is proved by not paying for the book. There is eye witness evidence from the security officer and Anna's own admission that she did not pay for the book.
9) Applying the case of *R v Ghosh*. Ordinary people would not consider her behaviour was honest. Nothing she did brings her within any of the definitions in s 2.
10) The book was found in Anna's bag.
11) She has made up a story about being stressed and just borrowing the book. If the law allowed the taking of property without permission as valid when that property is to be borrowed and returned there would be anarchy, our shops would be cleared and the businesses would have no legal foundation for stopping the taking without permissions.
12) Everyone gets stressed; does that mean that they are entitled to steal?
Conclusion: The concrete facts speak for themselves and are proof of her guilt.

Figure 14.2 Basic argument for the prosecution in the case of *R v Anna* showing relationships between inductive and deductive reasoning

inferences?' Does your favoured argument look strong or does a counter-argument stand up? This involves, among other things, using abductive reasoning to test your argument against potential alternatives. The best argument is constructed with full consideration of what the counter-argument might be. This also guards against the other party's argument catching you by surprise. Abductive reasoning as you may recall from Chapter 13 involves constructing opposing hypothetical theses. The evidence a lawyer has may suggest alternatives, and perhaps more plausible ones than his or her own proposition. Considering arguments around the data based on hypothetical matters the other party may raise demonstrates the creative aspects of argument construction.

As we have already discussed, inductive reasoning is the closest to everyday legal reasoning because it involves putting forward a conclusion that seems strong, based on inferences that provide evidence in favour of one party. Your final argument will consist of a range of propositions or assertions that will invariably be backed by evidence from cases and statutes as well as forensics and witnesses. The relationship between these components is shown in Figure 14.3.

Although the Figure 14.3 diagram looks simple enough it is necessary to bear in mind that the propositions may have alternative explanations and the evidence supporting these alternative explanations will need to be analysed.

At the level of factual analysis, deductive argument requires extension by tracking through the process of inductive reasoning, starting with the minor premise of the deductive argument. For most law problems, a cluster of arguments may need to be set up dealing with separate issues. In assessing your final argument you should also have engaged in the process of predicting what the other party may be arguing and factor this into your argument and refute it.

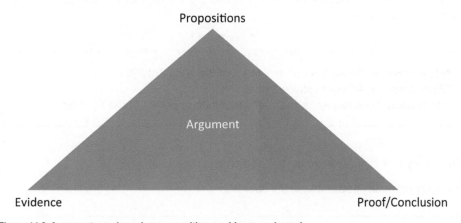

Figure 14.3 Arguments are based on propositions, evidence and proof

HOW DO YOU CRITIQUE DEDUCTIVE OR INDUCTIVE REASONING?

So far we have noted the following techniques for argument at the general level:

- the minor premise in a deductive argument becomes the thesis of inductive reasoning;
- the conclusion of a deductive argument is compelled and logically valid;
- the conclusion of a deductive argument may be incorrect because either the major or the minor premise or both are incorrect;
- the conclusion reached at the end of the process of inductive reasoning must be plausible;
- the conclusion reached at the end of the process of inductive reasoning must be contingent; another plausible conclusion may be reached on the information, facts, evidence and interpretation of law that has been used to forward the conclusion chosen;
- the conclusion reached at the end of the process of inductive reasoning forming the thesis proves or disproves the minor premise in the deductive reasoning process.

ATTACKING THE MAJOR PREMISE OF A DEDUCTIVE ARGUMENT

As the conclusion of a deductive argument is logically compelled, the conclusion itself cannot be attacked. However, the general assertion making up the major premise, or the particular assertion making up the minor premise, can both be targeted for critique and attack.

We will continue to use the case of *R v Anna* from the prosecution standpoint to illustrate these matters.

Major premise: Stealing is contrary to s 1 of the Theft Act 1968.
Minor premise: Anna has stolen a book.
Conclusion: Therefore Anna has committed theft under s 1 of the Theft Act.

How can the defence attack the major proposition?

The major proposition (premise) in the case is:

Major premise: Stealing is contrary to the s 1 of the Theft Act 1968.

The simple way to find out if this proposition is correct is to check s 1(1) of the Theft Act which states:

1(1) A person is guilty of theft if he dishonestly appropriates property belonging to another with the intention of permanently depriving the other of it; and 'thief' and 'steal' shall be construed accordingly.

As s 1(1) makes clear that the words theft and steal are interchangeable we can see that it applies to the situation of stealing a book which implies dishonesty, intentionality, the act of taking property belonging to someone else. Therefore in this case the general assertion in the major premise cannot be attacked as we have located the law and found it is correct to state that stealing is contrary to s 1(1) of the Theft Act.

How can the defence attack the minor proposition?

The minor premise always relates to the particular, in this case to Anna accused of stealing.

Minor premise: Anna has stolen a book.

This is the core issue in the case. The prosecution must prove this premise through the process of inductive reasoning using all available information, facts and the interpretation of the legal rule.

It is clear from the agreed facts that the *actus reus* of the office is proved:

- **Appropriates:** Anna has agreed she has taken the book without paying.
- **Property:** The book is property under s 4.
- **Belonging to another:** The book belongs to Discount Gold Store.

The only way in which the defence can attack the minor premise of the deductive argument is to use inductive reasoning to prove the opposite, that it is incorrect because 'Anna did not steal a book'.

As the *actus reus* is proved by Anna's own admission and that of the eye witness, the defence can only attack the two elements making up the *mens rea*, intention and dishonesty, arguing she was not dishonestly appropriating and she did not intend to keep the book. If just one of these two arguments on the *mens rea* is accepted then the prosecution for theft fails.

The prosecution can argue that the fact that Anna was seen taking the book, was stopped as she left the store and that the book was found in her bag demonstrates an 'intention to deprive permanently' (see points 1, 2 and 3 and 4 of the evidence for the inductive thesis of the prosecution set out in Figure 14.2).

The defence counters this argument by pointing to personal circumstances that potentially negate *both* dishonesty and intention. Anna insists she was not dishonest, but was only borrowing the book, and she did not intend to keep it but she was going to bring it back.

The importance of careful argument construction

You should now be able to appreciate the importance of careful construction of argument containing propositions backed by factual evidence to prove your legal position (in addition, of course, one needs to add the legal basis for the arguments found in the authority of decided cases). The essential quality of a well-structured argument is that it takes the reader or listener from its beginning to its end and makes them hold to the opinion that the argument is correct or the most plausible argument. Sometimes, the process of argument uses bridges from one fact to another that are not backed by evidence but inferred from one set of facts to a proposition. For example, 'You are wet – so it must be raining' is an inference based on your observation of facts. However, the person you are looking at could be wet because they fell in a pond.

It is not wrong to assert a proposition that is not backed by evidence to prove it, but an adjudicating body is not compelled to accept the validity of an unproved proposition. It is difficult to refute a proposition backed by strong evidence but of course evidence is *not* always strong: it may be tenuous, or medium-strong.

You must always consider the weak points in arguments. Most adjudicating bodies have elements of discretion and can accept the tenuous, but plausible, explanatory bridges from one proven fact to another fact that is not proven, as the argument progresses to conclusion. Any proposition that is pivotal for the case must be backed by evidence. Lawyers will tend to take the little jumps with plausibility and, hopefully, the big jumps with proven propositions!

Argument construction is not difficult if there has been meticulous preparation of information. The argument will be basic or elegant depending upon the development of skills, understanding of the law and the level of preparation, thought and reflection that has gone into the argument construction. What one gets back is proportional to the quality of what has gone in. A strong argument may ultimately be rejected if there is a fair amount of discretion, but the person who has forwarded it will know it is good. Indeed, often an adjudicator, even when deciding against an argument, will complement the argument-constructor on the art with which it was done.

The next section gives a guided case study to further assist the development of your skills of argument. The case study stays with the Theft Act, but uses another fictional case.

PUTTING IT ALL TOGETHER: A GUIDED CASE STUDY: *R V MARY*

Mary is accused of stealing £20 from one of her flatmates. We will imagine that the only evidence in the case are three statements that have been given to the police, two by Mary's flatmates, Andrew and William and one by Mary.

We will begin our consideration of *R v Mary* by considering three types of information:

(1)   the charge;
(2)   the governing legal rule(s);
(3)   the evidence.

(1) The charge

Mary has been charged with stealing a £20 note from William, one of her flatmates contrary to s 1(1) of the Theft Act 1968.

(2) The governing legal rule

Section 1(1) of the Theft Act 1968.

(3) Evidence

The following three witness statements have been taken from Mary and her two flatmates, William and Andrew and for the purposes of this case study they constitute the only evidence available. Please read these statements before continuing.

Statement 1: William

I share a flat with Andrew and Mary. I came home on Saturday afternoon and Mary asked me if she could borrow £20 because she wanted to buy a skirt. I didn't want to go out and get her money from the cash machine so I said 'No'. She asked me if I thought Andrew would mind if she borrowed the £20 note in his emergency funds jar in his room. Andrew was away. I said I couldn't speak for him. I didn't know. He is generous but can be difficult about his personal stuff. He wouldn't lend me his football shirt the other week. It just did not seem a good idea and I told her so. But I saw her go into his room and come out with the emergency funds jar. I saw her take the £20 note out of the jar, which was all that was in it, and leave a note in its place saying she would pay it back Monday.

Statement 2: Andrew

I came home late on Sunday night to the flat I share with William and Mary, two good friends. I was extremely tired. When I walked into the kitchen at about midnight I saw my emergency funds jar was on the kitchen table and it was empty. There should have been a £20 note in it and it should have been in my bedroom. It had no money in it just a note from Mary which said: 'Sorry – I had an emergency, need a skirt for my interview Monday, I'll put it back Monday night'. I was really angry – the money is mine for my emergencies. Mary knows that I don't like anyone walking into my bedroom. As far as I am concerned she stole my money. I don't believe she can pay it back Monday, or at all. She is unemployed and in debt. Perhaps if she had asked me personally I would have lent her the money to buy a skirt for her interview but she didn't.

Statement 3: Mary

I share a flat with Andrew and William who are good friends with me. On Saturday I heard I had an interview for a clerical job on Monday. I have been unemployed for six months and really needed a job. I thought it would be a good idea to get a new smart skirt for the interview. Andrew and William have been great about helping me out and even let me pay less rent. I was down to my last £10 on Saturday. I get unemployment money every Thursday. I thought that William might lend me some money but he wouldn't go down to the cash machine for me. Andrew is never like that, he always lends me money when I have asked him. I knew that if he was here he would give me the money. I decided to go into Andrew's room and take the £20 in Andrew's emergency fund jar. William did say it wasn't a good idea. I took it from Andrew's room and put a note in it saying: 'Sorry – I had an emergency, need a skirt for my interview Monday; I'll put it back Monday night'. I left it in the kitchen so he would know it was gone. I couldn't get anything. To cheer myself up I went to the cinema instead, then brought home a takeaway for me and William. When Andrew came home late Sunday he was unreasonable and shouted at me that I was a thief. He was furious that I had gone into his room. But he goes into my room all the time to get stuff he wants. I am really fed up with Andrew.

(1) Clarification of standpoint

In our scenario of *R v Mary* are two main, opposing assertions which are the two standpoints of the prosecution and the defence:

(1)   Mary *has* stolen £20 belonging to Andrew [the prosecution assertion].
(2)   Mary *has not* stolen £20 belonging to Andrew [the defence assertion].

(2) Analysis of the legal rule

As a student of law you also need to be aware of the particular definition of words or phrases in s 1 of the Theft Act and become aware of other sections of the same statute that are relevant in relation to the interpretation of s 1(1). You will remember from Figure 14.1 that with the exception of dishonesty, all the elements required to prove guilt under s 1(1) are defined in other sections of the statute. Dishonesty is determined by means of a case law test from the leading case of *R v Ghosh*. Intention to deprive the owner is construed from all the circumstances, including action in the absence of words.

(3) Analysis of the facts

The only information we have concerning the facts are the three statements. Therefore whatever standpoint you may be asked to take, your argument will use the facts as set out in the three statements, which constitute the evidence.

ACTIVITY 14.1: ANALYSING THE WITNESS STATEMENTS

You will adopt the standpoint of the prosecution. Carefully read the three witness statements in this case and highlight the key words and phrases that begin to allow you to break into them and locate the story, and the law. Bearing in mind the definition of theft in s 1(1) of the Theft Act make a list of facts in the statement that support the prosecution case.

Then answer the following questions:

(1)   What are the relevant facts?
(2)   What key phrases in the statements give you clues as to the application of the law?
(3)   Can you construct the deductive argument for the prosecution?
(4)   Can you construct the inductive argument for the prosecution?
(5)   Can you construct the opposing inductive argument for the defence?
(6)   Are there any conditions of doubt in your mind surrounding the wording of s 1(1) of the Theft Act which may apply (for example questions surrounding the presence of both *mens rea* and *actus reus*)?

Evaluation of your answers 1–6

Carefully consider Figure 14.4 which sets out the three statements of Andrew, William and Mary annotated with several text boxes to assist you to evaluate your answers to questions 1–6. The annotations consist of six text boxes A–F in Figure 14.4 and eight small text boxes labelled 'fact', all with arrows pointing to the relevant fact identified in the statements. Please read all annotations carefully and make sure that you can follow them.

Be sure to note not only what you got right, but what you missed. Think about why you may have missed a point.

Comment Box A in Figure 14.4 sets out the seven facts emerging from the statements.

Statement 1: William I share a flat with Andrew and Mary. I came home on Saturday afternoon and Mary asked me if she could borrow £20 because she wanted to buy a skirt. I didn't want to go out and get her money from the cash machine so I said 'No'. She asked me if I thought Andrew would mind if she borrowed the £20 note in his emergency funds jar in his room. Andrew was away. I said I couldn't speak for him. I didn't know. He is generous but can be difficult about his personal stuff. He wouldn't lend me his football shirt the other week. It just did not seem a good idea and I told her so. But I saw her go into his room and come out with the emergency funds jar. I saw her take the £20 note out of the jar which was all that was in it, and leave a note in it saying she would pay it back Monday.

COMMENT BOX A: Facts emerging from statements 1–3

1. Mary, William and Andrew share a flat and are good friends.
2. Saturday Mary takes '£20 note' from an emergency funds jar in Andrew's bedroom.
3. Andrew is away until Sunday.
4. Mary believes that Andrew would have given her money if she had asked.
5. Mary writes a note to Andrew and puts it in the jar stating that she will return the money on Monday night.
6. Andrew returns Sunday night and angrily accuses Mary of theft.
7. William sees Mary take the £20 note from Andrew's bedroom and leave a note.

FACT 3		FACT 5	FACT 7	FACT 1

COMMENT BOX B:
Testimonial Witness evidence from William that Mary took the £20 from Andrew's room.

FACT 2

FACT 4

Statement 2: Andrew I came home late on Sunday night to the flat I share with William and Mary, two good friends. I was extremely tired. When I walked into the kitchen at about midnight I saw my emergency funds jar was in the kitchen, and it was empty. There should have been a £20 note in it and it should have been in my bedroom. It had no money in it, just a note from Mary which said 'Sorry – I had an emergency, need a skirt for my interview Monday, I'll put it back Monday night'. I was really angry - the money is mine for my emergencies. Mary knows that I don't like anyone walking into my bedroom. As far as I am concerned she stole my money. I don't believe she can pay it back Monday, or at all. She is unemployed and in debt. Perhaps if she had asked me personally I would have lent her the money to buy a skirt for her interview but she didn't.

Statement 3: Mary

I share a flat with Andrew and William who are good friends with me. On Saturday I heard I had an interview for a clerical job on Monday. I have been unemployed for six months and really needed a job. I thought it would be a good idea to get a new smart skirt for the interview. Andrew and William have been great about helping me out and even let me pay less rent. I was down to my last £10 on Saturday.

I get unemployment money every Thursday. I thought that William might lend me some money but he wouldn't go down to the cash machine for me.

Andrew is never like that, he always lends me money when I have asked him. I knew that if he was here he would give me the money.

I decided to go into Andrew's room and take the £20 in Andrew's emergency fund jar. William did say it wasn't a good idea. I took it from Andrew's room and put a note in it saying, 'Sorry – I had an emergency, I need a skirt for my interview Monday, I'll put it back Monday night'.

I left it in the kitchen so he would know it was gone. I couldn't get anything. To cheer myself up I went to the cinema instead, then brought home a takeaway for me and William. When Andrew came home late Sunday he was unreasonable and shouted at me that I was a thief. He was furious that I had gone into his room. But he goes into my room all the time to get stuff he wants. I am really fed up with Andrew.

COMMENT BOX C: If Mary gets paid on Thursday and was down to her last £10 on Saturday. How could she pay the £20 back by Monday.

COMMENT BOX D: Mary believes that Andrew would have lent her the money; does this cast doubt on her 'dishonesty'? Does this mean she believed she had his permission to take the money and does that make any difference?

COMMENT BOX E: Admission by Mary that she took the £20 note from Andrew's room. This is an important admission of the one aspect of the *actus reus* appropriation.

COMMENT BOX F: Mary's note and her statement states that she will give the money back on Monday, the next day. Does this cast doubt on her intention to 'permanently deprive'?

FACT 2	FACT 5		FACT 6	FACT 3

Figure 14.4 Evaluation of activity

The analysis of *R v Mary*

Having considered the statements from the standpoint of the prosecution the following matters seem to have emerged:

- Has there been an appropriation? Mary alleges she acted in the certainty that Andrew would have lent her the money: in other words she had his implied permission.
- Has Mary been dishonest? Mary alleges she acted in the certainty that Andrew would have lent her the money: in other words she had his implied permission.
- Did Mary have an intention to permanently deprive? She said she was going to pay Andrew back the next day.

The prosecution will fail if the answer to any of the above questions is 'No' as all elements must be proved. The answer to each of the above questions lies in statute and case law. This is the moment to look for answers at the level of statutory sources and case law which we will do briefly. We will just make a few explorations to indicate how this matter can be pursued. But this book is about methods and skills – it is not a criminal law text and will not go into detail.

We will go through each element of theft in turn discussing them, identifying the questions about that element raised by the statements, looking to see if the Theft Act defines them and if so how, and referring to a small selection of relevant case law. This will give a fuller idea of how to flesh out your argument.

Element 1: Appropriates (actus reus)

- What is the legal meaning, if any, of 'appropriates'?
- Does the Theft Act define 'appropriates'?
- Is the meaning of 'appropriation' discussed in leading cases?

Section 3(1) of the Theft Act 1968 defines 'appropriation' as:

> Any assumption by a person of the rights of an owner, which includes coming by property innocently but then assuming the rights of an owner.

This all seems quite straightforward but difficult questions have been raised in cases concerning the issue of permission which negates the presence of appropriation.

For example in the case of *Lawrence v Metropolitan Police Commissioner*[11] a taxi driver picked up a passenger at the airport who did not understand much English. At his destination he did not understand the driver when he told him the amount of the fare charged. The passenger therefore offered his wallet to the driver and told him to take what he needed.

---

11 [1972] AC 626.

The taxi driver took more than the fare. At the trial the defence argued that he had permission to take money from the wallet and he was not found guilty. On appeal the Court of Appeal agreed with the prosecution argument that there was no implied consent to take money generally; the only implied consent was to take the correct fare.

In Gomez[12] the House of Lords held that it is possible for there to be an appropriation even when the owner has consented to the taking of money if there is evidence of coercion on the part of the defendant that induces the other to give him money.

Section 3(1) of the Theft Act defines 'appropriates' and also specifically refers to the situation where a person has come by property without stealing and later assumes the rights of an owner. Even if Mary believes she has permission to take the money for a skirt, does that implied permission cover her later use of the money for entertainment? Or was the implied consent conditional upon the precise use the money was put to?

The current position from the case law is that any act usurping the rights of the owner (or possessor) of the property amounts to an appropriation, even merely touching a piece of property. It is likely that 'appropriate' will be successfully proved.

Element 2: Property

- What is the legal meaning, if any, of 'property'?
- Does the Theft Act define 'property'?
- Is the meaning of 'property' discussed in leading cases?

Section 4 of the Theft Act defines 'property' and money is included under the general definition of property, although there have been discussions in the case law over whether it is the fact that money was taken, or the charge relates to the theft of those specific coins or notes.

Element 3: Belonging to another

- Does the money belong to another?

This is defined in s 5(1) of the statute and is quite is straightforward in this case as the money has been identified in all three statements as belonging to Andrew.

Element 4: Dishonesty (mens rea)

The appropriation of goods is not enough; it must have been a dishonest appropriation. Several questions are raised here:

- What is the legal meaning of 'dishonesty'? Does the Theft Act 1968 define 'dishonesty', and is the meaning of 'dishonesty' discussed in leading cases?

---

12 [1992] AC 442 (House of Lords).

- Does the legal definition include believing that you have permission to take something?
- Does the Theft Act deal with this aspect of honesty/dishonesty, and is this situation discussed in leading cases?
- What is the legal test (if any) for a reasonable belief that you have permission? Is it according to what other reasonable people would think (an objective test) or is it according to whatever Mary thought, no matter how unreasonable (a *very* subjective test)? Does the statute or the cases discuss this situation?
- Did Mary have conditional permission to take £20 for a skirt when she spent the money on something else? Does that matter? If she thought Andrew would give permission for the skirt does it matter that she went to the cinema and got a takeaway meal instead? Does the statute or cases discuss this situation?

The statute does not define the meaning of 'dishonesty' but in s 2 sets out three situations which are not dishonest. Section 2 of the Theft Act also makes clear that implied consent can negate a claim of dishonesty:

2(1) A person's appropriation of property belonging to another is not to be regarded as dishonest . . .
. . . (b) if he appropriates the property in the belief that he would have the other's consent if the other knew of the appropriation and the circumstances of it.

'Dishonesty' has been held by the courts to be an ordinary word, to be interpreted by the jury or the judge as a matter of fact. It does not carry a technical legal meaning. The question is, was Mary as a matter of fact dishonest in the circumstances?

In the leading case of *R v Ghosh* [1982] QB 1053 the Court of Appeal stated that the question whether a defendant is dishonest is to be determined by the use of a two part direction to the jury by the judge in relevant cases. The direction is composed of two questions and is referred to as the 'Ghosh test':

(1)   was what was done dishonest according to the ordinary standards of reasonable and honest people? If the answer is 'no' the defendant is not guilty as there is no proved dishonesty and a vital element of the *actus reus* is unproved. If the answer is 'yes' then the second question has to be asked;
(2)   did the defendant realise that reasonable and honest people regarded what he did as dishonest? If the answer is yes then the defendant is guilty.

In our case Mary may well find that the answer to the first question would come in as 'no' and she escapes liability. Should it not, the second question should be answered in the negative and she still escapes liability.

Do you think that most reasonable and honest people would regard that taking the money in the precise circumstances of *R v Mary* was not a dishonest act? Imagine that you are on the jury in this case: would you think that Mary had been dishonest?

Element 5: With the intention to deprive permanently (mens rea)

- What is the legal meaning of 'intention to deprive'? Does the statute or cases discuss this situation?
- Mary said that she did not intend permanently to deprive Andrew of his money. However, she said she would pay Andrew back on Monday, yet she clearly would have no money until Thursday. Does this matter?
- Does this suggest an intention to deprive permanently? Are there cases covering this?

    Intention is defined in s 6. There does not have to be a physical, permanent deprivation, just proof of an intention to deprive combined with the defendant treating the thing as his own to dispose of regardless of the other's rights. Borrowing is not theft unless there are exceptional situations in which it results in a taking and a disposal. However it is explored and defined in case law too.

The real-life, everyday legal problems you will be presented with in your academic studies are, of course, less obviously liable to provide the information required for the full factual analysis that we have engaged in here. However, in terms of knowing what to look out for at the level of facts and evidence, our discussion here will help you to develop a map of potential areas to be considered.

Your main role as a law student will be to construct arguments based on the facts of problems that are taken as given and asking you to discuss the application of the law to those facts.

CONCLUSION

By now you will realise the interconnections between all parts of legal reasoning from the correct diagnosis of the problem, application of relevant rules to that problem, utilising deductive reasoning to lay out basic positions and then using inductive reasoning to construct the final series of legal arguments concerning legal liability.

While there are many strands of thought about the theoretical aspects of legal reasoning, ultimately it is what happens in practice that allows us to make assumptions about English legal reasoning. We can see that argument by analogy is the most common form of argument construction in the English legal system, with the strength of the argument depending upon the degree of similarity between the cases. Arguments constructed should be tested by engaging in abductive reasoning. Overshadowing all of this is the importance of critical thinking to ensure the ultimate construction of viable argument.

CHAPTER SUMMARY

- There are many legal schools of philosophic debate, but there are four main ways of considering law from a philosophic perspective; natural, positivist, legal realism, critical legal studies.

- In natural law the ideology is of reason ascertainable by each person through their own rational enquiry.
- Positivism argues that there is no higher order of things discernible by reason; (secular or divine) law is created and maintained purely by power and will, and in this context the only matter of importance is that law is properly created.
- Legal realism maintains that law is what really happens-in-practice, at the level of the everyday.
- Each legal case revolves around the telling of stories. It can be overlooked that many contexts of law in action are also political, social, institutional, and/or religious.
- Schools of law have developed to critique its foundations. The critical legal theory movement argues that legal scholarship fails if it does not look at the power dimensions of the law.
- Good legal argument depends not only on correct reasoning for the application of law to facts but upon an individual's ability to test that argument by imagining other arguments, particularly those of the 'other side'.
- The preferred system of argument structure in the English legal system is 'argument by analogy', a form of inductive reasoning.
- Strict adherence to the doctrine of precedent is essential in the English legal system.
- Competent legal reasoning depends on the correct diagnosis of the problem, application of relevant rules to that problem utilising deductive reasoning to lay out basic positions and then using inductive reasoning to construct the final series of legal arguments concerning legal liability.

EUROPEAN LEGAL REASONING

15

LEARNING OUTCOMES

After reading this chapter you should be able to:

- Basically distinguish and compare English common law reasoning and civilian legal reasoning.
- Understand the process of judicial reasoning generally as used in the EU and in the European Court of Human Rights (ECtHR).
- Have a basic understanding of the problems surrounding interpretation in the Court of Justice of the EU (CJEU) and in particular with regard to the concurrent use of multiple languages.

INTRODUCTION

It is important to understand the different approaches to legal reasoning that occur in civilian legal systems. All of the founding member states of the EU have civilian legal systems with the exception of the English legal system which is a common law system. All signatories of the European Convention on Human Rights, again with the exception of the British and the Irish Republic, operate within a civilian legal method and reasoning. There are many differences between English common law reasoning and civilian legal reasoning and it is important that you are aware of these differences. Otherwise you will not properly understand EU cases in the CJEU, or EU written law, or cases heard in the ECtHR. It is the methodology of the civilian system that determines the method of drafting legislation and treaties as well as the methods for dealing with legal disputes before the courts. Whilst the EU does not have a code in the standard civilian sense its primary and secondary law is drafted in a manner more in keeping with the main attributes of a code, and not in a manner that is similar to the drafting of statutes in the English legal system.

As already discussed in the chapters on EU law one of the most important functions of the CJEU is to ensure uniformity in the interpretation of the primary and secondary law of the EU. We will engage with the idea of how the CJEU reasons by confining ourselves to the issue of interpretation. This is an area that is not much discussed in basic texts or even EU law set texts. This chapter therefore draws heavily on the articles by six academics and scholars who have in the last few years begun to address the issues of reasoning and interpretation in EU law.[1]

The chapter also considers the way in which decisions in the European Court of Human Rights slightly deviate from the approaches in the Court of Justice of the European Union but nonetheless remain civilian. The ECtHR is not part of the EU but it is the creation of treaties entered into by the Council of Europe.

THE DRAFTING OF LEGISLATION IN CIVILIAN LEGAL SYSTEMS

Civilian legal systems generally operate under legal codes covering all of the legal rules in all areas. Whatever is decided in cases in court the code as drafted remains the highest authority. If a court determines an issue in a certain way other courts do not necessarily have to follow it in other cases dealing with the same issue. However there are exceptions. The EU operates under a civil system of law and specifies that determinations in the CJEU on a matter of interpretation of a treaty or secondary legislation are binding on all national courts. While the CJEU itself could decide differently in another case, increasingly there are demands that it does not.

Civilian legal codes are drafted using clear and simple language and are expressed in highly generalised terms. The theory is that it is for those interpreting and applying the code to deduce from it the relevant legal rules and principles. Where courts are called upon

---

1   G Beck 'Letter: The legal reasoning: a response to Michal Bobek' (2014) 39(4), 579–581. *Bobek (2014)* 39 *EL Rev* 418, D Mattias 'Multilingual interpretation of CJEU case law: Rule and reality' *EL Review* 2014, 39(3), 295–315. U Sadl *EL Review* (2013) 9(2), 205–22. A Vermeule 'Constitutional amendments and constitutional common law' Harvard University Working Paper (2004) *Social Science Research Network*. K McAuliffe 'Precedent at the ECJ: the linguistic aspect' Law and language *Current Legal Issues* Vol 15 (2013).

to interpret legislation or articles in treaties they lean towards the teleological approach and will take into account broader social and economic issues.

English legislation is drafted in a detailed manner, with those drafting it trying to ensure that most situations can be covered. Due to the operation of the doctrine of binding precedent those drafting legislation will also be aware of words and phrases that have caused interpretational problems in court. They will seek to lessen opportunities for judicial interpretation, as it can change the nature of a legal rule in ways not intended by Parliament. English legislation is therefore characterised by the complexity of its structure and language. It is often accompanied by illustrations of how it should be applied in the statute, together with external explanatory notes issued with it.

THE GENERAL APPROACH TO LEGAL REASONING AND INTERPRETATION IN CIVILIAN LEGAL SYSTEMS

Firstly it is helpful to comment on several approaches to interpretation used generally by civilian law courts (some of which are used by judges in the English common law system, although you will not find them explicitly referred to).

The first approach can be termed 'the textual'. The court recognises that the text of the relevant part of the civilian code should be carefully examined to see if a meaning can emerge from it which resolves the dispute before the court without any necessity to engage in any further interpretation. This does sound similar to the English literal approach to statutory interpretation. But the English approach ignores contexts, specifying that all words have a clear and literal meaning. This is not the approach taken by the civilian courts.

If the textual approach does not lead to the resolution of the dispute the court will consider other methods of interpretation. When searching for the purpose of the legislation the court accepts the need to consult historical, social and economic sources. However, the open textured nature of interpretation in civilian systems means that even if the documents suggest a purpose for the relevant part of the code, the court does not necessarily have to accept that purpose.

Civil courts are also open to using a more contextualised reading of the text to ascertain meaning. Within the EU for example the CJEU will draw upon the legal systems of member states and what methods they use to deal with interpretational doubts. In the past the CJEU has taken the French civil code concept of 'acte clair' (meaning clear act, or 'it speaks for itself') when interpreting the word 'necessary' in Article 267 of TFEU.[2] This doctrine of 'acte clair' is most correctly also classified as a textual approach. As the UK is the only common law system within the European Union its legal doctrines are rarely seen as candidates for the adoption by the CJEU.

The most important method of interpretation used in civilian systems is the teleological, an approach finding some favour in the English legal system as we have discussed already in Chapters 2 and 11.

---

2   An article which deals with situations in which member states request a preliminary ruling.

In addition to using several approaches to interpretation, civilian systems also allow the consulting of the body of legal writing, and courts are prepared to be informed by and implement interpretational recommendations made in professional and academic texts. In the English legal system this is not accepted practice as a general rule. Academic work is not treated with respect or considered capable as being an authority for decision making. This view in fact is not a standard characteristic of common law systems. The American legal system is a common law system, but contemporary professional and academic writings are accorded great respect.

If a civilian court continues to have difficulties regarding the meaning of the relevant contested rule in a code it can turn to reliance on the general principles of the legal system. These will vary from one civilian legal system to another. Some codes explicitly state that the courts can resort to the use of general principles of law; others do not mention the issue of general principles. Where a code is silent the principles lead courts to be able to say that they have determined an interpretation in keeping with tradition and what the spirit of the law would say. How that 'spirit' is determined will differ.

In the EU a large number of general principles of law have been developed, for example to ensure justice, the cohesion of the EU, and the facilitation of business and free movement of workers. These are accorded legal authority. Within the English legal system the primary method of developing legal argument is through reasoning by analogy, a sub-species of inductive reasoning. There is close attention to the deconstruction of previous binding case law according to the doctrine of precedent. General legal principles do exist but do not carry the authority of law.

The civilian legal system encourages courts to deduce law from the generalised codes. Cases are not binding in the civilian system but are used as guidance in decision making. The need for statutory interpretation due to gaps in the codes is standard practice. The EU does not have a code but all of its laws are modelled on the civilian system and therefore the same deduction of law and meaning from generalised rules takes place. The level of abstraction and the lack of a concept of binding precedent mean that there is not much need for inductive reasoning, although it can be used if needed.

THE APPROACH TO REASONING AND INTERPRETATION BY THE CJEU

The CJEU is often criticised for the lack of explicit reasoned argument underlining its decisions, and for cases being decided that do not sit well with previous case law. It is also criticised for not explaining the reasons for the criteria the court develops and states must be applied in certain cases. Yet as already noted the EU system is based on the civilian legal system, with deduction favoured from general rules, and with loose adherence to precedent. Its overarching responsibility is to ensure the harmonisation of interpretation of EU law for national courts called to deal with EU law. It is inevitably placed in a difficult position by the fact that the policies of the EU and EU 'overlap in

---

3   U Sadl, case comment in *Ruiz Zambrano* as an illustration of how the Court of Justice of the European Union constructs its legal arguments. *EL Review* (2013) 9(2), 205–22, 205.

the decision making of the Court',[3] leading Sadl to maintain that in terms of the legal reasoning in the CJEU:

> 'Legal and policy arguments, it was argued, were justificatory reasons, and as long as they were universalisable, and as long as the outcomes 'made sense', i.e., being coherent with statute law and previous case law, the external factors that prompted the Court to rule as it did could safely be disregarded . . . Simpl(isticall)y put, the formulaic style of the Court, the vagueness of the reasons, the interpretative techniques and the open-endedness of answers bother some more than others.'[4]

Sadl analysed the rationale and strategies for decision making used by the court concentrating on the *Ruiz Zambrano* case 2011 which[5] raised an interesting issue relating to third country nationals whose children would have their enjoyment of their EU citizenship affected if their parents were not granted work and residency permits in the EU. With regard to the subsequent critique of the court's ruling there were two main issues. Some voiced concerns that the CJEU in this case used its power to interpret EU law to move it beyond the intentions of those who created it. Others however welcomed the ruling as indicating that the court took the issue of EU citizenship seriously.

As with much interpretation previous case law is treated as flexible and can certainly be made quite flexible. Addressing concerns that the court in the *Ruiz Zambrano* case was usurping the law makers Sadl argues that it was possible to look at the case law leading to the decision and see the court as 'consistently' breathing 'life into empty concepts'.[6] He maintains that this line of interpretation of the court's decision in *Ruiz Zambrano* made it possible for:

> 'The Court's reasoning, going beyond the wording of the text or the purposes of the Founders, could be defended by the outcome that the Court sought to achieve; i.e., to establish European citizenship as a fundamental status.'[7]

However the ruling could be heavily criticised stating that in its apparent disregard for consistency and case law member states are:

> 'continuously unable to rely on (legitimate!) limits and conditions, which they laid down in the treaties and subsequent legislation, and to which the rights of citizens were subject according to the treaty and Community legislation.'[8]

Sadl argues that even when judges in the CJEU do refer to previous decisions to justify their decisions they do not do so consistently. These previous cases are often removed from their original context and applied to new situations in a 'random' manner. His critique of the CJEU is that while it does tend to repeat formulas from previous cases, their use is

---

4   Ibid, 206.
5   Ibid, 206.
6   Ibid, 207.
7   Ibid, 207.
8   Ibid, 208.

not convincing because what the court is doing is using social policy to suit itself, without even acknowledging that the views put forward on these grounds are contested. The consequence of this is an inevitable superficiality in decision making that has more in common with policy making than legal analysis.

The CJEU is often accused of acting in a pro-union manner in its interpretations of union law and its final decision making, yet is this not its role?

The opinions in the CJEU leave us confused about the use of previous cases by the court. The court's reference to past cases has been criticised as no more than the random application of those cases used out of context. The court has been known to say that they created a principle of law in the previous case that must be kept to. However, equally they may say that a principle of law established in a previous case cannot bind a current court. While academics and lawyers can point to series of cases that tend to pay attention to an idea of precedent, they cannot point to an established practice consistently applied.

INTERPRETATION, LEGAL REASONING AND THE MULTIPLICITY OF LANGUAGES IN THE EU

One complication in relation to interpretation is the fact that the language of each member state is an official language of the EU. Therefore *all* documentation including treaties, legislation and opinions of the CJEU have to be translated into a variety of languages. As translation takes place the language can drift from the original source. The working language of the EU is French. Usually the translation of judgments is undertaken by non-native speakers which allows a large margin for error.[9] Most importantly, because of the range of the translations involved in a case, when presented with uncertainties about the law the court has the ability to engage in highly discretionary decision making.[10]

A particular complication can arise when there are disagreements about what language is binding for the judgment of the court. CJEU rules of procedure state that the judgment of the court is binding in the 'language of the case'. The everyday working language of the CJEU, including court hearings, remains in French. However, the rules of procedure make clear that once the language of the case is decided then it is *that* translation of the CJEU's judgment in the case which is the only 'authentic'[11] expression of the decision of the court.

You will not be surprised to note that there is often disagreement about what the official language of the case is, although in simple terms the idea is that the language of the case is determined by the plaintiff. In 2014 an entire edition of the *European Law Review* (*EL Review*)[12] was devoted to the issue of how the official language of a case is determined. It is important for this to be settled as inevitably decisions about the official language of a case also raise issues relating to precedent.

---

9 K McAuliffe 'Precedent at the ECJ: The Linguistic Aspect. Law and Language' *Current Legal Issues* (2013), Vol. 15. Available at SSRN: http://ssrn.com/abstract=2208710.

10 See D Mattias 'Multilingual Interpretation of CJEU Case Law: Rule and Reality' *EL Review* (2014) 39(3), 295–315, 302.

11 Ibid.

12 *EL Review* (2014), 39(3).

The articles in the *EL Review* outlined the views of a range of commentators in the area, and we will draw on Beck, Johnson, McAuliffe and Mattias[13] to get a flavour of the debate and the issues they raise.

Mattias[14] discusses recent examples of several national courts using four different approaches to determine the language in which the case is authoritative. An English Court of Appeal has held that since the CJEU conducts its proceedings in French then French is the 'language of the case', while the German Federal Administrative Court has held that the 'language of the case' is the language of those bringing the application (which in that case was Finnish). Most curiously a Danish Taxation Appeal Tribunal specifically stated that it would not refer to the French version of a relevant CJEU judgment on the grounds that it was the language of the CJEU. Nor did it refer to the German version of the judgment on the grounds that it *was* the 'language of the case'! Without explanation it did refer to the English and Danish translations of the judgment. Finally it points to the UK's HM Revenue and Customs arguing that 'all language versions of the judgment [are] equally authentic, consequently no particular weight should be given to the language of the case'.

This uncertainty as to which language is authoritative, despite clear guidance, as well as the lack of information concerning how the CJEU reaches its decisions makes the use of CJEU cases problematic. However, of course the fact that there are a range of ways of finding the language of the case may be said to give the national courts more leeway for discretion.

When determined to the agreement of relevant parties and institutions the language of the case is used for all of the documentation required in the case.

However, as noted above the working language of the CJEU is French and therefore all documentation and proceedings for the hearing are in French. Also French is the internal language of the court and the court will give its final judgment in French. This means that where another official language has been determined to be the 'language of the case', the final 'authentic' language of the case will actually be a translation.

French is not the language of the court as required by any legal regulation; it was a choice made by the CJEU on its creation, and it is now an entrenched part of its working life. But it has led to the situation where as a matter of fact (de facto) the final judgment is French, and as a matter of law the binding judgment (*de jure*) is a translation of the de facto judgment!

A duality that one can see immediately causes a number of interpretational problems.[15] Yet it is surprising that the CJEU does not comment on these matters with any authority and it is rarely noted by the Advocate-General in opinions to the court.

---

13 G. Beck 'Letter: The legal reasoning of the Court of Justice: a response to Michal Bobek' E.L. Rev. 2014, 39(4), 579-581; A.B. Johnson in his book, A treatise on Language (1836), quoted in A Vermeule, (2004) 'Constitutional amendments and constitutional common law', Harvard University Working Paper, Social Science Research Network; K. McAuliffe Precedent at the ECJ: The Linguistic Aspect. Law and Language, Current Legal Issues, Vol. 15, 2013, Forthcoming. Available at SSRN: http://ssrn.com/abstract=2208710 and D Mattias (2014) 'Multilingual Interpretation of CJEU Case Law: Rule and Reality' EL Review 39(3), 295–315, 228–9.

14 D Mattias 'Multilingual Interpretation of CJEU Case Law: Rule and Reality' *EL Review* (2014) 39(3), 295–315, 228–9.

15 See D Mattias 'Multilingual Interpretation of CJEU Case Law: Rule and Reality' *EL Review* (2014) 39(3), 295–315, 302.

Extra-legal strategies in decision making

Johnson[16] notes that Beck[17] argues that judges in the CJEU use a range of extra-legal strategies when coming to their final decisions in cases, such as:

- political issues;
- whether a number of member states have indicated opposition to the idea of what Mattias calls an 'integrationist stance'. The normal position is that the CJEU privileges an integrationist interpretation;
- the views of union institutions.

We have already noted that the CJEU has flexibility in decision making so that it can 'fill in the gaps'. Beck strenuously argues that when the court uses its interpretative strategies to actually change the meaning of clear wording in primary law (treaties) this is going far beyond any power that it has. He uses the case of *Pringle*[18] heard before a full court of 27 judges to make his point:

> . . . in Pringle the relevant Treaty rules were clear, yet the EU institutions and 12 national governments all maintained that 'no' meant 'yes' to the assumption of financial commitments. Judicial Realpolitik and the Court's integrationist pre-disposition, not Treaty language, meant there was never any question as to which way the judicial axe would fall: the Court would 'break the law to save the euro'.[19]

He continued:

> Pringle . . . shows that the relative weight the Court assigns to the various interpretative arguments cannot be reliably explained by interpretative methodology or the clarity and precision of the primary law, but only be 'reckoned' by taking further account of extra-legal steadying factors, in particular the Court's pro-Union tendency, its political realism and the 'constitutional' importance of the case. The Court has been a motor of integration, but it is also a politically astute court. It may defer in the face of strong national opposition, but, as Pringle shows, it will promote integration in opposition to the Treaties if Member States countenance judicial activism.[20]

Unlike judges operating within the English legal system, judges in the CJEU tend not to engage in historical referencing. Some conclude that the court's '. . . tendency to favour an integrationist solution to legal problems'[21] is an indication that the court prefers the

---

16 AB Johnson, in his book, *A Treatise on Language* (1836), quoted in A Vermeule, 'Constitutional amendments and constitutional common law' *Harvard University Working Paper* (2004), Social Science Research Network.

17 G Beck, 'Letter: The legal reasoning of the Court of Justice: a response to Michal Bobek' *EL Review* (2014) 39(4), 579–81.

18 Case C-370/12.

19 G Beck, 'Letter: 'The legal reasoning of the Court of Justice: a response to Michal Bobek' *EL Review* (2014) 39(4), 579–81, 581.

20 Ibid, 581.

21 M Bobek, 'Legal Reasoning of the Court of Justice of the EU' 39 *EL Review* (2014) 39, 418.

teleological approach, with the literal approach not much favoured because it has the potential to lead to inflexibility.

Mattias engaged in research to study judgments of the CJEU taken together with the opinions of Advocates-General presented to the court. He noted that there were:

> . . . four main approaches to the relationship between multilingualism and case law interpretation: emphasis on the language of the case (formalism); emphasis on the drafting language (realism); consulting both languages (dualism); or even relying on other languages (pragmatism) . . .[22]

The style of EU judgments

Numerous explanations have been put forward to explain the style of CJEU judgments. They are all shaped by the general open texture of EU law as drafted, as well as its multi-lingual dimensions discussed above. Both of these two issues give the CJEU great leeway in interpreting. But a continuing issue is the claim that clarity is lacking concerning the rationale for the decision. There is little detail given for the reasoning of the court, usually, by tradition, in keeping with civilian legal systems approaches, only giving one judgment which, again by tradition, contains no hint of any dissent among the judges in the court. This lack of information about why the court decided as it did has led to concerns over the apparent lack of transparency in this matter.

One way that the courts have attempted to overcome criticism is by issuing a shorter judgment. But surely this does not provide any rationale for judgment. There should be greater transparency given the place of the opinions of the CJEU as a source of law.

The use of past cases in the CJEU

It has seemed clear from the opinions of the judges in the CJEU that precedent does not operate in a binding manner in the EU legal system. Yet, when reading CJEU cases, it is clear that importance is indeed placed on past cases. Parties have to try to make predictions as to the way in which the court may react to their arguments, with very little to go on by way of the reasoning of the court in past cases.

Sadl noted in her research that although there were a large number of citations of previous cases these were used randomly, 'decoupled' from their facts. Yet parties to cases tend to see previous case law as establishing principles, although this is difficult to justify as the court does not have to give details of why it decided in such a way. Add this to the problem of which language is the language of the case and the one subject to linguistic analysis, it is often impossible for parties to make any prediction. However, the CJEU regularly uses language indicating that all lower courts (and therefore domestic courts of member states) must follow the case law of the CJEU.

---

22 D Mattias 'Multilingual Interpretation of CJEU Case Law: Rule and Reality' *EL Review* (2014) 39(3), 295–315, 228–9.

It would seem, however, that there are indications that the court is moving towards the more textual analysis of case judgments which is so familiar in the English legal system.

Mattias notes that many academics and professionals have begun to note this growing tendency to refer to previous case law.

> Tiresome concludes: 'The words of an opinion are not evidence of the law, as they once were. They are the law.' Building on this discussion, Komura has developed his theory of reasoning with previous decisions. The textualisation of **precedent** is evident in the approach to previous decisions by the CJEU, which tend to cut and paste passages of previous judgments. Assertions of the Court are treated as rules, akin to legislation, with even slight differences in wording seen as relevant. This is part of what Komura refers to as the legislative model of reasoning with previous decisions, based on a different idea of judicial authority as compared with the traditional case-bound model. In the latter model courts are adjudicating real disputes and their judgments are seen as experiments, suggested solutions for other courts to follow, no matter their position in the hierarchy of courts. The highest continental courts and the CJEU, on the other hand, are seen as superior authorities with the assignment to definitively determine the content of the law and control its application by lower courts.[23]

In light of the increasing textualisation of analysis of judgments in the CJEU, the words of the judgment are increasingly important and this brings us back to the issue of language usage, the working language of the court, the working language of the case, and the multilingual translations of the judgment. The judgments issued in some CJEU cases suggest that national and other courts should consult a range of language translations. Here you can imagine the endless difficulties. If a lawyer finds one translation more in keeping with his client's case he will press for that to be used, and the court may well follow.

Mattias points out the range of choice with regard to language in the following manner:

> 'brings flexibility, but the flipside of flexibility is uncertainty and arbitrariness . . . . When national courts employ different approaches to multilingual interpretation, as evidenced by the examples in the introduction, the uniformity of EU law is threatened'.[24]

LEGAL REASONING IN THE EUROPEAN COURT OF HUMAN RIGHTS

A large body of jurisprudence has been built up by the ECtHR, and this body must be followed by English judges. The Human Rights Act 1998 (HRA) imposes on judges a statutory duty to take note of the jurisprudence of the ECtHR. In their decision making the English judiciary consider that this imposed statutory duty indicates that they do not have to do

---

23 D Mattias, 'Multilingual Interpretation of CJEU Case Law: Rule and Reality' *EL Review* (2014) 39(3), 295–315 298.

24 Ibid, 315.

any more than 'note' it. They certainly do not have to apply it. But a UK citizen bringing a case in the English courts does have the right to bring a claim in the ECtHR if all appeals in the UK are exhausted. If they win that case then by virtue of Article 5 of the European Convention on Human Rights the government will have to pay all costs. Obviously it is politically undesirable to end up with more appeals under the HRA than before it.

Key issues with regard to legal reasoning in the ECtHR relate to how far there is discretion given to contracting states under the ECHR, and also how far differences between states should be taken into account when deciding issues on breach. The ECHR recognises state differences by specifically referring to the concept of a 'margin of appreciation'.

But when judges in national courts approach ECtHR cases for assistance in interpreting the articles that are the subject of an action in domestic courts they have been presented with the same range of issues causing complaints in the CJEU. The treaties are drafted generally and often in different styles. ECtHR issues only one judgment and as in the CJEU it contains no hint of dissent. But none of this is surprising as the ECtHR also works according to the traditions of the civilian system of law.

CONCLUSION

We have noted that the way in which the CJEU reasons, or does not, is the subject of a range of heated debates concerning the authority given to previous cases of the CJEU, the methods of determining the 'language of the case' and subsequent binding judgments. Key to most of these debates is the issue of language. The rationale it does give has been criticised for being too much inclined to EU social, economic and political policy rather than to the law and judgment in previous CJEU cases. However, in recent years research has indicated that a tendency to move towards greater analysis of previous cases by the CJEU has been developed in response to these criticisms of its decision making.

Similarly the European Court of Human Rights is also criticised for being too political and deciding delicate matters of human rights with far too much deference to the relevant contracting state.

Interestingly, exposure to the traditions of the civilian legal system has begun to impact on the English judiciary. Within the areas of EU law and the interpretation of the European Convention on Human Rights, English courts are tending to favour not only a more purposive approach to interpretation but also there is sympathy with the teleological approach. A trend is noticeable regarding using these methods of interpretation in legal disputes unrelated to the EU or human rights.

CHAPTER SUMMARY

■   The EU does not have a single code but all of its laws are modelled on the civilian system.

- Judges interpreting the code deduce the relevant legal rules and principles.
- Judges in the civilian legal system use three main approaches to interpretation, the 'textual', the 'purpose' of the law and teleological.
- The teleological approach is the most important method of interpretation.
- The CJEU will additionally draw upon the legal systems of member states and their methods of resolving interpretational doubts about law.
- Some codes state that courts can use general principles of law, others do not.
- In the EU the CJEU constructs legal principles which have legal authority.
- The CJEU is often criticised for the lack of explicit reasoned argument underlining its decisions.
- The CJEU do refer to previous decisions to justify their decisions but these references tend to lack consistency and are applied in a 'random' manner removed from their original context.
- A later CJEU does not have to follow the decision of a previous court case.
- The working language of the EU is French.
- The language of each member state is an official language of the EU.
- CJEU rules of procedure set out that each case has its own official language version, 'the language of the case'.
- There is often disagreement about what the official language of the case is.
- National courts applying EU law have taken different views on what constitutes the language of the case.
- The CJEU use a range of extra-legal strategies when interpreting, including views of member states and EU institutions.
- The style of reasoning of the CJEU is shaped by the general open texture of EU law as drafted, as well as its multilingual dimensions.
- The Human Rights Act 1998 imposes on judges a statutory duty to take note of the jurisprudence of the ECtHR.
- The ECtHR works within civil law but does not have its own civil law legal system; it is part of the order of international law however.
- Key issues with regard to legal reasoning in the ECtHR relate to how far there is discretion given to contracting states under the ECHR, and also how far differences between states should be taken into account when deciding issues on breach.
- The same range of complaints are levelled at decision making in the ECtHR as are levelled at the CJEU: that often the ECtHR issues only one judgment and as in the CJEU it contains no hint of dissent.

PART 5

GENERAL ACADEMIC SKILLS

Part 5 considers the often overlooked general skills of acquiring effective study, reading, writing, referencing, and reading and speaking skills. Although attitudes are changing in law schools all too often these general skills are assumed to be something the student arrives with and needs to develop alone with too little guidance from law lecturers. Furthermore it is assumed that the acquisition of competence in these general skills is easy. It is not: competence in the use of these general skills takes time and attention. Law brings its own technical language, its own methods of writing or speaking legal argument. These are underpinned by the competency of your general reading, writing and speaking.

Law as a discipline requires students to engage in large amounts of reading; you will soon come to think that your reading load is far in excess of that of your friends studying other subjects. Indeed – it will be greater. So it is important that you learn efficient ways to read, to improve your reading speeds and read material in differing ways for differing information.

The majority of your assessments will be set as continuous coursework (written essays, reports, reviews, or legal problem questions) and written examinations. It is therefore essential to ensure your English skills are good in terms of your writing and that you develop a clear academic written style, or voice. You need to also develop the ability to appropriately reference your work to demonstrate your growing competence as an academic student of law. Correct referencing also avoids any suggestion that you may have accidentally plagiarised.

Your legal oral skills development is also affected by general issues of personal confidence in public speaking, knowing how to use different spoken registers for different tasks. As you will see from the chapter on general oral skills there are many ways of ensuring that you gain confidence in your ability to speak in public.

Above all else effective study skills are key to your success on your degree programme and cannot be ignored or underestimated. They involve a range of issues including the role of lectures and seminars, the role of your teachers, how to improve your efficiency in learning, and how to develop a highly disciplined approach to your independent learning. The dedicated chapter on academic study skills looks at these issues and more.

In their totality the five chapters in this part aim to give you a firm foundation in all of these general skills so that your specialist legal study can develop to its full potential.

'What lies in our power to do lies
in our power not to do.'

Aristotle

After reading this chapter you should be able to:

- Appreciate the range of skills required to engage in competent study.
- Understand the concept of learning and teaching styles, recognising which you prefer.
- Identify inefficient study habits and take action to avoid them.
- Understand the structure of your degree programme and the cycles of academic life throughout the year and the term.
- Appreciate how courses and modules make up parts of the degree programme.
- Develop good independent learning habits.
- Appreciate the need to acquire excellent ICT skills and develop a plan to acquire them.
- Appreciate how to begin the process of personal development planning (PDP).

INTRODUCTION

This is a chapter designed to explain what study skills are, why you need them and how you acquire and develop them. Students generally do not consider *how* they study. The action of studying itself requires the acquisition of general skills that increase your ability to develop your subject specific knowledge and understanding. In order to efficiently learn, research, reflect, read and produce competent assessments and examinations you need to know *how* to study and how to self-manage your study.

For many students university simply happens to them. They do not make proper use of the opportunity to become independent learners, and do not succeed in acquiring a useful intellectual education which can open up the future in terms of life-changing career opportunities. Some students may see university as a necessary evil and do as little as possible. These students may leave university ill-prepared for the future with a worrying lack of self-awareness, and maybe a low degree classification that will not be of much use to them. Do not let your choices lead you to be in this position.

Studying is a highly disciplined enterprise and you, and no one else, are responsible for the choices you make concerning when, or if, you study. To meet deadlines and produce good quality assessments you need to allocate time in your weekly schedule to locate materials, date-plan for deadlines, internalise the content of your research, draft your assessments and submit them. Then when your assessments are returned you need to plan time to attentively read any constructive criticism given by your marker.

You should never be in the position of finding the allocation of your assessment marks (whether good or bad) a mystery. Many students do not realise that not only can they increase their grades by reading and acting on their tutor's comments about their work, they can book an appointment to speak to their tutor about how to improve their work, again increasing their ability to reach a higher level in their understanding. If you fail an assignment there is obviously room for improvement. If you get a 2.1 (60–69 per cent) there is still obvious room for improvement: you can aim to get a higher mark within the 2.1 range, or find out what you need to do to get a First. You need to focus on the skills needed to allow you to develop understanding and how to elegantly express that understanding through well written (or spoken) arguments supported by reference to academic and legal texts, presented in appropriate English.

This chapter gives you time to consider your overall goals and how you will achieve them. You may not have thought about your goals. Getting to university may have been a goal; the tendency once there can to be to make the mistake of not continuing to be goal orientated concerning what you want to achieve in the short and long term.

To assist with your organisation skills the general cycles of the academic year are discussed with suggestions concerning managing your lecture, seminar and independent study timetable; as well as your assessment or examination timetable.[1]

---

1   Exams and revision warrant special discussion and are covered in more detail in Chapter 23.

This chapter highlights the importance of understanding your department's preferred or mandatory communication protocols. It discusses appropriate ways of communicating with your tutors and fellow students as well as the importance of developing competency in the use of IT systems such as email, virtual learning environments (VLEs), internet searching and word processing.[2]

To assist your navigation of this chapter it has been divided into the following main sections:

- What are your goals?
- What is studying?
- How to engage in effective independent study.
- The importance of working with the teaching programme and the cycles of the standard university year.
- The range of skills required for successful legal study.

This is the time to consider the studies ahead of you.

Activity 16.1: What are your goals?

(1) Think about the following questions:

- **Why** are you at university?
- **What** do you want to achieve?
- **How** will you achieve it?

(2) Write down your answers to the three questions in (1) above and keep them in mind as you read this chapter. Also file them somewhere safe. You may need to remind yourself of your answers if you hit times of demotivation or lose self-confidence. Also they will need revision as you progress through the three years of your degree. They will certainly form the general core of any formal personal development planning that you are required, or you choose, to undertake.

WHAT IS STUDYING?

Students often think of studying as a passive process of soaking up and memorising what is handed out by the teacher. However, in fact studying is an active pursuit, and it is about learning about learning: learning about yourself, learning about your chosen academic subject area and learning *how* to learn.

---

2   The need to engage in competent library and IT research is generally referred to in the context of developing your skills base. For a detailed discussion of how to locate primary texts of law and secondary texts about law in print and online please refer back to Chapters 6–9 in Part 2.

The *Shorter Oxford English Dictionary* notes that the root of the English word 'study' is based on the Latin word 'studium' meaning 'zeal, painstaking application'. It goes on to define study in several helpful ways as:

- 'Thought . . . directed towards the accomplishment of a purpose.'[3]
- 'Application of the mind to the acquisition of learning . . . mental effort in the acquisition of learning.'[4]

Far from being a passive matter, study is dynamic and interactive. To study is to be knowingly engaged in the proactive process of searching for other ideas, weighing up possibilities and alternatives, criticising and evaluating.

Your role as a student is derived from the word 'study', with the Shorter Oxford English Dictionary defining a student as '. . . a person who is engaged in or addicted to study.'[5]

It is important therefore to spend time considering the range of skills required for your degree study. Active study enables you to learn.

Studying law at university

Many students beginning study at university find their new-found freedom strange, difficult to cope with, and easy to get lost in. Those arriving at university having been previously in employment or running a household will have been used to their weeks being structured around the requirements of others. Those arriving directly from school will be familiar with having their education highly structured by others on a daily basis. Mature students may think that university will be a little like their memories of school (both good and bad).

At university you will be taught in large and small groups. Your standard large group will be a lecture with 100–300 other students. In these circumstances not only does the lecturer not know you personally, they probably never will. You may be on a course where some small learning groups of five–eight students are student led, and you will only see the tutor when you are formally assessed on the presentation of your thoughts from those student led seminars.

A law degree is often seen as a dry and boring programme of study to those who do not know much about it. But the study of law will touch your imagination and provoke your emotions. You will learn how to exercise and make judgements concerning legal issues and to constantly engage with legal rules, ideas, theories, concepts and critiques. You will be taught to locate the assumptions on which ideas or theories are based, and to critically question these assumptions. You will need to develop an inquiring mind, one that is flexible and can take on new ideas and critically evaluate them in line with your views.

In order that you can reach a place of complex and sophisticated comprehension of the topic you are studying, you need to be constantly seeking to understand and decode what you are reading and then consider competing interpretations. You need to know what you think of the ideas of others, to justify the decisions you make about their strengths and weaknesses.

---

3   CT Onions, *Shorter Oxford English Dictionary* (3rd edn reprinted and revised, 1988) Vol 11, p 2159.
4   Ibid.
5   Ibid, p 2158.

WHAT IS LEARNING?

The purpose and outcome of study is learning and learning itself can be defined as the obtaining of knowledge about a skill or an art through personal study, reference to personal experience and teaching.[6] If your study skills are inadequate your learning (and therefore your knowledge and understanding) will be less competent than they may have been if you had displayed good study skills. Some students will say that they 'hate studying'. This is far too general and is muddling process with substance. They may hate law, not the process of learning law.

How do you like to learn?

Your personality has a major impact on how you learn so recognising some things about yourself and your learning will be of tremendous benefit.

Stop reading for a moment and think about how you approach the task of learning and why you study in a particular way. Did you positively choose that way of studying?

You may think that you do not have a particular way of learning: you just 'do it'. You read books, go to taught classes and write some notes, remember them and complete assignments and exams. But there is far more to learning. You need to process your reading and critique it. To do this you require good strategies for effective learning.

Students have different preferences for learning such as being:

- given all necessary information and memorising it;
- left to work alone to find out information for themselves.

Students also have different purposes for studying which predetermine the skills they need, for example only being interested in:

- grades and the skill needed for the best grades;
- doing the bare minimum to get a pass while they enjoy a great social life;
- doing what they can to achieve both a good degree and a balanced social life.

If you are going to make a choice, make sure you are informed about the consequences of your choices. Maybe you have never considered that you have learning styles or preferences.

Learning styles

According to learning theorists, there are several different learning styles, or preferences and many people have several learning styles or preferences depending on the tasks they are performing. Finding out which method or methods you prefer will give you your preferred learning style and this will assist you to get most out of your independent learning time.

---

6   CT Onions (ed) *The Shorter Oxford Dictionary on Historical Principles* (3rd edn, Clarendon Press, Oxford, 1988 revision and re print) Vol 1, 1191.

Below you will find three sets of learning style tables (Tables 16.1–16.3) which have been described by three different educational theorists (Table 16.1: Stella Cottrell,[7] Table 16.2: David Kolb[8] and Table 16.3: Peter Honey and Alan Mumford[9]). As you read each one consider if you use this style, or now you know about it would you consider using it? You will notice that several styles have similar features.

Cottrell's learning styles

Cottrell outlined four key learning styles: visual, auditory, kinaesthetic and interactive which are described in Table 16.1.

TABLE 16.1 COTTRELL'S LEARNING STYLES

Learning style	Description
Visual	Most happy learning from written information, diagrams and pictures. If they cannot take notes they will be stressed or de-motivated. Some visual learners will take their own notes even when they have been given pre-prepared ones. Written assessment works extremely well for visual learners. Some theorists split this group into those who relate best to print, and those who relate best to pictures, graphs and diagrams. Over half the population would fall into this learning style.
Auditory	Work best with oral skills. They like to listen to lectures, and may not take notes or write anything at all until after the lecture. If they see written information it will not make much sense until it is heard. One way in which this group find it easier to learn is to read aloud from their notes and books. Auditory learners can be particularly good speakers. About one-third of the population fall into this category.
Kinaesthetic	This style involves efficient learning through movement and/or touching. It relates to practical application such as watching others do something and then repeating it. Kinaesthetic learners are often thought particularly slow in grasping information but this only because popular teaching styles favour visual learners and, to a lesser extent, auditory learners. They may go to different physical places to memorise different information, classifying it in their head according to the place. Or they may pace or jog whilst learning. Very few people rely on kinaesthetic learning as their only preferred learning style.
Interactive	Like to learn through discussion with peers and teachers. This style is particularly well suited to small group learning. Many students will say that they enjoy learning this way, but if it is not backed up by notes of the session made by the student the learning can be lost.

7   S Cottrell *The Study Skills Handbook* (3rd edn, Palgrave Macmillan, Basingstoke, 2008).
8   D Kolb *Experiential Learning* (Englewood Cliff, Prentice Hall, 1984).
9   P Honey and A Mumford *The Manual of Learning Styles* (Peter Honey, Maidenhead, 1992), 5.

People tend to use the above preferences together when engaging in simple tasks such as rote learning. Verbal memory can be enhanced by uniting it with visual memory. Making notes and using differing colours to highlight, or using different patterns in your note taking, increases your ability to remember the text. You can also utilise kinaesthetic memory, for example, moving around and speaking aloud the text that you what you want to remember.[10]

Kolb's learning styles

Kolb classifies four main learning styles: the accommodator, converger, diverger and assimilator which are set out in Table 16.2.

Honey and Mumford's learning styles

Honey and Mumford, whose work was much influenced by Kolb, also identify four main learning styles: activist, reflector, theorist and pragmatist as indicated in Table 16.3.

TABLE 16.2 KOLB'S LEARNING STYLES

Learning style	Description
Accommodators	Are characterised by their ability to plan and to execute the plan. They are prepared to take risks, and get involved in new experiences, and are extremely able to adapt to new situations. They are not afraid to throw away theories that clearly do not fit the situations they see, and they have an instinctively intuitive ability to jump straight to the solution to a problem without following a step-by-step problem-solving methodology. They also rely extensively on gathering information from others. Whilst accommodators are socially relaxed they can be perceived as bossy or lacking in patience.
Divergers	Utilise their imagination to view situations from a range of different perspectives. They are good at any activity that requires the creation of sets of ideas, such as brainstorming. They are social, and tend to pursue their academic interests in the areas of the arts.
Convergers	Have a much stronger skill in the area of practical application of ideas. They are particularly good at locating answers when only one solution is correct. They tend to enjoy technical tasks, and excel at problem solving.
Assimilators	Have a major strength in the area of theoretical models. They can look at a range of seemingly disconnected facts and give an integrated explanation, if there is one to be found. They enjoy logical thought and, if a theory does not fit, they will carefully review the facts, and seek another theory.

10 Some students may be concerned that they have a bad memory, or believe that as you get older your ability to remember diminishes, and lose confidence. Mid-life memory loss is not substantiated by very much hard evidence. Mental processes do *change* with age and speed is lost, but we develop efficient strategies for the manipulation of data. Our application and understanding is enhanced. This more than makes up for the loss of speed which is hardly noticeable! The issue is how much the brain is *used* rather than the *age of the user*. To remember is to involve oneself in an active process.

TABLE 16.3 HONEY AND MUMFORD'S LEARNING STYLES

Learning style	Description
Activists	Prefer to learn 'by doing', so that their learning is based on experience. This is similar to Kolb's converger, and Cottrell's kinaesthetic learner. They are extremely open to new ways of doing things, but this can foster a tendency to be always moving on to new experiences. Activists can be easily seduced into thinking that the actual experience is the learning (which it is not). Experience cannot be turned into learning without reflection.
Reflectors	These are happy learning by observation, researching materials, reading them, reflecting on them and reaching conclusions. What can be a problem for these students is the tendency to collect too much information, making it difficult to reach a conclusion.
Theorists	Work best when constructing theories (explanations as to why something is as it is). They like to think things through logically, organising their views into theories like Kolb's assimilators. They can, on the negative side, jump to conclusions too quickly without taking care to reflect critically on their material and findings.
Pragmatist	Learn by translating what they know, whatever that may be, into practical experience which they experiment with in a range of situations. This is again similar to Kolb's assimilator. This preference for practical experience can also bring with it a tendency to jump to conclusions prior to the outcome of analysis.

Which learning style should you use, and should you stick to one?

Many learners only use one method of learning but educators consider that there is a benefit in trying all learning styles because different learning styles can be more, or less, suitable for different learning situations. For example, if we stay with Honey and Mumford (Table 16.3) the activist style is particularly useful when searching for data, such as the primary sources of law, law cases, legal rules and texts. Once data is retrieved you may find it more useful to adopt the reflector style, which is extremely productive for considering the tasks to be done (such as sorting, classifying and time-management). The pragmatist learning style is excellent when replicating learnt techniques and is therefore suitable for practising worked examples such as methods of problem solving. The theorist learning style is excellent for working towards understanding objectives and information, leading to summarising.

Activity 16.2: Finding out your learning style

Use Table 16.4 to tick the learning styles that you think you currently use and also the styles that you think would like to try. You can then make an effort to incorporate your

TABLE 16.4 WHAT IS YOUR STYLE OF LEARNING, AND WHAT ARE YOU WILLING TO TRY?

LEARNING STYLES	BRIEF DESCRIPTION OF LEARNING STYLE	YES: This is me	NO: This is not me	DON'T KNOW	I MIGHT TRY THIS
COTTRELL					
VISUAL	You like to deal with visual information (writing, diagrams, pictures). You like to take notes.				
AUDITORY	You like to deal with heard information and engage in oral skills. You may or may not take notes. You find it easiest to learn from hearing information.				
KINAESTHETIC	You like to learn through touching and moving, watching others and doing. Your learning recall is based on where you were at the time of the learning.				
INTERACTIVE	You like to learn through discussion groups with students and teachers.				
KOLB					
THE ACCOMMODATER	You are good at organising plans and sticking to them. You are prepared to take risks and adapt to new situations. You are good at taking information from others. You can be a bit bossy and/or impatient.				

TABLE 16.4—continued

LEARNING STYLES	BRIEF DESCRIPTION OF LEARNING STYLE	YES: This is me	NO: This is not me	DON'T KNOW	I MIGHT TRY THIS
THE DIVERGER	You will look at situations from a range of perspectives using your imagination.				
THE CONVERGER	You like to act from a practical perspective and apply ideas. You excel at problem solving. You enjoy problem solution with only one right answer.				
THE ASSIMILATOR	You are good at logical thought, devising theory and producing overarching explanations for a range of seemingly unconnected facts.				
HONEY AND MUMFORD					
THE ACTIVIST	You prefer to learn by doing. You are very open to new ways of doing things.				
THE REFLECTOR	You like to learn by observation, researching and reflecting.				
THE THEORIST	You like to construct theories. However, in the absence of supportive evidence, you have a habit of jumping to conclusions and this must be guarded against.				
THE PRAGMATIST	You like to translate knowledge into practical experience.				

chosen styles into your developing study strategies. You do not have to remember any labels. This is just a simple activity to highlight your existing learning styles and take the opportunity to experiment.

Why should you know your learning style?

Knowing your learning preferences is important because you will encounter lecturers and tutors who present different teaching methods and your preferred learning style may not be useful to you. You can use different learning styles to cope with the different teaching methods you will encounter, for example:

■ Lecturers will use oral presentation, PowerPoint slides, handouts, videos and audio clips to share information with you.
■ Lecturers will give you reading to go away and assimilate.
■ Your seminar or tutorial leaders will use small groups to engage in discussions and role plays. You will be asked to engage in investigative research.

You need to take as much as you can from all of these learning opportunities, regardless of your preferred style. University legal education relies heavily on lectures by the presentation of auditory information. If this is not your preferred learning style, then you need to consider what skills you must develop to ensure that you can learn from such presentations. If you need to learn from purely visual information and you naturally prefer auditory, again you need to consider how you can adapt to learn from this situation.

WHAT IS INDEPENDENT STUDY?

Students arrive at university by many different routes, straight from school, after a gap year or five to twenty years or more after they ceased formal education of any description. Both those arriving from school and those attending university as mature students do so with some expectation that it will be similar to the patterns of school life. Nearly all students are surprised by the expectation that they engage in many hours of independent study a week. If one assumes a learning week of 35 hours for a full time student during the two main teaching terms of the academic year they will spend at least 66 per cent of their time engaged in independent study. This statistic remains relative for a student studying part time as they pursue other activities during the week.

Life at university allows you the freedom to explore books and electronic learning resources – to prepare when you wish, and to discuss ideas with your peer group. We live in an age of 'lifelong learning' where more and more people of all ages become students either full time or part time, formally through structured degree programmes or more informally through MOOCs and other distance learning provisions. What they each have in common is that all students have to seize all of the learning opportunities offered and self-manage their own path through them.

Throughout the course of your law degree, independent studying will involve preparation for seminars or tutorials; engaging with pre-set questions and set reading; researching discussion topics; or completing coursework assignments, reports or presentations for formal assessment.

Your lecturers and seminar or tutorial leaders are generally academics who are not only teachers but are working on their own research and producing publications. Their role is to *guide* you through their module, giving you a blueprint to use to set the boundaries for you to determine your own independent study. This is an extremely different scenario from school organisation, where the teacher primarily teaches and pupils usually have exclusively taught classes and are expected to do directed home-based work out of school.

A required skill of the graduating university student is that they should demonstrate that they have developed a strong personal independency. This is seen as the marker of 'graduate-ness'. Employers will certainly be looking for evidence of this. The UK Quality Assurance Agency for Higher Education (the body that checks to ensure universities maintain their own academic standards and quality) require it to be instilled in students. One way of demonstrating you have this skill is to have good habits of independent study. It is not only essential for your academic and vocational education but also in the legal profession, organising the handling of their client's file.

HOW TO DEVELOP HABITS OF INDEPENDENT LEARNING

Independent learning involves the development of self-discipline: we are all different, you must not be concerned by others and their plans (or lack of them). You only need concern yourself with you. You need to take time and decide what works best for you in terms of learning.

Time management skills are essential for your development of good learning habits. Consider for a moment if you have a good track record of organising your time to get things done. In the past your teacher, your employer or your family may have given you a structure for planning your work. At university you will have to learn to do this for yourself, structuring task completion and also prioritising among tasks.

The efficient management of your independent study requires that you obtain the full range of information relating to being able to efficiently study which includes information on:

- your modules (syllabus/module outline, reading lists, handbooks, set texts);
- all assessment submission dates;
- your weekly/fortnightly/termly timetable of taught classes;
- term dates and the organisation of the academic year;
- using your department's virtual learning environment;
- using required IT (including word-processing packages);
- how to competently use the library;
- development of your English language skills and the ascertainment of your strengths and weaknesses.

Once you have pulled all of this information together, you will need to prioritise your time in terms of lecture attendance, seminar preparation, attendance and participation in seminars, submission of course work, revision and taking exams.

Always be aware of your own study priorities on a daily and weekly basis by keeping an organised digital or print diary. Look ahead and plan out the term, noting when assessments are set and when they are due for submission.

Being well organised in your management of class attendance, independent study and coursework submission will help ensure that you do not experience high stress levels.

THE CYCLES, PATTERNS AND SCHEDULES OF STANDARD UNIVERSITY STUDY

It is necessary to understand the organisation of your degree through all of its years, as well as the divisions of the academic year into terms or semesters. You cannot successfully manage your learning if you do not know the patterns of life at your university, what is expected of you and when it is expected.

The pattern of your degree

Full time students usually complete their studies within three years, although if placements are involved it can be four years. Part-time students usually take up to six years to complete their degrees, made up of two years part time study for each full time year of study. But students may be able to complete a part time degree sooner. Many universities will allow a part time student to study full time for part of the degree if the student is able to do so.

Modules

Each year you will take a range of modules and obtain credits at certain grades; these determine your degree result. In many universities year 1 grades do not count towards calculation of the final degree grade, but that may not be the case for all degrees. An often overlooked but important task for students is to understand how many modules are required for the completion of their degree, and which are compulsory and optional. If you want to gain a qualifying law degree for the purposes of professional exemptions you have to take as options subjects laid down by the professions.

You should aim to make links between the various modules on your degree course, rather than moving from one module to another without any regard for what has gone before.

For some modules such as employment law you will be required to draw on concepts learnt in previous years in the law of contract and law of tort modules (which may in your institution be called common law principles). Similarly make links between each individual topic within each module, seeing them as parts of a whole, and consider them in the context of other issues, such as social scientific analysis of law as well as legal analysis.

Each module that you study throughout your degree will carry a set number of credits towards your degree, with a degree being made up of 360 credits. Each year of your degree is therefore worth 120 credits and each course or module you study will contribute a specific number of credits to that total.

Many universities state that one full module is worth 20 credits, a half-weighted module will therefore be 10 credits and a double-weighted module will be 40 credits. In universities using a 20 credit system per full module you will study at least 18 modules throughout your degree, or 6 modules a year (120 credits). If you choose half-unit modules you will be engaging in more modules to make up the 120 credits of the year.

You will be required to complete a set number of compulsory courses or modules each year. Options usually have to be chosen in the induction week, if not before. Your choices here are important for a number of reasons. If you have a clear idea of the career path you want to follow after your studies (for example, you may want to practise corporate or commercial law), you may choose modules that are more closely aligned with that path. When you have ascertained what your optional modules are you should consider them carefully before making your choice. Many law schools have compulsory modules that they require all students to study. These may not coincide with the modules required by the professional bodies for your degree to count as a qualifying law degree for the purposes of entering the legal profession.

If a law student wishes to obtain a qualifying law degree the reality is that by the time compulsory courses for your department's law degree, plus those for the professions, are taken into account there is very little choice left to do other optional modules.

The cycle of the academic year

The academic year can be organised according to terms, or semesters. Terms split the academic year into three terms of 11–12 weeks separated by vacations, the semester system splits the academic year into two semesters of around 16–18 weeks again separated by vacation. The total number of weeks in the university teaching weeks is therefore in the region of 33–36 weeks. Some university departments hold exams at the end of each term or semester, others at the end of the academic year.

However university teaching rarely extends beyond weeks 22–24 of these teaching weeks, as time is set aside for revision and examinations. Generally all of the teaching and learning is squashed into the 22 weeks between September/October and March/April, a period that also includes around seven weeks of vacation time. The reality is that you are only taught for around six months of the year.

First year students can easily fail to get into proper study habits and independent learning until January or February by which time the taught year is half over and several modules are competed. In departments where modules are only one term in length students who take weeks to acclimatise upon arrival can find they are failing because they did not even realise modules ended in December: they thought they had more time to improve.

Each of these front-loaded 22–24 weeks contains lectures and seminars and in many weeks there will be assessment submission deadlines. It is this yearly pattern which determines the flow of your taught classes, independent study and free time.

Consideration of the pattern of your taught classes and assessments as well as vacations (when you will find you still need to be studying) allows you to see where you have spaces for independent study as well as paid employment if necessary and personal me-time.

It is equally important to understand the rhythm of your term/semester cycle and the timetable of weekly lectures, seminars and assessments. You will need to organise your study outside the classroom for seminars and assessments as well as increasing your general understanding of the subject. The discussion that follows discusses the termly pattern, as shown in Figure 16.1, but it can be adapted very easily to slot into the semester pattern if your institution uses it.

Zooming into this cycle in more detail, Table 16.5 sets out the months of the year and maps them against the standard academic activity taking place, so you can begin to see the rhythm of the academic year for the typical student. Not all university departments will have the same pattern but they will be similar. This will reinforce the comment above that you do not actually have a year to study; at best you have nine months. Of this time, only around six months will be spent with teachers in lectures and seminars.

Once you appreciate the structure of the entire academic year, you also need to understand how your time is divided at both termly and weekly levels. The next section looks at this micro-context and also engages in a discussion of personal management within the termly and weekly cycle. It is here, at the detailed level, that you are most likely to 'lose the plot'.

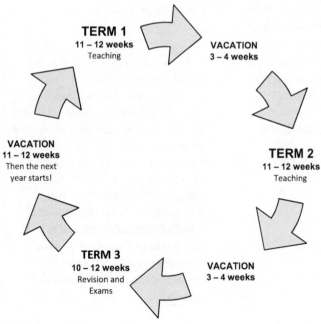

TERM 1
11 – 12 weeks
Teaching

VACATION
3 – 4 weeks

TERM 2
11 – 12 weeks
Teaching

VACATION
3 – 4 weeks

TERM 3
10 – 12 weeks
Revision and
Exams

VACATION
11 – 12 weeks
Then the next
year starts!

Figure 16.1 The cycle of the academic year

TABLE 16.5 TYPICAL ACADEMIC CYCLE FOR A YEAR 1 STUDENT ON A DEGREE DIVIDED INTO TERMS			
MONTHS	**OFFICIAL ACTIVITY**	**STUDENT TASKS**	**WEEKS**
SEPT	**TERM 1:** INDUCTION MAYBE START OF TEACHING	This is a whirlwind time of highs and lows for most students. Know what modules you are taking, times of lectures/seminars/tutorials and their venues and whether they are weekly or fortnightly. Choose any options. Get to grips with IT and the library.	**TERM 1 TEACHING TERM** 11–12 weeks
OCT	TEACHING BEGINS	Continue your induction; ask for assistance if you need it; do not suffer in silence as you will be lost. These are key weeks so make sure you get off to a good start. Your study timetable should be clear to you by mid-October.	
NOV	TEACHING There *may* be a 1 week reading week with no lectures. ASSESSMENTS: SUBMISSIONS POSSIBLE	Attendance at seminars and lectures should not be an issue, you should plan to be there. Use any reading week to catch up.	
DEC	TEACHING DRAWS TO AN END FROM AROUND 12–17. ASSESSMENTS: SUBMISSIONS POSSIBLE VACATION	As term draws to an end you may feel settled or unsettled. You may have catching up to do. It's not too late to make positive plans to change bad habits, develop good self-management skills and get on top of your work. A chat before leaving for vacation with your tutors can work miracles for your motivation. **[SEMESTERISED PROGRAMMES MAY HAVE EXAMS NOW OR PRIOR TO NEXT SEMESTER.] Speak to your personal tutor if you feel you need some general support or to your lecturers if you need subject specific support.**	**VACATION** 3–4 weeks

MONTHS	OFFICIAL ACTIVITY	STUDENT TASKS	WEEKS
JAN	VACATION/START OF TERM 2 This is the busiest term for teaching and assessment. ASSESSMENT: SUBMISSIONS MAY BE DUE WEEK 1 TERM 2.	Enjoy yourself in the vacation, and do take time out but ensure you continue planning and studying. Use the vacation to reflect on how you did in term 1, what worked and what did not. Term 2 is the make or break term.	
FEB	TEACHING: There may be a reading week with no teaching.	You can still make up for lost time if you work consistently. You should have your study plan in place but it is easy to lose motivation. **Speak to your personal tutor if you feel you need some general support or to your lecturers if you need subject specific support.**	**TERM 2 TEACHING TERM** 11–12 weeks **VACATION** 3–4 weeks
MAR	TEACHING: VACATION MAY START	It is important to keep going as the term approaches its end. You will be tired. This is a make or break term. It is easy to lose momentum and then fall behind.	
APR	VACATION: can start in March TERM 3 BEGINS	This is a make or break vacation in terms of exam success. You need to have a proper break and then ensure you do any necessary assessments, and plan your revision timetable in rough.	
MAY	REVISION AND EXAM SEASON	Look after your emotional and physical health in revision and exam season. If relevant go away from the university for a few weeks to revise when revision classes have ended. Everyone is different and you must do what is best for you. Some students panic more easily when surrounded by others revising. If this is you consider going somewhere else. **[SEMESTERISED PROGRAMMES MAY HAVE EXAMS NOW]**	**TERM 3: REVISION CLASSES** 1–2 weeks **PERSONAL REVISION AND EXAMS RESULTS: VACATION** 8–10 weeks Resits

TABLE 16.5—continued			
MONTHS	**OFFICIAL ACTIVITY**	**STUDENT TASKS**	**WEEKS**
JUN	EXAM SEASON	You just need to stay focused and move on if one exam seemed difficult. Put fears you have failed something behind you and keep your strength up for the next exam.	
JUL	VACATION AND EXAM RESULTS: If you failed any exam find out why from your tutors.	If you have failed any exams it is essential to see your tutor before they leave for the long vacation. Work hard for the resits and resolve to develop better revision strategies and independent management skills next year.	
AUG	VACATION	RESITS POSSIBLE	
SEPT	RESITS [NORMALLY] VACATION: **THE NEW ACADEMIC YEAR USUALLY STARTS MID TO END OF SEPTEMBER**		

Planning your weekly and termly timetable of taught classes and independent study

Let us suppose that you are studying the seven subjects shown below in Table 16.6 in your first year, and you are a full time student.

Taken together the seven different subjects equal 120 credits. It would seem from this list that you will study five modules in term 1 and four in term 2 (note that 3 and 5 run across both terms).

Note that the table gives you total and weekly expected teaching hours and total and weekly expected independent study. These translate differently into a weekly schedule depending upon whether the subject concerned is 20 or 10 credits (e.g. a full or a half module) and whether it is completed over one term or one year (which is effectively two terms taking into account revisions and exams etc.).

Often students only take into account the taught classes in terms of their timetable and the rest is haphazardly fitted in. This often has the consequence that learning is reduced to trying to do assessments as quickly as possible. This is not an efficient approach to study and often results in students failing to attain their potential. Lecturers and tutors do impress upon students the need to study but this is often ignored, or students become so worried they end up demotivated. The best plan is to take control of your learning as you are expected to do and then you will not fall into an exhausting cycle of overwork and underwork that does not give you the results you want.

We have entered the five hypothetical term 1 modules from Table 16.6 below onto a weekly timetable shown in Table 16.7. Many law schools will produce personal timetables

TABLE 16.6 HYPOTHETICAL YEAR 1 SUBJECT SHOWING TEACHING HOURS AND INDEPENDENT STUDY HOURS

Nos	Module showing number of assessments per term in brackets with exam indicated by (E)	Credits	Length of module in terms of 11 weeks	Total teaching hours per module required by module outline	Total independent study per module required by module outline	Predicted weekly teaching hours per module	Predicted weekly independent study per module
1	Contract (2) (E)	20	1	50	200	3	8
2	Critical legal studies (2)	20	1	50	200	3	6
3	English legal System and methods (4)	20	1 & 2	50	200	1.5	4
4	Philosophy (1)	10	1	25	100	1.5	3
5	Criminal law (2) (E)	20	1 & 2	50	200	2	5
6	Legal theory (1) (E)	10	2	25	100	1.5	6
7	Constitutional law (2) (E)	20	2	50	100	3	8

TABLE 16.6—continued

Nos	Module showing number of assessments per term in brackets with exam indicated by (E)	Credits	Length of module in terms of 11 weeks	Total teaching hours per module required by module outline	Total independent study per module required by module outline	Predicted weekly teaching hours per module	Predicted weekly independent study per module

Modules running in term 1: Modules 1, 2, 3, 4, 5,

Total taught classes per week term 1: 11

Total independent study a week term 1: 26

Total weekly study hours term 1: 37

Numbers of assessments due in term 1 (assuming yearly modules have assessments spread equally): 8

Modules running in term 2: 3, 5, 6, 7,

Total taught classes per week term 2: 8

Total independent study a week term 2: 23

Total weekly study hours term 2: 31

Numbers of assessments due in term 2 (assuming yearly modules have assessments spread equally): 6

ISSUES ARISING FROM THE ABOVE TIMETABLE

- The workload in term 1 is high when you are also settling in.
- The workload in term 2 is lower but by then several of your modules have finished.
- You may well have noted that your weekly independent study should be much higher if the required module hours of 100 or 200 hours' independent study are divided by 11 or 22.
  - a lot of independent study takes place in vacations;
  - many assessments are set over vacation periods. So vacations can use up a great deal of independent study;
  - some hours need to be reserved for revisions for exams;
  - hours are required for the extras needed to research and write assessments due in term time hours.

TABLE 16.7 TERM 1 PERSONAL WEEKLY TIMETABLE SHOWING FIXED POINTS FOR ATTENDING TAUGHT SESSIONS

TIME	MON	TUES	WEDS	THURS	FRI	THE WEEKEND
9–10		CRITICAL LEGAL STUDIES LECTURE Term 1 only Credits: 20	CRIMINAL LAW LECTURE Terms 1 & 2 Credits: 20	ELS & METHODS LECTURE Terms 1 and 2 Credits: 20	PHILOSOPHY LECTURE Term 1 only Credits: 10	
10–11			CONTRACT LAW			
11–12			LECTURE Term 1 only Credits: 20	ELS & methods seminars (every week) Terms 1 and 2 Credits: 20	Criminal law seminars (fortnightly) Terms 1 and 2 Credits: 20	
12–13	LUNCH	Contract law seminar (every week) Term 1 only	LUNCH	LUNCH	LUNCH	
13–14					Philosophy seminar (fortnightly) Term 1 only	
15–16						
16–17					Contract law seminar (every week) Term 1 only	
17–18		Critical legal studies seminar (fortnightly) Term 1 only				
18–19						
EVENING						

Figure 16.2 The personal weekly timetable with fixed points for classes

for students; others do not, and if this is the case you will need to do so. When you construct your own it is essential to put the venue as this can change from week to week. Most universities post electronic notices and/or send emails regarding room changes or lecture/seminar cancellations.

Our hypothetical timetable so far includes only the fixed times when you must be in classes, at least in term 1. The amount of study expected of you each week will vary according to whether your course or module is taught over one term or one year, and whether it is a whole unit or a half-unit module. Your module outline will state the number of taught hours and independent study hours they require. For a 20 credit module this is likely to be 50 teacher hours and 200 independent student hours. Make sure you read the small print.

If you look at the specimen personal weekly timetable for term 1 in Figure 16.2 you will see that our hypothetical student's timetable of five subjects just notes class times.

Once you have your class times you need to enter the times at which you propose to engage in independent study time, not forgetting that this takes place over the duration of the taught module, through 'vacation' periods in December/January and March/April, as well as increasing for revision for exams and around continuous assessment submissions. If you look back to Table 16.6 you will see that the weekly split of hours is given, with allowances for vacations etc. as noted in the 'ISSUES' section of the table.

The insertion of the independent study hours gives you term 1 of around 37 hours and term 2 of 31 hours a week. This leaves plenty of time for all the other things that need to be fitted in, including the need to engage in some paid employment.

Your tutors will usually guide you concerning the number of independent study hours required for a given subject. Once the fixed points are on the timetable, if you are working add in your paid employment requirements to your timetable. You may need to engage in paid employment in the daytime but then make sure that you allow study time in the evenings or weekends to compensate. If you play sports, training and playing time needs to be taken into account, in which case you will also need to rearrange your study hours.

If you carefully fill in the timetable with all of your commitments, you may find that you do not have as much free time as you thought if you want to succeed and get a good degree. But you will have enough free time to have fun.

Many management consultants additionally advise that crisis-time is built into your standard timetable planning. These are hours that are 'free' but 'in-waiting': in case you cannot study at the time allotted you can use a crisis-time bloc. There may also be a reading week or independent study week each mid-term when there is no teaching, allowing you to catch up, though this is not the case in all departments. The vacations also allow you some space to have a break as well as catch up with study or work on assessments that may be due.

As the third term is taken up with assessments, revision and exams, if you fall behind you need to take proper advice from your lecturers and tutors as to the best way of sorting out time problems.

Even if you are not formally examined until later in your degree, do not underestimate the importance of doing well in your first year. Law is a highly competitive profession to get into in terms of finding placements (which look good on your CV), obtaining places at law school and securing training contracts or pupillage. This type of competition demands focus and requires you to put in hours of studying. You need to get into good habits in your first year.

Often prospective employers and vocational stage institutions look at first year results even though they do not count towards the degree. Prospective law firms and vocational course providers will also be interested in your broader activity. What have you done to engage with the life of the university law school? Are you involved in the student law society? Are you involved in client counselling or mooting competitions? Have you completed any work placements? Have you been a student representative? What voluntary work have you done? By planning your time effectively, you can ensure you have time available to participate in appropriate activities which will enhance your job prospects.

THE RANGE OF SKILLS REQUIRED FOR SUCCESSFUL LEGAL STUDY

Table 16.8 sets out the wide range of skills that you need to develop for successful legal study. Do read these carefully; they are all interrelated and taken together impact your learning.

TABLE 16.8 THE SKILLS REQUIRED FOR THE SUCCESSFUL STUDY OF LAW	
Study skills	How to develop independent and highly efficient learning strategies including efficient filing systems which will tend to be both digital and hard copy.
IT skills	Efficient use of email, word-processing, being able to navigate virtual learning environments, competent internet search, e-library use, database manipulation. You will find plenty of online training materials and help on your university's web pages.
Communication skills	The ability to clearly and appropriately communicate with staff and fellow students in writing and orally. Competent understanding of the use of the electronic communication in your department.
Language skills	Competent understanding and use of general English and technical legal language. This requires a good grasp of vocabulary, grammar, punctuation and spelling. The quality of your language skills determines the effectiveness of your communication.

TABLE 16.8—continued	
Critical thinking skills	The ability to constantly question, seeking the underlying assumptions behind arguments, taking nothing for granted, seeking evidences for your assertions, questioning your own positions
Legal research skills	How to find law and texts about law through highly effective library search skills.
Legal method skills	Understanding strategies for finding, analysing and applying law.
Argumentative skills	Identification, construction and evaluation of argument.
Reading skills	How to read legal texts by engaging in active reading for sense; looking for markers in the text to aid reading; scanning for information; appreciating different methods of reading.
Writing skills	Writing efficient notes, summaries, essays, legal problem solutions, exams, reports and more.
Speaking (oral) skills	Being able to competently engage in debating, mock trials (mooting), mediation, negotiation, presentation.
Substantive law	Legal knowledge, for example of criminal law, contract law and so on.

You will by now realise that it is fatal to underestimate the importance of general study skills, and that your competent study requires competent English language skills, legal method skills, critical thinking skills and argument construction skills. You will not achieve your potential without engaging with these sets of skills.

It is essential to realise that deficiency in one group of skills can affect your performance in all areas, and therefore affect your grades. You may have a good ability to argue but you cannot express this competently in writing using grammatically correct English and using correct spellings.

Competent understanding of the use of the electronic communication in your department

Information relating to course requirements, timetable changes and assessment deadlines will be communicated to you by your department usually by means of electronic communication methods such as a virtual learning environment (VLE). Email will also be used a great deal. It is essential that you familiarise yourself with your department's preferred and mandatory communication systems and ensure that you set up a university email account. Most universities require students to register for the university, then register for the library, at which point they may use their library-user ID to register for access to IT communications.

You need to know how to make the best use of this and how to download and/or print material as required.

The types of electronic information you may be given from your department and your lecturers will refer to weekly, termly and yearly information, all of which are important. For example, you may be informed electronically of:

- your timetable of classes in a given subject, of tutorials and/or seminars;
- your timetable of examinations;
- your assessment timetable and protocols for the submission of work;
- the university's attendance policy and forms to use if you are sick or need leave of absence for reasons other than sickness;
- important regulations for your degree course.

MAKING THE BEST USE OF YOUR DEPARTMENT'S TEACHING ARRANGEMENTS

It is essential to properly use the offered teaching arrangements which are planned to give you the opportunities to learn from your teachers. Standard practice for university teaching arrangements on law degree programmes is the use of large lectures, small group work in seminars or tutorials (mostly with tutors, sometimes led by students) and limited one to one sessions with your lecturers or tutors.

Some students struggle to leave behind a teacher/pupil school mentality in both their expectations of and relationships with teachers. The standard term for the university teacher is either lecturer or tutor. Some of your lecturers will be in charge of the modules they teach, having overall responsibility for their design, recommended reading, and the construction of both assessments and the exam if there is one. Often a module will have a teaching team of several lecturers. A tutor refers to the role of leading small group meetings with students where they have pre-prepared work for discussion. So your criminal law lecturer could also be your small group tutor. Sometimes the tutor has no involvement in the teaching of the module in which they are tutor. This is usually because they are a lecturer on other modules. Where a team of lecturers and tutors are involved the lecturer in charge of the module will consult them concerning assessment design etc. It is useful to be aware of these basics.

We will look at:

- one to one learning opportunities with staff;
- lectures;
- seminars/tutorials.

One to one learning opportunities with staff

There are several types of one to one meeting you may have with lecturers or tutors:

- personal tutor meetings;
- a meeting with your subject lecturer or tutor prearranged by yourself or them; or
- taking the opportunity to attend a 'drop in' session during staff office hours.

Whatever the nature of the one to one session you need to go prepared, ensure you know what it is about in advance, listen in a focused manner during the meeting, remember what is said, make sense of it, note down important points, and ensure you leave understanding what you need to do next.

Lecturer office hours/drop in hour

Many lecturers/tutors have weekly office hours on a 'by-appointment' or a drop in basis when students can discuss issues surrounding their learning on the module. 'By appointment' means just that: prior to the office hour you contact the lecturer/tutor using their preferred contact methods to arrange a meeting.

These office hours are useful if you do not understand why you obtained a low grade for assessment, or if you are having difficulties with any topic or sub-topic. Ensure you go to these one to one sessions knowing what your issues are. If you are discussing your assessment performance, before you attend for your session you must re-read your work. Carefully re-read the question, and consider the feedback given by your marker linking it to your work and seeing if you understand what has been said. It is a waste of everyone's time when a student arrives without bothering to engage in pre-thought and just says 'Why is my mark so low? I thought it was OK'. Lecturers will have marked hundreds of pieces of work and although may recall your grade band they will not necessarily recall their detailed feedback. Therefore it is always sensible to take a copy of your coursework and any feedback given with you.

Lectures

Lectures are delivered to facilitate student learning. However, they are not all uniform in their purpose. Some lectures are designed to inform you about the general framework of a large or smaller area of your module. Other lectures focus on specific issues within a sub-topic of the overall module. The order in which lectures are delivered is carefully planned to give you the basic information you need to make sense of upcoming expected reading, seminar preparation and assessments.

Lectures can be thought of as a map of different areas, and are most definitely a shortcut to understanding the basics. Note I refer to the basics. No module can be passed on lectures alone. You need to engage with the required reading and with seminars. If you choose not to attend, do not be surprised if this choice is reflected in low assessment grades, and continuing lack of understanding.

Your active engagement with the lecture is vital. You may or may not wish to write lecture notes but it is usually a good idea to note basics and then read more widely on the topic after the lecture. If PowerPoint (ppt) slides are used: these can be downloaded in advance and used for adding notes.

SEMINARS/TUTORIALS

Usually in addition to lectures each module with have weekly or fortnightly tutor led small groups either called seminars or tutorials.

Traditionally, seminars were composed of larger groups of students (15+) who give seminar papers on pre-chosen topics by the lecturer. All the papers in a given seminar are related and the tutor facilitates discussion after they have been presented. Tutorials were much smaller than seminars (8+) but also led by tutors. Students are usually expected to engage in set reading and undertake exercises/tasks before the tutorial. The pre-work completed by students will then be the subject of discussion. Additional, more probing questions will be posed by the tutor to develop student understanding of the work they have prepared. You will be able to exchange your views with each other and the tutor.

However, many universities now blur the distinctions between the two types of small group. Running groups called tutorials or seminars having anything from 20–30 students.

Whatever the nature of the small group work in your modules, pre-work will be involved, and they will be led by a lecturer or tutor. At the end of all small group work whether labelled 'seminar' or 'tutorial' the tutor will draw your attention to any issues that should have been discussed and were omitted by you in your discussions. You are expected to take on board what is said in the small group and engage in any extra reading as you or the tutor consider necessary. It is a good idea to make sure that you leave each session with written notes relating to the correct approaches to the questions/tasks set.

Students often do not prepare at all or inadequately for these sessions, which is short sighted as they take you deeper into the subject. You can test your understanding and check you are on track in your views. So you will severely disadvantage yourself if you choose not to do the pre-set independent work. The seminar/tutorial is meant to be an active not a passive environment – make sure you can join in.

Your seminar/tutorial management is an important part of your independent learning development. If you neglect it you will again find your lack of understanding is reflected in low assessment grades.

Working in groups with fellow students (formally and informally)

The development of interpersonal skills through team working is one of the essential skills of a competent graduate. But team working is often demanding and challenging.

Many of you will have experienced some degree of team working prior to university, and it may have been a good or a bad experience. The fact is that success in life is very much down to your ability to engage at the appropriate time in competent interpersonal skills and to work as part of a team. In short, to get on with others, demonstrate you are a trustworthy team player, and demonstrate you can self-manage. These skills get you noticed, and you can be judged excellent or poor.

Many students working in teams or groups do not stop to consider the challenges of working with other people. They may feel angry (either passively or actively), or feel bullied, or they may themselves bully others. Notice that these are emotional issues. Emotions as well as lazy group members can demoralise other group members. Then the actual task they have to work on is de-prioritised whilst problems are resolved. It takes the development of good skills of listening and understanding, as well as appropriate levels of humility to respect the views of others. It takes self-discipline to prepare work for other students and to deal with those who are not 'pulling their weight'. But if this is done you will learn to manage people effectively and allow them to think and develop, and this quality is highly regarded in employment. The quality of group work and discussion will then result in very good work.

PERSONAL DEVELOPMENT PLANNING (PDP)

In academic life, both at school and university as well as professional life, PDPs are of increasing importance. We have already referred above to goals. A PDP assists you to develop towards your goals in a more formal manner. At root it involves stopping to think about your learning and how you are developing in your studies, including your good achievements such as assessment marks, and engaging in department or national competitions in law. It also involves planning your development at university and beyond from a personal, academic and career perspective.

Usually part of your department's VLE will be devoted to PDP and will guide you through the process. Building a PDP is a useful process because it allows you to develop focus. If you want to obtain a scholarship or to ensure a place at a good university for a master's degree or PhD, or obtain the ever dwindling supply of training contracts, you will need a 2.1 or a First. Often you need to demonstrate achievements outside the academic but related, such as relevant volunteering, internships or placements. So knowing this, it is not a good idea to miss lectures and seminars, attain low grades and be generally careless in your approach to studies. Nor is it a good idea to just do the basics and not seek placements etc.

PDP will help you to develop plans to develop independent learning, increase your grades or engage in extra-curricular activity. As you engage with the process you will find you become increasingly aware of your strengths and weaknesses in all areas. You will realise what you can change and then seek to identify specific skills sets that need development. Your tutors will be only too pleased to assist with your academic related development.

The formal process of PDP encourages you to keep a note of your achievements, and these are useful references when you are constructing a CV for further study or employment.

Students who have engaged in PDP maintain it is extremely useful in keeping them focused, and look at their learning preferences understanding why they have them and why it may be a good idea to try other learning styles. The more you engage in PDP in a flexible manner the more you genuinely take over the management of your present and future, and take, rather than miss opportunities.

Many law degree programmes integrate PDP into your skills training, as well as providing opportunities for work-based learning. All of these matters will be flagged by your department. If they are not then you can speak to the department's legal careers advisor or failing that to the university careers department.

The Legal Education and Training Review 2013 in its report 'Setting Standards: The Future of Legal Services Education and Training Regulation in England and Wales'[11] devotes much attention in Annex III to PDP in the profession. If you seriously are interested in a career in law it is a good idea to acquaint yourself with the contents of this report, or any update.

CONCLUSION

All of the areas considered in detail in this chapter are of comparable importance because they all work together to make you a successful and competent learner. Do not be worried by them, just be aware of them and perhaps use the framework of PDP to indicate where you think you are in each skill, and plan what you need to do to develop.

CHAPTER SUMMARY

- The student who takes control of their studies, considers their goals and how to achieve them and develops good habits of independent study will be able to realise their full potential.
- It is essential to understand the cycles of academic life through the year, your own personal teaching and assessment timetable so that you can effectively plan.
- Lectures, seminars/tutorials and one to one sessions with tutors are important to the development of your understanding.
- Studying involves the simultaneous use of a range of skills, self-management, development planning, reading/writing skills, IT skills, interpersonal skills and communication skills. Each has an important place in achieving a good degree.
- Awareness of learning and teaching styles, and recognising which you prefer, and the purposes of each develops flexibility and allows you to be an effective learner.
- Using personal development planning (PDP) will assist you in goal setting, self-awareness and in having a good resource to use for CVs for law school, training contracts, grants/scholarship applications and employment.

---

11 www.letr.org.uk/the-report accessed 19 November 2014.

GENERAL READING
SKILLS

17

'Reading is to the mind what exercise is to the body. It is wholesome and bracing for the mind to have its faculties kept on the stretch.'

Augustus Hare

LEARNING OUTCOMES

After reading this chapter you should be able to:

- Use a reading plan to efficiently understand a text.
- Competently use different methods of reading.
- Quickly identify whether a text is relevant to your needs.
- Identify the main and subsidiary issues in a text; outlining both propositions and evidence.
- Combine and compare arguments from several sources.
- Be confident in reading and using secondary texts.

INTRODUCTION

Reading involves several skills deployed together and as you improve those skills, you develop your reading ability. This chapter focuses on general reading skills. For study purposes, writing and reading[1] are inseparable groups of skills. If one of them is deficient it will affect the other. Your final written assessment or examination will only be as good as your ability to read and to write. You need to read to:

- understand the assessment or seminar task;
- competently undertake the literature research required;
- identify the arguments in the material;
- understand the arguments in the material;
- evaluate the arguments in the material;
- compare the arguments in the material;
- differentiate between information, description and argument;
- decide on your view and argument on the matters raised in your reading.

Students are required to read academic articles and books (as well as primary sources of law) for a range of reasons. For example you may wish to:

- obtain information about a topic;
- grasp the basics of an area of law;
- engage in analysis of the arguments forwarded by a particular author;
- critique the reasoning of judges in a case;
- acquire historical or political data on law;
- locate a range of different views about a case, statute, area, theory or method;
- obtain assistance in developing a sophisticated analysis of a topic or a case.

Your intellectual understanding of a topic will develop according to the depth of your reading. Notes from your reading will be the raw material that you use to write your assessments or collect your thoughts for a seminar.

You will be introduced to a general reading strategy that you can use to identify, understand, evaluate and compare arguments in the material you have read. If you read carelessly and fail to concentrate properly, it could impact the development of your understanding of a topic and affect your grade for assessed work.

READING SKILLS

We all read at different speeds; some may read slowly and others may read relatively quickly but have a very limited concentration span for reading. Whatever your reading

---

1 What you read is also often the result of legal research and if your legal research is deficient you will miss important texts and that too will affect your written assessments and development of understanding.

ability the study of law requires each student to engage in constant high volume reading. Luckily it is possible to learn effective reading habits and increase your reading speeds.

In brief you need to learn to read with an intended purpose in mind. Also you need to become familiar with different approaches to your reading, understanding when it is necessary to superficially read and when it is necessary to read for detail. You also need to be aware of your reading speed so that you can allocate the required time to a reading project, and if possible you need to know how to increase your reading skills without loss of any quality in your reading. We will now look at these issues in turn:

- Reading with a purpose.
- The three main approaches to reading.
- Reading speeds: how long does it take to read a text?

Reading with a purpose

Reading in the context of studying always requires reading for a purpose. All too often students see reading as passive, moving their eyes from one line to the next without necessarily stopping to join the words into sentences and derive meaning from those sentences as they form paragraphs. Some readers researching books for a specific purpose do not even write notes, or consider how they will remember everything of relevance in the absence of notes.[2]

Your purpose for reading comes out of your understanding of what you have been asked to do. When given assessment tasks you must correctly identify the limits of the question. For example, the facts of problem solution questions are often set in the areas between decided cases where there is an area of 'unknown', an area that the student is expected to talk about confidently. Therefore the competent identification of that 'unknown area' from the outset often determines the relevancy of your research texts and the quality of your final answer.

Reading with purpose means that you should be continually asking yourself:

'Am I reading this for description, information or analysis?';

'Am I seeking to find out basic things about the topic or am I trying to support propositions in my argument?'.

Effective competent reading can never be a purely passive act, because you need to engage in an active dialogue with the text. Your competency depends on a number of issues, including how motivated you are, and how well you can concentrate for a set period of time. It is also dependent on how quickly you read, and if speed means you are prone to careless reading that is a problem. Notice your inner dialogue as you read. Are you continually processing, reflecting, considering, agreeing or disagreeing with what you are reading? If you are not, then cultivate the ability to engage in these essential processes.

2   Competent strategies for note taking are discussed in Chapter 18.

The three main methods of approaching reading

It is vital that you know how to adapt your reading strategies to suit your purpose for reading a text. Not all texts have to be read in detail; some can be skimmed for relevancy or information.

There are three main approaches to reading:

- Scanning.
- Skimming.
- Detailed reading.

Probably you use all of these methods but have not put labels to them. Just as it is important to have a research plan, and a strategy for assessing the authority and the reliability of retrieved texts, it is essential to be familiar with the main three methods of approaching reading, and have a plan concerning when to deploy these methods.

Scanning

Think back to when you were last searching an index or contents pages: you know what you are looking for and will have scanned the text, that is you will have moved your eyes rapidly over sections of text only searching for the words you want, which tend to jump out as your brain is alerted to their location.

In relation to academic reading you often want to determine whether the text is useful, or if you know it is useful you want a quick overview prior to a more detailed reading. You can use the scanning method to read parts of a text to get a rough idea of its coverage which is excellent for assessing relevancy.

This requires reading:

- The contents page of a book if the whole book is relevant.
- Any abstract (summary of an article that appears above it).
- The introduction for a book or an article (or the preface for a book).
- The first and last paragraphs of any sections the article is divided into (or chapters in books) as writers tend to introduce and conclude in these).
- The conclusion to the article (or concluding chapter, if there is one, in a book).
- The index to the book.

Skimming

A skim read is just a quick read of the entire text for general meaning. Again you have probably already done this, when reading media or leisure information in print or online. Your eyes will ignore specific information, looking for general information that gives you an outline idea of what the main points of the information are. In academic reading you would be looking out for the main argument of the text.

You may think that there is no point doing this if you are going to have to read the text anyway but it is useful and an aid to understanding if you get a skim read overview of sections of text before you engage in a detailed reading of it. Or if you have read it in some detail and just want to skim over the text to recall a few details.

Skimming and scanning, although they are different methods, can both be used for determining the relevancy of a text, or getting an overview prior to a detailed reading.

Detailed reading

We will be concentrating on detailed reading in the following sections. When you are reading for detail it is important to read actively, not just passively turn pages taking in words without processing them in your mind. Have you noticed that sometimes when you are reading you are thinking about something else entirely? The best approach to detailed reading is to combine it with note taking as this increases your active engagement with the text and decreases your ability to think about something else while you are reading. Active engagement with the text you are reading improves concentration, retention of information read, and time taken to read.

Detailed reading and note taking

Not only do you usually need a summary of what you have read, but you need to double check that you have understood what you have read. You have to stop and think for a few seconds before writing your note of a section and this embeds as well as double checks your understanding.[3]

Reading speeds: how long does it take to read a text?

Not allowing enough time to read a text can be fatal to understanding. Often students have an over-optimistic view of how long it takes to read and understand an article or prescribed reading from a book. This means that they rarely get to a point of understanding which allows them to get the most out of the text they are reading. If you only allow 30 minutes to read an article that takes two hours to read properly you are setting up the conditions for your own failure. In order that you make sensible decisions about how much time to allow for reading you need to have an awareness of your standard reading speed.

Even fast readers can be slowed down by complex ideas and unfamiliar technical vocabulary. To get an indication of your academic reading speed, complete Activity 17.1: Finding your reading speed.

Increasing reading speeds

There are various ways in which you can increase your reading speeds, and just the fact that you are expected to read a lot when studying law will result in a steady increase in your reading skills as you gain more dexterity in your academic reading. However never sacrifice the content of what you are reading to increase your reading speed.

---

3   There are many strategies for actually making notes that we will consider in Chapter 18.

Activity 17.1: How to find out your reading speed for an academic text

This activity allows you to get a rough idea of your reading speed. It does this by guiding you through the reading of a self-chosen academic text (it could be a textbook or an article in an academic journal).

1. GENERAL INSTRUCTIONS

(1) Choose any academic book, law set textbook or academic journal article.
(2) Select any 4,500 word section (about 9 pages of single spaced text) about a topic that you are NOT familiar with.
(3) Using a 'post-it sticker' or some other device divide your 4,500 section into three 1,500 word sets, set 1, set 2 and set 3.

2. READING TASK INSTRUCTIONS (TO BE COMPLETED USING THE 3 SETS IN YOUR PRE-CHOSEN TEXT

(1) SET 1: Engage in a detailed reading without making notes. Note the start and finish time.
(2) SET 2: Engage in a detailed reading making notes. Note the start and finish time.
(3) SET 3: Skim read without notes to get a general sense of what is being said. Note the start and finish time.

3. WORKING OUT READING SPEEDS

(1) Standard calculation: Divide the *words read* by the *number of minutes taken to read* them.
Illustration: If it took you 5 minutes to read 1,500 words *without* note taking then
$1,500 \div 5 = 300$.
Therefore your reading speed is 300 words a minute (wpm).
(2) You now have all the necessary information to work out your reading speed for different tasks in 2.(1) – (3) above, that is, for a:
  (a) Detailed academic reading without note taking.
  (b) Detailed academic reading with note taking.
  (c) A 'quick' skim read for general sense without note taking.
(3) Finding your standard non-academic reading speed: **If you would like to find out your non-academic reading speed** repeat the reading exercise with fiction, non-fiction, media content, online and/or in print, using whatever is your normal reading strategy with one set of 1,500 words. The same formula applies for working out reading speed: words read divided by minutes taken to read.

4. WORKING OUT YOUR PREDICTED READING TIME FOR A TEXT

(1) Using the formula, and your knowledge of your reading speeds for different types of reading you can work out your predicted reading time for a text by noting its word count and the way in which you will be reading it.
(2) Predicting reading time when preparing for upcoming assessments is essential for planning the total time you need to finalise your assessment.

5. VARIABLES SLOWING READING SPEEDS

We are not machines; we do not always read at the same speed. Our environment or our current concerns can interfere with our ability to read efficiently. All of the following variables can slow your standard academic reading speed. If you are suffering from any of them you may need to adjust predicted reading speeds when planning work as well as attempt to resolve any troubling issues:

(1) Reading is online only (this may be preferred or disliked by the reader).

(2) Reading is in print (this may be preferred or disliked by the reader).

(3) The text contains complex sentence structures requiring consideration as to meaning.

(4) Text uses unfamiliar general vocabulary.

(5) Text uses unfamiliar legal vocabulary.

(6) Text includes complex ideas that require reader consideration as to meaning before proceeding.

(7) Readers not taking a break. You need to look up for a few seconds, or have 15–30 second breaks every 10–15 minutes. Taking short breaks can keep your speed good.

(8) The reader is tired, or unwell.

(9) Reader has a disability that affects the ability to see or comprehend text on paper or online.

(10) The reader is stressed.

Your reading speed can be increased by:

■ engaging in preparation prior to reading (we will be discussing this shortly);

■ having a reading plan;

■ choosing appropriate reading methods for the purpose of the reading.

You will find it useful to repeat Activity 17.1 six months after first doing it and you will no doubt find that your reading speed has improved.

Eye fix

You could also try to increase your reading speed by taking time to consider how long your eye views the text, technically, 'fixes' on each word as you read. Research has found that although eyes do move when reading they tend to do this in discreet sections of time called a 'fix'. A 'fix' is a time when your eye is not moving. Research has furthermore been able to demonstrate that it is relatively easy for an eye to 'fix' on around five words without losing overall understanding of those words in relation to their continuing reading of the text. By this I mean that all five words are simultaneously fixed and processed. To put the idea of five words in one eye 'fix' in a more concrete context, if your total reading speed is 300 wpm the eye fix would be two seconds for five words.

To increase reading speed therefore you need to consider how to increase the number of words your eye fixes on at a time. If you are not happy with your reading speed and would like to try extending your 'eye fix' try out Activity 17.2. Do be aware that the average reading speed for an adult is 240–300 wpm. Every person is different and reading speeds vary a lot from person to person.

Activity 17.2: One method for increasing reading speeds, increasing 'eye fix'

Nos	Instructions	Demonstration as required
1	Take a page of printed text and divide it into three equal columns numbered 1–3.	**COLUMNS** **1** — Take a page of printed text / Take anything that you **2** — and divide it into three equal / find makes a good pointer **3** — columns numbered 1–3 / and attempt to read each line
2	Take anything that you find makes a good pointer, and attempt to read each line of text by allowing your eye to fall only in column 2, the middle of each of the 3 sections of words indicated by your pointer. Try to read ALL of the words in each of the column '2s' in one view, or 'fixation' as you go down the page	**COLUMNS** **1** — Take a page of printed text / Take anything that you X **2** — and divide it into three equal / find makes a good pointer ↓ **3** — columns numbered 1–3 / and attempt to read each line X
3	Now repeat this using column 1. Try to read ALL of the words in all of the column '1s' in one view, or 'fixation' as you go down the page.	**COLUMNS** **1** — Take a page of printed text / Take anything that you ↓ **2** — and divide it into three equal / find makes a good pointer X **3** — columns numbered 1–3 / and attempt to read each line X

Nos	Instructions	Demonstration as required		
4	Now repeat this using column 3. Try to read ALL of the words in all of the column '3s' in one view, or 'fixation' as you go down the page.	**COLUMNS**		
		1	2	3
		Take a page of printed text	and divide it into three equal X	columns numbered 1–3 X
		X	X	↓
5	Now using only 3 eye 'fixes' read whole text in order across the 3 columns and down to the bottom of the page. It will seem awkward at first but you will build speed as you practise reading the text that you have split into 3 columns.	**COLUMNS**		
		1	2	3
		Take a page of printed text → →	and divide it into three equal → →	columns numbered 1–3 → →
6	When step 5 feels comfortable apply the method to text that has **not** been divided into 3 columns continuing to use only 3 eye fixes per line.	Take a page of printed text and divide it length ways into three equal columns numbered 1–3. Take anything that you find makes a good pointer, and attempt to read each line of text by allowing your eye to fall only in column 2, the middle of each of the three sections of words.		
7	When step 6 feels comfortable reduce the fixations to 2 per line. (An imaginary 2 columns rather than 3). You may need to begin by diving into columns.	**COLUMNS**		
		1		2
		Take a page of printed text and divide it into		three equal columns numbered 1–3.
		Take anything that you find makes a good		pointer, and attempt to read each line of text by
8	**When instruction 7 is a habit you will find that your reading time increases without any loss of efficiency.**			

Having now considered the three approaches to reading and the issue of reading speed we will now look at a strategy for efficient reading.

The four stages of reading: a strategy for efficient reading

It is useful to approach your university reading tasks by splitting each reading task into four main stages which together form a 'reading strategy'.

There are four main stages to any reading enterprise:

(1)   Preparation (prior to reading).
(2)   Choosing your reading method(s).
(3)   Understanding what you have read.
(4)   Critically evaluating your reading.

These are deceptively easy stages to set out but each stage can be challenging at the outset. Each of these four main stages can be further subdivided into sub-stages. For example 'preparation for reading' can be split into the sub-stages of 'reader intention' and 'text prediction'.

Understanding each of the main stages of reading, and their interconnection, is key to being able to effectively use the reading strategy. Table 17.1 sets out the four stage reading strategy showing each category's sub-stage. Consider it carefully as it provides the blueprint for you to follow when reading texts. We will be applying this reading strategy to the reading of an academic article in the next section of this chapter.

TABLE 17.1 A STRATEGY FOR COMPETENT READING			
STAGE 1 **Preparation prior to reading**	**STAGE 2** **Methods of reading** Note: Different reading purposes may require different reading techniques	**STAGE 3** **Understanding what is being read**	**STAGE 4** **Evaluating what you are reading**
Instructions	**Instructions**	**Instructions**	**Instructions**
1. **Reader goal(s)/ intention(s):** (1) What is my purpose in reading this text? (2) What do I want to get out of this text?	Note: Different reading purposes require different reading techniques. **1. Skimming:** Initially read very quickly and generally through text considering:	1. **Guessing words that you do not know:** (1) Do not expect to know all the words read. Even as a more extensive vocabulary is acquired, there will be words that are not known.	1. **Ascertaining the purpose of the writer:** This is crucial: (1) Are they discussing a specific problem? (2) Proposing a solution to a problem. (3) Comparing and contrasting ideas.

	(1) Publication date, gives a context and can indicate it is out of date! (2) The headings in the article, or chapter titles if a book. (3) Foreword, if any. (4) Abstract if an article or report. (5) Author details. (6) The introductory and concluding paragraphs of article/chapter.	(2) At this stage you can try guessing the meaning of words by identifying affixes and stems of words (see Chapter 18).	(4) Speaking of the present, future or past. (5) Does the writer want to inform or persuade you? Often a writer will seek to both inform and persuade.
2. Reader prediction of use and content of text: (1) What does the title of text suggest? (2) Choosing a text involves prediction that the text is relevant; that it will begin to answer some of the questions that you have in your mind.	**2. Scanning:** Often a secondary strategy (1) This activity assists in deciding the potential relevance of the text. (2) Unlike the general skim through, scanning involves quickly looking for specific words, phrases or information.	**2. Identifying ideas/ arguments:** (1) Main ideas will have been discovered in reading. (2) Return to the arguments in the text, re-check you have identified all the main arguments and evidences. Your understanding will now increase. (3) Careful reading here will identify secondary arguments.	**2. Evaluating the writer's arguments:** (1) Note how arguments are put together: Are points made backed up by reference to evidence? Or are they left to stand alone without evidence?

TABLE 17.1—continued			
	3. A detailed reading: (1) Identify primary and secondary arguments. (2) Classify the type of language used as figurative; journalistic; academic; etc. (3) Find out the meanings of unfamiliar words and phrases. Write a list of these and their meanings.	**3. Identifying overall text organisation:** How has the writer classified and structured the work?	**3. What do YOU think?** (1) Is the article well written? (2) Are the arguments plausible? (3) Are the arguments strong/weak?

As previously stated each of the four stages of the reading strategy is interconnected. This activity aims to develop your confidence in using the reading strategy to competently read an academic article.

Activity 17.3: Reading exercise designed to allow you to use the reading strategy when reading an academic article: JJ Weiler 'The European Union belongs to its citizens: Three immodest proposals' (1997) 22 EL Rev 150–156

Purpose for reading the article:

This article is being read in order to allow you use the reading strategy and to gain an appreciation of the range of skills that come together in its use to enable you to effectively and efficiently read an academic text.

Instructions:

1. Ensure that you have taken the time to properly consider and understand the four stage reading plan set out in Table 17.1. To assist you further Figure 17.1 gives a brief diagrammatic layout of the reading strategy.

2. Following the questions and instructions laid out in each of the four stages of the reading plan, read the article JJ Weiler 'The European Union belongs to its citizens: Three Immodest

Proposals' (1997) 22 *EL Rev* 150–156. It can be **located** online from Westlaw, or in print if your library holds the *European Law Review*.

Make careful, legible notes in answer to these questions/instructions. Make sure you use the same headings and make notes under each stage and sub-stage.

3. After you have completed your notes turn to the 'Guided demonstration of the reading strategy for JJ Weiler 'The European Union belongs to its Citizens'. You will find that guided demonstration contains extended discussion of language issues to assist you to learn about figurative language and the way in which words are constructed.

    Carefully read through it checking your notes against each of the stages and sub-stages, asking yourself as you finalise each new section the following questions:

(1) Are there omissions from my notes in any of the four stages or their sub-stages when they are compared with the demonstration? The text in blue particularly highlights what you should have in your notes.

(2) If there are omissions why are there omissions? Return to the article to resolve your gaps.

GUIDED DEMONSTRATION OF THE READING STRATEGY FOR JJ WEILER 'THE EUROPEAN UNION BELONGS TO ITS CITIZENS'

You will find commentary on each stage and sub-stage of the reading strategy below. Blue text gives a suggested answer to the questions asked, and you can check your notes against this to see if you located all of the necessary issues.

In some stages additional explanatory text is added to assist you to deal with and understand reading figurative language or guessing words.

Stage 1: Preparation prior to reading

Reader goal(s)/intention(s)

What do I want to get out of this text?

First, you need identify your reading goal(s) which can be most easily ascertained by asking a few questions. For example 'Why am I reading this text?' You may think that this is a ridiculous question to ask. Yet if you are consciously aware of your specific purpose in reading the text you will not become distracted by matters that are irrelevant to your purpose. In your studies you will read many texts, and for each one you need to know if you have to read in detail or just skim or scan to see if all or part of the text is relevant.

It is always important to decide why you are reading the text. Is it for background or core relevant material? Are there particular questions you hope it will answer? When you carefully think about what you are about to read it assists you to make the best use of the text.

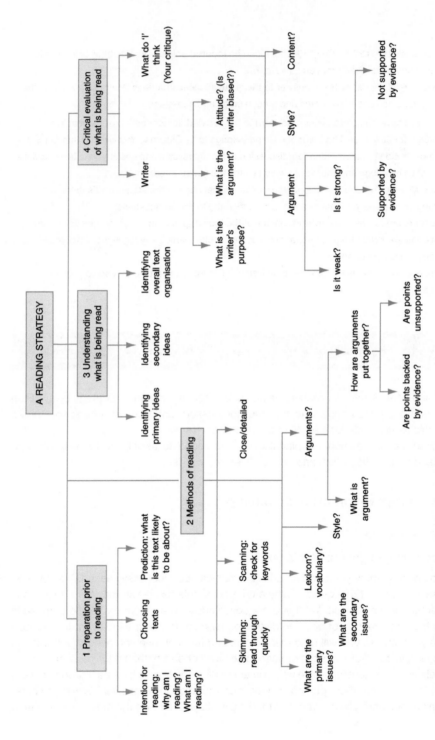

Figure 17.1 Interconnection between the four stages of reading

What do you want to get out of the text?

An appreciation of the range of skills that come together to assist you to understand the text.

Reader prediction of use and content of text

What does the title of the article suggest?

Next ask yourself, what does the title of my reading suggest? When you are trying to decide what to read as you are conducting your research, the title of the article itself is often useful. 'The EU Belongs to its Citizens, Three Immodest Proposals'; what does this title suggest to you?

What does the title of the article suggest? The title makes clear the article is about the European Union and it states that it 'belongs to its citizens'. So we note that the EU has citizens. Following directly on from this is the last phrase of the title, 'three immodest proposals'. The implication given is that EU does not belong to its citizens but that these three proposals, if put into action, could change that.

The author intends you to read the last phrase of the title as a deliberate 'play on words'. Usually, people will argue that they are only suggesting modest, small changes. This author is being controversial and states that he is putting forward 'three *immodest* proposals'. Immodest suggests they are outrageous or unacceptable to most modest people. The first part of the title 'the EU belongs to its citizens' sounds like a political slogan, a call to arms maybe. So the article, from its title, seems to be making the power of the EU citizen a contentious matter asking why the EU does not belong to its citizens, and suggesting proposals relating to the concept of coming closer to the reality of the EU belonging to its citizens.

Did you pick up on the unusual usage of 'immodest'? Or did you ignore the word and just read the title as 'three proposals . . .'? Picking up on various cues is an important aspect of understanding the text.

The 'preparatory' first stage is now completed.

Stage 2: Methods of reading

Different reading tasks require different methods of reading, which is why it is essential to know your 'reading intention' before beginning to read.

Skimming

This requires reading quickly through the article noting:

(1)   Publication date, this can often give a context for the article or suggest it is out of date!
(2)   Reading any headings.
(3)   Foreword, if any.
(4)   Abstract if an article or report.
(5)   Author details.
(6)   Reading the introductory and concluding paragraphs of the article.

(1) Publication date

The date of publication is 1997 and this immediately gives a context to the article in that today, you are reading it many years after the article was written. Changes may have occurred in that time. What do you know, if anything, about the EU now, and/or the EU in 1997? This can give valuable context to your reading. If you do not know, do not worry. You cannot know everything. These questions are intended to demonstrate once more how information and ideas are interconnected. An important treaty, Maastricht in 1997, introduced the European Union as an entity alongside what was then the European Community; the treaty also introduced the idea of citizens of member states being additionally citizens of the EU.

(2) Heading(s) and sub-heading(s)

The header(s) give clues as to the structure and content of the article.
The article is divided into four sections:

(1)   Introduction.
(2)   Proposal 1: the European Legislative Ballot.
(3)   Proposal 2: Lexcalibur – the European Public Square.
(4)   Proposal 3: limits to growth.

These headers give us the issues around the three immodest proposals and it is to be assumed that the introduction gives an overview of them, and the rationale for suggesting them.

(3) Author details

Author details are important: you need to know if you are reading a legal academic, or an academic from another discipline, whether the author is well known, if they are an academic or professional lawyer or a professional in another area, or a politician. You also want to know their job and location. All of this information can add credibility to an author making it more likely that they will be carefully attended to. You need to use the best evidence to support arguments you may make in your assessed work so you must be sure of the credentials of your author.

Author Details:

Name: J.H.H Weiler.
Title: Professor of Law and Jean Monnet Chair, Harvard University.
Job: Co-director, Academy of European Law, European University Institute Florence.

If you were studying the EU you would know that the 'Jean Monnet' in the Professorship title of J.H.H. Weiler, was one of the original architects of the European Community in 1957. The institution giving the professorship is Harvard, a prestigious American university with a renowned law school. Weiler's specific job is co-director of the Academy of European law in Florence. The author's job and title add weight to the potential authority of the argument to be set out in the article.

(4) Reading the introductory and concluding paragraphs of article

The introduction

What does a *skim read* of the introduction tell you? It is only eight paragraphs long. But the introduction is often one of the most important aspects of the text for a legal researcher. This is usually where the author gives the map of their argument. Many academic journals provide an abstract summarising the articles included which greatly assists in determining their potential relevance. Often it is enough for a skim to just read a few sentences in each of the paragraphs in an introduction. But as this article has only an eight paragraph introduction we will deal with all of it.

Activity 17.4: Reading the whole of the introduction in our article

If you did not read all of the introduction when making your notes read them now and note in précis the key point or points that each is stating.

Our skim read of the introduction notes the following

Para 1	Asks the reader to recall days of the Maastricht Treaty. Notes who was for and who against and raises doubts about understanding.
Para 2	Talks of: - street reaction relating back to title; - disempowerment of the individual European citizen.
Para 3	Gives three 'roots' of disempowerment: (i) democratic deficit;
Para 4	states second root. (ii) ever-increasing remoteness, opaqueness and inaccessibility of European governance;
Para 5	third root: (iii) competencies of the Union.
Para 6	One sentence: don't be surprised by the alienation.
Para 7	Says proposals of IGC 'very modest', with those who gain being governments, and consumers losing out.
Para 8	Says the author will give three proposals that can make a difference without a political fuss.

The three proposals:
- proposal 1: the European Legislative Ballot;
- proposal 2: Lexcalibur - the European Public Square;
- proposal 3: limits to growth.

This activity should have helped you to decide on the potential relevance of the text if that was the question in your mind for assessment purposes or seminar preparation.

Scanning

Unlike a general skim through, scanning involves quickly looking for specific words, phrases or information. This approach is useful for checking the potential relevance of any research materials retrieved for any academic task.

A detailed reading

A detailed reading will allow you to begin to identify primary and secondary or subsidiary arguments properly in the text. You should expect your detailed reading to be slower and more careful. Do make sure that you check out unfamiliar vocabulary. Some words and phrases will become clearer as more text is read. In our article, you might question:

(1)   The word 'Lexcalibur'. What does it mean? Where does it come from?

(2)   The phrase 'the European public square'. What does it mean?

Neither the word 'Lexcalibur' nor the phrase 'the European Public Square' can be found in a dictionary. However, their meanings unfold as you read the article.

Language used

The writer uses short sentences, slogans, rhetorical questions, and figurative language. He also invents words. For example, Lexcalibur.

Figurative language

One of the most frequently used language strategies in the article is that of figurative language, a poetic device in writing. It is generally assumed to be most used in literature or persuasive genres of writing outside the law. Because of its appeal to emotions it is maintained that figurative language is not used in the law, but in fact it is often used in legal texts and legal judgments in cases (it is not found in legislation). Before we go further and discuss the specific manifestations of figurative language in the article (which is in the form of alliteration and metaphor) please ensure you understand the basic meaning of figurative language and its main forms by looking at Table 17.2.

TABLE 17.2 THE MEANING OF FIGURATIVE LANGUAGE GENERALLY AND ITS MAIN FORMS: DESCRIPTIONS AND EXAMPLES	
Figurative language – General	**Description** Figurative language is the collective term for linguistic forms that describe one thing in terms of something else. Example: *The cakes were iced in many colours and looked like a rainbow.* The various forms of figurative language are outlined below.
FORMS OF FIGURATIVE LANGUAGE	**DESCRIPTION**
Alliteration	This is the repetition of the same initial letter, sound(s) or group of sounds, or repetition of a series words. Example: *I came, I saw, I conquered/You are fabulous, funny and fiery.*
Clichés	A cliché is a phrase commonly used as an expression that is so well used and known it is considered to be almost trite. Example: Time is money.
Hyperbole	This is a form of extreme exaggeration that is purely a matter of fantasy and used for emphasis: Example: *She was so hungry she said she could eat a horse.*

TABLE 17.2—continued	
Metaphor	Metaphor compares one thing with another either for emphasis or explanation or to describe the unknown by means of the known. The figure of speech in which a name or descriptive term is transferred to another object to which it is not properly applicable.[4] 'metaphor is that figure of speech whereby we speak about one thing in terms which are seen to be suggestive of another'[5] Soskice (1989:15). Example: *The kitchen was a war zone.*
Onomatopoeia	A word that when pronounced naturally produces a sound that is the object or action labelled by the word. Example: *Bubble*
Personification	This figure of speech has several meanings (1) As a perfect example of something e.g. John is the personification of an athlete. (2) Representing the abstract in humanity. (3) Applying human characteristics to animals or inanimate objects/concepts. *Example: 1. I love my car and she loves me, isn't she beautiful.* *Example: 2. The wind whispered through the trees.*
Simile	A simile uses the words 'like' or 'as' to compare one object or idea with another to suggest they are alike. Example: busy as a bee

Metaphor

The transference role of metaphor is deliberately intended to provide a means of describing the other object in novel terms. A more colloquial explanation of the functions of metaphor is as a poetic device to explore new ground by:

(1)   Giving a new perspective on something known.
(2)   Describing something that is not familiar, unknown, by applying to it a description from another thing that is familiar, known.
(3)   Extending the meaning attributable to a known thing.
(4)   Explaining problematic situations through the process of comparing them or describing them in relation to familiar situations.

---

4   GWS Friedrichsen, *The Shorter Oxford English Dictionary on Historical Principles* (3rd edn, Clarendon Press, 1973 (completely revised)) Vol 11, 1315.
5   J Soskice *Metaphors and Religious Language* (Oxford, Clarendon Press, 1987), 198, 15.

Legal texts always deny a place to passion and poetic language, seeking only to communicate the logical rational structured argument and explanation. But the ability of metaphor to be used to explore new ground is used frequently in legal texts. So it has an important function in texts where it is said not to have a legitimate place. Metaphor can be used to explain problematic situations by comparing them, or describing them, in relation to familiar situations.

Metaphor creates spaces for the imagination, and in these spaces, analogy occurs.[6] As we have already seen the core of legal reasoning is analogous reasoning, so perhaps this explains why metaphor may be found quite often in legal texts.

This signals the practical quality of metaphor as an aspect of language usage, but also signals its importance in the realm of understanding and interpretation. It is essential for you to understand that the use of metaphor by a writer, or indeed a speaker, always seeks to compel you, the listener, or the reader, to collude with the speaker/writer in the conveyance of sense via poetic language rather than the use of literal language.

A clear method of conceptual structuring can occur in the use of geographic or orientational metaphors (e.g. journeying) and, most usefully for you as you start the process of learning to interpret metaphors, tend to be culture-bound and therefore when you see, locate and interpret them often you gain valuable information about the prejudices of the writer.

Metaphoric themes can emerge by looking at several metaphors used by the writer in the text. For example if a dispute is referred to metaphorically as a 'war', then warring imagery may be randomly referred to recalling the fullness of the original use of the metaphor. If we 'buy in' to this interpretation we see the dispute as war, with all that war connotes. So we do not see it as a friendly disagreement, or even as a skirmish: no, we only see it in terms of a war.

Concentrating solely on reading for the moment a writer can first set up a metaphor in its full sense and then merely by making a passing reference to it later in the text, recall to the reader the immediacy and context of the full metaphor from its first use. Or a writer can extend or amplify their original use of a particular metaphor by referring to it in terms of a second metaphor. Here the reader will feel that the mere repetition has given weight to the idea carried by the first metaphor. Yet there is no actual increase in evidence for the proposition being forwarded. Just an increase of poetic language.

By choosing the initial metaphoric connection the writer launches their chosen metaphor from its normal source domain (war) to a pre-chosen target domain (kitchen). Noticing such choices can lead the reader to form an opinion about writer preference or bias.

How does metaphor work – the source domain and the target domain of a metaphor

So we have a process in which we could say that there is a source domain of descriptions/labels that the author believes that all readers will understand, a source domain that can be drawn on.

---

6   See G. Lakoff & M. Johnson, *Metaphors we live by* (1980 Chicago University of Chicago Press); J. Milbank, *Theology and Social theory*, (1990 Oxford, Blackwell. Oxford University Press); B.L Whorf *Language, thought, reality*, (1956 Massachusetts, M.I.T. Press).

Alliteration

One example sentence using alliteration is used below:

E.g. '. . . they are a mean, merciless, materialistic, money grabbing lot of people'.

As a figurative device it can be used together with metaphor. For example in the above sentence 'they' are described as money grabbers.

Example of the identification and interpretation of figurative language (alliteration, repetition and metaphor)

The following quotation in figurative language, Example 1, is taken from the summing up of Lord Justice Comyn in the defamation case of *Orme v Associated Daily Newspapers Group, inc.*[7] Although a short piece it demonstrates the use of metaphor, alliteration and repetition. The case was brought by the UK leader of an international religious group, the Unification church (often referred to pejoratively as Moonies) against the *Daily Mail* newspaper for serious allegations of malpractice in terms of recruitment of members for the group. Orme alleged that these allegations by implication would lower his reputation in the eyes of right thinking members of society because he was its leader.

The case was a civil case; however the plaintiff Orme has exercised a little known right to ask for a civil trial by jury. At the end of several months of hearing the judge began his summing up to the jury by saying:

'The defendants, the newspaper, say that these people the Moonies are no Church, they are not Christians; they are a mean, merciless, materialistic, money grabbing lot of people. Worse still, they capture and exploit young people. In attracting *them they use deceit*. When *they have them they use deceit*. To the outside world *they use deceit*. It all puts me in mind of that old nursery rhyme: "Come into the parlour said the spider to the fly". That is what the *Daily Mail* says about them; they are evil and wicked and must be stamped out.'[8]

This passage is set out below in Example 17.1 indicating alliteration (in bold black font), repetition (boxed) and metaphor (underlined).

EXAMPLE 17.1: THE SPIDER AND THE FLY

The defendants, the newspaper, say that these people the Moonies are no Church, they are not Christians; they are a **mean, merciless, materialistic, money** grabbing lot of people. Worse still, **they capture** and exploit **young people**. In attracting them *they use deceit*. When they have them *they use deceit*. To the outside world *they use deceit*. It all puts me in mind of that old nursery rhyme: **'Come into the parlour said the spider to the fly'**. That is what the Daily Mail says about them; they are evil and wicked and must be **stamped out**.[9]

---

7   *Orme v Associated Newspapers Group, Inc*. (1981) Transcript: Association of Official Shorthand Writers Ltd (TAOSW). Summing up 26–31 March.
8   (TAOSW 1981: 3–4).
9   Ibid.

mean, merciless, materialistic, money grabbing
In attracting them *they use deceit*.
When they have them *they use deceit*.
To the outside world *they use deceit*.

**Come into the parlour said the spider to the fly
stamped out**

Identification is the beginning of analysis, as we want to interpret the use of these metaphors in the text. We will do this by considering a few examples from the main text in Example 17.1. Example 17.2 just shows the metaphor of the spider and the fly and the notion of being stamped out, together with an explanation of what may be intended.

EXAMPLE 17.2: 'THE SPIDER AND THE FLY'

Verbatim metaphor from text	Explanation with interpretation
'Come into the parlour said the spider to the fly'.	This well-known story, contained in a children's nursery rhyme, has a spider saying to a fly 'come into my parlour', that parlour is sticky and the fly stuck fast becomes food for the spider. As used in context the metaphor casts the 'church' as the spider and the young person as the fly. This carries a memorable message that the church entraps the innocent and unwary.
That is what the *Daily Mail* says about them; they are evil and wicked and must be stamped out.[10]	Here the allusion is continued by the word 'stamps'. The church should be stamped out; as one would perhaps stamp on an insect – a spider for example.

The text in Example 17.3 is also drawn from the original text, in Example 17.3.

EXAMPLE 17.3: 'THE SPIDER AND THE FLY'; DEMONSTRATING ALLITERATION AND REPETITION

ALLITERATION

Verbatim quotation containing alliteration	Interpretation of the text
they are a	A list of negative labels for the plaintiffs, all
mean,	beginning with 'm'. Each emotional phrase

10 (TAOSW 1981: 3–4).

EXAMPLE 17.3—continued	
merciless, materialistic, money grabbing lot of people.	adds its weight to the one before. Seemingly increasingly the evidence is that this is what they are. But there is no increase of evidence, only a poetic increase of accusations.
REPETITION	
Verbatim quotation containing repetition	Interpretation of the text
In attracting them *they use deceit*. When they have them *they use deceit*. To the outside world *they use deceit*.	Repetition joined to alliteration gives an impression of evidence being increased in favour of statement. But it is just poetic thickening.

Joining Examples 17.2 and 17.3 we can see the effect of all of the figurative language in the extract in Example 17.1

EXAMPLE 17.4: THE SPIDER AND THE FLY – VERSION 2: THE ENTIRE TEXT EXTRACTED AND ANNOTATED			
Verbatim text	**Metaphor**	**Alliteration**	**Repetition**
'The defendants . . . say that . . . the Moonies are a . . . **mean, merciless, materialistic, money** grabbing lot of people.		mean, merciless, materialistic, money grabbing	
Worse still they **capture** and exploit young people.	capture		
In attracting them *they use deceit*. When they have them *they use deceit*. To the outside world *they use deceit*.		*d*eceit. *d*eceit. *d*eceit.	they use *deceit*. they use *deceit*. they use *deceit*.
It all puts me in mind of that old nursery rhyme. **[Come into the parlour said the spider to the fly']**.	**Come into the parlour said the spider to the fly'.**		
That is what the *Daily Mail* says about them; they are evil and wicked and must be **stamped out**.	stamped out		evil and wicked (through the use of synonyms).

Hopefully this has given you a good idea of how to deal with figurative language. So turning back to the article we can look at metaphor use.

Metaphors in the article 'The European Union belongs to its citizens'

Did you note the use of metaphors in your read-through of the introduction and the last lines of the end of the article? All too often readers ignore metaphors. But they can provide a useful 'other' reading for the interpretation of the article, and insight into the author's intention. They are not used by accident; they are chosen and deliberately used by the author.

Often readers do not follow the signposts to an argument that are located in the use of figurative language. They miss clues and connections because they are expressed in figurative language. They certainly do not take the opportunity to question the argument that is being formed, in part, by poetic language. They just ignore the poetic as if it provides no function at all. But if it did not have any function why would the author have used it?

Activity 17.4 will assist your understanding of metaphor by guiding you through a few answered questions about this metaphor found in the last sentence of the article 'the proof of the pudding is in the eating'.

Activity 17.4: Beginning to read and understand metaphors Deciphering 'The proof of the pudding is in the eating'

What is the source domain of the metaphor?	It is cooking. More precisely cooking pudding. This is an allusion to the proverb 'the proof of the pudding will be in the eating'. Proof as used there relates to the fact whatever is said about the pudding in terms of its excellence this is only proved by eating it and from that experience agreeing or disagreeing that it is excellent.
What is the target domain of the metaphor?	The target domain is the EU and the Intergovernmental Council's (IGC's) view on EU citizens.
What does the metaphor mean? What is the message that you the reader get from the metaphor?	The message is that no one will be able to prove the truth of the assertion of the IGC that 'the EU belongs to its citizens' until EU citizens take action and their viewpoint is taken into account. For that will indeed prove that the EU does indeed belong to its citizens.

Take a look at the breakdown of figurative language noted more widely in this article in Figure 17.2.

Political imagery	The Mandarins heralded
Mathematical imagery	'What's-in-it-for-me?' calculus
Architectural/geological	Shaky foundation
Nature imagery	Roots of disempowerment
Scientific imagery	The specific gravity of whom continues to decline
Nature imagery	The second root goes even deeper
Religious imagery	An apocryphal statement
Food imagery	It is End of Millennium Bread and Circus Governance
Elemental imagery	Could be shielded behind firewalls
Grand teleological style	Ours is a vision which tries to enhance human sovereignty, demystify technology and place it firmly as servant and not master
Food imagery	■ The European Court of Justice should welcome having this hot potato removed from its plate ■ The proof of the pudding will be in the eating

Figure 17.2 Examples of figurative language

Connecting and joining words/phrases

When reading be on the lookout for the following words and phrases that are used to hold together argument, indicate conclusions and also movement from one point to another in a text:

Activity 17.6: Being aware of cohesive and connecting words and phrases

Another	Incidentally	Smith's conclusion is dependent upon . . .
Another assumption	New work has claimed	While
But the evidence to date suggests	Now	The third postulate
Even though	On the other hand	There has been little support for the view that . . .
For example	One assumption	Therefore
However	Recent research has suggested	Thus
In reality	Research has demonstrated	Which

Stage 3: Understanding what is being read

There are a number of stages to work through to increase your understanding of the text, including:

Guessing words/phrases you do not know

Do not expect to know all the words you read. Even as a more extensive vocabulary is acquired, there will be words that are unfamiliar. You have been referred to the word Lexcalibur already. It is an invented word which signals both law in the use of 'lex' and the literary reference to the mystery that is King Arthur and his legendary sword, 'Excalibur'. It is co-joined to democratic 'deficit', 'competencies of the Union', 'specific gravity' and 'apocryphal statement'. Is he suggesting that law, as a sword, cuts through enemies, installing the good? This invented word is also functioning as metaphor.

The meaning of words can be guessed and double-checked in a dictionary but remember that unusual combinations of words may bring with them meanings not caught in a dictionary. Here informed guesses followed by plausible interpretation may be all you have to go on.

Guessing words by understanding the construction of English words (affixes)

You may have noticed that many words share the same parts. If you begin to understand how English words are constructed from different parts you can use this to make good guesses at unknown words. English words are made up of a changing combination of standard parts known as prefixes, suffices and word stems.

PREFIX + WORD STEM + SUFFIX = ENGLISH WORD

Many affixes are from other languages, particularly Latin. So if you can learn the Latin meaning of these Latin affixes you can have a good guess at the word. Table 17.4 sets outs standard prefixes and suffixes derived from other languages with their meanings, and Table 17.5 gives an indication of standard word stems and their meaning.

TABLE 17.3 THE CONSTITUENT PARTS OF ENGLISH WORDS

Word stem	Many English words share the **word stem**. The specific nature of the word is changed by adding a prefix or a suffix to that **word stem**.		
Affixes	The general term for prefixes and suffixes.		
Prefixes	These are letters attached before a word stem.		
Suffixes	These are letters attached after a word stem.		
EXAMPLE			
WORD	**PREFIX**	**STEM**	**SUFFIX**
Presupposing	pre	suppose	ing

TABLE 17.4 ENGLISH AFFIXES DERIVED FROM OTHER LANGUAGES (MAINLY LATIN, GREEK AND FRENCH) AND USED TO CONSTRUCT ENGLISH WORDS

PREFIX	TRANSLATION
ad-	to, towards
ante-	before
anti-	against
bi-	two
co, col, com, con-	with, or together
de-	away from
dis-	take away, not, deprive
em/en-	in, into
inter-	between
il-, im-, in-, ir-	not
syn-, sy-	same, together, similarly, like
SUFFIXES	**TRANSLATION**
-able, -ible,	can do, able
-al, -ical, -ial,	belonging to
-ation	state of, act
-ant	with force
-est	the more
-ist	one who does
-fy	to make, to form
-ment	concrete, thing
-ous	full of
-y	state of being
-able, -ible,	can do, able
-al, -ical, -ial,	belonging to

Try to answer the following questions in Table 17.5 about affixes with the information that you have been given. If you look at the above lists of prefixes and suffixes you will be able to answer these questions after further reading.

You can see from this short discussion that knowledge of affixes and stems will make it possible for you to understand an increasing number of English words.

TABLE 17.5 ILLUSTRATES HOW THE WORD STEM, THE CORE OF THE WORD, IS ALSO IN MANY CASES DERIVED FROM OTHER LANGUAGES.

Table 17.5: Stem words: derived from other languages (mainly Latin, Greek and French) and used to construct English words

Stem	English meaning
auto	self
bio	life
demo	people
geo	earth
homo	same
hyper	extra
judic	law
mis/mit	to send
mort	death

Words can be made up of several stems and affixes: e.g.

Stem Stem Stem Suffix

Autobiography = auto + bio + graph + y

self + life + write + state of being

TABLE 17.6 USING TRANSLATIONS OF AFFIXES TO GUESS AT THE MEANINGS OF WORDS

Legal means belonging to, or of, the law

Question

(1)   What type of affix is used to make the word **illegal**?
(2)   Give the affix.
(3)   Translate the meaning of the affix.
(4)   What does illegal mean?

(1)   What type of affix is used to make the word **legalist**?
(2)   Give the affix.
(3)   Translate the meaning of the affix.
(4)   What does **legalist** mean?

Relevant means 'having direct bearing on the matter in hand'

Question

(1)   What type of affix is used to make the word **irrelevant**?
(2)   Give the affix.
(3)   Translate the meaning of the affix.
(4)   What does **irrelevant** mean?

Identifying ideas/arguments

The main idea in the article is that a package of three proposals (a limited ballot by citizens concerning legislation, internet access to European decision making and establishment of a constitutional council), taken from research, initiated by the European Parliament, can make a real difference in increasing the power of the European citizen without creating a political drama.

Identifying the main argument

The argument presented by the author in this article has been divided into propositions (assertions, or statements building the argument) and the evidence supporting them, as outlined below. The first job when you approach the article is to look for the main propositions building argument, and then identify the supporting evidence for it, if there is any. At this point it is essential to note that many readers do not differentiate between proposition and evidence. This is a major error and leads to confusion and misunderstanding. A proposition is a statement being put forward. Strong propositions are given their strength by the evidence supporting them. A weak argument has no or little evidence. Therefore you must always differentiate between the two as indicated by Table 17.7.

TABLE 17.7 THE EVIDENCE SUPPORTING PROPOSITIONS 1–3 FORWARDED BY WEILER AND THE CONCLUSION DRAWN

PROPOSITION	EVIDENCE	CONCLUSION
1. Proposition 1, (para. 2) The Maastricht Treaty was not the remarkable diplomatic achievement it was claimed to be.	**Evidence:** street reaction apathetic, confused, hostile, fearful: (i) Danes voted against it; (ii) French approved it marginally (1 per cent); (iii) commentators at the time said that if there had been greater scrutiny in Great Britain and Germany the outcome would have been uncertain; (iv) those supporting it were just plain greedy.	A package of three proposals taken from research initiated by the European Parliament, dealing with the issues of democratic deficit, remoteness and the competencies of the union can make a real difference in increasing the power of the European citizen without creating a political drama.
2. Proposition 2, (para 3) There was a 'growing disillusionment with the European construct as a whole'.	**Evidence:** None given.	

PROPOSITION	EVIDENCE	CONCLUSION
3. **Proposition 3, located in paragraph 3:** The *'moral and political legitimacy'* of the European construct is in decline.	**Evidence:** There is 'a sense of disempowerment of the European citizen' which has many roots, but three stand out: (i) democratic deficit; paragraph 4; (ii) remoteness; paragraph 5; (iii) competencies of union. paragraph 6.	
Subsidiary arguments raised		
Potential clashes between the constitutional council and the function of the European Court of Justice.		

The summary of the argument as set out in the introduction (in paragraphs 1–3) is as follows: Did you manage to get all of the points?

'The Maastricht Treaty was not the diplomatic achievement it was claimed to be. The European citizen continues to be disempowered. There remains a growing disillusionment with the European Union as a whole which is suffering from a decline in its moral and political legitimacy. However, a package of three proposals (a limited ballot by citizens concerning legislation; internet access to European decision making; establishment of a constitutional council), taken from research, initiated by the European Parliament, can make a real difference to increase the power of the European citizen without creating a political drama.'

Identifying overall text organisation

Every writer has a different way of organising, classifying and structuring their work.

Here the author has clearly indicated their structure through headings and has discussed the points in the order indicated. Overall, the writer is: discussing a specific problem; and proposing a solution to that problem.

Stage 4: Evaluating what you are reading

You must always evaluate what you are reading as you are reading it, and this requires that you:

■ ascertain the purpose of the writer. The writer wants to inform about something and/ or support a particular point of view;
■ seek the strengths and weakness in the identified argument(s).

We have already discussed the purpose of this writer. Take time now to note down your evaluation of the main arguments and conclusion of the article (if you have not done so already) and then check your note against the following suggested evaluation of strength and weakness.

How to evaluate the strength and weakness of argument presented

Having ascertained the arguments, it is up to you to decide your view of the persuasiveness of the article, the strength of the argument and the evidence put forward supporting it. Your view of the argument of the writer will initially be limited by your lack of knowledge of the issues the author speaks of. But as you conduct more research, you will learn more about competing views and the area in general. Your view of the argument may then change or develop.

Sometimes you may need far more information before you can evaluate the writer's proposals concerning problems and solutions. You may not even agree with the problem itself. If a problem has been misdiagnosed, then the solution will not work. If the problem has been correctly identified, but the wrong causes attributed then, again, the solution will not work. In any text identifying problems and putting forward solutions in argument or description formats, the following questions need to be asked:

- Is it plausible to classify these circumstances as a problem?
- Is it plausible for the author to maintain that their stated causes of the problem are correct?
- Given the view on the above two questions, is it plausible for the author to offer these solutions?
- Is the author's conclusion plausible?
- Do I agree with the conclusion to the argument?
- If I do not, how do I attack it?
- Do I agree with all of the propositions that are the building blocks in this argument? Are the propositions strong or weak?

Try answering these questions in relation to the article on the European citizen. If there is any area where you feel you have a lack of understanding, ask yourself 'why?' Are there problems with the vocabulary, or the concepts, or is there too much assumed information? What is the attitude of the writer? Writers are usually biased towards a certain view in their writing, although on occasion a writer may be neutral. You must be able to gain skill in identifying a writer's attitude to the ideas he or she is discussing. You must at least know how to objectively ascertain whether the writer is neutral or biased.

What is clear, however, is that the detail that has been given in setting out the three proposals is not matched when indicating evidence to support propositions, perhaps because the writer feels that many of his propositions are self-evident. This would be a weakness of the article if you wished to use it for academic work.

Once you understand how to identify arguments in a text and the evidences supporting them then it is possible to consider their strengths and weakness. Consider Figure 17.3 below, do you agree with the allocations of weak or strong arguments?

- Is there enough information collected to properly cover the area?
- Have all of the arguments put forward been understood?
- Is there a lack of empirical/practical evidence to support theoretical positions?

It is vital to decide whether there is enough information and this is often a subjective matter.

Having read the article, it is possible to represent the argument as shown in Figure 17.3. This is a useful method of viewing all arguments uni-dimensionally, which our brain cannot do quite so easily with text!

Evidence for an essay 'Does the European Union Belong to its Citizens?'

If you were marshalling evidence for an essay entitled 'Does the European Union Belong to its Citizens?', it would be possible to incorporate the views of Weiler, and other authors – we will call them X, Y and Z – into the essay by slotting them into your diagram, as shown in Figure 17.4. Here we have annotated in Figure 17.4 whether fictional authors of articles X, Y or Z agree or disagree with Weiler's argument and evidences. In addition, you would look in leading textbooks to see if those authors had anything to add.

Having noted the areas of agreement and disagreement between the authors on the diagram, a clear view emerges of strong and weak arguments. Then, it is possible for you to come to a personal conclusion. If you do not feel able to come to a personal conclusion, ask yourself the following questions:

A brief conclusion to the above suggested essay is given in Figure 17.5. It centres on Weiler's article and the imaginary authors X, Y, Z. It illustrates how a competent reading strategy and note/diagrams can work together to bring clarity of thought and expression.

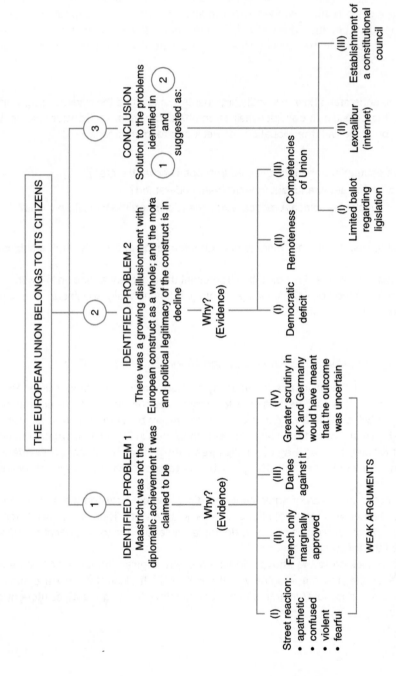

THE EUROPEAN UNION BELONGS TO ITS CITIZENS

1

IDENTIFIED PROBLEM 1
Maastricht was not the diplomatic achievement it was claimed to be

Why?
(Evidence)

(I)
Street reaction:
• apathetic
• confused
• violent
• fearful

(II)
French only marginally approved

(III)
Danes against it

(IV)
Greater scrutiny in UK and Germany would have meant that the outcome was uncertain

WEAK ARGUMENTS

2

IDENTIFIED PROBLEM 2
There was a growing disillusionment with European construct as a whole; and the mora and political legitimacy of the construct is in decline

Why?
(Evidence)

(I)
Democratic deficit

(II)
Remoteness

(III)
Competencies of Union

3

CONCLUSION
Solution to the problems identified in **1** and **2** suggested as:

(I)
Limited ballot regarding ligislation

(II)
Lexcalibur (internet)

(III)
Establishment of a constitutional council

Figure 17.3 Weiler's argument in diagrammatic form

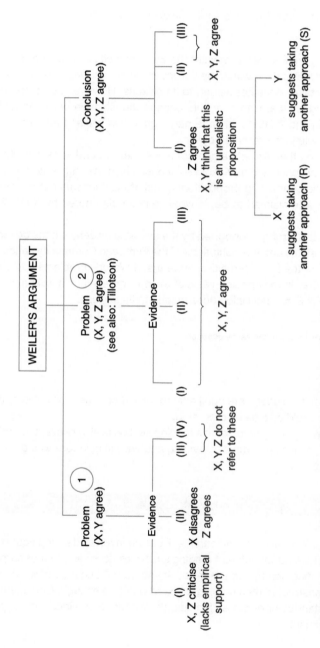

Figure 17.4 Comparing Weiler's argument with hypothetical other texts

'The European Union Belongs to its Citizens'. Discuss.

Conclusion

Weiler (1997) argues that at present the European citizen does not exert power over policy and law making within the European Union. This indicates that the European Union certainly does not belong to its citizens. However, as noted above, he convincingly argues that with very little change the situation could be rectified. X (1997), Y (1998) and Z (1998), in large part, agree with Weiler, both in terms of the problems and solutions presented by him.

It is suggested that Weller's argument is well set out and is essentially backed by supporting evidence and attainable solutions. It is further suggested that the evidence presented concerning proposition 1, that Maastricht was not the diplomatic achievement it was claimed to be, is weak, a point also noted by X (1997) and Y (1998).

Proposition 2 is strongly supported by the available evidence. If the governments of the member states and the institutions of the European Community seriously consider the issue of the European citizen in terms of Weiler's problems and solutions, it may well be that, in the opening years of the new millennium, it will be possible to maintain that the European Union does belong to its citizens.

Figure 17.5 Conclusion for a sample essay question

Textbooks are not included here but if a textbook did comment on a theory or give useful insights, these could also be incorporated.

As you may have realised much of this reading section is also relevant to understanding the processes of producing competent writing and we will now turn to a detailed consideration of writing skills.

CONCLUSION

Effective reading and writing are inseparable. Reading involves defining your purpose and acquiring the ability to adopt different reading strategies according to that purpose. Reading and understanding arguments are linked. If you do not understand what an argument is and how it is constructed then reading a text may not be enough. Consideration should be given to the standpoint of the author and the evidence provided (or not provided) to support their argument.

CHAPTER SUMMARY

■ Identify your purpose in reading texts and employ different methods of reading, scanning, skimming and detailed reading, according to your purpose.

Answer to questions posed in Table 17.6.

TABLE 17.6 USING TRANSLATIONS OF AFFIXES TO GUESS AT THE MEANINGS OF WORDS

Legal means belonging to, or of, the law

Question	Answer
1. What type of affix is used to make the word **illegal**? 2. Give the affix. 3. Translate the meaning of the affix. 4. What does illegal mean?	1. Prefix 2. il 3. not 4. Not belonging to the law which more specifically means an act that is not one that is legal.
1. What type of affix is used to make the word **legalist**? 2. Give the affix. 3. Translate the meaning of the affix. 4. What does **legalist** mean?	1. Suffix 2. ist 3. one who belongs 4. One who belongs to the law but usage has given this word an overtone of inflexibility, see standard dictionary definitions.

Relevant means 'having direct bearing on the matter in hand'.

Question	Answer
1. What type of affix is used to make the word **irrelevant**? 2. Give the affix. 3. Translate the meaning of the affix. 4. What does **irrelevant** mean.	1. prefix 2. ir 3. not 4. Not having a direct bearing on the matter in hand.

GENERAL WRITING SKILLS

18

'But words are things, and a small
drop of ink, falling like dew upon a
thought, produces that which makes
thousands, perhaps millions, think.'

Lord Byron

LEARNING OUTCOMES

After reading this chapter you should be able to:

- Explain the importance of good language skills for the study of law.
- Know how to increase your general and legal vocabulary.
- Understand the function of grammar and punctuation and know how to correctly use it.
- Begin to develop your own written voice.
- Coherently organise your writing according to purpose.

INTRODUCTION

The development of competent writing skills (appropriate use of grammar, punctuation, and vocabulary) and the development of a clear writing style cannot be overemphasised. This chapter considers strategies for competent use of language and writing usable notes from your reading or from lectures. Because of the importance of writing for law assessments, separate chapters in Part 6 'written and oral assessment' deal with writing law essays and with writing solutions to legal problem questions.

Like reading skills, writing skills can be undertaken for differing reasons. For example, you could be writing notes for your own personal use, or you could be writing an assessment.

Whatever your reason for writing you need to know how to use English grammar and punctuation appropriately. Badly written assessments can lower your grades despite the fact you are referring to acceptable sources, and setting up sound arguments backed by evidence. Sometimes badly written work obscures the argument or good idea being put forward and then you cannot get credit for them.

You need to take the time to *understand* the basic issues involved in the writing task:

- Development of your written voice.
- Learning the rules of academic writing.
- Grammar.
- Punctuation.
- Spelling.
- Use of technical language.

We will look at several of these issues in the following sections.

Developing your written voice: your writing style

For many students, finding their 'written voice' and developing their style is difficult. When you speak to others you do not have to consider how you might sound, or how you should say something, you just know. You automatically change your vocabulary, accent and tone of voice when speaking to different types of people (e.g. a close friend, an acquaintance, your family, or your lecturer). However, you may not be so accustomed to using and changing your written voice. It may be the case that you only write when you are being assessed in coursework or exams. Unlike the informality of emails, texting, instant messaging and social media, formal academic writing is a measured method of communicating, with clear rules of engagement that cover style as well as content. It has been described as a one-sided conversation with the reader. It can be difficult if you realise your writing does not sound right or you are told you need to change your style, especially if you do not understand why and how you could improve it.

Although academic writing uses formal structures and expression, you should avoid excessively formal language. Lakoff[1] identified the concept of hyper-correct language in speakers who resort to long words and archaic terms because they feel uncomfortably out of their comfort zone. The classic scenario is the witness in court who says: 'I immediately apprehended that the person was moving his arm in my direction with a clenched fist and he made contact with my left cheek towards the area of the chin, and I experienced a rush of pain. I noted that I had been the victim of a battery!' This can be most unconvincing heard orally in court and read in its written form. It is better to speak plainly and directly, 'Then the defendant punched me in the face.'

Look out for paragraphs where you are repeating phrases or ideas that you might have already used. Repetition in these circumstances suggests lack of time to properly edit your work. It is a difficult matter; how many different ways can you say 'argues' or 'states'?

If you can eradicate repetition you will make your writing more cohesive and interesting. Consider using words such as:

- for him the key issue is . . .
- she views,
- she considers that,
- they hold the view that,

as substitutions for 'argues' and 'states'. When you are comparing authors you can also note whether they agree with each other and when they do not.

Developing your written voice is exceptionally important. After all, it is the medium that will secure your degree. Take as many opportunities to engage in academic writing as possible, getting yourself used to the medium outside the assessment itself.

Activity 18.1: Finding your voice[2]

---

(1) Stop reading now; find a piece of paper and pen and start writing about anything for ten minutes, your favourite football team, your favourite celebrity etc. Do not at this point worry about style or grammar. But do use punctuation.

(2) When you have finished ***do not read*** over what you have written but put the paper to one side and keep on reading this book (or do something else).

(3) Later today or tomorrow return to the piece you have written. View it objectively, not as the writer of it. Do you consider that what you have read is well written? Evaluate your writing asking the following questions:
Are there phrases you like or dislike?
What worked and why?
What did not work and why?

---

1 R Lakoff *Language and Woman's Place* (Harper & Row, New York, 1975).
2 The idea for this exercise is taken from P Elbow *Writing with Power: Techniques for Mastering the Writing Process* (Galaxy books OUP, New York, 1981).

Activity 18.1—continued

> As you have been asked to write about anything you like with no further instruction it is likely that you will have adopted an informal style of writing. It will use abbreviations like 'didn't', 'don't', and may include street language or other colloquialisms. The 'voice' you discover will be your informal 'voice'.
>
> (4)   Keep trying this exercise until you feel comfortable with the idea of writing. You should start to find your voice.
>
> (5)   You can have more than one written voice. For academic writing you need to also develop a formal method of expressing your voice. This will not be too far removed from your informal written voice but it will need to keep to certain protocols such as not abbreviating. These protocols will be discussed later in this chapter.

One way to assess the effectiveness and quality of your writing may be to read it out aloud, so you can hear it and gain a different perspective on what you have written. You could record it and listen to it.

The requirements of formal academic language

Legal writing requires the use of formal language, but it must not be too formal. You do not want to fall into Lakoff's problem of hyper-correctness. We will run through the detail of what it means to be required to use formal language.

An objective style should be used, that does not in any shape or form refer to the person of the writer

You should avoid using the words 'I' or 'my'. This will take time to perfect but is well worth the effort. By objectifying, you in effect describe to the reader what the essay, the object, will do. The technical term for this is using the passive voice.

Instead of writing the phrase translate your phrase into objective language. This requirement to use objective language when communicating is not just about style. Whilst undergraduate students are expected to develop independent thoughts and views, in academic writing you should only express the views of those with authority (leading scholars and lawyers) on the issue. Any conclusion to your assessments needs to weigh up the academic and legal sources you have used in your argument. In terms of assessed academic writing your own views are not relevant except insofar as you state a preference for one accepted academic opinion over another. So you may give your view in objective terms by stating that 'It would seem that the views of X are supported by the evidence but the views of Y are not . . .' etc.

Gendered or gender neutral language?

You should also consider whether your writing style will be gender neutral. In the law, and often in the world at large, there is a convention that the masculine includes the feminine.[3] We are all accustomed to reading the male form as normal and it can be surprising if a writer discussing a hypothetical situation notes:

> 'Let us consider the thief, she may . . .' rather than 'Let us consider the thief, he may . . .'.

There are two schools of thought with regard to academic writing: either gendered language is discriminatory or it is not. You may choose your own style but it is worth finding out how your marker feels in case he or she is offended by gendered or gender-neutral language.

If you find language and style difficult, check to see if your university runs academic writing seminars.

Incorporating the work of others in your writing

Even when you are communicating the views of others, the language of your writing should not change. Rather than summarising each source separately and pushing it into your argument you need to consider the words used by your source and properly integrate your sources into a coherent argument. Here the value of good writtennotes is particularly important. *Your* written voice should be communicating the views of others.

Quotations must be used in a considered manner. A quoted sentence or two from a respected author may provide evidence to back up the argument you are constructing. Consider carefully whether you need to quote, and whether a referenced paraphrase of what the author has said would be better.

All too often quotations placed into the text by the writer appear haphazard and hang awkwardly in the text, serving no purpose. This often suggests that the student could not be bothered to précis the ideas in the quote. Often quotes are not grammatically linked to the writing piece and this too makes them read as out of place. You must think about why you want to quote the author. Then embed the quotation so it reads seamlessly in your work: even when you think the quote speaks for itself it has also to be introduced (and explained if necessary).

The structure and organisation of written work

It is not easy to organise your written work so that it communicates effectively in a clear flowing manner. The order in which you make your points is key to the effective communication of your ideas in writing.

Always read over your written work and ask yourself:

- Can I follow my own argument?
  - ☐ Is there a harmonious flow to the language and the ordering of the points and evidences?

---

3   Interpretation Act 1978, s 6.

☐   Is my argument well evidenced by reference to relevant academic source material?

☐   Are the points in the best order? If not think about what changes would present your argument more clearly.

■   Is my movement from one statement, proposition or point to the next logical? Or is it abrupt?

■   Are there any passages in my writing that seem to be confused?

■   Are there gaps in my argument? Have I jumped to conclusions?

☐   Are my paragraphs appropriate; does each new idea get its own paragraph? Do I have paragraphs?

Academic writing also demands formality. You should therefore avoid speaking in a colloquial manner or making asides in the text such as:

'personally I think that . . .'
'actually . . .'.
Nor should you use the informal language you may use to friends such as:
very, rather, little, quite a lot.

Grammar and punctuation

Key to good writing is the confident use of correct grammar and punctuation. We will look at each of these in turn. Understanding grammar, punctuation and spelling conventions will help you to produce good writing. These are the foundations to your effective communication and the development of your writing style.

Grammar

What is grammar?

A simple definition of grammar is:

A set of rules about the use of a language that describe:

(1) The standardised acceptable use of words.

(2) The acceptable methods for sentence construction (word order in a sentence); technically this is the study of syntax.

(3) The acceptable methods for word construction, dealing with the small parts of word; technically this is the study of morphology.

All languages have a grammar, sets of rules determining their appropriate use in the relevant community of language users. However, there is a general lack of precision about what the rules of English grammar might be. This is in part due to the fact that English is the result of many different language traditions. English also has a massive vocabulary, with extensive synonyms (words that mean the same thing).

What are morphology and syntax?

You will have noticed the use of technical words (syntax and morphology) in the above definition of grammar.

Morphology

Morphology in the context of language studies looks at how the smallest meaningful linguistic units, called morphemes, are formed into complete words. It also considers roots of words, word stems. We have already considered some aspects of small linguistic units carrying meaning when we considered affixes and word stems in Chapter 17.

Syntax

Syntax is that part of the overall grammar of a language that is particularly concerned with the rules of the language as they operate in various parts of the sentence. It is key for understanding what makes a sentence grammatically correct, for example in terms of appropriate word order in sentences and phrases.

Word order

By word order is meant issues such as where the verb(s) is/are placed in a sentence, as well as the other parts of the language such as definite and indefinite articles, propositions, nouns and adjectives etc.

The most vital aspect of syntax is the consideration of how parts of speech connect in a meaningful manner. If you have ever engaged in learning a language other than your native tongue you will know that it is key to understand the word structure of the new language.

Using correct word order conventions in your writing is important, if you do not your written and spoken language will be difficult or even impossible to follow. It will also lead to misunderstanding of points you are making and, as a consequence, to lower grades.

'If there were no rules then words would be put in any order, and it would be impossible to agree on what they were intended to communicate.' Think about the sentence you have just read; it makes sense because it follows familiar, internalised word order conventions for written English. But what if the above sentence was presented as follows:

No then what would be rules to put in words to communicate and they to agree on impossible were there it would be in order intended and if were any.

The example sentence above does not conform to understood rules of word order. Even knowing what is intended because you have read the sentence in the right order it is impossible to discern the meaning of this second version. Imagine the chaos with ad hoc punctuation as well! Language would fail as a communication system. The rules make it possible for an almost infinite number of sentences to be easily constructed and understood.

Comprehension of written and spoken language is completely down to the accepted, and therefore commonly understood, order of the sentence.

Why is knowledge of basic grammar important?

At university and professionally your English competency will be judged in part by your correct use of English grammar. Using the wrong tense of a verb, the wrong definite or indefinite article, the use of inappropriate verbs or the use of the wrong word will be seen as evidence of a lack of competency in written or oral English.

It is also worth bearing in mind that often the key to being able to understand a legal text is your ability to take the English it is written in apart for the purposes of interpretation and understanding. Knowledge of grammar is important for this task. For example, being able to identify the subject and the object of sentence, its main and subordinate clauses and its connectors are essential when dealing with English legislation. All of these important clues to breaking into a text are lost to you if you struggle with English grammar. Table 18.1 sets out most used grammatical terms, giving their meaning and function. An example is set out for your easy reference so that if you have any queries you can locate the answer.

What is punctuation?

It is the standard non-alphabetical symbols used to organise writing into grammatically correct sentences or phrases to bring out the meaning of the language used.

Why is it important to use correct punctuation?

The title of Lynne Truss' surprise bestseller on the subject of punctuation, *Eats, Shoots and Leaves*[4] shows the importance of correct punctuation in a memorable and entertaining manner. She describes the story of a panda who read in a book that a panda:

Eats, shoots and leaves.

This led to a tragedy as the panda went into a restaurant, ordered and ate a meal, took out a gun, began shooting and then left.

The punctuation was the cause of this drama. The comma was not required after the word 'eats' and if the entry had read that a panda:

Eats shoots and leaves.

---

4   L Truss *Eats, Shoots and Leaves: The Zero Tolerance Approach to Punctuation* (Profile Books, London, 2003).

TABLE 18.1 GRAMMAR: EXPLANATION OF TERMS AND DETAIL CONCERNING CONVENTIONAL USE OF GRAMMAR

General term for part of grammar	Function/definition	Example of the part of grammar	Example sentence
Articles	**A:** A is used when something is mentioned for the first time. **An:** Used when the article is immediately before a word starting with a vowel (a e i o u). **The:** Used when something is mentioned again.	A An The	There is nothing as good as a rasher of bacon. I ate an egg.
Adjective	This is a word that is known as a describing word. You would put it before the noun/pronoun it is describing. But it can also stand alone in a sentence unconnected to a noun. It gives more information about the noun. It can also make the meaning of a noun clearer.	Lazy Deliberate Pretty	The disgracefully and deliberately lazy decorators did not work quickly.
Adverb	The function of an adverb is to give the reader or hearer more information about the verb, an adjective or even another adverb. It will give information on issues such as when or how something happened. (It may assist you to think of an ADVERB in terms of ADDs to VERB)	Quickly, When Slowly Usually	The disgracefully and deliberately lazy decorators did not work quickly. Adverb
Conjunctions or linking words	These words join parts of speech and link ideas. They can be used at the beginning of a sentence linking it to the previous sentence (although it is generally considered bad grammar to begin a sentence with a joining word). Failure to use conjunctions results in abrupt sentences affecting the flow of your writing.	If But Because However	It should not really matter; however, if she does it again I shall be angry. John is studying today, he enjoys studying very much.

TABLE 18.1—continued			
General term for part of grammar	Function/definition	Example of the part of grammar	Example sentence
Consonant	These are letters that are not vowels.	B C D F etc.	
Infinitive	A verb with the word 'to' attached to it. With some verbs the 'to' is in fact not used.	To go	They decided **to go** on/**Can** you ring Mary?
Infinitives: split	(1) This occurs when a verb is detached from its infinitive 'to' by inserting a word between the infinitive and verb. Not good style in written academic work. (2) It can be avoided by placing the inserted word before the infinitive or after the verb stem.	Any word! e.g. courageously	(1) They decided **to** courageously **go** on. (2) They decided courageously **to go** on.
Nouns	Nouns are naming words for people, objects, animals, birds, things. They can be singular or plural and usually relate to the subject of the sentence. Articles can be used before a noun.		Are **lawyers** beneficial to modern society? The **lawyer** handed in his application.
Prepositions	These are words used together with nouns or pronouns, denoting place, time, position and method. They are there to indicate the relationship of one word to another. Certain words require the addition of a preposition and this is only learnt from experience.	To, With, From, At, Between, On, In, Near	My library book is **at** home. My assessment is **on** the computer.
Pronouns	(1) These words are used instead of a noun to refer to someone or something previously discussed. (2) Pronouns stop us having to revert to the noun which would sound awkward and boring.	He, She, They, We, You, It	(1) Tom crossed the road. **He** wanted to get to the other side. (2) 'John is cross that **he** is late' rather than 'John is cross that John is late'.

General term for part of grammar	Function/definition	Example of the part of grammar	Example sentence
Pronouns and gender	In the move away from sexist language, there is greater use of any, everyone, everybody, person, persons instead of the classic gendered pronouns she, he, him, her when speaking generally.	Any, Everyone Person, Persons	'All businesses rely on their chief executive, he must be able to. . .' Becomes 'All businesses rely on their chief executive who must be able to. . .'
Pronouns: relative pronouns	(1) Who is always the subject of a verb and whom is always the object of a verb or preposition. (2) When referring to non-humans 'Which' and 'that' should be used instead. (3) 'Which' and 'that' are interchangeable in most situations but not all.	Who or Whom, Which or That?	(1) I have seen Marcus, **who** is a third year student. (2) I have seen Marcus talking to John and Fred both of **whom** are students. (3) I just caught sight of the bear **which** was going into the cave.
Vowels	These are letters which are not consonants. In English these are a, e, i, o, u.		
Verbs	(1) A verb is used to discuss actions and states. Often referred to as 'doing'. (2) Formal English requires a verb for the construction of a sentence. (3) A verb has different tenses according to whether the verb relates to an action or state in the present, the past or the future.	Hate Love Write Enjoy	Verb: To study (1) John is studying (action) (2) John was studying (3) John will be studying

This would have told the panda that it was normal for him to eat shoots and leaves. Sense depended on where the comma was placed.

Punctuation provides sense for your writing and it is therefore an essential aspect of your written English. If you use punctuation correctly it will create a good impression of your ability as a writer. It is also important for the purposes of understanding your reading to have a grasp of the foundations of punctuation.

Used badly or hardly at all punctuation obscures sense, and this will affect your grades.

There are a number of conventions relating to punctuation that it is worth knowing and for your ease of reference these are set out in Table 18.2 which discusses the function of a range of punctuation symbols and gives examples of their use.

Often a source of distress and confusion, correct punctuation adds to the harmonious flow of your writing. Also it makes certain that your meaning is clearly understood. Punctuation symbols indicate pauses, by the use of commas, dashes, colons, etc, or inform the reader that someone is speaking by the use of quotation marks. It can also inform the reader that what they are reading is a direct quotation from another written

TABLE 18.2 PUNCTUATION SYMBOLS: NAMES, FUNCTIONS AND EXAMPLES

NAME/SYMBOL	FUNCTIONS AND EXAMPLES
APOSTROPHES '	These can denote: (1) **Contraction:** This joins the two words together to make one word. **EXAMPLE:** *'Haven't you understood?'* instead of *'Have you not understood?'* **Its or it's?:** Many people misunderstand when to use 'its' and when to use 'it's'. One way to ensure you do not make such a mistake is to understand that it's is a contraction and stands for 'it is'. So if 'it is' does not fit the sentence it is appropriate to use **its**, the possessive. (2) **Possession:** To show something belongs to somebody or there is a relationship between them. Placing of the apostrophe changes for singular or the plural noun: • A singular noun has the apostrophe placed before the addition of an 's': e.g. *The student's result was good.* (One student.) • A plural noun has the apostrophe placed after the addition of an 's': e.g. *The students' results were good.* (More than one student.) **EXAMPLE:** *The dog scratched its neck* **NOT** *The dog scratched it's neck.* You can clearly see the addition of 'it is' does not make sense in this sentence.

NAME/SYMBOL	FUNCTIONS AND EXAMPLES	
CAPITAL LETTERS (UPPER CASE) E.G. A B C D, ETC.	Use these only for (1) The first word in a sentence **e.g.** *The cat jumped over the dog* (2) Writing a proper name (place or person name) e.g. *Mary went to Rome.* (3) Writing words that derive from proper names: e.g. *Shakespearian, English.*	(4) For abbreviations known to all e.g. *EU*. (5) For things: e.g. *the Evening Standard* (6) Adjectives referring to places and people also begin with a capital letter. (7) Titles of people, books, plays, music, paintings begin with a capital and indeed it is usual to give a capital to the first, last and other words: e.g. *Queen Elisabeth; The Merchant of Venice.* In these situations small prepositional words (e.g. *to, of, in, at*) and conjunctives are not given a capital letter. (8) Words made from the capitals of the first letters of the name of an institutions etc: e.g. *CA = Court of Appeal.*
COMMA ,	The comma aids sense and clarity. It is used to: (1) List: Here the comma functions as the word 'and'. Do not put a comma before the last item in the list: use 'and', e.g. *Police, security, lawyers and judges.* (2) Punctuate relative clauses such as which or whose. (3) Split up a complex sentence. (4) Insert information. (5) Separate words that come after a noun to explain or describe it.	
SEMI COLON ;	This is used to keep parts of the sentence separate when a comma would not sufficiently indicate the break, and it is not appropriate to make both parts two separate sentences. A capital letter is not used after a semi-colon. E.g. The judge said, 'Will you get me a copy of the defendant's psychological profile; also I would like to hear in person from the psychologist and see the full medical report if I may'.	
COLON :	It can be used to: (1) Indicate that it is to be followed by information. E.g. *Law has a range of sources, for example: case law, legislation and custom.* (2) Link two clauses, for example a statement and a list. (3) Introduce an explanation to expand/explain/strengthen preceding statement.	

TABLE 18.2—continued	
NAME/SYMBOL	**FUNCTIONS AND EXAMPLES**
	(4) Introduce an explanation or reinforcement of a preceding statement (a dash – may be used instead).
	(5) Introduce a direct formal quote.
DASH –	A short line used to separate two words. A break that is less strong than a bracket, and stronger than a comma: they can be used:
	(1) As a pair separating a phrase from the rest of a sentence. Commas can also be used to do this.
	(2) At the beginning of a list or at the end of the list prior to making a comment about the list.
	(3) To indicate a strong pause that is followed by a strong point.
EXCLAMATION MARK !	Use at the end of a sentence, or after a word/phrase to indicate: surprise, anger, sorrow, commands, warnings, humour or a contentious statement. e.g.: *He won five million pounds! What!* If your exclamation forms a question use the exclamation mark. E.g. *Is it true, did he win five million pounds!*
	In non-academic work it is accepted that you can use one or even several exclamation marks (*!!!!*), or an exclamation mark plus a question on mark. (*Did he!?*) **NB:** However, an exclamation mark is not acceptable in formal academic writing.
FULL STOP . **('PERIOD' IN AMERICAN ENGLISH)**	This is used to divide groups of words:
	(1) A single full stop is used to end a sentence if there is no exclamation or question mark. (Note that the symbols for both of these include a full stop in their construction = ! ?) e.g. He was very happy with himself.
	(2) A set of three full stops (ellipsis) is used to indicate that words in an extract or quotation have been omitted. e.g. He said '*there is no more to be added . . . it is sad.*' (technically called 'ellipsis').
	(3) At the end of abbreviations or after titles in referencing where the relevant referencing system uses them.
HYPHEN -	This is a short line, shorter than a dash, that is inserted between two parts of a word and is used to:
	(1) Create compound words by joining two words that in their own right can be used alone.
	(2) Indicate that the beginning of a word with more than one syllable has been unexpectedly separated from the rest of it due to the necessity of a break.

NAME/SYMBOL	FUNCTIONS AND EXAMPLES
QUESTION MARK ?	Place it at the end of a sentence that is a question. E.g. *Why are you doing that?* Or put it in round brackets at the end of a sentence/phrase to indicate doubt e.g. *This is Fisherman's(?) Bay*. When direct speech is being reported use it at the end of a sentence inside the quotation marks. If reporting indirect speech including a question put it outside the quotation marks. A short request must be followed by a question mark; for a long request you can use a question mark or full stop.
QUOTATION MARKS ' ' & " "	These are often a source of confusion and the common rule is: Single quotation marks (' ') should be used for a first quotation of direct speech. E.g. Cedric said 'Come on, the way is clear.' Double quotation marks (" ") should be used for: (1) Any quotation occurring within a quotation, reporting of indirect speech. 'Yes you are correct. I heard Cedric say "Come on, the way is clear".' (2) Around the titles of poems, articles, radio and television programmes (although long titles tend now to be in italics). (3) Around words that you wish to indicate that you know are not correct or in doubt. E.g. *This "law" if it is a "law"*.
	(4) Punctuation marks come after the closing of quotation marks for the quotation of single words, or incomplete titles, or incomplete quotations. (5) Punctuation comes inside quotation marks for other instances (e.g. direct speech). (6) If you are quoting within a quote for clarity the normal convention is to use both types of quotation marks: it does not matter in these circumstances whether the outer set of quotation marks are single or double: e.g. *Mary heard Cedric say, 'So he said "I am here" but I thought that was odd.'/Mary heard Cedric say "So he said 'I am here' but I thought that was odd"*.
PARENTHESES BRACKETS ( ) / [ ]	Round brackets can be used around phrases in a sentence or whole sentences, to refer to a reference, or numbers (5), letters (v), or indicate interruptions. You use brackets around that part of a sentence that is not particularly about the subject matter of the sentence. 'The author Marcus Jones (not his real name) wrote prolifically.' A sentence adding information to the paragraph but not strictly relevant to what is being discussed can also be put in square brackets.

source. Certain punctuation symbols, such as exclamation marks and question marks, indicate that a controversial point is being made by the writer. Overall the correct use of punctuation aids the understanding of the reader, reduces situations of doubt about meaning and accentuates important or contentious points. It is therefore important for you to learn it and use it.

Vocabulary

Many students are concerned that their vocabulary is too small. You may recall an experience when you were talking to someone, or in a small group, and you did not understand most of the words you heard although you all spoke the same language.

You will need to acquire a large technical legal vocabulary and at the same time extend your ordinary English vocabulary.

An initial feeling of being overcome with too many unknown words is a natural first concern of law students. Do not worry. With persistent application your vocabularies, and therefore your general comprehension of legal texts, will expand. I have used the term 'vocabularies' because there is a difference between general and legal English.

Also in the study of law you will find that many ordinary, general English words will have a specialised meaning within English law. Words such as 'intention', 'negligence', 'recklessness', and 'knowingly' have been the object of much interpretative debate in law cases. At times legislation is enacted to try and clarify the meaning of these words, leading to more cases about their meaning.

Extending your general vocabulary

In academic life as well as in ordinary life people make unfounded value judgements about us. Because of its link to education vocabulary is routinely used to classify socio-economic status and make assumptions about a language user's intelligence. Promise yourself that you will not just ignore words you do not understand. If you do not understand the meaning of a word how can you know that it is all right to ignore it? An obvious thing that you can do is to keep an alpha ordered vocabulary. You should not assume that because you looked up a word once that you will remember its meaning months later. Ideally it should give the full range of meanings of the word, together with examples of using it in the different vocabularies in which it can occur. Words do change their meaning according to context. As your vocabulary will extend you will be able to use some of this new vocabulary in your academic discussions, or everyday discussions if appropriate.

As you concentrate upon extending your vocabulary, whether as a native English speaker, or reading English as another language, you will become aware that many words share the same parts. This knowledge can be used to assist you to understand new words. Recall the work on affixes and guessing words. But also recall that you should not assume that you have the correct meaning of the word from your guessing; you should also look it up.

Extending your technical legal vocabulary

The meaning of many technical legal words, and the appropriate words to use when referring to certain activities in law, will embed themselves in your memory as you will be using them often. Legal English also resorts to a large number of Latin phrases or tags which stand as shorthand for doctrines and methods of resolving disputes (e.g. *obiter, ratio*). These will be considered in more detail in the chapters on legal writing for essays and problem solutions. However, you can help yourself to learn this technical vocabulary by keeping an alpha listing of the meaning of such words (or phrases) so that in times of uncertainty about meaning you can just refer to your list.

Issues with spelling

There are many rules and exceptions in English with regard to spelling. Only a few of the more notorious issues are referred to here. Your computer will have a spell checker and it is well worth using it as a preliminary check for mistakes, but do check that it is set to British English and not American English. But do not accept a spelling without checking the computer has correctly understood your *use* of the word. The computer will flag up certain easily mistaken words (such as their/there) but not all.

What are the rules about adding suffixes to words or word stems ending in 'e'?

The following Table 18.3 sets out what you do with 'e' as many people have trouble deciding what to do with an e!

TABLE 18.3 WHAT DO YOU DO WITH AN 'E'?	
'e' rules	**Examples**
(1) Words ending in an 'e' lose that 'e' when the suffix added to the end of the word begins with a vowel (a,e,i,o,u).	Advise = advisory Educate = educat**ing**
(2) Words ending in an 'e' lose the 'e' when the suffix added to the end of the word is a 'y'.	Sauce = sauc**y**
(3) If the suffix begins with a consonant (that is any word that is NOT a vowel) the 'e' is generally retained: ly, ness, ment.	Sincere = sincere**ly** False = false**ly**
(4) *Sometimes* however the 'e' is dropped in front of a consonant.	Argue = Argument

Use dictionaries and thesauries

English dictionaries

Dictionaries are not just places to find out about spelling; they also give valuable detail on how to use a word, its derivation, how to pronounce it and what it means in differing contexts. For those students whose first language is not English the *Collins Cobuild English Dictionary 2014* (which has separate editions at beginner, intermediate and advanced level) gives you a sophisticated understanding of word usage. For native English speakers, as well as their online dictionary,[5] Collins also publish the *Collins English Paperback Dictionary and Thesaurus* set.[6] Another good dictionary provider is the *Oxford English Dictionary* series. You could consider the *Oxford English Dictionary Paperback*.[7] Oxford also has a good online presence which your library may subscribe to.[8]

A thesaurus

A thesaurus gives you synonyms, words meaning the same thing. If you feel that you are repeating a word too much, its capacity to give other words meaning the same thing is extremely useful. The most well-known thesaurus is *Roget's Thesaurus of English Words and Phrases* (penguin reference)[9] and now *Roget's Thesaurus of English Words and Phrases 150th-Anniversary International Edition*.[10] Both of these can also be accessed online.[11] Most are not in alpha order and you will need to read the classifications carefully. Collins however has got an alpha thesaurus, The *Collins Gem English Thesaurus*.[12] Oxford also provides the *Oxford Paperback Thesaurus*.[13]

Law dictionaries

Law dictionaries are invaluable for locating the meaning of technical terms. They will define main terms, as well as concepts and processes of the English legal system. They will include summaries of major areas of law. Many are in print and online and the online versions offer extra links to other reference sites. Your university department may have preferred law dictionaries that they wish you to use, and your library may have online subscriptions to these. Good law dictionaries would include the *Oxford Dictionary of Law*; it is available in print but the 7th edition is an online only edition 2014. Other online dictionaries of note will also be indicated by your library.

The HM Courts and Tribunal Service provides an alpha listing of the meanings for legal terms used in court.

Many libraries will stock a range of law dictionaries. Two particularly good options are *The Longman Dictionary of Law*[14] and *Osborn's Concise Law Dictionary*.[15]

---

5 www.collinsdictionary.com.
6 A new edition due in 2015.
7 C Soanes (7th edn, 2013).
8 www.oed.com.
9 2004.
10 George Davidson (Author, Editor) 2006.
11 www.thesaurus.com.
12 2012.
13 2013.
14 PH Richards, LB Curzon (Longman, 2011).
15 M Woodley (11th edn, Sweet and Maxwell, 2013).

Understanding the relationship between sentences and paragraphs

We have so far noted the importance of the use of correct grammar, punctuation, vocabulary and spelling. These all come together in the sentences, phrases and paragraphs that you choose when constructing your academic writing in response to tasks set by your lecturers. To use sentences and paragraphs properly you do need to understand the definition and function of them both. For your assistance these are set out in Table 18.4.

TABLE 18.4 UNDERSTANDING THE ROLE OF SENTENCES AND PARAGRAPHS IN THE CONSTRUCTION OF WRITING	
SENTENCE	
Definition	A sentence is a group of words grammatically linked containing a verb intending to communicate something.
Components parts	• **Verb:** Sentences must have a verb. There can be more than one verb in a sentence. • **Subject:** Sentences have a subject which is the word controlling the action implied by the verb. A subject can be a pronoun, noun (a proper name, or named concepts) and this can include prepositions such as 'this'. • **Object:** Sentences can have an object; again this can be a pronoun or a noun. • Sentences can also contain other grammatical units such as adverbs or adjectives. • Some would maintain that you should not start a sentence with a conjunction or words ending with the suffix 'ing'.
Verb	A verb is a word that discusses actions and states and it is often referred to as a 'doing' or 'being' word, e.g. running, happy, etc. A verb has different tenses according to whether it relates to an action or state in the **present** (present tense), the **past** (past tense) or the **future** (future tense). There are other tenses but you need not concern yourself with these now. The other words used in a sentence must agree with the tense of the verb they are in grammatical relation to. To check your understanding of tenses look at Examples 1 and 2 below. Adjectives and adverbs (as appropriate) joined to verbs in the sentence are indicated by dashes joining these words. Example 1. She loves-to-run but she hated-swimming-when-she-tried it = √ Example 2. She *love-to-run* but she *hates-swimming-when-she-try* it = X

TABLE 18.4—continued

SENTENCE

Subject	The subject of a sentence is the main focus of the sentence, what it is about. Often, but not always, it comes near the beginning of the sentence and determines the rest of the sentence. Sentences can have more than one subject. e.g. The barrister drafted the pleadings **subject verb object**
Object	Nouns in a sentence that are not the focus of the sentence are objects as they explain more about the subject and what they may be doing or thinking etc. Sentences can have more than one object. • A direct object is an object acted on by the subject: e.g. *The police officer caught the thief*. • An indirect object is where the object is indirectly affected by the action: e.g. *The police officer gave the thief a drink*.

PARAGRAPH

Definition	A group of sentences that are connected to each other because they deal with the same idea or point.
Component parts	Each paragraph will have a: • **Topic sentence** which is what the paragraph is discussing. • **'Body' sentence**s that give information following on from the topic sentence. Each new idea should be introduced in a new paragraph. • **Concluding sentence** is to smooth the way for the next paragraph, or to refer the reader back to the topic of the paragraph, or both.
Function/size	Each sentence in the paragraph should make sense in that paragraph; it should not be irrelevant, and sentences should be logically ordered within the sentence. There is no set size for a paragraph but ideally it should not be a page long, nor too small, but on some occasions a two sentence paragraph may be needed.

WRITING NOTES

Much of your independent study time will involve note taking; it is one of the most important tasks you will engage in. Your note taking includes all of the written records that you have made of what you have heard and what you have read.

They are a major contributing factor to your learning, for you will use them to assimilate and integrate information, critique concepts from a range of sources and translate them into arguments for your formal written work.

You will take notes for many reasons, to:

- Build up a body of materials that increases your knowledge.
- Form the basis for constructing exam answers and written (or oral) assessments.
- Help you express and understand concepts/ideas.
- Store information in a classified, ordered manner.

You will also take notes in different situations:

- From your reading.
- In lectures.
- In seminars.

It is very easy to lose sight of appropriate length for notes and write far too much. A note is designed to quickly recall more information to your mind. You do not want to wade through a large pile of notes therefore. It is also easy to write notes of irrelevant material if you do not apply your mind to the task in hand. Note taking, like reading, should be a dynamic not a passive activity.

Cottrell[16] suggests that asking the following questions can help you to decide what to note.

- Do you really need this information? If so, which bits?
- Will you really use it? When, and how?
- Have you noted similar information already?
- What questions do you want to answer with this information?

You also need to know how to use your notes by:

- Interconnecting your notes from lectures, seminars, books and articles using a reliable filing system.
- Using your notes effectively in your written work.

Note taking presents you with many challenges. You may find that:

- You make notes from a lot of background reading, but are then stuck when it comes to using them for your written work.
- You may feel overwhelmed in lectures; what do you note? Especially when every word seems factual and/or the lecturer is speaking too quickly for you to note. However, whilst in some schools teachers dictate notes, a lecturer is not dictating; they are speaking about the subject for you to note what you wish in view of handouts, reading and visual aids used in the lecture theatre.

---

16 S Cottrell *The Study Skills Handbook* (2nd edn, Palgrave Macmillan, Basingstoke, 2003), 126.

- You read slowly, and feel you cannot follow the sense of a text and write notes, and the notes you make are too detailed. As a consequence you fear that your note taking takes you far too long.
- After you have made a great deal of notes for an assessment you do not know which words are yours and which you copied out of the text directly, and find you are struggling because you now do not know if the ideas in them are yours or another writer's; this causes you to worry about falling into accidental plagiarism.
  - ☐ An easy way to avoid this is to give the title of the text and full reference as a header before you begin taking notes. Then make a note of any specific page you are noting. If you quote verbatim from a text in your notes ensure you use quotation marks. If you are summarising a set of ideas again clearly note whose ideas they are and the page number where they can be located. By giving the full reference and title of every text you note you also have the ability to quickly construct a sources list or bibliography for your writing.
  - ☐ By noting specific pages from the text in your notes it makes it easy to return to that place in the text maybe weeks later because your knowledge has increased and you now think that other information around that page could be important for your work.

Strategies for note taking

What should notes contain?

Always approach note taking by being clear about your purpose for noting. This should be easy enough for reading tasks if you are following a reading strategy and are reading for purpose. Given your purpose when you find texts of relevance you need to briefly cover the core facts or arguments, and to do so briefly. Long notes are no use to you.

You do not have to write your notes; you could consider underlining and highlighting words or phrases in your book that seem to be the core of the point being made. Only do this on your own books. If you do not want to write in your own books you could record the main headings in the text and give a few keywords in your notes about each chapter.

As you are reading and noting it is normal for questions, or thoughts about the text, to arise in your mind, and it is a good idea to record them in your notes. Your recorded good idea may be very useful for your later written work. Or they can prompt you to engage in more reading as follow up.

If it is possible write your notes on one side of paper only and then you can add in material covering the same area from other reading that you undertake later. When you have read a section it is a good idea to summarise it; the advice is to stop reading and take a few seconds to think about what you have just read and then summarise it in your own words, noting page numbers, and the author of any ideas. Then read back over the text to double check you did not miss any important points.

The structure of notes

You want to see at a glance core points, summaries, references, headings and sub-headings, and leave space to add in more information as you read and reflect on your developing understanding.

There are several ways that you can approach note taking and you need to be guided by the method(s) that suit you best, as the notes are for your benefit alone. You will soon learn the method you prefer. Some students find they use a variety of methods to suit the purpose for their note taking. We will look at the use of:

- Linear text.
- Diagrams.
- Mind maps.

Linear text

The majority of people use this method of writing notes. This involves writing notes in a sentence form, or bullet point form in the order that you are reading the text. If you use this method it is a good idea to get into the habit of using abbreviations. These should be kept short however, or you will become lost in detail.

Diagrams

There are several ways of constructing diagrams: we will consider spray and mind maps:

Spray

This operates on keywords that you have identified in the text. The keyword is put in the middle of the page and circled. Then you think of words that are connected to this key-word; these words could relate to concepts, facts, etc. They provide a way of you thinking more extensively about smaller sections of text.

For an example we have taken the keyword 'study'.

As you can see the diagram is random, and is only as good as your thoughts. You certainly need to know why you are creating the diagram or the exercise is unhelpful. But you can then see simultaneously areas where there are a lot of links and those where there are few. In academic terms you could do this looking at your essay as a whole noting gaps in evidences to support propositions.

Mind maps

These look at first glance to be a spray diagram; however there is a firmer patterning to the links and they are more structured:

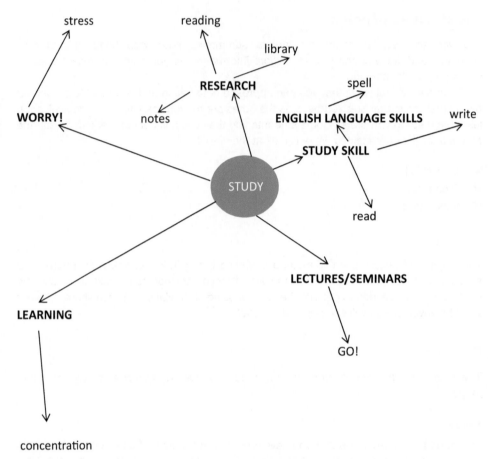

Figure 18.1 Example spray diagram using the keyword 'STUDY'

Notes from verbal presentations

When you are writing notes from text you have more control over your speed of work and choices about recording the information. However, for verbal presentations such as lectures, speeches, seminars and videos, note taking presents different challenges.

The presentation you are listening to may be disorganised which again creates difficulties for you. But even a well-organised presentation in a lecture requires you to engage in active listening skills (the note taking side of active reading skills). Active listening requires you to ask questions in your mind as you are listening and simultaneously noting. As you can imagine this skill of doing three things at once takes time to develop.

Students do ask lecturers to repeat points but it is often not looked upon too kindly. Usually lecturers in the university use PowerPoint slides which are posted on the VLE

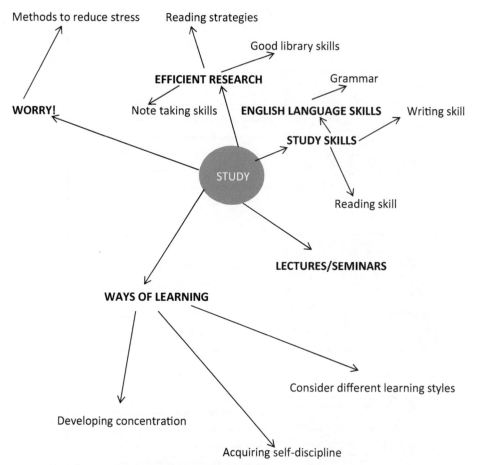

Figure 18.2 Example mind map using the keyword 'STUDY'

before the lecture. It is a good idea to print these out, using the three slide note taking option format in black and white to keep costs low. You can then write notes beside each slide as they are presented in the lecture and discussed. Just record key points and if references are mentioned that are not on the slide, note them. Equally if information is on the slide do not repeat it in your note. Figure 18.3 is a screenshot of PPT in handout mode showing three frames with lines.

After the lecture just make sure that you have an efficient method for highlighting further reading, any tasks you have been asked to do and file your notes. You might find that using different pens helps you identify areas you need to follow up for more information, or where you need to spend time trying to understand the point made. Read (or just flick through) a book on the subject of the lecture. Look for themes, issues, topics and headings. Look up any technical words you don't understand.

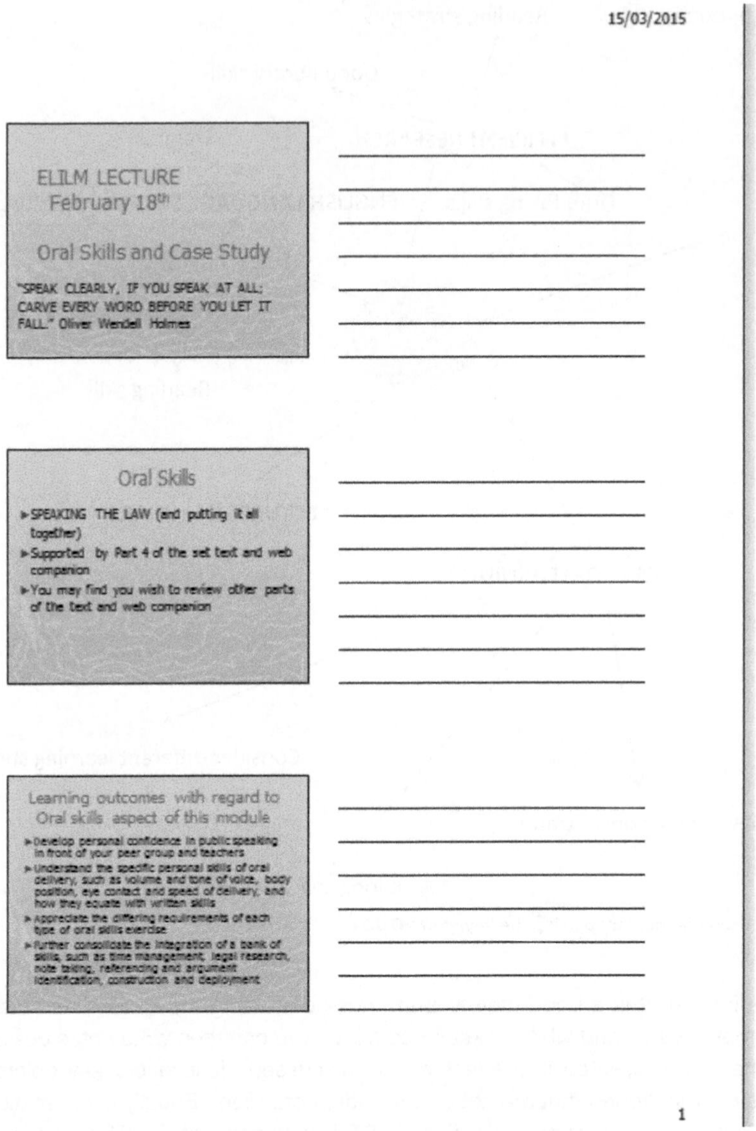

Figure 18.3 Screenshot of power point (ppt) printed in hand out mode

Note taking symbols and abbreviations

The idea behind symbols and abbreviations in note taking is to save yourself time enabling you to take efficient notes more quickly. You can use any symbols to mean anything for you as long as you remember what they stand for.

Abbreviations

You can devise a set of personal abbreviations of common English words that work for you. The table on p. 524 sets out a few suggestions. Can you think of others?

Questions arising in your mind as you write notes

If questions arise as you write notes put them in the notes either in another colour or on the back of the page of notes so that you can explore them more fully. If you do not write them down you will forget them and they are key to your development.

Any of the following matters may arise in your mind:

- an idea about a link to other issues;
- wondering if an interpretation other than the one you have read is better;
- a reference to follow up;
- some limitations that you think what you are reading may have but you need to check;
- some questions that your reading is raising in your mind;
- statistics that you need to look up.

Word	Symbol to use
Ecus	
And	&
At	@
Correct	√
Divide	÷
Equals/the same as	=
Half	½
Interesting	%
Less than	<
Minus, subtract, without	-
More than	>
Multiply	×
Pounds	£
Question/doubt	?
Surprise	!

Personal English abbreviations	
Abbreviation	**Standing for:**
cld or cd	Could
diff	Difficult
diffy	Difficulty
D'rent	Different
E/er	Employer
E/ee	Employee
govt	Government
Emer	Emergency
nec	Necessary
sld	Should
S'times	Sometimes
tho'	Though
w/i	Within
wld	Would
w/o	Without

Note-making templates

It is useful to develop a template for note taking so that it becomes second nature. Always give the full reference for the source, clearly head each different set of notes, and number all pages.

Notes should be clear, readable, and if possible use bullet points so that you can easily read connections between parts. You will find some excellent suggestions for templates and note taking at www.sas.calpoly.edu/asc/ssl/notetakingsystems.html.

CONCLUSION

Effective writing depends on your understanding of what you have read, your use of correct grammar, punctuation and spelling, as well as the development of an effective writing style using researched material that is appropriately referenced. We will deal with the general and specific aspects of writing competency for law assessments in Part 6. In the next chapter we consider the required formalities for competently referencing the sources used in your written work, so that you can ensure you do not accidentally plagiarise.

CHAPTER SUMMARY

- Find your written academic 'voice' and avoid hyper-correct language.
- Formal academic writing is a measured method of communicating, with clear rules of engagement that cover style as well as content.
- Eradicate repetition and make your writing more cohesive and interesting.
- Adopt an objective style and avoid using the words 'I' or 'my' in your writing.
- Ensure that you use the correctly referenced work (words, designs and ideas) of others in your writing.
- The order in which you make your points is part of the effective communication of your ideas in writing.
- Make sure you proof read carefully for errors of spelling, punctuation and grammar, as well as for the flow of your work through paragraphs and follow your department's conventions on referencing.[17]
- Most coursework will have word limits imposed and there may be penalties for exceeding them. Work out *before* you even start writing how many pages of your typing that amounts to.

---

17 Chapter 19 deals with referencing.

REFERENCING AND AVOIDING PLAGIARISM

19

LEARNING OUTCOMES

After reading this chapter you should be able to:

- Explain the purpose of referencing.
- Understand when a reference is required.
- Engage in consistent referencing of your source material.
- Understand how to use OSCOLA or Harvard referencing systems.
- Define 'plagiarism' and the ways in which it occurs.
- Understand how to avoid accidental plagiarism.

INTRODUCTION

This chapter considers how to ensure that your work is correctly, consistently and comprehensively referenced. When you submit work to the university for formal assessment you will be expected to describe, review, compare and critically analyse the work of academics, legal professionals and others and to use their work to support your own arguments. The university expects their work to be clearly distinguishable from your own work. To ensure that you can do this consistently and thoroughly you need to know how to reference your uses of the work of others. It is part of the skill of an undergraduate and graduate student that they learn to do this and deploy referencing in a way that enhances their work and their writing.

Several academic referencing systems exist and your university may even have set up its own preferred referencing system. The two main referencing systems used in UK law schools are OSCOLA (the Oxford System for the Citation of Legal Authorities) which is known as a footnote system and Harvard, an in-text system.

Many law schools use OSCOLA and some use Harvard. This chapter will briefly introduce the referencing protocols for both and make reference to sources where you can find more detail. Both referencing systems dictate the way in which references should be signalled inside the body of your text and laid out in detail outside the body of your text (e.g. as footnotes, endnotes, and in a bibliography).

If your institution does not enforce any particular style of referencing this does not mean that lecturers and your institution do not care about referencing. Nor does it mean that plagiarism is not an issue in that university – for it will be. In the absence of any stated preference by your institution it is advisable to adopt an accepted system of referencing rather than invent your own.

When explained, referencing can appear quite laborious and highly complex. Rest assured that it is not. Once you have understood the concept, and begun to use the system of referencing preferred by your academic institution or, if you have a choice, the system you prefer, the process of referencing your work will become an easy and automatic reflex.

Failure to meticulously reference your work can leave you open to an allegation of plagiarism. Plagiarism is the act of passing off as your own the work of another (e.g. their ideas, arguments, descriptions, critiques, statistics and illustrations). A finding of plagiarism has serious consequences for students and can jeopardise your degree programme. Accidental plagiarism, due to careless note taking leading to lack of appropriate referencing, as well as intentional plagiarism, will be pursued by the university, although penalties will usually differ. But for law students there are other serious consequences. The legal professional bodies require universities to inform them if a law student on a qualifying law degree has been called before a plagiarism panel and there has been a finding of plagiarism. This finding can be taken as evidence of a lack of good character and can therefore potentially have a negative impact on your future employment prospects and even your entry into the legal profession.

WHAT IS REFERENCING?

When writing your assessments you are expected to engage in research, locating texts to develop your understanding and referring to them in your work. When you write your assessment you are expected to competently and appropriately incorporate the knowledge you have gained from these sources into your written work. When you go over your notes from your source material you will need to make choices about how you will use it. Will you give a verbatim quotation from the source, or merely paraphrase that section from your source? Or will you restate the information in your source by summarising or by paraphrasing it? Whichever of these decisions you make you must give a reference to the source and pinpoint any required specific references.

When should you reference?

Whenever you use the work of another or quote directly from them in your writing, you must reference the source. If an idea has been set out at length in a chapter you will most likely just refer to the relevant chapter. If, however, the idea or argument you wish to use is set out in a few pages you can just refer to those few pages when you reference. These particular references are referred to as *pinpoint references* and they enable a reader to find the exact location in that other work. If you are indebted to the orientation of an entire book or article then you can consider stating this and noting the full work.

The requirement to reference does not stop with verbatim quotations but includes ideas, diagrams, tables, illustrations and the statistics which have been respectively designed, or collected and interpreted by others. Students often overlook the need to reference every time they refer to a legal rule. For example if you state 'it is a criminal offence to steal a book' you must give the pinpoint reference to the relevant legal prohibition (which is, of course, s 1 of the Theft Act 1968).[1]

If you are referring to issues discussed by a judge(s) in a case such as the development of a legal rule, or a matter of interpretation, you must give the full reference to that case and a pinpoint reference to the exact part of the judgment(s) developing the rule or interpretation.

Therefore when you discuss statements of law always ask yourself 'What is my authority for stating this?' then reference that authority. You can also ask yourself whether you wish to summarise the point or use a direct quotation and more will be said about this later in this chapter.

Many students speak of statistics in their work without referring to the source, but where did that statistic come from, and how do we know it is from a reputable academic or empirical source? Would you expect to take action based on unsubstantiated statistics?

---

1   Theft Act 1968, s 1.

I would hope not. You would want to know the source and then weigh up if it were a reputable source. You must give a reference to the report producing those statistics or to the author of the book or journal that cited such a statistic if they did not give the reference to the statistic. This latter situation would be a secondary source as you obtained the information from a source using the primary statistics.

When you are discussing legal definitions clearly they have an origin in a source beyond your own work. If they have been defined in case law or legislation that source must be cited. You can cite other sources for definitions such as a law dictionary or an article. But this should not be done to the exclusion of referring to the case law and legislation that has defined the legal concept.

If you know you have taken existing information from another author even though you have used your own words to communicate that information you must still reference your source for your summary. If you are not sure whether to reference or not, play safe and reference. Whilst you can be criticised for over referencing and it could lose you marks for presentation, if you have a genuine dilemma you cannot resolve it is better to err on the side of referencing caution.

It is generally considered appropriate not to reference factual information which everyone in a particular state or locality should know. This is because it is said to be common knowledge yet there are no general rules about what constitutes 'common knowledge'. It is often difficult to know what to do about referencing information that is said to be 'common knowledge' – that is, a fact everyone should know. For example if you write that David Cameron is the prime minister,[2] do you need to reference? Do you refer to the results of the last general election from the official record? What about a broader non-factual comment? If the information can be found in many places and is indeed known by many people then you need not reference it. But what does 'many' mean? If in real doubt it is best to seek advice from your tutors. Figure 19.1 provides a quick checklist of when to quote.

- Summarising the work of others.
- Paraphrasing the work of others.
- Using the exact words of others – direct quotation.
- Referring to statements of law.
- Referring to statistics.
- Referring to the execution of research.
- Referring to definitions in dictionaries and/or encyclopaedias.
- Referring to diagrams, tables, statistics prepared by others.
- Referring to any illustrations prepared by others.

Figure 19.1 Checklist for when to reference source material

---

2   Which he is at the time of writing.

Referencing systems

Your university department may have its own preferred method of referencing source materials. If it does have such a 'house style' you must ensure that you use it. You can ask your lecturers if you are in doubt about which method to use.

We will consider OSCOLA and Harvard, two widely used referencing systems. OSCOLA is known as a 'footnoting' system[3] and Harvard as an 'in-text' system that uses endnotes.[4] There are clear differences between the two and they should never be mixed in any one piece of writing. If you have a free choice consider the two systems and decide which you prefer.

How to use the referencing tools in your word processing package

Most, if not all, university departments now require written assessments to be word processed and electronically submitted. Word processing makes it easy to insert references for either OSCOLA, Harvard or other systems. Your word processor will have a referencing tool bar that will enable you to insert footnoting or endnoting referencing. It will place a superscript number in the body of your text that will automatically generate a footnote at the bottom of the page[5] or an endnote at the end of your writing if you are using Harvard. You choose which insertion is used. You can enter your reference immediately.

Each footnote or endnote is automatically kept in chronological sequence both in the text and at the bottom of the page or the end of the text. Each footnote or endnote can be deleted by highlighting the superscript marker in the body text and clicking on delete. The reference itself is also deleted and the remaining footnotes or endnotes in the entire document are automatically renumbered both in the body text and in the footnote or endnote. You can also use the general tools options to 'cut' and 'paste' to move your superscript number in your text.

It is extremely important to take the time to find out how your word processing package inserts references. Use the help icon in your word-processing package to assist you to learn how to insert references.

HOW TO USE THE OSCOLA SYSTEM OF REFERENCING

The OSCOLA[6] system was specifically developed in the UK to make it easier to deal with references required for primary legal source material. It also deals with references for secondary legal material well. It is a two part system that uses numerals in superscript in the text which refer to a footnote that appears at the bottom of the page prefaced by the same superscript number.

The OSCOLA system of referencing does not require a bibliography. However, if your lecturer requires a bibliography at the end of your work you need to prepare one and it must include all references to source materials that you have consulted in preparing your

---

3   A superscript number in the text matches a superscript number appearing at the bottom of the page, or at the foot of the page, hence 'footnote'.
4   Here in-text references are partial and full references are in notes at the end of a chapter, or a book, or an article, hence 'endnoting'.
5   Like this!
6   Oxford System for the Citation of Legal Authorities.

written work, including those that you did not specifically refer to by name in your work. This bibliography must be in alphabetical order using headings to separate academic texts, law cases and legislation.

How do I use OSCOLA?

In order to use OSCOLA, you need to know the answers to the following three questions:

(1) Where to place a raised numerical marker in your text.

(2) How to place the raised numerical marker using the referencing tools in your word processing package (e.g. in 'Word').

(3) What information is required to give a full reference to source material (this will vary according to the source material).

Each of these questions will now be considered in more detail.

Where to place a raised numerical marker in your text

As noted before, in OSCOLA a superscript marker is used to signal a footnote.[7] Conventionally the superscript number is placed outside the punctuation at the end of the sentence. However, it is now often the case that they are placed anywhere in the sentence. If you adopt this practice on occasion it must always be placed *after* the word or phrase it refers to, not before. The only rationale for placing the superscript number mid-sentence is to make clear which aspect of the sentence the source referenced refers to. This is certainly useful if you wish to make a comment about an author which appears in the middle of a sentence or you are referring to more than one author.

Some writers when wishing to refer to multiple authors put all superscript numbers at the end of the sentence, being careful to leave clear spaces between numbers. This is allowed in OSCOLA but do be careful as placing them all at the end of a sentence can create an imprecise and confusing situation if it is not clear exactly what any one reference applies to. See Figure 19.2 for examples.

Where to place the superscript numbers is a choice you need to make when considering where to place your markers to make best sense for the reader. You do not want to distract the reader by your referencing.

(1) Twining and Miers,[8] Webb[9] and Hanson[10] all agree referencing is important.

(2) Twining and Miers, Webb and Hanson all agree referencing is important.[11] [12] [13]

Figure 19.2 Examples of different placement of superscript footnote numerals in OSCOLA

7 Like this.
8 W Twining & D Miers *How to Do Things with Rules*.
9 J Webb *Learning Legal Rules*.
10 S Hanson *Legal Method, Skills and Reasoning*.
11 W Twining & D Miers *How to Do Things with Rules*.
12 J Webb *Learning Legal Rules*.
13 S Hanson *Legal Method, Skills and Reasoning*.

The footnote can give the full reference to the source used. If the full reference has previously been given it is only necessary to refer to your previous footnote.

Twining and Miers, Webb and Hanson all agree referencing is important.[14]

The information required to give a full OSCOLA reference for your source material

The information and conventions required for a full reference vary according to the type of material referenced (whether it is an internet source, print source or only one or the other).

Table 19.1 gives an indication of the types of source material that you will need to know how to reference.

Referencing primary source material

What is a legal citation?

'Citation' is a general term for the referral to all primary legal sources, for example 'a reference as to a legal statute, a previous law case, or a written authority, as precedent or justification'.[15]

UK cases

There are two types of citation used for UK cases, the neutral citation and a law report citation. They are completely independent of each other except for the fact that they both refer to a written record of the same law case.

TABLE 19.1 TYPES OF MATERIAL THAT WILL REQUIRE REFERENCING (NON-EXHAUSTIVE)	
PRIMARY LAW: TEXTS OF LAW	**SECONDARY SOURCES: TEXTS ABOUT LAW**
UK cases	Books
European Court of Human Rights cases	Academic journals
European Union cases	Professional journals
UK legislation	Internet only information from pressure groups, government agencies and departments etc.
European Union treaties and legislation	Multimedia/newspapers/film/video/photographic/ blogs
European Convention on Human Rights and associated protocols	Research reports
Laws from other legal systems	Parliamentary papers

14 See footnotes 18, 19, 20.
15 www.yourdictionary.com/citation accessed 20/2/15.

The neutral citation

This is the referencing system of the courts and is given to all cases post 2001. This includes the year, territorial jurisdiction, and a sequence number which denotes which judgment it is in that year in the relevant area (e.g. civil or criminal law), e.g.:

[2004] EWCA Civ 727

denotes that this citation is to the 727th judgment in the England and Wales Court of Appeal for the year 2004. The Supreme Court has UK wide jurisdiction and is denoted by the UKSC, United Kingdom Supreme Court.

The private report citation

The second type of citation is used for privately reported cases. This private law report citation will set out the year of the case, title of the law report, volume details and the page number for the first page of the report. Where there is no neutral citation in existence for the reported case because it is pre-2001, the court is given at the end of the citation in abbreviated form enclosed in brackets,

e.g. *R v Moloney* [1985] 2 AC 905 (HL).

For all references to private law reports you must give the neutral citation first (if there is one) followed by the references to the private report(s) of the case in order of their hierarchy of authority,

e.g. *R v Bree* [2007] EWCA Crim 804; [2008] QB 131; [2007] 3 WLR 600; [2007] 2 All ER 676; [2007] 2 Cr App R 13.

Citing UK cases

When dealing with cases the citation refers to the name of the parties, the year of the case, and if it is not reported the neutral citation giving court and number of the case in the year. If it is reported then it includes details of the private report (report title, volume number if any and page number). You may like to think of your law case citation as divided into two parts, the names of the parties, and the citation for its location. Each of these is inserted into the text in a different but connected way.

OSCOLA specifies that only the name of the case in italics with the superscript numeral should be put in the body of your text. It is the matching footnote that contains the cited location of the case. By way of example one can point to the case of *R v Bree*.[16] Note that the superscript marker immediately after *R v Bree* directs you to footnote 16, which as you can see, gives the citations for the reports where it can be located, beginning with the neutral citation, followed by other reports in accordance with the hierarchy of law reports.

---

16 [2007] EWCA Crim 804; [2008] QB 131; [2007] 3 WLR 600; [2007] 2 All ER 676; [2007] 2 Cr App R 13.

For OSCOLA it is not necessary to put the name of the case in your footnote as you have already noted it in your body text and tied it to the footnote by the body text superscript marker. However, many lecturers insist that students do so, and many students like to do so. You must always follow your lecturer's guidance if they give any.

Punctuation and citations

OSCOLA simplifies full referencing to case citations in the footnotes by stipulating that no punctuation is required at all in the reference. If the case reference relates to a pinpoint reference or to a specific judge then a full stop is placed after the pinpoint reference or reference to the judge – whichever constitutes the end of the reference.

Party names

Differences that you will encounter when using cases relate to party names. In private law areas individuals or companies are parties whether they are bringing the case or defending it and their names are used, for example *Smith v Jones* or *Smith v Jones Ltd*. In criminal law the Crown is the prosecutor and the naming convention is *R v Jones*.

The standard method always used for laying out the names of the parties is to use italics, including italicising the 'v' (the signification for the Latin word 'versus' meaning 'against') which comes between the names. For example:

Black-Clawson International v Papierwerke Waldof-Aschaffenburg [1975] AC 591.

The treatment of the *v* can change however, and you could find *v* rendered as v or *v*. But only italicising the *v* is valid for OSCOLA referencing.

Italics are used in all body text references to case names as well as in all footnote references and in any tables of cases that your lecturer may require at the end of coursework.

How the names of the parties are set out in the citation, and therefore in the OSCOLA reference can change. This change is either due to the differing area of law (e.g. criminal and civil cases) or because conventions for setting out names have changed in a given area over time.

OSCOLA referencing does not require case names to be repeated in the footnote reference if they are mentioned in the body text to which the reference superscript marker is attached. In reality however you will find that most writers tend to repeat the parties' names in the footnote.

Additionally there are conventions concerning when, and how, the names of parties to a case can be shortened for use in the body of your text.

Conventions for shortening names of parties in civil law

In the body of your text you may not wish to set out the full case name, and this is fine. But you need to use the conventional shortening not make one up. The rule is that you can only use the surname of the first party in the action as an abbreviation. It is important to have such a rule as shortening of case names is common and matters will be unduly compli-cated if different methods prevail. What is less easy to get used to is that customarily some famous leading cases will always be referred to by resort to both party names and others are conventionally shortened to the first party. You will just have to get used to these.

An interesting example is the case of *McAlister (or Donoghue) v Stevenson* [1932] AC 562. This is a famous civil law case in the area of the law of tort (the law relating to acci-dents). In the text this case is always referred to as *Donoghue v Stevenson*, but rarely referred to as *Donoghue*. Note too, that the first of the two named parties, McAlister, is again only rarely referred to in the text. If you were writing about negligence as developed within the law of tort and you decided to shorten this case to *Stevenson* no one would necessarily know the case you were referring to. If you somewhat exceptionally referred to '*Donoghue's case*' most people would know the case but feel that the shortening used was incorrect.

When the second name is rather long and the first party has a shorter name there will be a natural use of the first name only which then becomes common usage. For example the case of *Black-Clawson International v Papierwerke Waldof-Aschaffenburg* [1975] AC 591 is unsurprisingly referred to orally and in the body of text as '*Black-Clawson*', with '*International*' usually being dropped as well. When you are using cases in coursework you will of course be familiar with the area and the standard abbreviations of the names of the parties in the cases that you are dealing with.

Conventions for shortening names of parties in criminal law

When charged with an offence and subsequently indicted in court the offender is referred to as the defendant. It is the defendant who has committed a crime against the public and is therefore answering to the state for his or her actions. At one time the local police com-missioner was the formal prosecuting authority, and the first named party; however, now that the monarch is the formal head of state is used to denote the prosecuting authority and is the first named party to the case. Monarch is used in its generic Latin formulation of Regina (for Queen) or Rex (for King). A signification of R is now normal usage.

Can shortened names be used in your footnote citation?

You will think it tedious perhaps, but the standard rule is that the full reference should be used each time a footnote reference is required. This includes the full reference to the names of the parties. The only formal way around this, if you have already cited the full reference in a previous footnote, is to refer to that previous footnote. If a case report has a popularised name by which it is always known, and one that is not just a simple use of a first named party then you can use the full citation of the parties' names in the first full reference, placing the popularised name in brackets immediately after. The next time you reference you may use the shortened more popular name.

If there are several reports of the case you are referencing you could refer to all reports in your reference; however there is no need to do this as it is sufficient to refer to the most authoritative report according to the hierarchy of reporting.

The following five OSCOLA compliant case references illustrate the general issues raised so far concerning cases.

Example reference 1.

This reference to the case of *Adler v George*[17] is designed to demonstrate the appropriate referencing of a civil case without a neutral citation.

Example reference 2.

This reference to the case of *Evans v Amicus Healthcare Ltd*[18] is designed to demonstrate the referencing of a civil case with a neutral citation and a private report citation.

Example reference 3.

This reference to the case of *R v Moloney*[19] is designed to demonstrate the appropriate referencing of a criminal case without a neutral citation.

Example reference 4.

This reference to the case of *R v Rafferty*[20] is designed to demonstrate the appropriate referencing of a criminal case with a neutral citation.

Example Reference 5.

This reference to the case of *Black-Clawson*[21] is designed to demonstrate the use of shortening of party names. It is a well-known abbreviation of the full case name *Black-Clawson International v Papierwerke Waldof-Aschaffenburg*.

Figures 19.3–19.6 give more information on each full case name and citation.

Pinpoint referencing using cases

When using cases and referencing you may wish to directly quote what a judge has said in the body of your text. In this situation you will need to supply a pinpoint reference, as well as decide what you put in the body of the text, where you should place the superscript marker, and the format of the reference for your footnote.

---

17 [1964] 2 QB 7 (QB).
18 [2004] EWCA Civ 727; [2005] Fam 1.
19 [1985] 2 AC 905 (HL).
20 [2007] EWCA crim 1846; [2008] Crim LR 218.
21 [1975] AC 591.

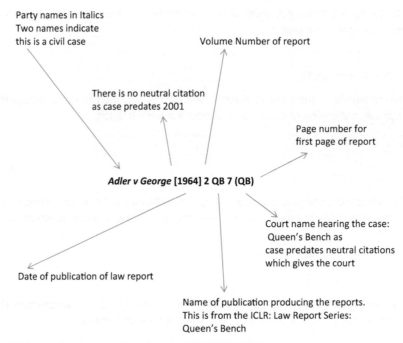

Party names in Italics
Two names indicate
this is a civil case

Volume Number of report

There is no neutral citation
as case predates 2001

Page number for
first page of report

Adler v George [1964] 2 QB 7 (QB)

Court name hearing the case:
Queen's Bench as
case predates neutral citations
which gives the court

Date of publication of law report

Name of publication producing the reports.
This is from the ICLR: Law Report Series:
Queen's Bench

Figure 19.3 Example reference 1: *Adler v George* [1964] 2 QB 7 (QB)

The convention for referencing a verbatim quotation from a judgment remains relatively consistent. If the case is reported you should only quote from the most authoritative law report. Place the text marker for the footnote at the end of the quotation, or after the introduction of the judge in the quotation.

The general rule for the verbatim quotation of text holds for quotes from law cases, reports, texts or any other form of text. A short quotation of two or three lines can be integrated into the text with the use of quotation marks as illustrated in Figure 19.7. A longer quotation of over three lines must be indicated by an indentation in the text allowing the quoted text to stand proud of the rest of the body text. There is no need for quotation marks as the position of the text makes clear it is a verbatim quotation. This is also demonstrated in Figure 19.7.

Referencing secondary sources

Books and journal articles

Books and journals articles can be authored by:

- a single author;
- multiple authors.

Again you will note that this reference has no punctuation, except for a semi-colon dividing the neutral citation, [2004] EWCA Civ 727, from the law report citation, [2005] Fam 1

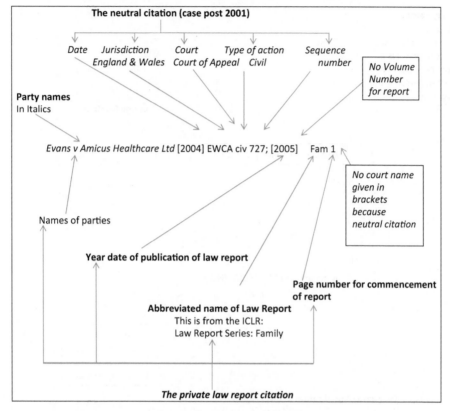

Figure 19.4 Example reference 2: *Evans v Amicus Healthcare Ltd* [2004] EWCA Civ 727; [2005] Fam 1

There are different types of reference that you may wish to make; for example you may wish to:

- Give a direct reference from the text you are reading – a verbatim quotation – here a pinpoint page reference is always required.
- Give an indirect reference – mentioning the author by name when a pinpoint reference may be required but not always.
- Give a specific reference to a viewpoint or argument which does not name the author when the reference is given to the author. If several authors of different texts are to be named they are separated by a semi-colon.

When referencing you may wish to refer to the entire book or just pinpoint one or more pages.

Again there is no punctuation

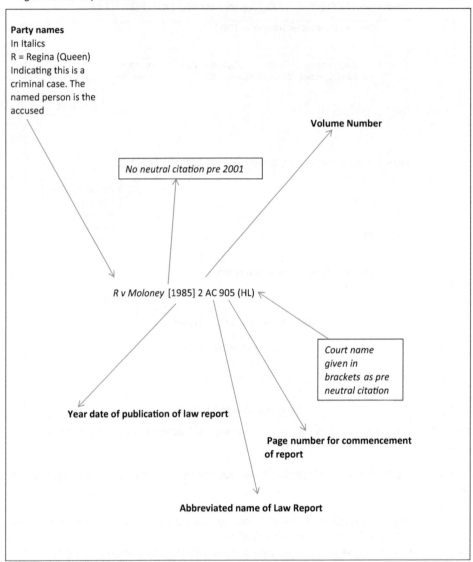

Party names
In Italics
R = Regina (Queen)
Indicating this is a
criminal case. The
named person is the
accused

Volume Number

No neutral citation pre 2001

R v Moloney [1985] 2 AC 905 (HL)

*Court name
given in
brackets as pre
neutral citation*

Year date of publication of law report

**Page number for commencement
of report**

Abbreviated name of Law Report

Figure 19.5 Example reference 3: *R v Moloney* [1985] 2 AC 905 (HL)

Again there is no punctuation and names are in italics. The neutral citation indicates it is a criminal case (Crim). It additionally appears in the specialist report series Criminal Law reports. The lack of any other reference suggests that this report, which is a review summary report and at the bottom of the hierarchy, is the only report of the case.

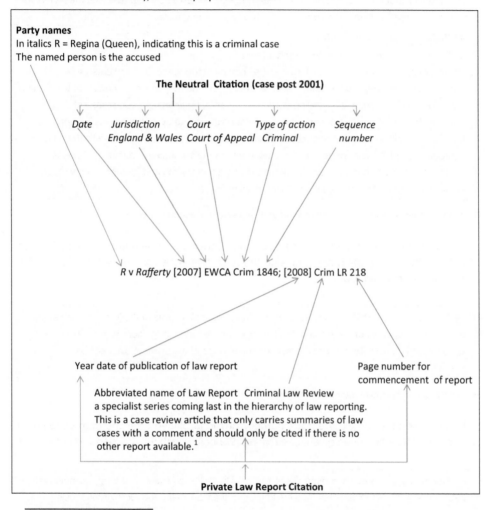

Party names
In italics R = Regina (Queen), indicating this is a criminal case
The named person is the accused

The Neutral Citation (case post 2001)

Date	Jurisdiction	Court	Type of action	Sequence
	England & Wales	Court of Appeal	Criminal	number

R v Rafferty [2007] EWCA Crim 1846; [2008] Crim LR 218

Year date of publication of law report

Page number for commencement of report

Abbreviated name of Law Report Criminal Law Review a specialist series coming last in the hierarchy of law reporting. This is a case review article that only carries summaries of law cases with a comment and should only be cited if there is no other report available.[1]

Private Law Report Citation

[1] The Criminal Appeal Reports, published by the private legal publishing company, Sweet and Maxwell, are the unofficial specialist series of law reports for criminal law which report cases in the Court of Appeal, House of Lords, and the Supreme Court.

Figure 19.6 Example reference 4: *R* v *Rafferty* [2007] EWCA Crim 1846; [2008] Crim LR 218

Example 1: Short quotation

In the case of *Costa v ENEL*[22] the court held that 'As opposed to other international treaties, the Treaty instituting the EEC has created its own order which was integrated with the national order of the member states the moment the Treaty came into force.'[23]

Example 2: Longer quotation

In the case of *Costa v ENEL*[24] the court held that:

As opposed to other international treaties, the Treaty instituting the EEC has created its own order which was integrated with the national order of the member states the moment the Treaty came into force; as such, it is binding upon them. In fact, by creating a community of unlimited duration, having its own institutions, its own personality and its own capacity in law, apart from having international standing and more particularly, real powers resulting from a limitation of competence or a transfer of powers from the states to the community, the member states, albeit within limited spheres, have restricted their sovereign rights and created a body of law applicable both to their nationals and to themselves.[25]

Figure 19.7 Demonstration of insertion of short and long verbatim quotations in text

If you want to refer to a specific page or pages, then the page number is incorporated into the footnote after the bracket closing the main reference for a book (see Figure 19.8 below and its attached footnote).

You can never underestimate the power of the word and the role of the library for the study of law. 'The key tools of the trade of the law student are found in the library, in the millions of words that constitute the body of the law and the millions of words that have been used to talk about the law.'[26]

Figure 19.8 Correct pinpoint reference for book

In the case of an article the page number or run is placed after the commencement page of the article has been given: see Figure 19.9 below with its attached footnote.

Numerous attempts have been made to consider the secularisation thesis; too many fail because they do not realise that they are inappropriately critiquing the roots of the thesis.[27]

Figure 19.9 Correct pinpoint reference for a journal article

Making direct and indirect references from books/articles

A direct reference uses verbatim text from the source, and it can be given with, or without, referring to the author in the body of your text. An indirect reference refers to the situation when you summarise the idea or thought of an author, with or without mentioning the author by name in the body of your text.

---

22 (Case 14/1964) *Costa v Ente Nazionale per l'Energia Elettrica (ENEL)* [1964] CMLR 425.
23 Ibid, p 456.
24 (Case 14/1964) *Costa v Ente Nazionale per l'Energia Elettrica (ENEL)* [1964] CMLR 425.
25 Ibid, p 456.
26 S Hanson *Legal Method, Skills and Reasoning* (3rd edn, Routledge-Cavendish, London 2010), 42.
27 S Hanson 'The Secularisation Thesis: Talking at Cross Purposes' (1997) 12(2) *JCR*, 191, 200.

Indirect referencing can cause students particular trouble. It helps if you place yourself into the shoes of an imaginary person reading your work. They may want to check out your sources for their own research. Are you using sufficient referencing to make it easy for them to locate your material?

Table 19.2 gives you a selection of scenarios that involve direct or indirect referencing and demonstrates appropriate referencing.

TABLE 19.2 MAKING DIRECT AND INDIRECT REFERENCING DECISIONS USING OSCOLA
Direct references: **Please read the three examples of referencing (1)–(3) with their matched footnotes 28–31**
Note: (1) You can either put the author('s) name(s) in the text before, or after, your quotation, In the footnote reference you can choose whether to use just a number to indicate the page after the publication year; or preface your number with a 'p' when you have used the author's name in the text as in example (1).   (2) Or you can use two footnotes, one after the first mention of the author and one after the quote as in example (2).   (3) If you do not put the author's name in the text then you must use a full reference as in example (3).
Examples of direct references:
(1) Hanson contentiously maintains that 'there is a danger that the daily process of *doing* the law blinds the "doers" (the practitioners) to the motivational influences of some institutional creators of law'.[28] Do you agree with this, or is it just empty rhetoric?
(2) Hanson[29] contentiously maintains that 'there is a danger that the daily process of *doing* the law blinds the "doers" (the practitioners) to the motivational influences of some institutional creators of law'.[30] Do you agree with this, or is it just empty rhetoric?
(3) It can be claimed that 'the daily process of *doing* the law blinds the "doers" (the practitioners) to the motivational influences of some institutional creators of law'.[31] Do you agree with this, or is it just empty rhetoric?
Please read the three examples of referencing (1)–(3) with their matched footnotes 32–35
You need to keep an ordered approach to your referencing when you are making an indirect reference to an author who may or may not be mentioned by name in your body text, and may or may not be mentioned alongside other authors. Please consider examples (1)–(3) carefully.
(1) Mention the author by name in the text when a general reference is appropriate. Hanson[32] generally argues that often practitioners as well as others just fail to note why law may have been enacted.

28 S Hanson *Legal Method, Skills and Reasoning* (3rd edn, Routledge-Cavendish, London, 2010), 377.
29 S Hanson *Legal Method, Skills and Reasoning* (3rd edn, Routledge-Cavendish, London, 2010).
30 Ibid, 377.
31 S Hanson *Legal Method, Skills and Reasoning* (3rd edn, Routledge-Cavendish, London, 2010), 377.
32 S Hanson *Legal Method, Skills and Reasoning* (3rd edn, Routledge-Cavendish, London. 2010).

TABLE 19.2—CONTINUED
(2) Mention the author by name in the text when a pinpoint reference to the place in the text is appropriate. Hanson[33] specifically notes that practitioners are blinded by the requirements of 'doing' and fail to see the motivations of those creating the law.
(3) Use appropriate referencing when referring to general agreement on approach by two authors named in your body text. In fact both Hanson[34] and Webb[35] would agree that it is essential to understand the process of rule handling.

Saving time? OSCOLA footnoting protocols when a full reference has already been given

There are times when you may be referring to the same source several times. It is quite tedious to have to replicate the full reference every time. Therefore many referencing systems provide you with accepted shorthand for giving less information in repeated references. There are four standard shortcut methods, and each one is a Latin abbreviation. These are set out in Figure 19.10; do note that OSCOLA only allows the use of two of these standard shortcuts.

Compiling bibliographies, tables of cases and tables of statutes using OSCOLA

A bibliography is a complete alphabetical list of all of your secondary sources, such as books, academic journals and parliamentary papers. For primary legal sources, tables of cases and legislation are prepared. A table of cases is a list of all the law cases referred to in a piece of work and separate tables are constructed for UK, European and/or international law. A table of legislation is a list of all the legislation referred to. Again separate tables are used for European treaties and in the case of the European Union, for European Union legislation.

You can either prepare your bibliography at the end of your research and writing project or compile it as you go along. It makes sense to compile it as you go along as this is more efficient. Just use an open running document as you are working and add sources as you use them. It should not contain any page number references as it is the correct citation to the whole work.

When compiling a bibliography the first name of the author is placed *after* the surname. Please place authors of articles, books and reports in one listing in alphabetical order according to surname. Place authors in date order if you are referring to more than one text written by the same author. Do not give pinpoint references in a bibliography, just the details of publication dates and location. If the reference is to an article give the first page.

---

33 S Hanson *Legal Method, Skills and Reasoning* (3rd edn, Routledge-Cavendish, London, 2010), 377.
34 S Hanson *Legal Method, Skills and Reasoning* (3rd edn, Routledge-Cavendish, London, 2010), 377.
35 J Holland J Webb, *Handling Legal Rules* (6th edn, OUP, Oxford, 2006).

Figure 19.10 Latin references as referencing shortcuts

Example of bibliographic listing

Hanson, S, 'The Secularisation Thesis: Talking at Cross Purposes' (1997) 12(2) *JCR*, 191.

Hanson, S, *Legal Method, Skills and Reasoning* (3rd edn, Routledge-Cavendish, London, 2010).

There is a KEY DIFFERENCE in OSCOLA between the method for referring to the names of authors in your footnotes and in your bibliography. In a footnote reference the author's first name comes before their surname, not after as it does for a bibliographic reference.

How to use the Harvard referencing system

The Harvard system uses an abbreviated in-text referencing to author, year of publication and page number with a reference list set out at the end of the text, or chapter in a book, or even the end of a book. This list is called an endnote or list of references.

For example, the following reference demonstrates a Harvard compliant reference from a book. You will see that the name of the author is placed in the text, with a bracket around the year of publication (2010) and a page reference number (377). The endnote reference is given and you can read it on p. 547.

> Hanson (2010: 377) contentiously maintains that 'there is a danger that the daily process of *doing* the law blinds the "doers" (the practitioners) to the motivational influences of some institutional creators of law.'[36]

In a book, the author can choose where the references are to be placed. For example in a book the author can choose to have them at the end of each chapter, at the end of each part or at the end of the book. But in an essay or a journal article the list of references, the endnotes, would always be at the end of the essay or article immediately before the bibliography if there is one.

The endnote reference list must refer to all the source materials you have referred to in your written work. Your bibliography is much broader than the reference list as it will include all the materials you consulted including those that may not have been referred to in your work. The range of your reading sources is an important aspect of the background to the written work and is therefore given.

In the Harvard system of referencing you have a choice about where you put the full citation of your source: in your endnotes or in your bibliography or in both. Harvard uses a two part process:

(1)   An in-text abbreviated reference to the source material.

(2)   The full reference placed in a list of endnotes and/or a bibliography.

The endnotes reference list is located either at the end of a chapter, or the end of the book. The role of a bibliography is to gather together in one place an alphabetically ordered list of all sources consulted for the written work. The endnotes just give the full citation for all sources noted in the text and are divided into sections in a longer work.[37]

The most complicated aspect of Harvard referencing is learning the conventions for the in-text referencing, and particularly the in-text referencing of books. Whilst the protocols for books are complex there are no hard and fast rules in the Harvard system for the in-text referencing of primary law (e.g. cases, legislation or treaties). You may either adapt Harvard as you wish, or adopt OSCOLA conventions in terms of the names of the parties or the statute in the body text, and then provide the full citation in the reference list. Cases, legislation and treaties can also appear as a table after the bibliography.

---

36 S Hanson (2010) *Legal Method, Skills and Reasoning* (3rd edn, London, Routledge-Cavendish).

37 OSCOLA has a three part process: the placing of a footnote marker in the text, the reference in the footnote and the reference in the bibliography.

With the exception of primary law materials, the Harvard system gives clear rules for the in-text reference and list of references for nearly all other imaginable sources. The full reference required for the endnotes or the bibliography is relatively straightforward and this will be considered after looking at the in-text referencing protocols.

The in-text reference

We now turn to consider the in-text referencing for the following source materials:

- Books.
- Academic journals.
- Law cases (both reported and unreported).
- Legislation.
- Newspapers.
- Law commission.
- Command papers.
- Parliamentary debates.
- Parliamentary papers.

In-text referencing protocols

As discussed above there are many ways in which you will want to directly and indirectly refer to and therefore reference your sources. You will want to make different types of in-text reference (e.g. direct, indirect or a specific reference to where a viewpoint is given). Also you may be dealing with sole or multiple authors.

When referencing you may wish to refer to the entire book generally or give a pinpoint reference. In the Harvard system you only need to note the author's surname in the text followed by the date of publication in round brackets. If you wish to pinpoint a specific page or pages within that book this information must appear immediately after the year date remaining within the round brackets, and separated from it by a comma. Use a 'p' for a one page reference or 'pp' to denote a several page reference as follows.

- Hanson (2009, p 45).
- Hanson (2009, pp 45–70).

Personally, I prefer the allowed Harvard variation of dropping the reference to the p or pp and using a colon ':' followed by the page reference. I think that this is a both a cleaner and quicker method of pinpoint referencing for example:

- Hanson (2009: 45).
- Hanson (2009: 45–70).

Below you will find examples of how to engage in direct and indirect in-text referencing for Harvard.

TABLE 19.3 SINGLE AUTHORS: MAKING DIRECT AND INDIRECT REFERENCING DECISIONS USING HARVARD

NOTE: When the author's name is mentioned in the narration as it is in the first two examples it is placed outside the brackets. When the author's name is not mentioned in the narration and is just in the text as the reference it is placed inside the brackets.

(1) A direct reference when you have used the author's name in the text.

 (a) *(i) Using a colon ':'*
- Herring (2009: 69) asserts that 'A powerful objection to the current law on assaults is that it is applied inconsistently.'

(ii) Using a 'p'
- Herring (2009, p 69) asserts that 'A powerful objection to the current law on assaults is that it is applied inconsistently.'

(b) A direct reference when you have not used the author's name in the text.
- It is quite usual to come across concerns about the rationality of the law on assault: 'A powerful objection to the current law on assaults is that it is applied inconsistently' (Herring, 2009: 69).

(2) An indirect reference when you have used the author's name in the text

(a) Mentioning the author by name in the text.
- Herring (2009) discusses a range of contentious issues within criminal law.

(b) Mentioning the author by name in the text when a pinpoint reference to the place in the text is appropriate.
- Herring (2009: 69) agrees with the view expressed by many commentators that the application of the law on assaults is unreliable and inconsistent.

(c) When mentioning two authors.
- Both Herring (2009: 69) and Padfield (2012) agree with the view expressed by many commentators that the application of the law on assaults is unreliable and inconsistent.

(3) An indirect reference to a sole author when you have not mentioned their name in the text: the reference is given to the author usually at the end of the sentence with their name enclosed within the brackets.
- Many commentators express the view that the law relating to assaults is inconsistently applied (Herring, 2009).

(4) An indirect reference to several authors when you have not mentioned their names in the body of your text: reference is usually given to the authors at the end of the sentence with their names enclosed within the brackets and a semi colon separating them.
- Many commentators express the view that the law relating to assaults is inconsistently applied (Herring, 2009; Padfield, 2012).

Slightly different protocols are used when dealing with multiple authors. The essence of the in-text citation remains the same, the name of the author(s) followed by the date of the publication enclosed in round brackets. However there are also differences of referencing based upon whether there are:

- Two authors.
- More than two authors.

For books with multiple authors, these three types of in-text reference can be set out as below.

TABLE 19.4 INDIRECT REFERENCE TO MULTIPLE AUTHORS
(1) Indirect reference to a book by two authors referred to by name in your text: You must separate the names of the two authors by the word 'and':   • Elliot and Quinn (2012) provide a good introduction to criminal law.
(2) Indirect reference to a book by two authors which is not referred to by name in your text: You must separate the names of the two authors by an '&' and place all information in brackets. If the reference is to come at the end of the sentence enclose the brackets within the punctuation of the sentence. The reference may also be placed anywhere within the sentence that you consider makes best sense to the reader.   • There are a range of good texts on criminal law for the student to choose from; the choice is often a highly personalised one (Elliot & Quinn, 2012).
(3) Indirect reference to a book mentioned in your text where there are more than two authors. You stick to the ordering of the authors in the book as published (which is usually alphabetical). List the authors separating them with a comma; however, place an 'and' before the last author.   • Davies, Croall and Tyrer (2010) provide an excellent complementary text for criminal law students seeking to expand their knowledge into the social scientific study of criminal justice.
(4) Indirect reference to a book not mentioned in your text where there are more than two authors. You stick to the ordering of the authors in the book as published (which is usually alphabetical). List the authors separating them with a comma; however, place an '&' before the last author. Enclose the entire reference within round brackets.   • A range of texts provide an excellent complementary text for criminal law students seeking to expand their knowledge into the social scientific study of criminal justice (Davies, Croall & Tyrer, 2010).
(5) Indirect reference to a book mentioned in your text where there are more than three authors. You need only quote the first author mentioned followed by 'et al.' meaning 'and others'. Can be in normal font or italics.

TABLE 19.5 MULTIPLE AUTHORS: MAKING REFERENCE TO MULTIPLE TEXTS BY ONE AUTHOR USING HARVARD
(1) Reference to several works by an author when their name is in your text. • Hanson (1999, 2003 and 2009) seeks to refine a particular approach to legal reasoning.
(2) Reference to several works by an author when their name is not in your text. • Many authors writing in the field of legal methods and reasoning seek to refine their approach to the subject (Hanson, 1999, 2003 and 2009).
(3) Reference to several works by an author in the same year when their name is in the text. • After the date in brackets allocate each work a lower case alphabetical indicator in alphabetical order. • Hanson (2007 a, b) has written about the language of law and its connection with religion.
(4) Reference to several works by an author in the same year when their name is not in the text. • Place author and date in brackets and after the date in brackets allocate each work a lower case alphabetical indicator in alphabetical order. • Law and language is increasingly an object of research (Hanson, 2007 a, b).

You may find that a particular author you have been reading has repeated or refined their argument in several books. All you need do in this case is refer to the different titles in chronological order in the in-text reference.

Often students are unsure about how to reference an author whose chapter has appeared in an edition of essays. The rule is that in your text you reference the author and the year of the volume but in your endnote and/or bibliography you give the full reference to the edited volume, including title and editor, plus the specific chapter title. This process is set out below as in Table 19.6 an example.

Referencing UK cases and legislation in Harvard

As noted there are no set conventions, and it is acceptable to follow the OSCOLA protocols for this. The in-text proper names are generally in italics as an in-text reference.

TABLE 19.6 DEALING WITH THE REFERENCING OF EDITED VOLUMES
In-text referencing of an author with a chapter in an edited collection. • Nathanson (1989) was one of the earliest writers to introduce students in the academy to drafting skills.

The endnote/bibliographic reference:
Whilst reading the in-text reference above one would assume that Nathanson was the sole author. However, the bibliographic entry which is listed below makes clear he is a contributor to an edited collection of articles. Nathanson, S (1989) 'Drafting a Legal Document'. In: Gold, N., Mackie, K. & Twining T. (eds) (1989) *Learning Lawyer's Skills* Butterworths, pp 139–148.

Shortcuts in Harvard referencing

Do refer back to Figure 19.10 relating to Latin references in the Harvard system. All four Latin shortcuts are acceptable in Harvard. That is:

- **Cf.:** From Latin **Confer** meaning to compare and consult so a reference stating Cf. Hanson n9 means compare this to what is said by Hanson in reference note 9.
- **Ibid:** From **Ibidem** meaning 'In the same place'. This is used to refer to the reference that is immediately before.
- **Loc. cit.:** From the Latin **loco citato** meaning 'in the place cited'.
- **Op. cit.:** From the Latin meaning **opere citato** 'in the work cited'.

PLAGIARISM

Many perceived problems that students have with plagiarism, particularly in relation to a fearfulness about 'doing it' and worrying about how to 'avoid it', come down to a complete misunderstanding of the purpose of referencing, and how to use methods of referencing.

What is plagiarism?

Each university will have its own preferred formal definition of plagiarism within its policy on the academic conduct of students. In essence, however, plagiarism is taking the work of another (e.g. ideas, illustrations, diagrams, statistics and words) and passing them off as your own. It can of course be completely avoided by making sure that you keep to the referencing protocols set out above. They render accidental plagiarism virtually impossible if you have kept careful notes of your research clearly indicating the work of others.

Now that you have worked through the pages on referencing you will be quite clear about the importance of referencing the ideas and work of another. This is important to give credit to those whose work you have read and considered when preparing your argument in your piece of work. Referencing correctly distinguishes clearly between the thoughts and words of another and your own thought and words. When you reference correctly, anyone reading your work can check out for themselves the sources you have used, to see if they agree or disagree with your interpretation of them.

Plagiarism is a form of intellectual theft, and a breach of university discipline in relation to your own work. The definitions of plagiarism do not have a built-in requirement of intention. Therefore even accidental plagiarism, due to bad habits with referencing or note taking, is still plagiarism nonetheless.

Sophisticated anti-plagiarism software is now used by the majority of universities. These enable not only thousands of databases to be searched but also enable universities, with suitable permissions, to access collections of assignments written for other public and private educational and providers and services.

You are liable to an accusation of plagiarism if you engage in any of the following activities in your written assignments without referencing the work of the original author. (This is still the case even if you were the original author, for example you rewrite, in a formally submitted assignment for your current education institution, sections from another assignment submitted formally for credit at your current or a previous educational institution).

- Summarising the work of others.
- Paraphrasing the work of others.
- Using the exact words of another – direct quotation.
- Referring to statements of law.
- Referring to statistics.
- Referring to the execution of research.
- Referring to definitions in dictionaries and/or encyclopaedias.

WHAT IS THE SANCTION FOR PLAGIARISM?

All universities are united in treating plagiarism as an extremely serious breach of university discipline. If the investigation process finds that you have committed plagiarism, a range of sanctions can be applied. Sanctions can range from a reduction of marks, insertion of a zero for that piece of work and in the most serious cases of intentional plagiarism, expulsion from the university.

A finding of plagiarism may be viewed as evidence of lack of good character by professional bodies such as the Law Society or the Bar Council. University law schools have an obligation to report findings of plagiarism to the Law Society and the Bar Counsel. A finding of plagiarism therefore can halt your career in law before it has begun. There is far too much at risk to engage in any form of intentional or accidental plagiarism.

CONCLUSION

You may find the task of referencing daunting because there seem to be so many rules. But if you think in terms of how to reference different types of documents you will quickly assimilate the information. Whilst it saves time to internalise the basics of referring to books, articles, internet sources, law reports, law transcripts and legislation you can look up any other document you come across in research and wish to reference on a 'need to know' basis. Both OSCOLA and Harvard have full manuals that will be available to you in your university library or on your library web pages and/or your VLE. Often you can download them for reference.

Plagiarism need not be a worry to you if you have good referencing protocols. You will not accidentally plagiarise if you understand referencing.

CHAPTER SUMMARY

- Students are expected to explain, compare and critique the work of others in their assessment and it is also expected that they will effectively and meticulously reference the work of others.
- Not only must verbatim (direct) quotations from work be referenced but so must all summaries indebted to a particular author or authors.
- The two main referencing systems used in UK law schools are OSCOLA and Harvard.
- Unlike Harvard the OSCOLA system is specifically designed to ease the complexity of English primary law referencing.
- Harvard offers no special method for referencing English primary law (or any form of law) and it is acceptable therefore to adapt the OSCOLA system if you are using Harvard.
- Your university may stipulate a particular system of referencing and if this is the case you must follow it.
- Plagiarism is using the work of others without referencing it.
- A finding of plagiarism, even accidental plagiarism, can seriously affect your studies.
- A law student is particularly affected as all incidents of plagiarism must be reported to the law professional bodies and can be looked upon as potential unfitness of character for the legal profession.
- Good referencing means that you will not accidentally plagiarise.

GENERAL
ORAL SKILLS

20

'Speak clearly, if you speak at all;
carve every word before you let
it fall.'

Oliver Wendell Holmes

LEARNING OUTCOMES

After reading this chapter you should be able to:

- Understand the specific personal skills of oral delivery, such as volume and tone of voice, body position, eye contact and speed of delivery, and how they equate with written skills.
- Appreciate the importance of understanding the skills sets required for differing types of oral skills exercise.
- Understand the issues involved in managing an oral skills exercise.
- Develop personal confidence in public speaking in front of your peer group and teachers.

INTRODUCTION

Any form of rounded academic education should ensure that graduates leave university with excellent communication skills. Legal education at the academic stage provides you with several different opportunities to develop your oral skills. In addition, should you intend to pursue a career in law, the vocational stage of legal training majors on assessing students as they engage in a large number of oral exercises that test competency in a range of differing types of oral communication skills, as well as the ability to apply legal rules or deliver legal information.

This chapter provides an introduction to general oral skills for personal development and assessment purposes. Part 6 includes specific chapters that each cover the types of oral skills exercises that law departments often use to develop student competency: presentations and debating, mooting, negotiation and mediation. Presentations, debating and negotiation are not unique to law and will be used on many degree programmes to assess student learning and development. Mooting, however, is unique to legal courses and mediation is an emerging area of assessment. If your department engages in national or international competitions in the areas of mooting and debating, or fields a team for the client counselling competition, you may be able to further develop your competency in these fields outside the classroom. Mediation is a relative newcomer to the group of oral skills that students are given the opportunity to gain competency in whilst at the academic stage of legal training.

ORAL SKILLS EXERCISES

The main types of oral skills exercises that you are liable to encounter on your law degree course are set out in Figure 20.1.

Some of these will be individual tasks only; others will require group work. Whatever the nature of the oral skills tasks their successful completion involves working on six key components (usually several at the same time):

- understanding the nature of the task;
- managing the task;
- research;
- content;
- delivery;
- teamwork.

Each of these six components are interconnected, as demonstrated in Figure 20.3 and a deficiency in one area can affect results for assessed exercises.

The research and content aspects of oral skills exercises generally require skills that are no different from those of research and content with regard to written exercises. The

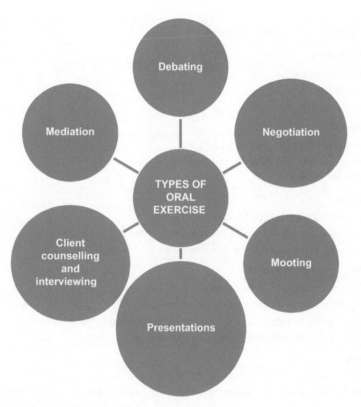

Figure 20.1 Types of oral skills exercises

main differences occur at the level of delivery in terms of style and language, and whether teamwork is involved.

The following sections work through each of the components in detail.

Understanding

There are several types of oral skills tasks and each has different requirements. You and your team (if there is one) must commit proper time to making sure you know exactly what the task is, what it is testing and drawing out all its issues. If you do not properly understand the task itself you will not obtain a good result.

Managing the task

There are two levels at which it is important to manage the task: the macro organisation of the order and timing of each sub-task that leads to the final product; and the micro organisation of ensuring the time limit for actual delivery is met.

Key components of oral skills exercises
(1) Understanding
• The nature of the task.   • The type of task.   • The requirements of the task.
(2) Managing
• Micro management of your personal time.   • Macro management of a team and the team's time.   • Managing your stress.
(3) Research
• Understanding the legal question posed by the task.   • Dividing the task into sub-tasks as appropriate for research.   • Researching the main issue and sub-issues.
(4) Content of oral skills exercise
• Ensuring content relevant to the question.   • Ensuring competent argument(s) put forward.   • Incorporating a rich range of sources to support argument(s) constructed.   • Using appropriate referencing – even oral skills work will require some referencing protocols.
(5) Delivery
• Use appropriate voice tone, speed of voice, and vocabulary.   • Support oral skills work with appropriate, high quality audio-visual aids for the audience (the marker).   • Deploy useful prompt cards.   • Produce an accurate copy of the full text of oral delivery for the marker.
(6) Team work
• Utilising different types of management and planning in the previous points.   • Working to ensure there is a good interpersonal relationship for the task.   • Managing team member performance.   • Managing the expectations of group members.

Figure 20.2 Summarises the nature of these six components

Overall task management

The degree of detail required by the oral skills exercise will be determined by the timescale you have been given. A five minute presentation cannot deliver the same level of detail as a 25-minute one. The longer you have the more detailed your presentation would have to be.

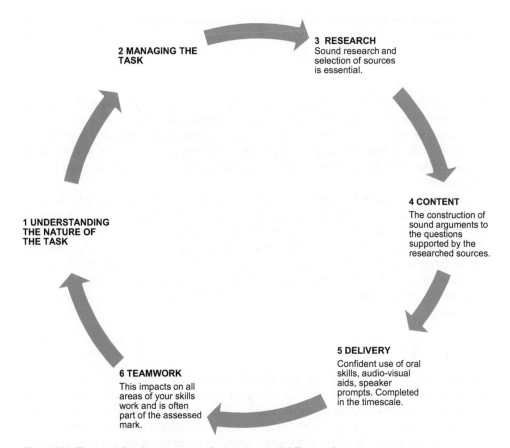

2 MANAGING THE TASK

3 RESEARCH
Sound research and selection of sources is essential.

4 CONTENT
The construction of sound arguments to the questions supported by the researched sources.

1 UNDERSTANDING THE NATURE OF THE TASK

5 DELIVERY
Confident use of oral skills, audio-visual aids, speaker prompts. Completed in the timescale.

6 TEAMWORK
This impacts on all areas of your skills work and is often part of the assessed mark.

Figure 20.3 The interrelated components of competent oral skills exercises

Also, an assessed oral exercise will be treated somewhat differently to a non-assessed exercise as it will be supplied with assessment criteria. These give details of what the marker is looking for in the finished exercise, and the skills levels required to obtain marks in each grade. You should be given a copy of the mark sheet and assessment criteria that the assessor will use, or be directed to a general mark sheet and general oral skills assessment criteria that are used for oral assessment.

The assessment criteria and the mark sheet are important documents to consider because they tell you what you have to do and how this should be demonstrated. You should also check the marks allocations as you will find out how many marks are available for content and argument construction, how many for teamwork if relevant and how many for the purely oral skills of tone of voice, speed of voice, use of appropriate formal language and so on.

Time limits

The 'time limit' given for any oral skills work can be viewed as having the same function as a 'word limit' in written work. But, while departmental regulations can often allow a 10 per cent leeway on word counts, time limits in oral assessments are rigorously applied and the student will be asked to stop speaking when the time is up. If crucial matters have not been dealt with this can have a detrimental effect on the overall mark awarded for the assessment.

The length of time that students are required to speak varies according to the purpose of the exercise and the level of study. A student nearing the end of their degree may be asked to speak for 25 minutes or longer. A student at the start of their studies may be asked to speak for 10 minutes alone, or to be a part of a group of students that in total only present for 10 minutes (so it is likely, depending on group size, that students speak for only 2–3 minutes each). Equally, however, a new law student could be asked to speak for 25 minutes. Whatever your time limit stick to it and plan your argument accordingly.

Managing stress

You may always find speaking in public difficult, but you can find ways to do it without everyone else knowing you are nervous. When we are stressed, our mouths dry out, so it is a good idea to have a glass of water available. A quick note to your marker, explaining the situation, should be enough for that to be allowed. Breathing exercises can help steady your nerves too. You will also find that if you feel you are in control of the exercise, knowing what it is about and where you fit, this will lessen your nerves.

Research

Understanding the question

You must ensure that you have properly and thoroughly understood the question. Researching the right area requires that you ascertain what the question is asking for. The issues here are no different to the type of investigations you were directed to engage in for law reports and secondary sources. Ask yourself what issues you think flow out of the question posed. Even if the topic is new to you, you can engage in prediction as the reading strategy in Chapter 17 suggests.

Whatever the exact nature of your oral skills exercise you will be called upon to deploy argument. You can only hold a plausible given position (for or against a proposal) if you know *what* the question is asking.

Delivery

Your oral skills exercise is a performance and your voice can be considered as an instrument. It matters therefore how loud or soft it is, how quickly or slowly you speak. Your voice is your expression of yourself to the outside world. You use it to express pain, joy, fear, nervousness, excitement and more. You can slow it down, speed it up, make it loud, make it almost inaudible or utter many different levels of sound in between. Your voice comes with its own particular resonance and accent, giving you a unique vocal stamp.

Listeners have optimum levels of understanding for voices, but they can also be rather easily put off by the sound of a particular voice. This can mean that they do not properly listen to you, which could be a problem if you are being assessed and your voice distracts your marker and they find it difficult to listen to. You need to use the right levels of audibility, changing your tone of voice to signal new ideas in much the way that you would signal a new paragraph in written work. Your body language should not be distracting, and you should not, as a way of dealing with nervousness, develop repetitive unconscious reactions, such as constantly flicking the same piece of hair out of your eyes or moving your hands too much. It is also possible not to move enough. Competent performance of language is a skill that needs to be acquired and this requires practice.

Think of times when you have listened to other people formally speaking; I am sure you will agree that you find it is a problem if they speak:

too quietly or too loudly.

Is it difficult to follow if their voice maintains a rather monotonous tone? Are you distracted by repetitive movements which are out of keeping with what the speaker is saying? Do you find it difficult to follow an argument if you are constantly drawn to irritating mannerisms such as foot-tapping or scratching?

It can be equally distracting and irritating for an audience to listen to vocal stutters, such as:

- errrrrrr;
- ummm;
- ahhhhh;
- errrr . . . ummmm . . . ah . . .

Have you noticed that some speakers will say 'er' or something similar every few words?

Often speakers are not aware of the impact of these verbal hiccups, but listeners, and markers, definitely are.

Body language

Slouching, leaning against furniture and putting your hands in your pockets can all be distracting. Do not let yourself down by using inappropriate body language for the circumstances.

TEAM WORKING

Oral skills exercises, whether assessed or non-assessed, will often involve team or group work. This brings into play another range of interpersonal skills and can be quite stressful, particularly if the exercise is assessed. Sometimes you will be allowed to choose your group, and sometimes (perhaps most often) your group will be neutrally allocated to you by your lecturer. Many of you will have experienced some degree of team working prior to university, and it may have been a good or a bad experience. The fact is that success in life is very much down to your ability to engage at the appropriate time in competent interpersonal skills and to work as part of a team. The development of interpersonal skills through team working is one of the essential skills of a competent graduate.

Many students working in teams or groups do not stop to consider the challenges of working with other people. It is important to note that everyone in the group may have different understandings of how to:

- work with others as part of a team;
- manage their own time;
- make sense of the material collected;
- make useful notes;
- make sense of the question;
- deliver an oral presentation.

Nothing can be more destructive to teamwork than self-appointed leaders inefficiently bullying others to do the work. The importance of commencing each team task as a group and considering what the task requires, how it will be managed and timed and who will do what, by when, cannot be over-emphasised.

Your course/module leader will have strategies for dealing with students who do not work well within a group. You need to carefully read instructions that you have been given for the group task to find out what you need to do in those circumstances.

CONCLUSION

As you will have noted, many general skills are combined to ensure that you can competently engage in assessed oral skills work. You need to understand these skills so that you can successfully join them to the specific skills that may be required for the different types of oral skills assessments that you will be involved in (e.g. presentation, mooting, negotiation, mediation). How you use your voice as well as your vocabulary are important aspects of oral skills work to competently deploy alongside the subject specific knowledge and specific oral skills required for the differing types of exercise.

Ultimately oral skills exercises depend on careful preparation just like any other assessment or developmental exercise. Oral skills exercises cannot be passed on the strength of your voice alone; you need to join the study skills habits you are developing together with your knowledge of legal research and when you have located your material you need to construct your argument. A good argument will take you a long way to success; join to that argument excellent pacing, clarity of expression, perfect timing, and to keep a connection with your audience you will be able to deliver good oral skills exercises. Chapters 23–27 consider in detail the development of your oral skills in relation to presentations, mooting, negotiation and mediation.

CHAPTER SUMMARY

- Competent oral skills involve skills relating to voice, language, confidence, team and subject knowledge.
- Any oral skills exercise tends to involve six general interrelated task components: understanding, managing, research, content, delivery and teamwork.
- It is essential to read assessment criteria and marks allocations as well as rigidly keep to set time limits for delivery.
- Your voice is important: ensure you can be heard, that you adopt an interesting tone and do not speak too quickly.
- Use the appropriate vocabulary for the task in hand, do not be formal when informality is required or informal when formality is required.
- Oral skills work can also depend on good interpersonal skills, especially those relating to team working.

PART 6

LAW ASSESSMENTS: WRITTEN AND ORAL

Part 6 is concerned with your competent performance in written and oral assessment throughout the degree programme, including your efficient revision and execution of examinations. Assessment and examinations test the whole range of your skills as they are performed by you in a series of one-off events throughout the years of your degree.

The quality of your language and your argument construction skills become essential as these are the vehicles that carry your legal work regardless of whether the assessment is written or oral. Your legal research skills allow you to locate the range of sources required for your work, but your skill in summarising, evaluating and critiquing those retrieved sources, and the demonstration of your critical thinking powers, are equally important. Your ability to comfortably use legal and academic as well as occasional legal professional resources will also be evaluated in assessments and examinations.

Law degrees are primarily assessed through written work. You may be asked to write a report or an essay or provide a solution to a legal problem. Chapters 21 and 22 exclusively consider law essays and problem solutions. The majority of law schools continuously assess students through the year as well as in set examinations which are invariably timed written occasions. Chapter 23 considers in detail specific issues to bear in mind when approaching revision and the day of an exam.

More law schools are now assessing general oral skills through presentations, and specialist legal skills through mooting, negotiation and mediation exercises and these are considered in Chapters 24–27.

All assessments test the developmental state of all of your skills and they must always be approached in a careful and timely manner. Taken together they also determine your degree classification.[1]

---

1 In some law schools year 1 does not count towards your degree classification, it is a qualifier. In some law schools, however, it may count.

WRITING LAW ESSAYS

21

LEARNING OUTCOMES

After reading this chapter you should be able to:

- Be aware of the appropriate way to structure an essay.
- Be clear about the importance of referencing, language usage and presentation.
- Be able to bring together the skills of research, analysis and argument construction and demonstrate competency in writing.

INTRODUCTION

This chapter considers the task of essay writing and suggests a method for constructing an essay. Most of your essays in your law modules will require you to show familiarity with handling legal rules and academic texts about law. This involves being able to develop an understanding of legal language. The characteristics of legal language will be considered at the beginning of this chapter.

The chapter then lays out an eight stage model for constructing an essay which if followed will ensure that you do not hand in work that has not been properly thought through. Students often spend far too little time preparing and thinking about the essay and then are concerned that they do not understand the question. But they are not incapable of understanding; it is just that they did not spend enough time thinking about *what* the question was asking and preparing the texts to be used.

Essay writing depends on your development of various skills set out in previous chapters: general language and writing skills, including finding your written voice,[1] referencing,[2] the development of good study skills,[3] reading[4] and research skills,[5] legal method and argument construction[6] as well as understanding the basic structure of essay writing. In addition it depends on the development of your understanding of the module that has set the essay.

A competent approach to legal research skills, argument construction and legal writing will allow you to produce work that demonstrates your understanding of an area. If you can synthesise your skills and create arguments rationally on the basis of existing theory, cases, statutes, and practice you should generate good results in the distinction category. Students who try to be creative but fail to produce any plausible evidence for their argument construct weak pieces of work that result in low grades.

CHARACTERISTICS OF LEGAL LANGUAGE

All academic disciplines have their own technical language, often expressed in Latin words and phrases and the law is no exception. In fact you may already know that English law uses unusual phrases and words many of which are in Latin. Some Latinised words or phrases are still used in legal documents because they are the product of a time during which those words were thought to be best practice. However, in addition there are still a large number of Latin phrases which could be described as technical terms. For example, within criminal law the physical and mental state elements of a crime are still referred to as the *actus reus* (guilty act) and *mens rea* (guilty mind) respectively. So much case law has been built up on the meanings of many of these Latin terms it is currently not thought viable to use English translations in case this introduces uncertainty into the interpretation

---

1   Chapter 18.
2   Chapter 19.
3   Chapter 16.
4   Chapter 17.
5   All of the chapters in Part 2.
6   Chapters 13 and 14.

of the law. However, many previously accepted Latin phrases have now been anglicised, such as an *ex parte* application which is now referred to as an 'application without notice'. Latin phrases should always be italicised. Table 21.1 sets out some standard Latin abbreviations used in standard academic writing as well as legal writing.

TABLE 21.1 GENERAL: LATIN ABBREVIATIONS USED IN STANDARD ACADEMIC WRITING AND LEGAL WRITING

Latin abbreviation	Latin full term	English terminology
c. or ca	*circa*	Approximately, about
cf.	*confer*	compare
e.g.	*exempli gratia*	for example, for instance
et al.	*et alii, et alia*	and other people/things
etc.	*et cetere*	and so on, and the rest
et. seq	*et sequens*	and the following pages
ibid	*ibidem*	in the same place (usually to refer to a reference)
i.e.	*id est*	that is, in other words
inter alia	*inter alia*	among other things
loc. cit.	*loco citato*	in the place mentioned
NB	*nota bene*	note well or carefully for important point
no	*numero*	number
op. cit.	*opere citato*	before in the work mentioned
passim	*passim*	at many points, recurrent
viz.	*videlicet*	namely (person or thing just referred to)
LEGAL		
Latin abbreviation	**Latin full term**	**English terminology**
Cur. adv. vult.	*Curia advisari vult*	The court wishes to be advised
Actus reus	*actus non facit reum nisi mens sit rea*	The guilty act/state: 'an act does not make a person guilty unless (their) mind is also guilty'
Mens rea	*actus non facit reum nisi mens sit rea*	The guilty mind 'an act does not make a person guilty unless (their) mind is also guilty'
Obiter	*Obiter dictum (obiter dicta plural)*	Comments made 'by the way' in a judgment and not key to the decision in that case. But they can be persuasive precedents under certain conditions

TABLE 21.1—continued		
Latin abbreviation	**Latin full term**	**English terminology**
Per incuriam		Without proper consideration or care, a situation where a court has given a decision ignoring or forgetting or being unaware of an applicable common law or statutory rule that should have been taken into account
Ratio	*Rationes decidendi (rationes decidendi plural)*	The reason for the decision. This is the binding part of a case, the binding precedent, and one that the judiciary must strictly follow under the doctrine of *stare decisis*
Stare decisis	*Stare decisis et non quieta movere*	To stand by decisions and not change/disturb them. This refers to the obligation of the judiciary to follow the doctrine of precedent
De minimis	*De minimis non curat lex*	The law can provide no remedy for a matter that is too trivial

English words that have come to develop a special meaning in law

A large number of perfectly ordinary English words have come to have a particular meaning within law, such as assault, battery, consideration, intention, reasonable, property, negligence, and reckless. It is wise to avoid using these terms informally in your writing; only use them if at all in their legal meaning to avoid any possible confusion in the mind of the reader.

THE IMPORTANCE OF WIDER READING AND CAREFUL NOTE TAKING

For all assessment your final work needs to demonstrate your understanding of the topic under discussion by your careful application and interpretation of your retrieved research materials. If you are pushed for time and only engage in limited research for your written coursework, it can be tempting to focus on finding and summarising articles that obviously answer the question at the more pedestrian level of description. If you only recount the facts and outcomes of cases, or summarise argument in texts, without demonstrating a critical awareness of the relevancy of the issues raised and an ability to apply them appropriately to your essay question your writing will not attract good grades. You need to use your materials to present an argument or a series of arguments supported by evidence in answer to the question.

Careful summarised notes of cases and texts that have identified arguments containing useful points and relevant quotations provide a good basis for argument construction as part of your response to the essay question.

It is essential to spend time thinking about what the question is asking, analysing the texts to be used and constructing an argument in answer to the question.

Good academic writing is a time-consuming task, and the time has to be found by you.

It takes *time* to properly:

understand the basic issues involved in the writing task;

appreciate the interconnectedness of the texts;

research sources;

compare texts, and compare your view with the view of other writers;

determine your views;

construct an argument in answer to the essay or problem.

If you choose not to engage in any reading beyond lecture notes and the textbook for your essay you would be missing out on some of the following valuable aids to writing your essay. You will remember some of these from Chapter 18:

- Academic disputes related to the area of relevance to your essay.
- Comments on the limitations in the arguments of others.
- Non-legal texts: legal, sociological, geographical, historical, political.
- Evidences to back your research as well as evidence that does not.
- Further references from reading that you can follow up.
- Interesting examples of practical research that tests theory.
- Other interpretations of the cases you are using.
- Recommendations of main findings of relevant research.

WHAT IS AN ESSAY?

In the university an essay is a relatively short piece of writing in response to a title given to the student by the lecturer, in which the student is expected to forward an argument or a series of arguments supported by evidence in answer to the matter(s) raised by the essay title.

Lecturers normally apply a word limit to the writing. Many first year essays can be 500–1,500 words. In later years some extended, or long essays, may be up to 5,000–10,000 words. Part of the skill of the essay writer is the ability to write appropriately to the word count.

What is the purpose of an essay?

An essay question is designed to test students' abilities in the following areas:

- Knowledge of the law or a law related issue.
- Ability to construct a sustained argument.
- Ability to apply primary legal texts and secondary academic texts to an issue.
- Knowledge of the grey areas of the law surrounding the cases decided in the given area under consideration.
- Knowledge of particular interpretational issues arising in the law under consideration.
- Ability to engage in critical reasoning.

What standard formats are used for essay questions?

Essay questions are set in one of the following formats:

(1)   A question requiring an answer.
(2)   A quotation that is given with the bland request to 'discuss'.
(3)   A quotation accompanied by a specific request to extract issues raised by the quotation.

Figure 21.1 sets out examples of essay titles to give you an idea of the formats used. There are a number of key activity words used in these below questions.

Question 1: Critically assess.
Question 2: Explain statement AND comment.
Question 3: Discuss the issues arising from quotation.
Question 4: Discuss SOLELY with reference to (1), (2) and (3).

These activity words/phrases determine your approach to the essay. If you do not give them sufficient attention then you will find your marks are low.

Because the instructions you are given with regard to an essay question can differ enormously, Table 21.2 sets out a range of standard words used in essay instructions and gives a definition of those words and an indication of what you are being asked to do.

Essay Question 1 Critically assess the view that the Equality Act 2010 has successfully dealt with the deficiencies of previous discrimination legislation.
Essay Question 2 'Damages are meant to put a claimant, so far as money can do it, in the same position as if the contract had been performed.' Explain this statement and comment.
Essay Question 3 'The English legal system is like a house that is not only too small, it is in need of repair. The question is do we build another extension and repair as necessary or pull the whole thing down and start again?' Discuss the issues arising from this quotation.
Essay Question 4 'In *R v Secretary of State ex p Factortame (No 1)* and *(No 2)* the English courts and the Court of Justice of the EU (GJEU) made it clear that not only do English courts have the power to suspend Acts of Parliament conflicting with European Union law but that European Union law demands that the provisions of lawfully enacted Acts of the UK Parliament be overturned and the CJEU can even dictate what national remedies should be available.' Discuss solely with reference to the following texts: (1) Extracts from *R v Factortame (No 1)*. (2) Extracts from *R v Factortame (No 2)*. (3) Extracts on the VLE from Tillotson, *European Community law: Text, Cases and Materials*.

Figure 21.1 Examples of essay questions

It is important to understand that, however an essay question is phrased, all essay questions require:

- Discussion of academic texts and in many cases legal texts.
- The construction of arguments in order to write the essay.
- The use of critical thinking.

Structuring your essay

Each type of essay question requires a different approach, but the same three part general structure is required. The standard structure is disarmingly simple and is quite likely to be one that you are already familiar with:

- A clear brief introduction.
- The main part (the body) of the essay setting out main and secondary arguments.
- A confident comprehensive conclusion.

TABLE 21.2 DEFINITION OF STANDARD WORDS USED IN ESSAY INSTRUCTIONS

Activity word	Definition
Account for	Give a detailed explanation of events with reasons for those events (what is it and why is it).
Account of	Give a detailed description, but just to tackle 'What', not 'why'.
Analyse	Break down one or several things into their various parts; and detail how these parts interact.
Argue	Maintaining a given position based on evidence.
Assess	Weigh up the strengths and weaknesses, the pros and cons of the issue(s) raised.
Clarify	Make clear: which could mean to intelligently simplify or explain a theory, institution or process; or to clearly differentiate between two things.
Comment on	Demonstrate understanding of what the question or quote is asking/ saying and then give your answer backed by evidence from academic sources.
Compare	Identify both similarities and differences between two things (this could be two judgments in two cases or the same case, or it could be between different ideas on legal reform).
Consider	Give your thoughtful view of a matter backing it with relevant academic evidence.
Contrast	Oppose several ideas, processes, judgments or texts, and bring out differences. While similarities should be noted the main thrust of this word is to speak of difference.
Critically evaluate	Careful consideration of an argument and its evidences drawing out hidden assumptions, and determining your view of the strengths and weaknesses of arguments and/or evidences. You should discuss any material that does not back you.
Criticise	Identify arguments about theory or cases, question existing beliefs and assumptions making a judgement based on the persuasiveness and authority of the sources you have located as the basis for your answer.
Define	Set out the meaning or the interpretation of a word or phrase; in law there may be competing meanings in which case you may be asked to give a view as to which is best.
Demonstrate	Show how something is done and give examples.

Activity word	Definition
Describe	Set out the main characteristics of an object or a concept; or give a chronological account of what is happening in a given situation.
Discuss	Conduct an investigation of an area to consider and evaluate the strengths and weaknesses of arguments coming to an overall conclusion on that area or process.
Elaborate	Information will have been given, in the question or a quotation; your job here is to add more detail to the given information.
Evaluate	Determine the value of something.
Examine	A meticulous look at the key issues related to a topic which you then need to critically evaluate.
Explain	An intelligent clear description of how something can be understood, defining words as needed.
Explore	Looking at a topic from differing analytic perspectives to present an argument backed by evidence.
Identify	Determine the main issues to be dealt with.
Illustrate	This is very much like 'explain', or even 'demonstrate'; you need to show how something works using evidence to back your explanation.
Interpret	Display your understanding of arguments, words, process, research or a given topic and discuss relationships between items and theories, by putting forward your view as to what they mean and ensuring that you support your view with evidence.
Justify	Put forward your views with reasoning and support it backed by academic evidence. Presenting an argument that is well considered and takes into account opposing positions.
Outline	This is a request to give a general, explanatory discussion of an area.
Review	Critically evaluate an area or topic assessing its strength and weakness with evidence. This is often a two part question, with a second part asking you to interpret or explain etc.
Show how	Similar to giving an account of (see above).
State	Lay out the main issues relating to a topic with reference to available evidence.
Summarise	Produce a brief précis of the relevant area only composed of relevant material or information.

Students are often not sure what they should put in each section and what the function of each section may be and so we will now briefly look at this tri-partite structure.

The function of the essay introduction

The role of the introduction is to clearly and succinctly set out the issues that the essay will discuss (and why). It will give very brief details of the argument(s) to be presented, and indicates the conclusion. It is important to 'begin with the end in mind' as it is the introduction that is key in guiding the reader through your work. It may help you to understand its importance if you think of it as a road map directing the reader to the conclusion and indicating how they will get there. The introduction is also the section in which you set out any areas you have chosen not to discuss giving your reasons for taking that course of action; often for reasons of word limit it is not viable to cover all potential areas.

The introduction should finalise when the main body of the essay is finished and your conclusions are clearer. You will need to check that the road map promised in your introduction is the one following in the main body and the conclusion. If it is not, because your views have changed, make sure this is reflected in changes to the introduction. Often students forget the promises they make in their introduction and just do not deliver because they lost their way in the essay.

The main body of the text (body text)

The main part of the essay is often referred to as the body of the text. Here, you will set out the propositions of your argument(s) in a carefully pre-planned manner with your propositions supported by evidence from the texts and cases that you have consulted.[7] It is absolutely essential to refer to case law, legislation, and textbooks and articles as appropriate in this main part of the essay or you will have nothing but unsupported claims that do not constitute an argument.

It is essential to understand that when writing assessed essays and exams you must use academic texts, such as academic journal articles and academic books. Even though you may be required to discuss primary legal texts in detail these are not academic but legal texts. You must use academic comment and review of primary law. Do remember that primary law and in particular law cases on their own are just law; they are in no way academic. It is particularly important to read academic journals as these are published much more quickly than a book (which could be a year or more out of date when published) and represent the latest thought in an area. An essay demands an academic response to the law.

It can take a long time to devise your argument and decide the best ordering of the body text; make sure you plan enough time to do this.

---

7   The chapters in Part 4 deal with argument construction.

The conclusion

The conclusion can do one of three things:

- Answer the specific question asked.
- Finalise your own decisions concerning the critique and review of information you have been given 'to discuss'.
- Present your final views on the issues you have been invited to extract for discussion.

The conclusion must align with your introduction and contain a very *brief* survey of your argument and the evidence supporting it, that also details its strengths and weaknesses before moving to your specific concluding response to the essay task.

METHOD FOR THE PREPARATION AND CONSTRUCTION OF ESSAYS

We have just looked at the standard structure of an essay (introduction, main body and conclusion). We will now look at a standardised eight stage model that can be followed and takes you from the moment you read the essay title to the finalisation of your essay for submission. Figure 21.2 sets out the model on the left hand side and the three part structure of the essay on the right hand side with a box in the middle encouraging you to constantly engage in critical reflection.

Each stage is designed to help you see the necessary ordering of breaking into the question, effectively researching the materials, thinking of argument construction and beginning to write with draft outline, draft version and final version. We will now take each of the headings in the figure and discuss the various issues in detail. As we track through each stage you may need to return to earlier chapters to recap on your skills.

Stage 1: Carefully reflect on the question

This is an exercise in basic English comprehension as well as an intellectual act, requiring a considered and methodical approach. You need to draw out all of the possible issues raised by your essay question. An effective way to begin to do this is to ask questions of your essay question, such as:

- What is being asked?
- How many issues are raised?

The actual essay question must be constantly borne in mind as texts are read and research is conducted. It is very useful to convert the question into a tree diagram that can be annotated as texts are collected.

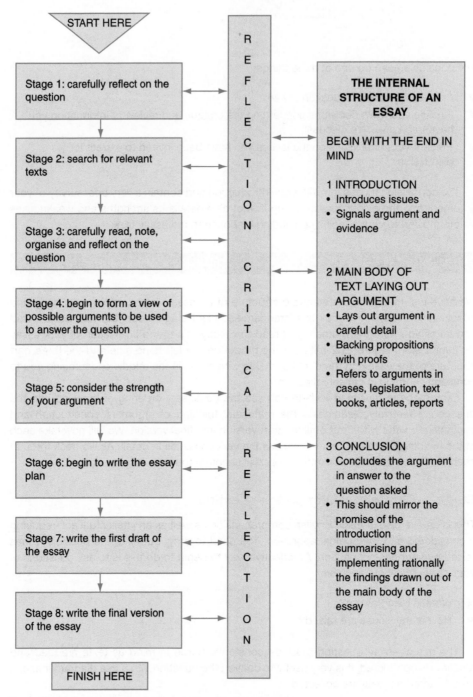

Figure 21.2 Method for the preparation and construction of essays

Let us look at one of the essay questions we gave in Figure 21.1 as an example:

Essay Question 3

'The English legal system is like a house that is not only too small, it is in need of repair. The question is do we build another extension and repair as necessary or pull the whole thing down and start again?' Discuss the issues arising from this quotation.

This is a standard quotation followed by a bland request to 'discuss the issues arising'. But you are not told what the issues are, so immediately you know that part of the test is your discovery of the 'issues arising'.

The quotation that you have been given is not referenced. It may be the case that it is an invented quotation by the lecturer. But equally it could be an actual non-attributed quotation that you might even come across when researching. If you do then you could mention its source.

You should also notice that this quotation presents itself as a metaphor. This should not be overlooked but engaged with. Our working definition of metaphor is that 'metaphor compares one thing with another either for emphasis or explanation or to describe the unknown by means of the known.'[8] Here it is used to describe one thing in terms of another.

The first thing to do is break down the metaphor into its parts. Then each part can be considered. You may have immediately understood that this is a question about reform and the nature of it, whether in parts or radical wholesale reform. If you did not, do not worry. Draw out your radial diagram as shown in Figure 21.3 but leave the centre empty (this is the core which joins all of the outlying circles). When you have added the metaphor in those circles you may well have found the core issue.

There are a number of options referred to in the metaphor; you just need to check back to see you caught them all. You may already know quite a bit about this area so you could move to each outlying circle and make it the centre of another diagram. When this is done it is time to move to stage 2.

The 'house' in question 3 is the English legal system and you are invited to further consider what the metaphoric terms 'repair', 'extension' and 'pulling down' might mean. Translating this back to our task in question 3 we need to look at our house, what is wrong, and then discuss what reforms (repairs) may have been put forward, whether new concepts or processes have been put forward to deal with issues (extension) or whether an entirely new legal system should be developed (pulling it down and starting again).

Throughout we should critique ideas about repair or extension, but ultimately the quote asks you to choose which of these suggestions is viable. That is a matter for you after the

---

8 See Chapter 17, Table 17.2.

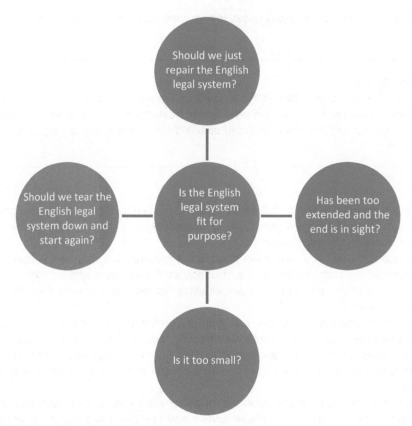

Figure 21.3 Radial diagram for essay question 3

relevant research and thought has gone into the question. But the metaphor also structures the main body of your essay and arguments, as well as the quote.

Another way of working out what the question is asking for is to actually annotate the words in it. This has been done in Figure 21.4 in relation to essay question 4 in Figure 21.1 above.

The notes given in Figure 21.4 make clear that at this stage of initial analysis of the question that the quotation forming the essay task contains an interpretation of the stated cases, which assertively states three issues. As you are asked to discuss the quotation you are expected to retrieve these issues and discuss whether they are correct or not. These are:

(1)   Did the courts in the cases referred to make it clear that they had the power to suspend an Act of Parliament?

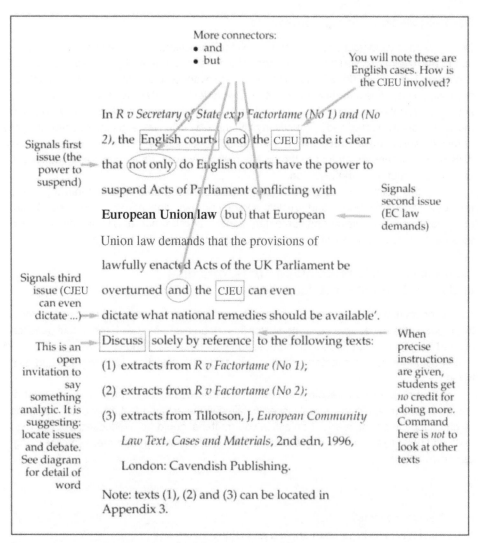

More connectors:
• and
• but

You will note these are English cases. How is the CJEU involved?

In *R v Secretary of State ex p Factortame (No 1) and (No 2)*, the English courts and the CJEU made it clear that not only do English courts have the power to suspend Acts of Parliament conflicting with **European Union law** but that European Union law demands that the provisions of lawfully enacted Acts of the UK Parliament be overturned and the CJEU can even dictate what national remedies should be available'.

Discuss solely by reference to the following texts:

(1) extracts from *R v Factortame (No 1)*;

(2) extracts from *R v Factortame (No 2)*;

(3) extracts from Tillotson, J, *European Community Law Text, Cases and Materials*, 2nd edn, 1996, London: Cavendish Publishing.

Note: texts (1), (2) and (3) can be located in Appendix 3.

Signals first issue (the power to suspend)

Signals second issue (EC law demands)

Signals third issue (CJEU can even dictate ...)

This is an open invitation to say something analytic. It is suggesting: locate issues and debate. See diagram for detail of word

When precise instructions are given, students get *no* credit for doing more. Command here is *not* to look at other texts

Figure 21.4 Annotated version of essay question 4

(2)   Did the courts maintain that European law can demand the overturning of a lawfully enacted Act of Parliament and if they did, is it correct to maintain that this is the case?

(3)   Did the Court of Justice of the EU say that they could 'dictate what national remedies should be available'?

Each of these three issues needs to be discussed in turn. Hopefully this demonstrates the importance of careful deconstruction of the essay question.

Stage 2: Search for relevant texts

Once you have used your preferred techniques to deconstruct your essay task it is important to make sure that you have understood the material at the level you were dealing with
it in class. This can be done by looking through relevant chapters in your set textbook, or
any recommended text (if there is no set text), your lecture notes, your seminar notes and
any personal notes you have made extending lecture and seminar work. You may even find
the source of any quote used in your essay title this way. Then re-read your question in light
of this superficial trawl through your class based material. See if what you have read has
developed your understanding of the question in any way. If it has, make any changes to
your deconstruction of the question.

It is at this point that you are well equipped to turn to research and begin to access
textbooks, academic books and articles, and any primary legal material you need. Do not
forget to refer to any relevant parliamentary papers, or other non-academic material such
as speeches, government or EU reports, and departmental or EU briefings.[9]

Stage 3: Carefully read, make notes, organise and reflect on the material collected

As you locate material that is relevant, save it, photocopy it and highlight it, or make notes.
It is a good idea to set up a separate file for this. Read everything with the actual question
in mind, and know what aspect of the question you are researching.

Extract arguments presented and then *reconsider* the question, both in parts and as a
whole.

The first task for your reading is asking the basic questions detailed below, whilst at
the same time recalling the actual issues detailed in the essay question you are doing the
research for. Otherwise relevant details in your material could be overlooked. As you read
texts you need to ask yourself questions which differ according to the text you are using,
as shown below.

Law cases

- What are the facts?
- What legal rules have been applied and why?
- How do the arguments presented assist in relation to the essay?
- What aspects of this case are relevant to my essay?

Textbooks

- Do I understand what I am reading?
- Does it fit with my understanding of the law or the topic?

---

9   Remember the reading strategy discussed in Chapter 17 and use skim, scanning methods to locate avail-
    able relevant texts. How to get the best out of your university library and research strategies for locating
    domestic and European legislation and cases as well as researching secondary materials are discussed in
    Chapters 6–9.

- Have I properly grasped the issues involved?
- What is of relevance to my essay?

Academic books and articles

- What is the writer's argument?
- Is it well supported by the evidence?
- Does the writer's argument support or deny my argument in the essay?
- What is of relevance to my essay?

It is also important to note whether there is a majority view developing in the texts concerning any of the issues raised by the essay question. Go back to any diagram of the essay question that you have made under Stage 1. Reference your texts on the diagram so that you can see which elements of your essay question you have a number of references for and where you have none or few. You can then seek to look for more texts in these areas.

Think about how your own views are developing on the various aspects of your question, but do keep an open mind. Your personal ideas may change as more research is conducted and some texts present persuasive arguments that you had not previously thought about.

What you are doing in this stage is methodically going through your retrieved materials, organising them (as relevant or not relevant) and then classifying whether they relate to part of the question or all of the question. Then you will make notes efficiently summarising. Using the strategies already discussed in earlier chapters you are breaking into these texts and sifting them, ready to think about your answer. As you read each text keep returning to the question so you do not drift off course. You will then be in a good position to turn to issues of analysis, evaluation and critique.

You may find that as you engage in reading your retrieved material it raises issues that require you to return to researching in order to investigate matters further.

Stage 4: Begin to form a view of possible arguments to be used to answer the question

Once the retrieved texts have been carefully prepared by ordering and summarising, then:

- Potential arguments can be reflected upon.
- Arguments can be compared.
- Differences of opinion expressed by judges and academics can be considered.

At this point, you can begin to have a personal view in answer to the essay task and begin to write. However do not begin writing until you:

- Understand each text as much as possible in isolation.
- Have considered and understood the interconnections between the texts.

Law cases and texts that conflict are as intimately interconnected as law cases and texts that agree with each other. You should organise your materials as follows:

- Materials containing arguments that are the same.
- Materials containing arguments that are different.
- Materials that are mixed in that in some areas they agree and some areas they disagree.

As Chapter 13 on the anatomy of argument demonstrates, no problem is ever a simple unitary one; problems come in bundles. Whilst questions posed may appear simple and unitary, they never are. Not only is there no such thing as a simple question, there is no such thing as a simple answer. All questions are complex and, of necessity, all answers are complex. It is never sufficient to give as an answer a purely descriptive commentary. No questions posed to test your understanding will only require description. They will require evaluation and critique as well. You need to make choices. Decide what issues are most relevant; and what can, and what cannot, be discussed in the answer to the question.

Texts which deny your argument are not to be ignored; they are to be dealt with. You can argue that they are unreliable (for example, you may argue that the argument is pure theory with no evidence to back it up); you can argue that it is one possible plausible inter-pretation but that you are presenting another equally plausible interpretation. If you cannot explain away an argument denying your view, then perhaps you should reconsider your view. How strong is your argument?

Your lecturer will know of texts that agree and disagree and will be looking to see if you have properly dealt with all the material.

Stage 5: Consider the strength of your argument

You should by now have a reasonably clear idea of how your argument may look. You will know what supporting evidence you have and where your argument lacks supporting evidence. You do not have to throw out weak arguments if they serve to build a broader picture and support a broader argument. But this must be in the context of well supported propositions or arguments. When you have considered all of your thoughts and potential arguments think carefully about how they apply to your essay, perhaps even returning to the essay the next day. Then refine your argument. Look back at your deconstruction of the question and deal with *each* assertion. Have you changed your views, have you seen more issues that you did not see before? Do your arguments or descriptions only relate to what you have been asked or are any irrelevant?

Stage 6: Begin to write the essay plan outline

Now you are ready to write an essay plan, by looking at:

- The diagram of the question you originally prepared.
- The notes of cases and other texts.
- The notes of your personal ideas/argument.

Produce an outline divided into three with sub-headers along the following lines:

Introduction

(1) Explain what you are being asked to do by the questions and how you intend to approach your essay.
(2) Deal with any matters you have decided not to deal with, giving reasons.
(3) Give the plan of the argument.

Body text

(1) Main argument(s) with evidence (propositions here may need to be backed by conclusions from secondary arguments).
(2) Secondary arguments with evidence.

Conclusion

(1) Brief survey of arguments and why they lead to the conclusion reached.
    You could use the following narrative signposts:
    'Therefore having carefully considered arguments 1, 2, 3, etc . . . it is possible to conclude that . . .'

Stage 7: Write the first draft of the essay

Although you will have an idea of what you are doing and where you are going and indeed what your answer is, it is a good idea to start your detailed first draft in the body of the text:

- Leave the intro at the outline plan stage
- Begin with the body text, the middle section, paying particular attention to the development of your main argument – is it supported by evidence?
- Review everything for your conclusion.
- Write the final version of the introduction last, ensuring that the body of the text and your conclusion do what your introduction says they will do.
- Then finalise your conclusion.
- When you have finished this, remember it is a draft not the final product. Read it through carefully.

- Ensure that every item referred to is appropriately referenced.
- If a bibliography is required ensure that it contains all referenced texts and all texts consulted for the essay but not referred to in the text.[10]

It is always worthwhile considering whether you need to search for any more texts. So allow time for this and go back and read the question again. As your understanding has developed through reading you may now spot issues in the question that you initially missed.

- Revise and produce a second draft going through the same steps as above.
- This time tackle issues of continuity between the introduction and the conclusion.

Stage 8: Write the final version of the essay

Carefully review your second draft:

- Consider whether there is a need to search for any more texts.
- Pay attention to the argument – does it clearly present itself?
- Pay particular attention to the conclusion and thoughts on the introduction.
- Review the argument. Is there evidence to back it up? Have opposing views been dealt with?

Then write the final draft:

- Proof read it carefully for spelling, grammar, word count.
- Double check *all* citations and references.
- Put it aside for a day if possible or a few hours if not and then carefully re-read and make any final changes.

A special note on presentation: editing, formatting and referencing

Students often neglect the presentation aspect of written work.[11] In addition to finding your voice, understanding the correct use of grammar, punctuation and spelling and refining your writing style; you should always allow time to edit and format your work. Make sure you read carefully for spelling, punctuation, grammar, and flow of your work through paragraphs. In addition, follow your department's conventions on referencing[12] and formatting. Your law department may require a certain font or line spacing to be used, and dictate whether you should only use one side of your paper.

If you have a free choice of font, choose one that is easy to read (this will keep your marker relaxed and happy). A font size of 12 is recommended as 14 tends to be too big and 10/11 too small. Keep your line spacing to 1.5 or 2 lines, as this again makes reading easier.

---

10 Referencing is dealt with in Chapter 19.
11 One of my students many years ago managed to hand in work with a dried-up baked bean stuck to it. The baked bean and the student were not well received.
12 Chapter 19 deals with referencing.

Cases and statutes should be formatted in order to make them stand out. Conventionally the names of cases are italicised, for example:

R v Briggs [1977] 1 WLR 605.

It is important, however, that you find out what your department requires and follow those specifications.

Be consistent in your use of headings and how they are displayed in your work and ensure that you number all of your pages. Only use headings if your essay is quite long, they assist with clarity and your lecturer has no objection to their use.

Word limits and editing

Most coursework will have a word limit imposed and there may be penalties for exceeding it. By one of life's strange ironies, students often rush to finish their coursework as quickly as possible complaining they cannot write enough, or they struggle with word limits saying they do not allow them to say enough! Your lecturer will know what is required and will have set your work having determined that the word limit is sufficient to allow the work to be competently completed. The word limit is part of the test.

If your word limit is 2,500 words, work out *before* you even start writing how many pages of your word processing that amounts to. This will vary according to the font you use and whether you use double, single or 1.5 spacing between lines. Then you will know how many pages you are aiming for and you should not be surprised by finding yourself 1,000 words over the limit at 2am on the day work is due in.

A single spaced word processed sheet of A4 paper using font size 12 will contain about 500 words. Therefore a 2,500 word essay would be five pages. If your introduction is around half a page and your conclusion maybe one page that leaves you three pages for your body text.

Make sure you allow yourself enough time to edit your work before it is due. Otherwise you may end up deleting highly relevant information, and retaining irrelevant information, in a desperate attempt to reach the right number of words at the last minute.

If you often exceed the number of words, consider whether your style of writing can be improved. Perhaps you are saying very little, in a lot of words. Practising sticking to the word limit can help you to refine your work, reflect on your style and become more succinct in your expression.

CONCLUSION

By now you will understand that your written work depends on your stage of development in a range of skills, particularly independent study, research, reading, writing and argument construction. You need to understand it, present it properly referenced using good English with an appropriate writing voice that obeys the protocols of academic writing but allows your own individual writing voice to show through. It is essential to take the time to retrieve sufficient materials to ensure you can write a well-balanced essay demonstrating your understanding of the question.

CHAPTER SUMMARY

- Your performance in written work depends on your stages of development in the whole range of skills, particularly reading, writing and argument construction.
- Whatever type of essay or problem question you are dealing with, the same type of information base is required for all questions. It is how this information, knowledge and understanding is drawn on to produce a particular written result that is important.
- Following standard methods for the preparation and construction of essay or problem question answers can help you effectively order the different tasks involved.
- Good written work requires an effective written voice, excellent grammar and appropriate choices of words.
- The referencing, formatting and presentation of your written work is as important as your grammar, spelling and punctuation and the vocabulary you use.

WRITING ANSWERS TO LEGAL PROBLEM QUESTIONS

LEARNING OUTCOMES

After reading this chapter you should be able to:

- Be aware of the approach to be adopted for writing solutions to legal problem questions.
- Develop greater confidence in your ability to tackle a problem question.
- Be able to structure a solution to a problem question effectively.
- Increase your understanding of the way in which the skills of general study, research, legal analysis, argument construction and writing skills work together to produce competent problem solutions.

INTRODUCTION

This chapter considers strategies for writing answers to problem questions. Generally students will prefer either essays or problem questions and will often maintain that they can, or cannot, 'do' a problem solution. However, the fact is that the same general information is required for essays and problem solutions. A problem solution tests whether you understand a particular area of law well and can apply it. But how can you answer an essay question if you do not understand the relevant area of law well first?

The structure of essays and solutions to problem questions do differ. Additionally, while essays require academic texts as their foundational proofs for all arguments forwarded, problem solutions primarily require the use of legal rules as the foundational texts. That is not to say that essays do not refer to legal rules but that these are not the final proofs in an academic legal argument for an essay.

To produce competent written answers to problem questions you need to have a good understanding of the way in which series of cases have developed areas of law, and how judgments by senior judges are of relevance in the development of legal argument. You also need to appreciate the relationship between legislation and cases and the role of statutory interpretation by the judiciary. If these matters are firmly understood you will be able to tackle a problem question confidently clearly demonstrating that understanding in the structure and content of your answer. Additionally marks are awarded for use of a correct method for problem solution, as well as the correct outcome.

A problem question at the academic stage of education is a fictitious legal dispute invariably drafted in such a way as to raise situations where there are conditions of doubt about facts, legal issues, or the interpretation of the law. The student will be asked to discuss the legal liability of one particular party, or all potential parties to the dispute. Using only the information given in the problem question as their guide, the student is required to identify, discuss and apply relevant legal rules to the issues raised by the problem question. Students are required to not only identify specific breaches of law but to be aware of any applicable defences and/or interpretational issues attaching to the law.

The student is expected to only refer to legal rules which invariably involve the discussion of law cases and refer to statements by judges in court. The student is not expected to refer to academic articles and textbooks, unless the judges in specific cases have referred to those articles or books in court (which is unlikely – but possible in certain defined situations). Books and articles can exceptionally be drawn upon if an aspect of the problem solution has been written about and never discussed by senior judiciary.

The problem question is raised in the context of one particular area of study and tests the student's awareness of current law, their ability to carefully analyse information they have been given and their competency in the construction of arguments, applying that law as they discuss the problem question and the issues it raises. Problem questions are often set in areas of doubt, so always be wary if you think the answer to the problem is simple and clear cut.

Problem questions bring together all of the skills of research, argumentation, critical analysis and application of law and demonstrate more than any other type of assessed task your aptitude for the legal profession. A key skill is also to retain the ability to see the problem from all sides, engaging in analogic reasoning, to check that you are aware of the potential arguments that can be put forward by all parties.

Problem questions bring the student very close to the work of the professional lawyer, as their job is to work towards resolving their clients' legal problems. Judges in cases listen to lawyers, and their job is to make a determination of liability to resolve the legal dispute. Developing problem solving skills assists you to develop your overall legal reasoning skills. You examine facts given to you, locate relevant legal rules and apply them to the facts to suggest ways of determining issues of legal liability.

Table 22.1 sets out two typical problem questions for you to get an idea of the way in which they can be structured.

As you can see from reading these questions they can vary in length and the complexity of facts presented. Question 1 presents relatively complex facts in terms of names, inter-actions and the timing of communications occurring over a very short time frame of a few hours. It is also quite long. Question 2 by contrast is short and divided into two parts, and the overall timescale of the facts given is seven days.

Often fact scenarios may seem clearly unrealistic, and you may feel that these events simply would not happen in the 'real' world. The person setting the problem is aware of this; it is merely a vehicle to get you to discuss legal issues and display your understanding and ability to engage in the correct methodology for answering a problem question.

What range of skills are tested and developed by problem questions?

Problem questions are specifically designed to test your developing abilities to research, handle and apply legal rules and construct legal arguments according to English legal reasoning protocols. Your ability to competently answer problem questions is affected by the development of your skills of general academic study, legal reasoning, as well as your developing skills specific to problem solutions. We will briefly list the sub-skills involved.

General academic study skills

- Independent study and time management.
- Library research skills.

TABLE 22.1 TWO SPECIMEN PROBLEM QUESTIONS

QUESTION 1

On 1 May at 9:30am Alfred, the sales manager of Baby's Little Friend (BLF) plc, a retailer of disposable baby nappies, sent an email to Marjory, the accounts manager at Baby Dream (BD) plc, a manufacturer of disposable baby nappies asking them to sell them 1,000 disposable nappies at their advertised price of 8p per nappy. At 10am on 1 May Marjory replies agreeing to supply BLF with the nappies and directing them to make the normal immediate full payment through BD's secure webpage. Alfred asks his assistant Margaret to do this at once which she tries to do at 10.10am through DB's secured webpage. However the BD server fails and payment is not made immediately. At 10.40am Marjory receives an email from Ivor, the sales director for InFix plc. They have run out of nappies and are now in a crisis trying to fill a big order for 1,200 nappies. Marjory replies by email stating that she cannot fill the order as BD only have 200 nappies having just agreed to sell 1,000 to another company. Ivor replies by email saying they are prepared to pay 12p a nappy. Marjory agrees to this immediately and emails Alfred at 10.55am revoking BD's acceptance of their order for 1,000 nappies at 8p per nappy. At 11.30am Alfred checks his email and sees the revocation email from Marjory; he is not pleased. Before he replies to Marjory he asks Margaret to confirm payment was made, Margaret tells Alfred that that due to the server problems the payment was not able to be sent until 11.40am and they still await notification of receipt from BD.

Advise BD plc as to any legal liability they may have incurred.

QUESTION 2

Cedric, a dealer in marble, has a 2kg quantity of rare green Ionian marble for sale. He has done business with Dorothy, a collector of fine green Ionian marble for five years. She normally pays £250 a kilo. He emailed her last Tuesday, asking if she would be interested in buying the marble. Dorothy emailed back within 15 minutes saying, 'Yes I will buy the 2kg of the green marble for the usual price of £500. If I hear nothing to the contrary I will consider it mine and bring the money (in cash), and collect it next Monday'. Cedric reads the email but does not reply to it.

Advise Dorothy as to her legal position in the following two situations:

(a) Cedric sells the 2kg of green marble to Timothy for £750.00 on Friday.

(b) Cedric puts the 2kg of green marble in a box labelled 'Marble for Dorothy £500 to pay, for collection and payment Monday.' Dorothy decided she did not want the marble after all and so she did not go to Cedric's on the next Monday. In the meantime Cedric lost out on a sale to Timothy who offered £750 for it on Friday.

■ General reading skills.

■ General writing skills (includes language usage in terms of vocabulary, grammar, punctuation and referencing).

■ Referencing primary legal source material.

☐ *Citing law cases*

It is essential to note:

– The court (Court of Appeal CA, Supreme Court).

– The names of judges giving important judgments in cases (which can be majority or dissenting or minority).

☐ *Citing legislation* ensuring you always refer to sections, sub-sections, paragraphs or sub-paragraphs as relevant.

☐ Cases and legislation should be in italics or underlined so they are clearly visible in the text.

Footnotes or endnotes (depending on your department's preferred referencing system) must be used to give the full citations of cases, and to give any quite relevant but not absolutely 'on point' comments. However footnotes/endnotes are not expected in examination conditions. You could for example use brackets in texts to indicate such matters. Nor are you expected to know page numbers for example in exams, just the name of the case, the court and the year of the case.

Legal reasoning skills

■ Understanding legal argument construction, and being able to construct a good argument backed by evidence.

■ Competent use of methods of legal reasoning according to the doctrine of precedent.

■ Understanding the relationship between cases and legislation.

Skills relating to legal problem solution

■ Factual organisation of a problem scenario usually with complex sets of dates, timings, actions, and multiple participants.

■ Identification of the legal issue or issues raised by the given factual scenario.

■ Knowledge of the law in a given area (e.g. criminal law, law of contract, employment law) so that you can identify legal issues relating to liability and any issues relating to defences.

■ Understanding of any interpretational doubts or gaps about the law revealed by decided cases in the area under consideration.

■ Ability to handle and apply case law and legislation to a problem.

■ The ability to manage and classify the given facts in a problem question and systematically apply the law to those facts.

METHODS FOR THE PREPARATION AND CONSTRUCTION OF ANSWERS TO PROBLEM QUESTIONS

The key to answering a problem question successfully lies in spotting the 'clues' to the legal issues to be discussed. Primarily the clues are in the facts you have been given in the problem. It is for you to apply your legal understanding to the facts and extract the issues. But also many of these clues are purely linguistic and organisational. You need to carefully consider any signposting words such as prepositions, or the use of any dates and times that may need to be unravelled and understood within the context of the set problem. You also need to be able to make reference to actions which need to be carefully considered.

At root in a problem question you are dealing with:

■   A fictitious fact situation involving a dispute disclosing legal issues that may result in legal liability being allocated to one or more of the social actors in the fact scenario.
■   Legal rules that need to be found, interpreted and applied to those legal issues.
■   Prediction of whether a particular social actor is likely to be legally liable for actions disclosed in the problem scenario.

Ideally what should be happening as you read your problem question is that certain facts, or groups of facts, should set off memories in your mind of cases with similar facts which you can then seek out.

METHODS FOR WRITING SOLUTIONS TO PROBLEM QUESTIONS

There are several methods recognised for outlining the issues that need to be dealt with in problem questions. The key skill is to adopt one technique and then methodically follow it through. As you gain experience you will find the method easier to use and your understanding of the analysis of legal problems will become more sophisticated. Once you have perfected your preferred technique you can use it for all problem questions in all of your subjects throughout your legal studies and beyond into a legal career. Table 22.2 sets out four suggested methods. In fact they are all similar and column 1, the description column, notes a four stage general approach. The last column gives an idea of how the four stages translate into a standardised structure for your written answer.

THE FOUR GENERAL STAGES OF PROBLEM SOLUTION METHODOLOGY

We will now go through each of the four generalised stages in column 1 of Table 22.2 to give you an idea of the matters to be discussed and action you can take to assist you to clarify issues. Until each stage is completed you cannot begin to determine the content of each part of the structure to your answer.

TABLE 22.2 INDICATION OF THE RANGES OF METHODS OF THE ANALYSIS OF PROBLEM QUESTIONS AND INDICATION OF IDEAL STRUCTURE OF YOUR FINAL ANSWER TO PROBLEM QUESTION

GENERAL DESCRIPTION OF EACH STAGE	SYNONYMS FOR VARIOUS METHODS				IDEAL STRUCTURE OF ANSWER TO PROBLEM QUESTION
	IRAC	IPAC	CLEO	PLAN	
STAGE 1: Identification of the legal issues arising from the facts in the problem question.	ISSUE	ISSUE	CLAIM	PROBLEM	**1. The introduction:** A brief discussion of the legal issues to be discussed in the main body of the answer noting any interpretational issues relating to identified legal rules. This encompasses material located in stages 1 and 2. Before this can be completed you need to engage in a careful reading of the problem question, extract the facts and through your factual analysis determine the legal issues, and through careful research determine relevant rules.
STAGE 2: Identification of all relevant legal rules	RULE	PRINCIPLE	LAW	LEGAL RULE	
STAGE 3: Application of relevant legal rules to the legal issues identified (including those relating to any defence or mitigation and discussion of any interpretational doubts concerning relevant legal rules)	APPLICATION	APPLICATION	EVALUATION	APPLICATION	**2. The main body of the answer:** The methodical deployment of your argument by setting out each legal issue separately and applying legal rules to it. Discussing likelihood of the applicability of any defences or mitigation. If more than one party is being discussed each issue and any defence etc. should be dealt with separately for each party. A key issue is the order in which you decide to lay out your argument in terms of primary and secondary issues. This uses the material collected at stages 1 and 2. Every point argued must be supported by available evidence. If no evidence is available the inferences must be clearly stated and your rationale for those inferences. Here you deploy your detailed legal analysis of the matters raised.
STAGE 4 Your determination of liability based on your prediction of the likely application of the law	CONCLUSION	CONCLUSION	OUTCOME	NOTE OUTCOME	**3. The conclusion:** Drawing out the conclusions in the main body you give your final likely determination of liability in relation to those parties you have been asked to discuss. This should be consistent with the matters raised in your introduction, and the arguments pursued in the main body of your text.

Stage 1: Identification of the legal issues arising from the facts in the problem question

Several sub-stages are involved here as follows:

Identification of all relevant facts given in the problem question

Key here is your meticulous attention to detail as you read the problem question. If you misunderstand the facts due to a careless reading you will also fail to pick up relevant legal issues. Depending on what you miss this could determine whether you pass the assessment. Some of the facts you are given will be highly relevant and others may not be that relevant at all. Again you need to make judgements about these matters based on your understanding of the law. For example in a shoplifting case the fact it is heavily raining may well not be a relevant fact, but it would be highly relevant in a dangerous driving prosecution.

You may find a simple flow chart of the facts and their ordering helps you to get a grasp of the issues; you can then place cases, etc. beside facts. This can be extremely helpful in allowing you to identify all relevant issues.

Identification of the primary and secondary legal issues raised by the facts

You have to ascertain this from the information and facts of the problem. This is part of the skill of answering problem questions. You will locate the law by going over your lecture notes, revisiting any relevant seminar work, reading sections in your textbooks, and reading the full text of relevant cases.

It is unwise to assume that all that you identify on a first reading (before engagement with stage 2 location of legal rules and other wider reading) is the sum total of the issues to be discussed. As you develop your understanding of the law you may well find that more legal issues become apparent.

Checking the capacity of the defendant or a litigant to be held liable

Issues of age and mental awareness for example can lead to a situation in which the law holds that a given defendant does not have the required capacity to be held liable for a breach of law.

Stage 2: Identification of all relevant legal rules

Determine the relevant legal rules relating to any breach of law

This will involve wider reading in textbooks as well as researching cases and legislation; the more careful your research the greater your understanding of the issues will become.

Stage 3: Application of relevant legal rules to the legal issues identified

Carefully consider doubts/interpretational issues and ask yourself what you consider to be the appropriate response to them

Problem questions usually involve issues relating to uncertainty, or gaps in the law. You need to locate these, research them, reading secondary legal texts as well as the law itself, and read relevant primary case law carefully. Then form a view based on existing law and predicted application of law in relation to those doubts or gaps

Discussion of applicable defences/mitigation

There are general defences to a range of breaches of civil and criminal law, as well as defences that are specific to given circumstances and breaches. You need to be aware of these when you are considering the answer to a problem question. If accepted these excuse the breach, or provide an accepted legal recognition of the act leading to the breach. In addition there may be certain information that the court can be asked to consider for example, specific circumstances existing at the time of the breach that may lead the court to lower damages awarded against a litigant or a sentence imposed on a defendant.

Decide the order in which you will discuss your identified legal issues.

Stage 4: Your determination of liability based on your prediction of the likely application of the law

Consider the strength of arguments for and against each point raised for answer and come to your view.

THE STRUCTURE OF YOUR FINAL WRITTEN ANSWER

It is important to develop a clear layout for your problem solution so that your arguments can be followed, and there is no danger of you forgetting to discuss an important issue. Obviously all sources must be appropriately referenced according to the system required by your department or in the absence of a departmental preference according to the system you prefer. Additionally you must seek to continue to develop a good third party voice for your written work. These general matters have been discussed in detail in earlier chapters.

When all of the matters in Stages 1–4 have been investigated and resolved to your satisfaction your answer needs to be carefully formatted and structured. The standard structure for this is set out in the last column of Table 22.2 and will be familiar to you from essay structure: (1) The introduction, (2) The main body of the answer and (3) The conclusion. Each of these will be discussed in turn, as the detail of each part of the structure is different to that for an essay.

(1) Introduction

Your introduction needs to make clear what legal issues are raised by the problem and how you will approach them. If the problem discloses more than one potential issue of liability then these must be discussed separately. It is far too easy to make a mistake and forget something if you discuss everything together. It is also quite easy in these circumstances to confuse the marker of your work too.

If you are discussing separate potential issues of liability it is also important to note any defences separately. However, do not be tempted to engage in an essay-style debate. A problem question requires a straightforward layout of legal issues and liability. Discussion of irrelevancies is therefore liable to be taken as a sign of confusion on the part of the student, or lack of knowledge.

(2) Main body: The worked out answer to problem question

This is where your legal argument is laid out in detail, each proposition backed with evidence if possible. Where the law is extremely uncertain it may be acceptable to refer to arguments in textbooks or articles but your main proof must be the law and its interpretation by the courts. This part of your answer may contain headings and sub-headings as appropriate for different heads of liability. It is certainly a good idea if the problem question involves several breaches of law and/or the discussion of the liability of several parties to an action, or several defendants are being prosecuted. This is a decision for you once you have determined the issues that need to be discussed.

You may not have considered that you were constructing legal arguments. However, you are. By the very act of applying legal rules to fact situations to provide a rationale for liability or non-liability of a relevant party you are creating legal argument.

(3) Conclusion

It is always best practice to give an overall conclusion which can just be a few lines. This ensures that you can sum up the important parts of your argument (which you have proved at length in your main body) to answer the problem question.

Figure 22.1 sets out the four stage method for approaching problem questions and the threefold structure for writing your answer to a problem question. Each stage of the process, and each aspect of the final written solution must be constantly subjected to your critical reflection.

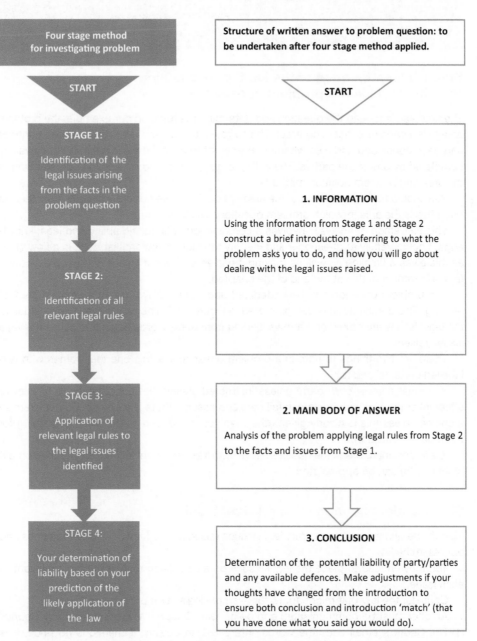

Figure 22.1 Four stage method of problem solution mapped against standard structure of written solution

Stage 1: Identification of the legal issues arising from the facts in the problem question

The first task is to read the question and determine the topic. In our example, the problem area of law chosen is that of contract. The narrower topics here relate to whether a contract had been concluded and if so whether an attempt to cancel the contract had been validly completed by one of the parties. The ability to do this is based on a solid understanding of the area and problem solution methods.

You should have a clear idea of the areas of doubt where currently the law is unclear, as often this is the area in which problem questions will be located.

This first stage of analysis involves a combination of linguistic ability and legal knowledge. Look carefully at question 2 and identify the facts given and list them in a flow chart as this gives a timeline as well as making it easier to pick out issues and people (you will find an example of this at the end of the chapter).

The problem question can be underlined and issues drawn out in a very simple first reading. This combination is demonstrated in Figure 22.2. The words that are the clues to the legal issues are boxed and arrows leading from these words begin to discuss the legal issues raised.

There are two things to note in a problem question like this one that comes with two labelled parts: (a) and (b):

You must answer *both* parts unless instructed clearly that candidates are to answer *either* (a) or (b). Many students can fail here and assume there is a choice. Do not exercise a choice unless this is clearly given otherwise you could lose half of the marks going for the problem question.

It is important to break the question down into its constituent issues, so that the context of (a) and (b) can be appreciated.

Stage 2: Identification of all relevant legal rules

Identify the primary and secondary legal issues raised by the facts, available defences and doubts in the law.

You may choose to place the legal issues on a tree diagram. List the facts relevant to each issue.

Consider the law that might apply, for example legislation or common law.

An offer must be communicated and be certain: *Gibson v Manchester County Council* (1978). Cedric's email uses the words 'interested' in buying. It mentions no price. It is hard to see how this could be an offer. If this is the case then Dorothy's email cannot be

IS THIS AN <u>OFFER TO SELL</u> OR JUST A <u>SERIOUS ENQUIRY</u> (AN INVITATION TO DEAL – TECHNICALLY 'TO TREAT') AS TO WHETHER DOROTHY WOULD LIKE TO BUY?

IS THIS AN OFFER TO BUY FOR £500, IN RESPONSE TO AN INVITATION TO TREAT, OR IS IT AN ACCEPTANCE OF THE OFFER TO SELL? CAN IT BE ASSUMED BOTH KNOW THE PRICE WOULD BE £250 PER kg AS USUAL?

Cedric, a dealer in marble, has a 2kg quantity of rare green Ionian marble for sale. He has done business with Dorothy, a collector of fine green Ionian marble for five years. She normally pays £250 a kilo. He emailed her last Tuesday, asking if she would be interested in buying the marble.

Dorothy emailed back within 15 minutes saying, 'Yes I will buy the 2kg of the green marble for the usual price of £500. If I hear nothing to the contrary I will consider it mine and bring the money (in cash), and collect it next Monday.'

IF DOROTHY'S EMAIL IS AN OFFER ARE THESE THE SPECIFIC TIME LIMITED CONDITIONS OF THE OFFER?

IF DOROTHY'S EMAIL IS A NEW OFFER: IS DOROTHY REFERRING TO NORMAL BUSINESS PRACTICE BETWEEN THEM, THAT DOES NOT REQUIRE CEDRIC TO COMMUNICATE HIS ACCEPTANCE OF HER OFFER?

Cedric reads the email but does not reply to it.

THE KEY QUESTION TO BE RESOLVED IS WHETHER THERE IS A CONTRACT IN EXISTENCE BETWEEN CEDRIC AND DOROTHY FOR THE SALE OF THE MARBLE, AND IF THERE IS WHO MADE THE OFFER, AND WHO MADE THE ACCEPTANCE? ONCE THIS IS DETERMINED FROM THE MAIN FACTS YOU ARE IN A GOOD POSITION TO ANSWER THE ACTUAL QUESTIONS SET OUT IN (a) AND (b)

Advise Dorothy as to her legal position in the following two situations:

(a) Cedric sells the 2kg of green marble to Timothy for £750.00 on Friday.

Much depends here on whether a clear offer and acceptance, along with an intention to create legal relations and clear consideration can be located. If it has, then Cedric is in breach of contact. If Dorothy's reply is an acceptance then the contract is concluded and Cedric is in breach. If Dorothy's reply is a counter offer then there is no communicated acceptance unless it can be shown none was needed in these circumstances.

(b) Cedric puts the 2kg of green marble in a box labelled 'Marble for Dorothy £500 to pay, for collection and payment Monday.' Dorothy decided she did not want the marble after all and so she did not go to Cedric's on the next Monday. In the meantime Cedric lost out on a sale to Timothy who offered £750 for it on Friday.

Much depends here on whether Dorothy's email is an acceptance in which case her change of mind constitutes a breach of contract. If her letter is a counter offer much depends on whether the fact Cedric has not communicated acceptance means that there is no contract? This may depend on business practice between the two and we have no information.

Figure 22.2 First breakdown of problem question: Initial questions that will begin a breakdown of questions to form legal issues and lay the foundation of a search through relevant case law

construed as an acceptance. However, Dorothy is clearly interested. We could argue that her response to Cedric's email is an offer in response to his invitation deal (technically 'to treat'), an offer that contains both a price and a method of acceptance. This offer is clear and communicated. But has that offer been accepted?

An acceptance of an offer must be communicated and will not normally be implied from silence. *Felthouse v Brindley* (1862).

The standard rule relating to an acceptance of an offer is that it must be communicated; however, case law does allow communication to be construed from conduct.

Can it be said that because in (b) Cedric puts the marble aside labelled for Dorothy with the price to pay he can be said to communicate acceptance in the circumstances by his conduct? To whom has he communicated his acceptance? How would Dorothy know? You will need to ask many similar questions and then check out law texts and primary legal rules to work towards an answer.

For every proposition you make you must refer to a law case in support. You cannot assert without legal authority to support you. However, as you become proficient it may be the case that there is a persuasive precedent you could use for a small point, including from a minority or even dissenting judgment.

We will not continue this demonstration as this is a legal method, not a contract, text, and enough has been set out to demonstrate the strategy of approaching problem questions and how, with the aid of diagrams, you can be reminded to lay out propositions, produce supporting case law and know where the doubts are. In an area of doubt, for example, on some occasions it may be enough to make a decision and back it by the state of uncertainty and any case support no matter how tenuous. What the reader, who is also your marker, is looking for is your skill in dealing with such legal issues with confidence, competently demonstrating your knowledge of the area and the relevant cases, and competently applying that knowledge. Each subject area will have its own areas of doubt and uncertainty and these are the areas to concentrate upon: the rules, the exceptions to the rules and the doubts. However, as a final demonstration Figure 22.3 begins to link propositions and cases.

Stage 3: Application of relevant legal rules to the legal issues identified

Consider each legal issue that you have raised, treating each potential liability and each potential party separately, and:

- Decide the order in which issues will be raised in your answer,
- Consider your view of uncertainties and gaps in the law in the area.
- Consider issues of interpretation and defence.

A doubt about the interpretation of the law is not a defence; it is a doubt about the law. Make sure you do not make this mistake, as dealing with these doubts requires different approaches.

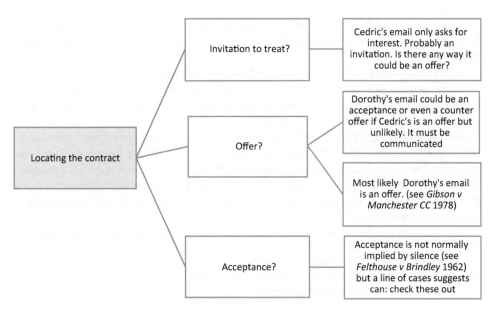

Figure 22.3 Locating the contract

In our example, it should be apparent that you need to have a view as to whether a contract has been concluded between Cedric and Dorothy, and if so when, before you can actually tackle questions (a) and (b). The answer to this is dependent upon whether an offer and an acceptance can be located. The issues to be considered can also be set out as a narrative where you should consider the effect of each component:

(1) Cedric emails Dorothy stating he has marble to sell and is she interested?
    Is it an offer or an invitation to treat?
    No price is mentioned. Is that normal business practice between them?

(2) Dorothy's email states yes, she would buy and gives price. Is that an acceptance or an offer?
    Is Dorothy's email an acceptance?
    Is Dorothy's email a statement of intention?
    Is Dorothy's email an offer?
    Can Dorothy waive the necessity for the communication of the acceptance if she so chooses?

(3) The problem question asks you to evaluate two responses to the these facts, the first (a) where Cedric ignored Dorothy's email letter and sold to someone else for a higher price; and the second (b) where he put the marble aside in response to the email putting a sticker on it saying sold and the price, but Dorothy did not collect it when she said she would and he missed out on selling it to someone else.

You are expected to consider the facts, legal issues and the uncertainties carefully, consulting case law and you would no doubt consult textbooks as well as case law concerning these matters.

With regard to part (a) if a contract has been formed, then Cedric is in breach of this contract when he sells the marble to Timothy. With regard to case law and commentators it does seem highly likely that, in these circumstances, no contract has been formed with Dorothy and Cedric is free to sell the marble.

With regard to part (b), if Dorothy has made an offer, not an acceptance, then Cedric has possibly accepted the offer when he takes the step of setting aside the marble, as it is possible to show acceptance by conduct. If this is the case, a contract has been formed and Dorothy is obliged to buy the marble. It needs to be noted that there are flaws and weaknesses in this particular question. There are, however, significant weaknesses in reaching this conclusion.

It should also be noticed that at present we have suggested issues but as yet we have no:

- Argument by way of linked propositions.
- Proofs (law cases) supporting or denying our propositions (or texts discussing areas where the law is unknown or uncertain).

Without a sustained argument backed by law cases there is no competent answer to the problem question.

Having used the word identification to sort out the legal issues they come down to the following:

(a)   Is Cedric's email an offer or an invitation to treat?
(b)   The answer to (a) determines the status of Dorothy's email – it is either a counter offer or an acceptance.

How do we approach answering (a) and (b)? Much revolves around the issue of communication.

Stage 4: Your determination of liability based on your prediction of the likely application of the law

The facts in a problem question can give rise to many issues but all of these may not be necessary to resolve the specific question(s) set in your problem. Problem questions tend to ask you to do one of two main things:

- discuss the issues raised in the problem scenario;
- advise one or all of the parties.

Both types of problem question require the same knowledge to answer them successfully. However, your approach to the answers will differ. In response to a question about discussing issues in general you must raise all the issues without privileging one party. Where you have been asked to advise one or all of the parties, you must raise all the issues but orientate your argument to the effect of those issues on the party, or parties, you are specifically asked to advise. Discussing, with reasons, the likely allocation of legal liability and the possibility of any available defences.

Once you have come to decisions and know that you have carefully followed each of the four stages you have all of the information required to produce a good written response to the problem question. This needs to be structured according to the standardised format of introduction, main body, and conclusion.

CONCLUSION

A problem solution does *not* require the discussing of academic articles and books (unless the book or article has been 'judicially recognised' in court). However, you will no doubt need to consult secondary academic texts to develop your understanding of the legal issues involved in your problem question. When you write your answer, however, all you are required to do is to engage in a discussion of relevant legal authority (cases) and statutory rules.

Whatever type of problem question you are dealing with, the same type of information base is required. It is how this information, knowledge and understanding are drawn on to produce a particular written result that is important.

Following standard methods for the preparation and construction of problem question answers can help you effectively order the different tasks involved. You can move on to your own preferred methods.

CHAPTER SUMMARY

- A problem question at the academic stage of education is a fictitious legal dispute invariably drafted in such a way as to raise situations where there are conditions of doubt about facts, legal issues, or the interpretation of the law.
- A problem solution tests whether you understand a particular area of law well and can apply it.
- Problem questions are often set in areas of doubt, so always be wary if you think the answer to the problem is simple and clear cut.
- You have to have a good understanding of the way in which series of cases have developed areas of law, how different judgments by leading senior judges can be of relevance in the development of legal argument, and you need to appreciate the relationship between legislation and case law, and the role of statutory interpretation by the judiciary.
- The student is expected to only refer to legal (unless the judges in specific cases have referred to academic articles or books in court, which is unlikely – but possible in certain defined situations).

- Problem questions bring together all of the skills of research, argumentation, critical analysis and application of law.

- Problem questions are specifically designed to test your developing abilities to research, handle and apply legal rules, construct argument and engage in competent writing.

- The key to answering a problem question successfully lies in spotting the 'clues' to the issues to be discussed. Many of these are purely linguistic and organisational, using prepositions, signposting words, and use of dates and times that may need to be unravelled.

- There are several methods recognised for outlining the issues that need to be dealt with in problem questions (IRAC, IPAC, CLEO, PLAN).

- All methods tend to involve the same four general stages.

  Stage 1: Identification of the legal issues arising from the facts in the problem question.

  Stage 2: Identification of all relevant legal rules.

  Stage 3: Application of relevant legal rules to the legal issues identified (including those relating to any defence or mitigation and discussion of any interpretational doubts concerning relevant legal rules).

  Stage 4: Your determination of liability based on your prediction of the likely application of the law.

- In many respects the threefold structure used of essays (introduction, main body and conclusion) can equally be used to structure a problem question solution:

  - Introduction to problem solution.
  - Main body of answer which relates to all of the issues raised in the introduction.
  - Conclusion.

- Following standard methods for the preparation and construction of problem question answers can help you effectively order the different tasks involved.

EXAMINATION STRATEGIES

23

LEARNING OUTCOMES

After reading this chapter you should be able to:

- Competently construct and follow a personal, and achievable, revision timetable.
- Use your lecturers' and tutors' revision sessions to best effect.
- Competently construct useful revision notes and diagrams.
- Work towards the best state of mind for the day of the exam.
- Efficiently plan which questions to answer in the exam.
- Efficiently draw planning diagrams for each question to be answered.
- Understand the best ways of quickly stating information of relevance if you do consider you are running out of time in the exam.

INTRODUCTION

This chapter aims to demonstrate that it is possible to predict to a certain extent what may or may not appear on the exam paper and to employ the same learnt information economically in different ways for problem and essay questions. It will also give ideas for ensuring that your revision management and in-exam-timing does not let you down. It looks at planning revision timetables, and tells you what examiners are really looking for. This chapter assists you to reach examinations in a good condition: fit for the task.

Few students like examinations. While there is a big debate within education concerning whether examinations are a good or a bad method of assessing students, the fact is that this is the main method of assessment that you will encounter on a law degree. Exams require stamina, good knowledge of your own psychology and careful pre-planning of your revision and in-exam strategies.

Whether you love, hate or do not mind exams, you may not realise that it is possible to prepare strategically for an exam and increase your likelihood of passing and obtaining a good grade.

FIND OUT ABOUT THE STRUCTURE OF YOUR EXAMS

There will normally be past examination papers available for the module or course that you are undertaking. If you are studying a new module, running on the degree for the first time, then it is highly likely that your lecturer will show you a specimen examination paper so that you know what the structure of your exam is likely to be. If your department uses electronic, multiple-choice exam systems your lecturer may well give you an opportunity to undergo a mock exam to clarify the approach used. Online examinations are not used much at present and can be taxing as many students are not used to reading questions and responding electronically within a set timescale. Again you will find that you will normally have the opportunity to engage with a draft online exam, although it may not be of the same length as the actual exam.

Whatever advance information you are given, you should note the number of questions on each exam paper, how many topics are covered and whether there is a tendency for questions to be split into two parts. These are usually a form of hybrid question as they will most often involve an essay-style question followed by a problem question. For example a hybrid question in the area of theft could contain a part 1 short essay question about dishonesty in theft, and a part 2 short problem question involving aspects of the meaning of dishonesty along with other issues perhaps. Usually the problem question is in the same area as the essay question. Past exam papers may also indicate if there is a tendency for one topic to be presented as a choice between two essays or problems with an 'either/or' choice being given. You must always carefully read such questions; all too

TABLE 23.1 A SAMPLE EXAM INVENTORY CHART

MODULE	QUESTIONS TO BE ANSWERED	QUESTIONS ON EXAM PAPER	COMPULSORY QUESTIONS?	LENGTH OF EXAM	TYPE OF EXAM			
					Closed book	Open book	Pre-seen	Unseen
Criminal law	2	9–11 changes each year	No	2 hours	√	x	x	√
Contract	3	8	No	3 hours	x	√	x	√
ELS	4	8	YES: Exam in two sections (a) and (b). One question in each section is compulsory and then a free choice	3 hours	√	x	x	√

often students incorrectly write an answer to both parts of an either/or question when they are only required to choose one or the other. The marker will only mark the first part. They lose marks overall as they will not have time to rectify their mistake in the exam, and will be one question short.

You must be absolutely clear in your mind concerning how much time you are given to answer the exam paper. A misunderstanding about timing can be fatal, because you cannot answer all questions required.

Traditional paper-based law exams tend to have essays and legal problem questions that need to be resolved. Some modules, however, do not lend themselves to any other form of question than essays. You must carefully note the rules (called the rubric) at the top of the exam paper to see if you are free to answer any type of question, or whether you need to answer a particular number of each type. For example you may be required to answer two problem questions and two essays. Or it may be the case that one question on the exam paper is compulsory and then you have a free choice. Or your exam paper may be divided into sections, in which case you need to be clear about what you are required to do in each section. You must find out all of this information weeks before the exam so that you can efficiently revise.

Additionally you must find out if you are allowed to take any books into the exam (this is called an open book exam). It is rare for level 4 exams (year 1) to be open book but it can occur. You may find that there are optional modules in levels 5 and 6 that are open book.

Finally exam papers can be 'unseen' and viewed for the first time in the exam hall, or 'pre-seen' which means they are released days or weeks in advance of the exam. This is less rare in level 4 exams but you can find some departments using this at levels 5 and 6.

Find out and make a note of the time, type and number of questions to be answered for each of your exams and note it down. Ultimately you must be guided by your lecturer, the module leader who will be setting the exam. At university your lecturers set all examinations for their subjects.

A sample chart summarising this information is a quick and useful reference for you and Table 23.1 is a hypothetical chart to demonstrate the utility of such a chart.

DRAWING UP A LIST OF POTENTIALLY EXAMINABLE TOPICS

It is your job to be sure that you are aware of all potentially examinable topics. Not all topics you study in your module will necessarily be examinable and appear on the paper. Usually topics that have been the object of continuous assessment will also not be on the exam paper. Studying past papers can give you an indication of previously featured topics. But do not assume that such topics will necessarily come up again. There is no substitute for surveying carefully the topics that are on your course syllabus for your year of study. It is always advisable to check with your lecturer if you are unclear about examinable topics. Lecturers are unlikely to answer leading questions such as 'Is the topic of theft coming up on the exam paper?' A better approach would be to ask 'Am I right to assume that theft is an examinable subject that could potentially be on the paper?'

When you are familiar with the topics on your module you need to look carefully at the ways in which each topic can appear on the exam papers (essays, problem questions, hybrid questions). Essays and problem questions can be quite wide ranging so become aware of what is normal on your course. It is also important to realise which topics tend to come up in conjunction with each other. Otherwise, even though you have revised a specific topic, you may not be able to answer the relevant question because you did not revise the topic that often accompanies it.

Drawing together information on your examinable topics

The best starting points for revision are your lecture and seminar notes. But of course the existence and condition of your notes over the term or year of the course will vary enormously. You may have missed some lectures or you may have lost relevant handouts. Much of this basic information should be on your department's virtually learning environment (VLE).

Some of you will have done the reading requested for tutorials and seminars and made notes in the seminar at the time. Some of you will not. You need to sort out what you have, what is missing, and see if you can take copies from other students. If you know you have lecture material missing it makes good sense to plan to do this in the last two weeks of term 2, before everyone leaves for the vacation. You can then check with friends about missing materials. Many law schools use a VLE and so you can easily download lecture PowerPoints. But do remember that lecturers say much more than is recorded on the PowerPoint (ppt) so it is a good idea to have a copy of the notes from a fellow student. Please choose someone with a reputation for comprehensive lecture notes.

Making an inventory of examinable topics so that you can choose your revision topics

You should prepare an inventory of examinable topics for each module or course, as shown in Table 23.2, for a hypothetical criminal law course. Your module outlines and syllabus will outline topics and sub-topics but be sure to consider all the information given to you by lecturers as well. Place the inventory at the beginning of your revision file for the module so you always know what will be required in the exam.

For each module or course you should consider how complete your existing knowledge is. Go through your inventory of examinable topics and consider each in turn.

STRESS AND EXAM PERFORMANCE

Few students like exams, but you do need to train yourself to be in the best frame of mind to sit them. Examiners do realise that examinations place pressure on students and the

TABLE 23.2 A SAMPLE HYPOTHETICAL EXAMINABLE TOPICS INVENTORY CHART FOR CRIMINAL LAW

Criminal law	Type of question			Is this an examinable topic?	
Topics covered in course	Problem question	Essays	Hybrid questions	YES – Lecturer has told me	NO – Lecturer has told me
The contexts of criminal law, • history, • media, • classifications of criminal acts • official statistics	x	√	x	√	
Principles and Policies • Criminalisation • Media • Women • *Actus reus* • *Mens rea*	x	√	x	√	
Defences	It will be involved in all problem questions	√	√ possible	√	
Murder	√	√	√	√	
Manslaughter	√	√	√	√	
Partial defences; loss of control Diminished responsibility	√	√	√	√	
Reform of the law of homicide	√	√	√	√	
GBH – Grievous bodily harm	√	√	√	√	

Sexual offences	√	√	√		√
Theft	√	√	√	√	
Burglary	√	√	√	√	
Handling	√	x	x		√
Robbery	x	x	x	√	
Criminal damage	x	x	x	√	
Guest lecture: Honour killings	x	x	x	**See next column**	**NB:** We have been told that it may be used to inform any essay questions on contexts, reform etc. in the area of murder/ manslaughter

ability to deal with this pressure is one of the first skills you need to work on. Exams require you to display your knowledge:

- in a specific area;
- on a specific day;
- at a specific time.

This is why students and lecturers often discuss exam 'performance', for exams require you to perform. It does not matter, for the purposes of the exam grade, how good you are before and after the exams. All that counts is what happens *during* the exam. That fact naturally causes pressure. Everything rests on your performance on the day.

While students worry ceaselessly about the idea of the exam and what questions will be on the paper, they tend to spend less time concerned about their emotional and physical state on the day of the exam. You need therefore to get in training and practise ways of defusing excessive stress, remaining in good health, studying consistently and developing a good examination strategy that works for you. It is a good idea to face your fears about failing the exam head on.

So – what happens if you fail? Well, life goes on, and you will plan to take the resit. Additionally you probably will not fail, because if you are reading this you are doing all in your power to plan to succeed.

ASSUMPTIONS ABOUT WHAT EXAMS ARE TESTING

There are some right and wrong assumptions concerning what the exam is testing. Some assumptions are true for some disciplines and not for others. You should take time to consider what your assumptions are. Read through the list of assumptions in Table 23.3 and tick the 'yes' or 'no' box to indicate whether you share each assumption or not.

Now go through the discussion below of each assumption and see where you were right and where you may have been wrong. Unconsciously your assumptions can determine your attitude to revision and if you only have a range of partially correct assumptions you may cause yourself difficulties in the exam. In reading through the explanations below you should begin to understand far more about what it is that the examiner is looking for.

Assumption 1: Exams are a test of how much information I can remember

To a limited extent examinations are a test of what you can remember. As you can only make links between the question and what you know, your memorised knowledge base is an important aspect of your examination performance. But your rote learning, or memorised

TABLE 23.3 TESTING YOUR ASSUMPTIONS ABOUT EXAMS

ASSUMPTION	YES	NO
Assumption 1: Exams are a test of how much information I can remember		
Assumption 2: Exams are a test of the quality of my reasoning powers		
Assumption 3: Exams are a test of my techniques for answering examination questions		
Assumption 4: Exams are a test of how well I can take apart an examination question		
Assumption 5: Exams test how quickly I can write in the time allowed		
Assumption 6: Exams test how well I can argue		
Assumption 7: Exams test how clever I am		

work is only the beginning of your answer. The examiner wants to see the proper use of your memorised information to form arguments in answer to the question.

Law exams require, in addition to knowledge of topics in set texts and articles, that you remember the detail of cases and legislation. As you need to know the case name, the court it was decided in, the names of the judges, the year of the case, the facts of the case and the reasoning in the case, memory is important. But the examiner wishes to see you demonstrate that you can use this knowledge of cases to form arguments. You do not get credit for laboriously setting out the details of irrelevant cases. Nor can you get full credit for relevant case details that you do not properly apply to a problem question. This merely demonstrates a lack of understanding. *Quality* in the application of your knowledge will achieve higher marks than a *quantity* of memorised learning being randomly listed without application to the question in hand. The careful deployment of a few leading cases and/or academic texts (depending on whether you are dealing with an essay or problem question) appropriately argued and discussed demonstrates confident understanding and application of knowledge to the issue in hand.

Assumption 2: Exams are a test of the quality of my reasoning powers

This is an absolutely correct assumption. The examiner is testing your reasoning powers and is interested in observing, through your answer, how you think. The examiner is looking to see you efficiently and confidently demonstrate the application of your knowledge in the construction of arguments. You need to choose relevant cases, legal rules and academic texts from your memory and use them to back up your arguments.

Assumption 3: Exams are a test of my techniques for answering examination questions

Again this is absolutely correct. The examiner is looking to see if you can sort the relevant from the irrelevant, and identify a good range of the correct issues. The examiner wishes to see you demonstrate that you can understand the topic and can think critically, write appropriately in terms of grammar, structure and spelling; and write confident and appropriate arguments in the time limit set by the exam.

Assumption 4: Exams are a test of how well I can take apart an examination question

Yes they are, and this ability is an essential skill. Without it you may well miss important aspects of the question and will not be able to properly answer it. You could then end up discussing irrelevant matters and setting out your rote learning without customising it to suit the question asked. Examiners dislike this very much and it can lose you marks.

Assumption 5: Exams test how quickly I can write in the time allowed

The answer is both yes and no. You are only given a limited time to answer questions in an exam and part of a successful exam strategy is being able to provide a competent answer and keep to that time limit. This is dependent on your knowledge and skills, but also your ability to write quickly and legibly. You need to know how much you can write in the time allotted for each question. The key here is to practise writing answers to past or mock exams using the time allocation that is given in the exam.

Time management in the examination is an important aspect of examination performance. You may know everything necessary but fail the exam because you just run out of time. Practise timed essay and problem questions, just as you would practise for singing, dancing or sport. In this way you increase your stamina, your speed of thought, your recall, and your handwriting speed. Legibility of handwriting is essential so that the marker can read your answer. All of your revision is useless if your handwriting cannot be read by the examiner. So practise fast legible writing. Quantity does *not* necessarily mean quality.

Assumption 6: Exams test how well I can argue

Absolutely, the quality of your argument construction can increase your grades at the top end of performance or make the difference between a pass or fail at the bottom. All exam essays and problem questions require a well-constructed argument. The competency of your *relevant* argument backed by proofs measured together with the breadth of your reading and legibility of your writing determines your grade.

(1) Correct identification of the issues raised by questions.
(2) Clearly identifiable argument(s) with an ultimate CONCLUSION in answer to the question ASKED by the examiner!
(3) The ability to support your argument(s) by reference to cases, relevant legislation, academic articles and texts of authority as required by question type.
(4) Evidence of critical thinking and understanding.
(5) Clear presentation: well-structured work in paragraphs, written in sentences rather than note form, and using legible handwriting. (However if you are running short of time then note form, or use of bullet points is an acceptable way of quickly noting your points for those vital last few marks.)
(6) Reference to material that demonstrates you have engaged in competent revision.
(7) Evidence of knowledge and understanding and the competent application of that knowledge and understanding to the question asked.

Figure 23.1 The range of skills that examiners look for

Assumption 7: Exams test how clever I am

It would be better to state that exams test your learning so far on the course. As such it can be said they test the acquisition of skills, knowledge and intelligence. However, they do much more than just measure intelligence. Exams assess a range of skills from memory and the ability to deconstruct questions correctly, through to rule handling and rule application to final construction of argument using sources to answer the question. Figure 23.1 summarises the full range of skills which examiners are looking for.

WHAT DOES YOUR UNIVERSITY LECTURER EXPECT YOU TO DEMONSTRATE IN YOUR EXAM?

Markers of exams expect your answers to demonstrate that you have read:

- relevant chapters in your set textbook;
- relevant law cases and statutes, as referred to in your set texts, lectures and seminars or located as a result of your independent study;
- a modest selection of academic journal articles: two or three articles for each topic if possible (these are to be used for essay questions only);
- relevant chapters in academic books.

But any essay with only primary law sources (cases and statutes) or just textbooks is lacking in competency. You are expected to use these *together* with academic materials such as academic journal articles or scholarly monographs. These academic sources are essential in an essay to back up your ideas and arguments. In the absence of any sources at all it will be difficult to reach a pass mark, but the addition of academic and legal sources immediately begins to give access to higher results.

Legal problem solutions do not require reference to academic articles/books. Indeed to do so is unacceptable unless the relevant text has been the object of 'judicial notice' in a case. Judicial notice describes a situation in which a judge openly refers to a writer in his or her judgment endorsing it as a source consulted in answering a difficult point.

It is unlikely that you will obtain a pass mark in a legal problem question if you do not refer to cases and to statutes.

With regard to statutes you must know:

- the correct name of the statute;
- year of enactment;
- the sections, sub-sections, paragraphs, and sub-paragraphs of the areas you have studied;
- the content of relevant sections etc.

For cases you need to be aware of:

- the names of judges;
- the facts;
- arguments presented by judges;
- the grounds of the action or the appeal and the outcome;
- the court;
- the year.

For each revision topic ensure that you draw up a list of relevant references to journals and cases/legislation from your lecture and seminar material. Pay particular attention to any handouts given out in exam/revision sessions. When you have decided what topics you will concentrate on you can then read selectively. Ideally, however, you will have earlier notes from your reading of these for seminars and assessments.

THE ART OF CAREFUL EXAM PREPARATION – REVISION

Note the word revision, means *re*-vision, i.e. re-seeing, looking again at work done. If you neglected to do the work in the first place you will not be engaging in revision; you will be learning for the first time. This generally takes longer than standard revision, so if you have missed material earlier in your course you will need to build extra time into your revision schedule.

It is not possible to overestimate the importance of planned, strategic topic picking and then careful, efficient revision of those topics. Once you know what examiners are looking for, you can use that information to strategically revise your work.

Preparing for examinations requires time, peer support from other students in the same position, and access to your lecturers, seminar leaders or subject tutors (at their allotted revision times) in order to ask any worrying questions you may have. Lecturers are busy people: be sure to respect their revision programme for the relevant module and their office hours. Do not expect their time and attention at other times due to your own disorganisation.

You need to plan revision time carefully, using it efficiently and effectively. It can be easy to do too little at the start and then too much too late. Or you can spend too much time on one area and miss the rest. Or even do too much revision for too long, effectively cancelling out that work by becoming exhausted, stressed and over-stretched. However, if you address revision properly and pace yourself you will be able to organise yourself appropriately.

To achieve optimum output and pacing it is important to engage in revision time management. Otherwise you may reach the examination with large amounts of material that has not been revised. Or large amounts of rote learning insufficiently understood and 'digested' so that you cannot properly and effectively deploy it.

Preparing a revision timetable

The following discussion assumes an end of academic year programme of examinations. Adjust timings if your exams are scheduled at other times of the year.

Revision time-management is an important aspect of ensuring peak examination performance. It is essential to draw up a revision timetable to monitor your progress and include in it every topic and subtopic you intend to revise. You should then annotate it with what you actually did revise. So, by the time of the exams, you know what you have *not* revised as well as what you have. It must also include times of your actual exams. You should also drop into that timetable paid employment and relaxation time.

Planned revision falls into two sections:

■ your main revision programme;
■ your 'recapping revision programme' in the day or days before the exam according to your preference.

In order to plot the basics on your revision timetable you first of all need to know your exam timetable and the spacing between your exams as this information predetermines your main, and your recapping, revision programmes.

You need to decide how many hours a standard revision session will be, and during what hours you will timetable revision. You can always make changes but you should start with a definite plan. The division of the day into morning, afternoon and evening sessions is a good place to begin. To assist you, in Figure 23.2 a chart has been set up that mirrors these first three natural dividers of the day (morning, afternoon and evening) to determine your revision sessions.

Session 1 (Morning)	9–1 : Break 2 x 15 minutes at least advisable
BREAK	1–2
Session 2: (Afternoon)	2–6 : Break 2 x 15 minutes at least advisable
BREAK	6–7
Session 3: (Evening)	7–9 Break 2 x 15 minutes at least advisable
Total revision in day	10 hours

Figure 23.2 Revision session timing

You will note that there is a one-hour break between each session, and each of the morning and afternoon sessions have two 15-minute breaks in the middle. Breaks are essential otherwise you will grind to a halt and lose motivation.

Table 23.4 sets out a hypothetical revision timetable that also includes paid employment, relaxation and exams. This revision table is for a hypothetical period 1 May to 15 June and covers nearly seven weeks. You may need longer and may need to use different dates. It allows for 236.5 revision hours spread over 76 revision sessions.

If the mere sight of it is liable to depress you, move on to the next section and come back to it another time.

The givens are put in first, the dates of your exams and the timings of any paid work, or any other occasions when you cannot study, for example family birthdays and special occasions. Relaxation time is also allocated on most days. The third session (see Figure 23.2) ends at 9pm so relaxation time is always available after that time. You can customise the sessions and times to suit you. You need to work with your best times, but be aware that there will be times when you have to revise when you are tired. When you are designing your revision plan do not leave too much to the last minute. You need to know yourself, act wisely and plan effectively so that you can draw up a realistic plan and stick to it. It may be a good idea to try and cut back on paid employment during revision and exams, if your pocket and your employer can cope.

It is sensible to allocate a specified revision session to each module. You may allocate less time to those with lower exam weightings. Whether you put a large number of same-subject revision together or split it up throughout your timetable is up to you. If you get easily bored by revision you will relate better to change.

A comments column allows for working out the weekly revision hours and study sessions and for any other notes, for instance if you have missed a session.

Compiling the list of topics that you will revise

Very few students can learn everything well, and attempting to learn everything can result in mediocre and patchy knowledge that reduces all of your revision to a superficial level. It is, however, possible to learn a few topics very well indeed. Since some exams are designed so that a limited series of topics comes up, many students will select the topics

TABLE 23.4 SAMPLE REVISION TIMETABLE

SESSIONS	TIME	MON	TUES	WEDS	THURS	FRI	SAT	SUN	TOTALS	
	Week 1	MAY 1	2	3	4	5	6	7		
1 Morning	9–1	3.5 hours	3.5 hours	RELAX	3.5 hours	3.5 hours	PAID WORK	RELAX	Revision Hours 39	Paid Work hours 14
2 Afternoon	2–6	3.5 hours	3.5 hours	3.5 hours	3.5 hours	3.5 hours		3.5 hours	Revision Sessions 12	Relax hours 12
3 Evening	7–9	PAID WORK	PAID WORK	2 hours	RELAX	PAID WORK	RELAX	2 hours		
	Week 2	8	9	10	11	12	13	14		
1 Morning	9–1	PAID WORK	3.5 hours	3.5 hours	3.5 hours	3.5 hours	PAID WORK	RELAX	Revision Hours 35.5	Paid Work hours 16
2 Afternoon	2–6	PAID WORK	3.5 hours	3.5 hours	3.5 hours	3.5 hours		3.5 hours	Revision Sessions 11	Relax hours 10
3 Evening	7–9	RELAX	PAID WORK	2 hours	RELAX	PAID WORK	RELAX	2 hours		
	Week 3	15	16	17	18	19	20	21		
1 Morning	9–1	3.5 hours	3.5 hours	3.5 hours	3.5 hours	3.5 hours	PAID WORK	RELAX	Revision Hours 41	Paid Work hours 16
2 Afternoon	2–6	3.5 hours	PAID WORK	3.5 hours	3.5 hours	3.5 hours		3.5 hours	Revision Sessions 13	Relax hours 8
3 Evening	7–9	RELAX	PAID WORK	2 hours	2 hours	PAID WORK	RELAX	2 hours		
	Week 4	22	23	24	25	26	27	28		
1 Morning	9–1	PAID WORK	3.5 hours	3.5 hours	3.5 hours	3.5 hours	PAID WORK	RELAX	Revision Hours 36	Paid Work hours 20
2 Afternoon	2–6	PAID WORK	3.5 hours	3.5 hours	3.5 hours	RELAX	PAID WORK	3.5 hours	Revision Sessions 12	Relax hours 10
3 Evening	7–9	2 hours	PAID WORK	2 hours	2 hours	PAID WORK	RELAX	2 hours		

TABLE 23.4—continued

SESSIONS	TIME	MON	TUES	WEDS	THURS	FRI	SAT	SUN	TOTALS	
	Week 5	29	30	31	JUNE 1	2	3	4		
1 Morning	9–1	3.5 hours	3.5 hours	3.5 hours	3.5 hours	3.5 hours	PAID WORK	RELAX	Revision Hours 44	Paid Work hours 14
2 Afternoon	2–6	3.5 hours	3.5 hours	3.5 hours	3.5 hours	3.5 hours	PAID WORK	3.5 hours	Revision Sessions 14	Relax hours 6
3 Evening	7–9	PAID WORK	PAID WORK	2 hours	2 hours	PAID WORK	RELAX	2 hours		
	Week 6	5	6	7	8	9	10	11		
1 Morning	9–1	RELAX	3.5 hours	3.5 hours	3.5 hours	EXAM	PAID WORK	RELAX	Revision Hours 31.5	Paid Work hours 8
2 Afternoon	2–6	3.5 hours	3.5 hours	3.5 hours	3.5 hours	3.5 hours	PAID WORK	3.5 hours	Revision Sessions 9	Relax hours 22
3 Evening	7–9	RELAX	RELAX	RELAX	RELAX	RELAX	RELAX	RELAX		Exam session 1
	Week 7	12	13	14	15	16	17	18		
1 Morning	9–1	EXAM	EXAM	EXAM	3.5 hours	3.5 hours	FINISHED		Revision Hours 19.5	Paid Work hours 0
2 Afternoon	2–6	EXAM	3.5 hours	3.5 hours	3.5 hours	EXAM			Revision Sessions 6	Relax hours 6
3 Evening	7–9	2 hours	RELAX	RELAX	RELAX	FINISHED				EXAMS 5 sessions

that they are going to revise, leaving some topics to one side. This process is part of the exam 'game-plan' or strategy. Topic picking is a difficult issue. Attitudes to it among both students and academics vary.

Above all else topic-picking involves knowing all the examinable topics in your module, and understanding your own strengths and weaknesses. It may also involve predicting what may, or may not, come up in the exam. You need to listen to information given to you from your lecturer and read what is said about the exam in your departmental and module subject guides, and any module revision guides issued by your lecturer or department.

The next step is to make strategic choices about the number of topics that you can revise in each of the subjects that you are studying. Only you can decide the number of topics to pick. You need to know how the topics splinter into a range of subtopics (for example, theft splits into issues of dishonesty that can be the object of an essay, as well as general problem questions). You also need to know the range of topics that could come up together. Here learning just one topic could mean that you cannot answer the question. For example, if you revise murder and not the partial defences, or indeed do not revise manslaughter, you might have difficulty in a problem question designed to test your knowledge of whether the defendant may be liable for murder or manslaughter, or whether a partial defence applies to murder.

You need to take sensible decisions. If you are convinced a topic will come up but it is a topic that you struggle with and have never understood, think carefully before choosing to revise it. Even if the topic is guaranteed to be in the exam, is there any guarantee that you will be able to understand it before the exam?

From the inventory of topics that you draw up for each module you will need to consider your state of understanding of topics and then choose those that you feel most confident about in terms of understanding. Obviously if some topics will form the foundation of a compulsory question you have no choice. Table 23.5 sets out a potential 'personal knowledge checklist' and again uses criminal law as our specimen module.

In our example Table 23.5 there are several areas that have not yet been covered by the student. There are also topics the student finds 'confusing'. They will need to decide whether it is worth spending the time getting up to speed on these topics or whether they should leave them. When making decisions about which topics to cover if you have a free choice and know what tends to come up and what does not you should make final choices based on your strengths and weaknesses. Also too many topics may be chosen: it looks like possibly nine areas could be chosen. Yet the paper contains eleven questions and students only need to answer two.

The value of this exercise lets you know if you are trying to cover too much, diluting the ability to learn more information about fewer topics in more depth.

For every topic that you do cover, it is best to prepare for both an essay and a problem question scenario, as you cannot always predict how a question will arise on the exam paper. Problem questions require quite extensive primary sources of law. Essay questions require academic sources and it is often necessary to discuss primary sources of law. It is important to realise that the same basic information is needed to do a problem question

TABLE 23.5 SAMPLE KNOWLEDGE SUMMARY FOR EXAMINABLE TOPICS

Criminal law	Coverage	Type of question I can do		Comment
Examinable Topics		Problem question	Essay	
The contexts of criminal law, • history, • media, • classifications of criminal acts • official statistics	x	-	-	But I only want to do an essay on classifications of criminal acts
Principles and Policies • Criminalisation • Media • Women • *Actus reus* • *Mens rea*	√	-	√	I only want to do criminalisation. I enjoyed the topic a lot. [I know I need to learn *actus reus* and *mens rea* for my individual offences of theft etc.]
Murder	√	√	?	
Manslaughter	√	√		
Partial defences Loss of control Diminished responsibility	√	√	√	I only want to do an essay on loss of control. I can use diminished responsibility for problem questions though.
Reform of the law of homicide	x	x	x	I missed this and won't do it. It has not come up often.
GBH – Grievous bodily harm	x	x	x	I find this too confusing.
Sexual offences	√	√	x	Interesting topic – Yes
Theft	√	√	√	I only want to do an essay on dishonesty, problem is that issues with appropriation may come up instead or with it. So I will have to learn both. Some of this is confusing to me.

Criminal law	Coverage	Type of question I can do		Comment
Examinable Topics		Problem question	Essay	
Burglary	x	√	x	We've been told this will only come up as a problem question, but it could also come up with criminal damage and/or theft. I do like this area.
Handling	x	x	x	I found this boring. I won't do it.
Robbery	√	√	x	Boring, I am not doing this.
Criminal damage		√	x	I didn't go to any lectures or seminars in this area but need to learn it if I am going to do burglary/theft.

and an essay question and it is best to revise a topic in order to answer whatever type of question comes up.

Assisting your memory

Once you have collated a full set of revision material from:

■ lecture notes;
■ seminar notes;
■ private study notes;
■ case notes;
■ articles/books,

you should condense all the information into key point form. You then need to ensure you understand these key points, and can remember them.

Memorising these key points can be difficult. However, although law exams cannot be simply passed by rote memory, you have to engage in memory tasks to commit to your mind the information you need to know in order to apply it to an exam question. You can engage in several different approaches for revision; some may not suit you but ideally you should engage in all of them. They assist in committing information to memory and putting you in a good position to pass the exam. Table 23.6 shows a range of different activities that relate to the learning styles discussed in Chapter 16. You will have your own preference for what works best.

TABLE 23.6 LEARNING STYLES AND MEMORY TACTICS FOR ENHANCING YOUR REVISION

LEARNING STYLES	EXAMPLE ACTIVITIES
KINAETHEST LEARNING STRATEGIES	• Link the information you are learning to doing different things. For instance, you could try learning different topics in different places to help recall.
VISUAL LEARNING STRATEGIES	• Construct diagrams of interconnections. • Construct a mind map.
	• Draw symbols or even pictures to help you remember cases. All you need in the exam is a trigger to release the door to your memory. Then you only need to learn the trigger. • Colour code narrative points if you wish.
	• Make revision flashcards: questions on one side and answers on the other. • Make revision flashcards: with case name on one side and the facts, reasoning and any precedent/interpretational point notes on the other. • Make some revision quizzes in the same way. • Making these up is of course part of the revision and memorising process.
HARNESSING AUDITORY LEARNING	• Speak your notes aloud. • Think of rhymes for different things. • Record your notes and listen to them. • Find a patient friend or relative and explain your topic to them.
FORMAL CHECKS	• Write answers to past or specimen exam papers under exam conditions in the time you will have in the exam. Check your answers in your textbook. • Remember that all of the conventions for good writing apply in an exam. • Check your answer for legible handwriting. Ask a friend if they can read it. • Check that you have provided evidence for each point in your argument. • Lecturers will often have specific timescales within which they will look at specimen answers so it is worth asking in good time if they will consider your draft answer.

How long before the exam should I start revising?

This is your decision and is influenced by a range of factors, including how fast you work, how consistently you have studied all year, how much new understanding you need to acquire and how many topics you struggle with. It is quite possible that when you have done your revision programme you will find that you have differing amounts of revision to do for each exam.

- DO NOT UNDERESTIMATE how much you need to do.
- DO NOT OVERESTIMATE what you can do in the time you have.
- PACE YOUR REVISION. If you push yourself too much and become too tired your brain will 'switch off' and you will find it extremely difficult to keep going with your revision. If you feel this happening, stop and take time to develop a more efficient plan.
- SLEEP. The temptation to revise late into the night is strong for some at exam time, but it is important to ensure you have enough sleep. Your brain is your major asset to be used in passing the exams. It needs sleep to be replenished.

From your inventory of topics for the course you will need to know which ones you can potentially tackle.

Revision activities and how to keep motivated (boredom sabotages revision!)

For many students, revision is not only stressful (because it reminds you that exams are looming); it is also boring. This means that however hard you try you may not remember what you revise as your brain has switched itself off.

(1) Answering practice exam questions.
(2) Switch topics several times in one revision session.
(3) Revise using a lot of small sessions (20/30 minutes) rather than a marathon session.
(4) List key points to each topic.
(5) Use diagrams to connect knowledge.
(6) Read, think, and then summarise in writing.
(7) Summarise notes, and re-summarise.
(8) Read case notes that you have made.
(9) Read and make notes on academic journal articles.
(10) Always aim for a page and no more of revised final notes that contain phrases to prompt your memory.

Figure 23.3 Revision activities

To avoid getting bored, find the revision activity that best suits you. There are many different revision activities to choose from, as shown in Figure 23.3. All of these make revision active. Consider whether any of these would work for you.

THE DAY OF THE EXAMINATION

You have done all the revising you can and now it is the day of the exam. It is worth thinking about what you need to know on the day and what habits you should try to acquire beforehand. Figure 23.4 lists some ways of staying unflustered and relaxed so you are able to perform at your best on the day.

If you finally realise that you have chosen to not properly prepare then there is no point over-stressing; you can only follow through with the exam and hope for some luck.

Strategies during the examination

It is important that you have a pre-plan of how you will divide up your time during the examination. Before the exam you need to have practised efficiently, producing draft answers in the actual time you will have in the exam.

If you have a two hour exam and only need to answer two questions you should allow reading time of 10 minutes at the start, and 10 minutes for edits, proofing review at the end. This means you have around 1 hour 40 minutes to write your two answers (50 minutes each). Some universities allow 15 minutes reading time under exam conditions immediately prior to the commencement of the exam.

Below are some suggestions for dividing up your time in a two hour exam without reading time prior to its commencement.

(1)   The first ten minutes: Read the *whole* paper through *carefully* and decide which
       questions you will answer. Check the length of the exam and the number of questions

(1) Be absolutely clear about the VENUE, DATE and TIME of your examination.
(2) Have a supply of **working** pens and pencils.
(3) Do not overwork the night before, or on the day of the exam.
(4) Eat and drink appropriately before the exam.
(5) Do not wait near the exam room if you are very nervous. You may pick up on the anxieties of others, or overhear students discussing what may or may not come up.
(6) Remember that you have revised to the best of your ability, you have good strategies and you will do your best.
(7) Some stress is normal so do not worry about feeling a little stressed.

Figure 23.4 Good habits on exam day

you are told to answer; check for compulsory questions. Make sure you know which questions are 'either/or' questions and which are asking you to do both parts of a question. Think about what the examiner is looking for in each question and whether you can deliver it. Check you have properly explored the language of the question so that you do not miss questions you are able to answer, or miss points in the questions you have decided to answer.

(2)   The next ten minutes could be used to plan answers to all of your chosen questions, *or* you could start your first question, planning each question as you go. Whichever process you use, planning time has to be incorporated into the time you have allotted for writing your answer to each question. Do not be tempted into writing without considered pre-planning of the question on a separate piece of paper. You can plan by making notes or drawing a diagram, and before the exam you need to think about how you will do this, and practise it when you do specimen papers under exam conditions. Invariably there will be a hierarchy in the questions you have picked to answer, with some topics you know well and some less well. Be rigorous, however, about moving on to the next question at the end of your allotted time for each question. This will open up the next set of marks for you. One brilliant answer rarely makes up for missed questions. Even a mediocre answer joined to a great one can push you into the next grade band. But if you continue to make your great question greater you are not really opening up the marks available to you. Each question has a set number of marks.

(3)   During the planning and writing process constantly refer back to the question to make absolutely certain you are addressing it. You are being tested on your structured and methodical approach to the questions you answer as well as on your knowledge and its application to the questions.

(4) Structuring essays

Make sure that each of your answers has a brief introduction, a main body and a conclusion. Also that you refer to academic journals in your answer, plus refer to any appropriate cases or legislation.

(5) Structuring problem answers

- Give a brief introduction stating ambit of problem.
- Do a flow chart of facts in your rough work to guide you.
- Answer each head of liability for each party separately.
- Ensure you make clear the rules that are relevant.
- State legal areas involved.
- Clearly set out issues.
- Apply statutes and cases methodically to each element.
- Do not forget defences unless told not to deal with them.
- Conclude for *each* party in relation to *each* head of liability.

Only refer to cases and legislation; do not refer to any academic text UNLESS it has received judicial notice in a case.

(6)   Rigidly stick to your pre-planned timing for each question.

(7)   Present your work so that it is easy for the examiner to follow, using the rules preferred in your department for drawing attention to law cases and statutes (for example underlining them).

(8)   Do leave time in the last ten minutes of the exam to recheck your whole paper for spelling and grammar. If you have been writing too fast you can leave out important linking words. This simple error can turn a great point into an incomprehensible point. Check all your sentences make sense. *Neatly* correct any problems. Make sure all rough work has a line drawn through it and you have correctly labelled your questions. This includes labelling parts of questions. If you think of extra materials or points, annotate your question: examiners will follow clear instructions from the exam candidate. You might also find that you remember a point of argument, or a case, or an article that you had originally forgotten when answering the question. You can always add this at the end (ensuring you signpost the examiner to the additional material with an asterisk or some other device).

(9)   At the end of the exam it may be a good idea to avoid those who are dissecting the paper to see what everyone else did, discussing whether they are wrong or right. This could needlessly upset you and even unnerve you before your next exam.

CONCLUSION

To be able to perform successfully in the exam requires sustained organisation on your part. You need to understand the structure of the exam and its relationship to the structure of your course. You need to understand what topics in your course are examinable topics that may come up in the exam. You also need to know your own capability with regard to the course, what you do understand and what you do not understand. This will enable you to properly devise a revision timetable, uniting understanding of the topics with any necessary rote learning required to apply the law and your academic sources to exam questions. Having properly revised you can then plan your in-exam strategy.

CHAPTER SUMMARY

■   Remember that exams are not unexpected events for which you cannot plan. It is essential to plan for them well in advance.

■   Be sure that you know what exams are designed to test.

■   Revision skills *and* tactics in the exam are an integral part of your skills. Indeed they are the summation of your year's work.

■   Ensure you know the examinable syllabus and have an idea of your competency in each topic.

- Be quite clear about how fast you write and what you can write in the time of the exam.
- Ensure your handwriting remains legible when writing to time limits under exam conditions by practising in advance answering questions in the required time.
- Revise strategically, engaging in topic picking if the exam is not composed of all compulsory questions.
- Keep a careful and disciplined watch on the time during the exam.
- Read the exam paper carefully and choose questions wisely.
- Read and follow all instructions.
- Answer the required number of questions.
- Plan each answer.
- Re-read each of your answers for sense, spelling and errors towards the end of the exam.
- Stay calm – otherwise your ability to think will be impaired.
- After the exam draw a line under it and move on to the next one.

PRESENTATION SKILLS

LEARNING OUTCOMES

After reading this chapter you should be able to:

- Understand the oral skills required to deliver a competent presentation.
- Appreciate the range of discrete tasks that need to be managed to deliver a presentation.
- Understand the importance of the editing process for the presentation.
- Efficiently use written prompts.
- Appreciate the need to have competent visual aids if required by the assessor.

INTRODUCTION

You will be required to deliver quite a few presentations during your degree studies, either as an individual or a team member, and some of these will be formally assessed. This chapter concentrates on the oral and management skills needed to deliver a good presentation. The nature of presentations will be explored and the chapter will go through the six key stages of:

(1)   Understanding the nature of the task.
(2)   Managing the task.
(3)   Research.
(4)   Content.
(5)   Delivery.
(6)   Teamwork (if applicable).

THE SIX STAGES OF THE PRESENTATION

Note: Issues relating to (6): teamwork will be woven throughout the discussion of stages (1)–(5).

(1) Understanding the nature of the task: what is a presentation?

A presentation is a time-limited oral argument put forward by a student or a group on a topic of relevance to your module. It is usually required to be accompanied by the student's use of audio-visual aids such as PowerPoint. It may be set by your tutor, or you may be asked to choose your own title for the presentation. Presentations can be assessed or non-assessed. Non-assessed presentations should always be viewed as a formative opportunity to get feedback on your presentation skills. Presentations can either stand alone or be designed to aid fuller and deeper discussion of a topic within the class in the context of a seminar.

The presentation is usually posed as a question, which can be broad, for example:

Should the English legal system allow cultural defence as a valid plea in relation to crime against the person?

Or narrow, for example:

Should the English legal system allow cultural defence as a valid plea to murder?

(2) Managing the task

Working backwards from the date of the presentation you need to determine how much time you have realistically to engage in research, how much time to deliberate over content, how much time you need to practise delivery and edit your presentation, and how much time you need to prepare any audio-visual aids such as PowerPoints (though this should be done after you have decided on the final format of your presentation as otherwise your slides may be out of line with your final product).

If you are working in a team, it is important that everyone understands the timescale and that measures are put in place to deal with those who do not prepare what they have been asked to do. This is all the more important if there are marks allocated to teamwork. It is a good idea to appoint someone different each week to coordinate everyone and check that they are going to be able to produce the required tasks in the agreed timescales. You may need to decide that some aspects of research should be covered by two group members in case one cannot complete the work.

Time limits

It is absolutely essential to practise the performance of the final presentation to ensure that it comes within the time limit. You will then have the opportunity to go for all of the marks available. It is not a good strategy to speak more quickly. This will mean that your audience and the marker will not properly hear or understand what you are saying and you will lose marks.

(3) Research

Imagine that your presentation question is:

> Should the English legal system allow a cultural defence as a valid plea in criminal cases?

This question asks you to reach a given position in a measured way. But it also requires certain issues to be explained. You need to split up your presentation question into discrete sections. Identifying the way that your question splits into other issues is important because it allows you to manage your time by deciding what has to be researched. It ensures that you do not overlook issues. If you are working in a team this will help you divide up tasks between you. Figure 24.1 sets out the demonstration presentation question above so that you can see how the issues arise from it.

If a team is involved you should *all* concentrate on splitting up the question into its issues, and then pool your findings. Several heads are always better than one – if *all* heads are thinking. Then each of your questions can be delegated to the team.

You must engage in focused and careful research through your institution's print and e-library collections. The depth of this research will be determined by the nature of the presentation. For instance, is it to start a seminar discussion, informing other members

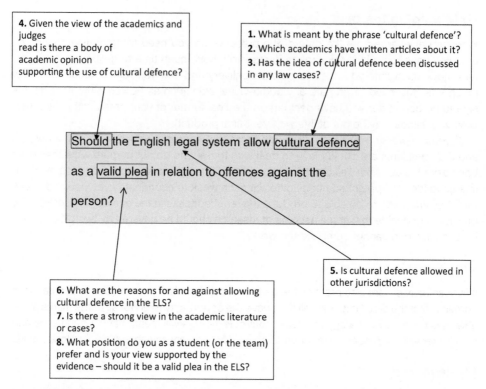

Figure 24.1 Eight initial questions flowing from a proper consideration of the demonstration presentation question: 'Should the English legal system allow a cultural defence as a valid plea in criminal cases?'

of the seminar group about descriptive issues? Or is it designed to demonstrate critical thinking? The depth of research will also be determined by whether the presentation is assessed or not. You must use judgement based on your understanding of the nature and purpose of the oral skills exercise. Also the length of the presentation is a guide. If it is only 5 minutes you cannot spend much time in detailed analysis. If it is 10–15 minutes you can.

If a team is involved, this is the point at which decisions are made concerning the allocation of certain sources to be researched. You need to have a risk assessment of the team and the likelihood of individuals executing any or all of the given tasks. If the team is arbitrarily put together then each student will have different skills and these should be discussed and borne in mind when tasks are being allocated.

Notes and sources

You should compile good notes, making sure that they are efficiently referenced so the original sources can be quickly located if needed. Of course, if it is an assessed presentation, your marker will also expect to hear your references.

Each team member should write legible notes and photocopy them for the group so that all information can be shared. Team members should be aware that each person's note taking skills may be very different. Therefore your team time management should bear this in mind and allow a few days for rechecking notes if necessary.

If your presentation is split into several different topic questions and team members have been allocated one each, this will obviously determine the sources for note taking.

(4) Content of the presentation

Overall, you are aiming to create a considered argument. There are several things that you can do to ensure the content of your presentation is academically acceptable and the argument well constructed.

Ensure that your presentation is relevant to the question

Read your notes and reflect on the question in light of the information that you have collected. Understanding can sometimes occur instantly, like a light being switched on. It is, however, more likely for understanding to dawn more slowly, as you think about issues, read your notes, ask yourself questions and reflect on the points that you do or do not understand. If you are team working, these tasks of reflection should occur individually and then as part of group discussions.

Ensure that you build competent arguments

Begin the process of building arguments based on your notes and your growing understanding. This text uses the follow definition of argument:

> An argument is a series of statements, some backed by evidence, some not, that are purposely presented in order to prove, or disprove, a given position.

Ensure your argument is mainly backed and is ordered.

It is also worth remembering that one piece of writing, and therefore one oral skills exercise, may require the setting up of several small arguments, the conclusion of each one going forward to form the overarching argument.

Here the use of good time management is essential as well. There is no point in having an excellent argument if you do not appropriately manage the time limits of the presentation and therefore cannot deliver your argument. Difficult decisions will need to be taken concerning what can be said and what cannot be said in the time. You will also be expected to refer to your evidence (academic texts, law, judges); how you decide to do this in view of existing time limits is important.

Often you will be asked to submit a written version of your presentation, unless it is recorded on film. This must contain all sources properly referenced. You need to know the differences between full referencing in a written format and referencing orally in a presentation.

(5) Delivery

A range of skills are involved with delivery of the presentation. The rationale for using the vehicle of a presentation to test your skills development is that competency in oral skills is an important aspect of being a well-rounded student. It acknowledges that the written genre is not the only forum in which you will be tested or called upon to act. Presentations begin the process of oral skills assessment for the law student. As you will find as you engage with them, a range of different skills must be added to your research, writing, reading and argument construction skills, in order to efficiently deliver an oral presentation. Above all your delivery must be well rehearsed but sound natural.

Never be tempted to read out your presentation. That is reading not presenting, and you will lose marks for it. Reading not only makes it impossible for you to maintain eye contact with your audience, which is an essential aspect of oral presentation, but your voice changes in tone and pacing, and there can often be a tendency to speed up and speak too quickly for your audience. When you are invited to a reading, it is to hear a well-known author read from their work of fiction for example, and it will be embellished with various performance skills for the spoken word. When you are asked to present, you are asked to look at your audience and speak to them, not read to them.

You will find that it is helpful to refer to the assessment criteria that you will have been given for an assessed presentation. You will find it will refer to the use of appropriate English; this means in terms of grammar and also in terms of technical vocabulary. It will also refer to pacing, that is, to the speed of your delivery, and to the tone of your voice. We will look at each of these in turn.

Your voice

Ensure that you speak clearly and do not engage in those grunts and 'er's' that so many speakers do. They are extremely distracting to an audience, but most importantly they interrupt sense and you can lose marks as a marker may well find that they cannot follow what you are saying. Read the following opening sentences of a student presentation and you will see how distracting it is.

Well er, The title er of my er presentation today is er 'Theft – and ummmm . . . Er . . . the problem with dishonesty'. Firstly I will er consider er the meaning of er . . . er . . . dishonesty . . . and, and, errr and errrrrr dis – honesty ah no err . . . I mean honesty, ummm, um as, as those words are er um ummm er as used in the er the Theft Act 1978.

What the speaker is intending to say, and probably what she had in her prompts and script, is much clearer when tidied up:

> The title of my presentation today is 'Theft – and the problem with dishonesty'. Firstly I will consider the meaning of dishonesty and dishonesty (no, I mean honesty) as those words are used in the Theft Act 1978.

Unfortunately nerves probably intervened and she found herself at the mercy of the families of 'er' and 'um'. Any student with a speaking disability should discuss presentations and other oral work with their tutor so that an appropriate manner of assessing in light of any disability can be found. Practise your oral skills exercise, asking fellow students or friends and family to listen; they will be able to assist you in eradicating these types of problems. The importance of such 'verbal editing' cannot be underestimated.

Part of the skill of speaking in public is to engage with the audience, and use your voice to supply the punctuation. This ensures your listeners maintain concentration and can understand. The tone of your voice should command the space given to you by others to speak. Even if you need to stop speaking to collect your thoughts, or to find a point in some notes, you need to command the silence. Do not appear to be embarrassed by stopping to check something. If appropriate, give an explanation of what you are doing, but do not apologise. Your tone should not in any way be condescending, too excitable, or indeed too obviously insecure or unhappy. You should speak at an appropriate speed. Recall times when you have been frustrated because you were unable to follow a speaker's point because they spoke far too quickly.

Regardless of the type of oral skills exercise, the aim of any communication is to actually communicate with the listener. You therefore need to plan both the argumentative layout of the content of your presentation and the way in which you will deliver it verbally for the listener. This can only come from practice, and from gathering feedback from others. If you ask people to explain constructively what was good and what did not work so well you will learn. Many universities have the facility for staff to video presentations. If you are videoed you may learn from watching yourself afterwards. Sometimes when we see mannerisms on screen that we think add to our effective communication it is clear that they add nothing and should be removed.

Try recording your presentation and listening dispassionately to your voice. Is your presentation delivered in a monosyllabic manner? Does your voice have emphasis? Is the delivery in a flat tone? Listen carefully to other students when they present. What do you like about how they communicate? Your task is to use your voice to carry your message successfully, letting it enhance your presentation. Above all, make sure that you form your words carefully. Do not mutter or mumble. Speak loudly enough to be heard but not so loudly that your voice is distracting.

Learn to change the speed at which you speak, making accommodation for the listener. You should also maintain reasonable eye contact with your audience to help maintain their attention.

Using appropriate high quality audio-visual aids

Presentations often require audio-visual aids for delivery in the form of PowerPoint slides or handouts. Be sure to practise your delivery with PowerPoint and try and check out the room beforehand so that you see where the equipment is in relation to the audience. Your university webpages will have instructions on PowerPoint and its use.

Using useful presenter prompts

Whilst you should have a good idea of what you are saying it is always sensible to have presenter prompts. For example, cards with trigger words on them so that if you forget something or lose your place you can easily find it again. Prompt cards allow you to glance down for a reminder of your next point. Be sure to write large enough for your audience to be able to read them.

Team issues on delivery

It is essential that a group presentation flows consistently. Ensure that you all have a copy of the whole presentation and work on making the moment where the next speaker stands and speaks as effortless and seamless as possible. Edit the presentation of the group as a whole unit, making sure each person knows what they have to do and by when.

CONCLUSION

The ability to be able to engage in competent general oral skills is an important academic and life skill. Presentations offer the opportunity for you to be able to test your general oral skills. Most students find presentations daunting and you will develop confidence as you engage in them and overcome your natural concerns about them as a mode of assessment of required performance. As you engage in them more regularly you will find they are invaluable in assisting you to improve your communication skills. Often presentations build in the opportunity for the marker to ask you one or two questions, and this allows you to practise that most important of all skills – competent thinking 'on your feet'.

CHAPTER SUMMARY

- A presentation is a time-limited oral argument put forward by a student or a group on a topic of relevance to your module. It is usually required to be accompanied by the student's use of audio-visual aids.

- Presentations can be split into six key stages: understanding the nature of the task, managing the task, research, content, delivery and teamwork (if applicable).
- If you are working in a team, it is important that everyone understands the timescale and that measures are put in place to deal with those who do not prepare what they have been asked to do.
- It is absolutely essential to practise the performance of the final presentation to ensure that it comes within the time limit.
- Presentation questions need to be split into discrete issues and sub-questions so that you do not overlook issues.
- If a team is involved you should *all* concentrate on splitting up the question into its issues, and then pool your findings. Then each of your questions can be delegated to the team.
- You must engage in focused and careful research through your institution's print and e-library collections. The depth of this research will be determined by the nature of the presentation.
- You should compile good notes, making sure that they are efficiently referenced so the original sources can be quickly located if needed. Each team member should write legible notes and photocopy them for the group so that all information can be shared. Team members should be aware that each person's note taking skills may be very different. Therefore your team time management should bear this in mind and allow a few days for rechecking notes if necessary.
- If your presentation is split into several different topic questions and team members have been allocated one each, this will obviously determine the sources for note taking.

Ensure that your presentation is relevant to the question

Ensure that you build competent arguments

- Ensure you have the time to deliver the argument by appropriately managing time limits.
- Any required written version of your presentation must contain all sources properly referenced.
- Practice your delivery in terms of your vocabulary, tone of voice and pacing.
- Never be tempted to read out your presentation. That is reading not presenting, and you will lose marks for it.
- Ensure that you refer to any assessment criteria that you will have been given for an assessed presentation. You will find it will refer to the use of appropriate English.
- Learn to change the speed at which you speak, making accommodation for the listener. You should also maintain reasonable eye contact with your audience to help maintain their attention.

Use appropriate high quality audio-visual aids

Use presenter prompts

- The ability to be able to engage in competent general oral skills is an important academic and life skill.
- Often presentations build in the opportunity for the marker to ask you one or two questions, and this allows you to practise that most important of all skills – competent thinking 'on your feet'.

MOOTING SKILLS

LEARNING OUTCOMES

After reading this chapter you should be able to understand:

- The range of skills involved in successful mooting.
- How to engage with the factual and legal analysis of the moot problem.
- The differing roles of senior and junior counsel.
- The general rules of engagement governing mooting (for example issues of timing, submissions and exchange of documentation).
- How to write a speech for oral delivery.

INTRODUCTION

Mooting is an excellent way of engaging in the development of your oral skills, your skills of fact and legal analysis as well as your ability to construct a good legal argument. Initially you will be guided through an explanation of what mooting is, and reasons why it is a good idea to moot. You will also look at the roles of the various participants in a moot, the rules of engagement governing the moot, turn taking in a moot, and the skeleton argument. You will then be guided through a four stage model for successful mooting, dealing with analysis of the moot problem, legal research, construction of legal argument and finally oral delivery of a moot speech.

There are many good online resources you can consult to watch examples of good mooting and obtain a range of invaluable tips on mooting, researching a moot and construction of your argument. A few of these are listed at the end of the book in further reading and useful websites.

WHAT IS MOOTING?

A moot is a competitive simulation of an appellate court hearing designed to test students' ability to orally present a well-structured legal argument in relation to narrow grounds of appeal based on a question of law. The setting can either be the Court of Appeal or the Supreme Court.

In addition to the grounds of appeal, mooters are given the facts of the original fictitious dispute and a fictitious procedural history. The appeal points argued could go either way and so everything depends upon the skill of the mooter.

It is conducted according to highly structured rules of engagement. A legal academic or professional lawyer role-plays the judge. Two teams of students role-play senior and junior counsel for the appellants and respondents. The presiding judge can stop counsel at any time in their submission and ask questions.

You may find that some modules you study require you to engage in a moot as part of your formal assessment. Additionally, most law schools will have a mooting society that runs an internal mooting competition early in the year. This is done to choose a team or teams to represent the law school in one of the national mooting competitions. Quite often year 1 students are surprisingly good at mooting and therefore 'newness' to law study does not automatically exclude you from being included in a mooting team. The winning mooting teams in national competitions are often required to travel abroad to represent their university in international mooting competitions.

'WHY SHOULD I MOOT?'

Mooting is a skill that is particularly associated with a serious intention to be a professional lawyer. It is therefore a great addition to your CV to state that you were an active member of your mooting society, particularly if you were on winning teams in national competitions.

As well as developing valuable communication skills, particularly oral skills, mooting also develops your ability to discriminate between legal arguments, determining which you consider to support your argument and which do not. It also refines your skills of fact management, legal research and argument construction. Mooting requires that you analyse legal rules and apply them efficiently and correctly to the grounds of appeal. As moots always involve working with others, mooting also develops the important graduate skill of team working.

But – I am too nervous to moot!

If this is your response, the first thing to say is that you are not alone. Many students find the idea of mooting particularly worrying because it requires public speaking, and the subjection to questioning by the judge. This does indeed put you on display and can make you feel vulnerable.

Some students cannot overcome this concern and they do not engage in mooting. However, if you wish to enter the legal profession you will find that at the vocational stage of training there will be many practical exercises and it is good to begin to engage with them earlier rather than later. You will then be more prepared. Also, if you do wish to enter the legal profession you need to be proficient in public speaking.

Mooting, like any other skill, can be learnt and academic staff and experienced student mooters will be only too pleased to assist you. You will be taught how to effectively deploy your oral skills, and how to speak in front of others. You will be instructed how to properly prepare your speech and how to deal with questioning. But the first step is yours; you need to take a deep breath and put yourself forward to moot. You may even enjoy it!

THE ROLES OF THE VARIOUS PARTICIPANTS IN A MOOT

There are many roles in a moot, and like other activities mooting requires quite a lot of behind the scenes administration to make it work smoothly, especially if mooting is being done as part of an internal or external mooting competition. Student law societies can have a sub-committee dealing with mooting, or there can be a freestanding mooting society. Members of academic staff will work alongside students organising mooting to assist with training and to role-play judges in moots. The following list of roles are, however, key.

The moot master[1]

The moot master is a key player in mooting. It is a position that is usually taken by a student who takes care of the overall management of mooting. Occasionally an academic member of staff may take on the role but this is not the normal course of events.

---

1 The word 'master' tends to be used regardless of the sex of the student undertaking the task, although the word 'mistress' has been used on occasion.

The moot master ensures judges are available to judge, usually setting up rotas of judges in competition times. It is their job to make sure that documentation the parties should give each other is indeed exchanged and copies given to the judge. Additionally they should ensure that any other documentation, required under the rules of engagement governing the moot, is duly produced and exchanged as necessary.

They also make sure that the room is properly laid out for mooting with the judge able to clearly see all counsel. The standard arrangement is for appellants and respondents to have their desks at an angle to the judge's desk. The appellants are to the left of the judge and the respondents to the right.

The judge

This is a key role as the judge not only decides which party 'wins' the legal point on appeal; they decide overall which team wins the moot. It is not necessarily the case that the team winning the legal point will win the moot. The judge will consider a range of issues from competent oral skills delivery (such as pace, tone, clarity, appropriate vocabulary and terms of address to the court and other counsel) to the construction of legal argument, depth of understanding of the material, and response to questioning.[2]

The clerk

Not all moots have a clerk, whose role is to assist the judge. This role is again taken by a student and their duties will involve passing authorities to the judge with page references already located and time keeping which can be particularly important in moots where judicial questioning periods are not part of the overall time count.

Counsel

Senior and junior counsel

Mooting teams consist of two students who are role playing either senior or junior counsel. It is customary for the more experienced mooter to be senior counsel and the less experienced mooter to be the junior. One of the main reasons for this is that senior counsel speaks first and for the less experienced mooter to speak first can be stressful. Also it is senior counsel for the appellant who deals with the right to reply. The skill of mooting is often in the manner in which the legal arguments to be forwarded are split between senior and junior counsel. Often both counsel will be equally experienced.

Care should be taken to decide which ground(s) of appeal is the more complex and then allocate roles accordingly.

---

2   All of these issues are discussed later in the chapter.

Counsel for the appellants

The appellants determine the agenda for the moot, as they have brought the appeal having lost the previous case. They go first setting out the reasons why the previous decision in the lower court was wrong.

As it is known that the respondents will counter argue it is good practice to incorporate into the submissions made potential rebuttals of positions that it is predicted the respondents will take. So when the respondents come to bring their case they need to deal with these rebuttals if indeed they have taken the positions assumed by the appellant.

Of course if the predictions are incorrect a respondent may 'play to the gallery' by feigning surprise that the appellants could have thought that such an argument would be presented by them.

Senior counsel for the appellants begins the moot by delivering the first speech. Because of this it is their responsibility to introduce their party and the respondents to the judge and set out the first point on appeal. Where a right of reply is allowed this will be done by senior council.

Junior counsel addresses the second point on appeal but as the junior finishes the case an overall summary will be included in their speech.

Counsel for the respondents

The winning side from the previous case responds to the points raised by the appellants, and responds to each point. Failure to respond to any point means in effect they concede, or are accepting the validity of that particular point. It is essential for the respondents to dispose of the appellant's points before proceeding to their own legal submissions. This can be particularly difficult if the appellants have correctly predicted their argument and rebutted it in their submission.

Senior counsel speaks first, opening the respondent's argument, and deals with the first point on appeal ensuring that all points raised by senior counsel for the appellants are rebutted. Again, junior counsel deals with the second point on appeal rebutting points made by junior counsel for the appellants. The junior closes the argument on behalf of the respondents.

THE GENERAL RULES OF ENGAGEMENT GOVERNING MOOTS

In this section the typical rules of engagement that must be followed in a moot are set out. However, while it is possible to generalise concerning the rules under which mooting will take place it is important to bear in mind that those organising moots can make changes. For example, they may change the timing of the moot, whether there is a 'right to reply' or the requirements of prior submission of material to the court and to the other side.

Case limitation

A limit on the number of cases that mooters can rely on as legal authorities is a customary part of the discipline of mooting. Ensure that you are aware of the case limits that form part of the rules of the moot. You do not want to exceed this and have a key case excluded by the judge.

Any case that is mentioned in the moot problem itself is deemed a court authority and does not count towards your limit. Also authorities used by the other side that you may choose to use as a line of support for your argument do not count as part of your case limit.

Time limits

Mooting is a time limited exercise. If counsel runs out of time before the end of the submissions to be made to the court it is going to affect the final outcome of the moot. In a competition this could mean losing the moot. It is normal for 15 minutes to be allocated to each side. The judge will ask counsel questions during their speech and usually time stops for the duration of the question and answer. However, in some moots a decision is made that time will not stop. This means that it is essential for the mooter to succinctly respond to questioning and move back as swiftly as possible to their actual speech.

Turn taking in a moot, the 'order of submissions'

There are two main models used for the ordering of counsel submissions in a moot. It is important that you ensure you know which model is being used for your moot as it could affect the manner in which you wish to present your submissions with your teammate. These are set out in Figures 25.1 and 25.2 below.

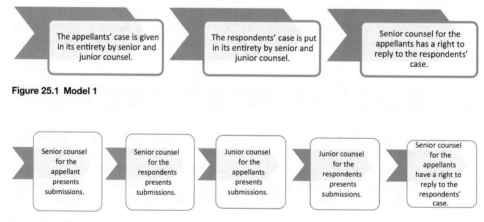

Figure 25.1 Model 1

Figure 25.2 Model 2

The 'right to reply'

From the two figures above you will have seen that the last stage in both models is the 'right to reply' to the respondent's case. Only the appellants have a 'right to reply'. This is because the respondents will have had the benefit of hearing the appellant's argument in its entirety prior to putting their own. They can therefore incorporate a response (if they deem it necessary) into their submissions to the court. The appellants have a right of reply because as they presented first they did not have the option to incorporate a response into their speech.

Some moots, particularly at the level of competitions, operate without the 'right of reply'. The reason put for this is that only senior counsel for the appellant has the right and this can put an undue burden on senior counsel.

Judicial questions to mooters

Whichever model is chosen by the moot organisers, the judge will stop counsel during their speeches to ask questions related to the submissions that they are making. These can range from queries concerning appropriate precedents, to requiring the mooter to engage in a detailed discussion of a legal point made or cases not addressed. Counsel must respond to the judge according to basic rules of court etiquette, and either give a detailed response or suggest that the question is not as central as the judge may consider.

The skeleton argument[3]

This is, as the word skeleton suggests, a basic outline of the legal submissions that are to be put by counsel. It will also contain a list of authorities to be relied upon. A copy is given to the judge and to the other party so that they have a preview of the way in which the argument is to be advanced.

Usually the skeleton argument must be given to counsel and the judge 24 hours before the moot, although in some national or international competitions a longer timescale is given. It is normally the master of moots who acts as the channel for delivery of the argument. It is good practice for internal competitions to keep to the 24 hour rule for delivery of skeleton arguments and/or list of authorities. Not all moots require a skeleton argument.

The respondents and appellant must carefully deal with the skeleton argument, familiarising themselves with the argument and the authorities to be relied upon. It is essential for them to measure their arguments against what they know of the appellant's argument. Ignore the skeleton argument at your peril. If you do not know the appellant's arguments as well as your own you will be at a disadvantage.

Read all the legal authorities that the other side intend to rely on. See if they can be used to support your argument too. Also you must be certain of the status of cases retrieved, particularly whether they are still 'good law'.

---

3   Not all moots require skeleton arguments, but most do.

Bundles

A bundle refers to a specific set of documents that mooters will be relying on in the legal submissions that they will be making. It will include a copy of the moot problem, the skeleton argument and copies of every case to be relied upon.

It is not necessary to copy cases that are authority for points that are not in dispute in the moot. You only need to copy cases used by the other side if you intend to also use them to support your argument. But make it clear this is one of your opponent's cases so that the judge does not include it in the count of cases you are allowed to use.

The cases must be put together in the same order as they appear in the skeleton argument. It is not acceptable to just copy the part that you will rely on; the entire case must be copied. Due to difficulties that can be encountered with page referencing, most mooters prefer to use the print version of a case for copying. Many case databases now include a pdf of the original case, but also many databases insert in the text the original page referencing. However, when paragraphs are also required in the reference, online versions do cause problems. In the moot the full reference to a case must be given and the judge will be referred to the copy in the bundle. It must be quick and easy to direct the judge appropriately to the right place.

There is a caveat to a bundle. You should only construct one if it is a real help to you. Competition moots do not normally require one. If you do prepare one then make sure it is an aid to you, not an obstruction.

When your bundle is completed in the correct order make sure you number each page to aid the judge in finding their way around your bundle. You may wish to consider using file dividers to separate the moot problem, skeleton argument and cases. Ensure you clearly guide the judge to the correct place in the bundle and then to the correct place in the case, for example:

'May I refer your ladyship to the words of Lord Atkin in the case of McAlister (or Donoghue) and Stevenson reported in the Appeal Cases for 1932 at page 562 which can be located in the cases section of the bundle, at bundle page 25.'

Dress codes

It is a requirement of moots that counsel wear wigs and gowns. These will be supplied by your university department. The normal expectation is that smart clothing of a subdued nature is worn under the gown. You do not want to wear anything that may cause the judge to make a comment about your dress.

Correct forms of address in relation to participants in the moot

It is essential to use the correct form of address for the judge, your teammate, and counsel for the other side. You should rehearse these forms of address until they become second nature. The last thing you want is to waste time trying to remember them. Smooth addresses are part of a good moot. These are dealt with later in the chapter.

Correct oral references to case citations

When reference is made to a law report during a speech, counsel must give a page and paragraph reference if there is one, and wait for the judge to find the place in the case before proceeding. The parties are named and it is most important to note that you never say 'versus' even though the 'v' separating the parties names is an abbreviation of the Latin word versus.

If you are referring to a civil case you would say 'and' as in Smith and Jones. If you are referring to a criminal case you would say – the crown 'against' as in the crown against Smith.

A MODEL FOR MOOTING

A model for ensuring that you prepare effectively and deliver a good speech is set out below in Figure 25.3.

All stages are of equal importance, if you fail to competently deconstruct the moot problem you will not engage in sufficient research. Your argument relies on correct interpretation of the moot problem and your research. Your oral delivery determines whether your argument is clearly followed by the judge.

Each of these main stages sub-divides and we will look at each stage in more detail.

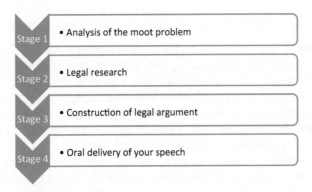

Figure 25.3 Model for approaching mooting

Stage 1 • Analysis of the moot problem

Stage 2 • Legal research

Stage 3 • Construction of legal argument

Stage 4 • Oral delivery of your speech

Stage 1: Analysis of the moot problem

Which court?

It is essential to know the court hearing the moot; this will determine a number of matters from terms of address to operation of the doctrine of precedent.

Understanding the procedural history of the moot

The procedural history is of importance as it will tell you what the decisions were of the initial trial court, and if applicable the Court of Appeal if you are mooting in the Supreme Court. It is essential to know how issues were treated at earlier stages. Also the focus of the appeal is highly likely to be much narrower than the issues in the original trial. It is not enough to know that a particular party won/lost in an earlier hearing; it is essential to know on what point or points they won/lost and why the court determined that they should win/lose, as well as to understand in detail the exact grounds for appeal.

Do not just consider the procedural history from your client's perspective, but additionally put yourself into the shoes of the other party and consider it from their perspective.

If you are acting for the party that won at trial, you can argue that the trial judge was surely best placed to decide as they did, being in command of the facts and being able to view witnesses, witness statements and other evidence. It is good practice to start your moot referring to the trial judge in these circumstances. The reasoning of a judge at first instance, or even at a prior appeal, is of importance to both parties as it sheds light on the rationale behind the decision. However, this is not to say that you should only deal with the judge's reasoning; you must move to the wider reasoning appropriate for the appeal as soon as you have dealt with the trial judge.

Clarification of which party you are representing in the moot

You may think that it is most unlikely that you would not know who you are representing. However, there is room for making a big and costly mistake. You will be told that you are acting for the appellants or the respondents. However, you cannot always tell from the case name which party is the appellant and which party is the respondent. It is not unknown for mooters to turn up ready to represent the wrong party with the consequence that they automatically forfeit the moot, wasting their time, the judge's time and the time of the other party. You do not want to find yourself in this position.

In civil cases the party names usually stay the same from the initial case, with the complainant's name first and the defendant's name second, for example *McAlister (or Donoghue) v Stevenson*. On appeal the name would remain the same. So there is no clue in the case name as to which party is the appellant. There can be exceptions to this so you need to read the moot problem very carefully to ensure who you are acting for.

For criminal cases the Crown is always listed as the first party, for example *R v B&B*, and therefore should the defendant appeal the party names will remain the same. If the prosecution appeals against a successful appeal by the defendant the case remains *R v B&B*. However, if the prosecution appeal from the finding of the trial court the name of the case changes from R (the Crown) to Director of Public Prosecutions (DPP) who deals with appeals for the Crown, for example *DPP v B&B*.

Should a party be unable to represent themselves you will find the name of the case listed as *Re Jones* which indicates this situation. This is most often used in family proceedings dealing with children, cases involving issues of mental health capacity and those claims related to deceased parties.

Analysis of the facts

It is of the utmost importance that you know and understand the facts of the moot problem. These are presented in detail in the moot problem and they are key for your understanding of the appeal points and the construction of your final legal argument forming the basis of your submissions to the court.

It is not unknown for mooters to make up facts to fill gaps or extend their argument. This is not acceptable. The facts in the moot problem are hypothetical but they are also the facts agreed or found in the trial and cannot be added to, changed, or be made the object of interpretation for any reason.

However, it is essential that you weave the facts as given to you by the moot problem into your argument on the point of law. Part of the skill of a mooter is the way in which they seek to apply generalised or abstract legal rules to a particular set of facts. Your legal argument therefore must be grounded in the facts and you should refer to them in your submissions. There can be a tendency amongst mooters to engage in a purely objectified discussion of the law relevant to the grounds of appeal without connecting it to the facts of the moot problem. It is this skill that allows you to argue persuasively, which is important because as already noted a moot is constructed out of issues that could be decided either way. If your argument is too abstract you are missing out on the ability to tie them to the facts and invite the judge to decide in your favour because of the relevance of your legal argument to the facts and the point on appeal. To argue in an abstract manner divorced from the facts of the moot problem is a common error. Make sure that it is not an error you make.

Many professional lawyers, as well as academics and students, will begin their analysis by drawing up a chronology of events (a timeline) in relation to the facts. You might be tempted to think that your moot does not require this as events occurred over a day or two. But you would be wrong: a timeline even of events taking place in a limited timescale can assist you to clarify matters. When you stand back and look at your timeline, issues that you have not so far thought of may spring to mind. As you read it over again as you retrieve relevant sources then you may well find issues that you had overlooked.

Read every sentence and phrase in a sentence attentively looking for issues that you may have overlooked. A moot has been specifically written to test you, therefore one implication is that no sentence is without merit or relevance. No aspect of the moot problem, and especially the facts, should be left without thorough analysis. This analysis should be repeated once you have engaged in your research as that will undoubtedly have improved your understanding and will allow you to make connections you could not make on a first reading.

Issues of fact and issues of law

The appeal will be on a narrow question of law; this means it relates to the construction and application of the law to the issue(s) raised in the grounds of appeal. Matters of fact cannot be entertained. This can be important if in your argument you seek to prove a point by reference to statistics etc. These are matters of fact and you may not add to matters of fact.

Court authorities

These are cases referred to in the actual moot problem itself. Both parties can refer to it and neither party has to include it in their list of limited allowed cases.

Analysis of the grounds of appeal

Having thoroughly understood the facts and the procedural history you need to turn your attention to the grounds of appeal. Different moots will in fact differ in the way in which the grounds of appeal are referred to. The grounds can be clearly set out or can be left for the mooters to infer them.

You need to ensure that you know the argument put by the appellant and that put by the respondent.

Stage 2: Legal research

Your final moot speech giving your legal submissions on the ground of appeal is only as good as the quality of your research. Many students see mooting as a display of advocacy skills and the ability to answer questions under pressure. However that display relies on a good legal argument based upon competent and extensive research.

While a moot problem involves an argument on a narrow ground of appeal based exclusively on a point of law it is also necessary for you to understand the wider legal context of the appeal. This will lead to focused legal research retrieving relevant material. Keep the facts and the grounds of appeal in your mind when researching and engaging in argument construction based on your research.

You need to consider in detail all judgments in relevant cases. Do not just read majority judgments but carefully consider any minority and dissenting judgments. As a moot problem is chosen specifically because it can be argued 'either way', it may be that you will obtain valuable points for your argument in dissenting or majority judgments. Although of course if there is a strong precedent and a clear majority view you will need to consider how best to introduce an argument from minority or dissenting judgments.

Questions to inform your legal research

Prior to commencing your legal research you should write yourself a list of questions based on your analysis of the facts and the grounds of appeal. This is a preliminary list which will inevitably be quite wide and generalised, identifying the main issues. However you will find that as you engage in research some of these questions will be resolved, some will be clearly seen as irrelevant, and a range of more detailed questions will emerge.

The statement of current law

Before you can begin to work out your argument on the grounds of appeal you need to be certain about what the current law on the matter is. This involves ascertaining and citing relevant legislation and case law. From here you need to go on and identify current controversies or issues in the area.

Resources to be accessed

You will be expected to consult *Halsbury's Laws of England*, case law, legislation, textbooks and articles in order to obtain enough information to draft your argument. What you will find is that you are gradually increasing your knowledge by initially sweeping broadly and then refining your research until you are reading articles on narrow legal points of relevance.

Halsbury's Laws of England

You may well recall that the best first port of call to get a clear view of the current law is *Halsbury's Laws* due to its encyclopaedic nature which allows you to look up subject areas of relevance to the moot and obtain the list of up to date relevant legislation and case law.

You should additionally note that most judges will actually expect you to cite *Halsbury's Laws* for definitions of key terms and concepts in the absence of legislation.

Having ascertained current law from *Halsbury's* it is essential to ensure you have a thorough overview of the area and for this you need to consult a textbook covering the overall subject of the moot. Do make sure that you use the best up to date textbook you can get your hands on. Members of staff teaching the area will be most willing to assist you.

As the moot is on a narrow point of law you will not have to research for too long. But it must be detailed. The textbook will also contain references and discussion on cases, legislation and other material of relevance. These should be read and incorporated into the argument.

Case law

Halsbury's will have identified the leading cases but this does not mean that you should not look elsewhere. As noted, read the case law carefully and if you notice points of relevance for your argument make a note. You must engage with every comment that does not support your case. You need to practise, giving the other side a robust and difficult time. Many lawyers and students use a two column table setting out points in a case supporting the appellant and points in a case supporting the respondent.

Reading case law effectively is set out in Chapter 10, for now it is enough to draw to attention the following list of matters you need to attend to when reading cases effectively:

- Date of case.
- Court.
- Jurisdiction.
- Procedural history.
- Legal issue(s) at trial and on appeal, as they can change.
- *Ratio*.
- Useful *obiter dicta*.
- Current status of the case (has it been overruled, distinguished, followed).
- Are the facts of the case similar to the moot problem?
- Citing the correct published version of the case according to the hierarchy of law reports.

The best way of ensuring that you have a firm grasp of the case is to make a detailed case note. But do not forget to check the current status of the case as it would be grounds for losing the moot if you attempt to rely on an overruled case.

The judge will not be impressed if you just cite all possible cases in your legal argument; you should refer to only those of most relevance. Nor will the judge be impressed if you fail to cite the most correct published version of the case. Errors of citation could be enough to lose you the moot.

When you have the other side's list of authorities it is a very good idea to make similar thorough case notes of those. Although of course your time to do that is limited.

Articles in journals

Journal articles can be either professional or academic (which further sub-divides into peer reviewed and non-peer reviewed journals). Before you attempt to read retrieved journal articles on narrow points you must fully understand the facts, applicable legal rules and the grounds of appeal in your moot. Some articles will discuss issues raised in a case or cases that you are interested in and you can use points made to formulate your legal submissions to the court. Some articles will look ahead at possible resolutions to difficult issues, and you may even find one that is exactly in keeping with the moot problems.

Do remember however that journals have differing standing according to whether they are professional or academic (peer reviewed or non-peer reviewed). This will affect the receptiveness of the judge to any argument you use. Additionally, it matters whether the article is written by an acknowledged specialist in the area or not. It is therefore worthwhile finding out some general information about the author of the article. Use the best article in terms of its support for your argument. Remember you should only quote an article if a judge in a given case has done so.

Making research notes and their organisation

As you locate relevant material you will make notes. You will have asked yourself a range of preliminary and more advanced questions and where appropriate you will have made a note of answers to these questions.

You will have consulted journal articles and again made notes of relevant factors in the articles ensuring that you have given page references in relation to discussion in the article where you may wish to consult the original. You should have a detailed but succinct case note for every case you are relying on and for court authorities. Make sure you reference paragraphs/page of report for important issues you may wish to return to the case for.

If you refer to a case or part of an article you will need to give the full pinpoint reference in court so it is essential to keep to a good referencing protocol.

It is important that you take notes, leaving enough spaces between lines or on the back of your page to make additions as your ideas and understanding change.

It is a good idea to put your notes in a file that is sub-divided into primary law (divided as necessary into legislation and cases) and secondary sources. You can sub-divide secondary sources as appropriate. Articles referring to specific issues in cases or legislation should be filed with the relevant case/legislation. Where articles refer to wider points they should be filed under a heading such as legal contexts.

The important issue is to make sure that your notes are brief but relevant and give you a good understanding of the wider and narrower legal contexts of the moot problem. These notes, together with any references you make to primary law, will determine the quality of your argument.

Construction of legal argument

Your legal argument

Having completed your research you will have several sets of notes from the various sources you have consulted. Your next task is to use them to address the points on appeal.

At the outset of your research you and your fellow teammate will have decided who is senior and who is junior counsel and who is dealing with which point. It is important however that you both fully understand the entire argument. Two heads are always better than one and your teammate may have comments to make that enable you to improve your submissions, and vice versa.

Initially however, you will each draft your response to the point on appeal that you are dealing with taking time to predict what you think your opponent's response will be. This will enable you to dismiss that response in your speech.

You will find that there are several legal points you wish to make; these are formally referred to as 'submissions to the court', and more commonly as 'submissions'. Each submission must be supported by primary law as well as necessary secondary texts that support your interpretation. Each submission should add weight to the one before and their arrangement is important. You are hoping that the judge will accept each submission. When both you and your teammate have completed your written submission you should come together to discuss them, redraft as necessary and ensure you have a streamlined argument.

Preparing the content of your speech in court

Writing and speaking

Written language is quite different from spoken language. Therefore you must ensure that your speech sounds correct when delivered in court orally. Language in a speech should be more direct; there can be a tendency to unnecessary complication in written English, and this sounds inappropriate in a speech that is to be spoken and heard.

Ensuring the judge follows and remembers your argument

You need to build into your speech memorability, and your submissions need to be sign-posted. This can be achieved by a quick recap of points just made and an indication of the next point, then using words indicating movement from one point to another. Standard comments in relation to movement in a speech are:

- Therefore . . .
- My next point . . .
- In summary . . .
- Turning to my next submission my first point is . . .
- To summarise my argument . . .

Oral delivery

Speed of delivery

The pace (speed) at which you are speaking can affect the capacity of the judge to follow your argument. You can speak too quickly or too slowly for your argument to be comprehensible for listeners.

Practising the delivery of your speech in front of friends and family will allow them to give you feedback on speed. It is never a good idea to speed up to deliver important points when you think you will run out of time.

Timing

All moots will have timed speeches by counsel. It is important to find out early whether the moot rules stop the clock when the judge is engaging in questioning or whether time still runs. If the clock is stopped there is no problem determining timing. If it is not stopped then you need to make some time allowance for judicial questioning when you are planning your speech.

When you have the time limit for your speech it is absolutely essential to keep to it. Timing limits are similar to word limits in an essay and going over in both will result in penalties. In a moot you will be stopped and it may be the case that there are key elements of your speech that you have not got time to discuss. It may even be fatal to the success of your argument that you ran out of time and were unable to deliver the complete argument on the grounds of appeal.

You should therefore make certain you have an easy way of keeping your eye on the time.

Be clear about who speaks when and who says what!

A moot is a stylised form of argument and we noted turn taking issues already. When it comes to delivery, senior and junior counsel not only speak in strict rotation but there are also specific tasks they must perform. Senior counsel introduces all counsel as well as themselves at the outset of the moot. Junior counsel must not only put their submissions to the second appeal point but they must also conclude the entire argument presented in the moot. Table 25.1 sets out the ordering of the legal argument and submissions and under 'comment' notes extra detail each counsel must give in addition to setting out the submissions for their specific ground of appeal. It assumes a situation when each side gives their argument in its entirety. You will however recall there can be situations in which the judge prefers to hear senior counsel for both sides followed by junior counsel for both sides.

Using correct forms of address when mooting

You will need to refer to your mooting teammate, counsel for the other side, the judge in the moot and to judges in the cases you are using. Mistakes will lose you points in the actual moot. Each of these will be considered. For the most part using the correct form of address is simply a matter to be committed to memory.

The judge in court and judges in the cases you are using

Judges are given various honours upon appointment. Whether this is a knighthood or peerage depends on the seniority of the office they are appointed to. Previous titles held

TABLE 25.1 ORDERING OF LEGAL ARGUMENT

Sections of legal argument	Senior counsel for appellants or respondents Appellant goes first	Junior counsel for the appellants and respondents Appellant goes first	Comment
Argument on the first grounds of appeal introduced.	√		Additionally senior counsel for the appellant will first introduce themselves and all counsel to the judge.
Legal submissions on first point outlined and then discussed in detail.	√		After listing submissions senior counsel for the appellants will ask the judge if she wishes to hear a brief summary of the facts. Then they will begin their legal submissions. Senior counsel for the respondent will only deal with a summary of the facts if the respondents are of the opinion that the appellant was mistaken in any of the factual information they gave to the court.
Conclusion to first point on appeal.	√		
Brief introduction to junior counsel.	√		
Argument on the second grounds of appeal introduced.		√	
Legal submission on the second grounds outlined and then discussed in detail.		√	
Conclusion to the second ground and overall conclusion to the grounds of appeal.		√	Junior counsel has the important role of concluding the argument on the appeal points.

by the judge are also taken into account when deciding what titles to give to a judge. This is why you will come across Barons and Viscounts as well as Lords in the appellate courts. However, in court all are referred to as My Lord.

The following Tables 25.2 and 25.3 indicate the correct forms of oral address in court for both the judge and judges in the court you are dealing with:[4]

The Court of Appeal

If there are two Lord Justices of Appeal with the same surname, then the junior Lord Justice will take their first name as part of their judicial title. When two or more Lord Justices are referred to at the same time in a law report, their post-nominal letters become LJJ.[5]

TABLE 25.2 JUDICIAL TITLES IN THE SUPREME COURT			
JUDICIAL OFFICE	**JUDICIAL TITLE IN FULL**	**ABBREVIATED TITLE USED IN THE LAW REPORTS**	**FORM OF ADDRESS TO BE USED IN COURT**
The President of the Supreme Court	The Right Honourable the President of the Supreme Court	Lord Smith P or Lady Smith P	My Lord or My Lady
Deputy President of the Supreme Court	The Right Honourable the Deputy President of the Supreme court	Lord Smith DP	My Lord
Male Justice of the Supreme Court	The Right Honourable Lord Smith	Lord Smith JSC If more than one Justice is referred to in a law report then the initials after the names are SCJJ e.g. Lord Smith and Lord Jones SCJJ. This remains the case with female Justices	My Lord Should there be two Justices of the Supreme Court with the same name then the junior judge in terms of time appointed will have the place of his peerage in the title. e.g. Lord Smith of Wincheap. This remains the case with female Justices
Female Justice of the Supreme Court	The Right Honourable Lady Smith	Lady Smith JSC	My Lady

4 *Oxford Standard Citations of Law Abbreviations* (4th edn, University of Oxford, Oxford, 2014), 19.
5 Ibid.

TABLE 25.3 JUDICIAL TITLES IN THE COURT OF APPEAL

JUDICIAL OFFICE	JUDICIAL TITLE IN FULL	ABBREVIATED TITLE USED IN THE LAW REPORTS	FORM OF ADDRESS TO BE USED IN COURT
The Lord Chief Justice of England and Wales if they are a peer	The Right Honourable the Lord Chief Justice of England and Wales	Lord Smith CJ or Lady Smith CJ	My Lord
Master of the Rolls and Records of the Chancery of England This office can carry a peerage but not always. This row deals with titles if the Master is appointed a peer	The Right Honourable the Master of the Rolls	Lord Smith MR or Lady Smith MR	My Lord
Master of the Rolls if office holder is not a peer	The Right Honourable the Master of the Rolls	Sir John Smith MR or Lady Joanna Smith MR	My Lord or My Lady
Male Lord Justice of Appeal	The Right Honourable Lord Justice Smith	Lord Smith JSC If more than one Justice is referred to in a law report then the initials after the names are SCJJ e.g. Lord Smith and Lord Jones SCJJ. This remains the case with female Justices	My Lord Should there be two Justices of the Supreme Court with the same name then the junior judge in terms of time appointed will have the place of his peerage in the title. e.g. Lord Smith of Wincheap. This remains the case with female Justices
Female Lady Justice of Appeal	The Right Honourable Lady Justice Smith	Lady Smith LJ	My Lady

Deliver your speech

Do not read it!

The judge expects you to deliver your speech, not read it. Additionally it is tedious to listen to someone reading a speech that should be orally delivered. You may not be aware of the fact that the voice changes when reading aloud from a pre-prepared text and when speaking without reading. A monotonous tone can creep into the voice when reading aloud.

A danger with reading your speech is that ultimately it makes you remember less about your argument. Should you lose your place when reading (because there has been a judicial intervention to ask a question) you may end up somewhat desperately looking for your place again. Marks will be deducted for counsel who persistently read.

You may not be able to deal efficiently with judicial questions if you rely on reading. You may need to rummage through your written text looking for information to help you answer the question. It is better to know, and understand, the contents of your speech without being tied to a script. You will find that you can respond much more readily to questions asked.

It is also particularly important to appear assured and confident in your delivery of the speech, even if you do not feel it.

When delivering your speech do use prompt notes

You will need to prepare a full written version of your speech to assist you to learn it. Whilst it is not a good idea to read this out or use it as a memory aid in the moot, you do not need to go into the moot with nothing in writing to refer to. You can take in a road map of your speech, listing your legal submissions, and under each submission listing the points you will make and cases you will refer to. Many students find it useful to use index cards rather than file paper; they are smaller and easier to handle. You can glance at them on the table. However, if you do this ensure that you can read your summary notes when standing! You can also hold them in your hand and turn them over or put them down as you finish with each point.

Your tone of voice

Your tone of voice is particularly important. You do not want to deliver the speech in a monotone voice, nor do you want to do so using too many variable tones. But it can be useful to practise the tone you will adopt. You need to find a comfortable general tone and then 'accent' tones. For example if you are saying 'I was most surprised' you may wish to express in your voice, in a measured way, the element of surprise. Changing your tone will increase your listeners' capacity to follow the argument that you are presenting. It will also alert the judge to important points in your argument or rebuttals being made. Do not just ask your teammate to listen and comment on your tone when delivering; it is a good idea to ask others to listen to you and give their view.

Pacing of your speaking voice for the speech

You will be dealing with the delivery of a time-limited speech and the temptation is to speak far too quickly in order to 'get it all in'. This is a temptation you must resist. When you are refining your speech take a steady pace. Not too slow as it can be a problem for listeners to follow a speech that is delivered far too slowly. As with pacing ask others to listen to you and give their view.

Dealing with judicial interventions

The judge can ask the participants questions during the moot. When this occurs the clock is normally stopped for the space of the question and answer but students can still find this particularly stressful. The manner in which you respond to questions establishes your command and comprehension of the legal area and also tests how you withstand pressure. Listen carefully, think before answering and take your time when you do answer.

It is quite likely that the judge may deliberately put forward an interpretation of a point of law that you do not agree with. Whilst you must continue to treat the judge with respect, if you do not agree you are allowed to disagree, in the correct format. For example, you could say, 'Whilst I am of course much obliged to your Lordship for drawing this to my attention, with great respect, I submit that the present case is distinguishable . . .' or 'If I may respectfully say . . .'. Even if you agree, you should be most polite in your agreement. Firmness and politeness is what is called for.

During questioning the judge may ask why you chose a particular case or article or whether you knew of another case or article so always when choosing your material be clear about why you choose it.

'Practice makes perfect'

Above all else, practise the delivery of your speech. Know the order of your main points and illustrations and just deliver your speech. You may find that each time it changes slightly, but that is not a bad thing. Such constant practice will ensure that you will not get lost during delivery, and during judicial interventions.

Some mooters like to write down the speech, using language appropriate for oral delivery, and then learn it by heart. This may work for you but it is not the best route to take. As already noted, reading creates a different dynamic.

CONCLUSION

Mooting is an oral exercise; however it brings all of your skills of research and legal analysis together to construct the arguments that you will orally deliver. It develops your confidence in public speaking and hones your legal skills, as it provides space for you to not only deliver a pre-written speech but to also respond to questioning from the judge and practise 'thinking on your feet'. As it relies upon efficient team working, mooting also develops your interpersonal skills. If you are clear that you wish to enter the legal profession you should take every opportunity to become involved in mooting. It will prepare you for the vocational stage of study as well as the profession you ultimately wish to enter.

CHAPTER SUMMARY

- A moot is a competitive simulation of an appellate court hearing designed to test students' ability to orally present a well-structured legal argument.
- Two teams of students role-play senior and junior counsel for the appellants and respondents.
- The judge determines who wins the legal point and who wins the moot. The judge can also intervene and ask the mooters questions.
- Counsel give their speeches in a strict order.
- Mooting is an activity that comes with a range of rules of engagement determining how the moot should be conducted (e.g. issues such as how many cases each side may rely on and the time limits for speeches). These can change between competitions so do be on guard.
- Customarily there is a limit to the number of cases that can be referred to.
- Any case that is mentioned in the mooting problem is a court authority.
- A skeleton argument may be required but not all moots require one.
- A bundle refers to a specific set of documents that mooters will be relying on in the legal submissions that they will be making. It will include a copy of the moot problem, the skeleton argument and copies of every case to be relied upon.
- Judges in the Supreme Court and the Court of Appeal are addressed as My Lord or My Lady.
- Co-counsel are addressed as 'my learned friend' and counsel for the other side as 'my learned colleague'.

NEGOTIATION SKILLS

After reading this chapter you should be able to:

- Develop personal confidence in speaking in public.
- Put into practice general oral skills such as volume of voice, tone of voice, body position, eye contact, pacing.
- Appreciate the skills requirements of negotiation (analysis of issues, client instructions, negotiation positions, team strategies, interpersonal skills, legal research, note taking, referencing, argument construction, in-negotiation strategies).

INTRODUCTION

Negotiation is one of several oral skills exercises that you may be required to engage with, not only for non-assessed skills development but also in relation to formal assessment. It depends on a fine balance of personal research, personal oral skills competency and good interpersonal team working skills. While mooting represents the litigation paradigm and the concept of court-based dispute resolution, negotiation introduces the ideology of alternative dispute resolution (ADR). This is the *alternative* to going to court or moving through the trial court process.[1] While the aim of a moot is to win (as is the aim of a court case), the aim of a negotiation is to reach a settlement with the other party.

As with mooting the discussion is conducted according to a range of agreed rules of engagement concerning who speaks first and appropriate turn taking. However, the setting is less formal.

WHAT IS NEGOTIATION?

At the academic stage of legal education negotiation, like mooting, is conducted as a role play between two teams, who act as legal advisors for the respective clients in a fictitious legal dispute. Unlike mooting, however, the subject matter of a negotiation can be far broader and conceptually different.

Students are seated, usually around a table, and while the language is formal and respectful primary legal sources are not quoted and speeches are not given. There is a conversational dialogue between the two sides as each seeks to implement their pre-planned strategies for obtaining the best deal for their client in light of their client's instructions.

Range of skills required for negotiation

As you may by now expect, negotiation requires you to integrate a large number of skills, including:

- personal management of the task;
- team management of the task and interpersonal skills;
- research;
- handling primary legal rules;
- managing facts and instructions from clients, and other documentation;
- competent note taking;
- writing pre-negotiation strategies;
- competent reporting back to the team;
- argument construction;
- oral skills;

---

1   ADR encompasses not only negotiation but also further mechanisms of mediation (when a trained facilitator allows the parties to interact with each other and reach a resolution) and arbitration. You will learn more about it on your English legal system course.

- handling the unforeseen within the negotiation;
- competent critical review post-negotiation.

The skills you bring with you to negotiation

It is highly likely that you come to the exercise of negotiation with some naturally acquired skills relevant to the task. These will have been deployed and developed just by being in the world, as part of a group of friends or family, in school, university or in the workplace.

Consider the last time that you made a bargain with someone to get something that only they could give you. You probably gave something or offered to do something as an incentive to get what you wanted from the other person. Maybe you wanted time off from your part-time job but thought your boss might refuse. You will have carefully chosen your time to ask for leave, and probably thought of what you could offer in return. Maybe there is a time in the week when you knew that your boss had trouble getting his staff to work. You might have suggested that if he gave you the time off that you wanted, then you would do one or two of those problem shifts straight away, or on your return to work. This situation would be a classic example of principled bargaining or negotiation because you need to continue your relationship with your boss.

All of this natural everyday activity involves flexibility. You need to think in advance about what barriers you might have to overcome before you get the 'yes', the object that you want. Often you may need to give something in order to get what you want. Usually you need to have an understanding of how the other person may be thinking, how they will view your request, what it is that you think they may object to, and how you can deal with this. All of this natural experience can be used to help you gain an understanding of formal legal negotiation.

THE TWO MAIN FORMS OF NEGOTIATION

Negotiation can take one of two major forms, positional and principled negotiation. Each form requires negotiators to adopt different stances. You can determine which type of negotiation is called for from the information you are given regarding your client's instructions to you. However, do not be caught unawares. While your client may think the negotiation is of one type, the other party may have different ideas.

Positional negotiation

Positional negotiation refers to a situation where both parties to the negotiation wish a settlement on purely financial grounds and do not wish to continue any relationship with each other. Because of these factors it can tend to be a more confrontational form of negotiation.

Principled negotiation

Principled negotiation refers to a situation where both parties not only wish a settlement of the current dispute (which may be seen in financial terms), but they also wish, or need, to continue their relationship. This form of negotiation requires a particular approach since the most amicable solution preserving the relationship may not constitute the best financial solution for one of the parties, or even both. However, often in these cases the continuance of the relationship is more important than financial issues. By the nature of its aims, principled negotiation tends to be more interactive and flexible in terms of outcome.

THE PROCESS OF A NEGOTIATION

You will not be surprised to be told that negotiation is a process. It begins before you and your team enter the room to negotiate and continues afterwards. To assist you to understand this it is best to view negotiation as a three stage activity involving:

(1) pre-negotiation planning;
(2) in-negotiation strategy;
(3) post-negotiation critical review.

This is demonstrated in Figure 26.1.
   As you can see, the greater part of the work takes place before the negotiation.
   There are several ways in which a negotiation can be set up for you by your lecturers, and a variety of 'paper trails' may be constructed for you. You may be given the time and opportunity to interview a fellow student role playing a live 'client', and here your job will be to extract the details of the dispute and your client's desired outcome for the negotiation. Or you may be given a written set of client instructions to work from. These written instructions should be relatively comprehensive, giving you all the information you require to look

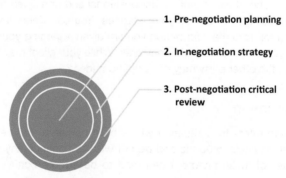

1. Pre-negotiation planning

2. In-negotiation strategy

3. Post-negotiation critical review

Figure 26.1 The three stages of negotiation

into the dispute. They may or may not be supplemented by other constructed documentation such as letters sent to your client or written by them, copies of any relevant contracts or copies of emails and file notes to and from your client.

GUIDED NARRATIVE ON THE STAGES IN A NEGOTIATION

The next pages will take you briefly through the steps in a typical negotiation. As with other skills there is no shortage of good guidance available. If you *are* to engage in negotiation you will be guided through your exercise by your tutor. Seen from a macro-level, the key steps for a negotiation are shown in Figure 26.2.

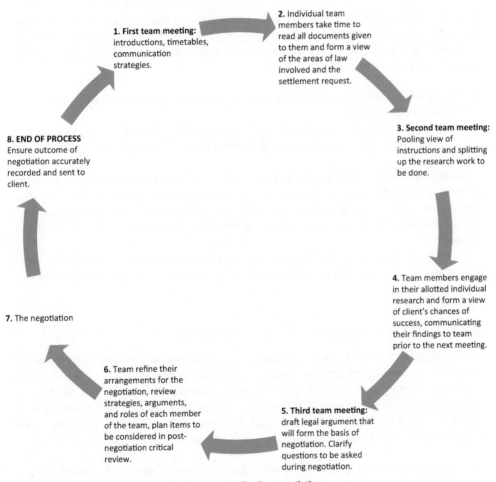

1. First team meeting: introductions, timetables, communication strategies.

2. Individual team members take time to read all documents given to them and form a view of the areas of law involved and the settlement request.

3. Second team meeting: Pooling view of instructions and splitting up the research work to be done.

4. Team members engage in their allotted individual research and form a view of client's chances of success, communicating their findings to team prior to the next meeting.

5. Third team meeting: draft legal argument that will form the basis of negotiation. Clarify questions to be asked during negotiation.

6. Team refine their arrangements for the negotiation, review strategies, arguments, and roles of each member of the team, plan items to be considered in post-negotiation critical review.

7. The negotiation

8. END OF PROCESS Ensure outcome of negotiation accurately recorded and sent to client.

Figure 26.2 The basic macro-level of arrangements for the negotiation

Pre-negotiation planning

The first task in any negotiation is to remember that you are part of a team. However, that does not mean you should not take responsibility for acquiring a general understanding of the area. The negotiation as an exercise, whether assessed or non-assessed, will succeed or fail on the basis of:

- each individual team member's independent management of the task;
- the overall team management of the task.

First meeting with your team and becoming familiar with the client instructions

There are usually just two or three students to a team, and you may not know each other before the task. It is a good idea to meet briefly right at the start, so that introductions can be made. You should then arrange a time to meet to discuss the negotiation, once each of you has had the time to consider:

- your client's written instructions, determining the area(s) of law involved and the potential issues raised;
- your client's instructions concerning the settlement they would find acceptable, and their willingness to compromise and if so their leeway for compromise.

Giving each team member proper time to consider the client instructions will avoid jumping to conclusions. It is important that each team member comes to their own view without being initially led by anyone else. This ensures that several minds have reviewed the instructions. If there are uncertainties in the team, a debate can begin about relevant issues.

There is no reason why you cannot in your first brief meeting agree that you will meet one or two hours later. The important issue is not to rush these important preliminary stages.

Second meeting with the team and allocation of tasks

A good discussion should take place concerning the areas of law thought to be involved, the nature of the dispute and the client's desired settlement. Ideally your team should reach a preliminary view as to the areas of law involved and then you can all decide how you will split the initial research between you. You all need to agree a timescale within which this initial research will be concluded. This will be determined by the date of the actual negotiation or times given to you by your lecturer. You can then work on:

- researching the area of law that is relevant to your part of your client's legal dispute. The best place to start is a textbook, to get an overview of the area. You can then look at primary legal sources as relevant. Follow any advice from your lecturer on this matter;

■ re-considering the facts of the dispute as set out by your client in light of your research and understanding of the general area of law;

■ considering, if you can at this point, the likely success of your client if the matter were to go to court, given your understanding of the law and the dispute.

Third team meeting and decisions concerning application of law, negotiating strategies and division of tasks in-negotiation

At the third team meeting you should:

■ Pool your research and discuss the likely success of your client, given your understanding of the law and the dispute, if the matter were to go to court. This information lets you know how advantageous it is for your client to settle. It also lets you know the likely response of the other side to your attempts to settle.

■ Consider your client's directions concerning their desires in relation to settlement. Is it solely a financial issue or are there other matters relating to relationships? Effectively, is this a positional or a principled negotiation?

■ Consider any incentives you can offer, such as continuing business relationships.

■ Draw up a plan for introducing issues during the negotiation. Decide which questions to ask, in which order and determine your best and worst acceptable outcome. Make a plan as to what to do if one of the team 'freezes' or begins to discuss a matter out of turn. Is there a leader who will interject?

■ Decide who is responsible for ensuring that at the end of the negotiation there is a clear note of the settlement (if there is one) or the next action to take (if there is no settlement). If there is a settlement your note of it should be compared to the other side's version. Make clear that any settlement has to be finally agreed by your client.

■ Ensure you have a proper strategy for good post-negotiation critical reflection.

As you discuss all of the matters above, you will agree as a team what further meetings may be required and what written notes have to be made and circulated.

In-negotiation strategy

The negotiation itself is a dynamic event. You cannot control everything and you do not know if the other team is going to be competent, efficient or professional. You do not necessarily know what it is that they are going to say or what their plan is, but your team should have thought about their likely strategies and plan. What you do know is your team strategy, where you fit within it and what your job is. Keep to this strategy and your job. Do not jettison it in a panic: you could place your team in jeopardy in the middle of the negotiation.

As a team you need to respond to the other team as required. This could mean taking control of the negotiation at appropriate points to ensure your strategy is worked out when it is needed. You may also need to change your strategy in response to the other team's behaviour and strategy.

At the micro-level you also need to consider the language that each of you uses. It must be appropriate, formal, professional and not peppered with legal terms.

When you turn to the actual negotiation itself, no matter how much time you have given to planning you will be surprised by the speed with which your allotted time passes. You need to have a clear view of the micro-dynamics of the negotiation and the processes it moves through to ensure you reach your goals. These are set out in Figure 26.3.

Figure 26.3 The micro-dynamics of the negotiation

Post-negotiation critical review

Reviewing the negotiation after it has taken place is an important learning tool. Indeed, critical reflection on any learning task is important as it allows you to achieve your full learning potential. Even if you felt the task went well, discussing the negotiation together as a team can help to tease out real problems and mistakes. You should take time to note which issues were the fault of the other team and which were down to you. However, mistakes by the other team might have caused you or your team to lose confidence. So it is important to discuss all of the issues. Many assessed negotiations will require your team to submit a post-negotiation review.

Agenda for post-negotiation review

It can be useful to have an agenda to discuss the different aspects of the negotiation. It could include:

Team-working issues

- Was a sensible timescale set up and implemented at team level?
- Did anyone fail to meet their obligations and cause a problem for the team? Could this have been avoided?
- Was there a good set of in-team interpersonal relationships for the task?
- Is there anything that could be done differently next time?
- Was there any team mismanagement of the task in terms of timing, preparation or in the negotiation itself? If so was this inevitable?
- Is there anything that could be done differently next time?

Individual issues

- Did you efficiently manage your own time?
- Do you consider that you put in adequate time and energy to the team?
- How did you respond in the team?

The appropriateness of the negotiation strategy – pre-planning

- Did the team follow the pre-planned strategy? If not, why not?
- Was the pre-planned strategy extensive enough?
- Did the team allow themselves enough pre-agreed flexibility?
- Did the team set sufficient 'best' and 'worst' case agreed settlements?
- Did the team set boundaries where they would not settle?
- Did anything unexpected occur? If so how successfully did the team deal with it?
- What would you and/or the team do differently next time re a strategy?

The negotiation outcome

- How successful was the outcome – was it the one you had planned for?
- If you did not want that outcome as a team is there anything that you or the team could have done differently to avoid it?
- Was the outcome you achieved the best that you could have got in the circumstances?

Proper attention to the completion of the post-negotiation review enables you to achieve a greater level of critical awareness of the process of negotiation. This will assist the continual development of your skills of negotiation.

CONCLUSION

Negotiation is a creative activity that provides you with the opportunity to work with a range of skills to refine your understanding of law. It refines your communication skills and team working skills, and continues to develop your argument construction skills. Your success in negotiation also depends on your research and analysis skills and your ability to read the client's instructions in a focused manner, enabling you to work towards the best settlement achievable. Negotiation encourages a sophisticated understanding of the relationship between facts of a dispute, applicable law, and client expectations.

Negotiation exercises are increasingly being used within the context of the academic stage of training because of their great value in allowing students to work within such broad skill sets. If you are able to engage in such exercises you will find that your understanding of these skills, your ability to handle legal rules and your ability to manage facts will be considerably enhanced. Since these skills are transferable, you will also be enhancing your understanding of other law subjects. You could even consider entering the national negotiation competition organised by the Centre for Effective Dispute Resolution (CEDR).[2]

CHAPTER SUMMARY

- Along with mediation, negotiation is a major form of alternative dispute resolution.
- Legal advisors, or other qualified negotiators, negotiate on behalf of their clients in accordance with their client's instructions, to reach a settlement of a legal dispute without the use of litigation strategies.
- At the academic stage of legal education an assessed or formative negotiation is conducted as a role play between two teams, who act as legal advisors for the respective clients in a fictitious legal dispute.
- Negotiation exercises test a number of skills sets from research, legal argument, independent study, management of documents through to oral skills, communication skills and team work.

---

2   This centre also trains practitioners in the areas of mediation and negotiation and it hosts an excellent website.

- Engagement with the process of negotiation encourages a sophisticated understanding of the relationship between facts of a dispute, applicable law, and client expectations.
- Negotiation exercises are increasingly being used within the context of the academic stage of training because of their great value in allowing students to work within such broad skill sets.
- There are two main forms of negotiation: positional and principled.
- Positional negotiation refers to a situation where both parties wish a settlement on purely financial grounds and do not wish to continue any relationship with each other.
- Principled negotiation refers to a situation where both parties not only wish a settlement of the current dispute but they also wish, or need, to continue their relationship.
- Negotiation is a process requiring careful pre-negotiation planning, in-negotiation strategies and post-negotiation review.

MEDIATION

Guest Chapter: Written by Mr Ben Waters, Founding Director of the Mediation Clinic, Canterbury Christ Church University.

'Discourage litigation. Persuade your neighbours to compromise whenever you can. As a peacemaker the lawyer has superior opportunity of being a good man. There will still be business enough.'

Abraham Lincoln

LEARNING OUTCOMES

After reading this chapter you should be able to:

- Appreciate the role of mediation in helping to resolve a wide range of disputes.
- Understand the structural process of mediation and its common phases as applicable to civil/commercial disputes.
- Gain an understanding of some of the specific core skills commonly used in mediation.
- Further consolidate some of the skills you have already acquired and apply them to a different context.

INTRODUCTION

Continuing the theme of communication skills acquisition, the study of mediation, whilst currently not widely embraced within the law student's curriculum at undergraduate level, is arguably an important way to introduce students to a dispute resolution process which is becoming more popular in the UK. Mediation is a process that will enable you to appreciate the importance of communication and in some cases perhaps give you an opportunity to acquire basic mediator skills to enable you to engage in peer mediation or even go on to further your practical skills competency through training with, for example, a community mediation service. In order to embed your skills there are also national and international student mediation competitions which are available for you to participate in.

Taking a broad approach to the teaching of dispute resolution provides a more accurate representation of the approaches taken in many common law jurisdictions. Through reading this chapter you will gain a sound understanding of the role of mediation within the dispute resolution continuum, develop an awareness of mediation principles and learn how to acquire some of the skills involved in both acting as a mediator and advising as a lawyer.

For parties who choose mediation as their dispute resolution process for the first time, it is helpful for them to understand that negotiation forms the basis of the mediation process. In the previous chapter you were introduced to the concept of negotiation and therefore have a sound platform upon which to build an understanding of mediation. The added dimension which affects the dynamic of a negotiation and transforms it into mediation is the introduction of a third party neutral called a mediator.

As well as bringing natural attributes to mediation, a good mediator will need to learn certain skills in order to facilitate the mediation process effectively. There are differing views on how interventionist a mediator should be and theorists tend to agree that there are two broad mediator style approaches: facilitative and evaluative. Whatever approach is favoured by the mediator, effective communication skills are required.

WHAT IS MEDIATION?

Simply put, mediation is facilitated negotiation. It is a voluntary process conducted confidentially whereby the parties to a dispute are empowered to resolve their differences in a structured yet informal environment with the assistance of an impartial facilitator: the mediator.

The foundational principles of mediation

It is important to remember that mediation is a wholly voluntary process; the parties must want to try mediation as an appropriate means to resolving their dispute rather than commencing or continuing litigation.

The mediation process is also confidential. The parties sign an agreement at the commencement of the mediation to be bound by confidentiality. Essentially this means that the parties agree not to repeat anything discussed during the course of the mediation. Similarly the process is accepted by the parties as being without prejudice, implying that if the dispute does not settle following the mediation and litigation commences or resumes, neither party can use any information disclosed during the course of the mediation in subsequent court proceedings.

The mediation process is facilitated by an impartial third party mediator, which brings a completely different dynamic to the negotiations which may have been conducted hitherto and which are more often than not bilateral. The mediator's task is not to take sides or pass judgement. In one sense mediation can be described as facilitated negotiation; the mediator assists the parties in finding a mutually acceptable solution to the dispute which may well have reached a position of stalemate.

The parties have full control over the process and the outcome; they can bring the mediation to a close at any time, and with the assistance of the mediator can explore a whole range of settlement options which are unavailable to a judge. All decision making rests with the parties and as such the process is both flexible and empowering.

Dispute resolution strategies can be viewed as being on a continuum ranging from 'consensual' (the most flexible forms of dispute resolution giving most power to the parties) to the adjudicative (the least flexible forms of dispute resolution with least power in the hands of the parties. This continuum is set out in Figure 27.1.

Negotiation----Mediation-----Arbitration------Litigation

CONSENSUAL   *ADJUDICATIVE*

Figure 27.1 The dispute resolution continuum

The further one moves towards the right hand side of the dispute resolution continuum the parties begin to lose control of their dispute. As a process, negotiation offers the most flexibility in terms of timing, forum and decision making, whereas litigation offers the least flexible process for decision making; it is formalised, governed by rules and the decision making lies with a judge and is therefore out of the control of the parties. Mediation offers a similar level of process flexibility as negotiation; whilst facilitated by a third party, the parties have full control over the decision making and it hence has a strongly consensual element associated with it.

THE MEDIATION PROCESS

The mediation process structure can vary depending on the type or subject matter of the dispute. Whether it be a commercial, community, workplace or family dispute the underlying mediation principles are generally the same and whatever the mediation forum, the mediator will use the same set of core skills.

The mediator will be chosen during the preparatory stage of the process. The type of mediator and their style can be important to the parties and their lawyers. Two broad mediator styles have been identified: evaluative and facilitative.[1] The evaluative mediator will be inclined to adopt a far more searching and probing style, often bringing their knowledge of the dispute area to the mediation; these mediators may be former judges, practising lawyers or come from a professional background with expertise relevant to the subject matter of the dispute. The facilitative mediator will be rather more inclined to let the parties work things out for themselves and assist, coach or guide them rather than evaluate the parties' theories, strengths or weaknesses.

Although the mediator will have overall control of the process structure, flexibility is a key factor and it is this principle of flexibility that very much sets mediation apart from many other dispute resolution processes. For the purpose of this chapter the model's application to civil/commercial disputes will be examined.

The phases of mediation

Once the necessary preparation for the mediation has been undertaken, which includes choice of mediator, the mediation process usually follows the same model progressing through four phases in sequence; from opening, exploration, bargaining through to the concluding phase. This is far from prescriptive, however, but for the purpose of simplification the four phase structure, demonstrated in Figure 27.2, will be adopted and explained.[2]

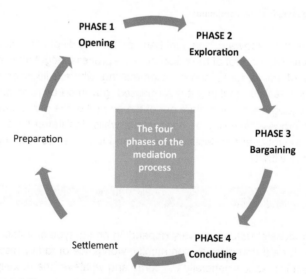

Figure 27.2 **Common civil/commercial mediation phases**

1   L Riskin 'Mediator Orientations, Strategies and Techniques', *Harvard Negotiation Law Review* (1997), 1(7).
2   The Centre for Effective Dispute Resolution (CEDR) works to the four phase model; see www.cedr.com/.

The four phases of a typical mediation

The next pages will take you briefly through the phases in a typical mediation as shown in Figure 27.2.

Phase 1: Opening

Once the mediator choice has been made and the parties are happy to proceed with mediation, it will be necessary for the mediator to contact the parties to clarify final arrangements such as position statements, an agreed bundle of paginated mediation documents, participant clarification, dietary requirements, directions to the venue etc. Fees (if any) should be dealt with in the pre-mediation agreement, which will also cover important aspects of the mediation process such as session length and confidentiality. All parties will have received a copy of the 'agreement to mediate' in advance. It is also important to ensure that those intending to be present at the mediation include a person from each side who has authority to make decisions about possible settlement.

On the day of the mediation, environment is important and the mediator should have an awareness of simple things such as the layout of the building, location of toilet facilities and hospitality provision. Familiarity with all these things helps to set the tone and creates a more relaxed atmosphere. It is vital that the mediator develops empathy from the outset, and your communication skills start here as mediator. This includes attentive listening and allowing the parties to be heard without interruption. Those attending mediation for the first time will often be nervous; they do not know what to expect and it may be the first time they have ever (or for some time) been face to face with their opponent. A safe and comfortable environment is therefore essential.

Each person present will usually at this stage be asked to sign the 'agreement to mediate'. The mediator (and co-mediator) should then go through introductions and clarify terms of address. Everyone should be thanked for making the effort to attend. The mediator should then describe what the parties might expect to experience during the course of the mediation and this includes an explanation of the principal aspects of the mediation process, that it is:

- voluntary;
- non-binding to the point of agreement;
- without prejudice;
- confidential;
- empowering in the sense that the parties come up with the solution.

The mediator should then explain their role and make clear to the parties that they are there to guide the discussion, to clarify the issues, not to judge (there are no rules of evidence), form a view or impose a decision. The mediator may point out to the parties that they may, on occasion, feel it necessary to act as 'devil's advocate' and in so doing may be required to ask some difficult questions. The mediator must remember to remain impartial through-out. Any ground rules for the mediation can also be agreed with the parties at this stage.

The parties will then be invited to make a short opening statement. They should be reminded by the mediator that these oral statements should be uninterrupted. The parties may then present their understanding of the case. This will be a good opportunity to hear some of the facts and issues which each side believes are important. It can provide an effective summary of the respective parties' positions and the parties should be encour-aged to address each other rather than the mediator(s).

It should be understood, however, that what are displayed by way of the positions held by the parties at the opening session will often only really be the 'tip of the iceberg' as far as the real interests behind those positions are concerned.

The opening phase should give the parties an opportunity to:

- learn about the mediation process and understand what is expected of them through engagement with it;
- set out their positions;
- listen to the other party's position.

Phase 2: Exploration

During what is described as the exploration phase of mediation, the mediator should have an opportunity to establish the interests behind the positions held by the respective parties through a series of meetings.[3] These meetings can be held either jointly or in private. It is well advised to make use of private meetings, sometimes called caucuses, when there is a requirement to tackle sensitive or challenging issues, examine the strengths and weak-nesses of a party's case and establish the parties' true interests and needs.

Joint meetings allow all parties to see and hear the information exchange. They can also save time. The mediator has control of the process so will decide what form the meet-ing should take.

Private meetings with the mediator can generate forward momentum in a mediation. The structure and components of such meetings can vary, however. Most commonly they will take place between the mediator and individually with a party. However, if the parties have lawyers present, there may be merit in meeting with the lawyers for both parties indi-vidually without their clients present. Caucuses can take place with the experts who may be present either alone or with the parties and their lawyers in attendance.

The extra confidentiality layer attributed to these caucus sessions ensures that the par-ties can speak freely and openly to the mediator and parties will be generally more pre-pared to share sensitive information in a confidential caucus setting than in a joint meeting.

Carefully managed joint meetings can allow all parties to see and hear what is happen-ing. In these meetings there is often the opportunity for useful information to be traded. There is, however, the potential for deadlock through positional behaviour and mediators should think carefully about the timing and reason for calling joint meetings. There is also

---

3 R Fisher and W Ury, *Getting to Yes* (2nd edn, Penguin Books Inc, New York, 1992), 40 provide a useful expla-nation of the relationship between positions and interests illustrated by the library dispute. See also C Moore, *The Mediation Process: Practical Strategies for Resolving Conflict* (4th edn, Jossey-Bass: San Francisco, CA 2014), ch 12.

the danger that the mediator might lose control of the process through for example an unexpected event occurring triggered by the parties being in the same space.

Overall the exploration phase of mediation should provide a really good opportunity for the mediator to build trust with the parties. This trust building process may then enable the parties to experience emotional release and can encourage them to express themselves openly. If approached skilfully, this phase will yield clarification of the real issues, reveal parties' needs rather than rights, expose hidden agendas and give the mediator the opportunity to 'reality test' some of the theories held by the parties.

This phase should enable development of potential strategies for settlement and facilitate continued forward momentum towards the next phase of the mediation process.

Throughout the exploration phase of the mediation, the mediator must remain impartial and is not seen as being an ally or perceived as being aligned with one party at the expense of another.

During the exploration phase the mediator should be able to encourage the parties to:

■   gain the trust of the parties;
■   focus on interests not positions;
■   examine the issues in detail;
■   determine the strengths and weaknesses of each party's arguments;
■   share information;
■   shift their positions.

Phase 3: Bargaining

Once the parties have shared sufficient information with each other and the mediator and they have accepted that the solution to their problem is not the other party's problem, they may be in a position to move towards the bargaining phase of mediation. In order for effective bargaining to take place the parties should have moved from their original positions. Arriving at this point in the mediation will usually be indicated by the parties' readiness and willingness to start making and trading offers. At this stage in the mediation the parties will start to negotiate possible terms of settlement.[4]

At the heart of any bargaining or negotiation process is a desire to achieve some kind of gain. You will have learnt that we negotiate in order to obtain something we cannot get for ourselves. Allied to this however may also be a desire to preserve a relationship. As we have seen in the previous chapter on negotiation, interests are the fundamental drivers of any negotiation and these are often distinct from the positions displayed by parties to mediation during the opening joint meeting. The interests underpinning them will have been explored and revealed in the exploration phase; it is then perhaps a measure of success in mediation as to how well a party's interests are met through effective bargaining.

There are no hard and fast rules as to how to move the bargaining forward from the exploration phase. The mediator should, through intuition and by observing the unfolding

---

4   CEDR maintain that for those new to mediation it is difficult to provide clear guidance on when this phase should begin, see *The CEDR Mediator Handbook* (4th edn), 89.

dynamics of the mediation, be able to assess the situation and then respond appropriately. Fundamentally however, the parties must have gained sufficient information up to that point in the mediation to enable the process to move into the next phase.

As well as helping the parties to select the alternative that seems best, the mediator's role during the bargaining phase may also involve providing encouragement on how bargaining might best be progressed. A good mediator can do this by:

- being creative;
- significantly influencing the negotiations;
- acting as a facilitator;
- taking offers and counter offers between the parties' rooms.

Throughout this phase the mediator should be carefully observing the effectiveness of the inter-party negotiations and at the same time be reminded of the importance of mediator impartiality. In turn the mediator should remind the parties that they must be responsible for owning the problem and the solution throughout.

With the mediator's help, the bargaining phase should give the parties an opportunity to:

- start trading offers;
- create rather than claim value;
- explore options for settlement;
- choose the more favourable options.
- think about tailoring an agreement to suit all parties' needs.

Phase 4: Concluding

With any dispute which arrives at mediation the overall goal is to meet the parties' interests. Perhaps therefore the measure of a satisfactory to good mediation outcome is how well these interests are met. A better outcome than one found elsewhere, i.e. than perhaps the best alternative to a negotiated agreement (or BATNA)[5] should include a creative solution that captures as much available value for each party as possible. It should be a legitimate solution so that none of the parties feel that they have been taken advantage of.

There must be a firm implementable and sustainable commitment, and perhaps an agreement that helps build the kind of relationship the parties want with each other in the future.

Any mediation settlement agreement must:

- be clear and not open to misinterpretation;
- be reached to the satisfaction of the parties and in that sense it will be self-determinate;

---

5   The idea of the BATNA was introduced by R Fisher and W Ury, ibid, 97.

- as much as possible, deal with all aspects of the dispute;
- be capable of being implemented and therefore must be workable and sustainable.

If these considerations are taken into account the mediation outcome should produce an agreement which avoids the need for further dispute.

The mediator's role during the concluding phase of the mediation is to ensure that the aspects mentioned above are brought about. Mediation is not concerned with achieving a settlement at all costs and the mediator should not be driven by the need for a successful outcome; remember this is the parties' dispute. Whilst every effort should be made to reach an agreement that covers all aspects of the dispute, sometimes not all issues can be dealt with and it may be that any outstanding issues can be the subject of ongoing negotiation. Research suggests that parties who take ownership of the problem and feel responsible for coming to their own resolution are more likely to honour the commitments they make.

Throughout the mediation and particularly during the concluding phase, the mediator should remain positive and encourage settlement opportunities wherever possible. This will inevitably involve the mediator liaising with the parties and helping them to draft the terms of the settlement agreement once they have reached terms. If the parties are represented, then their lawyers can usually take responsibility for drafting the settlement agreement, which can then be checked by the mediator once written up.

Of importance for the mediator is to ensure that there are no unforeseen obstacles regarding implementation of the settlement agreement; for instance are there deadlines, should there be a timetable and what happens in the event of default? When encouraging the parties towards settlement the mediator should be able to make use of some well-chosen active intervention techniques which will include the use of careful questioning about realistic options, on occasion playing 'devil's advocate' and providing helpful information so as to facilitate forward momentum.

As already mentioned, mediators should be in control of the process and it is this 'process-control' that can be a useful source of power when encouraging parties to move towards settlement. If properly in control of the mediation, the mediator can affect the perceptions, attitudes and behaviour of others present at the mediation.

The source of this mediator power may include associational status; some parties may be drawn to a mediator who is a lawyer or a former judge for instance. Mediators who have particular expertise in the field or area of the subject matter of the dispute may gain the trust and confidence of the parties and command respect. Intuitive or personal attributes should not be underestimated, and included in these natural skills is an ability to transmit messages in the right way or to use moral pressure without of course using duress or undue influence.

When a settlement has been reached the agreement should usually be evidenced in writing and signed by the parties. It should include:

- clarity of language, specificity, heads of agreement;
- reference to confidentiality;

- confirmation of the future dispute resolution process to be used in the event of the agreement breaking down;
- overall the agreement should be workable and one that the parties can live with.

MEDIATION SKILLS

An understanding of the mediation process and its place within the dispute resolution panorama is necessary before the skills a mediator requires can be acquired. Parties who decide to choose mediation as a process to attempt to find a resolution to their dispute may do so because they might have failed in their attempts to reach an agreement through negotiation.

Failed negotiations sometimes occur because communication has broken down; this may perhaps be due to the fact that the parties have become too entrenched or positional. Among other things, barriers to effective negotiation can be explained as being psychological, cognitive or even cultural.

Because much of mediation is about effective communication, without active participation in a process of communication, parties in dispute who choose to engage in mediation must be prepared to disclose information to the mediator and exchange information with their opponent. Without this facilitated communication information exchange, progress will not be made towards the possibility of a consensual voluntary agreement.

The skills you bring to mediation

Many of the skills that a mediator requires are centred around aspects of communication. We all have the ability to communicate; mediators have to be effective communicators and it is essential that they have a good command of language. Mediators should be prepared to encourage mediation participants to communicate in a positive way so as to develop forward momentum. The range of skills that a mediator is required to develop are set out in Figure 27.3.

We will consider the skills of Positivity, Questioning and Listening located in the communication skills set [B] in Figure 27.3. In relation to the skills of questioning and listening we will also consider their respective associated sub-skills of reality testing, brainstorming and reframing. They will be set out with their numbered headings enabling you to link them back to Figure 27.3.

Positivity: [B] 2

Mediators should whenever possible use positive language. They should encourage the parties to maintain a positive focus throughout the process and their role in using such positive language can be compared to coaching.

This positivity includes having the parties focus on interests and the underlying needs or requirements rather than positions. If relationships are important to the parties, then

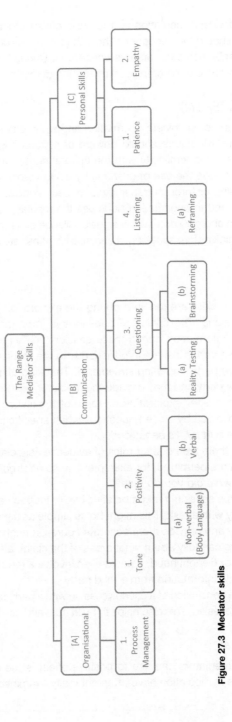

Figure 27.3 Mediator skills

they should be reminded that mediation is a future-focused process and any mediation settlement agreement should take account of how the parties would like the future to look as far as their relationship with each other is concerned. During the bargaining phase for instance, the positive focus can be employed by turning demands into options.

Non-verbal gestures: [B] 2 (a)

Non-verbal gestures can communicate information and when used can convey both positive and negative intent. Mediators should beware of cultural implications however and should be wise to have some familiarity with the cultural norms of those attending mediation. Mediators can manage the use of gestures by using verbal requests, by separating the parties and caucusing or through transmitting indirect signals. The use of silence can on occasion be helpful and through its judicious use the mediator can dictate the pace of the mediation discourse and give non-verbal signals. Silence can provide time for either the mediator or a party to think before speaking. It can also demonstrate interest and/or respect.

Questioning: [B] 3

Effective communication skills are required during the exploration phase and particularly during the caucus sessions. The choice of questions is important in order to maintain dialogue and draw out information during these sessions. Often the use of open ended questioning will enable a party to share information with the mediator, for example: 'what did you think of the other party's opening statement?' That kind of question will prompt an open response from the party and may provide the mediator with some useful information which can then lead to deeper exploration of some of the issues. An open questioning strategy can then be followed by closed questions when specific information is required, for example '*so you feel hurt by X's behaviour*'.

Unlike a court room there are no strict rules of evidence associated with mediation. As such leading questions are permitted, for example: '. . . *so after going to the supermarket and buying the goods, what did you do then?*'

At the end of a caucus session it might be sensible, or indeed necessary, for the mediator to provide the party with a task. This might be as simple as asking the party to look at the claim more carefully and provide more accurate figures. It might even involve requesting a party to think more carefully about what areas of the claim, after more detailed scrutiny, might be dropped or discontinued. It could even involve a request for a party to make a telephone call to obtain information from a third party.

It is also helpful at the conclusion of a caucus session with a party for the mediator to summarise the main points revealed. This also helps to build trust and confidence in the mediator.

Reality testing: [B] 3 (a)

One useful skill which mediators can use to positive effect is the idea of reality testing. Many parties who arrive at mediation have often not really examined the strengths of their case. This may be due to the lack of information or because they have not taken an objective view of the dispute. In testing the theories held by parties in relation to the strengths of their case, the mediator can use certain techniques to encourage this such as playing 'devil's advocate'.

One of the most difficult things to achieve for a mediator is to encourage parties to try to see the dispute from their opponent's perspective. If that can be achieved, then this can sometimes help to move the parties from entrenched positions. This does take skill and a certain amount of 'persuasion' on the part of the mediator. In no way must these kind of techniques be used to place pressure on a party or even hold them to ransom; such approaches would be in breach of the mediator's ethical code.

Brainstorming/option seeking: [B] 3 (b)

During the bargaining stage a number of different tactics can be used by the mediator to encourage the parties to search for settlement options. These may be utilised either in caucus or in joint session. With a view to making settlement easier to reach, brainstorming is a technique which can be of great assistance. The idea of brainstorming is to encourage the parties to look at the problem from different angles and reinforce those common interests already identified during exploration.

The parties will be required to think of alternative settlement options of differing strengths and appeal; the mediator may ask them for their preferences, perhaps invent a list of options to take if no agreement can be reached and then improve some of the more promising ideas and thus convert them into practical alternatives.

Listening skills: [B] 4

As a mediator it is essential to have good listening skills. Through attentive listening, a mediator will be able to:

- decode a verbal message;
- identify the emotion being expressed;
- be selective about words or phrases heard;
- be prepared to restate the 'feeling' content of the message accurately for affirmation, confirmation and clarification.

Mediators should also be prepared to use active or reflective listening techniques, such as nodding or smiling, when a party requires affirmation and throughout the exchange the mediator should maintain good eye contact with the party to whom they are listening.

Non-verbal gestures can communicate information. They can be both positive and negative. Mediators can manage the use of gestures by verbal requests, separation (caucuses) and indirect signals transmitted by the mediator. Beware of cultural implications however and in this regard mediators should be sensitive to cultural norms.

Good listening skills are essential as a mediator must be sure that they have heard exactly what the party who is talking has said. They must then be prepared to accurately verify what they have heard; in so doing the mediator must be able to additionally display personal skills of empathy and be able to demonstrate acceptance and acknowledgement of any emotions displayed by the speaker. This will then in turn allow the competent mediator to explore the reason for those emotions and uncover the underlying issues. Showing empathy can enable the parties to release tension through expression of emotion; it also gives the mediator an opportunity to manage the process through recognition of emotions by making appropriate responses.

Reframing: [B] 4 (a)

Mediators also use other techniques borrowed from therapeutic approaches such as active or productive reframing.[6] Reframing can be used to change the verbal presentation of an idea, concern, proposal or question[7] for example if a party says that 'Ever since my boss caused this problem I have been unable to concentrate at work' the mediator could actively reflect the content of that narrative by saying; 'so the problem you mention has really been affecting your work performance'.

Not only does this show to the party who has disclosed this information that they have been listened to by the mediator, but it can neutralise the language used by the party. In other words 'drawing the sting', so as to make the meaning of words appear less harsh or confrontational. The mediator intervening in such a way to modify language can help change a party's perceptions and behaviour and positive reframing techniques can sometimes achieve this.

Language variation or modification can:

- present claims in a different way;
- sometimes create a more a positive spin;
- de-personalise it.

Consider this phrase: 'I'm not going to agree to anything that deprives me of seeing my kids!' The mediator could reframe this statement by saying; 'so maintaining regular contact with your children is something that is important to you'.

It is undoubtedly much easier to reframe positions, interests and issues than it is to reframe values, moral codes or beliefs all of which can define a person.[8] However, during mediation the use of neutral words is often more appropriate than using those with connotations of conflict.

To test your developing understanding of the idea of reframing read Activity 27.1 and answer the questions that are posed by it in sections (a) and (b). Answers can be found at the end of the chapter.

---

6   See H Brown and A Marriott *ADR Principles and Practice* (3rd edn, Thomson/Sweet & Maxwell, London, 2011), 172 and Boulle & Nesic *Mediator Skills and Techniques: Triangle of Influence* (Bloomsbury, London, 2010), 151, who liken reframing to active listening. See also C Moore, supra n 3 at 237.

7   B Mayer *The Dynamics of Conflict Resolution* (Jossey-Bass, San Francisco, CA, 2000), 134. Most of the examples given in this chapter are what Mayer describes as detoxification reframing, which helps people get past their emotional response to the way someone's thoughts have been presented.

8   C Moore, supra n 3 at 239–43.

ACTIVITY 27.1: Reframing exercise

(a) Harsh 'conflict' words and phrases can be softened in order to remove the 'sting' which they might convey. This is called reframing. Reframe these words and phrases so as to soften their meaning;

Dispute/Conflict
Claims/Demands:
Opponent/Defendant:
Concede and compromise
It's a matter of principal/It is fundamental to the claim
You're a liar/I don't believe you

(b) Harsh statements – reframe these sentences so as to soften their meaning:

'The builder's a cowboy, he completely bodged the job.'
'The work done on my car has cost me a lot of money and it's useless to drive.'
'She's never going to see the kids again if she doesn't stop screwing money out of me.'
'The guy's an idiot, he's ignoring me and that's just plain rude; he just won't return my calls and refuses to speak to me to discuss the problem.'
'If he doesn't repair the car in one week I'm suing him.'

CONCLUSION

Mediation is a process orientated method of alternative dispute resolution within the wider dispute resolution continuum. Although it is a flexible dispute resolution process, it relies on certain core principles and, in the context of a civil/commercial type dispute, the mediator facilitating the mediation through a series of defined phases.

As with other areas of dispute resolution, mediation requires the application of specific skills. Some may already be possessed by the mediator and others can be acquired through learning.

Throughout the mediation process mediators should always:

- endeavour to be empathetic and patient;
- uphold the important ethical mediation principles such as impartiality (which includes being non-biased and non-aligned);
- remember to respect confidentiality.

An awareness of parties' emotions and their culture is important and mediators should wherever possible resist making assumptions or holding prejudices. Overall a good understanding of the mediation process structure is required in order to maintain effective process management.

CHAPTER SUMMARY

- Mediation is a voluntary process conducted confidentially which empowers the parties in dispute to resolve their differences with the assistance of an impartial facilitator: the mediator.

- The various dispute resolution strategies of negotiation, mediation, arbitration and litigation can be viewed as being on a continuum ranging from 'consensual' (the most flexible forms of dispute resolution giving most power to the parties) to the 'adjudicative' (the least flexible forms of dispute resolution with least power in the hands of the parties.

- Mediation offers a high level of flexibility in that although it is facilitated by a third party, the parties retain full control over the decision making process leading to settlement. Therefore it has a strongly consensual element associated with it.

- The mediation process structure varies according to the type and subject of the dispute but its underlying principles remain more or less the same.

- The choice of mediator is important as the mediator and their preferred style determine the contours of the mediation.

- Two broad mediator styles have been identified: evaluative and facilitative.

- The evaluative mediator (who is often an expert in the area or has legal expertise) adopts a more searching and probing style.

- The facilitative mediator tends to allow the parties to work things out for themselves and will assist, coach or guide them when required.

- It is possible to identify a basic four phase structure to most civil/commercial mediation involving opening, exploration, bargaining and conclusion.

- Mediators are required to develop an extensive range of skills circulating around organisational skills, communication skills and personal skills.

- Communication skills are key, and include the ability to remain positive, engage in effective listening and reframing, and develop good questioning skills. Mediators need to be able to draw out the parties into active engagement with the dispute resolution process.

ACTIVITY 27.1: SUGGESTED ANSWERS

(a) Harsh 'conflict' words and phrases can be softened in order to remove the 'sting' which they might convey. This is called reframing. The suggested reframed words and phrases are in *italics*:

Dispute/conflict – *disagreement* or *difference in opinion*
Claims/demands – *needs and requirements*
Opponent/defendant – *the person with whom I have a disagreement*
Concede – *compromise*

It's a matter of principle/it is fundamental to the claim
This is important to me.

You're a liar/I don't believe you
I find it difficult believing that this is correct.

(b) Harsh statements – The suggested reframed sentences are in *italics*:

'The builder's a cowboy, he completely bodged the job.'
I'm unhappy with the standard of workmanship. There are areas of the builder's work that were substandard.

'The work done on my car has cost me a lot of money and it's useless to drive.'
I would like to be compensated for the amount of money I have spent on this car or at least have the repairs done at no charge.

'She's never going to see the kids again if she doesn't stop screwing money out of me.'
We need to discuss the child contact arrangements and the level of maintenance payments.

'The guy's an idiot, he's ignoring me and that's just plain rude; he just won't return my calls and refuses to discuss the problem.'
I'm having difficulty speaking to him; can we try to talk this through so as to work out a solution?

'If he doesn't repair the car in one week I'm suing him.'
I think we need to discuss this before the matter escalates.

Notice that many of the reframing suggestions include elements of communication or interaction. Finding the time or courage to talk about a problem that is deteriorating can start a dialogue process which may ultimately lead to an agreement. The alternative is to ignore the situation and let the problem deteriorate further with worsening consequences.

CONCLUSIONS

This text has attempted to provide a clear view of the practicalities of studying law, focusing on the required skills of general study, reading legal texts, argument construction, writing and oral presentation. We have also discussed ways of developing good independent study habits and approaches to 'breaking into' texts to understand the flexibility and the inherent unreliability of language in a discipline that centres on the power of 'the word' and of language generally.

This brief conclusion finishes by signalling that only a partial understanding is reached if you do not consider the power inherent in any rule imbued with the authority of law. By this is meant the power inherent in law's context and status, its privileged authority over other institutions, and the power of those who interpret it and create it.

Law is applied, used or created by people acting in roles dealing with the memories of the law. Much time has been spent looking at mechanistic schemes for understanding legal words, legal texts, intertextual and intratextual links and the arguments for the outcome of the case. However, as Goodrich states, 'reading is never innocent'.[1]

There are vast dimensions of legal analysis untouched, ready to be tackled by politicians, philosophers, feminists, criminologists or sociologists. And there are a range of ever present, yet buried, motivational issues, such as why did the judge adopt that interpretation? Or which rationale for adopting that interpretation do 'I' believe? Was that legislation motivated by economics or welfare? We have considered a few raw legal arguments and have noted the reasons given to support outcomes. But valuable issues can also be raised by asking why the judge did not choose to take another plausible interpretation.

Judgments are the end result after parties and witnesses put their sides, via official and tortuous questioning. They take place in situations where rules of evidence, magistrates and judges control what is and what is not said, by whom, and how it is said. Lawyers, judges and officials control definitions too, as well as choosing interim and ultimate interpretations. Legal texts are never unambiguous representations of the law. They are the words from which interpretations flow. At the level of the obvious, the voice of consensus

---

1 P Goodrich *Reading the Law: Critical Introduction to Legal Method and Techniques* (Wiley-Blackwell, Oxford, 1986), 231.

states: 'we all know what this means, *don't we?*' Equally, this can be said in a tone of incredulity, or of ridicule: 'we all *know* what this means, don't we?'

In their texts judges build one official story, one official ending. But the story can often be very different, and so could the ending. The bricks for building are words. Despite our focus on study skills, English language skills, legal method skills and their interrelationship with substantive law and solving legal problems, it is the landscape that decides it all. The landscape of the officials, the institutions, politics, the judiciary, the police and policy all have an influence.

The critical thinker has to remain engaged not only in micro-questions within texts, but also in macro-questions at the level of law, politics and culture. This includes considering text as the product of a culture, continuing the search for underlying assumptions.

Much law degree study will revolve around 'fighting' with the language of, and arguments in, cases – reconciling, distinguishing and/or following them and explaining differences of interpretation where some might say there are no differences. Students learn a growing body of rules and, more and more, the overarching context of institutions and culture shrinks into the background. They may be interesting from an academic perspective, but cultural legal content has no place in the everyday life of the law and its mediation of competing interests. It is in the interest of these legal institutional values that the legal 'story' is the one that covers all. But there is a danger that the daily process of *doing* the law blinds the 'doers' (the practitioners) to the motivational influences of some institutional creators of law. The law as language is to be read, interpreted, questioned and seen in its fragmented contexts, to be the object of a healthy scepticism. It should not be invested with qualities it cannot control. Law is not justice, for indeed justice may demand that there be no law.

When deciding what words mean in court, judges make far-reaching decisions and maintain that they do so, not on grounds of morality, religion, justice or ethics, but purely as a true interpretation of the words. They support the orthodox view that law is a neutral instrument to achieve a moral society. Law is objective, rational and logical and one must believe in the ultimate good of the law and the ultimate ability of the law to determine what the law means. A problem can now be seen. As pointed out above, the law is not an autonomous neutral agent; it is used by people in a political and social role. Legal texts can be analysed as social texts created by social actors. Statutes are texts communicated via words created by politicians in compromise and interpreted by judges for a range of reasons, some explicit some not. Can discussions about law, therefore, ever be justifiably separated from discussions about power (especially since access to law making power is only available to players in the higher levels of politics or professionals in the higher judiciary)?

Law is not logical, nor does it have to be. There is social agreement that, for a range of reasons – political, social and moral – English law should be seen to be fair. But to apply a rule to a problem requires the clarification of the problem and proof that the facts of the problem as presented are the facts that occurred. Rules have developed which state what must be proved by testimonial or forensic evidence and when evidence itself must be backed up.

Due to the history of common law, its oral nature of proceedings, the breaking away of courts from the royal household, the ultimate ascendancy of statutory law and the complete reorganisation of the courts of England and Wales in 1875 and 1978, we now have a system of law which is based upon the reaction to arguments presented to those officials who decide which argument is legitimate, be they negotiators in offices, tribunals and juries, magistrates' or appellate courts. The legal system also continues to be challenged, stretched and changed by the new political and legal order of European Union and European Union law, as well as changes to the law relating to human rights.

As you finish your first year journey about beginnings and getting on the road, about study skills, language use, finding and handling legal rules, and after the study of the range of modules involved in getting your law degree, look forward to your next journey. Always try to keep the wider issues of law and its contexts and power in mind. As you develop through the stages of your academic legal study you will increasingly be called upon to ponder some of these issues and more; you will be required to spend more time tracing a critical pathway in your work. These are important tasks and may even become a life work for you.

FURTHER READING
AND USEFUL WEBSITES

FURTHER READING

Anderson T., Schum D. and Twining W. *Analysis of Evidence* (Cambridge: Cambridge University Press, 2005)

Beck G. 'Letter: The legal reasoning of the Court of Justice: a response to Michal Bobek' (2014) 39(4) *EL Review* 579–81

Bobek M. 'Legal Reasoning of the Court of Justice of the EU' (2014) 39 *EL Review* 418

Boulle L. and Nesic M. *Mediation: Principles, Process, Practice* (Butterworths, Bloomsbury Professional, London, 2010)

Chivers B. and Shoolbred MB. *A Student's Guide to Presentations* (SAGE Essential Study Skills Series, Sage Publications, London, 2007)

Clinch P. *Using a Law Library: A Student's Guide to Research Skills* (Blackwell, Oxford, 2001)

Costanzo M. *Essential Legal Skills Problem Solving* (Cavendish Publishing, London, 1994)

Cottrell S. *Critical Thinking Skills: Developing Effective Analysis and Argument* (Palgrave Macmillan, Basingstoke, 2005)

Cottrell S. *The Study Skills Handbook* (3rd edn, Palgrave Macmillan, Basingstoke, 2008)

Cottrell S. *Skills for Success, the Personal Development Planning Handbook* (Palgrave Macmillan, Basingstoke, 2010)

Fisher R. and Shapiro D. *Beyond Reason: Using Emotions as You Negotiate* (Viking/Penguin, 2005)

Fisher R. and Ury W. *Getting to Yes* (2nd edn, Penguin Books Inc, New York, NY, 1992)

Fisher R. and Ury W. *Getting to Yes: Negotiating an Agreement Without Giving In* (Random House, London, 2012)

Gatrell C. *Managing Part-time Study: A Guide for Undergraduates and Postgraduates* (Open University Press, Milton Keynes, 2006)

Gold N., Mackie K. and W. Twining *Learning Lawyers' Skills* (Butterworths, London, 1989)

Haigh R. *Legal English* (4th edn, Routledge, Oxford, 2015)

Hargreave S. *Study Skills for Dyslexic Students* (Sage, London, 2007)

Hill J. *A Practical Guide to Mooting* (Palgrave Macmillan, Basingstoke, 2009)

Holland J. and Webb J. *Learning Legal Rules* (8th edn, Oxford University Press, Oxford, 2013)

Hoult E. *Learning Support for Mature Students* (Sage, London, 2006)

Kee C. *The Art of Argument: a Guide to Mooting* (Cambridge University Press, Cambridge, 2006)

Knowles J. *Effective Legal Research* (3rd edn, Sweet and Maxwell, London, 2012)

Lawrence P. *Law on the Internet: A Practical Guide* (Sweet and Maxwell, London, 2000)

Mattias D. 'Multilingual interpretation of CJEU case law: rule and reality' (2014) 39(3) *EL Review* 295–315

McAuliffe K. 'Precedent at the ECJ: The Linguistic Aspect. Law and Language' (2013) 15 *Current Legal Issues* 483–493

McKay WR. and Charlton HE. *Legal English: How to Understand and Master the Language of Law* (Pearson Longman, Harlow, 2005)

Moore C. *The Mediation Process: Practical Strategies for Resolving Conflict*, (4th edn, Jossey-Bass, San Francisco, CA, 2014)

Northledge A. *The Good Study Guide* (2nd edn, Open University Press, Milton Keynes, 2005)

Pope D. and Hill D. *Mooting and Advocacy Skills* (2nd edn, Sweet & Maxwell, London, 2011)

Price G. and Maier P. *Effective Study Skills* (Pearson Education, Harlow, 2007)

Sadl U. 'Case Comment Ruiz Zambrano as an illustration of how the Court of Justice of the European Union constructs its legal arguments' (2013) 9(2) *EL Review* 205–22

Schum D. 'Alternative views of argument construction from a mass of evidence' 22 *Cardozo Law Review* 1461–502 (contains a valuable set of references within the discipline of law and in other disciplines concerning arguments)

Slapper G. and Kelly D. *The English Legal System 2015–2016* (16th edn, Routledge, Oxford, 2015)

Snape J. and Watt G. *How to Moot: a Student Guide to Mooting* (2nd edn, OUP, Oxford, 2010)

Stitt A. *Mediation: A Practical Guide* (Cavendish, London, 2004)

Sychin C. *Legal Method* (2nd edn, Sweet & Maxwell, London, 1999)

Thomas PA. and Knowles J. *How to Use a Law Library* (4th edn, Sweet and Maxwell, London, 2001)

Turner C. and Boylan-Kemp J. *Unlocking Legal Learning* (3rd edn, Hodder Education, London, 2012)

Twining W. and Miers D. *How to Do Things with Rules* (5th edn, CUP, Cambridge, 2010)

Vermeule A. 'Constitutional amendments and constitutional common law', Harvard University Working Paper (2004) *Social Science Research Network*

Webly L. *Legal Writing* (3rd edn, Routledge, Oxford, 2013)

Wigmore H. 'The problem of proof' (1913–14) 8 *Illinois Law Rev* 77

Wild C. and Weinstein S. *Smith and Keenan's English Law* (13th edn, Longman, Harlow, 2013)

USEFUL WEBSITES

Cardiff Index to Legal Abbreviations: http://www.legalabbrevs.cardiff.ac.uk

Council of Europe official site: http://www.coe.int

Equality and Human Rights Commission: http://www.equalityhumanrights.com

European Union official site: http://europa.eu

Legislation: http://www.legislation.gov.uk

OSCOLA official guide can be located at the following site: http://Denning.law.ox.ac.uk/published/oscola.shtml (with online tutorial and you will find advertised on this site that you can download a free pdf version: OSCOLA (4th edn, Hart, 2012)

UK Government: www.gov.uk

UK Parliament website: www.parliament.uk

Virtual training suite: http://www.vts.intute.ac.uk/he/tutorial/lawyers

ONLINE MOOTING RESOURCES

These sites will give you examples of moots, skeleton arguments, detailed pointers about dealing with judicial interventions, constructing bundles, delivery of your speech and much more.

Learnmore: http://learnmore.lawbore.net/index.php/Category:Mooting

Mooting Skills Guide by Slapper and Kelly: http://www.routledge.com/cw/slapper-9780415639989/s2/mooting/

Mooting Net: http://www.mooting.net

OUP: What is mooting?: http://global.oup.com/uk/academic/highereducation/law/mooting/more/

Oxford University Podcast on Mooting: http://podcasts.ox.ac.uk/mooting-short-introduction

YouTube: You can search for mooting guides; there are numerous videos to assist you to prepare

INDEX

abrogation 69, 341
academic year 446–454
accommodators 439
Acts of Parliament *see* statutes
acquis communautaire 102, 318–39
alliteration 484
analogous reasoning 384
appellate courts 40–2
argument 363–85; constructing 377–9;
    developing skills 365–7; meaning 364–5
argument by analogy 395–6

Bailii 194–5

cases in English legal system 172–7; case
    names 183–5; case note 270–2; case
    summaries 176–7; choosing legal
    authorities 179; citation not known,
    when 185; citations 179–90; full text
    cases 176–7; online 185–90; online
    databases 190–95; print collections
    185; private publishers, citations
    181–90; technical meanings of key
    words/phrases 174; terminology 173;
    unreported cases 176
civil law legal systems 316–317; common law,
    and 317command papers 214–15
common law 32–5
Council of Europe 72–4; institutions 74
Council of the European Union 100
Court of Justice of the European Union 51,
    101–2; approach to reasoning and
    interpretation 422–4; procedure 319–25;
    types of case 319–25
courts 38–47; generic terms 40; hierarchy 51–4

critical legal theory movement 391
critical thinking 367–72; critique of deductive
    or inductive reasoning 406; deductive
    argument: attacking major premise of
    406–8Current Law Statute Citator 141–2
Current Law Statutes 142
custom 37–8

deduction 381–82
domestic case law 31–55
domestic legislation 9–29; finding 12–13;
    locating 137–64 naming conventions
    11, 13; nature of 10–11; power of
    government to create 15; understanding
    279–313

Equality Act 2010: general layout 287; section 9
    289–92; section 13 296; section 19
    297–8
equity: development 35–7
essays 571–91; careful notetaking 574–5; final
    version 590–1; first draft 589–90; nature
    of 575–81; organisation of material 586;
    plan outline 589; possible arguments
    587–8 preparation and construction
    581–91; reflection 581; relevant facts
    587; strength of argument 589; wider
    reading 574–5
European citizens 89
European Commission 98–100
European Convention on Human Rights
    71–86; amendments and repeals 349;
    importance of up to date knowledge
    350; issues raised in relation to UK
    cases 358–9; leaving 77; legal impact

on English law 78–81; pilot judgments 77; protocols 78–81; rights contained in 346–9; structure and layout 345–6; UK and violations 80 locating European Convention on Human Rights 166
European Council 98
European Court of Human Rights 51, 74–6; legal reasoning 428–9; procedure 350–53 ECHR reports 198–9; online 198; print collections 196–8
European legal reasoning 419–30; general approach 421–22
European Parliament 101
European Union 87–102; consolidated versions of two founding treaties 2010 96–7; core functions 89–90; current treaties in force 97; founding treaties 89; institutions 97–102; interpretation 424–8; legal order 102; legal reasoning 424–8; multiplicity of languages 424–8; nature of 89
European Union law 87–116; citations 198; directives 343–5; directly applicable 106–8; enforcement 109–11; general principles 105; guided reading 325–3; hierarchy of legal norms 105; horizontal direct effect 107; legal effect 105–8; locating European treaties and secondary legislation 164–6; locating European Union law cases 196–9; primary: treaties 339–41; primary law 103; reading and understanding 317–18; regulations 342–3; secondary 340–45; secondary law 103–5; sources 102–3; supremacy 111–15; vertical direct effect 107
examination strategies 611–35; assumptions 618–21; day of examination 632–4; expectations of lecturer 621–22; potentially examinable topics 614–15; revision 622–32; stress 615–18; structure 612–14

factual analysis 397–402

government bill: drafting 18–19
Green Papers 18

habits of independent learning 444–5
Halsbury's Statutes 142–4
Halsbury's Statutes Citator 145
Hansard 309–10
Harvard referencing system 550–56; short cuts 556; UK cases and legislation 555
HeinOnline 211–12
House of Commons 14; passage of bill through 20–2
House of Lords 14; passage of bill through 22
Human Rights Act 1998 81–5, 353–9: background 81; Convention rights 357–8; current concerns 81; duties of English courts and tribunals 84; key sections 82–3; structure 356
hybrid acts 16

independent study 443–4
inductive argument 396–7
inference, use of 403–5
inferior courts 44–7
International Court of Justice 59
Internet: legal resources 121, 131; Internet retrieval: good practice 217–19; open access material: good practice 217–19

journals 207–12; article citations 208; HeinOnline 211–12; Lawtel 211; Lexis@ Library 211; title abbreviations 207–8, 209; Westlaw 208–11
Judicial Committee of the Privy Council 48
judicial titles in Court of Appeal 666
judicial titles in Supreme Court 665

Language skills; English affixes derived from other languages 490, stem words 491, figurative language 481–82, formal academic language 502–4, grammar 506–8, legal language: characteristics 572–74, metaphor 482–3, paragraphs 519–2017, punctuation 508–16, sentences 519–20, spelling 517–19, vocabulary 516–17
law dictionaries 518
law reporting: development 174–6

law reports 125; abbreviations 182; anatomy
239–42; basic reading of case 243–7;
breaking into difficult text 247–9;
detailed reading of judgment 249–72;
handling 236–8; hierarchy 177–8;
obtaining general overview 241–3;
relationship of electronic to print forms
178–9
Lawtel 211
learning 437–43; styles 437–43
lectures 458–9
legal argument 392–5
legal problem questions 593–609; guided
demonstration of basics 604–9; methods
for preparation and construction 597–8;
methods for writing solutions 598; skills
594–7; stages of solution methodology
598–601; structure of final written
answer 601–602
legal realism 390–1
legal reasoning 387–417; case study 409–16
legislation: 15; citations 139–40; consolidation
exercise 298; date in force 138–9;
drafting in civilian legal systems 420–21;
7; draft legislation 157; explanatory
notes 292–3; finding 136–impact of
changes to 293–5; layout of 281;
importance of latest version 288; layout
of individual sections 289; legislative
language: complexity 28, locating
domestic legislation 137–64;linking
series of sections 295–6; links between
sections 289; locating purpose of
section 289; ; online 145–54; overall
structure 283–8; passage through
Parliament 19–23; procedures 17–23;
print and electronic forms 152–6; public
domain sites 146–7; Race Relations
Act 1976 148–52; secondary legislation
154–66; statutes in print form 140–5;
terminology 137–8; using and handling
281–83; year of enactment 138
library: accessing e-library collection 126–7;
books 126; electronic collection 126–7;
electronic materials 127–31; journals
125; legislation 125; Parliamentary

papers 124–5; print materials 123–6;
public domain sites 131; reference
texts 124; thin resources 124; types of
resources 130
library catalogue 122–3, 212
logic 379–84

mediation 683–99; meaning 684–5; phases
686–94; process 685–92; skills 692–7
mooting 647–69; meaning 648; model 655–69;
participants 649–51; reasons for 648–9;
rules of engagement 651–55

natural law 389
negotiation 671–79; guided narrative in stages
675–80; main forms 673–4; meaning
672–3; process 674–5
neutrality and objectivity of law 299–302
notes, writing 520–28
notes from verbal presentations 524–8

oral skills 559–67; delivery 565–6; exercises
560–66; research 564; team working 566
ordering of legal argument 661–3
orders in council 16
OSCOLA 535–55; using 535–50
out of date law: retrieving 166

Parliament 14–15
parliamentary debates: finding 215–17
parliamentary papers 215
personal development planning 460–1
plagiarism 531–2, 555–6; meaning 555–6;
sanctions for 556
positivism 389–90
precedent, doctrine of 38, 227–36; effective
system, requirements for 228;
legislation, and 228; persuasive
227–8; practical implementation
236 understanding practice 235;
understanding theory 229–35
presentation skills 637–44; stages 638–44
primary legal materials: see legislation
and cases
primary legislation 15–23
Private Acts 15

private members' Acts 16–17
Public General Acts 15; 139; 142, 143, 153–154; measures, and 145public international law 58–9

reading skills 463–996; methods of approaching 466–7; purpose 465; speed 467–71; strategy for efficient reading 472–98
referencing 531–55; in–text 551–55; meaning 533; need for 533–34; systems 535
revision 622–32
Royal Assent 14, 23

secondary legislation 23–8; Parliamentary control over 25–6; procedure 26–8
secondary material 203–21; general issues 205–6; search strategies 206–7
secondary texts 132
seminars 459–60
set textbooks 213
skills required for successful legal study 455–6
standard university study 445–55
statute: see legislation, aids to 306–9; golden rule 304; literal rule 302–4; mischief rule 304–5; purposive rule 305; secondary legislation 310–11; statutory interpretation 299--311; teleological approach 305–6; use of rules 309–10
study skills 433–61

studying: meaning of 435–6
superior courts 42–4

teaching arrangements: making best use of 457–9
treaties 57–70; abrogation 69; accession 68–9; amending 67, 68; denunciation 69; definition 58; form 60; formalising 63; in force 66; layout 60–3; legal effect 58–69, 66–7; minimising dissent in negotiation process 64; names 67; new 68; official records 69–70; parties to 63; protocols 67; standard layout 339; subject matter 60; synonyms 60
Treaty of Amsterdam 1997 93
Treaty of Lisbon 2007 94
Treaty of Maastricht 1992 92–3
Treaty of Nice 2001 94
Treaty of Rome (No 2) 1957 91–2
tribunals 47–8; tier system 49–50
TSO official documents online 217

Vienna Convention on the Law of Treaties 1969 59

Westlaw 157–62, 190–3, 208–11
White Papers 18
writing skills 501–529; structure and organisation 505–20
writing style 502–504